This volume offers a new view of Joseph Haydn's instrumental music. It argues that many of his greatest and most characteristic instrumental works are "through-composed," in the sense that their several movements are bound together into a cycle. This cyclic integration is demonstrated in, for example, the "progressive" form of individual movements, structural and gestural links between the movements, and extramusical associations.

Central to the study is a detailed and comprehensive analysis of the "Farewell" Symphony, No. 45 in F-sharp minor (1772). The analysis differs from most others in its systematic use of different methods (Toveyan formalism, Schenkerian voice leading, Schoenbergian developing variation) to elucidate the work's overall coherence. The work's unique musical processes, in turn, suggest an interpretation of the entire piece (not merely the famous "farewell" finale) in terms of the familiar programmatic story of the musicians' wish to leave Castle Eszterháza.

CAMBRIDGE STUDIES IN MUSIC THEORY AND ANALYSIS

GENERAL EDITOR: IAN BENT

HAYDN'S "FAREWELL" SYMPHONY AND THE IDEA OF CLASSICAL STYLE

TITLES IN THIS SERIES

The first page of Haydn's autograph manuscript of the "Farewell" Symphony, showing the beginning of the Allegro assai (Budapest, National Schézényi Library, Music Division, Ms. Mus. I. 36. Reprinted by permission)

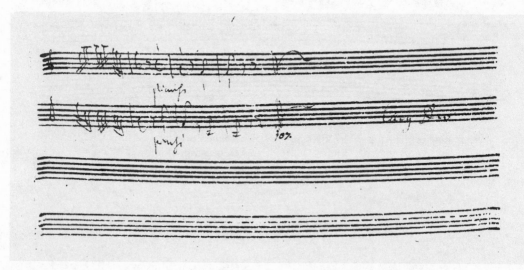

From the "farewell" finale: (*above*) the first structural cadence in F-sharp major (mm. 80–85) and the subsequent entry of the two principal violins; (*below*) the final measures

HAYDN'S "FAREWELL" SYMPHONY AND THE IDEA OF CLASSICAL STYLE

THROUGH-COMPOSITION AND CYCLIC INTEGRATION IN HIS INSTRUMENTAL MUSIC

JAMES WEBSTER

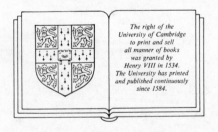

The right of the
University of Cambridge
to print and sell
all manner of books
was granted by
Henry VIII in 1534.
The University has printed
and published continuously
since 1584.

CAMBRIDGE UNIVERSITY PRESS

Cambridge

New York   Port Chester

Melbourne   Sydney

Published by the Press Syndicate of the University of Cambridge
The Pitt Building, Trumpington Street, Cambridge CB2 1RP
40 West 20th Street, New York, NY 10011–4211, USA
10 Stamford Road, Oakleigh, Melbourne 3166, Australia

© Cambridge University Press 1991

First published 1991

Printed in Great Britain at
the University Press, Cambridge

British Library cataloguing in publication data
Webster, James, *1942–*
Haydn's "Farewell" Symphony and the idea of classical
style: through–composition and cyclic integration in
his instrumental music. – (Cambridge studies in music
theory and analysis).
1. Austrian symphonies. Haydn, Joseph, 1732–1809
I. Title
784.184092

Library of Congress cataloguing in publication data
Webster, James, *1942–*
Haydn's "Farewell" Symphony and the idea of classical style:
through–composition and cyclic integration in his instrumental music
/ James Webster.
p.   cm. – (Cambridge studies in music theory and analysis)
Includes bibliographical references.
ISBN 0 521 38520 2
1. Haydn, Joseph, 1732–1809. Symphonies, H. I. 45, F♯ minor.
2. Haydn, Joseph, 1732–1809. Instrumental music. 3. Symphony – 18th
century. 4. Instrumental music – 18th century – History and
criticism. 5. Classicism in music. I. Title. II. Series.
ML410.H4W38 1991
784'.092 – dc20
90–1592 CIP

ISBN 0 521 38520 2 hardback

TO MARGARET

CONTENTS

PART II: CYCLIC ORGANIZATION IN HAYDN'S INSTRUMENTAL MUSIC

FOREWORD BY IAN BENT

Theory and analysis are in one sense reciprocals: if analysis opens up a musical structure or style to inspection, inventorying its components, identifying its connective forces, providing a description adequate to some live experience, then theory generalizes from such data, predicting what the analyst will find in other cases within a given structural or stylistic orbit, devising systems by which other works – as yet unwritten – might be generated. Conversely, if theory intuits how musical systems operate, then analysis furnishes feedback to such imaginative intuitions, rendering them more insightful. In this sence, they are like two hemispheres that fit together to form a globe (or cerebrum!), functioning deductively as investigation and abstraction, inductively as hypothesis and verification, and in practice forming a chain of alternating activities.

Professionally, on the other hand, "theory" now denotes a whole subdiscipline of the general field of musicology. Analysis often appears to be a subordinate category within the larger activity of theory. After all, there is theory that does not require analysis. Theorists may engage in building systems or formulating strategies for use by composers; and these almost by definition have no use for analysis. Others may conduct experimental research into the sound-materials of music or the cognitive processes of the human mind, to which analysis may be wholly inappropriate. And on the other hand, historians habitually use analysis as a tool for understanding the classes of compositions – repertories, "outputs," "periods," works, versions, sketches, and so forth – that they study. Professionally, then, our ideal image of twin hemispheres is replaced by an intersection: an area that exists in common between two subdisciplines. Seen from this viewpoint, analysis reciprocates in two directions: with certain kinds of theoretical enquiry, and with certain kinds of historical enquiry. In the former case, analysis has tended to be used in rather orthodox modes, in the latter in a more eclectic fashion; but that does not mean that analysis in the service of theory is necessarily more exact, more "scientific," than analysis in the service of history.

The above epistemological excursion is by no means irrelevant to the present series. Cambridge Studies in Music Theory and Analysis is intended to present the work of theorists and of analysts. It has been designed to include "pure" theory – that is, theoretical formulation with a minimum of analytical exemplification; "pure" analysis – that is, practical analysis with a minimum of theoretical underpinning; and writings that fall at points along the spectrum between the two extremes. In these capacities, it aims to illuminate music, as work and as process.

However, theory and analysis are not the exclusive preserves of the present day. As subjects in their own right, they are diachronic. The former is coeval with the very study of music itself, and extends far beyond the confines of Western culture; the latter, defined broadly, has several centuries of past practice. Moreover, they have been dynamic, not static fields throughout their histories. Consequently, studying earlier music through the eyes of its own contemporary theory helps us to escape (when we need to, not that we should make a dogma out of it) from the preconceptions of our own age. Studying earlier analyses does this too, and in a particularly sharply focused way; at the same time it gives us the opportunity to re-evaluate past analytical methods for present purposes, such as is happening currently, for example, with the long-despised methods of hermeneutic analysis of the late nineteenth century. The series thus includes editions and translations of major works of past theory, and also studies in the history of theory.

James Webster's study of Haydn's "Farewell" Symphony is a remarkable instance of analysis in the service of historical musicology. It is written by a professional music historian, and brings to bear upon its subject-matter a profound knowledge not only of Haydn's life and times, but also of his music and its sources, and of the music of Vienna in the late eighteenth and early nineteenth centuries. It is pluralistic in its analytical method ("multivalent" is Webster's word for his approach), and analysis runs through virtually the length and breadth of the book. It analyzes all the movements of the "Farewell" Symphony in detail, but it goes much further than that: it places a single analytical conception on the work as a whole, treating it as a through-composed entity. Nor does it stop there: it goes on to analyze other works by Haydn, and then to consider the larger implications of its findings, concluding with an important historiographical essay.

PREFACE

In 1985–86, while in Vienna on sabbatical, I received a pair of invitations to travel to Budapest to lecture on Haydn. This stimulated me to begin a long-postponed study of the "Farewell" Symphony, in part because I could combine it with an examination of Haydn's autograph manuscript (housed, like so many, in the National Széchényi Library in the same city). I am lastingly grateful to László Somfai and Katalin Komlós for extending these invitations (and for much else besides), as well as to Zoltán Felvy, director of the Institute of Musicology of the Hungarian Academy of Sciences, and György Króo, chairman of the Department of Musicology of the Ferenc Liszt Academy of Music, for financial and logistical support. I am equally grateful to Veronika Vavrinecz, head of the Music Division of the Library, for her unexcelled kindness and cooperation. Later, I gave related lectures at chapter meetings of the American Musicological Society – New York State–St. Lawrence (1988) and Greater New York (1989) – and at King's College, London (1988).

As background for the Budapest lectures, I carried out an extended analysis and interpretation of the symphony, as well as a largely independent study of the baffling D-major interlude in the Allegro assai. (For the latter, which incorporates several detailed discussions omitted from the present study, see the Introduction, n. 9.) I also made extensive studies of Haydn autograph materials that year in Vienna, particularly at the Gesellschaft der Musikfreunde in Wien (relevant in this context especially for the string quartets Op. 20); I remain most grateful to Dr. Otto Biba, director of the archive, for his exemplary assistance and support.

My 1986 account of the Farewell exemplified the familiar condition of being "too long for an article, but too short for a book." I therefore felt fortunate indeed to learn from Ian D. Bent the same autumn that the theory and analysis series he was then planning was to include a subseries devoted to self-sufficient monographic analyses of individual masterpieces, and that he would recommend publication of my study, including a brief exploration of its analytical and theoretical implications. Both at this initial stage and at every successive one, his many suggestions, and still more his unflagging interest and encouragement, were immensely helpful.

The reader will have observed the vast discrepancy between that image of a relatively short book devoted primarily to a single work, and the present volume. In the event, my "exploration of implications" grew alarmingly, at times uncontrollably, before it coalesced around the topics now covered in Part II: progressive form, through-

composition, and extramusical associations in Haydn's music; analyses and interpretations of a representative selection of his works in which these features are prominent;
and a historiographical conclusion focusing on "Classical style." The "implications"
are thus no longer primarily theoretical in nature, but constitute an extended essay
on Haydn's music and our reception of it (albeit still focusing on analytical and related
matters). I am profoundly grateful to Professor Bent, and to Penny Souster of the
Cambridge University Press, for their willingness to recommend publication of it in this
form, and for their forbearance during the long delay entailed by the revision.

It is a pleasure to acknowledge as well the assistance I have received from other
quarters. A full year's sabbatical in 1985–86 and a study leave in the autumn of 1989
granted by Cornell University made it possible to complete the volume without further
delays. Edward Murray and Roger Parker read the entirety of Part I and made many
valuable suggestions. Elaine Sisman and Richard Will read Chapter 7 and made available
unpublished research on Haydn's theatrical music and on Austrian program symphonies,
respectively; the latter also made helpful comments on the concluding chapter. Sonja
Gerlach generously shared unpublished studies on the chronology of Haydn's early
symphonies. Elizabeth Hudson, Parker, Don Michael Randel, Sisman, Jessica Waldoff,
and Will kept me honest regarding the relevance of literary criticism and historiography,
as did Wye Jamison Allanbrook and Mark Evan Bonds regarding the importance of
rhetoric. Neal Zaslaw as always shared his vast knowledge of the period; V. Kofi Agawu
provided last-minute advice and encouragement. Cliff Eisen checked some points regarding the autograph of the Farewell and provided information from the Union Catalog
of Eighteenth-Century Symphonies at New York University; Rebecca Harris-Warrick
located and described the Cimarosa source in Paris referred to in the Introduction.
Lenore Coral responded promptly and professionally to my requests at the Cornell
University Music Library; Jane Belonsoff and Estir Griffin went beyond the call of
duty in putting up with my incessant laser-printing and photocopying. Sarah Adams
checked references for me accommodatingly and efficiently. Kathryn Puffett not only
copy-edited the typescript with exemplary accuracy and thoroughness and supplied
additional references, but asked penetrating questions that helped me to focus my discussions of theoretical issues. Finally, I am deeply grateful to Eugene K. Wolf, whose
detailed reading of my concluding chapter under severe time pressure spared me from
numerous errors and infelicities. Of course, neither he nor anyone else is responsible for
the many that doubtless remain.

Words cannot express what I owe my wife Margaret for her encouragement and
support over a period of more than twenty years. I dedicate this book to her.

Earlier, I used the term "essay" in referring to this study. Despite its size and scope,
it retains more than a little of its original character – a sustained discussion of a single
masterpiece, and of its quasi-dialectical relations to our views of its composer and his
time. For example, the frequent references to the Farewell Symphony in Part II are not
limited to reminders of what was said in Part I, but incorporate new perspectives in
each successive chapter. Nor are critical strains absent, not even from the most densely

analytical passages. Impracticable as the suggestion must appear, I hope that this volume will be read in the spirit in which it was written: as a single-minded exploration of Haydn's through-compositional genius.

Ithaca, New York
March 1990

Cambridge University Press is grateful to the American Musicological Society for a subvention towards the production costs of this book.

AUTHOR'S NOTE

The "Farewell" Symphony has been published in critical editions by H. C. Robbins Landon (full-size: Doblinger; miniature score: *Critical Edition of the Complete Symphonies*, 12 vols. [Vienna: Universal, 1964–66], vol. 4, and also separately as Philharmonia, No. 745); and by C. G. Stellan-Mörner in *Joseph Haydn: Werke*, Series I, vol. 6 (Henle), with separate critical report. Since Haydn's autograph but no other authentic source is extant, the two editions are substantially identical. (For a facsimile of the autograph, see the Introduction, n. 2.)

When referring to the symphony as a whole, I use capital letters (as in the first sentence of this note), but when referring to the final movement alone, or to its procedures or the idea that lies behind it, I use "farewell" (lower-case). Especially in the former context, I usually drop the quotation marks. In addition, I often use the (capitalized) adjective Farewell alone as a substantive, again to designate the symphony as a whole.

I cite Haydn's symphonies by the traditional Mandyczewski numbers (which are replicated in Hoboken's Group I); keyboard sonatas by the traditional Päsler numbers (replicated in Group XVI); string quartets by the traditional opus designations; vocal works by title and key. Other instrumental works are cited by the full Hoboken number.

In analytical discussions, I use the following nomenclature: *Motives* are printed in italics, lower-case; they always begin with a letter: *a, b, b1, b1a, c,* etc. A lesser variant is indicated by a prime: in the sequence *d, d', d1, d1', d1a, d2,* etc., *d'* and *d1'* are relatively unimportant or temporary variants, compared even to *d1a. Theme* and *section numbers* are distinguished from motives in that they begin with a numeral, and are printed in bold-face.

All letter-names of pitches, chords, and keys are given in Roman type. The names of *individual pitches* follow the Helmholtz system, with middle C given as c^1 and changes at each octave: $C_1–B_1$, C–B, c–b, $c^1–b^1$, $c^2–b^2$, etc. *Pitch classes* are always given as capitals; where an ambiguity with an individual pitch in the C–B octave could arise, I make the distinction in the text. *Chords* and *keys* are usually capitalized (hence "D minor," not "d"); those with an accidental as part of the name are spelled out (F-sharp, A-flat), to distinguish them from pitch classes, which use accidental signs (F♯, A♭).

For the convenience of readers, when quoting Haydn's letters and other primary sources in translation I cite both my source for the original and (where available) a widely disseminated English translation. Nevertheless, many translations in this volume are my own (when these differ substantially from the cited translation, I so indicate).

LIST OF ABBREVIATIONS

AfMw	Archiv für Musikwissenschaft
AMZ	Allgemeine musikalische Zeitung
BzMw	Beiträge zur Musikwissenschaft
CM	Current Musicology
CMS	College Music Symposium
DJbMw	Deutsches Jahrbuch der Musikwissenschaft
H-S	Haydn-Studien
HYb	The Haydn Yearbook
JAMS	Journal of the American Musicological Society
JbP	Jahrbuch Peters
JHW	Joseph Haydn: Werke, ed. Joseph Haydn-Institut, Cologne
JM	The Journal of Musicology
JMR	Journal of Musicological Research
JMT	Journal of Music Theory
Mf	Die Musikforschung
MJb	Mozart-Jahrbuch
MQ	The Musical Quarterly
MR	The Music Review
Mth	Musiktheorie
MTS	Music Theory Spectrum
MusA	Music Analysis
19CMus	19th-Century Music
SM	Studia Musicologica
ZfM	Zeitschrift für Musik
ZfMw	Zeitschrift für Musikwissenschaft

INTRODUCTION

THE ORIGINS OF THE FAREWELL SYMPHONY

Every music-lover knows the story of Haydn's "Farewell" Symphony. Each year, the Esterházy court spent the warm season at Prince Nicolaus's new and splendid, but remote, summer castle "Eszterháza." With the exception of Haydn and a few other privileged individuals, the musicians were required to leave their families behind in Eisenstadt. (This much is independently documented.) Haydn's biographer Griesinger continues:

One year, against his usual custom, the prince determined to extend his stay in Eszterháza for several weeks. The ardent married men, thrown into utter consternation, turned to Haydn and asked him to help. Haydn hit upon the idea of writing a symphony in which, one after the other, the instruments fall silent. At the first opportunity, this symphony was performed in the prince's presence. Each of the musicians was instructed that, as soon as his part had come to an end, he should extinguish his light, pack up his music, and leave with his instrument under his arm. The prince and the audience at once understood the point of this pantomime; the next day came the order for the departure from Eszterháza. Thus Haydn related the occasion for the Farewell Symphony to me; the other version, that Haydn thereby dissuaded his prince from his intention to dissolve the entire *Kapelle*, . . . is to be sure more poetic, but not historically correct.[1]

Griesinger's general reliability, the story's correspondence with the musicians' documented situation, his (plausible) claim that Haydn was his source, and his explicit rejection of other versions – all this assures us that Haydn indeed composed a symphony which, at least in outline or in some essentials, corresponded to this program.[2] And this work can only be the one we know as No. 45 in F-sharp minor (1772).

To be sure, the nickname "Farewell" has nothing to do with Haydn; it stands neither in the autograph nor in any other eighteenth-century musical source, and apparently

---

[1] Georg August Griesinger, *Biographische Notizen über Joseph Haydn* (Leipzig, 1810), pp. 28–29; tr. in Vernon Gotwals, *Joseph Haydn: Eighteenth-Century Gentleman and Genius* (Madison, 1963), p. 19, and in H. C. Robbins Landon, *Haydn: Chronicle and Works* (5 vols., London and Bloomington, 1976–80), vol. 2, p. 180.

[2] For more information, including comments on the competing stories, see Anthony van Hoboken, *Joseph Haydn: Thematisches-Systematisches Werkverzeichnis*, vol. 1 (Mainz, 1957), under I:45; László Somfai's preface to a facsimile publication of the autograph (Budapest, 1959); *Joseph Haydn: Werke* (hereafter cited as *JHW*), edited by the Joseph Haydn-Institut, Cologne, under the direction of Georg Feder, Series I, vol. 6, *Sinfonien 1766–1772*, ed. C.-G. Stellan Mörner, pp. vii–viii; Landon, *Haydn*, vol. 2, pp. 180–82, 303, 758–59. Comments below on non-autograph sources and contemporary nicknames are also taken from Hoboken and JHW I/6.

originated in the 1780s, probably in France, following its publication by Sieber and a
review there in 1784. (As we will see in Chapter 4, its implications for the program are
in many respects actually misleading.) Nor does the autograph (the only surviving
authentic source) provide any indication of unusual goings-on such as blowing out
candles or leaving the hall. The title reads simply "Sinfonia in Fis minore" (see the
frontispiece), and Haydn's only verbal remark in the "farewell" movement is the single
phrase "nichts mehr," following the initial *envoi* solos (first oboe and second horn,
mm. 30–35).[3] As a whole, the autograph appears entirely normal: it consists of a single
paper-type and is entirely regular in gathering structure, with no missing or substituted
leaves, and Haydn (as usual) made no major corrections or alterations. In particular,
the Presto breaks off and the farewell movement begins in the middle of a gathering,
fol. 24ʳ, with no evidence of a change of mind or compositional plan, let alone that
one of the most extraordinary symphonic finales ever composed is about to get under way.

On the other hand, almost all later sources, both musical and anecdotal, specify that
the musicians are to get up and leave the hall. (These sources are described in Chapter 4.)
Many early manuscript copies amplify Haydn's "nichts mehr" with additional indications
at the end of each individual part, most commonly "geht ab" or the equivalent. The
citation of the autograph in the 1804 catalogue of Haydn's library includes the note,
"NB: where [they] depart one after the other"; in the catalogue of his effects made
after his death, the work is described as the symphony "with a joking finale, during
which, before the end, all the instrumentalists leave the orchestra one by one, except
for two violin players."[4] And the German nickname ("Abschiedssinfonie") was widely
disseminated in anecdotes by 1800; Griesinger himself uses it more than once. Nor is
there any doubt that Haydn's audience would have understood such a symphony in
programmatic terms (see Chapters 4 and 7).

Although Haydn (as usual) dated the autograph merely with the year (1772), an
unassuming document strongly suggests that the symphony indeed originated in the
autumn. On 22 October he authorized payment to a horn-maker for the delivery of
two special half-step slides ("Halbthönige Krummbögen"). As Paul Bryan pointed out,
these devices must have been used to lengthen standard horn crooks, in order to allow the
instruments to play in keys a semitone lower than normal. In 1772 Haydn composed
two symphonies (the only two in his *oeuvre*) for which such horn parts were required:
the Farewell, whose horns would have been transposed down from G to F-sharp; and
No. 46 in B, with horns transposed from C.[5] (In the Farewell, the horns play in F-sharp

[3] See the facsimile; the last four pages are also reproduced in Somfai, *Joseph Haydn: Sein Leben in zeitgenössischen Bildern*
(Kassel, 1966), pp. 56–57. I examined the autograph (Budapest, National Széchényi Library, Music Division, Ms. mus.
I. 36), as well as those of Haydn's other symphonies from 1772, Nos. 46 and 47, in November 1985; I am most grateful
to Veronika Vavrinecz, the director of the Music Division, for her kindness and cooperation. I also thank Cliff Eisen,
who later checked certain points for me.

[4] *JHW* I/6, critical report, p. 11; Landon, *Haydn*, vol. 5, pp. 316, 398.

[5] Bryan, "Haydn's Hornists," *H-S* 3 (1973–74), 58; cf. Sonja Gerlach, "Haydns Orchesterpartituren: Fragen der
Realisierung des Textes," *H-S* 5 (1982–85), 181. For the bill itself, see Arisztid Valkó, "Haydn magyarországi
müködése a levéltári akták tükrében," second series, in Bence Szabolcsi and Dénes Bartha, eds., *Haydn-Emlékére*
(Budapest, 1960), p. 557; transl. Landon, *Haydn*, vol. 2, p. 180.

only in the minuet and trio; in the other movements they are crooked in A and E.)
Both symphonies (which are a "pair" musically and programmatically; see Chapter 8)
must have been conceived before 22 October; the Farewell must have been completed and
performed no later than November, for the court had returned to Eisenstadt by the
Prince's name-day on 6 December.[6] And it is unlikely to have originated before October;
the anecdotes after all require that it originated in the autumn, and Haydn composed
almost exclusively with tangible expectations of imminent performance or prospects
for "outside" sales. (Confirmation of the precise date of composition from close study
of musical sources is unlikely. As is usual with Haydn's instrumental music, we have
no documentation regarding its performance at the Esterházy court. Each of the three
surviving symphony autographs of 1772, Nos. 45–47, is dated only to the year; each
is written on a different paper-type and is a uniform manuscript without substantial
revisions.)

ANALYSIS AND INTERPRETATION

The Farewell Symphony is not only Haydn's most popular pre-1780 composition, it is
also the most extraordinary – even in the context of his so-called "Sturm und Drang"
period from the later 1760s through c. 1772.[7] Its unusual features are by no means
restricted to the "farewell" movement. The key of F-sharp itself was most unusual;
the Farewell is the only known eighteenth-century symphony in that key.[8] It is so highly
organized as a cycle as to justify the epithet "through-composed"; the entire symphony
prepares, and is resolved by, the apotheosis of the "farewell" ending. And it is overtly
programmatic. After 1772, the earliest work that so much as approaches it in these
respects is Beethoven's Fifth Symphony.

[6] Landon, *Haydn*, vol. 2, p. 182. Landon concludes that the work must date from late November, but his basis for rejecting October or early November is merely his inference, from the fact that the normal stay in Eszterháza lasted through
October, that in that month the Prince could not yet have formed an intention to delay his return. (Although Haydn
was absent from Eszterháza on 31 October and 16 November, this does not prove that he was gone the entire two-and-
one-half weeks; in any case, he was present on 20 November.) Haydn's having ordered the horn crooks in mid-October
(if not earlier) implies that the composition was already under way.

[7] On this much-discussed subject see Barry S. Brook, "Sturm und Drang and the Romantic Period in Music,"
Studies in Romanticism 9 (1970), 269–84; Landon, *Haydn*, vol. 2, pp. 266–84; R. Larry Todd, "Joseph Haydn and the
Sturm und Drang: A Revaluation," *MR* 41 (1980), 172–96. On the symphonies in particular, see Landon, *The Symphonies of Joseph Haydn* (London, 1955), chaps. 7–8; Carolyn Gresham, "Stylistic Features of Haydn's Symphonies from
1768 to 1772," in Jens Peter Larsen, Howard Serwer, and James Webster, eds., *Haydn Studies: Proceedings of the International Haydn Conference, Washington, D.C., 1975* (New York, 1981; hereafter cited as *Haydn Studies*), pp. 431–34.

[8] Two other "F-sharp-minor" incipits are cited in Jan LaRue's *A Catalog of 18th-Century Symphonies*, vol. 1, *Thematic
Identifier* (Bloomington, 1988); both works are actually in D. No. 14367/C573 is the overture to Cimarosa's opera buffa
L'impresario in angustie (Naples, 1786); LaRue's informant mistranscribed the incipit (Paris, Bibliothèque nationale
[formerly Conservatoire], Ac. p. 3865), which has an erroneous key-signature of three sharps. No. 14369/G998 is
Adalbert Gyrowetz's Sinfonia Concertante for two violins and viola, Op. 33; the catalogue citation is from a mystify-
ing eighteenth-century incipit (Prague, National Museum, Music division, Lobkowitz collection, X.g.c:32), which
has nothing to do with his Op. 33. (No. 14368 is the Farewell itself.) I am grateful to Cliff Eisen for providing information on the union catalogue entries for these works, and to Rebecca Harris-Warrick for checking the Cimarosa source
in Paris. Joseph Martin Kraus composed a C-sharp minor symphony in 1782 (ed. Ingmar Bentsson and Bertil H. van
Boer, Jr., in *The Symphony in Sweden*, Part I, New York, 1982; *The Symphony 1720–1840*, vol. FII). It has no "special"
features comparable to the Farewell's.

One would suppose that so unusual and popular a work from such an important period in Haydn's career would have been much analyzed; but one would be wrong. Aside from a preliminary study of my own (and Landon's useful descriptive account), only one extended analysis has been published, and that of the opening movement alone (and not until 1990);[9] about the musically and programmatically central "farewell" movement, there is nothing at all save impressionistic discussions of the program (on these, see Chapter 4). The general level of insight in the literature may be judged from the characterization, in what is still the most widely disseminated life-and-works biography of Haydn, of the farewell movement as a mere "coda" to the Presto; and the statement by one of the greatest living authorities on the eighteenth-century symphony, in the standard musicological encyclopedia, that the work ends in A major.[10]

Part I of this study is therefore devoted to a comprehensive analysis of the Farewell Symphony – "comprehensive" in three different senses. First, it is detailed, in some contexts very detailed indeed; there is no other way to do justice to Haydn's art. (Those wishing an overview of the symphony's formal and aesthetic aspects may read pp. 13–20, 30, 39–45, 56–57, 71–82, 110–12, 116–19.) Secondly, depending on the context, I pursue different musical aspects: formal analysis, Schenkerian structural-tonal voice-leading, Schoenbergian "developing variation," phrase rhythm, and the (too often neglected) domains of instrumentation and register. In the long and detailed Chapters 2 and 3, the focus therefore changes from section to section. Motivic development is especially important in the Adagio and the "farewell" movement; formal disjunction in the Allegro assai and the minuet; the relation between foreground through-composition and repeated interruptions of a single background structure in the Presto and farewell; the search for coherent melody in the Adagio, minuet, and farewell; and so forth. Only in the farewell movement itself do all these aspects become essential (this constitutes part of its role as a culmination); this discussion is necessarily the most detailed of all.

This mixed analytical method has larger implications. The belief that a complex work can be understood on the basis of a single musical parameter is reductive: it privileges one aspect at the expense of others. The more theoretically self-conscious the method, the greater its pretensions to global explanation, the more it actually excludes. The only sane course is to pursue what is now (especially in opera studies) sometimes called "multivalent" analysis: to study each principal domain (form, musical ideas, tonal structure, rhythm, instrumentation, and so forth) independently, without regard for "unity," or the degree of congruence among their temporal patterns.[11] To be sure, this procedure

[9] Judith L. Schwartz, "Periodicity and Passion in the First Movement of Haydn's 'Farewell' Symphony," in Eugene K. Wolf and Edward H. Roesner, eds., *Studies in Musical Sources and Style: Essays in Honor of Jan LaRue* (Madison: A–R Editions, 1990), pp. 293–338. Webster, "The D-Major Interlude in Haydn's 'Farewell' Symphony," ibid., pp. 339–80. See also Landon, *Haydn*, vol. 2, pp. 302–03.

[10] Karl Geiringer, *Haydn: A Creative Life in Music*, 3rd edn. (Berkeley, 1982), p. 261; "Symphony," in *The New Grove Dictionary of Music and Musicians*, ed. Stanley Sadie (London, 1980), vol. 18, p. 450.

[11] I have explored these topics in "To Understand Verdi and Wagner We Must Understand Mozart," *19CMus* 11 (1987–88), 175–93, §I; compare Carolyn Abbate's and Roger Parker's introduction to *Analyzing Opera: Verdi and Wagner* (Berkeley, 1989), pp. 1–24. An early attempt to combine Schenkerian and Schoenbergian approaches was David Epstein, *Beyond Orpheus* (Cambridge, Mass., 1979); for an exemplary analysis of an instrumental movement along multivalent lines, see Christopher Wintle, "Kontra-Schenker: *Largo e Mesto* from Beethoven's Op. 10 No. 3,"

runs the risk of mindless eclecticism. One must therefore recombine the results into a comprehensive view – but (insofar as possible) without preconceptions as to the nature of the resulting form, and without Procrustean manipulations to ensure arrival at (say) an *Ursatz* or a *Grundgestalt*.

This point leads to the third "comprehensive" aspect of my analysis: I deal with the Farewell Symphony as a *through-composed* work. (This is another, indirect virtue of multivalent analysis. The more one thinks of the several domains within a movement independently, such that one's later "vertical" relation of them becomes a conscious analytical decision, the more one begins to ponder the temporal relations between different movements as well.) In the Farewell, many prominent features – musical ideas, tonal relations, destabilizing pitches and gestures, discontinuities of texture and topic, and so forth – develop throughout the work. Each movement, each aspect of a given movement (sonata form in the Allegro assai, tonal structure in the minuet and trio, motivic content in the "farewell"), demands to be understood in terms of its function in the entire symphony. Hence I frequently indicate the implications of an event for later ones, or its sources in earlier ones. This is another reason for the analytical density: Haydn articulates his trajectory towards resolution not merely through large-scale processes, but also through the cumulative effect of details. (One currently fashionable topic which I cannot pursue is the "compositional process." To be sure, Haydn often (perhaps always) made one or more drafts before writing the autograph fair copy, and those that survive do offer insight into his methods.[12] But as noted above, there are no corrections in the Farewell autograph except the occasional small detail; no sketches or drafts survive. I confess that I do not find this a limitation. The Farewell Symphony is a virtually inexhaustible masterpiece, the close study of which is a legitimate subject in its own right and needs no special justification.)

The Farewell Symphony also engages us because of its extramusical aspect: it demands not merely to be analyzed, but to be interpreted. (Of course, all analysis implicitly entails interpretation. My conviction that the Farewell Symphony is an appropriate subject for an entire book, my insistence on its through-composed character, reflect critical judgments as well as analytical results.) Throughout Chapters 1–3 I select musical features, and ways of describing them (including the occasional stimulus from recent literary theory), which are relevant to my reading of the program in Chapter 4. Admittedly, I do not conflate these approaches; notwithstanding the mutual dependence of analysis and criticism, it seems methodologically sounder to segregate those discussions which relate directly to observable musical events from those which are primarily interpretative. Nevertheless, I attempt to ground my hermeneutics in technical detail (see especially the final section of Chapter 3, "An apotheosis of ethereality," which

MusA 4 (1985), 145–82. On the historical contingency of the ideal of unity, see Carl Dahlhaus, "Some Models of Unity in Musical Form," *JMT* 19 (1975), 2–30.

12 Feder, "Bemerkungen zu Haydns Skizzen," *Beethoven-Jahrbuch*, 9 (1973–77), 69–86; Hollace Ann Schafer, "'A Wisely Ordered *Phantasie*': Joseph Haydn's Creative Process from the Sketches and Drafts for Instrumental Music," Ph.D. diss., Brandeis University 1987.

also serves as a transition to Chapter 4). For the program is there, and derives from Haydn himself; no analysis can afford to ignore it.

This issue has been much discussed of late. Many voices, of which Joseph Kerman's has perhaps been the loudest, are now raised in opposition to what is said to be the excessively narrow, "formalistic," "positivistic" character of most postwar analysis.[13] To be sure, all analysis entails interpretation (see above) – and not least by the style of presentation, the nature of the analytical "story" and the way it is told. (Every analysis, even a non-verbal one such as a Schenker graph or a table of motives, "tells a story," as surely as any narrative of Tovey's.[14]) As has recently become increasingly clear, eighteenth-century instrumental music was expressive – or, better, "rhetorical" – through and through: not only did it incorporate traditional "topical" associations, but musical form itself was understood on the basis of analogies with grammatical and oratorical rhetoric (see Chapter 5). Nor would any sensible person object in principle to interpretation (a preferable term to "criticism," which has too much the air of deciding between winners and losers) or even to hermeneutic readings. But the votaries of "criticism" protest too much, and in two senses. They fail to appreciate the overtly interpretative orientation of all the best analysts, notably including Schenker and what we may call the orthodox Schenkerian tradition.[15] Secondly, if all analysis is implicitly interpretative, so does every interpretation depend on analysis (even though this may remain unconscious). Hence even interpretative analyses should be carried out as rigorously as possible, and without preconceptions as to the result. Best of all would be to abandon the dichotomy (and the polemics) and to acknowledge analysis and interpretation – historical as well as hermeneutic – as ineluctably joined, as inseparable aspects of the understanding of artworks. The present volume is intended, in part, as a demonstration of this thesis.

THROUGH-COMPOSITION IN HAYDN'S MUSIC

No composition, not even the most unusual, exists in a vacuum. A comprehensive study of the Farewell Symphony leads directly to fundamental problems of both analysis and theory, and the historiography of eighteenth-century music. But this relationship is dialectical. The Farewell does not merely exemplify these larger issues, it virtually *creates* them – for, until now, they have gone largely unrecognized in Haydn studies. The significance of the artwork is grounded not only in its aesthetic qualities (however

---

[13] Kerman, "How We Got into Analysis, and How to Get Out," *Critical Inquiry* 7 (1980–81), 311–31; compare his *Contemplating Music* (Cambridge, Mass., 1985), chap. 3 *et passim*.

[14] Christopher Lewis, "Mirrors and Metaphors: Reflections on Schoenberg and Nineteenth-Century Tonality," *19CMus* 11 (1987–88), 26–42; V. Kofi Agawu, "Schenkerian Notation in Theory and Practice," *MusA* 8 (1989), 275–301; Fred Everett Maus, "Humanism and Musical Experience," Ph.D. diss., Princeton University, 1990, chap. 3, "Music as Narrative."

[15] A *Blumenlese*: Schenker's analyses of Schubert's "Ihr Bild," *Der Tonwille*, No. 1 (1922), pp. 46–49, and of Haydn's "Chaos" from *The Creation*, *Das Meisterwerk in der Musik*, 2 (1926), 159–70; Oswald Jonas, "The Relation of Word and Tone," in *Introduction to the Theory of Heinrich Schenker* (New York, 1982), pp. 149–61; Ernst Oster, "The Dramatic Character of the *Egmont Overture*," in David Beach, ed., *Aspects of Schenkerian Theory* (New Haven, 1983), pp. 209–22; Carl Schachter, "Motive and Text in Four Schubert Songs," ibid., pp. 61–76.

sterling) but in its ability, through alterations of our consciousness, to change our sense of the context of which it was a part, that which we call music history.[16]

Regarding analysis and theory: as stated above, nobody has attempted to account for the Farewell Symphony as a whole, in either technical or hermeneutic terms. Perhaps this lack of attention reflects the fatal influence of the program: it has doubtless "marginalized" the work for twentieth-century analysts, who, by and large, have restricted themselves to a relatively narrow repertory of works, thought to qualify as (or treated as) "absolute music." (In this respect, Kerman's strictures have been accurate and timely.) Be that as it may, the astonishing fact is that no multimovement work of Haydn's has ever been the subject of a comprehensive analysis on a monographic scale. The closest approach is Schenker's analysis of Sonata No. 52 in E-flat, to which should be compared Tovey's equally insightful essay on the same work.[17] Every other study of which I am aware is restricted to a single movement, a single analytical method, or both.

I insist on this point because the chief novelty of my analysis is its demonstration of the Farewell's cyclic integration. This phenomenon has not been much studied with respect to eighteenth-century instrumental music – not because it does not exist, but because the analytical attitudes and traditions required to see it have developed chiefly with respect to nineteenth- and twentieth-century music. The few studies of this sort devoted to Haydn concentrate on single musical aspects: most commonly motivic continuity, less often tonal organization, and hardly ever rhetorical or "narrative" content. Those who write about "weight" and "balance" among the several movements usually limit their remarks on thematic continuity to elementary similarities among headmotives; none attempts to reveal deeper tonal processes. Devotees of "motivic unity" betray little concern for formal or psychological coherence, let alone structural voice-leading. On the other hand, the Schenkerian tradition has virtually ignored the issue of multimovement relationships.

A symptom of this neglect is that we do not have a generally accepted term to denote the kind of multimovement coherence that characterizes the Farewell. In general usage, a "through-composed" work is one based on run-on movements without internal repetitions. (The distinction is especially characteristic of the literature on the art-song, where such works are contrasted with strophic settings.) But the Farewell has internal repetitions aplenty, and only the two finales are run-on. Although the term "cycle" is used in some contexts to denote a multimovement work, the term "cyclic" most often refers to the use of recurring themes (often in transformation) in different movements; nothing of this kind is at work here (or in later eighteenth-century music generally). (A phrase like "totally organized" would claim too much, and has too many associations with serial music.) I therefore use both terms mentioned above, in general with the following connotations: "through-composed" for dynamic or gestural phenomena (run-on movements, recalls, unresolved instabilities, lack of closure, and so forth); "cyclic integration" or "organization" for aspects of musical construction and technique (com-

[16] Dahlhaus, *Foundations of Music History* (Cambridge, 1983), chaps. 1–3, 7.
[17] Schenker, "Haydn: Sonata Es-Dur," *Der Tonwille*, No. 3 (1922), pp. 3–21; Tovey, *Essays in Musical Analysis: Chamber Music* (London, 1944), pp. 93–105.

monalities of material, tonal relations, and the like). But in Haydn these domains cannot be meaningfully dissociated, and the reader must not expect total consistency of usage.

Part II of this study explores the nature and extent of Haydn's integration of instrumental cycles. It is organized around three main topics (each of which could be the subject of an independent volume). In Chapter 5, I explore his "progressive" (nonsymmetrical) musical form in individual movements. Instability, continual development, freely recomposed recapitulations – not to mention wit, surprise, irony, and the rest – are central aspects of his art, in all contexts (not merely in through-composed works). Although they are found in all periods of his career, they undergo a quantum leap in frequency and importance beginning in the late 1760s (that is, with the "Sturm und Drang"). They must however be understood in terms of the dominant formal and psychological conceptions of music in Haydn's time; these can be subsumed under the category of *rhetoric*. Its importance has been underrated, both because the notion of "Classical style" is biased in favor of the opposite virtues (balance, symmetry, recapitulation, "architectonic form," and so forth), and because of the theoretical bias in favor of "absolute music." All this is directly relevant to through-composition: many of Haydn's destabilizing techniques, his methods of maintaining a forward drive throughout a movement, are in principle the same as those which relate separate movements to each other.

Chapter 6 focuses on Haydn's techniques of cyclic integration. One of these is to manipulate the conventions of genre: to include more movements than usual; to use an incongruous type of movement in a given context; to break the larger continuity for a change of topic or a thematic recall. Another, familiar in nineteenth-century works, is to articulate the finale as a culmination (not merely an ending). Two or more movements can of course be run-on; in many cases (not all), this creates a through-compositional effect. More familiar as organizing techniques (albeit described primarily with respect to nineteenth- and twentieth-century music) are commonalities in musical material and tonal organization. Haydn's particular brand of thematicism resembles that described by Schoenberg under the term "developing variation"; it is a pervasive aspect of his style, from the very earliest years to the end of his life. He used tonality to integrate the cycle in two primary ways: by articulating an overall progression (for example, from minor to major), and by repeated juxtapositions of remote keys and sonorities. Again, he first systematically explored these techniques towards 1770, primarily in works in the minor mode; he integrated remote-key juxtapositions into the major only towards the end of his life. (This distinction calls into question the common notion that Haydn's tendency to end minor-mode movements in the major is mere "cheerfulness.") The relation of these integrative techniques to more general aspects of his style is broader, and their psychological import deeper, than has been recognized.

In Chapter 7, we turn to a different, but no less effective, method of organizing the cycle: extramusical associations. Haydn's aesthetics, like those of his contemporaries, were oriented around vocal music. His instrumental works having such associations refer to the times of day and the seasons, religious observance, theatrical and incidental music, "exotic" cultures, and "characteristic" topics like the pastoral and the *chasse*. These associations are impressive for their seriousness and their cultural importance; they document yet another aspect of Haydn's rhetoric – his moral earnestness. (To be sure, this trait is not incompatible with his vaunted humor; but because of the latter's notoriety, it has been undervalued.) Furthermore, the majority of his "integrative" innovations on the technical level originated in the 1760s and 1770s, specifically in symphonies with extramusical associations. In the 1780s and 1790s, although the incidence of overtly programmatic works declines, his rhetorical impulse was transformed into what has been called "moral enlightenment": the symphony became a vehicle for the sublime.

Chapter 8, finally, brings these themes together – and returns to the study of individual compositions – by analyzing a dozen works which exemplify Haydn's integration of the cycle, drawn from all periods of his life and all the main instrumental genres. Their goals and methods vary tremendously: early symphonies that manipulate the conventional movement patterns while exhibiting ongoing thematic continuity; a sonata that is run-on from beginning to end; through-composed string quartets with culmination-finales; a symphony that rivals the Farewell in using all available methods of relating the movements, and in so doing recreates its own musical past; tonal organization and the rhetoric of the sublime. As a result, and in conformity to my preference for mixed, non-reductive methods, the analytical approaches in this chapter are varied as well. Finally, a number of these works entail extramusical associations; they will provide ample opportunity to explore further the dialectic of analysis and interpretation in understanding Haydn's music. The variety, the chronological and generic distribution, and the quality of these compositions confirm the thesis that cyclic integration was central to Haydn's art.

HAYDN AND "CLASSICAL STYLE"

The Farewell Symphony, composed in 1772, is through-composed, exhibits the most consummate level of compositional skill, and places its techniques and mastery in the service of a musical program. Furthermore, despite its radicalism it is not isolated; its techniques are common in Haydn's *oeuvre*, and a number of other works approach it in their degree of cyclic organization. These insights suggest that we need to revise our views of Haydn's development as a composer, his historical role, and his relation to "Classical style."

The concept "Classical style" (I must use quotation-marks) is an anachronism. Haydn was understood in his own time as *modern*, a bold pioneer; his progressive form and destabilizing rhetoric are incompatible with the shibboleths of balance, symmetry, architectonic form, and the rest. He and Mozart were not thought of as "classics" until early in the nineteenth century; not until 1900 did Adolf Sandberger, Guido Adler, and Wilhelm Fischer promulgate the concept "Classical style" in its full conceptual and ideological meaning. Technically, it was held to depend on *thematische Arbeit* (as a synthesis of harmony and counterpoint) and periodic phrasing (as a flexible successor to Baroque *Fortspinnung*). But, in a remarkable conflation, Haydn's personal development was described in the same terms; he was said to have first mastered these techniques in the string quartets Op. 33 (1781). With this conjunction, the die was cast: just as the ideology of "Classical style" denigrates all earlier instrumental music as limited (in various ways), so all of Haydn's music from before 1780 (or in some cases before 1770) has been typed as "immature" and "experimental." Such attitudes relegate the composer of the Farewell Symphony – forty years old, in his twelfth year as Esterházy Kapellmeister, with hundreds of successful works to his credit – to a "pre-Classical" ghetto, when they do not do worse by trivializing it as the work of that good-natured jokester, "Papa Haydn."[18]

That this is no idle concern emerges clearly from Charles Rosen's otherwise brilliant discussions of Haydn in *The Classical Style* (New York, 1971). Rosen criticizes the music from before 1780 (including the Farewell) so harshly as to suggest that some "ideological" animus has skewed his judgement. Indeed, his arguments match those adduced by Adler, Fischer, and the other turn-of-the-century inventors of "Classical style," and which are also found throughout the professional Haydn literature. Hence my concluding chapter examines the language and ideology of this traditional concept of "Classical style." This proves to be simplistically and teleologically *evolutionist* in its assumption of inevitable progress towards a historical synthesis; the traditional views of Haydn's early "immaturity" and "experimentation" reflect the same evolutionism, and are equally untenable. Appealing to the results of this study, I will argue that all of Haydn's music, including that from his earliest years, is masterly, and completely adequate to its purposes both generically and aesthetically.

The results of this study also have important implications for our understanding of Haydn's relations to later music. His through-composed works call into question the notion that coherent multimovement instrumental cycles were unknown before Beethoven, as well as the related notions that programmatic music and "ethical" concerns among composers were not important in the later eighteenth century. I therefore conclude by comparing recent pronouncements on these matters in the Beethoven literature with the image of Haydn's music developed here. Beethoven's understanding of through-composition and, more generally, his combination of freely developing rhetoric with the highest compositional technique – all this he learned from Haydn. The most telling single example of these relationships is the Farewell Symphony.

---

[18] On Haydn's personality, and the function of such myths in misunderstandings of his style, see Feder, "Joseph Haydn als Mensch und Musiker," in Gerda Mraz, ed., *Joseph Haydn und seine Zeit* (Jahrbuch für österreichische Kulturgeschichte, 2), pp. 43–56; Webster, "Prospects for Haydn Biography After Landon," *MQ* 68 (1982), 490, 493–95; W. Dean Sutcliffe, "Haydn's Musical Personality," *The Musical Times* 130 (1989), 341–44.

PART I

THE FAREWELL SYMPHONY

1

THE CONSTRUCTION OF THE WHOLE

A THROUGH-COMPOSED SYMPHONY

The Farewell Symphony is arguably Haydn's most extraordinary composition. It is his only symphony in five real movements – Allegro assai, Adagio, minuet and trio, Presto, and the "farewell" movement itself. The last two movements constitute a through-composed *double finale*, unique in Haydn's symphonies; the concluding movement is not only an adagio, but ends in a different key from that in which it begins. (The term "double finale" is explicated below; Haydn's other symphonies which alter the usual cyclic patterns are described in Chapters 6–8.) The symphony also has an unusual and complex tonal scheme, involving three different structural tonics, F-sharp minor, A major, and F-sharp major; the double finale alone incorporates all three. A contemporary listener could have inferred the existence of an extramusical basis for the work directly from these disruptions of normal generic expectations – as easily as for Haydn's Symphony No. 60, "Il distratto," in six eccentric movements; or Beethoven's "Pastoral" Symphony in five, the last three run-on.

The Presto and the farewell movement constitute a run-on movement pair; that is, two contiguous movements, each of which articulates a complete formal design, except that the first breaks off towards the end or closes on the dominant, the second following *attacca*. The Presto is in sonata form (except for breaking off at the last moment); the farewell movement, despite beginning and ending in different keys, executes a complete form as well. (Neither movement is a mere introduction, coda, or "frame"; if either were, we would speak instead of a compound [single] movement.) On the other hand, the Presto does not attain closure; a single background structure (in the Schenkerian sense), several times interrupted, governs the entire complex. Hence the overall cyclic pattern is ambiguous. The length, independence, and formal elaboration of the two concluding movements, the profound contrast between them, and the programmatic associations of the farewell imply that the symphony is in five movements, with two finales; first, a conventional type, which however is not in last position; then an unconventional one, which concludes the work. The resulting form could be diagramed as follows:

F	S	M	Fn$_1$	Fn$_2$
i	III	I	i	III–I

13

On the other hand, the fact of its being a symphony, the evaded closure of the Presto, the single *Ursatz* and tonic governing both finales, the tonal mobility of the farewell movement, and the fact that, if independent, it would have to be construed as a "second slow movement" or a "second finale" – all this implies a four-movement pattern, with a single (compound) finale:

F	S	M	Fn$_1$–Fn$_2$
i	III	I	i———I

(The ambiguity is even reflected in published scores. Landon begins counting measure-numbers over again at the beginning of the farewell movement, whereas JHW continues a single numbering for both movements. Haydn's autograph gives only a single barline and fermata at the end of the Presto and continues to the farewell movement without a turn of page; this could be thought to support the latter interpretation.) In order to account for this duality of generic function, but without privileging either possibility, I use the term "double finale" to refer to the Presto and farewell movement when dealing with them as a unit. (The aspects of cyclic patterning adumbrated in this paragraph are discussed in Chapter 6.)

Beyond this, however, the symphony is essentially through-composed (in the sense described in the Introduction). From beginning to end, it "composes out" a single idea: to project the unusual and "difficult" key of F-sharp minor as something inherently unstable, which demands, and receives, resolution by the tonic major. The major does not arrive as a sudden, overwhelming revelation, like "And There Was Light" in *The Creation*, or as a cheerful reversion to second-group material originally presented in the relative major, as in many late Haydn sonata-form movements. Rather, it is the result of a *process* – gradual, complex, and yet systematic – from instability to stability, from closure denied to closure achieved. This process involves every aspect of the music: large-scale ideas, "developing variation," tonality, structural voice-leading, cadential dis-position, rhythm, form, instrumentation, dynamics – as well as gesture, rhetoric, aesthetic qualities, and psychological content. Indeed, it continues throughout the double finale; musical closure and aesthetic resolution alike are withheld until the final "farewell" section in F-sharp major. The Farewell Symphony is inherently dynamic.

The farewell movement articulates another "progressive" principle, that of a systematic decrease in instrumentation and volume of sound. The little "farewell" solos (described in the first section of Chapter 3) occur in a consistent order: first the winds (one oboe and one horn, on each of two occasions), then the strings, from lowest to highest. The special character of the farewell ending derives in large measure from this unusual correlation of strong formal and tonal resolution with an almost insubstantial texture – a "negative climax" at the end of the work.

It seems likely that Haydn intended not only the final section (mm. 86–107) to be performed by soloists (as seems essential on both practical and poetic grounds) but the preceding section (mm. 68–85) as well. The autograph names the four violin parts "Violino 1mo/Violino 2do/Violino 3^{zo}/Violino 4to"; it makes no distinction between

solo parts and ordinary ones. (In Haydn's very small ensemble, such a distinction
would in any case have been less consequential than we tend to assume.[1]) The penultimate
section is scored for the third and fourth violins (the first and second pausing and
putting on their mutes), accompanied at first by viola and cello, then by viola
alone. These accompanimental parts must surely have been performed by soloists, on
two grounds: the Esterházy ensemble at this time included only one cellist and
(most often) one violist; and both parts here make their "farewells" – a procedure which
makes sense only if each is a soloist. This already implies a soloistic ensemble; choral
performance of two melodic parts over a one-on-a-part bass would make little sense.
Furthermore, given the normal maximum of eight violinists and violists together,
there would not have been sufficient players for two on each of four violin parts, plus
the viola. (Admittedly, there could have been a total of six violinsts: two principals,
and two ripienists on each of the third and fourth parts.) Finally, the aesthetically decisive
entry of soloistic music makes the most sense if correlated with the wonderful, long-
delayed arrival of the tonic major. (Until this point, the first and third and the second
and fourth violin parts double each other, producing the usual two parts *de facto*.)
The "negative climax" at the end will remain well articulated by the use of mutes, the
departure of the viola, and the higher register.

Example 1.1 Farewell Symphony: overview

This progression from instability to resolution is carried out by means of an unusual
double cycle, which involves the tonal plan, dynamics, rhythmic activity, instrumentation,
and register. (See Example 1.1, an overview of the entire work.) The most obvious
parallelism between the two cycles involves an ordered sequence of three keys: F-sharp
minor, A major, and F-sharp major. In the first cycle, this sequence comprises the Allegro
assai (F-sharp minor), the Adagio (A major), and the minuet (F-sharp major); in the
second, the Presto (F-sharp minor) and the two parts of the farewell movement, which
begins in A and ends in F-sharp major. In addition, each cycle incorporates an extended

---

[1] My remarks on Haydn's ensemble are drawn from Gerlach, "Haydns Orchestermusiker von 1761 bis 1774,"
   H-S 4 (1976–80), 45, 47, and "Haydns Orchesterpartituren," *H-S* 5 (1982–85), 170, 176 and n. 32.

diminuendo from loud to very soft, and from a fast, agitated style to a slower, calmer one. Both movements in F-sharp major feature reduced or omitted bass. The minuet begins and ends with violins alone; its concluding tag is structurally identical to the violin afterbeats following the final "farewell" cadence (see Example 1.2). Both concluding gestures are *pianissimo*, occupy two bars in triple meter preceded by an upbeat, and both begin on c#², skip immediately to a#¹, and close with a# in the bass, projecting the

Example 1.2

(a) End of minuet

(b) End of symphony

tonic triad in first inversion rather than root position. Hence the "farewell" aesthetic itself is prepared, over the course of the symphony, by this double large-scale diminuendo.

At the same time, the articulation of this progression in two cycles, rather than just one, reflects the overall progression from instability to stability. In the first three movements, the forces of tonal and rhythmic coherence seem almost to break down; no other movement by Haydn (I would guess no other eighteenth-century symphony movement) exhibits the savagery of the Allegro assai; the wistful ambiguities of mode and form in the minuet and trio cannot be reconciled. All three movements are tonally unstable and have inadequate closure. An inexplicable, disruptive event in the Allegro assai is the extended and apparently isolated *piano* interlude in D major (mm. 108ff) which constitutes the entire second half of the development; it, too, reveals its true significance only at the very end of the symphony.[2] The double finale necessarily moves in the direction of clarity and resolution, in material, tonality, form, lack of disjunction, indeed in every respect (see the beginning of Chapter 3). Despite the parallelism, the end of the symphony is "more so" – that is, less – than the end of the minuet; two solo violins, muted, unaccompanied, for fifteen Adagio measures. As a "negative climax," it has never been surpassed.

[2] The discussions of the D-major interlude in this volume summarize my detailed treatment in the article cited in the Introduction, n. 9.

MAJOR/MINOR EQUIVALENCE AND
REMOTE THIRD-RELATIONS

Any true conflation of the major and minor forms of the tonic is inherently chromatic and will alter the tonal language of any work of which it is a basis. (I leave *tierces de picardie* and all merely "cheerful" major-mode endings of minor-mode works out of account.) It implies major/minor mixtures, and by extension foreground chromatic relations of all types; the repertory of normally related keys (those bearing a diatonic relation to either tonic) will include many that are remote from each other. The Farewell Symphony consistenly exploits both modes. Major/minor juxtapositions and distantly related sonorities dominate on the structural level (see again Example 1.1). The first and most prominent movement is in the minor, as is the other fast movement; on the other hand, the symphony not only ends in the major, with the minuet and trio in that key as well, but as a whole is far more heavily weighted towards the major than any other Haydn minor-mode work before 1780, except the somewhat mysterious Symphony No. 34 in D minor (and major).[3] The use of two different major keys, each as the governing tonic of two separate movements (counting the farewell movement as bipartite), is unprecedented. The structural keys (those used for form-defining cadences and prominent appearances of the main themes) range from A minor to C-sharp major, a total of seven steps on the circle of fifths; more distant sonorities are touched on in passing.

Within this expanded tonality, A major plays a complex mediating role. It is of course the relative major of F-sharp minor; but it also indirectly relates to F-sharp major, insofar as both are major keys and provide relief from the minor. The farewell movement itself begins in A and ends in F-sharp. In addition, when F-sharp minor and major govern complete movements or sections, A major always stands between them – as if to prevent them from colliding head-on. (When they do make direct contact, in the minuet and trio, the consequences are unsettling indeed.) The key of A also shares with both forms of F-sharp the pitch class C♯, which provides melodic continuity throughout the symphony; this is indicated schematically (and without Schenkerian implications) in Example 1.1.

Except at the beginning of the second movement, whenever A major is a governing tonic, it is *indirectly* related to the preceding and following chord or key. Haydn always emphasizes the common-tone function of C♯ at the joins in question. The end of the Adagio is only distantly related to the minuet in F-sharp major; the implied progression (Example 1.1) involves the chromatic move from A to A♯ in the upper parts, and root motion down a third from A to F♯. In the foreground (see Example 1.3), c♯[2] is the last melody note of the Adagio (first oboe and first horn, doubled below by the violins) and the first note of the minuet, emphasized by entering unaccompanied. Furthermore, the critical new pitch class A♯ enters as the sole accompanimental pitch on the next

---

[3] Bernhard Rywosch, *Beiträge zur Entwicklung in Joseph Haydns Symphonik 1759–1780* (Turbenthal, 1934), pp. 94–95; Landon, *Symphonies*, pp. 338–39. On Haydn's use of the minor mode generally, see the last section of Chapter 6.

Example 1.3 End of Adagio–Beginning of minuet

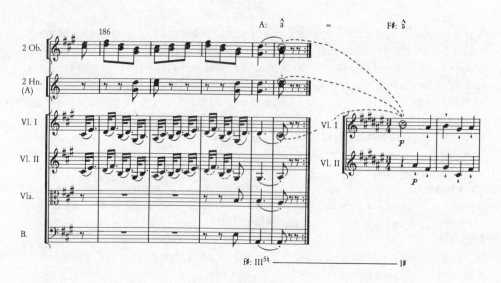

beat; the melody then skips directly to it as well. In the farewell movement, the remote key relation A–F-sharp is further mediated by the sonority of C-sharp major, which prepares both its parts. It is in fact as surprising to hear the familiar A major at its beginning as the remote tonic major at the end, not merely because it introduces an unexpected and drastic change of subject, but owing to its remote preparation (see Example 1.4): from the point of view of A, a half-cadence on III# (V/vi). (We will examine Haydn's general use of remote progressions within and between movements in Chapters 5 and 6.) In this movement, A major thus relates to two different remote sonorities, each a third away: C-sharp major and F-sharp major. The addition of C-sharp entails another chromatic move, E to E#; see Example 1.1.

Major/minor confrontations, modulations by thirds, and remote key relations are common in the foreground as well. Many peculiar features of the Allegro assai in particular make sense only in this context. In the second group of the exposition, two different keys appear: first A major (and minor) and then C-sharp minor (see again Example 1.1). In all Haydn's symphonies, string quartets, piano trios, and keyboard sonatas, this is the only opening movement or finale in the minor whose exposition goal is the dominant minor (rather than the relative major). (Occasionally, a complete second group in the relative, with closure, is followed by a retransition via the dominant major chord, as in both outer movements of Symphony No. 44 in E minor; this is quite different.) What is more, this use of *two* keys, constituting what I have elsewhere called a "double second group,"[4] is found nowhere else in Haydn and, so far as I know, in on Austrian sonata-form movement before Beethoven. (It is found in minuets; but that is another

---

[4] "Schubert's Sonata Form and Brahms's First Maturity," *19CMus* 2 (1978–79), 18–35; 3 (1979–80), 52–71.

Example 1.4 End of Presto–Beginning of Farewell movement

story.) To be sure, both III and v are normal key relations; the three keys of the exposition are generated straightforwardly by arpeggiation of the tonic triad. But in addition to its effect of instability, this procedure has a structural point: the two roots involved, A and C♯ (III and V), are precisely those which, in conjunction with the tonic, govern the entire symphony. Thus A holds sway at the beginning of the development with a complete statement of the main theme, and C♯ returns prominently in the recapitulation; the development of the Adagio, unusually, establishes two "main" keys rather than just one, namely F-sharp minor and C-sharp minor; and the Presto, after the customary A major in the second group, places virtually the entire development in the dominant minor (again very unusual). And, as already explained, the entire double finale is governed by these three roots.

Even the D-major interlude conforms to the rest of the symphony in this respect (see Example 1.5). It is preceded by the dominant of B minor (mm. 106–07) and a G.P.; the quiet theme enters immediately in D, without transition or dominant preparation. This is a close aesthetic counterpart of the join between the end of the Presto and the beginning of the farewell (Example 1.4): a tumultuous *forte* passage which breaks off on an unresolved dominant, followed by a drastic and unexpected change of topic, a completely new, *piano* theme. The two joins are tonally related as well. Both entail a remote juxtaposition with root motion by downward third and chromatic substitution (here A for A♯). The two keys thus prepared are themselves closely related: D and A, submediant and mediant.

Even more important, that unresolved dominant preceding the interlude is the chord of F-sharp major – the first appearance of this crucial sonority in the symphony, precisely halfway through the development (thirty-five bars out of sixty-nine; indeed, not counting repeats, almost exactly halfway through the movement [107 out of 209]). Moreover, the end of the interlude (Example 1.5b) moves directly back to F-sharp minor, again without any intervening root-position dominant (merely vii⁶); D major thus functions as a third-related "embellishing chord" to both tonic chords, major and minor. Hence the tonic major remains unresolved – which is to say, it is brought into a close, but of course merely "potential," tonal relation with F-sharp *minor* at the reprise. There is also a gestural link with the very end of the movement (see Example 1.5c): except for their mode, the three "conventional" offbeat chords (motive *c1*) that end both halves (so defined) are effectively identical. Within the Allegro assai, the D-major interlude thus mediates the "difficult" relation between tonic minor and major, and it does so precisely when this "problem" – the point of the whole work – is adumbrated for the first time. As we will see, it does much more besides.

DEVELOPING VARIATION

The progressive character of the Farewell Symphony also depends on the thematic content; the fate of the chief motives is in fact one of the primary sources of its coherence. Haydn's technique is that known – in studies of nineteenth- and twentieth-century music – as "developing variation." (This term and the concepts associated with

Example 1.5 Allegro assai, D-major interlude:

(a) Beginning

Ex. 1.5 (*cont.*)

(b) End

Ex. 1.5 (*cont.*)

(c) End of movement

(d) Beginning: structural voice-leading

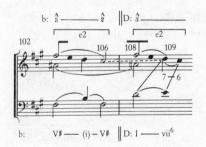

it are problematical. I postpone discussion of this issue to Chapter 6, in the section "Thematicism," and proceed for now on a heuristic basis.) In every Haydn movement, the material develops constantly. What is more, any given motivic type, once established, can develop not only within its "own" domain but in interaction with others, in the middleground as well as the foreground, subliminally as well as overtly. That which develops includes not only patterns of pitch and rhythm, but "abstract" parameters such as types of musical motion (for example, step vs. skip), rhythmic profile (for example, onbeat vs. offbeat), and the effects of destabilizing pitches; and it takes place on any and all structural levels. The intermingling of all these elements not only ensures variety, but is potentially form-defining as well.

In the Farewell, this multi-domain process is sustained throughout all five movements. Three complexes of motives carry the action: *triadic* figures (labeled *a1*, *a2*, and so on in all examples); *descending stepwise* progressions (*e*); and *repetitions* (*c*), primarily *offbeat* figures. (A conspectus of this material is given in Example 1.6; it should be studied in conjunction with the detailed analyses in Chapters 2 and 3 and the qualifying remarks on thematicism in Chapter 6.) The reader may well wonder how such "little" motives, at once common and unspecific, can govern an entire symphony. In the first place, the Farewell is notable for its absence of coherent stepwise melody; under such circumstances, rhetorical continuity necessarily devolves onto the motivic level. Moreover, each of these motive-types stands for a basic form of musical motion – *a* = arpeggiation; *e* = linear melody; *c* = rhythmic activity – and these elements, as suggested above, become primary bearers of significant content. (At the same time, one should not push such resemblances too far; the limits are suggested on pp. 203–04, in the final paragraphs of the section "Thematicism.")

Without unduly compromising the analyses to follow, I indicate here a few salient aspects of the symphony's motivic development. In the Allegro assai, the nearly total absence of linear melody is striking. In the exposition, the only motivically significant stepwise progressions come in the second group: the two-bar dissonance–resolution pairs in the bass (*e*, mm. 44ff), the answering four-bar descent in the violins (*e2*), and the bass theme following a deceptive cadence (m. 56). Both inherently (m. 56, for example, derives directly from the stormy *a* headmotive[5]) and owing to the violent context, these attempts at melody are doomed to fail. The D-major interlude, to be sure, is largely governed by *c* and *e* motives from the exposition; but it is aesthetically so divorced from the context that the effect is merely that of another failure, even more devastatingly ineffectual. The Adagio is ambiguous: it is difficult to "breathe" the two-note motive *a5* across the middle of each bar, but the stepwise *e3* at first does not attract attention; it remains "latent." Its potential emerges only at the clinching structural cadence of the second group (mm. 69–71), a change prepared during the long second group, which is dominated by stepwise *e* material. The "tag" ending of each half of the minuet, for violins alone, also derives from the main theme of the Allegro assai. Furthermore, it relates to the Adagio; to note only the most obvious similarity, the two-bar opening phrase on *a5*, with offbeat bass, is similar to mm. 1–2 of the Adagio (and identical to a variant at the beginning of the second group, mm. 29–30).

---

[5] Rywosch, p. 94, notes this derivation from *a*, as well as that in the minuet, mm. 11–12.

Example 1.6 Principal motive-complexes

	a (triadic)	a c (repeated; offbeat)	e (stepwise)
		X	
Headmotive			
Main-theme cadence	X	X	
Transition		X	
Second group	(X)	X	X
Second group	X		X
Second group (following deceptive cadence)	X		(X)

Ex. 1.6 (cont.)

Ex. 1.6 (*cont.*)

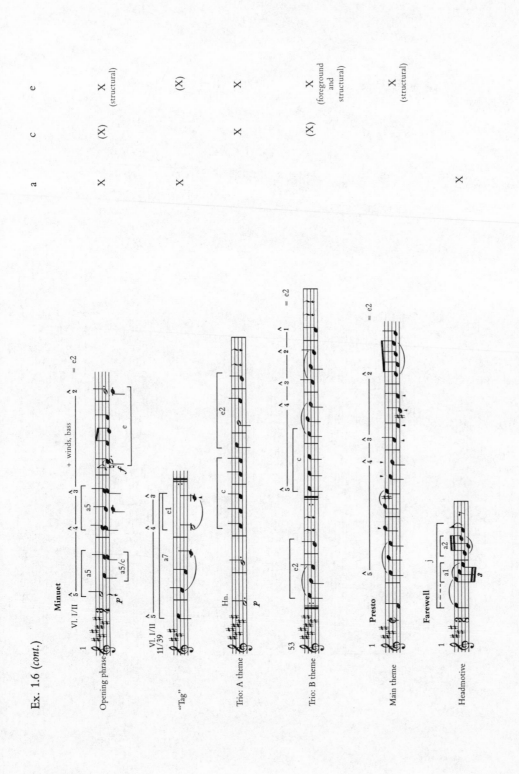

Ex. 1.6 (*cont.*)

In the farewell movement, motives from the first three movements assume new guises appropriate to the changed context and the progress towards resolution. The headmotive sounds new, but its first two bars are a compressed variant of the triadic motives of the main theme of the Allegro assai: straightforwardly descending $a1$, then complex $a2$; that is, $a1$–$a2$=theme–cadence. The answering cadential phrase becomes fabulously intricate, as do various later ideas derived from it; at the same time, however, it incorporates a clear middleground $e2$ descent from $\hat{5}$ to $\hat{2}$, of a type already familiar from the opening themes of the minuet, trio, and Presto (indicated in Example 1.6). The motivic synthesis in mm. 8–10 (which will require an entire paragraph to describe) takes on added significance from its association with the very strong half cadence, the first such form-defining event in the movement. Much of the remainder of the farewell movement further develops these conjoined motives.

The final F-sharp section, by contrast, "liquidates" this material into basic musical figures, representative of fundamental processes. The destabilizing bass c motives disappear. The triadic a motives increasingly dominate in the foreground, with increasing internal consistency: $a8$ in mm. 90 and 92; $a1$ in 94, 96, 97; $a2$ in 101–02. The two structural cadences of the section concentrate, in turn, on each of these primary triadic motives – motives which originated in the opening theme of the Allegro assai. Motive $a1$ (m. 94) descends to the deceptive cadence in 95; $a2$ creates the final structural cadence in 102–03. The basic pattern thus recurs at the crux of the entire symphony: $a1$ comes first, but $a2$ takes over at the cadence. What is more, these a cadences create coherent stepwise $e2$s, which repeatedly cadence on the tonic, in the background as well as the middleground (every earlier descent of this type stops on $\hat{2}$). At the end of the Farewell Symphony, the triadic motives become transformed into pure melody – one of the most important of the many respects in which this music resolves the prevailing tension and instability.

2

INSTABILITY

The first three movements of the Farewell Symphony are unstable throughout. This instability is heard in almost every aspect of the music: weak and problematical articulations of keys and cadences, the violence of the minor mode itself (which also troubles the major-mode movements), a lack of coherent stepwise melody, and ambiguities of form and structural voice leading. Tonal and rhetorical coherence, which ordinarily governs Haydn's music even at his wittiest and most original, seems at times almost to break down.

ALLEGRO ASSAI

The Exposition

The Allegro assai in particular is remarkably unstable. Most of its keys are not prepared by root-position dominants; most emphasize first-inversion tonics at the expense of the root position. Almost every full cadence is harmonically weak or rhythmically subverted. The rhythm is mechanically, almost obsessively regular. The only contrast, the only melody worthy of the name, is the D-major interlude; but this passage is not only formally problematic, it is not nearly as stable or lyrical as it seems to be.

The Main Theme The violent opening theme (shown in Example 2.1), with its syncopations, chromaticism, slashing descending triadic motives, unison tremolos, and the rest, has often been described. Unlike most of Haydn's opening themes in this period (those of Symphonies Nos. 44 in E minor and 46 in B, for example), it has no overt internal contrast and is almost entirely triadic. This alone is significant: the lack of clear stepwise melody will prove to be a central "problem" in the work. A more immediate difficulty, however, is the relation of the theme to its cadence. The first three phrases, all 4 (2+2) bars, are continuous, harmonically explicit, and full in texture. But the cadential phrase suddenly dissolves into bare octaves, the winds dropping out; the high register above $d^2/c\#^2$ is abandoned, and the true bass register below f#/e# is absent at the actual cadence (mm. 14–15a); even the pervasive syncopations become absorbed into the faster, but undifferentiated tremolo. The discontinuity is reinforced by a change in form of the principal submotive, from the straightforwardly descending *a1* to the more complex,

Example 2.1 Allegro assai, main theme

(a) Foreground

Ex. 2.1 (*cont.*)

(b) Middleground (literal)

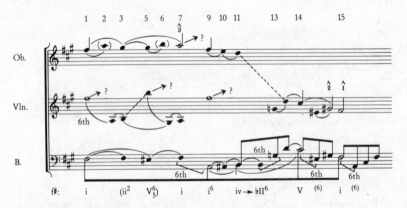

(c) Middleground (orthodox)

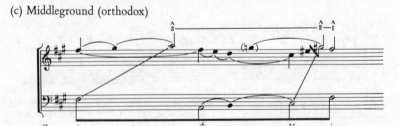

contour-changing *a2*. All this undercuts the apparent symmetry: the theme divides not so much 8+8 (as the return to the tonic in m. 9 might imply) as 12+4: harmonic syncopations–unison tremolo; *a1–a2*; theme–cadence. The effect is heightened by the sudden stop at the end and the G.P. separating the cadence from the *piano* counterstatement. (The cadential phrase is discontinuous in a larger sense as well: unison tremolos are heard nowhere else in the symphony, except in the thematic restatement at the beginning of the development.)

This textural and motivic discontinuity reflects the failure of the opening theme to project meaningful linear and registral connections (see Example 2.1b). In the violins, the slashing b² (m. 5) does not relate to anything in register, and f♯² is ignored after m. 7; only oboe I connects b² to a² and leads f♯² down to d² (mm. 9–12), where, however, it breaks off, leaving the violins to resolve d² to c♯². The oboe mounts purposefully from f♯² to a² over the tonic in mm. 1–8, implying 3̂ as a local headnote, but a² never appears in the violins; in particular, it remains divorced from the melodic cadence g♯¹–f♯¹ (mm. 14–15), and hence no middleground 3̂–2̂–1̂ descent occurs in register. In the double finale, this specific registral difficulty – 3̂ and/or 2̂ left "hanging," higher than the cadence – will even dominate in the background.

The bass and the harmonic progression are equally problematic. The satisfyingly low register of mm. 9–12 is strangely abandoned at the cadence; the high dominant c♯¹ (m. 14) leaves the low subdominant B undisplaced in register, and is therefore insufficiently weighty to resolve the theme as a whole. Furthermore, both this dominant and the ensuing tonic are immediately undercut by leaps of a sixth down to their respective thirds, e♯ and A. The latter pitch in particular is strongly articulated a sixth below the tonic f♯ (mm. 8–9, 15); this first-inversion construction appears on every bass scale-degree from m. 9 on: i⁶–ᵇII⁶–V⁽⁶⁾–i⁽⁶⁾. In fact, the apparently conventional afterbeat figure in mm. 15–16 is a diminution of the bass of the entire theme: f♯–A–c♯–f♯. (Perhaps this disposition is adumbrated by the plunge from f♯² all the way down to a in the beginning of the melody.) All this implies that the Allegro assai will have difficulty asserting its tonic, particularly in the low register; that functional dominants will be weak (particularly C♯ with respect to B); and that first-inversion triads will be unusually prominent, especially A below the tonic. These features recur in other movements. The minuet fails to establish a strong root-position tonic at the beginning, moving instead from I⁶ to V; in the Presto, low A in the bass will repeatedly be linked to high c♯¹ rather than c♯. (This audibly "problematizes" the relations between III and V as structural bass sonorities, outlined in Chapter 1.) All of these instabilities persist throughout the first three movements, and in some cases beyond. (One could rewrite Example 2.1b as an orthodox Schenkerian voice-leading graph, as in (c); but the latter underplays these registral and instrumental complexities, which are so important to the aesthetic of this theme.)

The second group: stability denied The entire second group avoids firm cadences (see Example 2.2, an overview of the form, and Example 2.3, a motivic and harmonic analysis of the second group). The first arrival on A major occurs in the transition, on theme **2** (m. 23, based on **1**), but it is rhythmically undermined by the downbeat rest

Example 2.2 Allegro assai: form

Exposition

1Gr	Tr		2Gr			Cl.		
1	1	1/2	3	1/2	4	5	6	7
1	17	21	29	38	49–50 53	56	60	65

Development

Cl.	Dev.				Intl.
7	1	2	2′	5	
71	73	88	96	102	108

Recapitulation

1Gr	(Tr)	2Gr		Cl.		
1 (dev.)	1/2	3	4	5	6	7
142	157 169	179	189	195	199	204

f♯: i ——— III (V/iii) ——— iii♭ ——— v ——— III ——— iv – V/iv ——— VI ——— i ——— (V   iv)

Note: Brackets denote passages marked off by caesuras; the music enclosed within each bracket is continuous. A vertical mark within a bracket (e.g. at 3, m. 29) denotes an elided cadence.

Example 2.3 Allegro assai: transition and second group

Ex. 2.3 (*cont.*)

in the bass, and hence we must push on towards the local dominant at m. 26. But its potential is also dissipated: theme **3** (mm. 29–37) avoids root-position sonorities entirely, and the new tonic is once again projected merely as a first-inversion triad (mm. 29, 31, 33). Just as, in the opening theme, the bass in some senses articulated A more strongly than F♯, so here it articulates C♯ more strongly than A; just as we have now arrived at the tonal area a third higher, thus foreshadowed, so will III in its turn soon give way to the dominant minor. A powerful rising sequence (mm. 33–37), still based on first-inversion triads, heads purposefully towards a root-position A major, but the arrival (m. 38) is brutally undercut by an unexpected eruption of the main theme (in its transitional form **1/2**) in the remote key of A minor. This violent event – another major/minor mixture – destroys A major as a tonic for the rest of the exposition; astonishingly, it has never really been established. Another rising sequence, still tonicizing first-inversion triads (mm. 42, 45, 47), leads towards C-sharp minor; but its arrival (m. 49) is only another sixth chord, prepared only by V^6 and vii^6. (The high b$\sharp^2$ in m. 48 links enharmonically with the earlier destabilizing high c^3 in A minor.) In this new key enters the new theme **4**, descending to the root-position c$\sharp$ in the bass (m. 53), which however is still rhythmically weak, merely a step in a sequence, and supports only $\hat{3}$ in the melody.

At last, in m. 55, comes a strong cadence with a melodic descent to the tonic – but it lands on the submediant! (That the first real arrival onto a root-position A major should be a deceptive cadence, long after the key of A has disappeared, can only be understood as deliberate irony.) Nor does the bass theme **5** (mm. 56–59, a variant of *a*) offer contrast or relief; the music remains as restless as ever, still prolonging the dominant. Both **5** and the continuation **6** revert merely to first-inversion tonics (mm. 57c, 59c, 61, 63). The only perfect authentic cadence in the entire exposition is that in C-sharp in mm. 64–65 – note the similarity between the two pre-cadential bars 54 and 64; the deceptive cadence is literally "made good." There is no tonal or rhythmic stability until this final event, which is followed only by 2+2 bars of cadential reinforcement over a tonic pedal (theme **7**). Thus A major suffers an unprecedented fate. This "inevitable" second-group key, otherwise invariable in Haydn's fast sonata-form movements (see Chapter 1), so broadly hinted at by the low As of the main theme, so clearly prepared contextually in the transition and theme **3**, is *made* to fail; it is a mere transition on the way to the dominant. The principle of instability, ordinarily understood as a rhythmic and gestural aspect of the foreground, is inscribed in the tonal structure itself.

Not that foreground rhythmic instability is absent! The movement is dominated by a two-bar rhythmic module, implied by the subdivisions of the main-theme phrases (Example 2.1: motive *a* vs. *d*; harmonic rhythm).[1] From m. 21 to the end of the exposition (Example 2.3), all the phrases are two measures long, except the rising sequence in mm. 33–38; even the falling sequence in mm. 50–53 (which moves bar-by-bar) does not contradict the overpowering two-bar pattern. Of course, the two-bar phrases vary in internal construction. Many of those based on the main theme (mm. 21–26, 38–43) are single-harmony constituents of larger phrases; others remain independent, and combine into four- or six-bar units only through repetition and elision (mm. 29–32, 44–49, 54–61, 65–72). For example, the bass theme **5** (mm. 56–57, 58–59) closes onto i^6 on the last beat of mm. 57 and 59; it remains "modular," separate (emphasized by the *piano* echo). The only notable disruption of two-bar periodicity comes (again) at the rising sequence mm. 33–38, which suspends the prevailing pattern of a strong measure every other bar (mm. 29, 31, 33); the A-minor arrival establishes the "opposite" bars 38, 40, 42 as strong. Even the four-bar phrase at the structural cadence, mm. 62–65, grows out of a repetition of mm. 60–61.[2]

---

[1] My rhythmic analyses throughout this study are (freely) adapted from the principles developed by Edward T. Cone in *Musical Form and Musical Performance* (New York, 1968).

[2] Schwartz ("Periodicity and Passion," introduction and §II) calls the deceptive cadence in m. 55 the strongest of the exposition, and interprets mm. 56–72 (*sic*) as a "closing theme," constructed as a "broken double period" with an elided cadence at m. 64 (*sic*). All this ignores the structural cadence in m. 65.

This almost mechanical phrasing combines with the prevailing instability to create a rhythm which can only be called obsessive. Following the abrupt halt in m. 16, the momentum never lets up. Every harmonic arrival in A is elided or undermined: the full cadence in m. 23 by the bass rest and new motive $c1$, the first-inversion cadence in m. 29 by the continued offbeat motives and elision, the A minor in m. 38 by elision, and so forth. Nor do the C-sharp arrivals in mm. 49 and 53 bring stability; even the structural cadence in m. 65 is elided to its own continuation, as is the (re-)transition to the repetition and to the development. Indeed (again ironically) the only break in the action comes at the deceptive cadence in m. 55 – the only one which is not a local tonic. With the exception of the D-major interlude (see below), this modular two-bar rhythm persists until the end of the movement. Unlike the tonality, it is not unstable; it is too uniform for that. But it is equally destabilizing: driven, incessant, unstoppable. (This insistent two-bar phrasing is very unusual, even in Haydn's so-called "Sturm und Drang" period. For example, the opening theme of Symphony No. 44 in E minor contrasts the *forte* unison motto with a sighing *piano* answer and a more *Fortspinnung*-like development towards a half-cadence (mm. 1–2, 3–4, 5ff); that of No. 46 in B is periodic but asymmetrical (2+2, 2+7); that of No. 47 in G is a systematic buildup of instrumentation, register, and harmony; that of No. 52 in C minor is non-periodic, but still based on contrasting phrases. The examples could be multiplied; we return to the general subject in the conclusion.)

Two-bar phrasing also characterizes the Adagio and minuet. The main theme of the Adagio, a large antecedent-consequent period (8+8), employs two-bar phrases throughout (see Example 2.11). The minuet (Examples 2.14, 2.15) is organized almost exclusively in two-bar units (most prominently, the decisive opening phrase and closing "tag" for violins alone); only the cadential phrases (mm. 7–10, 30–34, 35–38, 57–60) and the six-bar horn calls at the beginning and end of the trio are longer or more supple (and even they are compatible with the two-bar norm). (Of course, two-bar phrasing was not unusual in Haydn's minuets.) In this context, the second group of the Adagio is especially poignant: it is the symphony's first (and not entirely successful) attempt to liberate itself from mechanical two-bar phrasing.

At the same time, a remarkable rhythmic continuity cuts across this duple obsession: the "Farewell" is Haydn's only symphony with three successive movements in pure triple meter. (By the qualification "pure" I mean to exclude 6/8, which is duple with a triple subdivision of the beat.) The only partial exceptions are No. 6, *Le matin*, where, however, the opening Allegro is preceded by a slow introduction in 4/4 and the Andante framed by an Adagio in 4/4; and No. 31, the "Hornsignal," where it is a 6/8 Adagio that bridges the Allegro and the minuet. It scarcely seems a coincidence that all three of these symphonies have explicit extramusical associations. Hence we may suppose that Haydn intended the unprecedented "triple"-style as an organizing feature of the Farewell – especially in combination with the obsessively "duple" phrasing. Indeed they create a powerful, if perhaps in part abstract disjunction, one more aspect of the stylistic instability of the whole.

The D-major interlude and the irony of melody

We have already noted the lack of clear stepwise melodies in the Allegro assai. Therefore, the "material" basis of its ideas – its rhetoric – must reside in smaller musical motives. This adds to the difficulty; not only are these motives less "memorable" than ordinary themes, but (as outlined in Chapter 1) they develop in multifarious, often subtle or only indirectly apperceptible ways. The stormy Allegro assai is based almost exclusively on the powerful descending triadic motive a and agitated, repeated-eighth c motives (the pervasive syncopations b doing nothing to relieve the tension). The triadic derivatives of a require no special comment, save to reiterate the change from the straightforward $a1$ in the first three phrases of the main theme to the more complex $a2$ at the cadence. The complexity of Haydn's developing variation is evident in the transition (Example 2.3, mm. 21–29). Motive d (mm. 23–24), which originated in the main theme, harbors the "latent" offbeat motive $c1$. This submotive combines with the repeated eighths of c to generate the agitated offbeat octave-leap $c2$ (m. 23, bass); this not only rhythmically undermines the cadence (as just described), but immediately proceeds in invertible counterpoint with $c1$ and d. In the second group proper, $c2$ develops into the even wilder form $c3$ (m. 29); new forms of these offbeat c motives appear throughout the symphony. (Notice that $c3$ incorporates the triadic descent $a1$; if it did not develop directly out of $c2$, one would doubtless call it an a motive.)

The nearly total absence of linear melody is striking. In the main theme, stepwise connections hardly occur; even in the cadential phrase, the only melodic steps are the isolated pairs d^2–$c\sharp^2$ and $g\sharp^1$–$f\sharp^1$. (These successions, to be sure, relate to structural melodic steps elsewhere in the symphony.) The second group is equally harsh. The only motivically significant stepwise progressions are the e motives in mm. 44–54; the bass $a3$ (m. 56) is hardly more stable.[3] These fragments scarcely satisfy our desire for melody; e appears only in the bass, within an unstable rising sequence; $e2$ must struggle against the harshly dissonant $e1$ motives in the second violins; nor is $a3$ anything like a "second theme" (as it is occasionally called), in view of its unstable rising ductus and the persistent themeless syncopations above (b). To be sure, before the late 1770s Haydn rarely composed "second themes" of the type later recognized by sonata-form theory;[4] nevertheless, the anti-lyrical tone in this movement exceeds that in any other. (Even in the almost equally violent No. 52 in C minor, the second group pauses twice for a restful *piano* theme.)

But what about the mysterious D-major interlude – surely this is nothing if not melodic? Indeed it is; astonishingly, however (given its apparent lack of relation to the context), it has been prepared on the motivic level (Example 2.4).[5] Motive f in its normal form

---

[3] Its derivation from the main theme is noted by Rywosch, p. 94; Landon (*Haydn*, vol. 2, p. 302), noting the "theme-less" syncopated b motive in the violins, describes it as a "call to the barricades."

[4] Webster, "When did Haydn Begin to Write 'Beautiful' Melodies?" *Haydn Studies*, pp. 385–88.

[5] Rosen (*Sonata Forms* [New York, 1980], p. 160) and Schwartz ("Periodicity and Passion," §II) have also noted the relation between what I call $c3$ and f.

Example 2.4 Allegro assai: D-major interlude

Ex. 2.4 (*cont.*)

Ex. 2.4 (*cont.*)

(mm. 110–11) maintains the offbeat-eighth, over-the-barline rhythm of the longer form of *c3* (compare Example 2.3, mm. 29–30); the appoggiatura resolution, which distantly varies m. 30, is simply *e1*. Meanwhile, the accompaniment is *c1* – itself just heard prominently in the F-sharp half cadence of mm. 106–07 (compare Example 1.5a). Beyond this, the interlude begins with an immediate (if disguised) pitch repetition: its initial phrase (mm. 108–09) is a variant of mm. 104–06 (see Example 1.5d). There motive *a3* impinges tangentially, as it were, on the high pedal f♯² and leads it down to c♯² over the prolonged dominant harmony – that is, it becomes motive *e2*. But motive *f* in mm. 108–09 incorporates the identical descent, harmonized as I–vii⁶ in D. (The eighth notes *within* m. 108 are another, hurried form of *e2*.) Also, the interlude's prominent first-inversion triads in rising sequence relate to similar patterns in the second group (Example 2.3, mm. 33–37, 42–49).

But motivic continuity can go only so far; aesthetically, the interlude remains divorced from its context. As described in Chapter 1, its D-major tonality is locally unintegrated. In addition, the interlude "floats" in the air, without foundation: the bass drops out, lifting us from the sixteen-foot octave (double basses) to the four-foot (violas), made even more insubstantial by the open-string d¹; even though the bass reenters in the second phrase, the damage has been done. The transition back to the reprise is equally high and unstable, the basses skipping down a full ninth across the G.P. The *piano* legato ductus is without parallel in the movement. The indirect tonal relations, the style, and the instrumental-registral projection render the interlude not only non-structural and unintegrated, but almost "otherworldly." It is hardly surprising that it has been found perplexing; even its basic character seems elusive.⁶ Landon, frankly baffled, calls it a second theme out of season; Rosen invokes a red herring, namely Sammartini's "trio"-like development sections. Schwartz's description of it as a "minuet," characterized by "polish and control" and "utter clarity of form and texture," at least conforms to its outward style; but as we shall see, this too misses the mark.⁷

Haydn's aim is different: to introduce the possibility of lyrical coherence, but to reveal it as paradoxical and hence unattainable. The interlude turns out to be everything other than what it seems. It comprises four similar eight-bar phrases (see Example 2.4), of which the last modulates away from D to prepare the reprise; the tempo remains very fast, close to one-in-a-bar (reinforced by the harmonic rhythm). Each two-bar motive *f* (see the phrase-analysis above the music) leads from a weak measure to a strong one, marked by the change of harmony across the barline and the long appoggiatura on *e1*. But these self-contained motives are not congruent with the upbeat accompaniment motives *c1* (analysis *below* the music), which function statically within each harmony and create "opposing" strong measures, in interlocking alternation with the melody. Each eight-bar phrase is a "sentence" (*Satz*), in which the interlocking 2+2's

---

⁶ See, in addition to the authors cited below, Rywosch, p. 94; Somfai, introduction to the facsimile of the autograph; Geiringer, p. 261; Orin Moe, "The Implied Model in Classical Music," *CM* No. 23(1977), pp. 51–52.

⁷ Landon, *Symphonies*, p. 320; *Haydn*, vol. 2, p. 302; Rosen, *Sonata Forms*, pp. 156–60; Schwartz, "Periodicity and Passion," §III. Compare Webster, "D-Major Interlude."

are followed by a rhythmically unified four-bar cadential phrase.[8] (To this extent, the interlude does fulfill the promise of its style; the prevailing two-bar module becomes both lyrical and supple.) The first, second, and fourth phrases begin on the tonic and rise by stepwise bass through first-inversion triads; but the third begins on the dominant with a complex elision to the end of phrase 2 – the bass entry in m. 123, which at first sounds like a mere "filler" motive, actually initiates phrase 3 – and hence creates the effect of contrast by intensification. The interlude is so fast as to seem almost breathless, and yet so smooth, quiet, and regular as never to run out of breath. Its phrasing and form seem crystal clear, yet it supports nothing more than a floating, insubstantial embellishing chord. There is nothing like it anywhere else in Haydn.

Its formal construction is also problematical. The first three phrases (which come to a full close in m. 131) exhibit a thoroughgoing lack of congruence among the musical parameters: the basic material and the harmony of the incipits create the pattern aab; the cadential structure, aba; and the use of registers and presence or absence of the bass, abb! A further complication is that the contrasting dominant beginning of the third phrase creates a different pattern of intensification and release, hinting at a more complex overall form a|a|ba or a|b|ba. (Such intensification within a "third" phrase is fundamental to late eighteenth-century thematic construction; it has been little studied except by Dénes Bartha.[9]) Additional problems arise with respect to the formal relations among the phrases. Is the second phrase to be heard as a consequent to the first, as their almost identical incipits and parallel construction would suggest, producing a phrase-grouping 1+2|3; or should it go with the third phrase, as the elision across the dominant and their V–I cadence structure imply, in a higher-level intensification-resolution pair, 1|2–3? Or, more complex yet, we might note the "antiperiod" relationship between the first two phrases and read the entire three-phrase theme as a "double period" with compressed consequent:

$$
\begin{array}{c|c||c}
\text{a} & \text{a} & \text{b—a} \\[4pt]
\text{I} & \text{V} & \text{V—I}
\end{array}
$$

(An antiperiod is a period whose consequent cadences *off* the tonic and hence is more "open" than the antecedent: e.g., –I, –V (or –V, –V/V). Although such constructions are common in the Classical period, they too have been little studied.[10])

In short, the interlude will not parse. Nor would it help to appeal to the final phrase, which is overtly unstable and leads back towards F-sharp minor and the maelstrom. Just as it floats in the air, just as its surface regularity is incompatible with its breathless

[8] On the "sentence," a Schoenbergian concept, see Erwin Ratz, *Einführung in die musikalische Formenlehre* (Vienna, 1951), pp. 22–25; Walter Frisch, *Brahms and the Principle of Developing Variation* (Berkeley, 1984), pp. 11–18.

[9] For example, "Song Form and the Concept of 'Quatrain,'" *Haydn Studies*, pp. 353–55 (with further references).

[10] A few comments are found in Wilhelm Fischer, "Zur Entwicklungsgeschichte des Wiener klassischen Stils," *Studien zur Musikwissenschaft*, 3 (1915), 25–29, types 4 and 5, and "Zwei neapolitanische Melodietypen bei Mozart und Haydn," *Mozart-Jahrbuch*, 1960–61, pp. 7–21 ("umgekehrte Periode"); Eugene K. Wolf, *The Symphonies of Johann Stamitz: A Study in the Formation of the Classic Style* (Utrecht and Antwerp; The Hague and Boston, 1981), pp. 195; 220, n. 58; 347.

pace, so its construction is inherently self-contradictory. The modulating fourth phrase only manifests what has implicitly been the case all along: the interlude could never achieve closure. Its paradoxical construction and aesthetic negate its lyrical, melodic character; it is too self-contradictory to be effective. This negation also compromises its prominent four-note stepwise descent *e2*, which, as we have seen, stands for the possibility of melody in this movement. But after having first appeared in a hostile context (mm. 50–53) where it cannot actualize this potential, it now introduces an ostensibly lyrical interlude whose very meaning is questionable. Genuine stepwise melody is now established as a central "problem" of the Farewell Symphony. The interlude can best be understood as another example of irony. It pretends to be in repose, but is in fact breathless and unbalanced; it sounds isolated and divorced from the context, but is in fact integrated motivically and tonally. On a subliminal level, it incorporates and extends the principle of instability which, it is now clear, governs the entire Allegro assai – the remainder of which is more violent than ever. Since the interlude remains unexplained, never returning, it too forms part of the "problem" of the work. Its resolution can only come *elsewhere* – on a level which involves the entire symphony.

A climax of violence

Even the recapitulation maintains the violence and instability.[11] The last phrase of the interlude (Example 2.4, mm. 132ff) develops the rising first-inversion triads into an unstable, modulating sequence, now rising in diminished chords all the way to the edge of the abyss – $g\#^1$ in the bass and d^3 in the violins – whereupon everything stops, and we suddenly plunge back down into the reprise. This is lack of preparation with a vengeance! Until the violins' accented halt at the top of an inversion of motive *a*, there is no hint of the main theme. Everything is still too high: the melody skips down a sixth across the G.P., the bass more than an octave, into a completely different register. Despite the presence of the leading-tone, it is very weak harmonic preparation: there is no prolongation of the dominant (merely a move from VI to vii⁶), no dominant root, in fact no C♯ whatever. The entire interlude remains non-structural, reinforcing its stylistic disjunction.

With F-sharp minor having been so weakly prepared, the recapitulation which now begins is potentially unstable – and it is unstable in fact (see Example 2.5). In an outright refusal to acknowledge the formal meaning of the reprise (which even here is a "double return," to the main theme and to the tonic), the second phrase at once propels us into a modulating, chromatic, dissonant passage. (Note for example the searing second horn e^1 in mm. 150–51, a minor ninth over the bass; Haydn added it in the autograph as an afterthought.) This is an extreme example of what Rosen calls a "secondary development": an unstable extension within the recapitulation of a first group (indeed this passage develops *a* motives exclusively).[12] This makes perfect sense: the interlude occupied

[11] Schwartz ("Periodicity and Passion," §IV) emphasizes this as well, going so far as to interpret the abrupt juxtaposition of the interlude and the reprise as a representation of the sublime. (On this concept in Haydn's symphonies, see Chapters 5, 7, 8.)

[12] *Sonata Forms*, pp. 104–10, 276–80.

Example 2.5 Allegro assai: recapitulation

1

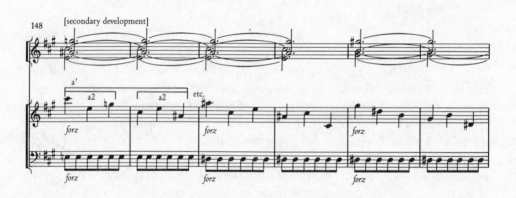

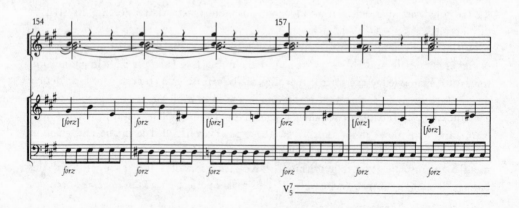

Ex. 2.5 (*cont.*)

Ex. 2.5 (cont.)

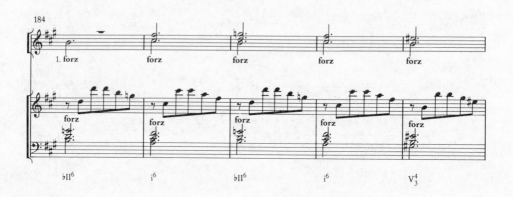

fully half the time between the end of the exposition and the reprise. Hence, even though the latter enters at Haydn's usual proportional location (about two-thirds of the way through the movement),[13] development of the material has been drastically curtailed. From this viewpoint, the inadequate tonal preparation for the reprise is highly appropriate: the last thing we want is a conventional recapitulation.

But a meaningful restoration of F-sharp minor, and hence any meaningful recapitulation of the second group in terms of the "sonata principle" – that important material and form-defining cadences first heard outside the tonic must later be "grounded" in the tonic[14] – depends on strong dominant preparation. Accordingly, the secondary development drives towards a long dominant pedal (mm. 157ff); this is in fact the first functioning dominant in the normal register, rather than an octave higher as in mm. 14 and 65–72. In view of the absence of C♯ at the end of the interlude, this passage *is* the tonal retransition. Hence we confidently await the long-delayed return of F-sharp minor – but we are wrong again. The dynamics abruptly drop to *pianissimo* (m. 163), the dominant mysteriously turns minor, and soon moves bewilderingly to a new outburst of the main theme in B minor (m. 169). But again this is "consequential," to use Cone's term,[15] and for three reasons. First, the "hanging" dominant of B minor preceding the D-major interlude is now (distantly) resolved. Secondly, the subdominant is an entirely appropriate tonal region in a secondary development. And finally, this passage recapitulates the transition (mm. 169–82 = 21–32); the initial motive *a*, erupting from a low-register *piano* or *pianissimo* onto high b², is identical in both. At the same time, it also recapitulates the later A-minor outburst (m. 38), which was at the very close pitch level c³. Because the latter can have no force in the present minor-key context, and is accounted for by the close resemblance of this B-minor statement, it is not recapitulated at all. Except for this cut, the recapitulation is regular from m. 169 on.

But "regular" still means unstable (see again Example 2.5). B minor undermines the preceding dominant pedal; this large-scale dysfunctionality of the dominant – moving to $\hat{4}$ instead of the tonic – reappears locally "diminuted" in the next preparation for F-sharp minor (m. 179 = 29). C♯ in the bass (m. 175) supports only the minor dominant, and the functional (major) dominant – once again too high – is only V², over $\hat{4}$ (m. 178 = 28). (The registral bass discontinuity between low B and high c♯¹ in the opening theme thus reverberates here in the middleground, precisely at the return to the tonic.) We are now *in medias res* of the second group, but theme **3** still articulates only i⁶. Even the Neapolitan in mm. 183–89 – the most savage passage in this entire savage movement, along with mm. 146–62; note the constant Beethovenian *fz*s in both – prolongs i⁶ alone. As in the exposition, no perfect cadence is heard until five bars before the end (mm. 203–04 = 64–65); even this one fights shy of any dominant lower than c♯¹. (To be sure, the bass theme **5** has just articulated the dominant in the lower octave.) Most extraordinary, with the exception of the unsatisfactory unison conclusion of the main theme at the beginning, this is the only perfect cadence in F-sharp in the entire movement. Instability persists up to the very end.

[13] This assertion is based on unpublished studies of the proportions in Haydn's sonata-form movements.

[14] The term "sonata principle" was first adumbrated in Cone, *Form and Performance*.

[15] "Twelfth Night," *Musiktheorie*, 1 (1986), 44–48, 50–52; tr. in *JMR* 7 (1986–88), 136–41, 147–49.

Structural voice-leading and progressive form

Although later movements will be more complex in this respect, the Allegro assai unambiguously establishes A ($\hat{3}$) as the background headnote (see Example 2.6; a middleground graph of the exposition is given in 2.7). The oboe line from f#^{2} to a^2 at the beginning (mm. 1–7) has all the earmarks of an initial ascent; $\hat{5}$ appears only in m. 14, and cannot descend here by step. The a^2 is prolonged through the A-major and A-minor passages of the second group until m. 50, where – precisely at the arrival of C-sharp minor – it recurs in the first violins and is led down by step, bar by bar, to c#^{2} (m. 55). The first four notes of this descent, a^2–e^2, are the dotted half notes which create motive *e2* in mm. 50–53, the first genuinely "melodic" event in the movement. Of course, the background only moves to $\hat{2}$ (g#^{2}); it is immediately rearticulated by the powerful syncopated g#^{2} over theme **5** in the bass (mm. 56–59). This tonal/motivic constellation – a background fall from $\hat{3}$ to $\hat{2}$ created by motive *e2* in the foreground – will be of fundamental importance in the minuet, the Presto, and the farewell movement.

In the development and especially the recapitulation, however, the background voice leading becomes problematical. In my view, the weakness of the tonic in the recapitulation prevents the initial $\hat{3}$/i from ever being "recaptured" in the background. According to this reading, the entire movement articulates an *un*interrupted

$$\hat{3}-\hat{2}-\hat{1}$$
$$\text{i–V–i}$$

The structural dominant is prolonged all the way from the second group of the exposition to the final cadence, as shown in Example 2.6. This must be one of the most extreme "delayed structural downbeats" in all music.[16] In addition, this type of through-composed background is unusual in late eighteenth-century music; one usually finds an interruption structure, based on a "dividing" $\hat{2}$/V and recapture of the initial sonority at the reprise, with the entire recapitulation executing a complete *Ursatz*, as shown in Example 3.10b (through m. 51) or 3.12b. But this structure can only arise when a strong root-position dominant defines the end of the background "antecedent" (usually the end of the exposition or the development), followed by a strongly articulated, stable return to the tonic which constitutes the beginning of the "consequent" (the recapitulation). Precisely these features are lacking in the Allegro assai; its progressive, end-oriented form is mirrored in a unitary, undivided background. The Presto, by contrast, does exhibit an interruption structure of this type – until the end.

(Most Schenkerians today analyze interruption structures as comprising two equal members, with the "consequent" *entirely in the background* and *temporally separate* from the "antecedent," as suggested in Example 2.6c(1). Schenker himself preferred a more nearly unitary form, in which the consequent is a *middleground prolongation* that is *embedded within* the background [Example 2.6c(2)]. However, although his theoretical treatment of this point was clear, his analytical notation of interruption structures varied wildly,

---

[16] On this concept, see Cone, "Analysis Today," *MQ* 46 (1960), 174–75, 181–83; Robert P. Morgan, "The Delayed Structural Downbeat and its Effect on the Tonal and Rhythmic Structure of Sonata Form Recapitulation," Ph.D. diss, Princeton University, 1969.

Example 2.6 Allegro assai: background and deep middleground

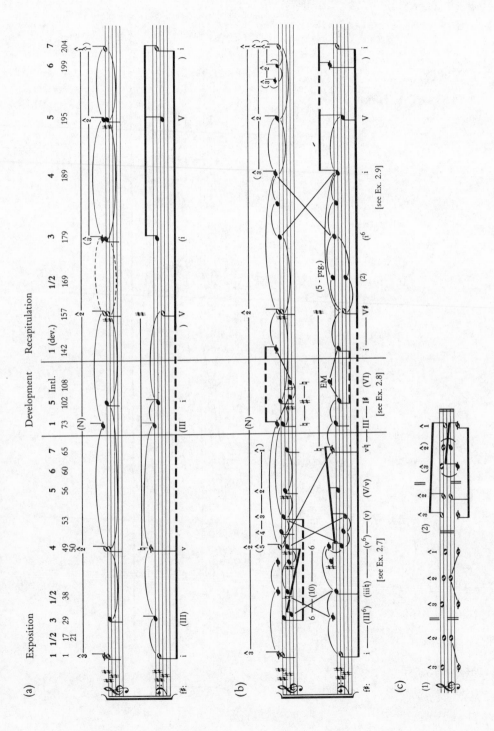

Example 2.7 Allegro assai: exposition, middleground

from "equal," non-overlapping antecedent-consequent pairs to graphs in which the consequent is so thoroughly "embedded" as to suggest a plain linear progression in the middleground.[17] This variability is no defect; rather, it testifies to Schenker's empirical, "artistic" sensitivity to individual works (which he understandably de-emphasized in the text of his theoretical tract, *Free Composition*). It also relativizes his dogmatic assertion that all sonata-form movements are based on interruptions, and implicitly justifies my through-composed reading of Haydn's Allegro assai – not that special pleading would be necessary in the case of this radically unusual music.[18] This entire complex of questions warrants a detailed study.

As this volume amply testifies, I am in fundamental sympathy with Schenkerian analysis. At the same time, I am skeptical. As explained in the Introduction, it is only one approach among many, which must ordinarily be combined with others in order to achieve adequate understanding of a work. I also reject the claims of orthodoxy: if art is free, as Haydn said, so (within more modest limits) are analysis and criticism. My appeal to Haydn as an authority is pertinent: to a degree arguably matched by no other composer of his stature, his art is based on freedom, irregularity, unpredictability. In analyzing his music one ignores "what happens," in the most literal, tangible sense, at one's peril; perhaps even more than with other composers, *one must preserve the integrity of the foreground*. For example, Haydn often subverts closure at the end of a movement, as in the Allegro assai here (see below), the Largo of Symphony No. 64 (Example 5.4), or the Adagio of No. 49 (Example 8.4), or (as here) has no root-position dominant preceding a recapitulation. Conventional analyses showing ordinary background sonorities in such passages would falsify these effects. In the first movement of the "Oxford" Symphony (Example 5.7), Haydn overtly problematizes the join between introduction and allegro; my middleground graph reflects this in a manner that – rightly – violates Schenker's norms of contrapuntal voice leading. In other contexts, for example with respect to Symphonies 49 (Example 8.4) and 99 (Example 8.23), I suggest alternative readings, without insisting that we must decide whether (say) $\hat{3}$ or $\hat{5}$ is the background headnote. I hope that this heterodox approach will be taken as constructive criticism from "within" Schenkerian theory, which, as Arnold Whittall has suggested, is more likely to be fruitful than ignorant polemics from outside the tradition.[19])

This uninterrupted fundamental structure entails a massive, twofold prolongation of the dominant across the entire development and recapitulation. In the deep middleground (Example 2.6a), the bass twice arpeggiates from C♯ through triad-pitches: down from c♯[1] through a and f♯ (mm. 73, 102) in the first prolongation, with low c♯ regained at m. 157;

---

[17] *Free Composition* (2 vols., New York, 1979), vol. 1, pp. 36–40, §87–99; vol. 2, Exx. 21–26 (my Ex. 2.6c replicates his Ex. 21). See Ernst Oster's important gloss, p. 37, n. 7. For a large-scale sonata-form graph that is appropriately ambiguous as to whether the recapitulation is an interruption or, like my Example 2.6a, a through-composed structure, see Ex. 154/4 (the first movement of Beethoven's "Appassionata" Sonata), whose reprise is on the dominant.

[18] Schenker's assertion is found in *Free Composition*, §312. Oster (p. 139) cites several sonata-form movements, some graphed by Schenker in the same work, which do not exhibit the canonical interruption structure. To this list one could add numerous analyses in *Das Meisterwerk in der Musik*, most prominently of Mozart's G Minor Symphony (vol. 2, 1926). The first edition of the *Harmonielehre* (1906), as is well known, named the author merely as "an artist."

[19] In a review of Epstein's *Beyond Orpheus*, in *JMT* 25 (1981), 325.

to f♯ alone (m. 179) in the second, with c♯ at m. 195. The melody regains a² each time, but only as a neighbor to $\hat{2}$ (m. 73) or as the beginning of a subsidiary $\hat{3}$–$\hat{2}$–$\hat{1}$ descent (m. 179; see *Free Composition*, as just cited). The first prolongation (Examples 2.6 and 2.8)

Example 2.8 Allegro assai: development, middleground

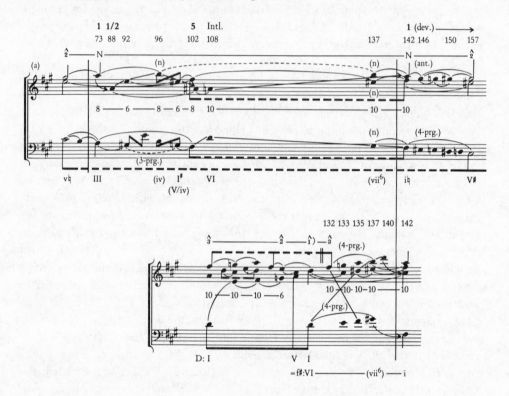

transforms C-sharp minor, the dominant key, into C-sharp major, the dominant chord, as is common in minor-mode development sections; except that, as already described, the latter is not attained until the secondary development (m. 157). A in the bass coincides with the A-major restatement of the main theme in the beginning of the development, while F♯ supports the first appearance of the sonority of F-sharp major, which prepares the D-major interlude. As described above, the interlude is an embellishing chord to I in the bass (its relation to the larger context is shown in Example 2.8b); in the melody, however, D major already cancels the raised third degree A♯, preparing A in the reprise. VI is thus not a large-scale neighbor to the dominant, as would ordinarily be the case; it is reabsorbed into the (modally altered) F-sharp whence it came – a non-structural function appropriate to the otherworldly effect of the interlude. At the same time, because no strong major dominant has yet appeared, the thematic reprise does not recapture $\hat{3}$/i in the background; a² is still a neighbor to the prevailing $\hat{2}$. The pedal in the secondary development then completes the transformation of the dominant into the major, with E♯ in place of E; for all its remote, dissonant sonorities, the progression from i to V (mm. 142–57) is a straightforward chromatic descent in the bass (see the end of Example 2.8).

The second prolongation of the dominant (see the right-hand segment of Example 2.6 and Example 2.9) runs from the secondary development to the final cadence – the

Example 2.9 Allegro assai: recapitulation, middleground

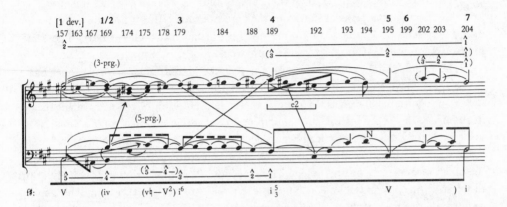

only tonic cadence since mm. 14–15, and the only one in the movement with independent melody and bass parts. (The tonic in m. 192 [Example 2.5] is not a true cadence; it is rhythmically too active, and the entire phrase is heading for the deceptive cadence in mm. 193–94.) The bass simply elaborates the dominant with the subsidiary tonic F♯, entering at m. 179 (*sic*; Example 2.6b) as root-position tonic support for 3̂ at the beginning of the second group. In the foreground, however (Examples 2.6b and 2.9), this 3̂/i is displaced forward to m. 189 and the recapitulation of theme **4**, by means of a middleground voice-exchange on the triad pitches. The resultant i⁶ sonority supports the savage first-inversion recapitulation of theme **3** (mm. 179–88); this i⁶ is prepared by a passing 4̂, harmonized as the B-minor transition (m. 169), which undermines the preceding structural dominant. This bass 5̂–4̂–3̂ progression then recurs in diminution (Example 2.9), beginning again as the *minor* dominant (m. 175), which reverts to the major only at the last moment and in last inversion (m. 178).

The foreground displacement of the root-position tonic forward to m. 189 allows the melodic 3̂ to reappear in the same context as that in which it descended to 2̂ in the exposition, namely the beginning of theme **4**; once again, four weighty dotted half notes (motive *e2*) descend from a² (mm. 189–92). (Compare mm. 189–92 in Examples 2.5 and 2.9 with mm. 50–53 in Examples 2.3 and 2.7.) The deep middleground moves from 3̂ to 2̂ and back are thus consistently correlated with important foreground events. Even the development participates: the move to I³♯ (mm. 102ff) is introduced by the second-group theme **5**, and the transition to the interlude, as we have seen, is articulated by *e2*. Finally, the middleground elaboration of 3̂/i as two sonorities, i⁶–i (mm. 179, 189), permits the second bass prolongation to "imitate" the first by *descending* to A: the background C♯ from the secondary development is transferred back up to c♯¹ in m. 175, from where it descends in a fifth-progression all the way to f♯ in m. 189.

The pervasive tendency towards chromatic progressions and first-inversion sonorities on all levels also accounts for many unusual features of the exposition. The interval of the third in the bass (see Chapter 1) is critical. Important sonorities are consistently articulated so as to emphasize their own third degrees at the expense of their roots. The double second group itself throws the background interval A–C♯ into relief, along with the destabilizing transformation of the apparent goal (III, a third above the tonic) into a way-station on the road to the dominant (the next-higher third). The same pitch-class interval, A–C♯, governs every important progression in the double finale.

In the middleground (Example 2.6b), the melodic a¹ and c♯² arise in an inner part, as the roots above the first-inversion arrivals on III⁶ and v⁶ (mm. 29, 49; "6–6"). The important additional chromatic element is the violent eruption of c² on the main theme in A minor (m. 38). This mixture anticipates the diatonic c♯² of m. 49, a connection made explicit by the enharmonically equivalent leading-tone b♯¹, just one measure before (m. 48). In the foreground (Example 2.7), these inner-part pitches are transferred into the upper octave; the consistent stepwise connections in register from a² (mm. [29], 36) through b² (m. 37) and c³=b♯² (mm. 38, 48) to c♯³ (m. 49) create a rising third-span, connecting the two anchors a² and c♯³. (In other contexts, this c♯³ might be taken as a background headnote, prepared by a long initial ascent from f♯² in the opening theme, and descending – still without interruption – through 4̂ in mm. 96–101 and 3̂ in mm. 102–56. But voice-leading problems and a lack of convincing background support for the putative 4̂ [b² in mm. 96–101], as well as the motivic-structural role of e2 on A–G♯, as described above, militate against this interpretation.) In turn, the bass anchors C♯ and E (mm. 29, 49) form partial arpeggiations in both second-group keys (3̂–5̂ in A; 1̂–3̂ in C-sharp minor). Meanwhile, the root-position tonic A (m. 38) *fails* to govern the passage: it is undermined by the destabilizing minor-mode outburst above it – and c³ soon turns into the dissonant b♯². In turn, each of the successive high points is approached by foreground ascents from 5̂ (e²) in an inner voice: a² by fourth-progression in mm. [26]27–29; b²/c³ by sixth-progression in mm. 33–38; b♯²/c♯³ in a rhyming, "mock" sixth-progression in mm. 43–49. The latter two ascents are accompanied by parallel progressions in the bass – again, all in first inversion. The rising sequences, first-inversion chords, and structural rising thirds in the bass are thus determined both developmentally on the musical surface, and by these complex middleground prolongations.

A denial of closure

In the Allegro assai of the Farewell Symphony, the ambiguity and instability in both foreground and background, united with the surface violence, almost abrogate Haydn's customary tonal and rhetorical coherence. In the exposition, A major fails to be established; even C-sharp minor barely attains closure. Can the tonic itself feel any less under siege? Its cadence in the main theme is undermined registrally, and to an extent structurally; in the development it is juxtaposed with a functionally ambiguous major *Doppelgänger* and a non-functional, otherworldly interlude; its attempted reprise lasts barely four bars, and even the succeeding strong dominant is dissipated into the subdominant; its return at last, in the recapitulation of the second group, is still only in first inversion and buffeted by *fortissimo* Neapolitans. And after all this, a single little cadence (mm. 203–04), with a high dominant bass lasting only one (very fast) beat, must round off this entire huge, violent, tonally wide-ranging movement! It is asking too much. The Allegro assai may cadence in the tonic at the end of a regular second-group recapitulation, but it does not achieve closure. The instability remains; it will be resolved, if at all, only at some later time. With this extraordinary step, the die is cast for the course of the entire symphony.

ADAGIO: MOTIVIC TRANSFORMATION AND EXPRESSIVE MELODY

The second and third movements are also unstable, albeit in different ways from the Allegro assai (and each other). To be sure, the Adagio substantially eases the tension. It is squarely in the relative A major; the tonic and dominant keys are firmly established; its main theme is a stable antecedent-consequent period; coherent stepwise melodic motion becomes prominent. As shown in Example 2.10, it is in very clear sonata form.

Example 2.10 Adagio: form

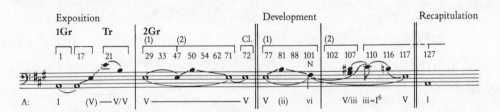

(This "bass-line graph," like Examples 5.8 and 8.21a, is not a Schenkerian analysis and should not be read as such, notwithstanding certain apparent similarities of notation.) The movement also achieves meaningful rhythmic and tonal resolution at the end of the exposition and recapitulation. Nevertheless, all is not well: the melodies remain troubled by rhythmic disunity and cannot articulate their own cadences, and the entire second group is burdened with major/minor chromaticism.

A fundamental basis of the sense of resolution at the end is developing variation, which continues from the Allegro assai into this movement (and throughout the symphony). (An overview of the material as it appears in the exposition is given in Example 2.11.) The quasi-hocketing opening theme (mm. 1–2) is not as simple as it appears: it conjoins two of the principal motivic complexes (triadic *a* and offbeat *c*). The

Example 2.11 Adagio: exposition

Ex. 2.11 (*cont.*)

two-note figure *a5* begins on the beat, is confined within the bar, and states the interval of a third; its identity as a motive is confirmed by its unified harmonic support in each bar (I$^{[6]}$ in m. 1, V^2 in m. 2). But it is difficult to "breathe" this motive across the middle of each bar, with the punctuating rest in the melody and the offbeat attack in the bass; furthermore, an alternative reading exists in the stepwise progression from c#^{2} to b^1 across the barline: this can only be an *e* motive (*e3*). But this motive is merely "latent" in this context of distinct, sequentially repeated, strongly harmonic *a5*s (for example, the possibility of resolving g#^{1} by step to a^1 in mm. 2–3 is studiously avoided). The hocketing bass exhibits a similar hybrid character, which however involves the offbeat, rhythmically unstable *c* domain (its relation to *c* emerges clearly in the plain repeated notes of m. 2). The label *a5/c* in m. 1 acknowledges this hybrid character (compare *c3* in the Allegro assai, mm. 29ff: Example 2.3). But when the motive moves by *step*, as it does as early as

m. 5 (=13), it can only be understood as a different hybrid, *c/e*. Both motives will play important roles later in this movement, as well as in others. The opening theme of the Adagio thus unassumingly projects a complex motivic combination in the context of a coherent periodic theme; this conjunction also becomes more important in the "farewell" movement.

For the moment, however, the hybrid, hocketing motives tend to destabilize things, a tendency reinforced by other aspects of the theme. The two-bar phrase module persists. Rhythmic congruence between melody and bass is systematically avoided, especially at cadences: in mm. 1 and 3 the bass rests on the downbeat, and then enters merely on $\hat{3}$; the cadences in mm. 4 and 6 are rhythmically weak; even that in m. 16, the end of the period, is undermined by another missing downbeat. These alternating attacks are maintained in the transition (mm. 21–28), and the original disunified pattern returns at the beginning of the second group (m. 29). Thereafter, suspensions take over: within descending eighth notes in mm. 33–36; in a painfully slow, continually unresolved ascent in mm. 37–40; indeed, throughout the second group. Particularly troubling is the cadence to this long paragraph, mm. 45–46: the melody resumes the upbeat *e4* syncopations before the resolution, on d#^{1}. Far from being a conventional decoration, this motive not only rhythmically subverts this cadence but is developed without break into the beginning of the next paragraph (still in Example 2.11); indeed, it dominates the remainder of the second group until the structural cadence in mm. 69–71.

In addition, the second group is full of unstable major/minor mixtures; its very beginning, on the main theme (m. 29), is immediately compromised by a repetition in the minor (m. 31). This is no conventional echo; the syncopated continuation (mm. 33–37) is too troubled for that (it also renounces the incessant skip-appoggiaturas of the main theme, a manifestation of Haydn's sprightly profundity which has by now gone on long enough). Following the evaded cadence in mm. 45–46, the sighing descent *e2* takes over, once again with an immediate minor echo (mm. 47–48, 49–50). The two extensions of this motive (mm. 50–52, 62–64) are especially poignant; see the barely disguised parallel fifths in mm. 50–52 and the augmented triad in mm. 62–64, both still shot through with major/minor ambiguity. They color the entire paragraph, surrounding the mysterious chromatic purple patch in mm. 54–61. In the recapitulation, the latter passage is expanded to a remarkable chromatic descent underneath d#, #$\hat{4}$ (shown in Example 2.12). This is also "consequential": it recalls the chromatic bass descent to the dominant in the Allegro assai, mm. 146–62; indeed, in the development of this movement, mm. 105–09, we have already heard a chromatic descent to a dominant underneath d#^{2} (see Example 2.12d). (It is tempting to imagine this dominant resolving, in m. 110, to C-sharp *major*: see the accidentals above the notes in Example 2.12d. The remote sharp-side sonority would be very fresh, and would fit the chromatic language of the movement. The echo in m. 112, analogous to the major/minor echoes at the beginning of the second group, would then restore the diatonic minor key – transformed, however (as appropriate in a development), into a stable echo of an unstable headmotive. But Haydn actually used such remote third-related sonorities as tonics only late in life; see Chapter 6.)

These chromatic mixtures also destabilize the second group, in conjunction with

Example 2.12 Adagio: "purple patches"

(a): Second group

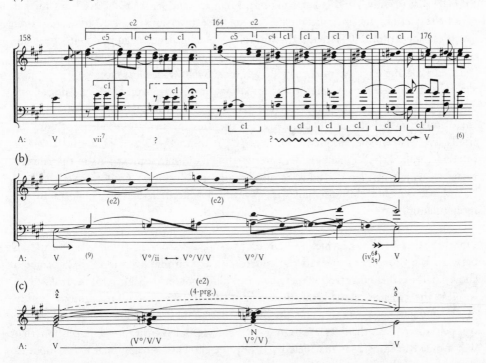

(b)

(c)

(d): Development

evasions of direct tonal progressions comparable to those in the Allegro assai. The dominant in mm. 36–40 is based only on the weak inversions V^6 and V^2; the bass leading-tone $d\sharp^1$ never resolves and is left hanging in register, and its weird octave leaps further cloud the picture; the melodic pitches above these inversions resolve "too late," over a bassless abyss (mm. 40–41); the rhythmically evaded cadence in mm. 45–46 conspicuously fails to resolve the hanging melodic a^1 (m. 45) until the continuation (m. 47), when the next paragraph is already under way. Such evaded cadences continue until the end of the second group; the entire passage mm. 50–66 prolongs the dominant, elaborated by the first-inversion $d\sharp$ (the basis of the chromatic mystification), until the diatonic resolution onto I^6 (mm. 66–69) prepares the structural cadence. (Note the similarity between the chromatic motives *f2′* in mm. 42–43 and *f2* in the D-major interlude, mm. 121–22 [Example 2.4], in the same harmonic context.) As in the Allegro assai, we enjoy neither rhythmic resolution nor tonal closure until the very end of the exposition; and this instability is, again, reproduced in heightened form in the recapitulation.

On the other hand, the chief motive *a5/e3* undergoes a remarkable transformation between the opening theme and the end of the exposition. Even mm. 1–2, as noted above, harbor the potentially "melodic" *e3*. This potential begins to be realized as early as the cadence of the same theme, mm. 15–16: the change of harmony within m. 15 juxtaposes $g\sharp^1$ and a^1, and the strong harmonic progression across the barline compels us to hear them as a progression. This completes the literal resolution that was avoided in mm. 2–3; the melody, if not yet the bass, already realizes the upbeat-downbeat, tonally directed implication of this motive. Motive *e3* becomes even stronger later on. The transition shows *e* as explicitly legato (mm. 21–24), and thus encourages an interpretation of m. 27 as *e1*, continuing with *e3* across the barline. But the bass still hesitates; it is only at the clinching structural cadence of the second group (mm. 69–71) that both outer parts join in rhythmic unison on the coherent, upbeat-downbeat *e3* motive. (Bars 69 and 70 could no longer even theoretically constitute the harmonically stable *a5*; the harmony changes *within* each bar, and the melodic third is expanded to non-triadic fourths.) The exposition thus moves from downbeat triadic fragments, resting-in-themselves yet rhythmically unstable, to upbeat-downbeat, goal-directed melodic steps, supported by active harmonic progressions and informed by strong rhythmic unity – yet all on "the same" motive (note the return of the skip-appoggiaturas). (This kind of motivic-rhythmic transformation from the beginning to the end of an exposition is common in Haydn.[20] In the recapitulation, this cadence resolves $g\sharp^1$–a^1 itself; see Example 1.3. As that example also shows, the codetta – based on the incipiently transitional new theme from m. 17 – confirms the change: its motives are also upbeat-downbeat, and move by step across the barlines.) In this gradual realization of *e3*'s potential, developing variation is thus a *constituent* of the form, just as it is in Brahms. Still better is to come, in the farewell music.

[20] Thrasybulos Georgiades, "Zur Musiksprache der Wiener Klassiker," *MJb* 1951, pp. 50–59.

This change is prepared during the long second group, which is dominated by legato and syncopated versions of *e* material (still Example 2.11). They are adumbrated in the transition (mm. 21–24), based on the original form of *e* from the Allegro assai: two-note, full-bar descending steps (cf. Example 2.3, mm. 44–49). The legato ductus takes over for good with the new motive *e4* (mm. 34–35), emphasized by the first expressively syncopated note in the movement; it engenders not only the bare passage mm. 37–44, but the entire poignant, minor-colored paragraph mm. 47–69. Especially important is a new progression just following the evaded cadence at mm. 45–46 (evaded, indeed, by means of *e4*). The resumption of activity (mm. 47–48) links two consecutive *e4*s into a descending motive of four notes; that is, it creates a new version of *e2* – now for the first time a "real" motive, with its own expressive character. Essential here is the chromatic rise in the bass to V, emphasizing ♯4̂ (this *e2*+bass progression will be of great importance in both finales). We have already learned to associate *e2* with potentially structural melodic motion; its prominent exposure on a strong dominant now raises the possibility of its eventual resolution onto the tonic – of a union of melodic coherence and tonal closure. In principle, this could take either of two forms (see Example 2.13):

Example 2.13 Possible resolutions of motive *e2*

transposition down a step while maintaining the motivic identity of *e2* as a four-note figure, with the consequent phrase consisting essentially of V–I, with or without elaboration (two possible forms are shown in Example 2.13a); or an extension of the motive to five notes rather than four, with recapture of the initial 5̂ and a complete I–V–I progression (Example 2.13b).[21] Both forms of resolution will prove vitally important in the minuet and the farewell movement, in both foreground and background.

In this movement, however, neither form of closure is granted to this motive. To be sure, following the chromatic mystification, mm. 65–68 bring *e2* in the bass underneath

---

[21] Ex. 2.13 is adapted from Schenker, Exx. 87/5 and 88/1–4. (Schenker does not illustrate the "motivic" type of consequent beginning on 4̂; but it is common enough – as we will see.)

e4 in the melody, always one step behind in voice exchange. This diatonic legato, within the otherwise chromatic second group, prepares the resolution on *e3* at the structural cadence. But *e2* does not participate in that resolution: it is relegated to the weak inversions IV$_6$–I^6. On the other hand, these bars (mm. 65–68) establish another important idea: a distinctive "rocking" motion, resulting from the voice exchanges and alternating weak inversions. This entails a delay on $\hat{4}$ in the bass (m. 68), which accommodates the transformation of IV into V^2, "dissolving" the rocking motion so that the ensuing move to I^6 (m. 69) can initiate the structural cadence itself. (In the Allegro assai, $\hat{4}$ has already inhibited the resolution of dominants to root-position tonics: mm. 21–26 vs. 27–28 and 56 vs. 57 [Example 2.3], and especially mm. 157–66 vs. 169–70, and 175–76 vs. 178–79 [Examples 2.5 and 2.9]; this "reverse" emphasis was first heard in the opening theme [Example 2.1, mm. 11–12 vs. 14]. This progression will play an even more important role towards the end of the other adagio movement, in the climactic F-sharp-major farewell section.)

Overall, then, the Adagio melodies remain troubled. They become important in the foreground; the expressive *e2* comes into its own, even generating the transformation of the principal motive *a5/e3* at the cadence. But *e2* itself can play no role in this modest triumph; it cannot even resolve its own dominant. The possibility of melody has now been given too clearly to be suppressed, and it has been shown to have potential as a force for coherence. But it cannot yet articulate such coherence on its own.

MINUET AND TRIO: AMBIGUITY

In the minuet and trio, we finally hear F-sharp major as a key, and clear stepwise melodic descents to the tonic in both foreground and background. But the key of F-sharp is projected tentatively, and still clouded by minor-mode mixtures; both the structural voice leading and the form are ambiguous. We still experience no sense of resolution.

The minuet

The first two bars (see Example 2.14a) are *piano* for the violins alone, without bass, and they avoid stable projection of the new tonic root in favor of $\hat{5}$ and $\hat{3}$. The initial attack is an unaccompanied c♯^{2}, reflecting the end of the Adagio (see Example 1.3); the accompaniment enters on a♯^{1}, to which the melody itself immediately moves, both by skip in m. 1 and by step in mm. 1–2 as a whole; the tonic in the second violin arrives only on the last beat of each measure. Only in m. 3 do the other instruments enter – but the *forte* D in the bass disrupts the delicate melodic play. This abrupt entry on a mixture from the minor, creating a harsh augmented fifth with respect to the just-achieved a♯^{1}, is a rude shock. (This juxtaposition reflects the D-major interlude in the Allegro assai, which provocatively followed the first F-sharp-major sonority in the symphony. The interlude was not only contextually unintegrated, but its root D could not resolve normally to the dominant; now, at last, it does – but only after again destabilizing things!) The combination of this tentative opening and this obtrusive

Example 2.14 Minuet

(a)

(b)

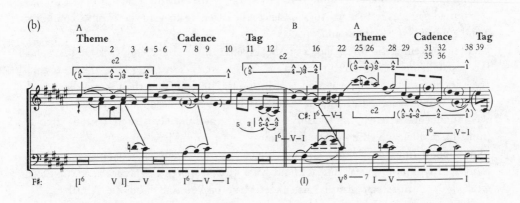

(c)

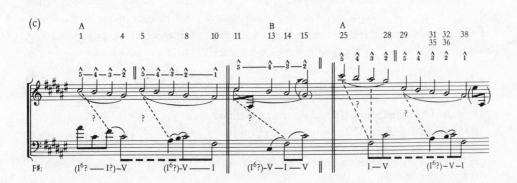

interruption throws F-sharp major under a cloud: it finally appears as a tonic, but it cannot resolve the prevailing tension.

The "tag" ending of each half of the minuet (Example 2.14, mm. 11–12 [=39–40]) is remarkable. Following the structural cadences (mm. 10, 38), the violins end each section, and thus the movement as a whole, as they began it: quiet and unaccompanied, the dynamics indeed intensified into *pianissimo* (a mark which is always significant for Haydn at the end of a movement; see Chapter 5). As noted in Chapter 1, this descending, two-bar, essentially triadic gesture (*a*7) varies the opening theme of the Allegro assai (*a*); in this sense, the entire cycle (the first three movements) concludes where it began – transformed from fierce agitation to wistful insubstantiality. But the tag also recapitulates the pitch content of the opening of the minuet itself: $\hat{5}$–$\hat{4}$–$\hat{3}$, spread over two measures. This striking unaccompanied motive is heard six times (if not indeed eight, as in most "historical" performances), always in the same exposed formal context; its aesthetic – a quiet, insubstantial ending – is surely destined to play a significant role later on. The minuet also relates to the Adagio. The opening phrase is an almost literal transposition of the earlier movement's second phrase (see Example 2.11, mm. 3–4); it is even closer to the second-group variant (mm. 29–30) – which immediately proceeds to a minor-mode mixture, just like m. 3 here. And the A section repeats, as it were in diminution, the motivic-rhythmic progression of the entire Adagio exposition: following this similar opening, mm. 7–10 proceed, like the Adagio second group, through syncopated passages to the structural cadence; the latter, again as in the Adagio, combines *a* and *e* motives in rhythmic unison.

Given the emphasis on $\hat{3}$ and $\hat{5}$ at the expense of the tonic, the lack of bass, and the destabilizing minor mixture in m. 3, it is scarcely surprising that the structural voice leading of this section is odd (see Example 2.14b, an unorthodox middleground analysis which reflects this unusual effect). The potential headnote is uncertain: is it the prominent, repeated, motivically significant, rhythmically strong takeoff pitch $\hat{5}$ (mm. 1a, 5, 10c), which however never enjoys root-position bass support; or the $\hat{3}$ with tonic support (mm. 1c, 2c, 6c), towards which the motive always gravitates, but which is always rhythmically weak and without bass? If we suppose the latter, these high and weak $\hat{3}/\mathrm{I}$ sonorities can scarcely articulate a true background headnote. Until m. 10, every F♯ is rhythmically weak and confined to the inner parts; even the second bass entry (m. 7) is only on I⁶. The root-position tonic at the structural cadence (m. 10=38), just before the tag, can only be the *concluding* background $\hat{1}/\mathrm{I}$ (whether of the A section or of the entire minuet). Hence the entire A section is an augmentation of the opening two bars, I⁶–V–I, and its background comprises merely two chords,

$$\begin{array}{lcl} \hat{2}-\hat{1} & & (\hat{5}-\hat{4}-\hat{3})-\hat{2}-\hat{1} \\ \mathrm{V}-\mathrm{I} & \text{elaborated as} & (\mathrm{I}^6-\mathrm{V}-\mathrm{I})-\mathrm{V}-\mathrm{I} \end{array}$$

(see again Example 2.14b). (Schenker acknowledged such "incomplete" progressions in the foreground and middleground, for "smoothness";[22] in the background, however,

---

[22] See *Free Composition*, §244–245 (Chopin's Op. 28, No. 2; figure 110, a3). Another often-cited example is Brahms's Intermezzo in B-flat, Op. 76, No. 4.

he admitted them only to the ghetto of preludes and waltzes, not into large-scale movements in sonata style.)

As described earlier, the tag ending of the A section recaptures the high initial c♯^{2}.
From here, the foreground motive a5 carries the four-note descent e2, with the same
harmonization I^6–V–I–V, *across* the double-bar to m. 16. ($\hat{2}$ is delayed and transferred to
the upper octave, but the connection is clear.) The B section is thus governed by another
$\hat{2}$/V preceded by unstable $\hat{5}$/$\hat{3}$ play. To be sure, the $\hat{3}$/I in m. 14 is a vigorous *forte*, with
bass; but the root-position tonic is still rhythmically weak and fails to coincide with $\hat{3}$,
and the phrase still carries through to the dominant. This dominant is tonicized for more
than eight bars, with a full cadence in m. 22, before preparing the reprise at m. 25.
And the reprise is stronger in every way than the beginning: *forte*; for full ensemble
including the bass; the oboes, first horn, and first and second violins united on the
melody in the highest registers. It is thus a modest example of what Kerman has called
"thematic completion": a withholding of the definitive or only satisfying version of an
important idea until near the end.[23] Hence mm. 25–26 finally provide a background
tonic, projected as strongly as the following dominant (mm. 27–28), which leads directly
to the paired cadential phrases and the final $\hat{1}$/I. The deceptive cadence in m. 34 is no mere
rhythmic extension: the bass d♯^{1} cancels that disruptive d^1 (just heard again), a diatonic
emphasis without which closure would not be possible. These closing phrases (including
mm. 7–10) are also the only ones to alter the prevailing two-bar module to integrated
four-bar cadences.

The minuet thus exhibits a markedly progressive structure. The opening A section is
weak and tentative, the B section in the dominant clearer and stronger, the reprise
strongest of all. In addition, the A|B–A form of the voice leading is not congruent with
the surface form (see Example 2.14c). Because the first structural progression is complete in m. 10, the tag, which returns to $\hat{5}$, actually initiates the next descent, running
across the double bar into the B section. Only at the end is its aesthetic effect – an
"after-event" – congruent with its structural function.

The trio

The trio (Example 2.15) is also in F-sharp major. (This is unusual; ordinarily, when a
Haydn minuet is in the opposite mode from the first movement, the trio reverts to the
original mode.) It begins with a theme for solo horns (mm. 41–46), which Landon
calls a variant of the so-called "Lamentation" chant melody Haydn used in several
instrumental works.[24] Once again we begin without bass (although to be sure many
trios feature reduced scoring); once again we head straight for a half cadence by means

[23] In "Beethoven," *The New Grove*, vol. 2, p. 381; repr. in Kerman and Alan Tyson, *The New Grove Beethoven* (New York
and London, 1983), pp. 106–7. (He has used the term "thematic completion" itself, as far as I know, only in unpublished papers.)

[24] Landon, *Symphonies*, pp. 190, 289–93, 339. But in this case Haydn did not label the incipit or place it in an overtly
religious context, as he did in Symphony No. 26 and the divertimento Hob. II:23; nor does its similarity to the chant
melody extend beyond the rise from $\hat{1}$ to repeated notes on $\hat{3}$.

Example 2.15 Trio

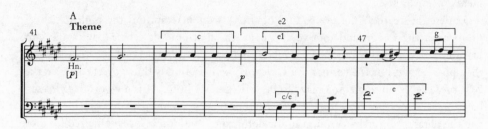

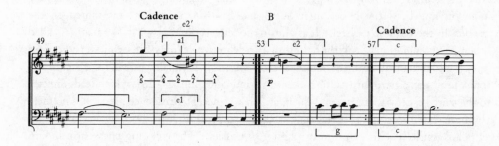

Ex. 2.15 (cont.)

of motive *e2* descending from $\hat{5}$ to $\hat{2}$. Now, however, the theme is longer (six bars); and its half cadence immediately generates a modulation to the dominant (mm. 47–52), where the A section ends with a full cadence. The B section is unusual in that it is based on a different theme, presented twice, and with a strange juxtaposition of major and minor. It first appears as a complete eight-bar sentence in the major (2+2+4), ending with a full cadence in m. 60. Hence it is odd to hear it immediately repeated in the minor, again ending with a full cadence. (The *forte–piano* phrases in mm. 65–68 recall the rude interruption in mm. 3–4 of the minuet, especially d²–c♯² in mm. 67–68.) These two cadences in mm. 60 and 70 are the clearest and strongest in the entire symphony to this point, and the first ones that so much as touch low F♯ in the bass. But their large-scale mixture of major and minor confirms what the minuet only hinted at: the minor mode has not been overcome. The non-congruence between these modal mixtures and the calm repetitions and firm cadences is itself destabilizing, and forestalls what otherwise might be a sense of resolution. (In this respect, the effect is like that of the D-major interlude.)

In addition, the form is highly unusual; in the middle, the B section "takes over" from the lamentation theme. The usual construction (even in Haydn) of this kind of trio would be A|B–A (not ABA), with each section of comparable length; B would be a contrast or intensification on or in the dominant, and would *resolve into* the reprise: say, 12|8–10 or 12|10–12. (If the B section were substantially extended, it would be over a dominant pedal.) Here, however, both B periods cadence in the tonic; mm. 61–70 are not a recapitulation at all, but a modally varied repetition of B. To be sure, the lamentation theme finally returns; but it has been absent a long time, it follows the two strong perfect cadences, and it is very soft. (Admittedly, the full scoring provides a measure of "thematic completion.") It sounds more like a wistful recall than a form-defining reprise. On the other hand, its cadence (mm. 75–76) recapitulates *both* dominant cadences from the first part: mm. 45–46 on the dominant (compare the rhythm of *e2*, both times beginning on c♯²–b¹ following motive *c*); and the closing mm. 51–52 in the dominant (compare the bass motive *e1* and the pitch content of the melody, an exact transposition down a fifth). Although the sonata principle is thus observed in miniature, the horn theme makes an incongruous frame to the static, tonally stable, but unintegrated major/minor B section.

Ambiguities

In one crucial respect, the minuet and trio achieve more than either of the previous movements: the descending stepwise motive *e2* comes into its own as the foreground and background vehicle of melodic resolution. In the minuet (Example 2.14), it creates all of the structural $\hat{2}$/V sonorities, the last of which is incorporated into a satisfyingly complete background progression. (If one prefers the more orthodox $\hat{5}$-line interpretation shown in Example 2.14c, the minuet resolves these *e2*s as five-note background motives descending from $\hat{5}$ – one of the two possible forms of such a resolution; compare Example 2.13b.) And in the trio (Example 2.15), *e2* not only dominates in the fore-ground, for example at the first half-cadence (mm. 45–46), but in the modally mixed B section it unequivocally resolves down to the tonic in the background as well. In the major period, mm. 57–60 bring the first unbroken stepwise descent from $\hat{5}$ to $\hat{1}$ in the entire symphony, over a strongly articulated perfect authentic cadence (compare again Example 2.13b); the ensuing minor period, again for the first time in the symphony, resolves with an unadorned four-note descent to $\hat{1}$, harmonized by an equally strong cadence (the "other" potential resolution, as in Example 2.13a). The potential of *e2* to serve as the carrier of significant melody is finally realized – during the first movement in the tonic major.

But these melodic resolutions take place in a context of ambiguous background voice leading. The minuet may have an incomplete background, with no initial tonic (Example 2.14b). A different analysis, based on the motivic descents from C♯, is shown in Example 2.14c. Even here, however, the putative headnote $\hat{5}$ suffers from inadequate bass support (described above); it never coincides with a root-position tonic. Only the beginning of the reprise – the thematic completion – enjoys root-position bass support in the correct register. A further problem with this suggested interruption structure of both A sections is that the consequent phrase (mm. 5–10, 29–38) never regains a meaningful root-position tonic; this implies that the initial sonority is not recaptured. This structural ambiguity makes the entire minuet sound unfocused, an especially strange effect in the context of its clear $\hat{5}$–$\hat{2}$, $\hat{5}$–$\hat{1}$ melodic organization in the foreground.

The background voice leading in the trio also exhibits odd disjunctions (see Example 2.14b); the ambiguity between $\hat{3}$ and $\hat{5}$ is still present. The horn theme reiterates a♯[1] as if nothing could compromise it, yet *e2* again takes off from c♯[2]; the bass, coming in at the last minute, is again no help. In the B section, however, $\hat{5}$ serves as the headnote for six *e2* descents in a row, preparing not only each $\hat{2}$/V but both perfect cadences in mm. 60 and 70; no comparable emphasis on $\hat{3}$ is heard. Also, the major-mode cadence (mm. 57–60) resembles the minuet in being harmonized as I⁶–V–I, with no root-position tonic until the cadence. The subsequent minor-mode cadence, to be sure, reaches the tonic under the last $\hat{5}$ (m. 68), but this seems much too late in a "periodic" form for an *initial* background sonority, even one preceded by an initial ascent from $\hat{1}$ or $\hat{3}$. What is worse, the recapitulation of the horn theme incorporates the only unambiguous background progression in the trio, initial low F# and all – but it can only be based on $\hat{3}$! ($\hat{5}$ has "nowhere to go" in mm. 71–76; see Example 2.15b.) The trio is as ambiguous in structure as it is unintegrated in form.

Although they close this "cycle" in the tonic major, the minuet and trio remain clouded. The major mode cannot suppress echoes of the minor, rudely disruptive in the minuet, wistfully unintegrated in the trio. The melodic entries are off-tonic and have no bass. Even their ostensibly clear structures are ambiguous, both formally and in terms of the underlying voice leading. (In addition, the minuet consistently uses both *piano* and *forte*; it is the only movement in the symphony that must shuttle uneasily between the two basic dynamic levels.) And the last thing we hear is the minuet's off-tonic tag.

A PROMISE OF RESOLUTION

The first three movements of the Farewell Symphony seem consistent only in their abnormality. Each projects its tonic in an incomplete or unstable manner, reaching closure only at the last moment – indeed, in the Allegro assai, failing to articulate it persuasively at all. Its violence and rhythmic obsession are not resolved by the Adagio or the minuet; both movements are shot through with ambiguities, and neither succeeds in banishing the minor. The D-major interlude remains a mystery; the use of triple meter in three consecutive symphony movements is unprecedented. The structural voice leading of all three movements is problematical: the Allegro assai is based on an unusual background progression, with an almost impossibly long central dominant and a comparably "delayed" structural downbeat; despite the clear foreground cadences, $\hat{3}/\hat{5}$ ambiguity begins and ends both the minuet and trio.

The first three movements exhibit a basic ambiguity as to the role of the pitch class C# ($\hat{5}$). (To be sure, in minor-mode movements it is often difficult to decide whether $\hat{3}$ or $\hat{5}$ should be taken as the headnote.[25]) Despite its conceptual and common-tone importance (as suggested in Example 1.1), $\hat{5}$ seems not to function as a "universal" background headnote: in the Allegro assai, only $\hat{3}$ seems plausible; in the minuet, the ambiguity between a prominent but unsupported $\hat{5}$ and a vertically well-supported but contextually weak $\hat{3}$ is never resolved. This ambiguity is then confirmed by the final tag: $\hat{5}$–$\hat{3}$ without bass. (The Adagio, in A major, is a different case. If C# were the universal headnote, this movement would have a $\hat{3}$-line; the opening theme [Example 2.11] shows at once that, again, either $\hat{3}$ or $\hat{5}$ is possible. We will take up the issue of A-major backgrounds within

---

[25] Schenker's *Free Composition* and other late writings, which of course include many analyses of minor-mode movements, do not focus on the specific differences between major and minor backgrounds (in §98, he never states that the *point* of Ex. 26 is that it's in the minor!). Schachter discusses the issue in "A Commentary on Schenker's *Free Composition*," *JMT* 25 (1981), 126–28, but only in the context of defending Schenker's liking for $\hat{5}$-lines against recent attacks. A comprehensive study is wanting.

an overall context of F-sharp in the "farewell" movement, in conjunction with the appearance of A in the middle of the through-composed double finale.)

The instability of the first three movements, their alternatingly violent and troubled style, the dissociative effect of the D-major interlude, and the ambiguous form of the minuet and trio create a special kind of musical world – a world in which all the events point *beyond*: beyond any cadences yet heard, towards different music, towards stability and resolution – in a word, towards the end of the symphony. At this point, however, the end is not in view; indeed it can hardly be imagined on the basis of what we have heard so far. To be sure, progress has been made, not only from minor to major, but also towards the possibility of stepwise melody: from unrealized potential (in the Allegro assai) and irrelevant daydreaming (in the D-major interlude), through clear functioning (though still no structural role) in the Adagio, to basic background and foreground significance (though insufficient coherence) in the minuet and trio. This gradual emergence of melody in the context of an implied resolution to the major cuts across the prevailing instability and ambiguity, and suggests the possibility of more meaningful resolutions to come. The double finale will create new patterns, of decreasing tension and increasing stability. At the end, the programmatic "farewell" music will bring about an apotheosis: a transfiguration of the difficult musical language of the symphony.

3

RESOLUTION

THE FORM OF THE DOUBLE FINALE

The second cycle of the Farewell Symphony comprises the Presto and the unique Adagio farewell movement, which together make up the double finale. (The rationale for this term has been given in Chapter 1; see also the discussion of eighteenth-century genre patterns in Chapter 6.) It is entirely progressive – not merely in being through-composed and in the "action" of the "farewells," but also in thematic development and formal and tonal structure. The farewell music has never been analyzed; a brief overview at the beginning of this chapter may therefore be helpful. However, its form can be understood only in conjunction with the Presto: the movement pair is not only run-on, but governed by a single background progression (see Example 3.5 below). The Presto, in many respects a typical "Sturm und Drang" symphonic finale, is in very clear sonata form, except that the recapitulation breaks off at the last minute without attaining closure; this disruption leads to a structural dominant, which does not resolve, but progresses indirectly to A major and the farewell movement (this join is shown in Example 1.4). The latter is in two main parts: a binary movement in A (mm. 1–55), and a compressed recapitulation and conclusion in F-sharp major (mm. 68–107); they are linked by a modulating transition (mm. 55–67), which "recaptures" the unresolved structural dominant from the end of the Presto. (Throughout this discussion I use Landon's measure numbering for the farewell movement; the corresponding numbers in *JHW* are higher by 150.) Hence the concluding F-sharp-major section provides tonal resolution for the entire double finale. The opening root-position F-sharp-major triad (m. 68) resolves the structural dominant in the foreground (it is the first strong V–I cadence in F-sharp since mm. 136–38 of the Presto, still in the minor). Most importantly, the repeated strong cadences towards the end (mm. 85, 103) grant us the long-awaited musical and gestural closure – at the very end of the symphony and in the tonic major, and there alone. This integrated form is further articulated by the linked pair of structural roots A and C♯, which govern all the background and middleground progressions, especially the (in this context) so essential transitions.

Musical stability vs. progressive form

In many respects, this complex movement-pair repeats the pattern of the first three movements: F-sharp minor moves via A major to the tonic major; full scoring with primarily *forte* dynamics yields to *pianissimo* solo violins; and so on. But in other ways it is utterly different. Both movements point towards the end as towards an apotheosis. They are not merely through-composed in the obvious sense of breaking off and being linked by transitions; they systematically postpone closure until the final section in F-sharp major – and this ending, unlike that in the minuet, *resolves* the music which precedes it. The complex themes (many of which continue to develop familiar motives) are eventually liquidated into "pure" triadic and scalar motives – fundamental musical entities. The tonal articulations become increasingly coherent and increasingly diatonic, most of all in F-sharp major at the end. The "farewell" procedure is progressive in its own right; the gradual and systematic reduction of the ensemble to two muted solo violins creates a unique "negative climax" at the end of the symphony.

On the other hand – and this is especially striking in the context of the first three movements – the surface musical language becomes "normal." The basic material is clear and stable. The Presto (at last) is in duple meter (Example 3.1). Its opening theme

Example 3.1 Presto, main theme

(at last) is a balanced antecedent-consequent period based on four-measure phrases; this tames the contrast between *piano* and *forte*, harmony and unison texture. The outer parts emphasize the stable scale degrees of $\hat{1}$ and $\hat{5}$ and the stable intervals of fourth and fifth. (Hardly any melodic leaps between $\hat{1}$ and $\hat{5}$ occur in the first three movements, none in the main thematic material.) Melody and bass proceed without rhythmic conflict; in the antecedent the bass marks every downbeat with a firm half note. Most important, both phrases lead to strong, rhythmically unified, root-position cadences. The octaves in mm. 5–6 are only a medial contrast; the cadence restores full texture. (The main theme of the Allegro assai was not a period, and its destabilization affected the cadence itself.) Although the low A in m. 6 recalls mm. 9–14 of the earlier movement, both phrases exhibit clear, well-supported downward step motion; the half cadence in m. 4 (at last) places a functioning dominant of F-sharp minor in a proper bass register. Most important, this stable opening theme, including the strong tonic cadence, is immediately repeated in its entirety. Given the return to the tonic minor and the very fast tempo, it would be difficult to imagine a stronger contrast to the Allegro assai.

The farewell movement also begins with a prominent melodic fifth. In many ways, it resembles the earlier Adagio (see Example 3.2): in key, tempo, and meter, as well as a

Example 3.2 Farewell movement and Adagio: thematic relations

tendency towards short phrases. Indeed, its first ten bars amount to a "subliminal" recomposition of the first eight bars of the Adagio (only the half-cadences diverge). On the other hand, its rhythmic gestures and mood are quite different. It begins in rhythmic unison, with the bass on the downbeat; the initial cadences in mm. 2 and 4 arrive together in melody and bass; that in m. 10 is even stronger. Even the offbeat melodic motives in mm. 7–8 are contained within strong bass downbeats; they retain little of the unstable, disruptive quality of the earlier *c* motives. The calm, moderate harmonic rhythm (primarily quarters and eighths) remains steady, yet supple; strong cadences appear frequently, but they are modulated in metric placement and "weight." There are no subverted cadences or disoriented bass lines like those in the Adagio, mm. 36–42 and 45–47, no passages of mystification like 160–76. At the end, the stable, clarified character of F-sharp major differs fundamentally from its tentative and clouded mien in the minuet and trio.

Many other important features of both movements are more neutral, less provocative, than before. Dominants arrive in root position and lead to root-position tonics. The form of the Presto is simple, that of the farewell movement complex but intelligible; in both, the paragraph structure is crystal clear. The surface rhythm is straightforward; for example, in the Presto there are hardly any syncopations, merely a few "fourth-species" suspensions in mm. 24ff and (by implication) the offbeat attacks in mm. 31ff; in the farewell movement, there are no syncopations whatever. There are no major/minor mixtures; the A-major farewell section never so much as hints at A minor. Indeed, there are few chromatic notes of any kind; except for the bass in transition passages, none is of more than local significance. Each movement modulates to only one key in the exposition; there are no remote keys. The development of the Presto harbors no new themes, evaded cadences, or other disquieting novelties. Both finales exhibit a clear and regular reprise of the main theme in the tonic, prepared by a clear and strong dominant; in the Presto this reprise even includes the perfect cadence at the end of the theme (m. 105), so that the entire recapitulation is tonally grounded from the beginning.

The second cycle thus has a different "internal rhythm" from the first. Each of the first three movements is different from the others; they remain separate, unintegrated. They have in common only their instability, their postponement of (inadequate) closure to the last moment; their only suggestion of increasing coherence – the emergence of melody within a change from minor to major – is not realized. The two finales are paradoxical in the "opposite" way. Their musical language is stable, almost conventional; they are clear and comprehensible throughout; every note implies that satisfactory closure will be achieved. Nevertheless, they are through-composed, welded into a single structure (and a single psychological progression); in this respect they are by far the more unorthodox half of the symphony. The liquidation of the thematic material and the increasingly strong tonal coherence create a new and different *kind* of F-sharp major at the end of the symphony: not a distant or abstract idea presented hesitantly, but a concrete tonal and expressive reality.

Presto

The movement is in very clear sonata form (see Example 3.3); its main theme has been described above. The four-bar transition theme (Example 3.1, mm. 17–20) grows out of the headmotive, in the varied form *h2* already associated with unison texture, and modulates directly to the dominant of A. The second group (shown in part in Example 3.7a below; the recapitulation in 3.7b) comprises four themes (**a–d**), unvaryingly loud

Example 3.3 Presto: form

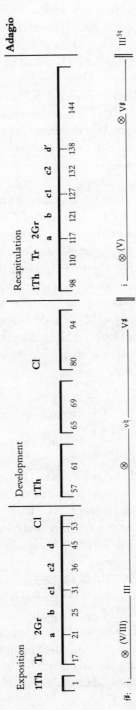

and almost breathless, linked into a single paragraph whose cadences become progressively stronger. (No such integrated progression was heard in the exposition of the Allegro assai.) The first, imitative theme **a** (mm. 21–24) includes no root-position dominants and cadences essentially on I⁶; the rushing eighth notes of the next theme **b** arrive on a root-position tonic (m. 31), but the harmony is merely a circle-of-fifths sequence, and the melody only attains $\hat{3}$ (C♯). In contrast, the driving, implicitly syncopated theme **c** (Example 3.7a) leads, via additional rushing eighths, to a very strong cadence (m. 45), but the momentum continues unbroken through theme **d**, whose nearly identical cadence (mm. 52–53) is the structural goal of the entire paragraph. The closing theme (mm. 53–56) clinches this arrival with four additional root-position V–I cadences, in the accelerating rhythm characteristic of such confirmations. This headlong rush towards unambiguous closure sets up the decisive disruption at the end of the movement.

The development falls into two parts. The first (mm. 57–80) explores the main theme and centers around the dominant minor; this unusual key-emphasis, following the second group in A, further exploits the overall A/C♯ tonal organization. The second part (mm. 81–97) is based (again unusually) on the closing theme; it passes through A major and even the tonic on its way to the home dominant. The recapitulation then proceeds regularly – *too* regularly. For the overwhelming drive towards the structural cadence is subverted at the end of the *third* second-group theme **c** (see p. 95); although **d** follows, it is deformed into an unstable transition back to the dominant. The structural cadence of the second group (m. 53) is never recapitulated; closure is denied, symmetry undermined; the "sonata principle" itself is compromised. The closing theme obviously can play no role; perhaps this accounts for its prominence towards the end of the development.

The farewell movement

The farewell movement is in two parts, in A (mm. 1–55) and in F-sharp (mm. 68–107), linked by a modulating transition (see the upper part of Example 3.4); each part is divided into two sections of roughly equal length. (The material is shown in Examples 3.8, 3.11–3.13, an overview of the form and the background voice leading in 3.5, and detailed voice-leading diagrams in 3.10 through 3.13. Each of these examples is explicated in the appropriate place below.) The A-major part is in binary form, 31+24, with a compressed and reordered second half. The first half (shown in Example 3.8) is an exposition: main theme, transition, second theme with structural cadence, and closing theme. Each theme is bipartite, constructed essentially as theme–cadence. The main theme (6+4) comprises three short downbeat phrases (aba) – the three full cadences in a row are again unusually stable – and a contrasting offbeat phrase, ending on a strong half cadence. (Insofar as it "begins over again" in m. 5, it could also be construed as an antiperiod: 2+2 cadencing on I, 2+4 on V.) The transition (mm. 11–18) immediately transforms this half cadence into the dominant key, and leads to an equally strong cadence on V/V; its first phrase develops the original headmotive, but the continuation (mm. 15–16) adds the chromatic

Example 3.4 Farewell movement: form

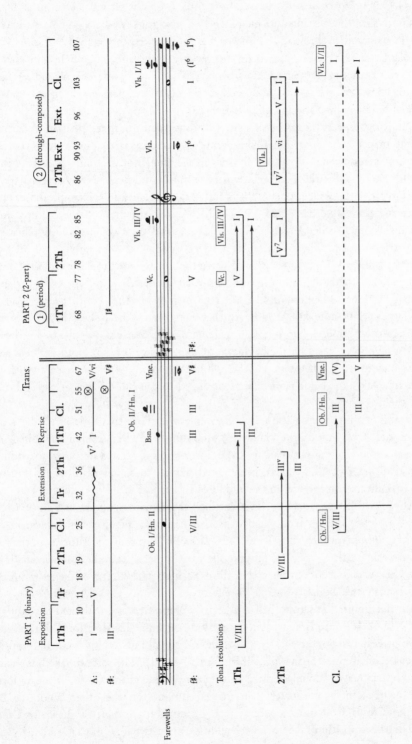

eighths b$\sharp^1$ and e$\sharp^1$ (motive *e8*), derived from mm. 7–8. The second theme (mm. 18c–25) begins with a motivically intricate melody over a "rocking" V^2–I^6, V$^6_5$–I bass; the cadence reverts to the familiar chromatic neighbors and the plain descending scale of mm. 17–18. The balance is remarkable: the main theme and transition, whose headmotives are related, constitute an antiperiod moving to V/V and preparing the second group; at the same time the transition and second theme, with parallel cadences, make an antecedent-consequent period in the dominant.

But in other respects the entire exposition is continuous. Each member arises harmonically out of the preceding one (main-theme cadence and transition on V, transition cadence and second theme on V/V); all develop the same motives; only the second theme ends with an authentic cadence. The rhythm is supple and flexible: the three paragraphs differ from each other in length (10+8+7) and phrase organization (Example 3.8). Despite its three successive two-bar phrases with full cadences, the main theme has no taint of "mechanism"; each cadence falls on an afterbeat, and no two in succession have the same metric position. The transition is a clear sentence, (2+2)+4, but the small-scale consequent (mm. 13–14) is linked seamlessly to the somewhat chromatic cadential phrase. And the second theme is the most complex of all, in detail as well as phrase structure. Each main *m* motive begins off the beat (the melody on the sixteenth-note level, the bass on the eighth-note level). Nor are they congruent: the offbeat bass *c/e* motives are contained within each bar, but each melodic motive cascades over the barline beyond the next downbeat – until, at the beginning of the cadence (m. 23), both aspects reverse, the bass moving to A on the downbeat, while the melody breathes. Even the strongly confirmatory closing theme (mm. 25–31) is elided to the full cadence at the end of the second theme.

Now this closing theme features concertante solos for the oboes and the second horn; in fact, they initiate the "farewell" procedure itself. As Landon has noted, each player has a solo just before departing (here, first oboe and second horn – crooked in E!). But in addition (what has never been noted), these solos are essential to the form. (They are indicated on the staff in the middle of Example 3.4, along with the "exit" pitch for each departing instrument.) In particular, the remaining oboe and horn (in A!) also solo on the closing theme, and depart, *in the tonic, during the recapitulation of the same closing theme* (mm. 51–55). These two "farewells" are thus constituents of the form. Far from being mere jokes, or programmatic gimmicks, they create a thematic and instrumental parallel between the end of the exposition and the end of the recapitulation. They articulate the "sonata principle" itself.

Up to this point, the second half has been a compressed and reordered recapitulation (Example 3.4). It comprises two ten-bar periods: in mm. 32–41, a tonal retransition is fused to a recapitulation of the second theme on the dominant; they not only precede, but prepare, the reprise of the main theme (mm. 42–51). The second half thus includes the highly articulated "double return" of the main theme characteristic of sonata form – despite being somewhat shorter than the exposition. On the other hand, the main theme now leads to a full cadence, which is actually a variant of the second-theme cadence in the exposition, likewise at the end (Examples 3.8–3.9: mm. 49–50=23–24 *and*

9–10; the chromatic neighbors in mm. 49–50 ensure the connection). Hence the sonata principle applies to the structural cadence of the second section as much as to the "farewell" codetta.

Now only the strings are left. The violone (double-bass) leads the transition (mm. 55–67, Example 3.11) in a rhythmically subtle rising sequence from A through B minor to C♯, and then he, too, departs. (His "farewell" is also based on the closing theme.) This C♯ is of course the home dominant; as we have seen, it rhymes tonally with the end of the Presto. (The transitions to these two dominants are structurally related as composings-out of the fundamental A/C♯ relationship; see Example 3.5 below.) The entire A-major farewell music is thus, in one sense, a vast interpolation between these two dominants.

The concluding F-sharp-major music comprises a compressed and varied recapitulation of the A-major music; a second, primarily new, section of the same length; and a repetition of the closing theme (18+18+4). The first section (mm. 68–85, Example 3.12) features the third and fourth violin parts. (It seems possible that, like the two principals at the end, they too were performed by soloists; see pp. 14–15. The aesthetically decisive entry of soloistic music would make the most sense if correlated with the wonderful, long-delayed arrival of the tonic major.)

The section is constructed as a large-scale antecedent-consequent period (mm. 68–77, 78–85). The antecedent is a literal transposition of the main theme (mm. 68–77=1–10); the bass is the cello, who completes the half cadence on C♯ and then departs. The consequent, with only the viola on the bass, begins with the first phrase of the second theme (mm. 78–81=19–22); it culminates in a synthesis of first-theme and second-theme motives (mm. 82–85, examined below), with a very strong, form-defining perfect cadence on the octave f♯/f♯^{1}, embellished by an e♯^{1} appoggiatura. This period thus recapitulates the essential material of both the first group and the second group from the A-major part of the movement.

The third and fourth violins now yield to the two principals, muted, who mount into the highest registers and lead the movement to a close (Example 3.13). Because the essential material has already been heard in the tonic and has led to a structural cadence, this section is free to vary and eventually liquidate the motives. (It also extends F-sharp major to a sufficient length to balance the A-major section.) At first the viola still takes the bass; a repetition and extension of the second theme (mm. 86ff) lead to his departure in m. 93 (oddly, in the middle of the paragraph). The two violins, now completely alone, head for another strong cadence in mm. 94–95 – but it proves to be a deceptive cadence onto d♯^{1}/f♯^{1}, again with an e♯^{1} appoggiatura in the melody. Hence we have another extension, until the second structural cadence finally arrives in m. 103. Both cadences (mm. 82–85 and 100–03) are again supple, integrated four-bar phrases. But this one is the most "perfect" of all: a unison; the only cadence in the F-sharp-major farewell music without embellishment; indeed, except for the problematical ones in the trio, the only F-sharp-major full cadence onto a rhythmic unison downbeat anywhere in the symphony. But even now, the form is not complete, because the closing theme has not been recapitulated in the tonic. And so the violins rescale the heights to bring it safely down to earth as well.

The construction of this movement (Example 3.4) is as rigorous as its aesthetic intent is original. The roughly equal parts of the binary form in A (25+20) lead to a precisely balanced two-part form in F-sharp (18+18), the "farewell" codettas confirming each section. As indicated at the bottom of Example 3.4, every structural half cadence is matched by an appropriate full cadence – not only within the A-major part, but between A and F-sharp. The latter point is crucial: F-sharp major can only be a believable tonic at the end if it functions as the place of resolution. (This principle remains operative in Haydn and Mozart whether or not a movement exhibits an outwardly symmetrical construction such as sonata form.[1]) The resolution of the structural dominant by F-sharp major in mm. 67–68 is the first such occurrence since the entry of the reprise in the Presto (which was still in the minor). Not only is the main theme resolved within A major (half cadence in m. 10, full cadence in m. 51), but this ordered pair of cadences is itself resolved into F-sharp, within a balanced antecedent-consequent period (half cadence in m. 77, full cadence in m. 85). The second theme appears twice in the A-major section, first in the dominant key (mm. 19ff) and then on the home dominant (mm. 36ff); it also appears twice in F-sharp (mm. 78ff and 86ff), within two paragraphs both of which cadence "perfectly." And the closing theme is resolved both within A major and with respect to F-sharp – and all three times it is the very last item, or codetta, directly elided to the structural cadence. Indeed, this theme *is* the farewell melody, from its introduction in the oboes and horns, through the double-bass transition, to its ethereal ending of the symphony in the two solo muted violins. F-sharp minor, A major, the structural dominants, the entire double finale – all are subsumed within F-sharp major at the end. Everything is rounded off. The form is as logical and coherent as in any other movement by Haydn.

MOTIVIC LIQUIDATION, BACKGROUND STRUCTURE, AND CLOSURE

The sense of resolution at the end of the Farewell Symphony does not derive merely from the foreground form and tonality. The complex motivic content becomes liquidated into fundamental musical entities (pure scales and triads). And the entire double finale is governed by a single background tonal structure (see Example 3.5), three times interrupted by dividing structural dominants: twice in the Presto, at the end of the development and when it breaks off at the end, and in the transition between the two farewell sections. In the farewell movement, the disjunctions and ambiguities of the first three movements are overcome: the material and the tonal structure almost seem to interpenetrate.

---

[1] See Tovey on Haydn's quartet Op. 20 No. 2 in "Haydn's Chamber Music," in *Essays and Lectures on Music* (London, 1949), pp. 41–43; Rosen, *The Classical Style* (New York and London, 1971), pp. 72–78, 289–302; and *Sonata Forms*, pp. 104–05, 272–80. See also Chapters 5 and 8 below.

Example 3.5 Double finale: structural voice-leading

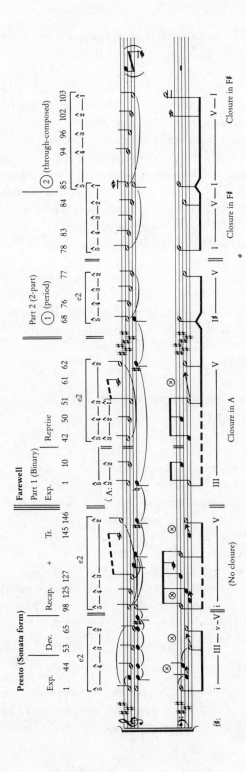

Presto

The Presto differs from the Allegro assai not merely in harmony, rhythm, and phrasing; the material of the main theme (shown in Example 3.1) is also new, and the movement develops primarily out of its motives *g2* and *h*. Moreover, disregarding for the moment the lack of closure at the end, the background of the Presto is an unproblematical interruption structure (see again Example 3.5), as different from that of the difficult Allegro assai as are its style and form. And $\hat{5}$ (c#²) is strongly articulated at once in the foreground (see Example 3.1): $\hat{1}$ leaps explosively up to it on the initial downbeat, where it receives root-position tonic support and is prolonged for most of the first two bars. To be sure, a¹ arrives on the downbeat of m. 3 over a root-position tonic, and in the consequent it is the only triad pitch to be recovered in register (mm. 6–7). But in m. 3 it is descended *to*, an unlikely initial articulation of a headnote, and in m. 6 it is a mere unison; no triad pitch receives root-position support in the consequent. Hence the a¹ in m. 6 prolongs $\hat{2}$/V (from m. 4) as a neighbor; the theme carries out an uninterrupted $\hat{5}$–$\hat{1}$ progression.

Equally important, the clear descent from $\hat{5}$ to $\hat{2}$ in the antecedent (Example 3.1) reasserts *e2* as a structural melodic motive. In fact, except for the stronger support of $\hat{5}$, its middleground is identical to the first four bars of the minuet (cf. Example 2.14b); even the bass D recurs (having learned better manners), in the same tonal and rhythmic position within the phrase. Thus *e2*, whose harmonic support was inadequate in the minuet and ambiguous in the trio, now initiates the Presto in a clear, tonally stable, antecedent-consequent theme. These melodic *e2* descents will dominate the entire double finale, on all levels – most prominently, and with the greatest structural significance, in the F-sharp-major farewell music.

The transition varies the opening phrase structurally as well as motivically (see Example 3.1): a four-bar phrase from the tonic to $\hat{2}$/V, except that "V" is now the dominant of A. This theme brings a significant new variant of motive *e2* in the bass (labeled *x*): it rises chromatically to the dominant, rather than falling diatonically from it. The derivation is confirmed by its introduction as a pair of two-note motives; *e2* was so constructed on its first "motivic" appearance, in the Adagio: the presence in both passages of the leading-tone #$\hat{4}$ in the bass, on motive *e3* in the identical rhythmic position, is telling (see Example 2.11, mm. 47–48, and imagine it transposed to A, as in the recapitulation). Here motive *x* connects the "pivot" pitch class C# to the new dominant E; this resembles the second group of the Allegro assai, where C#–E formed the bass of the middleground III⁶–v⁶ progression (Example 2.6). Functioning on all levels, *x* governs every transition in the double finale (see Example 3.6), including the most important one of all, that between the two parts of the farewell movement (Example 3.11). In so doing, it remains chromatic; it is in fact the only significant chromatic element in either movement.

However, all the later *x*s prepare the *home* dominant, connecting the structural triad pitches A and C# ($\hat{3}$ and $\hat{5}$ in the bass). Like motive *h2* of the Presto theme (which it develops), *x* is another consequence of the initial disruptive event of the symphony:

Example 3.6 Presto: transitional motive x

(a)

(b)

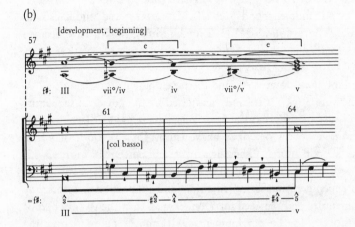

(c)

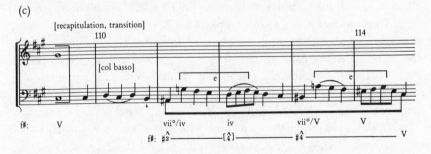

(d)

the low A and unison texture from mm. 9–14 of the Allegro assai. Up to this point, however, every structural bass connection between $\hat{3}$ and $\hat{5}$ in F-sharp minor – even mm. 6–7 of the Presto – has been unsatisfying in register (either C♯ or both pitches have been "too high," in the octave around middle C) and has generated unstable foreground events ("first-inversion" keys, the double second group, non-resolving dominants, and so forth). In the double finale, however, the pitch classes A and C♯ function together in powerful structural progressions, linking clear and stable background sonorities; in the climactic "farewell" transition, for the first and only time, they will create a coherent progression in the lowest bass register. Meanwhile, over x, the transition melody imitates the original antecedent phrase not only motivically, but in arriving on $\hat{2}$ (g♯¹) in m. 20 (Example 3.1). On the other hand, this g♯¹ arrives not from c♯², but from a¹ (the transition melody uses no middleground $\hat{5}$ at all). The unresolved middleground motive is thus the two-note progression a¹–g♯¹ ($\hat{3}$–$\hat{2}$ in the tonic); it will have decisive consequences later on.

The second group carries the *Urlinie* down to $\hat{3}$, and the development leads it on to $\hat{2}$/V (see Example 3.5). The headnote $\hat{5}$ (c♯²) is strongly reasserted by the powerful sequential descent to it in m. 31, over root-position A as the new tonic. The remainder (see Example 3.7a) leads to the two strong cadences described above (mm. 45, 53), both of which lead down through b¹ over V to a¹ over I. (There is a structural descent in mm. 43–45: the explicit $\hat{3}$–$\hat{2}$–$\hat{1}$ in the very audible first horn. The impression that the second group is not complete here thus depends primarily on rhythmic and proportional factors: the continuing whirlwind momentum and the need for a longer span than the twenty bars of the main theme and transition.) In the development, $\hat{3}$/III moves on to $\hat{2}$ over the dominant, the first of the three structural "interruptions" in the double finale. As is often the case, $\hat{2}$/V appears first as the dominant minor key (C-sharp minor, mm. 65–80), with E♮ later raised to E♯ to produce the home dominant (mm. 94–97). The development as a whole thus mirrors the original transition: $\hat{3}$–$\hat{2}$ in the melody, and III–V in the bass; indeed, motive x explicitly carries the foreground transition to C-sharp minor in mm. 61–65 (see Example 3.6b).

The recapitulation (Example 3.7b and c) recaptures $\hat{5}$ (mm. 98 and 106) and prolongs it through the initial second-group theme **a** (mm. 116–20), where it begins its background descent towards $\hat{1}$. (Once again, the bass is x: [A]–A♯–B–B♯–c♯; cf. Example 3.6c.) Before the descent begins, however, c♯² is transferred up to c♯³ by the strong oboe pedal in mm. 116–20, the violins following at m. 120. (This register transfer has been prepared by previous events. In the exposition, all the background melodic events take place in the tonal space f♯¹–c♯², which therefore seems established as the obligatory register. In the development, however, the upper octave f♯²–c♯³ increasingly takes over; I call this henceforth simply the "high register," the former the "low register.") But the *Urlinie* fails to descend to the tonic. To be sure, the second group appears to articulate such a descent in mm. 125–38: b² (mm. 125–26) is supported by V⁷ at the end of the circle of fifths, and a² (second oboe, completing the sequence in m. 127) by the tonic, prolonged by voice exchange through m. 136; then follows a very clear, bar-by-bar

Example 3.7 Presto, second group:

(a) Exposition, later sections

Ex. 3.7a (*cont.*)

Ex. 3.7a (*cont.*)

Ex. 3.7 (*cont.*)

(b) Recapitulation

Ex. 3.7b (*cont*)

Ex. 3.7b (*cont.*)

Ex. 3.7b (*cont.*)

Ex. 3.7b (*cont.*)

(c) Recapitulation, middleground

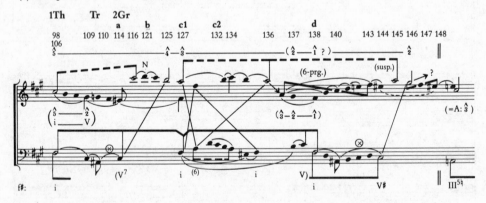

a^2–$g\sharp^1$–$f\sharp^1$ descent at the cadence in mm. 136–38. But the cadence does not effect closure. First, the high octave is abruptly abandoned: a^2 in m. 136 (first oboe, first violins) is conspicuously left hanging, and the ostensibly conclusive $\hat{3}$–$\hat{2}$–$\hat{1}$ is relegated to the low register. Secondly, the winds, which have been playing uninterruptedly since m. 116, fall silent, the oboes and first horn break off entirely, and the second horn (in E) merely reiterates the tonic $f\sharp^1$. $\hat{2}$ is conspicuous by its absence, despite the ready availability of $g\sharp^1$ in the same instrument (compare mm. 126–27). The formal and rhythmic disruption of theme **d** which follows is a "consequence" of this tonal and registral disruption.

(Haydn's winds, in particular the horns, often articulate background structure in this way. In the first Adagio of this symphony, for example, after being withheld throughout the exposition and development, they enter at the reprise of the main theme, articulating a rise from $\hat{1}$ to $\hat{3}$. And this ascent is never led back down: at the final cadences, the first horn twice insists on the same $c\sharp^2$, preparing the striking common-tone link to the minuet (cf. Example 1.3). In the minuet, the horns reflect and create the ambiguous background: except in the trio, they never cadence onto $\hat{1}$ – something almost unheard of when horns are crooked in the tonic key. And, as we have seen, the horns play a central formal role in the farewell movement.)

The cogency of leaving high a^2 hanging in m. 136 becomes apparent in the unstable transition on the remaining second-group theme **d** (still Example 3.7bc): all potentially structural notes higher than $f\sharp^2$ are avoided until the dominant (m. 144). Then, and only then, the violins and first oboe regain a^2; from there, the oboe again descends on an explicit four-note *e2* motive (a^2–$e\sharp^2$). (The bass move to V is a version of *x*; see Example 3.6d.) This descent from a^2 to $e\sharp^2$ rhymes with mm. 92–94 at the end of the development (the same pitches in the same instrument, also in the context of a structural dominant); it also resembles mm. 3–4 and 17–20 of the Presto, mm. 3–4 of the minuet and, most of all, the first appearances of *e2* in the symphony, in the Allegro assai, mm. 50–53 and 189–92 (Examples 2.7 and 2.9). These likewise involved the background and deep middleground in the high register; nothing similar has been heard in F-sharp minor – until these transitions.

The prominent return of this highly charged melodic gesture at such an important point brings hitherto unsatisfactorily resolved concerns to the fore once again. Nevertheless, for the time being it again merely arrives at $\hat{2}$ ($g\sharp^2$) in the background, and is again left hanging. The normal dominant interruption at the end of the development thus rhymes with an equally powerful, but highly unusual interruption at the end of the Presto. What is more, with the first half of the farewell movement squarely in A major, $\hat{2}$ will have no opportunity to descend to the tonic in the background until the key of F-sharp returns. The only possible location for tonal closure will be the final farewell section in the tonic major.

The farewell movement

The abrupt entry of the farewell music in A major (Example 1.4) is disruptive not only aesthetically and formally, but tonally and structurally. The high background $\hat{3}$–$\hat{2}$

over the dominant at the end of the Presto is left hanging (Examples 3.5 and 1.4). Again there is a registral discontinuity: as implied by the initial theme, the obligatory register of the A-major farewell music is lower, a^1–e^2, with no stepwise connection to $g\sharp^2$. And in any event, the putative background pitch class G$\sharp$ can play no role in the key of A ($\hat{8}$-line analyses being a thing of the past except in a few small-scale, unitary pieces[2]). Similarly, the foreground leading-tone $e\sharp^2$ can only move chromatically to e^2.

The farewell music resolves all these difficulties – the role of G$\sharp$–A, the registral discontinuities, and the ambiguities of $\hat{3}$ and $\hat{5}$ as headnote – but in a complex way. The main theme headnote could be either $\hat{3}$ or $\hat{5}$; C$\sharp$ ($\hat{3}$) does not emerge clearly as the governing melodic pitch until the final cadence in A major (Example 3.9). (On theoretical grounds, of course, E is unlikely: given – again – the almost total absence of $\hat{8}$-lines in large movements in sonata style, it cannot form part of any normal *Urlinie* in F-sharp. C$\sharp$, on the other hand, can obviously be a headnote in connection with either tonic.) But given that we do hear $\hat{3}$ as the A-major headnote, when the same theme opens the F-sharp-major section, we will naturally hear it descending from $\hat{3}$ as well: i.e., from the critical new pitch class A$\sharp$. However, this would create an inconsistency with respect to the Presto, which initiated the "single background progression" of the double finale with a clear C$\sharp$ headnote. Haydn solves this problem (we should recall that he never consciously thought in these terms) by changing the *continuation* of the farewell theme, in such a way that it is reinterpreted as descending from $\hat{5}$. Throughout, we have heard C$\sharp$ as a common tone in foreground connections, and perhaps "notionally" in the background as well (cf. Examples 1.1, 1.3, 1.4); now, it governs both major keys, as $\hat{3}$ in A and $\hat{5}$ in F-sharp, in the single background progression of the double finale (Example 3.5). At the same time, this prominence of C$\sharp$ as the pitch-class $\hat{3}$ in A major allows A$\sharp$ – $\hat{3}$ in transposition – to remain prominent and vital in F-sharp too. In this way, the ambiguity between $\hat{3}$ and $\hat{5}$ that has plagued the entire symphony is resolved.

To understand these tonal processes, however, we must analyze the motivic development in detail. In distinction to the Presto, the farewell movement returns to motives from the first three movements; however, they assume new guises appropriate to the changed context and the progress towards resolution. The motives develop continually, becoming at times fabulously intricate – until, at the end, the "opposite" process asserts itself: a motivic liquidation into simple triadic and scalar figures. These new, conclusive forms are associated with equally clear (and unprecedented) melodic descents to the tonic, based on the familiar figure *e2*. This transformation of difficult material into "pure" motives which incorporate fundamental musical processes is a major source of the ending's satisfying effect.

A major The A-major material is shown in Example 3.8. The opening idea sounds new: motive *j* (mm. 1–2) begins squarely on a long downbeat, before dissolving without haste into the measured triplet sixteenths that constitute the virtually unbroken surface rhythm of the movement. (This melodic pattern is a stylized representation of the older *messa di voce*, which Haydn employed in purer form at the beginning of several early

---

[2] As even Schachter admits ("A Commentary," pp. 126–28).

slow movements.) Nevertheless, its first two bars are a compressed variant of the essential triadic motives of the main theme of the Allegro assai: it begins (m. 1) with the straight-forwardly descending *a1*, but the next bar brings the more complex *a2* (cf. Example 1.6). The pattern is the same: *a1–a2*=theme–cadence. Like the final dominant in the Presto, this reversion to original *a* motives with their original functions implies that the farewell movement will return to basic, still unresolved musical issues. (The two perfect cadences in the second and final F-sharp major section will recompose this relationship between *a1* and *a2* in a startling new way.) But these motivic parallels do not attract attention (on this issue, see pp. 203–04). This prefigures the ending in another way: the often difficult ideas of the symphony will resolve unobtrusively, their fate (as it were) subsumed

Example 3.8 Farewell movement: exposition

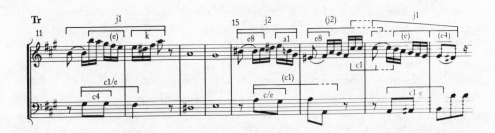

Ex. 3.8 (*cont.*)

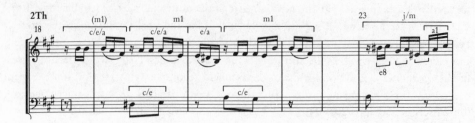

within more fundamental musical processes. Furthermore, and again in contrast to the Allegro assai, the main theme incorporates prominent stepwise melodic motion in mm. 3–4, as well as briefer two-note connections in mm. 1–2 and 9–10. The theme thus suggests the possibility of an ultimate rapprochement between triadic and melodic motion.

The answering cadential phrase, mm. 7–10, introduces a crucial new offbeat motive, *m*. In mm. 7 and 8, the repeated-note *c1* is at first decorated with the simple chromatic neighbor *e8*, producing the three-note *e8/c*; then m. 9 brings an extraordinary synthesis. The static *e8* changes into the diatonic appoggiatura *e9*, which *moves* within each beat; the resultant three-note motive on the second beat combines the stepwise-descending character of *e* and the triadic, self-contained nature of *a1* (hence *e/a*). (This configuration, *e/a*, is unquestionably relevant as a motive: it is immediately repeated in downward sequence; we have just heard both its constituents, *e8* and *a1*, in the two preceding bars; and *a1* immediately recurs in m. 10.) What is more, the longer five-note offbeat figure on the first two beats of m. 9 (whose cogency will also soon become apparent) can only answer to the comic-sounding appellation *c/e/a*! All three primary motivic complexes of the symphony – offbeat repeated notes, triadic arpeggiation, and directed stepwise descent – combine in this unassuming triplet figure. (The importance of a *five*-note figure is guaranteed by the more obvious *c1/e8*, just heard twice in mm. 7–8, in the same position within the bar.) This synthesis takes on added significance from its association with the very strong half-cadence in mm. 9–10, the first such articulation in the movement, and from the overall shape of mm. 9–10, a descent from e^2 to b^2 – that is, motive e2. The complex motivic structure at this cadence actually creates a melodic-structural event. (Those who feel that these motivic "syntheses" may be too clever by half, or that I may be claiming too much for them, may wish to consult pp. 203–04.)

The antecedent-consequent relation between transition and second theme (see the preceding section on the form of the finale, pp. 78–80) is reflected in their further joint development of these ideas. The transition begins with the opening motive j, but its second, cadential phrase combines this motive with the chromatic neighbor e8 in augmentation. (It was also a cadential phrase, mm. 7–10, in which e8 was introduced.) The bass develops the offbeat and stepwise c/e motives, and continues to do so well into the F-sharp-major section. The intricate second theme is based on the complex c/e/a figure from m. 9. (Any doubts one may have had as to the significance of this motive are put to rest by its recurrence as the leading idea at this thematically sensitive place; its first appearance, in mm. 18–19, is further emphasized by rests on both sides and an immediate varied repetition.) The cadence, however (mm. 23–25), rhymes strongly with that of the transition (mm. 15–18): see the chromatic neighbors (e8) on both $b\sharp^1$ and $e\sharp^1$ over ii^6, and the diatonically descending scales in mm. 17 and 24. However, alone among the six phrases so far, this cadence combines the onbeat, "thematic" form j and the offbeat, "cadential" form m – and it does so at the structural cadence of the entire exposition.

In the closing theme (the first oboe/horn "farewell"), the oboe takes up another complex motive, labeled m2/j1 (Example 3.8, m. 25; compare mm. 7, 17, and 24); the new diatonicism is appropriate to its cadential function. The inclusion of a4, for the first time in the melody, creates another (admittedly subtle) contextual link with the Allegro assai, where a4 was also introduced in the closing theme (compare Example 3.8, m. 26, with Example 2.3, mm. 65–69). The foreground melodic descent from $\hat{5}$ to $\hat{1}$ echoes the straightforward cadences at the end of the transition and second theme (mm. 17 and 24). Thus each of the four exposition paragraphs ends with a strongly supported descending melodic cadence (middleground in mm. 9–10, foreground in the others). The second A-major section brings further syntheses. The formerly separate transition and second theme are combined in a single paragraph (mm. 32–35 + 36–41), which precedes (and prepares) the reprise. And (as described pp. 80–81) the main theme now ends with a full cadence (shown in Example 3.9), which at the same time varies the second-theme cadence; the reprise "grounds" both primary paragraphs from the exposition. (An even more remarkable synthesis of these two themes at a structural cadence will occur in F-sharp major.)

Regarding structural voice leading, the A-major section is again based on an interruption structure (see Examples 3.5 and 3.10). The first half is of course the exposition, with the dividing dominant represented by the transition, second theme, and closing theme in E, and closure articulated by the structural cadence in mm. 24–25 and its confirmation in mm. 25–31. The first paragraph of the second section (transition and second theme, mm. 32–41), as is usual, transforms the dominant key back into V^7, preparing the reprise; the final descent occurs during the reprise of the main theme.

Example 3.9 Farewell movement, A-major section: structural cadence

(a)

The voice-leading analyses show c♯² as the headnote, with the prominent e² above
it thrown up from an inner part; however, as stated above, this relationship does not
become clear until the final cadence in mm. 50–51. In the opening theme, both c♯² and
e² are potential headnotes (compare Examples 3.8 and 3.10): the latter is prolonged
until the cadential descent in mm. 9–10; c♯² twice descends to a¹, as if in anticipatory
diminution of a background. The "form-defining" cadence in mm. 9–10 is structurally
undecidable. If e² is construed as the headnote, it strongly and coherently descends to
$\hat{2}$/V by means of the key melodic motive *e2*. But c♯² can lead to $\hat{2}$/V just as well, after e²
has "coalesced" down into it by means of the all-embracing *c/e/a* motive analyzed above.
(Although one could construe an e² headnote as descending $\hat{4}$/V⁷–$\hat{3}$/I in m. 4, and from
there on to $\hat{2}$, the return to the beginning in m. 5 and the prominent e² in m. 8 would
be unclear.) This "coalescing" of $\hat{5}$ down into $\hat{3}$, just before the latter's descent to a
cadence on $\hat{2}$/V, has already been heard in the minuet and trio (see Examples 2.14 and
2.15); it will be important in the F-sharp-major music as well.

But the reprise of the main theme at the end of the A-major music seems to establish
$\hat{3}$ (c♯²) as the headnote (see again Example 3.9). Since the original state of affairs (following the interruption) is restored only at this point, the headnote – whatever it is –
must descend to the tonic during this paragraph. But as we have seen, e² and c♯² are
both prolonged through the first eight bars of the theme (unless e² descends to c♯² in
m. 45=4). Hence the background descent to the tonic can take place only during the
cadence in mm. 50–51 – and a descent from e² is impossible. The single bar 50 would
have to incorporate $\hat{4}$ over the bass ii⁶, and on through $\hat{3}$ and $\hat{2}$ over V – all in the back-

Example 3.10 Farewell movement, A-major section: structural voice-leading

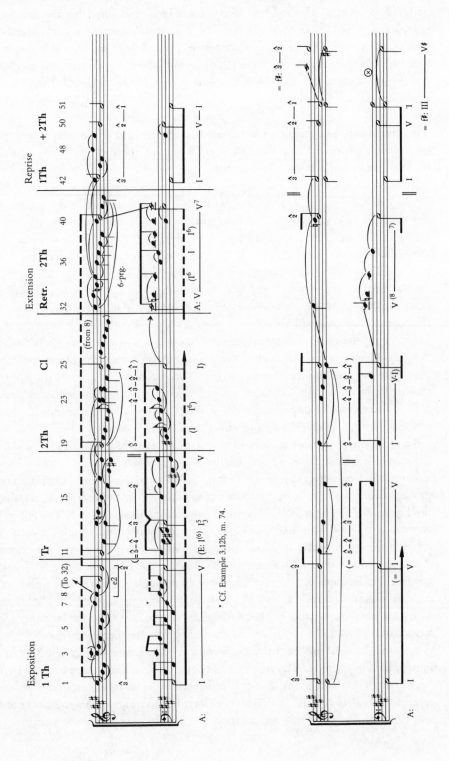

ground – in order for $\hat{1}$ to arrive at the cadence. It is too much to ask. Even if e^2 could be heard to move to d^2, the latter note is not displaced at all within the cadential time span, let alone led down to a^1. On the other hand $c\#^2$ unambiguously descends to the tonic; $\hat{2}$ lasts the entire measure, is articulated over both ii^6 and V, and is connected to both the preceding $\hat{3}$ and the ensuing $\hat{1}$. The hints from the opening theme (and from theory) are thus confirmed: C$\#$ is the governing melodic pitch class of the A-major farewell music.

The transition The transition between the A-major and the F-sharp-major parts of the farewell movement (see Example 3.11) is one of the most wonderful passages in the symphony, and a key to the structure of the double finale. It grows directly out of the closing theme in A; the leading violone part takes over *m3* (compare Example 3.8, m. 26 [=52, 54]). But it organizes the melody on a larger scale: the legato, upbeat-downbeat *e3* motive now rules, in weighty, separately articulated eighth-note pairs, falling in the small but rising sequentially in the large. And, just as in mm. 47–48 in the second movement (Example 2.11), two successive *e3*s in downward sequence produce *e2*, the most important melodic motive of all (mm. 55–57); in addition, the interlocking *e2*s in the melody and bass, descending from $\hat{6}$ to $\hat{3}$ "out of phase," recompose mm. 65–68 of the same movement. Structurally (Example 3.11b), the transition transfers the just-achieved background tonic a^1 back into the upper octave, where we left it at the end of the Presto; reinterpreted as $\hat{3}$ in F-sharp, it descends by step to $g\#^2$ over the newly arrived dominant. The transition thus confirms the role of e^2 as an inner-part pitch in the background of the A major music: it is in the alto, and rises chromatically to the new leading-tone $e\#^2$, underneath the unambiguously structural $\hat{3}$–$\hat{2}$. (This reverses the disposition at the end of the Presto, where the indirect resolution of the dominant forced $e\#^2$ down to e^2.)

The basic progression is prolonged by 5–6 sequences (Example 3.11c) and elaborated chromatically (Example 3.11d); the latter stage introduces the two most important foreground *e3* appoggiaturas, g^2–$f\#^2$ (=mm. 58–61) and a^2–$g\#^2$ (mm. 61–65). (The same pair of chromatic steps in the melody accompanied x in the two III–V transitions in the Presto; see Example 3.6bc. The most important of them, A–G$\#$, also governed the original transition (Examples 3.1 and 3.6).) The stage shown in Example 3.11d also generates the rising chromatic sequence x in the bass, which governs the tonicizations of B minor and C-sharp. The appoggiaturas can also be understood in a different way, however (see Example 3.11e): as arising from an arpeggiation of the two upper voices in 3.11d as a compound melody, and hence as standing for passing-tones in a lower register. This guarantees the cogency of the background leap from a^1 to a^2: the latter note literally arises from below. (The earlier and comparable g^2 creates the rising melodic line in the foreground, by breaking the pattern of four-note *e2* descents; see Example 3.11a, m. 58.) Finally, the foreground (3.11f) adds new appoggiaturas, in diminution of those in (d) and (e), to every other note in (d). The only difference is the subtle elision of the "redundant" repetition of g^2–$f\#^2$ ("NB" in 3.11f), which creates the supple phrasing at the B-minor join (mm. 58–59). The two-bar phrasing is restored, however, by the repetition of the

Example 3.11 Farewell movement: transition

(a)

(b)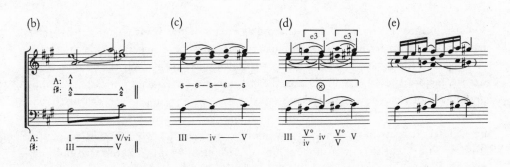

(c)

(d)

(e)

(f)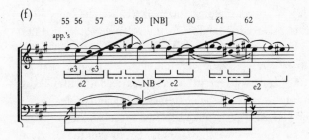

climactic a^2–$g^{\sharp2}$ immediately on its arrival (mm. 61–63). This "extra" repetition, making a total of three statements of motive *e3* on these notes precisely at the arrival of the structural dominant, clarifies their fundamental role beyond doubt.

As noted above, the bass is the final incarnation of motive *x*, chromatically linking the structural roots A and C♯. But another vital aspect of this transition is symbolized by the leading role of the violone itself. For the first time in the symphony, the bass progression III–V is placed in an appropriately low register. The violone begins (m. 55) on low A_1 (notated A) and ends on C♯ (notated c♯), the latter prolonged for six bars. The last transition is also the weightiest. Beyond that, the two finales are welded into a single structure, not merely because they are through-composed, but because the same musical processes animate them from within. Both transitions (at the end of the Presto and here) prepare a background $\hat{2}/V$ by the combination of *e2* in the melody and the rising chromatic sequence *x* in the bass. It is heard here for the last time, and prolonged longer and in a more complex manner than anywhere else. (In mm. 63–64 and 65–66, the steps $b^{\sharp1}$–$c^{\sharp2}$ over the barline stand for the harmonically congruent steps $f^{\sharp2}$–$e^{\sharp2}$, but in the alto; if actually heard in the melody, where they notionally belong, they would complete motive *e2* in the foreground, as in mm. 145–48 of the Presto. See Example 3.11f.) In both transitions, the structural a^2 picks up an unresolved earlier background $\hat{3}$; in both, it rises into the upper register from below. The hanging $\hat{2}/V$ at the end of the Presto redoubles its force upon its rhyming recapture here, in the middle of the farewell music. Hence any ensuing cadence onto an F♯ root, any strong melodic descent to $\hat{1}$, will resolve the tonal structure of the entire double finale. As was foreshadowed in the minuet and trio, the essential melodic component of this resolution is the stepwise descending motive *e2*. But how ambiguous and unsatisfying was its effect then, and how wonderful the entry of F-sharp major that now follows!

F-sharp major The concluding F-sharp-major part of the farewell movement grants final resolution, in terms of both the material and the tonal structure. The first of its two sections (see Example 3.12) chiefly repeats the first theme and the second theme from A major; its only new material is the cadence in mm. 82–85 – but this is the most profound motivic synthesis in the movement. It is based primarily on the first-theme cadence (mm. 74–77): *m* reappears in its original form in mm. 82 and 84, while the first and third beats of 83 bring a new motive, marked "!", which is related to *c/e/a* from m. 76, except it is even more complex. Although, as in *c/e/a*, the two-note sub-motives *e9* move by step within the beat and thus lead the melody down, the three notes as a whole imitate *e8/c* (cf. m. 82), albeit in diatonic inversion (hence the label *e9/c*). That is, unlike *c/e/a*, this motive is not triadic at all. On the other hand, *e9/c* differs from *e8/c* in that it is not embedded within the larger five-note *c1/e8*: there are no offbeats or upbeats; it is closed off by the preceding and following *a1* motives and the rest on the downbeat of m. 84; the sequential repetition from 83a to 83c reinforces its independence. But m. 82 also relates to the second theme, which it concludes, developing both the *c/e/a* motives and the stepwise bass.

Furthermore, the harmonies *move*, not only on each beat of m. 83, but on the last beats

Example 3.12 Farewell movement, F♯-major section: 1st paragraph

(a)

(b)

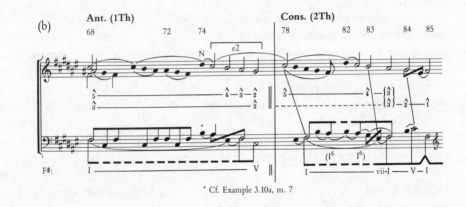

* Cf. Example 3.10a, m. 7

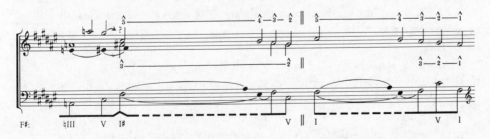

of mm. 82 and 84 as well, rather than remaining static within each bar as in mm. 74–75. This significantly changes the character of the cadential phrase: it is active, fluid; there is even a suggestion of hemiola. This difference has been subtly prepared in the immediately preceding recapitulation of the first theme (mm. 74–75). In A major (Example 3.8, mm. 7–8), this root-position IV skipped firmly to a root-position tonic; now, by contrast, it glides smoothly to I⁶ ("*" in both examples). In m. 82, the same fluid IV–I⁶ progression, with the same motivic content and the same melodic neighbor ($\hat{6}$–$\hat{5}$), initiates the faster and more complex harmonic motion of the cadence. This cadence integrates not only the three motivic complexes *a*, *c*, and *e*, but also the form: it resolves both the first theme and the second theme, by leading the latter to its (expected) cadence while rewriting the cadence of the former. And it is the first perfect cadence in F-sharp major! Not merely because of its motivic synthesis, not merely because of this remarkable multiple function, this phrase is perhaps the most beautiful in the symphony.

The second and final F-sharp section (see Example 3.13) begins with another statement of the second theme, but then liquidates the material into increasingly pure forms. The various complex motives largely disappear – not only *c/e/a* and "!", but even the simple *c/e* in the bass; after m. 89, the incessant, subtly destabilizing downbeat rests disappear. The triadic *a* motives dominate in the foreground, with increasing internal consistency: *a8* (from the closing theme, related to *a4*) in mm. 90 and 92; then *a1* in 94, 96, 97; finally *a2* in 101–02. The scale passages in mm. 100, 103, 104 are purely diatonic and no longer even change direction; the new, "rocking" quarter-eighth *e1* motives in mm. 90, 92, and 96–99 are equally pure and equally consistent. Indeed the two remaining cadences concentrate, in turn, on each of the two primary triadic motives from the opening bars of this movement – that is to say, from the beginning of the symphony. Three consecutive *a1*s in m. 94 descend to the deceptive cadence in m. 95 (and more follow in mm. 96–99); five consecutive *a2*s create the final structural cadence in mm. 101–02. The crucial motivic pattern thus recurs at the crux of the entire work: *a1* comes first and is more thematic, but *a2* takes over at the cadence. Storm and stress, motivic complexity: both achieve an inviolable resolution in the transfigured simplicity of these final descents.

But they are structural melodic descents as well. The triplet motives still create coherent stepwise *e2*s on the eighth-note level, but now these repeatedly reach the tonic. The *e2* half cadence at the end of the first theme (Example 3.12, mm. 76–77) repeats mm. 9–10, which at that time enjoyed no resolution (the following phrases modulated into the dominant). Now, however, it is resolved by the miraculous cadence in mm. 82–85, where the synthesis of both themes is wedded to the first clear descent of *e2* all the way from $\hat{5}$ to $\hat{1}$ in the key of F-sharp, since its unsatisfactory appearances in the trio.

The rocking stepwise bass of m. 82, with its implication of *e1* in quarter-eighth rhythm harmonized as IV–I⁶, takes over in the final section (Example 3.13): mm. 90–93 proceed IV–V²–I⁶ (the identical pitches as in m. 82, in both melody and bass) and thus prepare the deceptive cadence in mm. 94–95; mm. 96–101, still rocking, prepare the perfect cadence in mm. 102–03. (A similar progression prepared the structural cadences

Example 3.13 Farewell movement, F#-major section: 2nd paragraph

Ex. 3.13 (cont.)

(b)

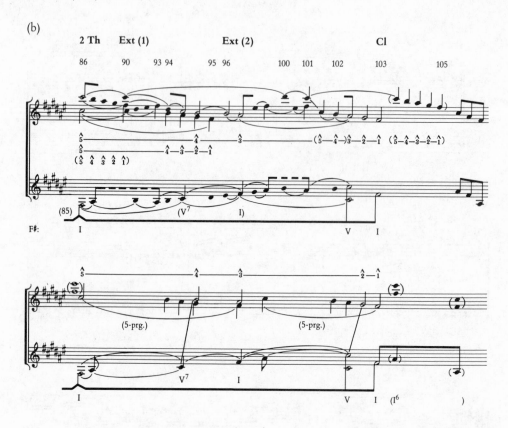

in the first Adagio; see Example 2.11, mm. 65–69. Even the lengthened $\hat{4}$ in mm. 100–01 here, returning to I⁶ "one more time" when the cadence already seems at hand, is the same.) And both cadences, in their purified motivic simplicity, incorporate *e2* on the eighth-note level. The deceptive cadence (mm. 94–95) is particularly striking: the stepwise $\hat{6}$–$\hat{5}$–$\hat{4}$ in the melody (m. 94) implies resolution to $\hat{3}$, completing a four-note motive *e2*. This is however undercut by the skip down to low $\hat{7}$–$\hat{8}$ over the bass d♯¹, even though a♯¹ would have been compatible with the submediant harmony. (To be sure, Haydn wanted the rhyme with m. 85 on the appoggiatura e♯¹.) Instead, b¹ is notionally suspended into m. 96, where it does resolve – but only after the next phrase has begun. (This resolution introduces the new rocking motive, *a1* being transferred into the bass.) At last, *a2* rounds off the paragraph by stepwise $\hat{5}$–$\hat{1}$ descent, as clear and elemental as that in mm. 82–85. The triadic motives liquidate themselves into pure melody.

In the larger tonal structure up to this point, much has implied that A♯ ($\hat{3}$) will be the headnote in F-sharp major. Both interruptive transitions have strongly emphasized A in minor; the final section opens with a literal transposition of music in which $\hat{3}$ was the headnote; finally, $\hat{3}$ is the raised third degree, the critical new tonal element in the long hoped-for tonic major. And yet C♯ proves to be the headnote. This reinterpretation is achieved straightforwardly (Example 3.12). Measures 1–10 are repeated literally in mm. 68–77; as before, the half cadence at the end could imply either a $\hat{3}$-line or a $\hat{5}$-line, and its tonal meaning therefore depends on the sequel. But this sequel culminates in that miraculous cadence of mm. 82–85, in which an unadorned descent to $\hat{1}$ in F-sharp major, articulated by all three chief motivic elements, takes off from $\hat{5}$, which has been prolonged over a root-position tonic ever since m. 78. This reinterpretation confirms what was implied in A major: the foreground common-tone $\hat{5}$ (C♯) (cf. Example 1.1) is the head-note of the entire double finale, in all three keys.

As if to banish all possible doubt, the second F-sharp-major paragraph offers a cornuco-pia of four additional descents from $\hat{5}$, overlapping on different levels (Example 3.13b): (1) mm. 86–103 in the background, low register: c♯² in mm. 86–94 connects to b¹ at the deceptive cadence in mm. 94–96, resolving to a♯¹ in m. 96 (and repeated several times thereafter), until the final descent in mm. 101–03; (2) mm. 86–89 in the fore-ground, high register, on the second theme; (3) mm. 86–95 in the middleground, low register: c♯² in mm. 86ff connects to $\hat{4}$–$\hat{3}$–$\hat{2}$–$\hat{1}$ on the last sixteenth of each *a1* motive in mm. 94–95; (4) the foreground descent from c♯² in mm. 101–03, resolving to the tonic along with the background descent itself. (Schenker often showed complex overlapping descents of this type.[3]) Poetically, the codetta then gives us $\hat{5}$–$\hat{1}$ "one more time," as if by reflection – one of several descents to $\hat{1}$ in the highest register, which resolve the hanging $\hat{3}$–$\hat{2}$s from the end of the Presto and the transition from A major. The back-ground descent, however, remains in the lower register. Because it is governed by this undivided progression, the paragraph is not an antecedent-consequent period (as was mm. 67–85), but a unitary tonal structure. The sense of coherence, of overcoming divisions of all kinds, continues to the very end, manifested in the background voice leading itself.

As in the preceding paragraph, however, $\hat{3}$ is also thrown into relief. In the preceding paragraph (Example 3.12), $\hat{4}$ is supported only by the leading-tone e♯ in the bass (mm. 76. 83), which lends the descent from $\hat{5}$ to $\hat{3}$ a certain lability. In the final paragraph, however (Example 3.13), $\hat{4}$ receives strong root-position support from the c♯¹ in m. 94, and thus participates in the crucial deceptive cadence in mm. 94–95.[4] Hence $\hat{3}$ is also emphasized, remains in motion, owing to the delayed resolution; by the time a♯¹ is gained in m. 96, the next phrase is already under way. This $\hat{3}$ is therefore also prolonged until, in m. 102, it coalesces with the foreground descent from $\hat{5}$ (m. 101), whereupon both lines complete the structural cadence "in unison." $\hat{3}$ thus still functions as a kind of nodal point within descents from $\hat{5}$, which still culminate in three-chord foreground progressions, $\hat{3}$/I – $\hat{2}$/V – $\hat{1}$/I (like many passages in the minuet and trio, the main theme of the Presto, and the final cadence of the earlier F-sharp-major paragraph). Insofar as these

---

[3] For example, *Free Composition*, Exx. 48/1, 88d, 154/3.

[4] Contrary to a widespread view, Schenker did not require that the dissonant $\hat{4}$ in a $\hat{5}$-line receive consonant sup-port in the middleground. See *Free Composition*, §35, 69 (and compare for example Ex. 40/8); Schachter, "A Com-mentary," pp. 125–26.

complex relations now coexist in a context of gestural resolution, the final section also grounds the deeper, almost "philosophical" conflicts between $\hat{5}$ and $\hat{3}$, between structural pitch and prominent melody note, which have been present throughout the symphony.

To be sure, the old bass preference for $\hat{3}$ and the concomitant I⁶–V–I progressions are still in evidence. Following its perfect cadence on f♯ at the end of the first F-sharp-major paragraph (m. 85), the viola bass avoids any pitch lower than a♯, and in particular restricts the tonic to the higher f♯¹. Indeed its exit pitch, unlike that of all the other significant instrumental "farewells," is placed in the middle of a phrase (m. 93) – and it too is merely a♯. The second violin seamlessly takes over the bass on the same pitch, from where it rises, remarkably, in unbroken step motion all the way to the structural dominant at c♯² (m. 102b). (Even this second-violin bass is thus organized around a diatonic version of x, $\hat{3}$ up to $\hat{5}$ as extremes of range and contour; again, the dominant is a tenth above $\hat{3}$.) The violin bass even crosses over the melody at the moment of dominant arrival (the second beat of m. 102), before recrossing for the final cadence; the pitch-class content of this part crossing is precisely $\hat{5}$ and $\hat{3}$ – the two most "sensitive" notes in the symphony, in the very register where they have most often been prominent and problematical. (Of course, this does not compromise the *functions* of $\hat{3}$ as melody note or $\hat{5}$ as bass, any more than the second violin b in m. 84 undermines the dominant c♯¹ at the previous structural cadence.[5])

What is more, as shown on the middle staff of Example 3.4, every bass "exit" pitch in F-sharp is off the tonic: C♯ (notated c♯) for the violone; c♯ for the cello; a♯ for the viola; and, perhaps most striking, a♯ for the second violin as well, at the very end. The entire codetta (mm. 103–07) projects I⁶ (a♯ on the bass), rather than a root-position tonic (see Examples 3.4, 3.13). All this recalls the final tag of the minuet: not merely the high register, the solo violins without bass, the pianissimo; but the pitch structure and even the rhythm – c♯² on top as an upbeat, a♯¹ across the barline, and finally a♯ on the bottom (cf. Example 1.2). That tag, heard six (or eight) times, concluded the only other F-sharp-major music in the symphony. When it now recurs almost literally at the end, we grasp that this unique double finale is a similar cycle, closely if complexly related to the first: a recomposition of the first three movements into a new kind of music, transfigured, perfect.

AN APOTHEOSIS OF ETHEREALITY

The farewell movement reverts to basic motives not heard since the Allegro assai, liquidating them into pure musical essences, in a context of tonal resolution and closure. Beyond this, however, it completes an aesthetic progression towards ethereality. The instruments exit in a consistent order: first the winds, then the strings, the latter from lowest to highest. The music becomes increasingly high and soft, the texture increasingly transparent; at the end, the two muted solo violins seem almost insubstantial. As they

---

[5] On bass part-crossings in Haydn, see Webster, "The Bass Part in Haydn's Early String Quartets," *MQ* 63 (1977), 402–16.

cross and recross at the final cadence, even the aural distinction between melody and bass disappears.

The music also becomes increasingly diatonic. In the A-major section, the cadential phrases incorporate chromatic neighbors (Example 3.8, mm. 7–10, 15–16, 23); the transition from A to F-sharp (Example 3.11) is chromatic even in the middleground. But the first A-major cadence itself incorporates a progression towards diatonicism. The chromatic neighbors in mm. 7–8 turn into diatonic appoggiaturas in m. 9, animating the structural descent to the half cadence in m. 10 – the first form-defining event in the movement. And a similar progression towards diatonicism governs the F-sharp-major section as a whole. The repetition of that half-cadence in mm. 74–77 leads to the same chromatic neighbors in the wonderful cadence which concludes the first period (mm. 82–85; Example 3.12). But from that point on, throughout the entire concluding section for the two principal violins, there is not a single chromatic note – not a single accidental! The pitch content of the farewell movement thus mirrors the progression of the entire symphony, from instability to stability. (The proof lies in its difference from the minuet, in which F-sharp major was destabilized by D♮, a lack of root-position tonic support, and unintegrated minor-mode passages in the trio.) All the musical parameters – *pianissimo*, two solo muted violins, the lack of bass, the distant tonal region – unite to create this unique resolution, not so much "lonely," as Landon describes it (*Haydn*, vol. 2, p. 252), as poignant, insubstantial, ethereal. This ethereality is the aesthetic counterpart to the resolution of instability and the transfiguration of the motives into essences.

However, this might seem to create a new problem. How can such high, insubstantial music, in such a difficult key, provide satisfactory closure? What is the aesthetic relation of this ethereal F-sharp major to the rest of the symphony? In fact, it has been prepared, and precisely by the most problematical earlier passage in the work. The D-major interlude in the Allegro assai provided the first link between F-sharp minor and F-sharp major (see Chapter 1). But it also adumbrated the aesthetics of the farewell ending: scored for strings alone; beginning without bass and ending in the four-foot register (thus remaining insubstantial in the mind's ear); soft, legato, tuneful; regular in phrasing. Most important, its discontinuity, its lack of integration, meant that its world of symmetrical beauty was itself "left hanging." It staked a claim to eventual resolution – a claim which until now has remained unfulfilled.

The minuet, to be sure, with its unaccompanied beginning and especially its concluding off-tonic violin tag, confirmed the association between F-sharp major and high, bassless music; but as far as resolution is concerned, it scarcely represented an improvement on the interlude. At the end of the Presto, however, the remote third-progression which introduced the interlude, F-sharp major to D, returns in transposition to prepare the beginning of the farewell movement in A major – a shock despite the familiarity of the key. And in the middle of that movement, A major leads in turn to that very sonority of F-sharp major, miraculously transformed into the tonal goal of the entire symphony – inevitable despite its remoteness. This close contextual association renders audible the underlying tonal relation between A and D, such that the final resolution of A into F-sharp major in a sense "grounds" the tonal tension of the D-major interlude itself.

This resolution has been carefully prepared. D, scale-degree $\hat{6}$ in F-sharp minor, would ordinarily function as a neighbor to the dominant (as in mm. 13–14 of the Allegro assai; Example 2.1) and as the root of deceptive cadences (as in mm. 193–94; Example 2.5). But the interlude denies any such normal functioning of $\hat{6}$. And the next prominent appearance of D in an F-sharp context is overtly disruptive: the rude bass entry in m. 3 of the minuet. This minor mixture also remains unintegrated at first; there is no further $\hat{6}$ in the bass (except its repetition at the reprise) until its replacement by d♯¹ at the deceptive cadence (m. 34), just before the structural cadence in m. 38 – the final cadence in Cycle 1. This pair of cadences on ♯$\hat{6}$ and I prepares the ultimate triumph of diatonicism at the end. At precisely the analogous place in Cycle 2 – just before the final cadence of the farewell movement – we hear another deceptive cadence onto d♯¹ (m. 95; Example 3.13), which also resolves prominent earlier Ds: m. 3 of the Presto (which rhymes with m. 3 of the minuet), and especially the transition from the Presto to the farewell movement, m. 143 (Example 1.4). Since, from that point forward, the key of F-sharp is not heard again until in m. 68 of the farewell movement, D still needs to be replaced by D♯. But, astonishingly, the deceptive cadence in m. 95 is the only bass $\hat{6}$ in the entire F-sharp-major farewell music. That note, and it alone, resolves minor $\hat{6}$ into the major, as it helps to establish the long-range connections between the minuet and the "farewell," between the endings of both cycles: instability yielding to stability.

Just as the D-major interlude is prepared by F-sharp major, the tonal goal of the entire symphony, so the interlude's aesthetic character prefigures the "farewells." At the end, its register, style, and mood, which have remained unintegrated and unexplained for four-and-one-half movements lasting twenty-five minutes, recur – in the tonic. Though not even hinting at a thematic recall, the ending thus implicitly *recapitulates* the interlude; the "sonata principle" is affirmed, over the course of the entire symphony. The symphony is through-composed; its entire dynamic is resolved in this ethereal apotheosis. There has never been a more stunning triumph of long-range musical planning.

Nevertheless, as an ending, it is not "easy"; it hovers between the apparently opposed values of structural closure and insubstantiality; our attempted synthesis of them into a reassuringly unified state will be fragile at best, not easily sustained. This multivalence, this resistance to a univalent conclusion, almost forces us to move "outside" the work "as such" – which is to say, to reinterpret it on the basis of the external program.

4

THE PROGRAM

The Farewell Symphony's paradoxical ending in an apotheosis of ethereality leads directly to a programmatic interpretation. As outlined in the Introduction, its authentic status as program music requires us to try to understand it in this sense; to regard it as a mere concatenation of notes (however remarkable), or an abstract poetic utterance (however satisfying), would be to ignore its historical and intrinsic significance. In any case, the symphony's programmatic aspect will foster our sense of its overall coherence; the story we tell about it will create a narrative thread, binding the movements together perhaps more powerfully, if also more subjectively, than their common thematic and tonal relationships, their drive towards long-postponed closure. Of course, the narrative must be compatible with our analysis; it must have an "objective correlative" (T. S. Eliot's phrase) "in" the work. On the other hand, it need not correspond in every detail: if the principle of multivalence has any validity at all, it applies not only within an analysis, but even more on the "higher" level of the relation between structural and hermeneutic understanding. (These topics are further adumbrated at the beginning and end of Chapter 7.)

RECEPTION

Programmatic works were common both in Haydn's *milieu* and his own output (see Chapter 7). To be sure, as far as we know for certain he composed only one symphony (No. 60, "Il distratto") on a program in the "strong" nineteenth-century sense of disseminating a work, and asking it to be understood, in association with a narrative (as in Berlioz's *Symphonie fantastique*) or a literary title or idea (as in many concert overtures and tone-poems). The majority of his symphonies in this class would be better described as having extramusical associations, or as belonging to a "characteristic" type such as the pastoral or the *chasse*, or indeed merely as having a popular nickname.[1] (As noted in the Introduction, "Farewell" itself is only a nickname; as we will see, it does not well represent the symphony's program.) Indeed Beethoven's familiar expression regarding the "Pastoral" Symphony, "more the expression of feeling than depiction," would have been as respectable in 1772 as it was in 1808, although composers then would have been less defensive than Beethoven about accusations of "tone-painting."

---

[1] On these distinction, see Walter Wiora, *Das musikalische Kunstwerk* (Tutzing, 1983), pp. 146–55; and Chapter 7 below.

Admittedly, we have no direct knowledge of how the Farewell Symphony was understood on its original presentation, let alone what (if anything) of the program was communicated to Haydn's listeners. Only the written anecdotal tradition, which did not begin until the 1780s, testifies that the performance had the desired effect. A hardened skeptic might assert that perhaps Haydn intended nothing unusual at all, that the stories are mere legends which he endorsed in his dotage. But within the anecdotal tradition, positive outcomes are universal: the reliable Griesinger testifies, appealing to Haydn's authority, that "the prince and the audience at once understood the point of this pantomime; the next day came the order for the departure from Eszterháza" (p. 1). (A different sort of "reception" is evidenced by other symphonies influenced by the Farewell; see p. 227.)

The later reception of the work exhibits an interesting confusion (or dialectic) between "serious" and "comic" interpretations. On the whole, eighteenth-century readings were serious. The earliest surviving notice, from the *Mercure de France* in 1784, is mixed: it describes the farewell theme as "a sad and lugubrious melody," but the entire movement as a "joke" (*plaisanterie*).[2] A casual anecdote in the *Preßburger Zeitung* from 1787 proposes the scenario that, owing to a dispute with princely bureaucrats, the musicians had resigned, and that the symphony was their "farewell" to the court! It claims further that the work was "very famous and well-loved" and that it "was performed at the court in Vienna, in the concert spirituel in Paris, and for the Queen [of England] at St. James."[3] The former assertion seems exaggerated: at that time it had been printed only in Paris; and the manuscript dissemination was not very much greater than for other Haydn symphonies from the same period.[4] No evidence for performances at the Hapsburg or the Hanoverian courts has ever been reported.

A later anecdote published in the *Allgemeine musikalische Zeitung* (1799) transmits the wholly implausible story (which Griesinger even felt constrained to refute) of Esterházy's having had to dissolve the *Kapelle* because of economic hardship. The portrait of Haydn is already proto-Romantic: "Haydn, so inexhaustible in musical imagination and invention . . . also put out his light and, much moved, departed with a noble gait." The author concludes by asking rhetorically why Haydn never published this "interesting work," whereupon the editor replies in a footnote:

At the least, the symphony is fairly well known. This stroke of genius in fact makes a great effect. I heard this symphony performed on the occasion of the last assembly of a certain musical institution. When in the finale at first some of the winds departed, one was amused; many in the audience even found it comical. But when even the essential instruments stopped playing, put out their lights, and departed quietly and slowly – then everyone became anxious and afraid. And when, at the end, even the double bass fell silent, and only the violins – now only one single violin was left, sounding faintly, and then died: well, the audience went out so quietly and so moved, that it was as if all musical pleasure had passed away for them forever.[5]

---

[2] Quoted in Landon, *Haydn*, vol. 2, p. 181.

[3] Marianne Pandi and Fritz Schmidt, "Musik zur Zeit Haydns und Beethovens in der Preßburger Zeitung," *HYb* 8 (1971), 189–90.

[4] Approximately 35 MSS before 1800, as compared to 20–25 for other symphonies; see *JHW* I/6, critical report.

[5] *AMZ*, vol. 2, No. 1 (2 October 1799), cols. 14–15.

And Nicolas Framery, in his 1810 biographical note of Pleyel, perpetuates the notion of the musicians' resignation but attributes their anger to insupportable behavior on the part of Prince Nicolaus himself, portrayed as subject to fits of melancholy, which it was Haydn's duty to ameliorate by the production of new symphonies![6] (His source was presumably Pleyel, who – according to a tradition which, so far as I see, is not documented – came to study with Haydn precisely in the year 1772.) Be this as it may, these accounts agree in treating Haydn's programmatic intentions seriously, and in assuming that the work succeeded in its effect.

In the nineteenth century, the worm turned. As early as 1809, the catalogue of Haydn's effects (quoted in the Introduction) described it as the symphony "with a joking finale." Griesinger (1810) refers to Haydn's "naive playfulness, or what the British call *humor*. . . . This mood exhibits itself very strongly in his compositions. . . . Just so, the Farewell Symphony (which I mentioned above) is a [well] executed musical joke."[7] Griesinger began as an intimate of Haydn's, but he was a contemporary of Beethoven's and eventually became a member of his musical party; his opinions reflect the somewhat ambivalent attitudes towards Haydn in the first decade of the nineteenth century.[8] With the triumph of Romantic musical aesthetics, Haydn's very different kind of seriousness was outmoded; by a perverse synecdoche, his comic *Laune* was taken to represent his entire style; "Papa Haydn" was born. Even Mendelssohn's comment following his "historical" performance in 1838 – "It is a curiously melancholy little piece" – seems divided between respect and the gentle contempt of familiarity, as does Schumann's remark, reviewing this concert, "the musicians . . . put out their lights and left quietly; nor did anyone laugh, for there was nothing to laugh about" – when juxtaposed with his generally patronizing attitude towards Haydn.[9] (Mendelssohn commits the interesting error – a Romantic Freudian slip? – of referring to the ending as being in F-sharp *minor*.)

The century-and-a-quarter from Mendelssohn to Landon and Rosen produced no worthwhile commentary; even Arnold Schering's promising assertion that, if the finale is programmatic, the entire symphony must be related to it, leads merely to a banal, depressingly literalistic interpretation.[10] And (as noted in the Introduction) there has still been no attempt to interpret the symphony as a whole in terms of the program. But insofar as our analysis has taught us to take the Farewell Symphony seriously again, we are no worse off than Haydn's contemporaries. To be persuasive, however, the interpretation must account for salient features *throughout*, not merely a few piquant details in the farewell movement. On the other hand, no more than an analysis must it be "global"

---

[6] Quoted in Landon, *Haydn*, vol. 2, pp. 758–59.

[7] Griesinger, p. 107 (Gotwals, p. 57).

[8] Webster, "The Falling-out Between Haydn and Beethoven: The Evidence of the Sources," in Lewis Lockwood and Phyllis Benjamin, eds., *Beethoven Essays: Studies in Honor of Elliot Forbes* (Cambridge, Mass., 1984), pp. 18, 26–28.

[9] Susanne Großmann-Vendray, *Felix Mendelssohn Bartholdy und die Musik der Vergangenheit* (Regensburg, 1969), p. 161 (cf. Landon, *Haydn*, vol. 2, p. 303); Schumann, *Gesammelte Schriften über Musik und Musiker*, 4th ed. (Leipzig, 1891), vol. 1, p. 100n.

[10] "Bemerkungen zu J. Haydns Programmsinfonien," *JbP* 46 (1939), 23–24.

or exhaustive; not every movement, not every disruption, need be part of the story.[11] It will suffice to demonstrate how the program can function as a governing metaphor for understanding the symphony, enlightening (we may hope), but open-ended both in nuance and in extent.

I make no pretense of penetrating the thickets of current theorizing about narratives in music, even though it might be made relevant to discussion of the Farewell (see Chapter 8, with respect to Symphony No. 46). I simply assume that the through-compositional rhetoric of the symphony has its own coherence, which can be brought into relation to the program, and that we can verbalize that relation. This verbalization will of course be a narrative, but it will be "about" the symphony; I do not suggest that any narrative resides "in" the work, let alone that the music itself "narrates" the story. My narrative will focus on our *feelings* – the principal mode in which eighteenth-century musicians verbalized about musical expressiveness – or, more precisely, my interpreta-tion of feelings I attribute to the "persona" I find in the work.[12] This may be more than most of Haydn's listeners would have done, and it is certainly more self-conscious; but it is not different in principle.

AN INTERPRETATION

The basic point is obvious enough, and it governs the whole work. The "persona" comprises Haydn's musicians (taken collectively). With winter approaching, they are stuck in the barren splendor of Eszterháza castle; they desperately want to go home to their families. Their frustration is vividly projected by the unstable, passionately unfulfilled Allegro assai in F-sharp minor. But F-sharp minor is no ordinary key. Not only was it "difficult" – to tune, and for intonation in the strings – it was literally unheard of as an overall tonic in late eighteenth-century orchestral music (see the Introduction). F-sharp minor thus represents a remote and inhospitable part of the musical universe – just as Eszterháza lay in a remote and inhospitable district. (Haydn himself sometimes called it an *Einöde*, a wasteland: "Here I sit in my wasteland"; "[Do] not be frightened away from consoling me occasionally by your pleasant letters, for they comfort me in my wasteland."[13]) The musicians' plight is thus not only suggested by the style of the first movement, but is tangibly present in the very musical "system" on which the symphony is based. Equally obviously, their yearning for home is symbolized by the parallel major, the only sonority which can really resolve the tension and dissonance of a minor key. But this key is F-sharp major – extremely distant (six steps from C on the circle of fifths), a region almost never dreamed of, let alone attained, by late eighteenth-century orchestral musicians.

Indeed, during the second half of the eighteenth century composers systematically

---

[11] The perceived need for explanations to be exhaustive is a historically contingent prejudice. See Dahlhaus, "Some Models of Unity," §3–4.

[12] On musical "personae," see Cone, *The Composer's Voice* (Berkeley, 1974).

[13] Letters to Marianne von Genzinger, 9 February and 30 May 1790, quoted in Landon, *Haydn*, vol. 2, pp. 737, 741; for the originals see Bartha, ed., *Joseph Haydn: Gesammelte Briefe und Aufzeichnungen* (Kassel, 1965), pp. 228, 235.

avoided sharp-side minor keys in orchestral music. (This applied even in the opera, where the range of *Affekten* needed to be as wide as feasible. For example, in Haydn's twelve Italian operas for the Esterházy court, there are only two arias in sharp-side minor keys: *La fedeltà premiata*, No. 18, Amorante's "Vanne, fuggi" in B and *Armida*, No. 20d, the heroine's "Odio, furor" in E.) This inhibition presumably reflected difficulties of intonation for the strings and (regarding B and F-sharp) the general unavailability of horns in keys "sharper" than E. Very occasionally, interior movements of cyclic works for or with orchestra are set in F-sharp minor, even by the (in this respect) conservative Mozart (the Adagio of the Piano Concerto in A K. 488). And of course Haydn did compose chamber and especially keyboard works in sharp-side minor keys (see pp. 223–24).

F-sharp minor was "difficult" in an aesthetic sense as well, as is obvious from eighteenth-century comments on "key characteristics."[14] (It differed from other sharp-side minor keys chiefly in degree, not in kind.) Mattheson (1713) described it as "lead[ing] to great distress, abandoned, singular, and misanthropic"; Laborde (1780) said that both minor and major were "scarcely ever used"; Schubart (1784) characterized it as "gloomy: it tugs at passion as a dog biting a dress; resentment and discontent; it languishes ever for the calm of A major or for the triumphant happiness of D major"; Knecht (1792) as "melancholy." Other writers, including Rousseau (*c.* 1794, 1768), Lacombe (1758), and Galeazzi (1796), omitted it from lists of key characteristics altogether. Even more omitted F-sharp major. Mattheson included it among those keys whose characteristics "are too little known and must be left to posterity to be determined"; Grétry (1797) said that it is "hard, because overloaded with accidentals." On the other hand, two writers describe F-sharp major in terms that are not irrelevant to the Farewell's ending: Schubart (mentioning it only in the guise of G-flat) opines, "Triumph over difficulty, free sigh of relief uttered when hurdles are surmounted; echo of a soul which has fiercely struggled and finally conquered"; and an anonymous correspondent writing in Cramer's *Magazin der Musik* in 1786 asserts, "A splendid mixture of a noble and, because of its infrequent use, a strange, lofty pride, fit to put the listener in admiring awe." In this context, it is reasonable to suppose that Haydn intended F-sharp minor to signify a state of extreme frustration, F-sharp major one of "otherworldly" resolution.

The Farewell Symphony, then, deals with the idea (not the "depiction"!) of the musicians' journey home from the wilderness of F-sharp minor to their safe and comfortable family hearths in Eisenstadt – represented, however, by the unimaginably distant key of F-sharp major. If this is "home," they can hardly even recall it; it will be reachable (if at all) only at the end of a long and arduous journey (during which their difficulties of intonation will only increase!). To appreciate Haydn's tonal point, one need only consider how different is the effect of transforming tonic minor into tonic major in, say, the key of C – as when he employed this radiant, "purest" of all keys to symbolize the creation of Light out of Chaos.

---

[14] The following comments are synthesized from Rita Steblin, *A History of Key Characteristics in the Eighteenth and Early Nineteenth Centuries* (Ann Arbor, 1983), pp. 133, 270–73 *et passim*; compare her "Key Characteristics and Haydn's Operas," in Eva Badura-Skoda, ed., *Joseph Haydn: International Congress Vienna 1982* (Munich, 1986), pp. 91–100.

Within this context, the musicians' progress towards their tonic major home can be read directly from the various uses of the major mode in the symphony. In the wild desert of the Allegro assai, no major key can function. Our first glimpse, in the second group, is of that conventional oasis, the relative major. But it cannot establish itself; its tonic triad cannot put down roots; it is soon undermined by its remote parallel key, A minor. Only minor keys can survive here! And so we end up in C-sharp minor. (Note that unique formal features of this movement, such as the double second group and the dominant minor close of the exposition, are consistent with the programmatic interpretation.)

The next structural major-mode sonorities to be introduced are F-sharp, at the half-cadence midway through the development, and D, the key of the interlude. We have already seen that the former serves as a harbinger of the overall itinerary. But the key of D, astonishingly, makes sense as well. The musicians are still searching for rest, for the major mode; but by now they are *in extremis*, lost in the barren wastes; the major will never be provided by "normal" means. And this D major is anything but normal: it is the "wrong" key to be home, in the "wrong" place. Worse, it has no basis in reality: no dominant preparation, no bass, no apparent relation to the context, no coherent form. In short, the interlude is a *mirage*. (The more closely they approach it – the more we try to analyze it! – the more nearly it disappears into thin air.) At the same time, however, it uncannily prefigures the ultimate musical and aesthetic resolution; like a mirage, it represents precisely that which they most desire: their arrival home.

The Adagio is in A major. It is beautiful; but it is long and languorous, and still troubled by rhythmic disunity, minor mixtures, and chromaticism. In the minuet, we are vouchsafed our first vision of our real goal, F-sharp major as a tonic. But it is still shot through with disquieting reminders of the minor-mode wasteland, and is projected tentatively and without bass; this "home" does not have a firm foundation! The trio's horn-call is an audible symbol of their longing (whether or not it counts as Haydn's "lamentation" theme). Nor has there been a real progression: the first three movements are not truly linked; they merely project "beyond" themselves, towards a goal not yet attained. It will take more effort than this to arrive home. As a whole, the first cycle thus "rehearses" the journey, without actually attempting it.

The rehearsal was not in vain. F-sharp minor in the Presto, though still stormy, is no longer terrifying; perhaps it can be endured. Indeed, the second cycle undertakes the journey, traverses all the steps along the way: the keys become structurally integrated, with clear phrasing, organized transitions, strong dominants, firm cadences, background melodic descents, and the rest. It is particularly satisfying that A major, originally a "false" image of home, is a stage on this journey: the first part of the farewell movement is firmly enclosed between two strong dominant pillars; it is a place of resolution in its own right, before being incorporated into the F-sharp recapitulation. At the end, F-sharp major is established by its own dominant, repeatedly confirmed by strong cadences and structural melodic descents, purged of all dissonance and chromaticism, and informed by pure and directly expressive musical ideas. It is no longer a mirage; Haydn's musicians have earned the right to call it "home."

And yet, this music has no bass and mounts increasingly high; at the end it can hardly be heard. F-sharp remains distant, not present here and now, not "real." Can it be that Haydn's musicians don't arrive home after all? Indeed it can: they have not yet even undertaken the journey; they are still in Eszterháza, performing the symphony for their prince, who has by no means yet changed his mind. Just as, technically and aesthetically, the resolution at the end is indeterminate – can closure outweigh insubstantiality? – so the Farewell Symphony's image of home remains a desire, forever unattainable.

Haydn's symphony does not *represent* the journey (which would be pretty vulgar: picturesque scenery, neighing horses, the coach getting stuck in the mud, greetings of the happy wives and children). Rather, it engenders a psychological progression that corresponds to our feelings about a desperately longed-for journey home – a much more appropriate topic for musical illustration. As we listen, the setting is the condition of absence; our goal is merely a cherished hope. That is why the ending is so high and without foundation. (And that is why the nickname is illogical; the symphony has nothing to do with a "farewell" – except a farewell to Eszterháza, but that would have been music in a different style! In view of the program and the character of the last movement, it would be more appropriate to call it the "Absence" Symphony, or the "Symphony of Longing" – or, in view of the action at the end, the "Departure" Symphony. But perhaps this merely proves that logic should not always be granted the last word.)

The insubstantiality of the ending does not compromise its psychological truth. On the contrary, feelings of homesickness are well-nigh universal. (Perhaps the continual "rocking" motives towards the end [mm. 78–81, 86–99; see pp. 106–08] even connote a lullaby – as if our yearning for distant hearths were atavistic; that is, childlike.) Haydn invokes his musicians' longing so vividly that Prince Esterházy himself – however little his personal comfort may have been at stake – listening to this music, in the wastelands of Eszterháza with winter approaching, surely did not remain immune. And that is why, more than two centuries later, we believe in the happy ending: we too respond to the genius of Haydn's musical vision, that miraculous balance of absence and fulfillment, of desire gratified only in hope. Of course, what is "in" the music is merely a succession of sounds. The unattainable vision arises in our feelings alone; the happy ending of the Farewell Symphony exists only in the stories we tell about it.

PART II

CYCLIC ORGANIZATION IN HAYDN'S
INSTRUMENTAL MUSIC

5

PROGRESSIVE FORM AND THE
RHETORIC OF INSTABILITY

The through-composed character of the Farewell Symphony calls into question the traditional notion that strongly integrated multimovement instrumental cycles were more or less unknown until Beethoven. Moreover, for all its uniqueness, it is not an isolated case. Other Haydn works exhibit nearly as great a degree of through-composition; many individual techniques found in the Farewell are actually common in his music. Part II of this study examines the nature and extent of Haydn's integration of the instrumental cycle. In this chapter, I consider his tendency towards progressive, non-symmetrical form in individual movements – not only a characteristic feature of his art in its own right, but also of fundamental importance for through-composition on a larger scale. In the central sections of this chapter, I focus on the symphony and on the years c. 1765–74: that is, the immediate chronological and generic context of the Farewell itself, including Haydn's expressive period known under the rubric "Sturm und Drang." (In this connection, I have divided his symphonies through 1774 into chronological groups and subgroups, as indicated in Table 5.1.[1])

GESTURE AND RHETORIC

Owing to the ideology of "Classical style" (see the concluding chapter), the Haydn literature has focused too much on form-as-shape (balance, symmetry, sonata form, the metaphors of architecture), and too little on form-as-process – the dynamic development of musical ideas in time – as described with respect to the music of later periods by authors such as Ernst Kurth and B. V. Asaf'ev.[2] (In German, this distinction is often rendered by the separate terms *Form* and *Formung*.) In addition to Tovey, with his emphasis on "drama" and the rhythmic and psychological effects of tonality, the honorable

---

[1] See Feder's work-list in *The New Grove*; Landon, *Haydn*, vol. 1, pp. 280–83, 552–53; vol. 2, pp. 284–86; Larsen, "Haydn's Early Symphonies: The Problem of Dating," in Allan W. Atlas, ed., *Music in the Classic Period: Essays in Honor of Barry S. Brook* (New York, 1985), pp. 117–31; Gerlach, "Haydns 'chronologische' Sinfonienliste für Breitkopf & Härtel," *H-S* 6/2 (1988), 116–29; "Welche stilistischen Kriterien können zur genaueren Datierung von Haydns frühen Sinfonien beitragen?" *Jahrbuch für österreichische Kulturgeschichte*, vol. 13 (in press); and "Fragen zur Chronologie von Haydns frühen Sinfonien," unpubl. typescript, 1987. Throughout Part II, I draw on this literature in matters of chronology without further citation.

[2] An exception is Kurt Westphal, *Der Begriff der musikalischen Form in der Wiener Klassik: Versuch einer Grundlegung der Theorie der musikalischen Formung* (Leipzig, 1935). See also Friedrich Blume, "Fortspinnung und Entwicklung," *JbP* 36 (1929), 51–70.

Table 5.1. *Chronological groupings of Haydn's symphonies through 1774*

Period	Symphonies	Works	Sonata movements
Through 1765	1–25, 27–33, 36, 37, 40, 72, 107, 108	38	104
–1761	1, 2, 4, 5, 10, 11, 15, 27, 32, 33, 37, 107	12	35
1761–65	6–9, 12, 13, 21–24, 28–31, 36, 40, 72	17	44
Uncertain	3, 14, 16–20, 25, 108	9	25
c. 1765–66?	34, 39	2	5
1766–74	26, 35, 38, 41–52, 54–60, 63ᵃ, 64, 65	25	69
1766–69	26, 35, 38, 41, 48, 49, 58, 59	8	23
1770–72	42–47, 52	7	20
1773–74	50, 54–57, 60	6	17
(?1770–73)	51, 63ᵃ, 64, 65	4	9

ᵃ First version (finale only relevant to this study)

exceptions among recent writings in English are Edward T. Cone's studies of tonal phrasing and large-scale rhythm; Charles Rosen's analysis of relations between motif and form, and the destabilizing effects of foreign or disruptive notes and intervals; and Leonard B. Meyer's "implication-realization" model of musical processes.[3] Some promising recent attempts to apply concepts derived from literature and aesthetics, for example narrative theory, are too recent and tentative to evaluate;[4] characteristically, these authors have so far not considered so much as a single movement by Haydn. (The literature on C. P. E. Bach, whose reception has been in many respects anti-"Classical," is more open-minded about asymmetry.[5])

The common thread among the writers just named is a focus on what may be called the dynamic role of gesture in tonal music. This can function in many domains – rhythm, phrase construction, non-congruence among different musical domains or among apparently parallel formal units, the blurring of formal boundaries, denials of closure, contrasts of all kinds (dynamics, orchestration, material, "topos" and *Affekt*), and so forth. These gestures are often correlated with tonal instabilities, such as an emphasis on the third or the fifth scale-degree or a non-triad pitch at the expense of the tonic, or on a dissonance or chromatic element. In such cases, the "progressive" effect is correspondingly stronger, and can govern entire sections or movements. Schoenberg stressed this: "Every tone which is added to a beginning tone makes the meaning of that tone doubtful. . . . There is produced a state of unrest, of imbalance which grows throughout most of the piece. . . . The method by which balance is restored seems to me the real *idea* of the composition." His disciple Rudolph Réti attempted to demonstrate this

---

[3] Cone, *Form and Performance*; Rosen, *Classical Style*; Meyer, *Explaining Music* (Chicago, 1973).

[4] For example, Fred Everett Maus, "Music as Drama," *MTS* 10 (1988), 56–73; Carolyn Abbate, "What the Sorcerer Said," *19CMus* 12 (1988–89), 221–30. I return to this topic in Chapter 8, in connection with Symphony 46.

[5] See, for example, Pamela Fox, "The Stylistic Anomalies of C. P. E. Bach's Nonconstancy," in Stephen L. Clark, ed., *C. P. E. Bach Studies* (New York, 1988), pp. 105–31.

process in the first movement of Mozart's G-minor Symphony.[6] Neither applied the idea
to Haydn; all the more welcome are Rosen's recent analyses of the long-range effects of
initially destabilizing pitches in Haydn's later string quartets (*Classical Style*, pp. 115–36).

Furthermore, to an extent rarely acknowledged, Haydn's musical "persona" – to be
distinguished from the personality of the historical figure Joseph Haydn – is irregular,
eccentric, infused with *Willkür* (the willful arbitrariness and capriciousness beloved of
the German Romantic ironists). (One example of this trait among hundreds is the coda of
the finale of Symphony No. 102 in B-flat.) Not for nothing did turn-of-the-century critics
compare him to great literary ironists like Sterne and Jean Paul.[7] Even in the formal
domain, Haydn's art of making musical events imply something "beyond" themselves
forces us constantly to guess what will happen next, with the inevitable consequence
that we are wrong, and wrong again, often until the very end of the movement. In a
fundamental sense, his music is "about" this sense of potential, and the unexpected
ways in which it is realized, as for example in the finale of the string quartet Op. 54
No. 2 (see Chapter 8).

In the eighteenth century, these "gestural" aspects of music were understood as part
of a more general quality that has since become unfamiliar to us: that of *rhetoric*.
Every musician of the period believed in the expressive powers of music. Much instrumental music of the time entailed extramusical associations; these are explored in
Chapter 7. But eighteenth-century musical rhetoric incorporated two additional aspects,
at once fundamental and nearly universal. First, every instrumental work was composed and understood within a context of genre, *Affekt*, and "topoi" (topics), which in
principle enabled its ideas and gestures to be located within a network of traditional
associations, including dance types and distinctions of social status.[8] Any given musical
attribute could be a "sign" of some extramusical association or formal function;[9] the
set of available signs in a given context often incorporated all relevant possibilities,
permitting a repertory of meanings to develop through binary oppositions among its
elements – in short, creating an intuitively understood *system*, which we may study in
structuralist or semiotic terms.[10] Analysis based on these insights has been especially fruitful with respect to the so-called "rhythmic topoi": the system of dance-meters, tempi,

---

[6] Schoenberg, *Style and Idea* (London, 1975; Berkeley, 1984), p. 123; Réti, *The Thematic Process in Music* (New York, 1951), chap. 5.

[7] Gretchen A. Wheelock, "Wit, Humor, and the Instrumental Music of Joseph Haydn," Ph.D. diss., Yale University, 1979; Hartmut Krones, "Das 'hohe Komische' bei Joseph Haydn," *Österreichische Musikzeitschrift*, 38 (1983), 2–8; Howard Irving, "Haydn and Laurence Sterne: Similarities in Eighteenth-Century Literary and Musical Wit," *CM* No. 40 (1985), pp. 34–49. On "personae," see Cone, *The Composer's Voice*. An unpublished study of mine on irony in Haydn dates from 1977.

[8] Leonard G. Ratner, *Classic Music* (New York, 1980), parts I–II; Krones, "Rhetorik und rhetorische Symbolik in der Musik um 1800: Vom Weiterleben eines Prinzips," *Mth* 3 (1988), 117–40; Wye Jamison Allanbrook, "'Ear-Tickling Nonsense': A New Context for Musical Expression in Mozart's 'Haydn' Quartets," *The St. John's Review* 38 (1988), 1–24.

[9] For example, Janet M. Levy, "Texture as a Sign in Classic and Early Romantic Music," *JAMS* 35 (1982), 482–531.

[10] Agawu, *Playing with Signs: A Semiotic Interpretation of Classic Music* (Princeton: Princeton University Press, forthcoming).

and rhythmic/motivic dispositions of musical material.[11] Hence an instrumental composition's patternings in time are always potentially meaningful, whether by association with implied referents, by analogy with temporal progressions in other domains, or even understood as a rhythmic/motoric equivalent to the human passions.[12] Such associations enable us to link the technical and the aesthetic domains of music, in a viable eighteenth-century analogue to E. T. A. Hoffmann's linking of them in Beethoven.

Secondly, the eighteenth-century sense of musical form itself was "rhetorical."[13] It was not limited (as musicologists have tended to assume) to elementary notions of musical "figures" analogous to those of rhetoric, or correspondences between the parts of a composition and the parts of an oration. On the contrary, it made a general analogy between events in a composition and "the possible means of persuasion with respect to any subject" (Aristotle). The very vocabulary of eighteenth-century theories of form ("period," "sentence," "phrase," and so on) was grammatical: as the ends of verbal grammar were communication and persuasion, so the purpose of musical "grammar" was the effective working-out of musical ideas. To be sure, theorists and composers alike observed the principle – to revert to modern sonata-form terminology – that the chief ideas from the second group should be recapitulated in the tonic. Nevertheless, a movement was said to be governed by a single basic idea, and a composer's task was to develop that idea intelligibly – that is, with convincing rhetoric. Instability, unexpected juxtapositions, and outrageous humor could as well find their place in this rhetorically based style as a beautiful melody or a complex contrapuntal development.

All this will have encouraged Haydn to base a movement on a single main idea, but to develop it constantly, inventing ever-new variations, maintaining both its continuity and the novelty to the end. (The common musicological interpretation of this tendency as "exceptional" is possible only on the basis of anachronistically dualistic notions of sonata form.) His own account of his compositional methods implies this relationship:

Once I had seized upon an idea, my whole effort was to develop and sustain it [*sie auszuführen und zu souteniren*] according to the rules of the art. . . . Many of our younger composers . . . tack one little idea onto another; they break off before they have scarcely begun, and so nothing remains in the heart after one has heard it.[14]

Haydn's concept of developing his idea (note the singular), of "sustaining" it throughout a movement, implies continuity not only of material and rhythm, but of rhetoric and expression; otherwise, "nothing remains in the heart." Such music may be asymmetrical, and develop continually until the end. In Haydn, this development may compromise, even abrogate, conventional formal divisions. Potentially, these correlations

---

[11] Allanbrook, *Rhythmic Gesture in Mozart: "Le nozze di Figaro" and "Don Giovanni"* (Chicago, 1983), introduction and part I.

[12] See, for example, John Neubauer, *The Emancipation of Music from Language* (New Haven, 1986), pp. 157–67.

[13] Mark Evan Bonds, "Haydn's False Recapitulations and the Perception of Sonata Form in the Eighteenth Century," Ph.D. diss., Harvard University, 1988, chap. 2, "The Rhetorical Perception of Form"; George Robert Barth, "The Fortepianist as Orator: Beethoven and the Transformation of the Declamatory Style," D.M.A. essay, Cornell University, 1988.

[14] Griesinger, p. 114 (Gotwals, p. 61).

between material and meaning could also function *between* movements, providing a dynamic progression throughout an entire symphony. On the threshold of Romanticism stood Haydn's "Chaos–Light" sequence at the beginning of *The Creation*: a musical progression across three movements from paradoxical disorder to triumphant order; a perceptible and memorable analogy to that which is unfathomable, unthinkable; a "representation" of the origins of the universe and of history. Without rhetoric, without dynamic musical "forming," this music – all of Haydn's music – would not have been possible.

DESTABILIZATION

Openings

Haydn often begins a movement with a gesture of destabilization. Rosen has brilliantly analyzed a number of quartet beginnings of this type: Op. 50 No. 1 in B-flat, with its diminished seventh entering over the cello's naked tonic pedal; Op. 50 No. 6 in D, with its unaccompanied violin e^2 plunging down to g^1, harmonized as V_5^6; Op. 55 No. 3 in B-flat, with its sudden halt on a chromatic e^1, and diminished-octave leap to the next phrase.[15] (He might well have added an even more extreme, and earlier, example: Op. 33 No. 4 in B-flat, which begins unmediated on the last inversion of the dominant seventh, $V^2–I^6$, an astonishing stroke not risked again until Beethoven's *Prometheus*.) And Haydn always exploits these destabilizing notes or intervals throughout the movement. Another destabilizing aspect of his style is his penchant for irregular, asymmetrical phrasing.[16] In this respect, the Farewell Symphony is not unusual; comparably irregular opening themes are found, for example, in the chronologically neighboring Nos. 43 in E-flat, 47 in G, and 52 in C minor. They too entail a disjunction between a non-periodic main section and an abrupt cadence, especially No. 43 (see the conclusion, pp. 336–40). No. 47 is dynamically non-periodic in its relentless buildup of the winds over the intermittent string ostinato, and its astonishing transformation into the minor at the recapitulation.[17]

But destabilizing openings need not entail dissonance or irregular phrasing; it suffices to avoid the tonic in the bass. The most familiar examples of this type are the related, tonally ambiguous openings of the quartets Op. 33 No. 1 and Op. 64 No. 2, both in B minor. The former exploits this ambiguity throughout the first movement. Despite the considerable literature,[18] this feature has never been properly described, for two reasons:

---

[15] *The Classical Style*, pp. 120–36.

[16] Landon, *Symphonies*, pp. 238, 244–48, 319 *et passim*; Ludwig Finscher, *Studien zur Geschichte des Streichquartetts*, vol. 1, *Die Entstehung des klassischen Streichquartetts: Von den Vorformen zur Grundlegung durch Joseph Haydn* (Kassel, 1974), pp. 195–99, 219–25, 246–53; Rosen, *Classical Style*, pp. 146–51; Schwartz, "Thematic Asymmetry in First Movements of Haydn's Early Symphonies," in *Haydn Studies*, pp. 501–09; Webster, "'Beautiful' Melodies."

[17] Landon, *Symphonies*, pp. 326–27.

[18] Tovey, "Haydn's Chamber Music," pp. 49–50; elaborated in "Brahms's Chamber Music," *Essays and Lectures*, pp. 266–67; Rosen, *Classical Style*, pp. 114–16, 120; Landon, *Haydn*, vol. 2, pp. 580, 657; Keller, *The Great Haydn Quartets* (New York, 1986), pp. 64–65, 150–52.

first, every published account is based on the corrupt traditional modern texts (which horribly bowdlerize the crucial passages) rather than the accurate text in *JHW* XII/3; secondly, none pursues the consequences of Haydn's ambiguous opening throughout the movement as a whole.

The essential points are illustrated in Example 5.1. The first violinist will have initially understood mm. 1–2 (theme **1a**) in D major, ending with a half cadence on the leading-tone. (No names of keys appeared in the sources; minor-mode quartets on the sharp side were very unusual around 1780.) The opening phrase is given by the two violins alone; the initial sonority, $f\sharp^1/d^2$, is an incomplete triad, not even in root position; it could equally well be I^6 in D or III^6 in B minor. (The corrupt texts give the second violin double stops $f\sharp^1/a^1$ in the first half of m. 1, destroying the ambiguity.) This ambig-uous sonority is prolonged until the melodic cadence to $c\sharp^2$ in m. 2; only here, when $f\sharp^1$ becomes the root of a fifth, do we hear a putative dominant and hence begin to orient ourselves towards B minor. (The second violin could equally well move to a^1, the dominant of D, at the end of m. 2.) The cello entry on $f\sharp$ (theme **1b**), supporting a dominant seventh chord, then clinches the issue. Nevertheless (as Rosen notes), the ambiguity between D and B minor reverberates in the augmented-octave clash, A vs. A$\sharp$, between cello and upper parts in mm. 3–4. Furthermore, deceptive resolutions in mm. 4 and 7 postpone the cadence until m. 11. In this moderate tempo, and in light of the initial ambiguity, this is a long wait – and precisely at this moment of tonic arrival, Haydn changes the subject, to the entirely new theme **2**. This implies that B minor can be established only as the result of a long and difficult process, and that complex, in part disjunctive relationships between the material and the tonal structure will characterize the movement.

Example 5.1 String Quartet Op. 33/1/i: B minor vs. D major
(a)

Ex. 5.1 (*cont.*)

(b)

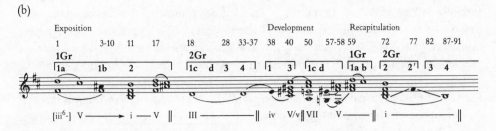

(c)

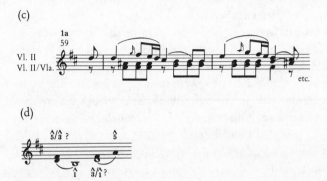

(d)

The new theme leads to a strong half-cadence (mm. 16–17), rhyming with the original half-cadence from m. 2. The second group follows directly, without transition, and with the original melody (**1c**); although such "monothematicism" is common in Haydn, this case is unique. First, consistent with the original ambiguity, the melody appears not in transposition, but on the original pitch level. Secondly, it is harmonized as the strongest imaginable D major, anchored by the the cello's rock-solid low D. (This is the cello's lowest note in the entire exposition, matched only by the final chord.) And (as Tovey points out) this firm D major throws an entirely new light on the opening bars when they are heard again in the exposition repeat: they now sound as if they were still "unambiguously" in D.

Finally, Haydn articulates the beginning of the recapitulation with one last D-major/B-minor trick (which, owing to the corrupt texts, has gone unnoticed). Dominant preparation for B minor is strong and unambiguous (mm. 57–58), emphasized by an augmented-sixth chord. The reprise (Example 5.1c) reverts to the high register of the beginning, the cello again pausing; the melody is unaltered, the bass (in the viola) essentially so. But one tiny change effects a stunning reversal. The second violin completes the triad; it even resolves the original ambiguity, by providing the "missing" leading-tone a♯¹ – but in so doing it creates an *augmented* triad! This new harmonization may be logical, but it is implicitly destabilizing, indeed explicitly dissonant; it miraculously recapitulates the original fluidity and complexity as well. (The corrupt scores and parts give the bowdlerization a¹ in place of Haydn's a♯¹.)

Moreover – and this is the "rhetorical" point – Haydn reinterprets the formal function of theme **2** (see Example 5.1b). In the exposition, it grew out of the first group by elision, precisely at the arrival of B minor; it resolved an ambiguity. In the recapitulation, however, mm. 3–10 (**1b**) are expanded and altered, including a longer and much stronger dominant (mm. 69–71), which serves as the goal of the paragraph and ends with a caesura. Its cadence has therefore become the formal equivalent of mm. 16–17 from the exposition; that is, the end of theme **1** now has the section-ending function which in the exposition was entrusted to the new, powerful **2**. In fact, the entire retransition and first-group recapitulation prolong the dominant; there is no bass tonic anywhere. Tonally, theme **2** (m. 72) therefore again restores B minor: it is a delayed structural downbeat. But its formal function is no longer that of the cadence of the first paragraph, but the beginning of the second group. (Its later expansion into a contrapuntal climax, **2′** in mm. 77–81, is an appropriate textural and rhetorical realization of this higher status.) This reinterpretation follows "consequently" from the original premise: theme **2** always resolves the instability and ambiguity of **1**. The omission of any recapitulation of the second-group version of the main theme (**1cd**) is triply motivated: it has already been heard in the tonic, at the reprise; an analogue to mm. 18–19 in D would violate the principle of never stating this theme strongly in B minor; finally, much of this material has appeared in the development, in related keys (see mm. 50–56).

The opening sonority D/F♯ thus governs the entire movement. The initial state of affairs is tentative: there is no bass, only violins; the implied harmony is not in root position; the tonality is ambiguous. The "missing" pitch could be either A or A♯; these possibilities precisely incorporate the chief distinction between D major and B minor (compare mm. 3–4); as we have seen, this ambiguity remains central throughout. Just as, locally, the opening sonority reveals itself as the upper notes of a B-minor tonic only gradually, so, in the large, theme **1** leads to **2** (and in the recapitulation to **3** and **4** as well); only these later themes are truly "in" B minor. As in the case of the D-major interlude of the Farewell, this can only be understood as a kind of irony, composed into an (apparently) non-referential instrumental work.

Perhaps the earliest example of this type of tonal instability is found in Op. 17 No. 4 in C minor, with ambiguous effects comparable to those in Op. 33 No. 1.[19] Its technical basis is twofold: (1) an emphasis on scale-degrees $\hat{3}$ and $\hat{5}$ at the expense of the tonic and (2) high-register basses or absence of the bass part. It is especially common in the minor mode, where the non-tonic-triad pitches $\hat{3}$ and $\hat{5}$ can imply the stable key of the mediant, which has the identical scale and key-signature, and (in Haydn) is almost always destined to be the key of the second group. In the major, however, neither the mediant (which could be implied by $\hat{3}$ and $\hat{5}$ alone) nor the relative minor (by $\hat{3}$ and $\hat{1}$) has any comparable importance. The distinction emerges clearly if we consider another famous quartet from Op. 33: No. 3 in C. From a structural/tonal viewpoint, it begins identically to No. 1: the bare sixth e^1/c^2 is an inversion, incomplete, without bass. But the tonic is

---

[19] Cf. Tovey, "Haydn's Chamber Music," p. 33; Landon, *Haydn*, vol. 2, p. 322.

clear from the beginning – nobody will think of III⁶ in A minor – and when the cello enters at the climax of the phrase, it rockets up from the open-string low C. Hence the opening "bass" 3̂ promotes, not tonal *ambiguity*, but tonal *instability* (it is off-tonic and suspended in midair).

A crucial aspect of these openings is the restriction of the initial gesture to the upper parts. When the music projects the tonic in root position, it remains unambiguous; the ensuing bass entry clarifies what we already "know." But when the opening sonority is incomplete, off the tonic, or ambiguous, the differences between its tonal implications and those of the later bass entry usually have long-range consequences, as in the first movement of Op. 33 No. 1. These unstable openings deserve study in their own right; in this context, a brief survey of Haydn's symphonies through the period of the *Farewell* must suffice (see Table 5.2). A clear chronological distinction obtains: tonally unstable openings appear in only two pre-1765 symphony movements, or less than 2 percent; from 1766 through 1774, they are proportionately ten times as common. Most of the off-tonic upper-register openings (first column) articulate I⁶, as in Op. 33 No. 3; that in Symphony No. 65 anticipates the B-minor/D-major play of Op. 33 No. 1.

The Andante of Symphony No. 35 in B-flat (1767) is a wonderful early example of Haydn's tonal wit. Although the subdominant key E-flat is unremarkable, the opening phrase is deceptive tonally (see Example 5.2). The violins fall from B♭ to F (5̂–2̂),

Example 5.2 Symphony No. 35/ii: tonal ambiguity and resolution

elaborated by A♮; however, with the close of the Allegro di molto still in our ears, this can only be understood in B-flat, as 8̂–5̂. To be sure, the bass enters on the tonic E♭ – but as a dissonance: the harmony continues in B-flat (V²–I⁶). The first hint of E-flat as a key is the chromatic sequence to V²–I⁶ of its subdominant, A-flat (m. 3), which is incompatible with B-flat as a tonic; clarity, however, does not arrive until the cadence (in m. 5, be it noted). Later appearances of this motive confirm Haydn's purposeful intent. The development transforms convention into wit: as was customary, it begins with the theme in the dominant B-flat (thus confirming what the beginning had denied). But the first melody note is displaced from F to E♭, and this creates an inversely deceptive tonal relationship from that at the beginning: there, the unaccompanied B♭ proved to be 5̂ of the key a fifth below; here, the unaccompanied E♭ is the subdominant of the key a fifth above – but at the same time it is the originally suppressed tonic! Further

Table 5.2. *Off-tonic openings in Haydn symphony movements (through 1774)*

Mvt.	No bass; opening gesture long or ♯ I^5_3	Bass entry on $\hat{3}$ or $\hat{5}$; offbeat or middleground	Bass dissonant or ♯ $\hat{1}/\hat{3}/\hat{5}$	Remarks
9/ii			$\hat{7}=V^6_5$	
14/iv	Long=I⁶			Contrapuntal
26/M		i⁶ middleground+offbeat		Hocketing; see pp. 243–44
35/ii	I? V?		$\hat{1}=V^2/V$	See Example 5.2
39/ii		I⁶ offbeat		3/8 slow movement as in 45/ii
/M		i⁶ offbeat		
42/ii		I⁶ offbeat		3/8 Adagio; hocketing; cf. 45/ii
/Tr	Long	V⁷ middleground		Becomes dominant key
43/Tr			V^7/vi (I)	Cf. following double bar
/iv			V^7–vi	
45/ii		I⁶ offbeat		3/8 Adagio; hocketing; cf. 42/ii
/M	I⁶–V–I (offbeat)	V⁷ middleground	♭$\hat{6}$–V	Cf. 42/ii; 45/ii
/Tr	Long; I⁶–V–I	V^6_5–V middleground	$\hat{7}=V^6_5$	
46/M	Long	I⁶ offbeat		See Example 8.5
/iv	V⁽⁷⁾		$\hat{4}=V^2$	See Examples 8.6, 8.7
[/M₂]	I⁶	Offbeat	V^6–V, vi–I⁶	See Example 8.8
47/Tr	Long	I⁶ middleground		*Al rovescio* play
/iv				
52/M			$\hat{4}=V^2$	Cf. trio: V⁷
56/ii		I⁶ offbeat	$\hat{4}=V^2$	
58/i		I⁶ offbeat		
/M		I⁶ offbeat		
59/ii				(Middleground too?)
65/ii	IV⁶? vi?		V⁷	Cf. Op. 33/1/i (Example 5.1)

unexpected transformations occur at the reprise. Finally, as a codetta, the theme returns one more time, *pianissimo* (Example 5.2). At last, everything is stable: the bass enters on the beat; the initial melodic goal F is harmonized with a diatonic ii⁶; and the bass harmonizes the melodic $\hat{1}$ of the third bar of the theme, for the first and only time, with a root-position tonic. (The progression is the same as that in the Adagio of the Farewell: ambiguity yields to stable clarity.)

Table 5.2 omits off-tonic beginnings of purely local significance. The second column lists (a) those off-*beat* bass entries that are rhythmically and tonally unstable (even if they proceed directly to $\hat{1}$) and (b) off-*tonic* entries with background or middleground significance. The only examples of the latter type are the minuet of Symphony No. 26 (see pp. 243–44) and the finale of No. 47; the latter resembles the first movement of Op. 33 No. 1 in that the root-position tonic enters as the *forte* cadence of the entire *piano* opening paragraph (m. 19) and is elided to the sequel. The offbeat bass entries comprise a distinct compositional type: every example listed in Table 5.2 is in triple meter and begins on the third degree in the bass, harmonized as I⁶. The Adagio of Symphony No. 42 (1771) is remarkably similar to its counterpart in the Farewell: keys, tempi, meters, initial bass and melody notes with subsequent voice exchange, and (to an extent) even the "hocketing" rhythmic relationships are the same. Of course, being by Haydn, the two movements then go their separate ways; as a whole, No. 42 avoids yearning chromaticism and vast phrase extensions. But Haydn's original version of a rhythmically obscure, written-out *decelerando* on an unstable V/V chord – "dies war vor gar zu gelehrte Ohren," he wrote in the autograph after altering it ("this was for entirely too learned ears")[20] – is as *recherché* as anything in the Farewell. The difference is that, a year later, he had discovered a convincing context for this degree of esotericism.

When the bass enters on a dissonance or a non-tonic-triad pitch (Table 5.2, third column), the opening melodic gesture is often brief and unproblematical, and the bass merely continues the progression towards a cadence. Among the several bass entries on $\hat{4}$=V², only that in the minuet of Symphony No. 52 in C minor does not soon lead to a strong root-position cadence: the bass downbeat is only i⁶, the answering motive is already on the dominant, and the sequel moves directly into the dominant key. (Comparable dissonant or off-tonic bass entries are found in many string quartets. In Opp. 33 No. 4, first movement; 50 No. 1, trio; 50 No. 2, minuet; 50 No. 5, first movement: minuet, trio; and 50 No. 6, first movement: the unstable opening becomes a primary constituent of the movement, comparable to the role of D/F♯ in the first movement of Op. 33 No. 1.[21])

Developments and reprises

Once set in motion, the forces of instability and ambiguity animate many later events, at least until that point at which (in Schoenberg's phrase) "balance is restored." Because the events in question seem to have relatively little direct bearing on our larger subject –

[20] Often quoted; for example, Landon, *Symphonies*, p. 325.
[21] On the first-movement expositions of Op. 50 Nos. 5 and 6, see Rosen, *Classical Style*, pp. 125–29, 131–32.

the relations among *different* movements – we must pass over the fascinating aspects of instability in Haydn's second groups. By contrast, certain tonal events in his development sections, and especially in the retransition and the beginning of the recapitulation, are of direct relevance for his sense of through-composition.

There is no comprehensive account of Haydn's development sections, early or late, in the symphonies or in any other genre.[22] To oversimplify drastically, his developments up through the mid-1760s tend to have three main sections: (1) a short paragraph, usually based on the opening theme, beginning in or around the dominant, and perhaps also including an "immediate reprise" (another statement of the opening theme, in the tonic);[23] (2) a "main" section (occasionally there are two distinct central sections), usually longer than the preceding one, in some movements modulating widely, in others centering around a single key, sometimes restating exposition material more or less bodily, at others fragmenting and developing it, but in any case usually cadencing in a related key about two-thirds or three-quarters of the way through; (3) a retransition. (In these early works, Haydn already employs both of Heinrich Christoph Koch's primary models for development sections: relatively stable and unvaried presentation of ideas from the exposition; or "continual dissection" and recombination of motives during ongoing modulations. Often, of course, he combines both in the same development.[24]) Chronologically, Haydn's symphony developments up to the mid-1760s execute this plan primarily with diatonic key relations, whereas from the late 1760s on, and increasingly after 1770, he includes chromatic progressions and remote keys. (In the 1780s and 1790s, the three-part plan itself is replaced by a variety of constructions.)

Obviously, these features are subject to the widest possible variation. In many cases, such variations affect the form of the whole movement, by blurring the function of large units, or the location of their boundaries. An obvious example is the so-called "false recapitulation."[25] An ambiguity as to the location of the structural cadence at the end of the exposition (let alone an outright subversion), making the process of development begin before the double-bar, is uncommon in Haydn; one example is the first movement of the String Quartet in A, Op. 55 No. 1. On the other hand such blurrings at the reprise are a central aspect of his formal sense (see below).

Remote harmonic juxtapositions In a substantial number of early and middle symphony development sections, Haydn directly juxtaposes remotely related sonorities. The keys entailed are not themselves remote; rather, the dominant of one key confronts the tonic of another across a caesura, or at a structural location such as the double bar,

[22] A good start on the early symphonies – albeit discussing the manipulation of material more than principles of tonal and sectional construction, and so far not followed up – is John Vinton, "The Development Section in Early Viennese Symphonies: a Re-valuation," *MR* 24 (1963), 13–22. See also Harold L. Andrews, "The Submediant in Haydn's Development Sections," in *Haydn Studies*, pp. 465–71.

[23] The immediate reprise is a much-misunderstood phenomenon, which modern writers tend either to conflate with the "false recapitulation," or to see as a defect in form. See Webster, "Binary Variants of Sonata Form in Early Haydn Instrumental Music," in Eva Badura-Skoda, ed., *Haydn Congress Vienna 1982*, p. 128; Bonds, pp. 220–24.

[24] Koch, *Versuch einer Anleitung zur Composition*, vol. 3 (Leipzig, 1793; facs. repr. Hildesheim, 1969), pp. 307–11, 403–19; tr. Nancy K. Baker as *Introductory Essay on Composition* (New Haven, 1983), pp. 199–201, 237–44.

[25] See Bonds, introduction and chaps. 4, 6.

Table 5.3. *Half-cadence caesuras with remote continuations in Haydn symphony developments through 1774*

Passage		Location	Type	Tonal relationship	Subsequent material[a]
7/i	85–87	Middle	1	V/vi–V^7/IV–iii	88=1P?; 91=2Pb (m. 26)
31/i	70–71	Early	1	V/vi–I (=V/IV)	K (2P) (m. 54)
42/i	88–89	Early	1	V/vi–I	1P
42/ii	107–09	Retransition	3	vi$^6_4$–V^0/ii–ii^6–V^2–I	1P
43/i	109–13	Early	1	V/vi–I	1P
45/i	106–08	Middle	1	V/iv–VI	New
46/i	68–70	Early	1	V^6/vi–I	1P
48/i	93–95	Early	3	V/vi–IV	3S (m. 53)
48/ii	50–52	Retransition	1	V/vi–I	2P
49/ii	71–72	Middle	1	V/v–VII	T (m. 14)
50/iv	85–88	Early	1	V/ii–IV	1P
	126–27	Retransition	1	V/vi–I	1P
51/i	80–89	Beginning	2	V–V/vi	K (2P) (77–78 [6–7])
	107–08	Middle	1	V/ii–IV	1P
54/i	64–65	Beginning	2	V–V/vi	1Pa
54/ii	74–75	Retransition	1	V/vi–I	1P
55/i	66–67	Beginning	2	V–V/vi	1P
	84–97	Early	3	V/iii–I	1P
56/i	99–100	Beginning	2	V–V^6/vi	1Pa2 (m. 4)
	[159–65	Retransition	1	V/vi–(V^7)–I	1P]
57/i	117–18	Beginning	2	V–V/vi	1P'
64/iv	109–13	Retransition	1	V^9/vi–I	1P
65/i	58–64	Early	(3)	V/vi–(ii$^6_5$–V)–I	1Pb (m. 2)
65/iv	42–44	Early	3	V/vi–IV	1P'

[a] The letters in this column and the fourth column of Table 5.4 are adapted from Jan LaRue, *Guidelines for Style Analysis* (New York: Norton, 1970).

creating an indirect or elliptical progression. These juxtapositions are often aesthetically shocking. (Of course, these are by no means the only chromatic progressions or harmonic surprises in Haydn's developments during this period. I focus on them here because of their relevance to the issue of through-composition.)

The remote successions across half-cadence caesuras in Haydn's symphony developments to 1774 are listed in Table 5.3. The caesura may occupy any of five possible locations (see the second column), which correspond to his development structure described above: "beginning" (across the double bar itself); "early" (the end of the initial period or short paragraph); "middle" (a break within the main section, or between two main sections); "end main" (the primary cadence late in the development, found only in later works); and "retransition" (acrose the join to the reprise). In addition, we may distinguish three types of root-motion across the caesura, shown schematically from the point of view of C major in Example 5.3. (1) In the most common type, the bass skips down a *major* third to a new *tonic*, while the raised third above the cadential root descends chromatically to a perfect fifth above the new root. This progression occurs on various

Example 5.3 Types of indirect tonal resolution

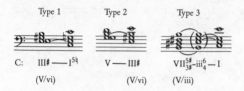

scale degrees, of which the most common is III♯–I (V/vi–I). (2) The bass skips down
a *minor* third to a new *dominant*. This usually occurs at the beginning, where the dominant
at the end of the exposition is juxtaposed with V/vi (V–III♯). (3) The bass moves up by
step, most often from $\hat{7}$ to $\hat{8}$, harmonized as V/iii(iii$_4^6$)–I.

The chronological distinction noted above with respect to the unstable openings
applies here as well: these remote juxtapositions occur in only two of 104 pre-1766
symphony development sections (Nos. 7 and 31, first movements), but in about
one-quarter of the 1766–74 movements – more precisely, beginning about 1768, the
date of Symphony No. 49 (and perhaps No. 48 as well). Another indication of their
increasing importance is that five early-1770s developments include two each, at different locations (Nos. 50 finale, 51 first movement, 54 second movement, 55 first
movement, and 56 first movement). This destabilizing resource is thus specifically
correlated with Haydn's "Sturm und Drang" period and its aftermath (it is in fact
more common after the expressive high-water mark of 1772 than before). The same
chronological distinction can be observed in his string quartets: only one passage of
this type is found in the ten early works (in Op. 2 No. 4 in F),[26] compared to at least eight
in the eighteen quartets of Opp. 9, 17, and 20.

The majority of these progressions fall into clear types (cited in boldface in the third
column of Table 5.3 and illustrated in Example 5.3). The clearest, because strongly
correlated with location, stylistic function, and chronology, is Type 2, the descent of
a minor third V–III♯ (V–V/vi). The five examples, in Symphonies 51 and 54–57, are
all from 1774 (51: *c.* 1773–74), all in first movements, and all at the beginning of the
development. Although (except in No. 51) the material is based on the main theme,
tonally these progressions move from stability (end of the exposition) to instability.
For Haydn, they doubtless represented a solution to what must have been becoming
an increasingly urgent compositional problem: to find new ways of beginning the
development section, other than the conventional restatement of the main theme in the
dominant. These developments begin in a tonally discontinuous manner but, as if in
compensation, remain thematically linked: at once disconcerting and familiar, startling
and cogent. The importance of such multiple layerings for Haydn's continuing development as a composer is obvious. Familiar later examples of recomposed main themes

---

[26] See Tovey, "Haydn's Chamber Music," pp. 19–20; Webster, "Freedom of Form in Haydn's Early String Quartets," in
Haydn Studies, pp. 527–30.

at the beginning of development sections include the tonally unexpected, rhythmically displaced C major in the first movement of the "Surprise" Symphony, and the dominant pedal on D in No. 98 in B-flat. The latter, in fact, is tonally identical to the 1770 examples just cited, and its surprising deceptive resolution to E-flat (m. 141) has earlier counterparts in Nos. 51, m. 89, and 55, mm. 84–97. In addition, Haydn always relates his initial remote sonority to subsequent features, usually by means of further surprises – for example, again in No. 55.[27]

The most common type of remote juxtaposition, however, is Type 1, involving the fall of a major third. It occurs in three locations: "early" (at the end of the initial period), in the "middle" of a bipartite development, and in the "retransition" (directly preparing the recapitulation). The majority incorporate the root succession V/vi–I (two others are transposed down a fifth, on V/ii–IV). The function of these juxtapositions follows directly from these facts of tonal orientation and location. In the context of a development section, a tonic sonority necessarily represents a reprise (even if no return of the opening theme is entailed); these reprises are prepared indirectly, by the dominant of the mediant, with common-tone $\hat{3}$. If the progression occurs early in the development, it leads to an "immediate reprise"; if in the middle, to a false recapitulation; if in the retransition, it prepares the recapitulation itself.

Around 1770, Haydn began to exploit these V/vi–I progressions as a normal type of retransition to the recapitulation (see below). In other development sections, we find them at the end of the initial paragraph: the first movements of Symphonies 31, 42, 43, 46 and 65, and the finale of No. 50 (note that the use of this particular location is concentrated in first movements). In Nos. 42, 43, 46, and 50, they prepare immediate reprises; in No. 31, however, the *closing* theme follows the caesura, while in No. 65 the drop of a third prepares the second phrase of the opening theme, *piano* on ii$_5^6$, eventually cadencing onto a root-position tonic. In No. 46 in B, the caesura falls instead on a first-inversion triad, with the local leading-tone Fx in the bass (m. 68). The two progressions of this type that use V/ii–IV differ in appropriate ways. The finale of No. 50 has an immediate reprise; the orientation around the subdominant avoids redundancy with the true recapitulation, which is prepared by the same progression on V/vi–I (shown in Example 6.4). Indeed, this movement is the only one in the repertory with two Type 1 progressions. In the opening movement of No. 51, finally, V/ii–IV occurs near the middle of the development, as a "true" false recapitulation in the subdominant. The variety of Haydn's repeated uses of the same device is remarkable.

The remaining three Type 1 progressions occur in the middle of the development; they cannot be reduced to uniform subtypes. In *Le midi*, the tonic root (mm. 86–87) is harmonized deceptively as V[7]/IV and soon reveals itself as an augmented-sixth chord in E minor. The other two occur in movements in the minor mode. The falling third progression, harmonized as V[#]–III, is characteristic of Haydn's minor-mode *expositions*: when the first group ends on the dominant with a caesura, the second group (or transi-

---

[27] On this development section see Rosen, *Sonata Forms*, pp. 150–54.

tion) often begins directly in the relative major. So it is in the Allegro di molto second movement of Symphony No. 49 (mm. 13–14); the same passage in transposition generates a remote juxtaposition in the development (mm. 71–72). The other example is none other than the F♯–D juxtaposition which introduces the interlude in the Allegro assai of the Farewell. (It is worth noting how few of Haydn's minor-mode "Sturm und Drang" symphony movements incorporate this new tonal and formal resource. The minor was indeed significant for his expansion of key relations in this period, but primarily in the context of overall tonal organization; see Chapter 6.)

The third and last type of remote juxtaposition involves root motion up a step; five passages are listed in Table 5.3. In two of these (the second movement of No. 42 and the first of No. 65), the upward step motion is combined with a more powerful downward third progression (Type 1); they have been cited above. Of the remaining three, the first movement of No. 48 in C and the finale of No. 65 in A are tonally identical, V/vi–IV; both occur at immediate reprises (in No. 48, however, this reprise is subverted by an unexpected, unstable theme). In the first movement of No. 55 in E-flat, there is instead a middleground progression from V/iii to I (bass D–E♭, mm. 84–97); this resembles similar development progressions in works in the related key of B-flat, Symphony No. 51 and Op. 33 No. 4.

Unusual and "weak" preparations for the reprise A crucial aspect of the Allegro assai of the Farewell Symphony is the weak harmonic preparation for the recapitulation. This too has its counterparts elsewhere: in many Haydn early and middle symphony movements, of various types and styles, the preparation lies "off" the dominant, or is otherwise harmonically indirect (see Table 5.4). For the sake of brevity and clarity, I deal here only with "true" recapitulations in unambiguous sonata-form movements. I also adopt a terminological distinction between a *reprise* (a return of the opening idea, in any context), and a *recapitulation* (the entire section in question or, when no ambiguity can arise, the return of other material in the tonic).[28] The chronological profile of these veiled reprises is the same as that already noted for off-tonic openings and remote juxtapositions in developments: there are relatively few before 1761, more in the first half of the 1760s, and a virtual explosion in the late 1760s and early 1770s.

As always, Haydn's variety of resource is astonishing. The chord of preparation may appear on any degree of the scale; even ♯$\hat{4}$ makes an appearance. The chords themselves include not only all the inversions of the dominant and various third-related chords built on $\hat{3}$ and $\hat{6}$, but others which might be supposed to have no cogent preparatory function: ii (the first movement of Symphony No. 43 and the finale of No. 56); III⁶ in minor (No. 52 finale); V⁹/vi (No. 64 finale); and V⁶/v in minor (No. 49, first

---

[28] The issues of principle are briefly described, in the context of all of Haydn's early instrumental music, in Webster, "Sonata/Binary." On retransitions in general, see Beth Shamgar, "On Locating the Retransition in Classic Sonata Form," *MR* 42 (1981), 130–43. On Haydn's reprises, see Heino Schwarting, "Ungewöhnliche Repriseneintritte in Haydns späterer Instrumentalmusik," *AfMw* 17 (1960), 168–82; Shamgar, "Rhythmic Interplay in the Retransitions of Haydn's Piano Sonatas," *JM* 3 (1984), 55–68; Bonds, chaps. 4–5.

Table 5.4. *Haydn symphony movements in sonata form with preparations for the reprise other than root-position dominants (through 1774)*

Location	Tonal disposition	Caesura?	Material of retransition	Remarks
Before 1761				
107/iii, 42–43	V^4_3–I	No	1P'	V m. 41b, but not articulated or prolonged
108/i, 32–33	V^4_3–I	No	T (m. 9–10)	T omitted in recapitulation
/iv, 59–60	I | I	Yes	1Pa'	Sequence: ii⁶–V⁶, V–I (full stop) | Reprise
37/i, 109–10	I^6–I^6	(Yes)	2P (m. 13–16)	Location of beginning of recapitulation unclear: m. 110 (1Pb' [=4]+1Sa [=14])? m. 118 (1S' [=17])? m. 127 (1Pb' [=5])? Strong dominants preceding mm. 118, 127 only, not 110; material throughout this movement highly variable
1761–65				
7/ii, 23–24	[See remark]	No	1Pa' (m. 22–23) (cf. 1, 19)	Double-concerto movement. Reprise is to 2P (m. 24ab=3) entering on IV (m. 23cd), then V–I as 2P emerges
8/i, 172–73	I | I	Yes	1S' (m. 41)	Structural V (mm. 152–64) leads to "retransition," which comes to a full stop on I
21/ii, 65–66	$V^{(6)}_{5}$–I	(Yes)	1Pa'	Fast second movement
[23/i, 92–96]	vi–(V⁷)–I	Yes (92)	2P (m. 9)	Reprise is to 2P (m. 66=10); 1P returns as if a coda (m. 95)
/ii, 65–66	I | I	Yes	2P (m. 30)	Caesura on vi m. 92; retransition links by sequence Retransition=sequence, iv–ii–I; tonic arrival precedes reprise as full stop
/iv, 57–59	$V^6_{[5]}$–I	Yes	1P	No caesura to m. 59 (=1); p continuation (=2) retrospectively creates caesura on the phrase-level: Retr. | Reprise
24/ii, 43–45	V⁶–I	No	1S (m. 14)	Dominant prolonged, but only as V⁶ (V²); retransition leads directly to 2S (m. 45=18), on IV; 1P omitted
40/i, 88–89	V⁶–I	Yes	1Pb' (m. 6) (cf. 62, 74)	

Table 5.4 (cont.)

Location	Tonal disposition	Caesura?	Material of retransition	Remarks
1766–c. 1770				
26/i, 79–80	V^6_5–I	(Yes)	[Athematic]	Minor dominant main development key; full cadence and implied caesura m. 74
41/iv, 89–90	V^2–I^6	(Yes)	2P (m. 8)	Movement begins without bass; mm. 92–93 (=3–4): V–I
48/ii, 50–51	V/vi–I	Yes	T (m. 12)	Remote, V/vi–I; cf. Table 5.3. Reprise is to 2P See pp. 262–64
49/i, 61–62	V^6/v–i [sic]	Yes	1P	Sequence, v–iii–i; third member (in i, mm. 98–99) = local transition to 1P. See pp. 266–67
/ii, 97–100	III–V^6–i	(Yes)	4S (m. 37)	
c. 1770–1774				
42/ii, 110–11	V^5_3(?)–V^2–I^6	(Yes)	T (m. 22–24)	Middleground: remote, V/vi–I; cf. Table 5.3
43/i, 160–62	ii–I	No	1P	Retransition=sequence, IV–ii–I. (Cf. Op. 20/4/i)
/ii, 80–81	V^6_5–I	(Yes)	2S (m. 25)	
/iv, 100–05	vi–[V–I^6]–V	No	1S (m. 34)	Movement begins without bass; final V (m. 105) = m. 2
44/i, 100–01	V^5_3–I	(Yes)	1S' (m. 20)	
/iii, 57–58	V^5_3–I	(Yes)	1Sa2' (m. 17) (cf. upbeat/9)	Reprise is to 1S; 1P omitted
45/i, 140–42	VI–(vii^6)–i	Yes	Interlude	Many non-root-positions throughout; see pp. 281–83
46/i, 104–05	vii^6–I	No	4Sb (m. 45)	Movement begins on I^6 without bass; see pp. 270–74
/iv, 95–96	I^6–I^6	No	2S' (m. 35)	
50/iv, 125–27	V/vi–i	Yes	2Sc' (m. 41–43)	Remote, V/vi–I; cf. Table 5.3 and see pp. 210–11
51/i, 148–49	I^6–I^6	Yes	1S" (m. 38)	Reprise is to 2P (m. 5), originally on I^6; 1P follows, but in the counterstatement form (157=13)
52/ii, 116–17	V^2–I^5_3 [sic]	(Yes)	3Sd (m. 69–72)	Cf. 54/iv
/iv, 99–101	III^6–i	(Yes)	1Pa	Middleground: iv–III–i
54/ii, 74–75	V/vi–I	Yes	1S (m. 17)	Remote, V/vi–I; cf. Table 5.3
/iv, 97–98	V^2–I^5_3 [sic]	Yes	2S (m. 38)	Middleground: remote, V/vi–I. Cf. 52/ii. Cf. also Opp. 20/3 and 74/3, in G minor (p. 318)
[56/i, 154–65]	V/vi–(V^7)–I	(Yes)	2Sa2 (m. 55–56)	Middleground: remote, V/vi–I; cf. p. 143
/iv, 85–86	ii–I	Yes	1Pa	Note f–p play on contrasting motives

Table 5.4 (*cont.*)

Location	Tonal disposition	Caesura?	Material of retransition	Remarks
58/i, 94–95	$V^2 - I^6$	(No)	1Pa (m. 5, bass)	Cadence vi m. 89; sequential retrans.; m. 96 (=1): $I^6 - I$
60/i, 157–58	$V^4_3 - (V^7) - I$	Yes	2Sb (m. 71)	Mm. 158–59 = opening = $V^7 - I$
/ii, 79–80	iii $- I$	Yes	Ka1 (m. 43)	
64/i, 101–02	$ii^6 - (V^6_5) - I$	(Yes)	1Pby (m. 3, bass)	Middleground: vi $- I$. Note horns m. 101b
/iv, 109–13	V^9/vi $- I$	Yes	3S (m. 52)	Middleground: remote, V/vi $- I$; cf. Table 5.3
65/i, 89 [*sic*]	(ii $-$)$V^6_5 - (V) - I$	No	3S (m. 37)+ 1Pa' (m. 10–11)	Retransition: 3S on IV (mm. 83–86), 1Pa' on ii $- I$; reprise: 1P'+3P (89ff=10ff, not 1ff)

movement). Nor are the weak harmonic progressions restricted to straightforward inversions of the root succession V–I moving by step in the bass. A number of odd and indirect progressions appear as well: V^2–I_3^5; the remote juxtaposition V/vi–I; and a truly weird, elliptical V^6/v–i progression in the opening Adagio of Symphony No. 49 in F minor (see Chapter 8). Also relevant to the topic of indirectly prepared reprises are Haydn's run-on returns from trios to minuets, described later in this chapter.

The most common remote reprise preparation involves descent by a major third, described above as Type 1 in development sections. In this context, the only possible tonal orientation is V/vi–I (III♯–I): the reprise in the tonic follows a structural half-cadence on the dominant of the relative minor. We thus have yet another middle-period Haydn manipulation of a formal convention, the structural caesura towards the end of the development. Earlier in his *oeuvre*, such caesuras usually appeared either towards the end of the development, on a full cadence, or at the very end, as a half-cadence on the home dominant. The novelty thus lay in what might be seen as a tonal/formal ellipsis: the caesura still occurs on a type of dominant and now directly precedes the reprise, but it has been transformed into an indirect tonal preparation.

This method of preparing a return to the tonic was common throughout the middle and late Baroque. The most familiar example is doubtless Bach's Brandenburg Concerto No. 3 in G, in which a skeletal iv^6–V♯ of E minor stands for the entire middle movement; the finale is thus prepared by the familiar V/vi–I.[29] (In the context of Baroque tonality and style, this progression may not have seemed remote in the later sense of a distant, chromatic relation.) Around 1770, however, the sense of this progression seems to have changed into a sophisticated variation of the (by then) all-too-conventional dominant retransition, a kind of alternative dominant (and not merely a variant of the earlier full cadence in the relative minor).[30] To a far greater extent than is generally recognized, in fact, it remained common throughout the Classical period; both Haydn and Mozart often employed it.[31] V/vi is often the structural goal of the entire development in full-fledged, late sonata movements; examples include the first movements of Haydn's string quartets Op. 54 No. 3 in E and Op. 64 No. 6 in E-flat, the slow movement of Symphony No. 99, the finale of the "Drum Roll" Symphony, and the Kyrie of his last mass, the *Harmoniemesse*, as well as many works of Mozart.[32] Another common procedure, especially in Mozart, is to follow the caesura on V/vi with a very brief, usually contrasting transition via a passing dominant, as in the opening Allegro of the E-flat Symphony K. 543.

Characteristically, the secondary literature focuses exclusively on Haydn's late music in this connection. In fact, however, he began to exploit the V/vi–I retransition as a

[29] Jan LaRue, "Bifocal Tonality: An Explanation for Ambiguous Baroque Cadences," in *Essays on Music in Honor of Archibald Thompson Davison by his Associates* (Cambridge, Mass., 1957), pp. 173–84.

[30] As Rosen assumes in the otherwise useful discussion in *Sonata Forms*, pp. 255–62.

[31] Contrary to LaRue, "Bifocal Tonality," p. 177.

[32] See also David Beach, "A Recurring Pattern in Mozart's Music," *JMT* 27 (1983), 1–30; Channan Willner, "Chromaticism and the Mediant in Four Late Haydn Works," *Theory and Practice*, 13 (1988), 79–114.

normal resource around 1770. It appears in six symphony movements (as well as in other genres) from the first half of the decade, in all three primary movement types: the slow movements of Nos. 42, 48, and 54, the finales of Nos. 50 and 64, and the first movement of No. 56. The juxtapositions in Nos. 48, 50, 54, and 64 are direct and unmediated; those in Nos. 42 and 56 are elaborated by subsidiary transitional harmonies. Even in the four unmediated examples, Haydn does not repeat himself. Those in the slow movements of Nos. 48 in C and 54 in G are straightforward common-tone modulations. But only the latter prepares a normal recapitulation of the opening theme; in No. 48 we begin instead with the *second* first-group theme (m. 52=9), the opening theme being withheld until m. 58, following a strong dominant half cadence. The finale of No. 50 in C, mm. 125–27, is a shocking juxtaposition (see Example 6.4). In the finale of No. 64 in A, finally, the V/vi of the development is no longer a simple triad, but a dominant ninth chord (the horns astonishingly project the seventh, c♯/b¹); then everybody but the violins drops out, leaving the third b¹/d² to resolve to c♯² at the moment of recapitulation. Even though this return is not actually based on a melodic common-tone, the progression V/vi–I remains its imaginary contextual basis. Perhaps it was already becoming a convention in its own right.

In other movements Haydn employs a variant of this technique, namely a brief linking retransition. In the Adagio of Symphony No. 42, the relative minor (F-sharp minor) governs the second half of the development; the local dominants culminate on a tonic six-four on C♯ in m. 107, which however resolves deceptively through B minor (iv=ii) and proceeds directly to the reprise (m. 111). The dominant in m. 110 is too weak to override the larger progression from C♯ in mm. 98–107 (as is only logical: the very first bass note in the movement, faithfully reproduced on the second eighth of m. 111, was also C♯). But if the contextually disjunct linking passage includes a root-position dominant, the latter may supersede even the strongest preceding emphasis on V/vi. In the first movement of Symphony No. 56 in C, for example, a loud passage beginning in E minor (m. 134) reaches its goal on the dominant of A minor at m. 154, extended tonally through the first six bars of the ensuing *piano* retransition. As the two-bar phrases continue, the harmony moves III♯–iii–V⁷–I; even though mm. 163–64 remain *piano*, the re-entry of the basses and horns and the dominant seventh signal the reprise. An even more sophisticated exploitation of the same ambiguity, also in C, is found in the first movement of Op. 33 No. 3. It will be recalled that this movement begins off the tonic on I⁶ without bass. The development then exploits the implications of E as bass by emphasizing E minor (iii); see mm. 73, 83, 96–97, 98, 107–08. Although m. 108 is the beginning of the thematic reprise (equivalent to m. 1), it is astonishingly still in E minor; C major does not arrive until m. 111, as the goal of the progression iii–V[2][4]/3–I – that is, the equivalent of m. 4, the location of the cello's original confirming low C![33] Haydn's keyboard sonatas from this period also have retransitions of this type. In the opening movement of Hob. XVI:25 in E-flat (1773), he goes so far as to aim the development at the leading-tone D (V/iii); following a pedal and caesura

---

[33] Because of the part-crossing, the identity of the inversion in m. 110 is ambiguous. On this subject, see Webster, "The Bass Part," pp. 402–16.

(mm. 48–50), the reprise enters by simply moving up a step (note the avoidance of parallel fifths). (In the larger context, one may choose to hear the ensuing strong half cadence in m. 52 as linked to that D, its third, and hence as subsuming the reprise-tonic in m. 51.) Later, Haydn essayed this half-step retransition most often in the key of D (for example, the third movement of Op. 33 No. 1 and the finales of Symphonies 93 and 104); Beethoven perpetuated this tradition, again most often in D (for example, the first movement of Op. 18 No. 3 and both outer movements of Symphony No. 2).

Many of Haydn's early and middle retransitions are based on "weak" harmonic progressions (also listed in Table 5.4). They fall into various types: non-root-position inversions of the dominant (for example, the finale of Symphony No. 107 and the first movement of 108); and sequential retransitions, usually iii–ii–I, with or without intervening dominants, a type also found in Sammartini.[34] Two odd reprise preparations move V^2–I_3^5 ($\hat{4}$–$\hat{1}$ in the bass): the Andante of Symphony No. 52 in C minor and the finale of No. 54 in G. The "opposite" type of weak preparation arises when the retransition reaches a full cadence on a root-position *tonic*, just before the thematic reprise. This occurs only in early works: the finale of Symphony No. 108, the first of No. 8, the second of No. 23, and the first of No. 37 (on I^6). These cadences sound awkward to modern listeners: the caesura on the tonic prevents the moment of reprise from resolving the development, either tonally or rhythmically.

By contrast, Haydn's later weak and sequential retransitions are pointedly inventive, usually relate to larger issues in the same movements, and often lead to an outright blurring of the boundary between development and reprise, a procedure ordinarily thought to be more characteristic of Brahms and other composers from the last phase of tonal sonata form.[35] (Two examples are Op. 33 No. 3 in C, just described, and Op. 50 No. 1 in B-flat.[36]) Two movements from the early 1770s which fuse the end of the development and the beginning of the reprise on a first-inversion tonic have *begun* on I^6. One is the finale of Symphony No. 46 in B (discussed in Chapter 8). In the first movement of No. 51 in B-flat, the first group establishes D as a mysterious bass pitch class, and the entire development plays with D and E♭; the retransition naturally continues the story, in such a way that the recapitulation begins with the *second* theme from the first group (mm. 148ff = 4ff). Similarly, the sequential retransition in Symphony No. 43 (whose opening theme oddly emphasizes I^6; see the concluding chapter) simply moves down by sequence, IV–ii–I (mm. 152–62), with no secondary dominants or other modulatory gestures. The Allegro di molto of the String Quartet Op. 20 No. 4 in D, which also features an unusual and quiet opening theme, has a similar sequential retransition on the subdominant side, but it slips into the dominant at the last minute.

[34] Bathia Churgin, "The Italian Symphonic Background to Haydn's Early Symphonies and Opera Overtures," in *Haydn Studies*, pp. 334–35.

[35] On blurred reprises in Brahms, see Rosen, *Sonata Forms*, pp. 322–27; Webster, "The General and the Particular in Brahms's Later Sonata Forms," in George Bozarth, ed., *Brahms Studies: International Brahms Conference, Washington, D.C., 1983* (London, 1990), §V.

[36] On the retransition in the first movement of Op. 50 No. 1, see Janet M. Levy, "Gesture, Form, and Syntax in Haydn's Music," in *Haydn Studies*, p. 360; and the discussion on p. 362.

Not surprisingly, many of Haydn's unconventional retransitions involve jokes; these need no special emphasis here. On the other hand, his most astonishingly elliptical retransition in this period occurs in a most serious context indeed: the opening Adagio of Symphony No. 49 (see Chapter 8).

But a reprise may function in a destabilizing manner even when it enjoys strong dominant preparation and is unambiguously announced by a caesura. A stunning example is found in the first movement of Symphony No. 47 in G, in which the main theme is unexpectedly transformed into the tonic minor and recomposed (a passage Landon justly singles out for praise). This "reverse" type of progressive reprise (major to minor) dates from the same year, 1772, as the kinetically frustrated recapitulation in the Allegro assai of the Farewell. Thus (to conclude this section) in the late 1760s and early 1770s Haydn learned to manipulate the conventions of development sections in different ways; such manipulation remained a central element of his style from that time forward. In general, the more unexpected and original the result, the more closely it relates to significant features elsewhere in the movement. This point is critical for the issue of through-composition: in principle, such relations can equally well be extended to embrace elements in different movements. At the same time, every Haydn development section is individual – and none more so than the Allegro assai of the Farewell, with its spectacular example of the D-major interlude. Its juxtaposition of the tonal degrees V/iv–VI is the only example of its kind in any Haydn development (at least up to 1780). No other passage has so profound an effect on the form: the F-sharp major cadence prepares, not a reprise, but something new, unprecedented, baffling, which remains a mystery until the end of the symphony. Nevertheless, the technical elements entailed are but intensifications of principles Haydn regularly employed. The dialectic of the uniqueness of the individual work and the continuity of an artist's development is rarely as manifest.

Endings

Compromises of closure The sense of closure is arguably the most essential structural attribute of tonal music. In this it is sharply distinguished from the other arts, none of which can even approach its power to create a sense of satisfactory finality.[37] The belief in "organic unity," so characteristic of twentieth-century analysis in all the arts, is in music both a cause and a result of the importance of closure. Tovey often wrote about the special "perfection" he believed was characteristic of "consummate [musical] master-works" alone.[38] Schoenberg, when describing opening destabilizations (see above), insisted on the eventual restoration of "balance" in successful works and invoked in support the mystical concept of the *Grundgestalt* (see p. 195). Schenker went so far as to claim that everything in a movement following the arrival of the background on

---

[37] On closure in literature, see Frank Kermode, *The Sense of an Ending* (New York, 1967), emphasizing eschatology; Barbara Herrnstein Smith, *Poetic Closure* (Chicago, 1968), form and overt content; Peter Brooks, *Reading for the Plot* (New York, 1984), chaps. 1 and 4, narrative and the unconscious.

[38] For example, "Musical Form and Matter," in *Essays and Lectures*, pp. 160–82.

$\hat{1}/\text{I}$ is mere "coda," no matter what its relation to events in the foreground;[39] but then his concept of the "background" is no less mystical. But musical closure also has its paradoxical aspects. How can one understand so apparently powerful an organizing force, let alone describe it, when its elements are mere sounds heard in time, which can be studied only in memory as prompted by a score? To what extent is the sense of necessity we feel at the end of many movements by the greatest tonal composers a merely psychological effect? Some contemporary writers have focused on the problems entailed by organicist notions of this kind, without presuming to voice definitive answers;[40] an especially promising current forum is opera studies.[41] But in the context of the Farewell Symphony, it seems natural to inquire more generally into Haydn's undermining of closure at the end of instrumental movements as well.

Even in this respect, the Farewell merely radicalizes techniques that Haydn regularly employed.[42] (See Table 5.5. I focus solely on movements which do end, with a full cadence and pause; *attacca* and run-on movements are described in Chapter 6.) Closure can be weakened by an avoidance of root-position V–I cadences, of melodic resolution to the tonic, or of "strong" rhythmic organization; an insufficiency of dynamics, register, or instrumental forces; or the absence of appropriate "signs" of finality.[43] As a generalization, we may say simply that closure is weakened whenever there is no sufficiently strong "structural downbeat" (Cone) on the tonic sufficiently close to the end (of course, this can only be evaluated in context). For example, depending on the scale, the final structural downbeat can be followed by one or more tonic chords, several V–I cadences, or even a brief paragraph, all without compromising closure. For the purely "confirming" function of the latter to remain unambiguous, however, this material must ordinarily be elided to the structural cadence, without caesura; see, for example, the Farewell, Presto, mm. 53–56, and finale, mm. 103–07.

Off-tonic melodic cadences Ordinarily, confirming cadences or motivic repetitions following the structural downbeat are unproblematical, even if they emphasize $\hat{3}$ in the melody. Nevertheless, surprises do occur. The final cadences in the second movement of Symphony No. 34 are harmonized, astonishingly, as V_3^4 (with $\hat{2}$ in the bass), rather than V^7. (The same is true in the first movement of the late String Quartet in G Op. 64 No. 4, with a very strange part-crossing that makes the first violin the bass.) The concluding melodic $\hat{1}$–$\hat{2}$–$\hat{3}$ in the finale of Symphony No. 35 in B-flat (1767) is perhaps Haydn's earliest symphonic example of what would soon become a familiar joke: to end a movement with its opening phrase. The fourth movement of No. 55 and the fifth of No. 60 (both 1774) are similar; the effect of destabilization in the latter is even stronger, owing to the acceleration to allegro (perhaps a reflection of the stage action

[39] *Free Composition*, p. 129, §304.

[40] For example, Cone, *Form and Performance*, pp. 17–23, 88–98; Meyer, *Explaining Music*, chap. 4; Agawu, "Concepts of Closure and Chopin's Opus 28," *MTS* 9 (1987), 1–17.

[41] The issues are surveyed in Webster, "To Understand Verdi"; Abbate and Parker, "On Analyzing Opera."

[42] Haydn's movement endings are surveyed in Jürgen Neubacher, *Finis coronat opus: Untersuchungen zur Technik der Schlußgestaltung in der Instrumentalmusik Joseph Haydns* (Tutzing, 1986).

[43] On stylistic "signs" in tonal music, see Agawu, *Playing with Signs*; Levy, "Texture as a Sign."

this music originally accompanied). Slightly longer passages we may call "codettas"; even they do not ordinarily compromise the structural cadence (see Symphonies 13, finale; 45, second movement; 48, minuet; 55, finale; and 59, first movement).

Endings on $\hat{5}$ in the melody (rather than $\hat{3}$) are very rare. The finale of Symphony No. 23 in G (1764) ends with a composed-out ritardando to *pizzicato*, all on $\hat{5}/I$; this is the earliest of Haydn's few symphonic conclusions with *pianissimo* (see below), and arguably his first overtly joking ending.[44] The only other ending on a prominent melodic $\hat{5}$, in the opening Presto of No. 59 in A (late 1760s?), takes place over a tonic pedal, inflected by an essentially unresolved $\flat\hat{7}$. (The ending of the Allegro in the chronologically neighboring No. 58 in F is similar: $\flat\hat{7}$ is prominent over a tonic pedal, in the context of an unexpected drop to *piano*; here, however, a final *forte* cadence restores the balance.) Occasionally a movement actually ends on an afterbeat I^6 chord (always without bass), as in the end of the Farewell Symphony. The delicately farcical "echo" Andante molto of the slightly earlier No. 38 in C ends in the same way; it is remarkable that the identical ending on I^6 can function effectively in such different aesthetic contexts.

Weakened structural cadences Occasionally, the final dominant may be so brief or insubstantial that the entire structural cadence seems vitiated, as in the Allegro assai of the Farewell. Comparable effects occur in two other symphony movements from the early 1770s, the opening movements of Nos. 51 and 54. In the former, the long passage following the very strong cadence in mm. 179–80 seems to have a stronger aesthetic than structural role. The quiet hocketing theme (mm. 181ff) reaches another cadence (mm. 187–88), but only in the strings; the repetition is diverted *through* the quiet dominant in m. 198 to the *fortissimo* eruption on V^2 in m. 199; and when the dominant returns (m. 205) it is, oddly, once again quiet and in the strings alone. The effect is hard to pin down. In No. 54, first movement, the last strong cadence appears in mm. 204–05,[45] and every following dominant is weak: *piano* in the answering cadence (m. 210), *piano* and relegated to the violas following the diminished-seventh fermata (m. 226); the final flourishes offer no dominant in the bass, merely a tonic pedal. (In other movements from this period the structural dominant, though very strong, seems to come too early; I discuss these below, in connection with free recapitulations.)

In two extraordinary slow movements, the final structural cadence is compromised in the opposite manner: a strong, unambiguous dominant *fails* to resolve to the tonic convincingly. One is the opening Adagio of Symphony No. 49 in F minor (1768, see Chapter 8). The other is arguably the strangest movement Haydn ever composed, the Largo of Symphony No. 64 in A ("Tempora mutantur," *c.* 1773?; possibly a theatrical movement).[46] I cannot analyze this amazing piece in detail here; relevant to the ending, however, are the continual interruptions on six-four chords over the dominant, and

---

[44] As suggested by Landon (*Symphonies*, p. 250).

[45] Landon's miniature score edition, exceptionally, begins counting measures from "1" again at the beginning of the Presto, resulting in numbers which are seventeen "too low"; the numbers given here are those in *JHW*.

[46] The nickname may well not be authentic; see Chapter 7. Further on this movement, see Elaine R. Sisman, "Haydn's Theater Symphonies," *JAMS* 43 (1990), 326–31.

Table 5.5. *Haydn symphony movements with early or problematical closure (through 1774)*

Movement	Relation to structural downbeat	Harmonic type at end	Remarks
Before 1761			
11/ii	Early V (sustained)	Unison $\hat{5}$–$\hat{1}$	Long V pedal mm. 139–52 [–61?]; V–I only mm. 161–62 (deceptive cadence 159–60 continues bass sequence); no melodic descent to $\hat{1}$ (except horn. I)
1761–65			
13/iv	Codetta (=exp.)	I–V–$\hat{3}$/I	Closure at m. 159; cadence m. 165 p, high bass, no V; $\hat{3}$ thereafter (even downbeat 169); cf. end exposition (m. 56 low A; 60 $\hat{1}$ not $\hat{3}$)
23/iv	Coda	$\hat{5}$/I	Joke: twofold closure, f at m. 79, p at m. 87 (=end exposition); joke ending pp pizz. $\hat{5}$ m. 96.
31/i	Codetta	$\hat{3}$/I	Closure at m. 154; codetta (on 1P) reverts to $\hat{3}$. See p. 246
/iv	Codetta	$\hat{3}$/I	Closure at m. 164; codetta reverts to 1P from first movement
1766–c. 1770			
34/ii	Afterbeat variant	I–V$^4_3$–$\hat{3}$/I	Closure at m. 90; $\hat{3}$ through end (94); final cadences V$^4_3$, not V^7
35/iv	Afterbeat variant	I–V–$\hat{3}$/I	Closure at mm. 132 (f) and 140 (p; codetta); final f $\hat{1}$-$\hat{2}$-$\hat{3}$ (140–41) on opening motive (cf. end exposition: f chords all $\hat{1}$)
38/ii	Codetta (=exp.) High pp	I^6	"Echo" movement (V.I normal, V.II with mutes); closure m. 95; concluding "tags" violins alone, similar to end of Farewell
48/M	Codetta; pp	$\hat{3}$/I$^{\text{I-V-I}}$	Closure at m. 40; extension $\hat{8}$-$\hat{3}$ (end 44). Cf. – in the same key and from the same period – the minuets of quartets Opp. 9/3, 17/4
49/i	Fails to resolve V	I$^{\text{V/IV–IV–vii–I}}$	$^4_6$ m. 91 (f, with winds) resolves pp, strings alone. See p. 264
58/i	Codetta	I$^{8\text{-}\flat7\text{-}6\text{-}5}$	Closure at m. 134 (=end exposition); end m. 145
59/i	Codetta (=exp.)		Closure at mm. 113 (*re* bass), 119 (*re* melody and form); $\flat7$/I thereafter never really resolved (no $\sharp7$ anywhere); pp ending

Table 5.5. (*cont.*)

Movement	Relation to structural downbeat	Harmonic type at end	Remarks
c. 1770–1774			
45/i	No V in 2Gr recap	Weak V	Cadence at m. 204, but insufficient (end 209)
/ii	Codetta	I–V–3̂/I	Closure at m. 185; codetta reestablishes 3̂ (end 190)
/M	"Tag"; high *pp*	I⁶	Closure at m. 38 (end 40)
/iv			Closure denied
/v	Codetta; high *pp*	I⁶	Closure bassless (mm. 85 viola; 103 violin II); codetta follows (end 107)
50/i	Early closure	Unison 5̂ – 1̂	Only root-position dominant at end (m. 148c) very fast, no independent melody. (mm. 151-52=3̂ afterbeat)
51/i	Early closure	Weak V	Final paragraph 21 bars (mm. 189–209); only root-position dominant (205) *pp*, no winds
/M	Very early V	V_3^4	Final dominant (m. 15) V_3^4 (gimmicky bass part)
52/iv	Very early V	Unison 5̂ – 1̂	Entire second group (mm. 131–88) without root-position 2̂/V – 1̂/i (unless 186?)
54/i	Early closure	Weak V	No loud V – I root-position bass after m. 204: 210–11 soft, strings alone; 215 subverted; 220, 226, 228, 230 no bass V
55/iv	Codetta	I–V–3̂/I	Closure at m. 171 (=30); motivic tags without bass; final cadence (179) restores 3̂
60/v	Afterbeat variant	I–V–3̂/I	Closure at mm. 71, 75; Allegro conclusion leads to 3̂ at end (78)
64/ii	??	V–?–I^{I-V-I}	See pp. 149–51

the discontinuities in register and scoring (mm. 4, 7, 12–14, 38, 41–43, 74–76). Hence when the theme is stated for the last time, the pause on I_4^6 in m. 94 is familiar enough (see Example 5.4). The dominant is transferred to the horns in mm. 96–97; from there it moves to the lower neighbors $\hat{4}$ and $\sharp\hat{4}$ in mm. 98–100; the implied dominant in m. 101 is heard in the violins alone, much higher, and only in last inversion ($\hat{4}$ again, as in m. 98). The gestural/registral bass (basses and horns) thus moves V–♭II⁶–V⁰/V–I ($\hat{5}$–$\hat{4}$–$\sharp\hat{4}$–$\hat{1}$). Of course, the very low tonic pedal at m. 102, with the diminished-seventh harmonies above (clear "signs" of ending), does resolve the dominant from mm. 94–97. But to leave it at that, or to claim (as some Schenkerians might) that the insubstantial V² in m. 101 implies a bass root A (perhaps by "voice-leading" from the melodic D in m. 94 and the bass G–G♯ in mm. 98–99), would falsify more than it would explain: the entire movement is based on the principle that "normal" procedures are abrogated.

Pianissimo endings One of the most remarkable aspects of the Farewell Symphony is its construction as a pair of extended decrescendos (Cycle 1 and Cycle 2) culminating in the systematic dying-away at the end. The aesthetic issue of quiet endings in the Classical period has scarcely been investigated.[47] They are by no means rare in Haydn, even in works which, as a whole, are loud and agitated, or those in the minor. They include jokes, of course; indeed his earliest known joke ending, the finale of Symphony No. 23 in G, ends *pianissimo*, as does his most notorious example, the finale of Op. 33 No. 2 in E-flat. The latter impinges on a second type, better described as witty, because it involves the common twist of ending a movement with its own opening phrase. (The earliest known example of this type is the finale of the divertimento Hob. II:8 in D, from *c.* 1761–62.[48]) But Haydn also writes quiet endings that represent an *intensification*: the strain on the performers to maintain vitality while playing softly, and on the listeners to maintain their concentration under a decreasing level of physical stimulation, seems to enhance his expressive design. This effect is especially common when he prescribes *pianissimo*, a marking that often seems to have had deep meaning for him, serving as a sort of reverse climax. (We are thus leaving the world of overt destabilizations, in favor of a richer aesthetic tradition, of special relevance in the context of the Farewell Symphony.)

Indisputable indications of the significance of *pianissimo* endings in this period can be found in Haydn's sacred vocal music. One example is the stunning (and through-composed) *Salve regina* in G minor (1771). Another is the *Agnus Dei* of the "Little Organ Mass" (*Missa St^i Joannis de Deo*; mid-1770s). Haydn twice breaks off the *fortissimo* long-note headmotive on a deceptive cadence (mm. 52, 61), both times following with imitative, slightly chromatic cadences on "Dona nobis pacem," first *piano*, then *pianissimo*. As the final stroke, he transforms the latter motive into a diatonic *perdendosi* accompaniment to the chorus, singing the words "dona" and "pacem" *pianissimo* on the hitherto *fortissimo* long-note "Agnus" motive.

---

[47] Except in Neubaucher, pp. 236–46.

[48] Webster, "Haydns frühe Ensemble-Divertimenti: Geschlossene Gattung, meisterhafter Satz," read at a symposium of the Gesellschaft für Musikforschung (Eichstätt, 1988); unpublished.

Example 5.4 Symphony No. 64, Largo: conclusion

Ex. 5.4 (*cont.*)

In the symphonies, by contrast, *pianissimo* finale endings are unusual; I have located only four before 1780 – of which at least three entail extramusical associations. The joke in No. 23 (1764) has already been cited. The next example is the laconic close of the minuet/finale of the religious No. 26 in D minor (late 1760s, described on pp. 243–44); still later comes No. 73 in D, "La chasse" (1781), whose finale recycles the overture to Haydn's opera *La fedeltà premiata*, including its contented dying away at the end. The only *pianissimo* ending to a first movement is the long, subdominant-inflected tonic pedal at the end of the opening movement of No. 59 in A ("Feuer" [late 1760s] – again, possibly adapted from incidental music). In two additional works with extramusical associations, an essentially *pianissimo* finale ending is "confirmed" (in reverse) by a single *forte* cadence: No. 67 in F (*c.* 1774–75), with a very unusual fast–slow–fast finale (whose middle section incorporates a quotation from Haydn's *Missa S^{ti} Nicolai*); and No. 46 in B (1772, described in Chapter 8).

During this period, Haydn cultivated the expressive *pianissimo* close most intensively in the string quartet (see Table 5.6): in the three sets from around 1770, twenty-five movements (more than one-third) end this way, fourteen in Op. 20 alone (more than half). (In Opp. 1 and 2, only slow movements close in this way.) Already in both Op. 9 and Op. 17 every movement-type is included; in the latter set, the witty *pianissimo* ending of the finale – and hence of the entire work – almost becomes a mannerism.

Table 5.6. *Pianissimo endings in Haydn string quartets through Op. 20*

Work	Movement	Context	Content	Remarks
1/1 (Bb)	Adagio	"Frame"	Cadence	Extension beyond "frame" at beginning
1/3 (D)	First	=end exp.	Tonic pedal	Slow opening movement
2/1 (A)	Adagio	=end exp.	Tonic pedal	Cf. Op. 2/2 (E), Adagio (*piano*)
2/4 (F)	Adagio	=end exp.	Tonic pedal	Minor mode
9/3 (G)	Largo	=end exp.	[Tonic pedal]	Obbligato cello on prominent motive
9/4 (d)	Adagio	=end exp.	Tonic pedal	
9/5 (Bb)	Largo	=end exp.	Cadence	Resolves last, unstable phrase of K
9/6 (A)	Finale	End coda	Tonic pedal	Presto 6/8
	Minuet	New codetta	Tonic pedal	
17/1 (E)	Finale	End coda	Cadence	Coda=delayed recap. of mm. 13ff; pp=only statement of mm. 23–27 (3P) on I
17/3 (Eb)	Minuet	Reprise of P	Cadence	Witty reinterpretation *Tierce de picardie*
17/4 (c)	First	End coda	Tonic pedal	"Recitative," in tonic minor; mm. 76–80 recapitulate 41–45
17/5 (G)	Adagio	=end exp.	Tonic pedal	Witty recall of opening motive
	Finale	New codetta	[Tonic pedal]	
20/1 (Eb)	First	=end exp.	Tonic pedal	"Affetuoso e sostenuto"; model for Mozart (K. 428/iii)
20/2 (C)	First	=end exp.	Cadences	Registral-motivic intensification
	Adagio	[See Remark]	V pedal	"Capriccio," in the minor (many dynamic contrasts); ends on V and leads to minuet
	Minuet	Codetta	Cadence	Special effect following Adagio; trio also pp
20/3 (g)	First	[Coda]	[Tonic pedal]	[Cadence] Coda-like extension within pp on long V^4_3, cadence *f–p*
	[Minuet]	Codetta	Cadences	"Perdendosi", trio ends pp
	Slow	=end exp.		
	Finale	≈ end exp.	[Cadences]	Cello motivic; intensifies end exposition

Table 5.6. (*cont.*)

Work	Movement	Context	Content	Remarks
20/4 (D)	First	Codetta	Tonic pedal	"Grounds" earlier retransitions in I
	Slow	End coda	Cadence	"Un poco adagio e affetuoso"; only cadence in very long coda, after dynamic contrasts
20/5 (f)	First	End coda	Cadence	Long, far-ranging coda; *piano assai*
20/6 (A)	First	≈ end exp.	Tonic pedal	"Allegro di molto e scherzando"
	Adagio	= end exp.	Cadence	
	Minuet	Delayed repr.	Cadence	Trio "sopra una corda"

(The famous joking finale endings of later years, such as Op. 33 Nos. 2 in E-flat and 3 in C, or Op. 54 No. 1 in G, had thus already emerged around 1770.) But Haydn also explores *pianissimo* endings in darker contexts: the first movements of both Op. 17 No. 4 in C minor and Op. 20 No. 5 in F minor, and both outer movements of Op. 20 No. 3 in G minor – a work in which every movement ends *pianissimo* (if we count the *perdendosi* of the minuet). No. 2 in C is almost equally consistent. These "negative culminations," expressed in widely differing styles and moods, became a fundamental aspect of Haydn's aesthetics in Op. 20 – a set composed in the same year (1772) that saw his greatest stroke of genius along these lines: the prolonged *decrescendo* which is the basis of the entire Farewell Symphony double finale. It is thus no coincidence that the "farewell" movement increasingly aspires to the condition of chamber music – and beyond, to one of pure insubstantiality. And, as this work makes clear, denial of closure is in a more general sense a powerful force for destabilization, which can lead to stronger links among movements in the cycle than would otherwise be possible.

THROUGH-COMPOSITION

We now examine individual movements with distinct sections that project complex or run-on relationships. These movements are of two types: minuets and trios, and introduction–allegros. In both, Haydn sometimes alters or manipulates conventional principles of construction, creating a tonal, gestural, or psychological progression across what would ordinarily function as a strong boundary. (We are now beginning to move from instability as a general aspect of composition, operating primarily within single movements, to overt integration of the cycle; this topic thus serves as a transition to our survey of Haydn's overtly through-composed works. His other compound movements in two tempi are not "types" in this sense, but individuals or pairs; see Chapter 6. Also postponed until Chapter 6 is a consideration of thematic relations within compound movements, including those discussed in other respects here.)

Minuets and trios

A substantial number of minuets in Haydn's symphonies and quartets include through-composed features; they are listed in Table 5.7. The simplest case occurs when the repetition of the first part of a minuet or trio is varied in scoring, dynamics, or rhythmic figuration, or in the inner parts, and hence must be written out. Examples are the minuets of the Quartets Op. 50 No. 1 (the repeat sign from m. 16 back to m. 1 found in many printed editions is spurious) and Op. 77 No. 1, and Symphonies 100 and 104. Occasionally the material itself is varied, without compromising the binary form (as in the trio of Symphony No. 46), or the join at a double bar is handled differently on first and second playings (trios of Op. 76 No. 4 and Op. 77 No. 1; the latter is written out from beginning to end). One of Haydn's more notorious jokes belongs in this category: in the trio of the "Clock" Symphony, No. 101, the strings refuse to change harmony under the solo flute melody in mm. 86–87, only to "correct" their "error" in

Table 5.7. *Through-composed elements in minuets of Haydn symphonies and string quartets*

Work	Location	Remarks
Symphonies		
18 (G)	Minuet (repr.)	"Tempo di menuet"; *da capo* written out, without repetitions; coda follows
30 (C)	[Entire]	"Tempo di Menuet, più tosto Allegretto." Notated form: M—Tr₁(V)—Tr₂(vi)—M—Coda. No repetition-signs in notated minuet *da capo*. No indication of additional minuet *da capo* between the two trios
43 (Eb)	Trio	Begins in vi; i.e. already modulating from I to V. Second part begins identically but reverts to I. Cf. Mozart Quartet K. 428, also in Eb
46 (B)	Trio	See pp. 269–70
[47 (G)	Both	Second part=first part played *al rovescio*]
50 (C)	Trio + Retr.	See pp. 206–09
57 (D)	Trio	See p. 158
58 (F)	Trio	In tonic minor; no change of key signature. (Cf. Op. 50 No. 5, also in f)
[81 (G)	Trio	See p. 159
93 (D)	Trio	See pp. 158–59
97 (C)	Both	Written-out repetitions throughout (changes in scoring); see p. 158
99 (Eb)	Trio	See pp. 327–28
100 (G)	Minuet	First part: written-out repetition (*forte–piano*)
101 (D)	Trio	See pp. 157–58
104 (D)	Minuet	First part: written-out repetition (*forte–piano*)
	Trio	Remote key (♭VI). Begins by implying brief transition (mm. 53–4), which is however part of repetition-structure; followed by retransition onto V/i
String quartets		
9/1 (C)	Trio	In tonic minor; second part not repeated; ends on V/i, minuet *attacca* in I
17/2 (F)	Trio	Second part of trio incomplete and run-on to minuet; see p. 161
17/5 (G)ᵃ	Trio	In tonic minor; second part not repeated;ᵃ ends on V⁶₅ (V²)/i;ᵃ minuet *attacca* in Iᵃ
20/1 (Eb)	Trio	Second part of trio incomplete and run-on to minuet; see p. 161
20/2 (C)	Trio	Second part of trio incomplete and run-on to minuet; see pp. 298–99
20/3 (g)ᵃ	Trio	Second part of trio incomplete and run-on to minuet;ᵃ see p. 161

Table 5.7. (*cont.*)

Work	Location	Remarks
50/1 (B♭)[a]	Minuet	First part: written-out repetition[a] (changes in scoring)
50/5 (F)[a]	Trio	See pp. 159–60
55/2 (f)	Minuet	First part: written-out repetition (contrapuntal buildup)
74/1 (C)	Trio	Remote key (VI♭); coda reverts to V/vi, minuet *attacca* in I (remote)
74/2 (F)	Trio	Remote key (♭VI); coda reverts to home dominant (V/i); minuet *attacca* in I. Cf. Op. 77/2 (also in F)
76/4 (B♭)	Minuet	Cadences directly into trio by elision
	Trio	First part: written-out repetition (viola/cello tied over m. 51)
76/6 (E♭)	Trio	Written-out repetitions throughout (continual contrapuntal variations)
77/1 (G)[a,b]	Minuet	First part: written-out repetition (more active inner parts). Codetta "answer" phrase (not "1st ending") cadences directly into trio[a]
	Trio	Remote key (♭VI); written-out repeats; no closure (VI = an augmented sixth on ♭6̂, moving to V/i); minuet *attacca* in I
77/2 (F)[b]	Trio	Remote key (♭VI); coda (*pp*) modulates to V/i; minuet *attacca* in I. Cf. Op. 74/2 (also in F)

[a] Traditional texts (Eulenburg, Peters, etc.) corrupt; correct readings only in JHW or autograph facsimiles.
[b] On Op. 77, see also pp. 213–18.

the repetition (mm. 102–03). Finally, in two quartets a written-out repetition fosters a systematic contrapuntal buildup: the first part of the minuet of Op. 55 No. 2 in F minor, and Tovey's favorite trio, that of Op. 76 No. 6 in E-flat, which develops continuously towards a climax at the end.[49] And in Symphony No. 97, the entire movement is written out in full (except for the minuet *da capo*), in order to accommodate a continual development of the dynamics, rhythmic motives, and instrumentation, which leads to an amazing quiet climax of orchestration at the end of the trio.[50] The last three examples palpably synthesize through-composed and binary form.

Occasionally, Haydn seems deliberately to "fool" us as to the formal divisions in a trio. In Symphony No. 57 in D (1774), the trio is in the tonic minor. But it begins with a twofold statement, *forte–piano*, of the unison cadential motive of the minuet; the actual tune comes in B-flat in m. 55, with the same motive still in the bass. Hence the four bars on the tonic sound more like a transition than part of the binary repeat structure (gesturally, they *are* transitional). The trio of Symphony No. 81 in G (*c.* 1783–84) has the following remarkable form:

mm. 45–52		53–60	61–68		69–76	77–84	
: a	:	: b	a		b	a	:
I		vi–V	I		vi–V	i	

Given the regular eight-bar phrasing and the context, the return of the **b**-phrase (mm. 69–76) following the repetition of **a** (mm. 61–68) already sounds like the repetition of the entire second part; but the sudden appearance of **a** in the tonic minor (mm. 77–84) upsets this illusion. If anything, we still believe that we are in a written-out, altered repetition, rather than (as proves to be the case) the very long second half of an asymmetrical form. But even as early as the string quartet Op. 9 No. 5 in B-flat (*c.* 1769–70), Haydn begins the very short trio with a variant of the phrase that twice began the **b** section of the minuet (mm. 29–32 ≈ 9–12) – as if we were hearing that section a third time – but in a new form which could equally well be a codetta to the minuet as a whole. To complete the joke, this phrase concludes the trio after all (mm. 40–44). Although these examples look simple on paper, they are at first almost impossible to grasp by ear. And in other contexts Haydn indulges this kind of formal manipulation on the largest possible scale; for example, the finale of the Quartet Op. 54 No. 2 (see Chapter 8).

The three trios just described turn out to exhibit (rounded) binary form with formal repetitions. But in two remarkable late trios, the first part is inherently asymmetrical and unstable. The trio of Symphony No. 93 in D (1791) is based on the alternation of a thundering four-bar unison tonic D in the winds and brass and a quiet answering phrase for the strings. But the quiet answering phrases ignore the tonic: each one

---

[49] "Haydn's Chamber Music," p. 64.
[50] See Rosen, *Classical Style*, pp. 342–43.

interprets the loud D as a consonant common-tone in a different key – until the third
time, when the strings leap in "prematurely" and transform D into a *dissonance*, V_5^6/V,
whose resolution forces the music into the dominant. (The second half brings further
surprises, but these prove to be compatible with repetition.) An even more astonishing
stroke governs the trio of the String Quartet in F, Op. 50 No. 5 (1787; see Example 5.5).
The opening unaccompanied motive of the minuet appears several times, always on
the dominant, the last time with a remarkable unresolved hemiola. The trio begins
with the same motive in all four instruments in unison; we expect it to behave the
same way. It is therefore one of the greatest shocks in tonal music when, without
warning, the entire ensemble crashes down onto D♭ (m. 44), modulates from there
directly into A-flat major, and cadences in that key. And indeed the trio turns out to
be in F *minor* (but with no change of key-signature). (Traditional modern editions bowdlerize this passage in a ghastly manner:[51] a key-signature of four flats for the trio;
a dynamic mark of *forte* at the very beginning; D♭ in place of D in mm. 42–43 – and,
inevitably, repeat signs for mm. 42–55!)

Example 5.5 String Quartet Op. 50/5/iii: major vs. minor

---

[51] The correct reading as given in Example 5.5 was established by Feder and myself in work on *JHW* XII/4, still
unpublished.

Ex. 5.5 (*cont.*)

A number of Haydn's minuets and trios are actually run-on. In the very late Op. 76 No. 4 in B-flat and Op. 77 No. 1 in G, the minuet cadences directly into the trio by elision.[52] More common, however, is a run-on relation between the end of the trio and the *da capo* of the minuet. This occurs in two different forms, from different periods in Haydn's career. The earlier group is found in six string quartets, all from the "Sturm und Drang." Each trio changes key: to the tonic minor in Op. 9 No. 1, Op. 17 No. 5, and Op. 20 No. 2; the relative minor in Op. 17 No. 2; the subdominant in Op. 20 No. 1; and the submediant in Op. 20 No. 3 (whose overall tonic is minor). (The latter three are the only trios in these *opera* which are not in the tonic or the parallel major or minor.) In all six trios, the second half not only is asymmetrical (non-repeating and lacking closure), but never returns to the tonic at all; the minuet reprise follows directly on an open, unresolved sonority. Still more remarkably, only two of these final sonorities

[52] Op. 77 is also bowdlerized in modern editions; in the absence of *JHW*, see Somfai's facsimile edition of the autograph (Budapest, 1972; repr. 1980).

are the home dominant in root position (Opp. 9 No. 1 and 20 No. 2 – both, interestingly, in C, with the trio in the tonic minor). In Op. 17 No. 5 in G, the trio is also in the tonic minor, but the dominant at the end appears only in weak inversions, V_5^6 and V^2; the latter chord links directly with mm. 2–3 in the reprise. (Again, all traditional modern editions are corrupt; only *JHW* presents an accurate text.) In Op. 20 No. 3 in G minor, the trio is in the submediant E-flat; the second half moves by sequence to C minor, and to a pedal on its dominant, G major – from where Haydn leaps directly back to the minuet in G minor. In Op. 20 No. 1 in E-flat, the second part of the trio (in A-flat) cadences on the dominant of F minor; here we unexpectedly hear the first phrase of the minuet, very high and (presumably) *piano*. Like its model, this phrase pauses on V_5^6 (of ii), whereupon the minuet itself takes over, in the tonic E-flat (and presumably *forte*); the bass progression e^1–e♭ is anything but stable.[53] The minuet and trio are welded together not merely by the run-on effect and the commonality of material, but by the dreamy insubstantiality of the trio itself, which is so leisurely, so self-absorbed, that a completion of its design would unduly compromise the larger sense of action.

In Op. 17 No. 2 in F, finally, the trio is in D minor. The first half modulates not to the usual relative major or dominant minor, but to the submediant B-flat. The second part then continues sequentially to the local dominant on A – from where, astonishingly, the common-tone a^1 leads directly back to the minuet in F. (This presumably explains B-flat at the end of the first part: any hint of F there would ruin the reprise.) This harmonic move, V/vi–I, is the same one we have noted in sonata-form developments, where it is especially characteristic precisely as a preparation for reprises. As we shall see, this progression in this context was a primary source of Haydn's later cultivation of remote key relations.

Haydn's other run-on trio endings are found in late works: the quartets Op. 74 Nos. 1 and 2 and Op. 77 Nos. 1 and 2, and Symphonies 99 and 104. Even more than the earlier group, they constitute a "type," determined conjointly by tonality: they occur in every symphony- and quartet-trio in a remote key – and only in those. Unlike the earlier ones, these trios exhibit a regular binary design; the second part usually attains full and firm closure in the tonic, and it is always repeated. The run-on effect results instead from a retransition, which usually prepares the minuet reprise by reverting to the home dominant (see both symphonies, as well as both quartets in F, Opp. 74 No. 2 and 77 No. 2).

The remaining trios vary this plan. In Op. 74 No. 1 in C – the earliest of these works (see the discussion of Symphony No. 99 in Chapter 8) – the retransition is entirely on the dominant of A minor; the melody soon establishes e^2 and e^1, from where the minuet enters directly by common-tone modulation, V/vi–I. It is thus structurally identical to the reprise in Op. 17 No. 2. It scarcely seems coincidental that Haydn's first use of a remote *key* for an independent section in a quartet or symphony should harken back to what had long been his favorite method of relating a remote *sonority* to

---

[53] On "implied" dynamics of the type found in this passage, see Webster, "The Significance of Haydn's String Quartet Autographs for Performance Practice," in Christoph Wolff and Robert Riggs, eds., *The String Quartets of Haydn, Mozart, and Beethoven: Studies of the Autograph Manuscripts* (Cambridge, Mass., 1980), pp. 71–73.

the tonic, including examples in the identical formal context. Aesthetically, of course, this trio is very different from Op. 17 No. 2, owing to the sweet C♯ of the remote A major, in contrast to the blandness of D minor with respect to F. (This suggests another key-related similarity in Haydn: the trio of the only other late quartet in C, the "Emperor," Op. 76 No. 3, indulges in the same sweet A major. But its trio is in the ordinary relative A minor; the remote A major enters as a surprise substitute reprise, before yielding to the true reprise. And the only symphony to use a run-on minuet reprise, No. 50, uses this progression in this key as well; see Example 6.3.) In Op. 77 No. 1 in G, the trio is through-composed – and eccentric in the extreme. It is apparently in E-flat (♭VI), but this key enters merely as a deceptive cadence at the end of the minuet and is never confirmed by its own dominant; the retransition confirms the point (compare Example 6.5). (The young Beethoven imitated Haydn in this regard; many of his trios have incomplete second parts with run-on lead-backs to the minuet.)

Introduction–Allegro movements

In most of Haydn's symphonies of the 1780s and 1790s, the slow introduction is related to the following fast movement; in general, the later the work, the closer and more pervasive the relations.[54] This is especially true of the much-discussed thematic and motivic continuities (for these, see Chapter 6). What has rarely been described, however, is that some Haydn introductions relate to the allegro in *dynamic* fashion: they are run-on, or the join is articulated by an unexpected or deceptive harmonic progression.[55] In other cases, a striking gesture may return later in the allegro; a simple example is found in Symphony No. 93 in D, where the chromatic progression vii⁶/V–iv⁶–V⁷ at the end of the introduction (mm. 18–20) recurs at the climax of the (very free) recapitulation (mm. 247–49) – a passage which seems unmotivated until one notices this connection. The much more famous recall of the "Drum Roll" introduction differs to be sure in its "pregnant" preparation, the change of tempo, and the extent of the actual quotation; but the principle remains the same. Such connections, governing an entire movement, cannot be understood on the basis of material relations alone.

The conceptual background of such devices was the usual introduction plan of the time: this comprises, essentially, a stable tonic passage at the beginning and a stable dominant passage at the end, with or without intervening material or clear paragraph divisions. The concluding dominant usually arrives forcefully on a "strong" measure, and is extended by a pedal or neighboring harmonies, often colored by the minor; the

---

[54] On Haydn's symphonic introductions in general, see Hans Joachim Therstappen, *Joseph Haydns sinfonisches Vermächtnis* (Wolfenbüttel, 1941), pp. 21–32; Landon, *Symphonies*, pp. 217–18, 240, 321, 356, 373, 408–10, 572–75; Gail Ellsworth Menk, "The Symphonic Introductions of Joseph Haydn," Ph.D. diss., University of Iowa, 1960; Rudolf Klinkhammer, *Die langsame Einleitung in der Instrumentalmusik der Klassik und Romantik* (Regensburg, 1971), chaps. 1–2; Marianne Danckwardt, *Die langsame Einleitung: Ihre Herkunft und ihr Bau bei Haydn und Mozart*, 2 vols. (Tutzing, 1977), vol. 1, pp. 19–60; Peter Benary, "Die langsamen Einleitungen in Joseph Haydns Londoner Sinfonien," in Anke Bingmann et al., eds., *Studien zur Instrumentalmusik: Festschrift Lothar Hoffmann-Erbrecht zum 60. Geburtstag* (Tutzing, 1988), pp. 239–51.

[55] See Klinkhammer, pp. 32–43.

final sonority (or the following rest) is usually emphasized by a fermata, suspending regular musical time at the critical moment. This structural dominant is the goal of the entire introduction, which therefore constitutes a large-scale half cadence, or "antecedent"; it is *separated* from what follows. The allegro is thus not merely a contrast, not merely a local resolution; its first theme (or even the entire first group) is a large-scale "consequent" to the introduction as a whole.

This outwardly simple and conventional form could support original ideas and grand rhetorical gestures. In Haydn's late introductions, a mixture of contrasting rhetorical "topoi" is correlated with an avoidance of symmetrical melodies and regular periods (except perhaps at the beginning), in favor of short, contrasting, irregularly-phrased motives, juxtaposed in unexpected or apparently incommensurable ways (Symphony No. 97, mm. 1 vs. 2–4; No. 102, mm. 1, 6 vs. 2–5, 7–10; No. 103, drum roll vs. bass theme vs. later high instruments). The aesthetic result was nothing less than an invocation of the sublime – a transfer, towards the end of the eighteenth century, of this concept from the domains of poetry and aesthetics, as represented by writers such as Burke and Kant, to that of instrumental music, as adumbrated by Sulzer and worked out by Michaelis and Hoffmann; an equivalent of what, in Beethoven's day, had already become an overt cultivation of contradiction and paradox.[56] From the point of view of through-composition, the resulting "pregnant" effect, the air of "potential," is of obvious significance: these tensions can find resolution only outside their place of origin, in the ensuing allegro – or perhaps even later.

In Haydn's through-composed introduction-allegro movements, the join is blurred by one or both of two distinct, but related procedures: the harmonic progression deviates from the customary –V‖I– (Symphonies 60, 73, 88, 90, 92, 94, 99, and 103); or the two sections are actually run-on (Nos. 86, 97 and, to a lesser extent, 94 and 104). (In this discussion I still take for granted commonalities of material [see Chapter 6]; they are especially important in Nos. 90, 97, 98, and 103. Only in No. 97 and especially No. 103 do thematic recalls in the allegro affect or disrupt its course; the former is discussed below, the latter in Chapter 8, pp. 330–31.)

In the simplest altered harmonic progressions, the introduction still ends on the dominant, but the allegro begins off the tonic. In Nos. 60 and 88 the latter begins on the dominant itself (admittedly of purely local significance); in Nos. 73 ("La chasse"), 86, and 94 ("Surprise"), however, the allegro resolves the preceding dominant deceptively (to IV in No. 73; to $V_{[5]}^6$/ii in Nos. 86 and 94). This sonority is for violins alone and proceeds by sequence to a tonic arrival in the fourth bar of the allegro, where (except in 73) the full orchestra joins in, *forte*. (Note the similarity to Haydn's earlier bassless quartet beginnings, such as Op. 33 Nos. 1 and 3 and Op. 64 No. 2, where the cello provides a real bass only at the cadence of the initial phrase.) Often, as if by way of compensation,

---

[56] Peter Gülke, "Introduktion als Widerspruch im System," *DJbMw* 14 (1970), 5–40. On the sublime in the musical aesthetics of Haydn's time, see the excerpts by the authors named, as well as the editors' introduction, in Peter le Huray and James Day, eds., *Music and Aesthetics in the Eighteenth and Early-Nineteenth Centuries* (Cambridge, 1981); Carl Dahlhaus, "E. T. A. Hoffmanns Beethoven-Kritik und die Ästhetik des Erhabenen," *AfMw* 38 (1981), 167–81.

this strong tonic is massively extended, usually with a pedal in the bass. In the "Surprise," Haydn creates strong links between the beginning of the Vivace assai and the remainder of the movement. The goal chord of the introduction is V^7; its naked dissonant seventh c^2 is resolved by the first melody note of the Vivace assai, b^1 ($\hat{3}$). The link is rhythmic as well as tonal: unusually, there is no fermata, and the run-on character is notationally reinforced by the "extra" half-measure at the beginning of the Vivace. The unexpected harmonization by sequence beginning off the tonic (V/ii–ii; V–I) transforms B from the expected stable tone of resolution into a locally mobile one; it is thus "marked" for further exploitation. (Already cogent is the resolution of the "hanging" *forte* high c^3 [m. 16] to b^2, precisely at the first Vivace *forte*.) Every subsequent return to the opening theme (except the immediate one at mm. 38–39) is prepared not by the dominant, but by B itself: see the repeat of the exposition (mm. 105–07 and back to the beginning), the beginning of the development (mm. 105–10), and the retransition (mm. 152–58). In addition, the theme itself is weak in closure in all its appearances except the very last (mm. 219–28) – characteristically, a passage lacking any counterpart in the exposition. On this gestural level as well, the movement is dynamic rather than symmetrical.[57]

In two pairs of late works, Symphonies 90 and 92, and 99 (effectually) and 103, the introductions actually end off the dominant. Nos. 99 and 103 comprise the two E-flat works from the second London set; both point the introduction towards $\hat{3}$ (G), harmonized as the dominant of C minor (see Chapter 8). Nos. 90 and 92 both belong to an undeclared "opus" (Symphonies 90–92, from 1788–89); in both, the goal chord of the introduction is a predominant based on $\sharp\hat{4}$, which resolves to the *dominant* across the double-bar. In some respects these transitions resemble those just described: the allegro begins "in medias res," *piano* and for strings alone; the structural tonic arrives at the cadence four or five bars later, with changes of dynamics and texture (texture and instrumentation in No. 90). However, the tonal meaning is different: the structural dominant is displaced forward into the allegro; in its place at the fermata appears an unstable and (in Schenkerian terms) inessential sonority. (Both movements have thematic connections as well, especially obvious in No. 90. No. 92 is discussed at length below.)

Other Haydn introductions are rhythmically run-on to the allegro. Instead of being a goal, the dominant progresses "through" the double-bar to the initial tonic of the allegro, in tempo, and without fermata or "empty" beats or measures. This tonic both resolves the introduction, completing a tonal span reaching back to the beginning and, by elision, functions as the "takeoff" sonority of the allegro. Haydn's most thoroughly run-on introduction of this type is that to the Vivace of Symphony No. 97 in C; the movements are thematically linked as well. The surprising and memorable diminished seventh in m. 2, arising out of *forte–piano* pulsations on a bare tonic C, was doubtless a primary source of the chromatic appoggiatura chords that are so characteristic of musical Romanticism. But Haydn's goal-directed progressions, his initially unmediated contrast between a fully harmonized legato theme and nakedly rhythmic tonics, are different from (say)

---

[57] Cf. Guy A. Marco, "A Musical Task in the Surprise Symphony," *JAMS* 11 (1958), 41–44.

Schubert.[58] The structural dominant (m. 9), recaptured within the theme itself (m. 13), resolves without break to the overwhelming *fortissimo* unison tonic of the Vivace – which at the same time is merely an intensification of the opening sonority. Hence, despite all contrast, the Romantic introduction theme remains an essential aspect of how the Vivace came into being. It is thus in the highest degree "consequential" that it recurs in the Vivace, at the end of the exposition (m. 99), that in the recapitulation (m. 240) it modulates as far as the Neapolitan D-flat, and that this excursion eventually leads to the final, triumphant reprise of the unison triadic main theme.

No other Haydn introduction is run-on to this extent. The introduction-allegro join in Symphony No. 86 in D is continuous rhythmically: the pulsing octave dominants in the final bar lead without break or fermata to the Allegro, and the repeated notes (present since m. 9) prepare both the high bass of mm. 22–25 and the three-note *fortissimo* motives in mm. 26ff. No. 104 in D includes an unusual transition. The final full measure (16) is very like the equivalent bar in No. 97: the tonic six-four arrival on the downbeat and resolution to the dominant within the measure imply the entry of the tonic itself, without pause or fermata, simultaneously with the double bar and change of tempo. To be sure, there is no fermata; but Haydn notates an odd, fragmentary "empty" measure, only one beat long.[59] It is as if he wished to relate the introduction to the allegro in both ways: run-on and in tempo, and separated by a caesura. Perhaps he had by this time begun to feel the need for more complex large-scale rhythmic relations between introduction and allegro, to complement the material and tonal links he had already developed. But after his return to Vienna he composed no more symphonies, and hence no more slow instrumental introductions – except in the very different context of mass Kyries, and the most tremendous example of all, the "Chaos" in *The Creation*.

Free recapitulations

In many sonata-form movements, Haydn substantially recomposes the recapitulation.[60] This is well known; here too, however, chronological distinctions are necessary. Except for a brief efflorescence in occasional pre-Esterházy works, Haydn preferred a "decided symmetry" (Tovey) during the 1760s and 1770s, before overt freedom emerged with a vengeance towards 1780 (for example, in the first movement of Op. 33 No. 1, discussed at the beginning of this chapter). But a subtle, hitherto unremarked discontinuity affected certain recapitulations of the 1770s, for example in the first movements of Symphonies 50, 51, and 54 (see again Table 5.5). The structural cadence seems to arrive well before the end, within the second group proper, yet the remaining events nonetheless parallel those of the exposition. Tonality and form seem out of phase: the structure achieves closure

---

[58] On Romantic appoggiatura chords, see Kerman, "A Romantic Detail in Schubert's *Schwanengesang*," *MQ* 48 (1962), 36–49. Thrasybulos Georgiades compares this passage with the opening of Schubert's String Quintet in C, in *Schubert: Musik und Lyrik* (Göttingen, 1967), pp. 158–63.

[59] So in the autograph, and without second thoughts; see the facsimile, ed. Wolfgang Goldhahn (Berlin, 1983).

[60] See Tovey, "Haydn's Chamber Music," pp. 54–56 *et passim*; Wolf, "The Recapitulations in Haydn's London Symphonies," *MQ* 52 (1966), 71–89; Webster, "Freedom of Form"; Ethan Haimo, "Haydn's Altered Reprise," *JMT* 32 (1988), 335–51.

before the recapitulation is complete. Or, to put it a different way suggested by Schenkerian theory, the last paragraph of the thematic recapitulation may be a structural coda.[61] Such disjunctions are characteristic not so much of the "Sturm und Drang" as of the period immediately following. They must therefore represent the first stage of Haydn's later asymmetry-within-symmetry of wholesale recomposition: a separating out of the tonal and formal senses of "recapitulation." For that is the deeper meaning of his later freedom: the tonal structure and proportions are perfectly recapitulated, while the material – the rhetoric – develops to the very end.

   This recapitulatory freedom is often bound up with the gradual increase in importance, within the movement, of an originally subsidiary musical idea, or even a tiny motive (as in the well-known example of Symphony No. 104, in which the unassuming motive first heard in the third and fourth bars of the Allegro dominates the development and occasions the biggest climax of the recapitulation). The most common type relates to one of Haydn's special features of form: the so-called "three-part" exposition. This centers around a long, unstable *Entwicklungspartie* or "expansion section" in the middle, preceded by a short first group in the tonic and followed by a short, contrasting, *piano* theme and codetta in the dominant.[62] In this context, the *piano* towards the end is not so much a "second theme" in the nineteenth-century sense as a "closing theme": it comes more or less three-quarters of the way through, following and confirming the first structural cadence in the dominant. What has not been emphasized is that in these cases the closing *piano* theme often becomes increasingly important in the development and recapitulation (as in Symphony No. 80 (p. 167)). And this in turn becomes a source of Haydn's dynamic form.

   More generally, such procedures coexist with, and in some cases even override, the formal function of the second-group recapitulation as generally understood. Ratner's two-reprise form (based on eighteenth-century theory), Cone's "sonata principle," Rosen's "grounding of structural dissonance" – these interpretations assume an essential congruence between the events of the second-group exposition outside the tonic, and their repetition in the tonic; this congruence is the basis for the sense of "resolution" invoked. None is adequate for late Haydn. Even Tovey, the only theorist who accepts Haydn's free recapitulations as fundamentally normal, never offers a general explanation, other than the somewhat misleading concept "synthesis of recapitulation and coda"[63] – misleading, because Haydn's recapitulations are not codas. (Classical-period codas, including Beethoven's, *follow* recapitulatory closure; they do not take its place.) The real meaning of Haydn's freedom is, again, the infusion of a sense of process into a context of formal and tonal symmetry; he continues to "compose out" the potential of his ideas to the very end.

---

[61] *Free Composition*, I, 129, §304.
[62] Larsen, "Sonatenformprobleme," in Anna Amalie Abert and Wilhelm Pfannkuch, eds., *Festschrift Friedrich Blume zum 70. Geburtstag* (Kassel, 1963), pp. 221–30; Michelle Fillion, "Sonata-Exposition Procedures in Haydn's Keyboard Sonatas," in *Haydn Studies*, pp. 475–81.
[63] "Haydn's Chamber Music," pp. 47, 54–56.

SYMPHONIES NOS. 80 AND 92, FIRST MOVEMENTS

I conclude this chapter by considering two Haydn symphony movements which exhibit progressive form, without depending on run-on sections, recalls, and the like. In the first movement of No. 80 in D minor (*c.* 1783–84), the exposition, resolutely unstable up to this point, closes with a trivial-sounding, dotted-rhythmed dance tune in F, which seems completely out of context; it is not even a decent antecedent-consequent period. However, it immediately astonishes us across the double bar (and a two-bar G.P.) by dropping down a major third to the remote key of D-flat. Following a digression, it recurs in E-flat (in m. 79, following a half-cadence), and is then fragmented and sequenced just as if it were a main theme (m. 83; the actual first theme joins in at m. 93). The dance tune soon reappears in A major (m. 110); this is a bit of a puzzle, for A is not closely related to D minor (and Haydn ordinarily does not use the dominant major as a key). But just as at the end of the exposition, it comes to a full stop and another two-bar G.P – and, in the best joke so far, again drops a major third, into the very key of F in which the development began! Only thereafter do we revert to the main theme and the recapitulation.

Thus the entire development is based on this cheap tune. Not only does the process begin and end in the key of F, but the two drops of a third across the G.P.s create a circle of major thirds (F–D-flat, A–F). What is more, the initial members of the two downward-third leaps, F and A, articulate the two chief related scale-degrees to the overall tonic (III and V$^\sharp$), while the remaining member is the leading-tone (D♭ = C♯). In a sense, the development thus actually begins *before* the double bar, with the dance tune in F. The reprise abruptly emerges out of the second F-major statement (mm. 125–28; compare the Allegro assai of the Farewell); there is no tonal stability until the D major of the second group. And so the tune, saucy as ever, closes the movement in the tonic major. But *what* is thus recapitulated? Not merely this tune's original appearance in the exposition, but the tonal tension of the development itself, dominated by this very theme in all manner of peculiar keys, whose only common thread was their relation to D. The most subtle point is that the conclusion in D major "grounds" the otherwise problematical A major far more strongly than the tonic minor ever could.

A stunning example of Haydn's through-composition in a single movement, which touches on most of the subjects covered in this chapter, is the first movement of Symphony No. 92 ("Oxford," 1789). The slow introduction opens with what sounds like the antecedent of a normal period (theme **1**, mm. 1–4; see Example 5.6). But the following phrase cadences even more strongly on the dominant (m. 8) – is this then an antiperiod? – ; and worse yet, so does the third (m. 12). At least, the latter D-chord seems unambiguously established as a structural dominant. Now, however (theme **2**), it unexpectedly leads to a chromatic neighbor E♭, supporting iv⁶ (m. 13); and E♭ returns (m. 16) as the bass of an augmented-sixth chord, prolonged across the double bar to the Allegro spiritoso. The mood becomes ominous; iv⁶ is troubled by a dissonant d^1, suspended and then descending chromatically; g^2 floats insubstantially far above; as

Example 5.6 Symphony No. 92/i: principal motives

soon as the bass returns to D, e♭³ is heard in the high flute. The augmented sixth is sustained to excruciating length, the rhythm becoming increasingly obscure; it culminates in an unsupported diminished seventh (m. 20). Under these conditions it is difficult for the dominant established in mm. 4–12 to maintain its apparent structural role. Is the governing bass pitch of mm. 13–15 the D in m. 14, resolving the iv⁶ – or is E♭ in m. 13 stronger than the dominant, linking directly with the big E♭ in mm. 16–20? (Compare the alternative middleground graphs given as Example 5.7a and b.)

Another important factor is the gradual increase in prominence of C♯. At first an ordinary chromatic neighbor in an inner part (m. 8, second violins), it becomes a prominent melodic passing-tone (m. 11, first violins), a disquieting chromatic descent (m. 13), and the most prominent note of the critical augmented-sixth chord; in the last bar, naked and followed by silence, it seems to bear the weight of the entire introduction. In fact, as suggested in Example 5.7c, the entire introduction may best be understood as prolonging this descending chromatic "motive": $\hat{5}$ (d²), established at the beginning, descends to a¹ (mm. [8], 12) only in the middleground; it is recaptured in mm. 14–15, from where it descends chromatically to c♯² over E♭, and on to c² at the beginning of the Allegro. (According to orthodox Schenkerian notions of voice-leading, the melodic c² in m. 21, which is dissonant over D, is "really" a passing-tone from an "implied" d² that enters consonantly with the bass and resolves c♯² "correctly" as a leading-tone; see Example 5.7d. This would be inappropriate here; a Schenkerian analysis of music which problematizes tonality and form – as when Haydn's five-bar-long, naked, dissonant C♯ proceeds directly to the dissonant C♮, at the formally most significant passage in the movement – is useful only insofar as it shows such events as related to comparably unusual and "difficult" events in the deep middleground, as in Example 5.7c.)

By this reading, there is no structural dominant in the introduction at all. Instead, this dominant is withheld until the beginning of the Allegro, supporting the c² which resolves c♯². Even more destabilizing is that this sonority – which supports the main theme itself – is dissonant; indeed, this dissonance propels the music forward throughout the movement. The relation is reinforced by prominent motivic connections:[64] the threefold downbeat repetition of *a* that opens the introduction accompanies the first allegro measure, and this motive remains important throughout; and the first and most prominent stepwise motive, the descending fifth *b* (mm. 2–3, second violins, and elsewhere), is the opening melodic motive of the Allegro, at the same pitch level and with the same harmony as in mm. 6–7. (As we have seen, this motive animates the entire introduction as well, on every level.) Equally important is the structural motive of the tritone (mm. 6–7), which leads to the succession g²–c♯²/c²–f♯¹ at the join, an "unfolding" of the underlying chromatic descent (see Example 5.7e).

Haydn exploits the dominant-seventh harmony of his opening theme and its chromatic preparation throughout the Allegro spiritoso (a formal diagram is given as Example 5.8; as in Example 2.10, this bass-line graph should not be read as a Schenkerian analysis).

---

[64] Some of these are suggested by Landon, *Symphonies*, p. 410; Raimund Bard, *Untersuchungen zur motivischen Arbeit in Haydns sinfonischem Spätwerk* (Kassel, 1982), pp. 117–18.

Example 5.7 Symphony No. 92/i: introduction

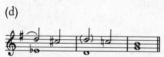

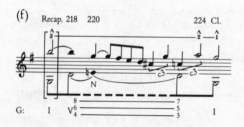

Example 5.8 Symphony No. 92/i: form

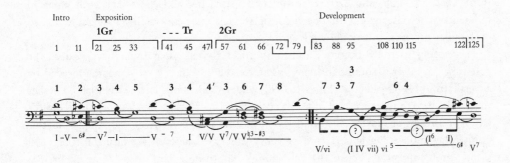

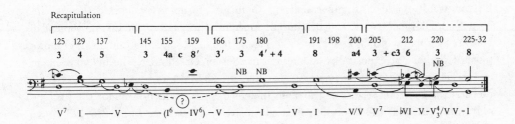

Locally, it resolves to the *forte* $\hat{3}$/I, shown as **4** in Example 5.6; compare the similar resolution in the fourth bar of the Vivace in the "Surprise." The returns in the exposition transform a cadence *in* the dominant (with C♯) back to the dominant seventh (mm. 36–38 to 39–42, mm. 79–82 to 21). As a whole, the exposition can only be called perfunctory; the perky closing theme **8** comes even sooner, and is even shorter, than usual. But, again analogously to the "Surprise," the retransition to the recapitulation (mm. 122–24) is based not on the home dominant, but on *a sonority which prepares that of the opening theme* – that is, V/V, with C♯. (The plain dominant could have no force as a preparation in this context, any more than in the introduction.) Now follows one of Haydn's most extraordinary recapitulations. It is the longest, proportionally, in his entire *oeuvre*: more than half the entire Allegro, 108 measures of 212 (the brief exposition is 62 bars, or 29 percent; the very brief development only 42, or 20 percent). This great length results from a wholesale recomposition of the second group – constructed, however, not as Tovey's "synthesis of recapitulation and coda," but as a series of departures from and returns to the extraordinary main theme on the dominant.[65] It is already suspicious that both its first-group appearances return (m. 125=21, m. 145=41, except for the minor-mode coloring); such repetitions are among the most common locations

---

[65] This feature is noted by Rosen, *Classical Style*, pp. 160–62, without being related to the movement as a whole.

for recapitulatory cuts. But in the second group, which in the exposition had but a single thematic statement (m. 57), Haydn brings no fewer than four separate reprises (mm. 166, 176, 205, and 220), each different in scoring and effect, and each prepared differently; they alternate with a bewildering succession of contrasting passages, all based on familiar motives, but nonetheless new.

The closing theme **8** becomes more important as well. It appears twice; indeed the first time (m. 191) it sounds in many ways like the end of the movement: preceded by a very strong I_4^6–V cadence (mm. 189–90) and rounded off with cadential flourishes (mm. 198–99; compare the end of the exposition, mm. 79–80). In addition, the recapitulation is already proportionally longer than normal, 43 percent of the Allegro to this point (Haydn's average is about 35 percent). But we have not yet heard all the main second-group material; hence the "clinching" eighth-notes (m. 200, compare m. 81) develop by sequence back to V/V and yet another statement of the main theme. This leads further to a surprise plunge into E-flat (m. 212), which is however a recapitulation of the similar outburst in D minor **(6)** from the exposition (m. 61). ("Surprise" outbursts on E-flat towards the end of movements in G major are an unrecognized, key-specific "topos" in Haydn, Mozart, and Beethoven, apparently initiated in the first movement of Haydn's Symphony No. 8, *Le soir*, m. 206. Haydn also liked sudden outbursts in D minor towards the end of expositions and recapitulations in D; compare the first movement of No. 96, m. 194; and the finale of No. 104, m. 287.) More importantly, this E-flat prepares the climactic reprise of the main theme (m. 220), which now, for the first and only time, enters as the resolution of a conclusive I_4^6–V^7 cadence (mm. 218–19, shown in Example 5.7f; compare mm. 189–90) – harmonized, however, as the very V/V which hitherto has always prepared the plain dominant seventh for this very motive! (To be sure, Haydn often brings a climactic statement of the main theme on V/V at the very end of a movement – for example, the first movements of the string quartets Op. 33 No. 3 in C and Op. 54 No. 1 in G; they relate in different, equally interesting ways to their particular contexts.) The introduction casts its shadow in other ways as well: both surprises in this second part of the recapitulation, E-flat in m. 212 and V/V here, re-establish $\hat{6}$ as neighbor to V in the bass. Best of all, the prominent tritone g^2–$c\sharp^2$ in mm. 220ff precisely recalls mm. 17 and 19 (noted above), whose resolution to the other tritone across the double bar was the source of all the energy in the first place. Now, mm. 223–25 finally resolve this progression normally, for the first and only time.

This unique recapitulation "composes out" – in a rhetorical sense as well as a Schenkerian one – the "premise" of the unusual join at the end of the introduction. Since the main theme is built on the dominant, the reprises likewise continually prepare and attain the dominant. Hence the movement risks never being able to reach closure on a structural tonic! Perhaps this even explains the unusual proportions. Given that the governing sonority is V^7, the usual sonata-form dynamic – a dramatic move to the dominant key in the second group and a postponement of its resolution back to the tonic by means of the development – would have little significance. In this movement, the adventure of resolving the dominant can take place only *within* the recapitulation. That is why the second group is so perfunctory, the development so short, the recapitulation so long; why, despite its gestures of finality, the initial recapitulation of the closing theme is insufficient; why the final thematic reprise is *off* V^7. As a direct consequence of the unique opening, the entire structure resolves only at the end. The same spirit animates hundreds of other movements throughout Haydn's *oeuvre*. His form is inherently dynamic.

6

INTEGRATION OF THE CYCLE

In this chapter, we turn to the central topic of Haydn's integration of multimovement instrumental cycles. But we must begin with a few *caveats*. Only a small minority of his works are overtly through-composed, in the manner of the Farewell Symphony. More common is to find tangible links between only two movements, or within only one musical domain (motives, tonality, gesture). And one must avoid the false assumptions that Haydn's most strongly integrated works are better than the others, or that he and his contemporaries necessarily intended or desired such integration in terms that would be intelligible today. (For our results must be intelligible today. Any viable historical study entails a synthesis of ideas from the period under investigation with others from the historian's own time.) Nevertheless, Haydn's truly cyclic works are so remarkable, and his techniques of relating the individual movements so important for his style in general, that a systematic survey is needed – especially since none has ever been attempted.

To what extent is a Haydn symphony more than a succession of separate and independent movements, related only by pleasing contrasts and continuities within the conventional generic patterns of the time? Why, in a given location in a given work, is only *this* movement the "right" one? If the Farewell Symphony is as strongly through-composed as I have suggested, why does its first Adagio resemble the slow movement of No. 42 in key, meter, and opening melodic and rhythmic motives; why could they not be exchanged? Both Symphonies 93 and 96 were composed in London in 1791, are in D, open with almost identical descending triadic motives (each of which is said to generate many subsequent motives), have their slow movements in the subdominant, and have formally simple, dance-like finales in 2/4 featuring a prominent two-note opening upbeat which is the basis for witty returns. Why could one not make valid new symphonies by arbitrarily selecting the first movement of one, the slow movement of the other, and so forth? What about the slow movements of Mozart's "Linz" and "Jupiter" symphonies, both in F and involving triple meter; or (ignoring for now the difference in scoring) the finales of the "Dissonant" Quartet K. 465 and the Quintet in C K. 515, so similar in style, meter, tempo, and thematic construction?

But if movements cannot thus be arbitrarily exchanged, if each must be as it is and occupy the position it does, how do we understand and describe the "necessity" entailed? The most common term in such discussions is "unity." What is actually meant by the assertion that a Haydn symphony is unified? Is this sense of unity subjective, arbitrary, conventional – essentially a rationalization of the favored status of privileged works – or does it have an identifiable psychological or technical basis? Given its intellectual roots in organicist thinking of the nineteenth and earlier twentieth centuries, what is the rationale for claiming "unity" as a constituent of eighteenth-century instrumental music, or maintaining it as a theoretical category today? If on the other hand it is dropped in favor of "coherence" or some other less loaded term (as I have done in Part I), are the problems eliminated, transferred to a less obviously objectionable domain, or merely clouded by a semantic distinction without a difference? They cannot be dismissed by invoking the supposed distinction between conventional eighteenth-century genres and individual nineteenth-century creations. Neither the ideology of "Classical style" nor Haydn's and Mozart's reputations could survive a demonstration that the movements in their works could arbitrarily be exchanged (as suggested above), or that their overall coherence is restricted to that circumscribed by the conventional genre-patterns.

Still another apparent difficulty lies in the eighteenth-century practice (which actually lasted well into the nineteenth) of performing the movements of symphonies separately, whether entirely alone or intermingled with arias, concertos, and so forth.[1] How common it actually was in Haydn's time generally, let alone at the Esterházy court (where no documentation survives as to the actual events of musical performances), remains unclear. The once widespread belief that his London symphonies were regularly performed in this manner is now discredited; it was based on a misinterpretation of the term "Finale," used in London concert programs to designate the last item (not the final movement of a work begun earlier), and on an overhasty generalization from Haydn's performance of the "Military" Symphony in this way at his own benefit concert in 1795 – an exceptional context by any standard.[2] Similarly, Mozart's often-quoted description of an "academy" in Vienna (letter of 29 March 1783 to his father) began with "the new Haffner Symphony" and concluded with "the last movement of the first symphony." This has been interpreted as meaning that the symphony was performed in fragments, with the first three movements at the beginning and the finale at the end, but it is equally possible that the entire symphony was heard at the beginning and the finale was *repeated* at the end, in effect as an encore. In any case, we are no more bound by this (to our taste) Philistine practice than we are constrained, by the fact that listeners of the time came and went freely during opera overtures and other numbers, to deny that the overture to *Don Giovanni* has a function in that opera as a whole.

I make no pretense of having answers to the larger questions raised above. But I do claim, on the empirical basis of musical experience and common sense, that a high level of through-compositional organization is present in many works of Haydn. To provide a context for assessing this claim, this chapter surveys the literature on and the plausibility of the relevant aspects of cyclic organization of late eighteenth-century instrumental works. These seem to be three in number: abrogation of the conventions of genre by

[1] Christoph-Hellmut Mahling, "Zur Frage der 'Einheit' der Symphonie," in Mahling, ed., *Über Sinfonien: Beiträge zu einer musikalischen Gattung* (Tutzing, 1979), pp. 21–28.

[2] He wrote out the program for this concert in his (lost) Fourth London Notebook, from which it was transcribed by Griesinger, p. 53 (Gotwals, p. 31; Landon, *Haydn*, vol. 3, p. 309).

which the movements are ordinarily understood as separate and distinct (by running them together, or by overt gestural similarities); relations among the musical ideas; and tonal organization. A fourth basis for overall coherence, equally important but quite different, comprises extramusical associations or a program; this topic is reserved for Chapter 7. In Chapter 8, finally, we examine a number of individual works in detail.

THE BACKGROUND OF GENRE

Any hypothesis of cyclic integration must take account of the conventions of genre which Haydn and his audiences took for granted. Within any given geographical and stylistic context, each main genre was defined not only by instrumentation, but by norms regarding the number of movements, their types, and their ordering. (I confine myself to the Austrian–Bohemian realm in Haydn's time. Since eighteenth-century musical writings say little about this subject, my assertions are based primarily on induction and a critical reading of the scholarly literature.[3] They must be understood as generalizations only, offered in order to provide the necessary context for the discussion to follow.)

Around mid-century most symphonies were in three movements; gradually, albeit not uniformly, four movements became usual and remained the normal maximum. (The programmatic character of the Farewell Symphony and Beethoven's "Pastoral," for example, can be inferred directly from their five-movement structures, which include run-on movements.) Haydn's ensemble divertimenti (in various scorings), including his earliest string quartets, were usually in five movements; later string quartets and allied genres in four, occasionally in three (especially if they were popular in style).[4] Concerti were almost always in three movements, as were the majority of keyboard works, and a great many diverse chamber scorings.

Furthermore, a given movement ordinarily belonged to one of a limited number of types:

F	opening (or interior) fast or moderate movement in sonata style
S	interior (or opening) slow movement in sonata style
M or TdiM	minuet and trio or *tempo di menuetto*
Var	theme and variations (by function: S [any location] or Fn)
Song	A B A and the like (by position: usually interior S or Fn)
Fn	fast finale (usually "lighter" than an earlier fast movement)
FN	weighty finale (e.g., a fugue)

[3] Therstappen, pp. 145–63; Landon, *Symphonies*, chap. 6; William S. Newman, *The Sonata in the Classic Era* (Chapel Hill, N.C., 1963), pp. 133–43; Warren Kirkendale, *Fugue and Fugato in Rococo and Classical Chamber Music* (Durham, N.C., 1979), pp. 55, 58–59; Finscher, *Streichquartett*, vol. 1, pp. 98–102, 142–45, 152–55, 193–94, 205–06, 216–19, 233–35, 241–46, 272–75; Feder, "Die beiden Pole im Instrumentalschaffen des jungen Haydn," in Vera Schwarz, ed., *Der junge Haydn* (Graz, 1972), pp. 192–201; Somfai, "Vom Barock zur Klassik: Umgestaltung der Proportionen und des Gleichgewichts in zyklischen Werken Joseph Haydns," in Gerda Mraz, ed., *Joseph Haydn und seine Zeit* (Eisenstadt, 1972), pp. 64–72, and "Opus-Planung und Neuerung bei Haydn," *SM* 22 (1980), 87–110; Webster, "Towards a History of Viennese Chamber Music in the Early Classical Period," *JAMS* 27 (1974), 226–27.

[4] On "popular" quartets in Vienna during the 1780s, see Finscher, *Streichquartett*, vol. 1, pp. 270–75.

Obviously, these movement-types overlap in some respects. Indeed – and this principle engenders both flexibility and ambiguity – they are in part defined not by any absolute characteristics, but by their relations to the other movements in the same work. For example, only "finales" were restricted to a given position (and substantially defined by it); "fast" movements could appear in either first or second position, "slow" movements in first, second or third; minuets were common everywhere except in first position, and variations could appear anywhere.

Nevertheless, there was one overriding principle: that of contrast between successive movements. The tempo almost always changes (unless a dance movement is involved, for example fast minuet to finale, in which case the rhythmic and formal contrast suffices). Usually meter and *Affekt* are contrasted; slow movements and trios are often in a different key; and the formal design, texture, and (in works other than those for strings or winds alone) instrumentation may change as well. Two additional restrictions are that there is only one "slow" movement in cycles of five movements or fewer (although a "slow" binary/sonata or A B A can be combined with a variation movement in moderate tempo) and only one minuet in those of four or fewer. In addition, this post-1750 period should not be confused with earlier ones dominated by the "church sonata" pattern

$$
\begin{array}{c|c|c|c}
S & F & S & Fn \\
\hline
I & I & (x) & I
\end{array}
$$

that is, with two slow movements. (In generic schemes such as this one, a movement that was always or almost always in the tonic is labeled "I"; if it was in a different key (including the parallel major or minor), it is labeled "x," or "(x)" if the key contrast was optional.) Hence in cycles with four or fewer movements, only "fast" movements could appear more than once in a given work, and they were almost always in the tonic.

Even in his earlier years, Haydn's most common pattern in symphonies was the four-movement

$$
\begin{array}{c|c|c|c}
F & S & M & Fn \\
\hline
I & x & I & I
\end{array}
$$

But there were other four-movement patterns as well. In the 1750s and 1760s he began seven symphonies with slow movements in sonata style (Nos. 5, 11, 18, 21, 22, 34, and 49). Since there could be no other 'slow' movement (in the generic sense), the remaining movements were necessarily fast, minuet, and finale; according to the principle of contrast, the resultant cyclic pattern was

$$
\begin{array}{c|c|c|c}
S & F & M & Fn \\
\hline
I & I & I & I
\end{array}
$$

(Note the differences from the older church-sonata pattern: only one slow movement; minuet in third position; all movements in the tonic. No. 18 comprises only S-F-M.)

If however the opening movement (whether in sonata style or a theme and variations) was moderate in tempo, it ordinarily was not "the" slow movement, which therefore came later. In order to maximize contrast following the opening moderato, the minuet was usually placed second:

$$
\begin{array}{c|c|c|c}
\text{F} & \text{M} & \text{S} & \text{Fn} \\
\hline
\text{I} & \text{I} & \text{x} & \text{I}
\end{array}
$$

This pattern is especially characteristic of Haydn's string quartets before 1790; it is also found in many of Mozart's quartets and quintets of the 1780s, and even Beethoven's Opp. 18 No. 5, 59 No. 1, and 135. It is less common in symphonies; even so, it occurs in four early and two middle Haydn symphonies – Nos. 108 ("B"), 15, 32, 37, 44, and 68 – as well as late Beethoven works, including the gigantic Ninth Symphony and the "Hammerklavier" Sonata. (In certain works in this pattern, the opening movement is fast, rather than moderate; here the minuet's contrast of style, form, and texture was evidently thought sufficient.) Three-movement symphonies remained common through the 1760s, either in the form

$$
\begin{array}{c|c|c}
\text{F} & \text{S} & \text{Fn} \\
\hline
\text{I} & \text{x} & \text{I}
\end{array}
$$

or with a minuet (Haydn's Nos. 9, 18, 25, 26, 30).

Haydn's solo and accompanied keyboard sonatas (like those of all eighteenth-century composers) were based primarily on cycles of two and three movements, rather than four. The most common pattern was the three-movement one just cited, also found in the concerto and some symphonies. Common as well were several "galant" three-movement patterns (as I call them), comprising a fast movement, a slow movement, and a minuet or *tempo di menuetto*, in various permutations. They tend to read like subsets of four-movement cycles:

$$
\begin{array}{c|c|c}
\text{F} & \text{S} & \text{M} \\
\hline
\text{I} & \text{x} & \text{I}
\end{array}
\qquad
\begin{array}{c|c|c}
\text{S} & \text{M} & \text{Fn} \\
\hline
\text{I} & \text{(x)} & \text{I}
\end{array}
\qquad
\begin{array}{c|c|c}
\text{S} & \text{F} & \text{M} \\
\hline
\text{I} & \text{I} & \text{I}
\end{array}
\qquad
\begin{array}{c|c|c}
\text{F} & \text{M} & \text{Var.} \\
\hline
\text{I} & \text{(x)} & \text{I}
\end{array}
$$

The galant effect is often emphasized by relatively simple outward form and style – even, for example, in the minuet/finale of Haydn's late and sophisticated "Genzinger" sonata, Hob. XVI:49 in E-flat. Finally, various two-movement patterns with both movements in the tonic were important, primarily S | F and F | M. The type was not necessarily "easy": Sonatas 18 in B-flat, 44 in G minor, and 48 in C, as well as numerous two-movement trios, are as strong and original as their three-movement counterparts. Nor was it in any sense "immature": Sonata No. 48 and, again, all the two-movement trios date from the mid-1780s through the mid-1790s, the culmination of Haydn's career as a composer of instrumental music.

CYCLIC FORM?

From eighteenth-century views to ours

There is little direct evidence of eighteenth-century views on the integration of multi-movement instrumental works. To judge from the literature, instrumental music was still understood primarily along Aristotelian lines, as an imitation of human passions or of a verbal model (explicit or implicit).[5] This orientation entailed the opinion that any work, insofar as it was not programmatic or literary, projected a single dominant feeling. Hence, except for the commonplace notion of "unity within diversity," late eighteenth-century theorists had no conceptual vocabulary for describing the relations of temporally separate, dissimilar movements.[6] Although they often refer to the need for unity (*Einheit*) in the abstract, in practice they discuss only individual movements, list conventional genre-patterns (and associated moods), and assert that the last movement had more or less to revert to the feeling of the first. Apparently, only Johann Nikolaus Forkel attempted (in 1783) to justify the succession of different feelings awakened by a multimovement work, as a reflection of the natural process of the soul's changing passions.[7] Such a sequence can indeed progress, can end in a different state from the initial one; moreover, corresponding "inner" relations among the movements must exist. Forkel illustrates these ideas with a description of a C. P. E. Bach "Kenner und Lieb-haber" sonata in F minor (Wq. 57/6, Helm 173), whose three movements contain [*enthalten*], respectively, "a certain impatience," "examination and reflection" on that feeling, and the resultant "somewhat melancholy relief" (*ein gewisses Unwillen, Betrachtung und Überlegung, etwas melancholische Beruhigung*).

But even Forkel says nothing about the *nature* of those "inner relations." That step was taken – decisively – early in the nineteenth century. In his famous review (1810) of Beethoven's Symphony No. 5, E. T. A. Hoffmann invokes Shakespeare, in terms that will have been familiar to the bard's defenders against the French rationalists' charge that his plays lacked unity:

How little the peculiar nature of music was recognized by the instrumental composers who tried to represent definable feelings or even events through their music and thus attempted to treat

---

[5] Many excerpts from primary sources are presented in translation, with commentary, in le Huray and Day. On the change from "imitative" to "expressive" theories towards 1800, see Meyer H. Abrams, *The Mirror and the Lamp* (New York, 1953), chaps. 2–4; Carl Dahlhaus, *The Idea of Absolute Music* (Chicago, 1989), and *Esthetics of Music* (Cambridge, 1982), chaps. 4–6; Bellamy Hosler, *Changing Aesthetic Views of Instrumental Music in 18th-Century Germany* (Ann Arbor, 1981); James Anderson Winn, *Unsuspected Eloquence* (New Haven, 1981), chap. 5; Neubauer, *Emancipation*.

[6] The remainder of this section draws on Mahling, "Einheit"; Wilhelm Seidel, "Schnell – Langsam – Schnell: Zur 'klassischen' Theorie des instrumentalen Zyklus," *Mth* 1 (1986), 205–16, and "Die ältere Zyklustheorie, überdacht im Blick auf Beethovens Werk," in Sieghard Brandenburg and Helmut Loos, eds., *Beiträge zu Beethovens Kammermusik: Symposion Bonn 1984* (Munich, 1987), pp. 273–82.

[7] "Ueber eine Sonate aus Carl Phil. Emanuel Bachs dritter Sonatensammlung für Kenner und Liebhaber, in F moll," *Musikalischer Almanach für Deutschland auf das Jahr 1784* (Leipzig, 1783), pp. 22–38; cf. Seidel, "Theorie des Zyklus," pp. 206–07.

their art, which stands in direct opposition to plastic art, in a plastic way!. . . [They] are ludicrous aberrations which ought to be punished by burial in oblivion. Just as the esthetic surveyors have often complained of a complete lack of true unity and inner coherence in Shakespeare, while only those of deeper vision have witnessed the springing forth of a beautiful tree, buds and leaves, blossoms and fruits, from a germinal seed – so too will only a very deep penetration into the inner structure of Beethoven's music reveal the great extent of the master's self-possession [*Besonnenheit*]. Such self-possession is inseparable from true genius. . . .

The movements . . . seem to be linked together in a fantastic way. . . . The heart of every sensitive listener, however, will certainly be deeply and intimately moved by an enduring feeling . . . of foreboding, indescribable longing – which remains until the final chord. . . . Besides the internal arrangement of the instrumentation, . . . it is particularly the intimate relationship of the individual themes to one another which produces the unity that firmly maintains a single feeling in the listener's heart.[8]

As suggested by the last full sentence in each paragraph, Hoffmann consistently accounts for the unity of the work on both technical and psychological grounds. (His invocation of the "listener's heart" at the end recalls Haydn's "Nothing remains in the heart," quoted at the beginning of Chapter 5 (p. 125). As this similarity implies, both eighteenth- and nineteenth-century musical aesthetics saw a link between unity and feeling. The difference is that Haydn – apparently – was speaking of surface continuity within a single movement, whereas Hoffmann explicitly discusses the integration of independent movements having outwardly contrasting material.) During the same period, even the older, conservative Ernst Ludwig Gerber could write:

Haydn and his worthy followers . . . often fill . . . many pages with [developments of] a single phrase of two or four measures; . . . thereby they achieve that admirable unity in their artworks, which gives the whole, despite its manifold parts (If I may be permitted this comparison), the appearance of an egg, whose unending [*unendliche*], but thoroughly homogeneous parts likewise form an indivisible whole. . . . This method of composing symphonies on a *single main idea*, which Haydn invented . . . , is the *non plus ultra* of the most modern art, the highest and most splendid [type] of instrumental composition. . . . This method raises the symphony to a self-sufficient whole, in that it no longer is cobbled together from patches found here and there, or from imitations – or even quotations – of texted music (song).[9]

By the time of the aesthetician G. F. Fink (1835), these thoughts had become dogma:

The whole must have a definite and firmly maintained character, which connects the various parts with one another in their innermost relations, so that – as in Beethoven's symphonies, whose often entirely heterogeneous-appearing individual movements nevertheless, on closer inspection, are generated from a single element – everything aims at *one* given goal, and unifies itself into the expression of *one* inner idea of the spirit.[10]

---

[8] *Allgemeine musikalische Zeitung*, 12 (1809–10), 633–34, 658; transl. F. John Adams, Jr., in Elliot Forbes, ed., *Beethoven: Symphony No. 5 in C minor* (New York, 1971), pp. 151, 162–63. Compare Dahlhaus, "Hoffmanns Beethoven-Kritik"; Robin Wallace, *Beethoven's Critics: Aesthetic Dilemmas and Resolutions During the Composer's Lifetime* (Cambridge, 1986), pp. 20–26 and chap. 5.

[9] "Eine freundliche Vorstellung über gearbeitete Instrumentalmusik, besonders über Symphonien," *AMZ* 15 (1812–13), 475.

[10] "Ueber die Sinfonie," *AMZ* 37 (1834–35), 557–58.

The writers have the organic metaphor well in mind, with its corollary of "growth" from a "cell" (Hoffmann: "the springing forth of a tree, buds and leaves, blossoms and fruits, from a germinal seed"; Gerber: "it is a whole, like an egg"). Noteworthy is Hoffmann's and Gerber's explicit distancing of modern symphonies from older sorts of instrumental music, which were merely "cobbled together," dependent on imitation or on vocal models (Gerber); and "ought to be punished by oblivion" (Hoffmann). The concept of unity, the increasingly marginal status of overtly programmatic music, and the rise of "absolute," autonomous instrumental music, were mutually determined.

But these attitudes still did not adumbrate a *theory* of the relations between movements. This found its clearest nineteenth-century formulation in Adolf Bernhard Marx's *Die Lehre von der musikalischen Komposition* (Leipzig, 1845; I follow Seidel's summary). The movements are still understood primarily as separate, independent entities, but they are joined into a cycle on the basis of relationships among tempo and key, meter and formal type, content and "idea." Both tempo and key are symmetrically organized: an initial state is established, a contrasting state intervenes, and the finale returns to the beginning: fast–slow–fast, tonic–non-tonic–tonic. This assures coherence, because not only is each pattern symmetrical, but the patterns themselves are congruent. Variety of meter and form fosters diversity; this diversity is a desirable elaboration within the underlying cyclic symmetry. Content and idea also relate dialectically as diversity and unity. The material of each movement is strongly profiled and distinct from the others. Hence the overarching progression in many works (like Fink, Marx is thinking of Beethoven) cannot be located in the "material" realm, but only by positing an underlying "idea" that guarantees overall unity. (In this respect, Hoffmann was still a guiding spirit.)

The deficiencies of this theory are evident. The last two criteria belong to the realm of aesthetics; nor is their relationship to the others clear. But the technical criteria themselves are inadequate. Except for the idea of the cycle itself, with its (conventional) corollary of diversity-within-unity, they hardly go beyond what was taken for granted in the eighteenth century. The model of a three-part, symmetrical construction cannot account for the minuet/scherzo (for which various pseudo-explanations were devised), or three-movement works built on other principles (Beethoven's Op. 109), let alone those in two movements (Op. 111) or five or more. It disprivileges many important eighteenth-century patterns, such as two-movement keyboard works and three-movement works with a minuet (see the two Beethoven sonatas just cited, whose basis in traditional notions of genre remains to this day underappreciated in the Beethoven literature). Finally, it is helpless to explain the many works which *are* essays in culmination.

However, except when they appeal to the quite different domains of tonality and thematic relations, modern theories of cyclic organization are scarcely more impressive. Tovey's, remarkably, is almost exclusively psychological (his famous demonstration of tonal coherence in Beethoven's C-sharp Minor Quartet being as exceptional as that work itself).

Why do the classical sonatas maintain this scheme of self-centred movements with no community of theme? The answer to this lies in the relation between their time-scale and their emotional content. . . . The individual movements, while complete as designs, raise emotional issues which each movement is unable to satisfy without the others. The first movement of Beethoven's . . . *Appassionata* Sonata . . . whirls us through an immense tragedy in eight minutes. The movement is irrevocably completed; but our emotional reactions have not yet more than begun. We need the unutterable calm of the slow movement. . . . A foreign chord replaces that of its cadence; the vision is broken and the finale rushes headlong to the end of a tragic fate.[11]

And Tovey continues by propounding two familiar theses, both confirming his skepticism regarding the unity of eighteenth-century cycles: a denial of the importance of thematic allusions in sonata style, and an assertion that Haydn's and Mozart's "comic" art was incapable of encompassing an emotionally adequate finale to a "tragic" work. It is no better with contemporary musicologists (I am still postponing tonality and thematicism); they hardly go beyond a generalized concern with "weight" and "balance" among individual movements.[12] Very recently, Fred Everett Maus has interpreted Tovey's account quoted above in terms of the distinction, familiar from the theory of narrative, between "story" and "discourse":

Tovey claims that . . . each of the outer movements, at least, forms a complete story. There is no plot continuation from one movement to the next. The juxtaposition of the movements is not, itself, part of any story. It is a feature of the discourse, introduced in order to provide a satisfying experience for a listener. . . . Breaks between movements can imply that a composition persists through a change of story.[13]

In short, individual movements are "stories," but the relations between them are the subject of a meta-story, a narration "about" them. This seems at once confusing (who tells the narrative – the composer? the listener? – and what does it say?), and promising: any method for simultaneously understanding the movements in the cycle as separate, autonomous structures and as members of a temporally determined "plot" is worth pursuing. We will return to it in connection with one of Haydn's most unusual works, Symphony No. 46 in B (see Chapter 8). Whether the distinction will prove generally applicable in ordinary eighteenth-century cycles is perhaps less clear.

In sum, a judicious combination of relevant notions of cyclic organization from all periods, from Haydn's time to ours, seems most likely to lead to satisfactory explanations. Eighteenth-century conventions of genre; nineteenth-century cycle theory; the traditional modern interest in continuities of material and tonality; and recent explorations of rhythm, gesture, topos, and narrative – all have a role to play. Thus David Schulenberg, modifying Forkel's psychological interpretation of C. P. E. Bach's sonata, achieves a balanced view by adducing as well the run-on transition between the second and third movements, and (modest) motivic connections, while being careful not to claim too much.[14] A comparably varied approach will be found my analyses of Haydn in Chapter 8 below.

---

[11] "Sonata Forms," in *Musical Articles from the Encyclopaedia Britannica* (London, 1944), pp. 229–30.

[12] For example, Friedrich Blume, "Josef Haydn's künstlerische Persönlichkeit in seinen Streichquartetten," *JbP* 38 (1931), 24–48; Finscher, *Streichquartett*, vol. 1, pp. 152–54, 205–07, 216–19, 233–37, 245–46; Somfai, "Opus-Planung und Neuerung."

[13] Maus, "Humanism," pp. 140–41.

[14] Schulenberg, *The Instrumental Music of Carl Philipp Emanuel Bach* (Ann Arbor, 1984), pp. 138–40.

The "finale problem"

Another aspect of the coherence of multimovement cycles is the role of the finale, especially in its potential function as a culmination. Other things equal, a work in which the finale is articulated as a climax or resolution will seem more highly organized than one with a traditional sonata-rondo or minuet/variations. Hence an efficient method of investigating cyclic coherence in general is to examine finales. (The development of the four-movement symphony may have entailed, not so much the insertion of a minuet into the F–S–F pattern, as is usually assumed, as the addition of a finale to the traditional three-movement pattern ending with a minuet.[15] To the extent that this was so, it is appropriate to think of the finale as having posed a new problem of style, weight, and contrast with respect to the other movements.)

The conventional view is that three distinct types of multimovement cycle, each with its characteristic type of finale, succeeded each other from the eighteenth century into the nineteenth. In the earlier eighteenth century, a conventional or arbitrary succession ended merely with the "last" movement (even if it was a spirited windup). In the late eighteenth and early nineteenth centuries, a balance among diverse movements led to a contrasting but equal pendant to the first. Taking their cue from Beethoven, more and more nineteenth-century composers created overarching progressions, leading to the finale as climax or apotheosis.[16]

Haydn himself indirectly testified to this changing aesthetic. Regarding the finale of Symphony No. 93, he wrote from London to his confidante Madame Genzinger (?2 March 1792),

I cannot send Your Grace the symphony which is dedicated to you . . . because I intend to alter the last movement of it, and to improve it, since it is too weak compared with the preceding movements. I was persuaded of this myself, and by the public as well, when I produced it the first time, . . . notwithstanding which it [the symphony] made the most profound impression on the audience.[17]

The nature of any changes Haydn actually made cannot be determined, as the autograph is lost, and the surviving sources all transmit the same version. As Landon emphasizes, in its present form the finale does not seem in any way inadequate.[18]

---

[15] Larsen, "Some Observations on the Development and Characteristics of Viennese Classical Instrumental Music," *SM* 9 (1967), 136.

[16] Karl H. Wörner, *Das Zeitalter der thematischen Prozesse in der Geschichte der Musik* (Regensburg, 1969), chap. 1, "Finalcharakter"; Bernd Sponheuer, "Haydns Arbeit am Finalproblem," *AfMw* 34 (1977), 199–224, especially the introductory section.

[17] ". . .ich [kann] dermahlen die für Euer gnaden gewidmete neue Sinfonien . . . nicht übermachen . . . weil ich willens bin, das lezte Stück von derselben abzuändern, und zu verschönern, da solches in rücksicht der Ersteren Stücke zu schwach ist, ich wurde dessen sowohl von mir selbst als auch von dem Publico überzeugt, da ich dieselbe . . . zum erstenmahl producirte; Sie machte aber ungeacht dessen den tiefesten Eindruck auf die Zuhörer." *Briefe*, No. 174, pp. 279–80; Landon, *Haydn*, vol. 3, p. 521.

[18] Landon, *Haydn*, vol. 3, pp. 521–22. On Haydn's finales generally, see Therstappen, pp. 139–51; Finscher, *Streichquartett*, vol. 1, pp. 203–05, 213–16, 231–33; 253–56. (Despite his apostrophization of a "problem," Sponheuer does not directly address the issue of the relations between Haydn's finales and the other movements of the same works.)

Unquestionably, apotheosis-finales have been composed mainly in the nineteenth and twentieth centuries. The paradigmatic example remains Beethoven's Symphony No. 5, which impressed his contemporaries as revolutionary in just this way; to us, the Ninth Symphony and the C-sharp Minor Quartet, and perhaps the "Hammerklavier" and Op. 110 Sonatas, seem equally end-oriented, as does the B-flat Quartet Op. 130 in its original form ending with the *Grosse Fuge*. These works also suggest the chief methods of producing a through-composed effect, and of articulating the finale as a culmination: run-on movements (the Fifth and Op. 131); recalls of earlier movements (both symphonies); the transformation of minor into major (both symphonies; Op. 131 ends with an expanded Picardy third); prominent and unusual tonal relations (C major in every movement of the Fifth, B-flat in the Ninth, the Neapolitan in Op. 131); an impression of incompleteness or unfulfilled potential before the finale (the concentration, lack of contrast, and abruptness of the Allegro con brio in the Fifth; the lack of strong dominants and of sonata form in Op. 131); a mood of tension or irresolution (the Fifth). The finale must grant that which has been promised: it must have a problematical or "searching" introduction, where possible with thematic recalls; exceed the other movements in length and complexity; establish the major mode, break the tension, articulate sonata form if the other movements were simple, or a compendious super-form if they were long; or, if all else fails, bring in voices which sing of brotherhood. Finally, although overtures (which are single, usually compound, movements) are not properly part of our subject, Beethoven's *Leonore* Nos. 2 and 3 and *Egmont* had an immense influence on nineteenth-century composers' sense of musical climax.

But the features on which such effects depend were by no means unknown during the eighteenth century. The older church-sonata tradition not only maintained a serious tone throughout, but included run-on movement-pairs and fugal finales, a tradition which remained common in Austrian chamber music well past 1770.[19] In view of the status of the "learned" style, and the high level of contrapuntal density entailed, the possibility that fugal finales were heard as culminations cannot be dismissed. Run-on movements ending with climactic fugues were also common in large-scale Mass settings, particularly in Glorias and Credos. In addition, it was common in Austria to set the concluding "Dona nobis pacem" as a repetition of earlier music, most often drawn from the Kyrie; this created a potentially "cyclic" form governing an entire five-movement work lasting half an hour or more and programmatically organized by its coherent liturgical function. Haydn's only example is the *Missa S[ti] Nicolai* of 1772 – the same year as the Farewell itself.[20] Indeed, many mid-century Austrian symphonies were related to the so-called "intrada" church music tradition.[21] Haydn concluded one relatively early symphony, No. 40 (1763), with a formal fugue. And he surely intended an effect of

---

[19] Kirkendale, *Fugue and Fugato;* regarding the importance of this context for Haydn's chamber music, see pp. 137–43.

[20] Bruce C. MacIntyre, *The Viennese Concerted Mass of the Early Classic Period* (Ann Arbor, 1986), pp. 232–42, 304–62, 414, 515–18, 564. (The widespread notion that this mass was composed for Prince Esterhazy's name-day – "Nicolaus," 6 December, a month or so following the Farewell premiere – has no documentary support.)

[21] Larsen, "Zur Entstehung der österreichischen Symphonietradition (ca. 1750–1775)," *HYb* 10 (1978), 76, 78.

culmination with the fugal finales in Op. 20 (see Chapter 8 and the conclusion) and Op. 50 No. 4 (Chapter 8).

In the 1780s and 1790s, by contrast, Haydn's and Mozart's use of fugue in instrumental finales usually took the form of fugato passages, or sonata movements written in contrapuntal texture. This enrichment was analogous to the creation of the sonata-rondo: whether in texture or in form, the finale became more complex than before, capable of balancing a serious opening movement, but without necessarily abandoning its traditionally lighter character. Haydn's most familiar example is perhaps the recapitulation fugato in the "Clock" Symphony, No. 101 (mm. 189ff). Occasionally, Mozart synthesized the galant and the learned so thoroughly and with such brilliance that the finale actually outweighs the opening movement; if the finales of the G-major Quartet K. 387 and (especially) the "Jupiter" Symphony are not culminations, it is difficult to know what to call them. Here too, however, the same tendencies existed earlier. Haydn composed numerous earlier symphony finales in which fugal passages are integrated into a sonata-form structure, as in Symphony No. 13 (1763), or alternate with homophonic ones, as in Nos. 3 (pre-Esterházy?) and 70 (c. 1778–79).

The conventional three-stage view of the development of the finale must therefore be qualified. Not only were many of the individual features associated with culmination-finales present by 1750, but a few works from the second half of the century exhibit the type fully formed. In Haydn's *oeuvre* these include not only the Farewell Symphony, but No. 46 as well, and the string quartets Opp. 20 No. 2, 50 No. 4, 54 No. 2, and 74 No. 3 (see Chapter 8). Doubtless there were others – many of which may not yet have been recognized, because traditional musicological biases have inhibited the search for them.

Gesture

Relatedness of movements by gesture can be of two kinds: striking similarities of procedure which go beyond the usual and conventional, or systematic differentiation between some movements and others. The latter possibility is easier to notice; apotheosis-finales themselves are a clear example. Occasionally Haydn makes a comparable distinction somewhere else within a work. A familiar example is Symphony No. 88 in G (1787): the trumpets and drums are withheld from both the first movement and the first section of the Largo, so that their blazing entry in the later *fortissimo* passages (mm. 41, 76, 107) is all the more effective; they return in the minuet and the finale. (But does this stroke "organize" the symphony? Do the first movement and the first part of the Largo in any sense constitute an "introduction" to the remainder? Such questions have never even been asked.) These entries might also have had extramusical associations. "Largo" is Haydn's slowest tempo, which he uses but sparingly; a number of other largo movements are either explicitly programmatic or very unusual; see Symphony No. 64 and the quartets Opp. 74 No. 3 ("Largo assai") and 76 No. 5 (both in very remote keys) – not to mention the "Chaos."

In general, however, similarities of gesture and rhetoric are more difficult to pin down:

the search for them does not move in familiar channels, and it is notoriously difficult to talk about these aspects of music.[22] An interesting exception involves C. P. E. Bach: although thematic links and (especially) transitions between movements are common in his music, the literature focuses instead on the disruptive and eccentric in his style; these, paradoxically, are taken as elements of continuity. Even Schulenberg's balanced and intelligent survey (see note 14) treats the possibility of unification in a markedly diffident manner. In any case, no other eighteenth-century composer except Haydn went so far as Bach in elevating instability to a governing principle, and Bach never matched Haydn's feat of binding this degree of instability into coherent form, never achieved the level of through-composition found in the Farewell. Perhaps the recent interest in "topoi" and the semiotics of eighteenth-century music will lead to a better understanding of rhetorical continuity from one movement to another; it might even provide a method for linking the technical and the aesthetic domains, as Hoffmann attempted to do in the early nineteenth century. Until these aspects of single movements are better understood, however, this larger-scale project will remain impracticable.

An incontrovertible means of linking separate movements is for one to *recall* material from another. The effect is especially strong when the tempi and meters contrast, so that the movement in progress must break off – as in the "Dona ut Kyrie" mass finales just mentioned. In instrumental music, Beethoven's Symphony No. 5 is again the paradigmatic example; its scherzo-recall, as always in Beethoven, has both formal and aesthetic functions. And again, Haydn anticipated him. In the first movement of Symphony No. 31 in D, "Hornsignal" (1765), the opening theme is withheld from the recapitulation, to appear at the very end as a brief coda; more important, it returns at the end of the finale, to close the symphony as it began (see pp. 246–47). Symphony No. 46 in B (1772) brings a truly astonishing stroke: the Presto finale is interrupted near the end for a reprise of the minuet, after which it resumes and concludes (see Chapter 8). As far as I know, this is the only recall in any eighteenth-century symphony comparable to that in Beethoven's Fifth.

RUN-ON MOVEMENT PAIRS AND COMPOUND MOVEMENTS

One type of gesture which fundamentally – and objectively – fosters multi-movement continuity is the use of run-on or *attacca* relations between successive movements. (This is also a rhythmic phenomenon: the larger the scale, the more rhythm and gesture approach each other.) As I use it, the term "run-on pair" designates two contiguous movements, each of which articulates (or strongly implies) a complete formal design; the first breaks off at the last moment or closes on the dominant, the second following *attacca*, without pause. An example is the Presto and the concluding Adagio in the Farewell Symphony. Related to these are "compound" (single) movements with discrete

---

[22] For example, Raimund Bard's recent "'Tendenzen' zur zyklischen Gestaltung in Haydns Londoner Sinfonien," in Christoph-Hellmut Mahling and Sigrid Wiesmann, eds., *Bericht über den internationalen musikwissenschaftlichen Kongress Bayreuth 1981* (Kassel, 1984), pp. 379–83, is unpersuasive.

sections in different tempi. The chief intrinsic distinction is that in the latter, at most one section may articulate a complete formal design; the other(s) must be fragmentary, dependent either on the main section or on each other. The most common types of compound movement are Introduction-Allegros and finales with *stretto* codas (on the former, see Chapter 5). (Still another related case comprises minuets and trios. These are actually double-faced: two separate movements, each usually complete in itself, which nonetheless "count" as one. As we have seen, they are frequently run-on or otherwise exhibit through-compositional features.) Although Haydn composed both compound and run-on movements with some frequency, in all the major instrumental genres and throughout his life, they have never been systematically described. (This failing reflects musicologists' general lack of interest in through-composition in eighteenth-century music.)

In addition to the intrinsic distinction just noted, an equally strong contextual distinction lies in the system of generic patterns described at the beginning of this chapter. A symphony beginning with an introduction and allegro is always described as having four movements, never five. A slow passage that follows three complete movements, of which one is a slow movement, is almost always an introduction to a finale – even if it as weighty and expressive as the second Adagio in Mozart's G-minor String Quintet. (Again: nobody describes this as a five-movement work.) Continuity of material or the formal plan can also be determinant. For example, an ABA pattern can rarely be heard as anything other than a single, compound movement: the recapitulatory return to earlier material binds the whole together, and the law of contrast prevents the second A from being understood as a "different" movement from the first. (It is in part for this reason that mere recalls of earlier movements, as in Haydn's Symphonies 31 and 46 and Beethoven's Fifth and Ninth, are not heard as abrogating the four-movement pattern; a separate movement must be stronger, longer, more independent – as in Haydn's farewell movement, or the storm in Beethoven's "Pastoral.")

Keyboard music

Most of Haydn's keyboard music was destined in the first instance for private patrons. This, along with its relatively improvisatory style, fostered a greater variety of cyclic patterns than was permissible in the string quartet or symphony. Modern writers have devoted correspondingly more attention to the run-on movement-pairs in his keyboard music than in other genres;[23] even so, there is no general account of them. These are listed in Table 6.1. Fifteen works are involved, eight sonatas and seven trios; this represents about one sixth of the extant works in these genres – a far from negligible repertory. Inexplicably, the works including run-on pairs stand only in the keys of D, E-flat, E (minor and major), A-flat, and A, but not C, F, or G, or any other minor key. Hardly

[23] See, for example, Hermann Abert, "Joseph Haydns Klaviersonaten," *ZfMw* 3 (1920–21), 536; Tovey, "Haydn's Chamber Music," p. 59; Rosen, *Classical Style*, pp. 351, 356–65; A. Peter Brown, *Joseph Haydn's Keyboard Music: Sources and Style* (Bloomington, 1986), pp. 291, 306, 310, 320–23, 336 *et passim*. A wealth of material is contained in Somfai's brilliant 1979 monograph (in Hungarian), now being readied for publication in English (Univ. of Chicago Press).

Table 6.1. *Run-on movement pairs in Haydn keyboard sonatas and trios*

Work	Movement-plan	Remarks
Sonatas (Hob. XVI)		
24 (D)	F | S——Fn I | i–V–I	Adagio: sonata without development, compressed recapitulation Finale: long, rondo-like theme; one variation; free variation-coda
30 (A)	F–S————TdiM I–Mod.–V–I	Entire work run-on (see Chap. 8)
31 (E)	Mod. | S——Fn I | i–V–I	Allegretto: binary/sonata; contrapuntal, pseudo-Baroque Variation finale
33 (D)	F | S——TdiM I | i–V–I	Adagio: sonata form Tempo di minuetto: double variations
34 (e)	F | S——Fn i | III–V–i	Adagio: sonata form Finale: double variations ("innocentemente")
37 (D)	I | S——Fn I | i–V–I	Largo: binary; sarabande-like, passionate Finale: variation-rondo ("innocentemente")
38 (Eb)	Mod. | S——M I | vi–V–I	Adagio: sonata form, "veränderte Reprise" exposition (no closure) Finale: short minuet
47 (e)	S——F | TdiM i–V–I | I	Opening Adagio: sonata form Allegro: sonata form
Trios (Hob. XV)		
7 (D)	Var. | S——Fn I | i–V–I	Andante: binary Finale: big rondo (two-note upbeat; short sections)
14 (Ab)	F | S——Fn I | ♭VI–V–I	Adagio: A-B-A (*minore* in E minor), *with* closure, plus transition Finale: big sonata form
16 (D)	F | S——Fn I | i–V–I	Andantino: sonata with very short development Finale: big rondo
18 (A)	F | S——Fn I | i–V–I	Andante: Variation ABA (B in tonic major) Finale: sonata without development (big, rondo-like theme, "Polonaise")
24 (D)	F | S——Fn I | i–V–I	Andante: miniature sonata Finale: ABA, minuet-like; "Allegro ma dolce"
29 (Eb)	Mod. | S————Fn I | ♭VI–I–V–I	Andantino ed innocentemente: AA' BB'; B' returns to Eb Finale: sonata form; presto assai "in the German Style" (Allemande)
30 (Eb)	F | S————Fn I | VI♯–V/vi–I	Andante: A B (in V) A' B'; remote preparation of . . . Finale: A B+Dev A Coda; quasi-Allemande

more transparent is Haydn's motive for *always* incorporating the run-on pair in D major (so long as the cyclic pattern permits it at all), but doing so in only some of the works in each of the other keys named. (This is by no means the only "key-related" correspondence we will notice in Haydn.)

All fifteen works are in three movements (or so it appears); all but two (Sonatas 30 and 47) follow the movement-pattern

$$
\begin{array}{c|c}
\text{F/Mod} & \text{S—Fn} \\[2mm]
\text{I} & \text{x—I}
\end{array}
$$

and in all but Trios 7 and 29, the first movement is in sonata form. (In the relatively early Sonata No. 47, the first two movements are run-on; Sonata No. 30 is entirely through-composed [see Chapter 8]. But even in the former, the opening movement is slow, the second fast – both are in sonata form – and so the *attacca* relation remains associated with the tempo sequence slow–fast.) About two thirds of the time, the dominant which ends the earlier movement is provided with a fermata (presumably suggesting an *Eingang*), and the measure ends with a double bar.[24] When either or both are missing – the fermata in Sonatas 30 (end of second movement), 31, 33, and 34 and Trio No. 14; the double bar in Sonatas 24, 30 (end of first movement), and 33, and Trio No. 16 – the run-on effect is potentially stronger. Haydn must have envisioned it as especially abrupt in Sonatas 24 and 33 and Trio 16, in which the final bar of the slow movement is incomplete and has no barline at all, and is "completed" by the upbeat of the ensuing fast movement. (Once again: all three works are in D.) A remark such as "Attacca subito" appears about half the time.

In most of the thirteen works exhibiting this standard *attacca* relation, the slow movement is brief and relatively simple in form and texture; substantial length or complexity would presumably inhibit the run-on effect. And it almost always contrasts strongly in mood with the outer movements: Haydn eschews the customary subdominant and dominant, using instead either the tonic minor (when the overall tonic is on the sharp side) or one or another submediant (when on the flat side). Sonata No. 34, the only work truly in a minor key, employs the mediant; the slow movement in No. 30 is overtly transitional. Trios 14, 29, and 30 use remote major-mode variants of the submediant (VI$^{\sharp}$ or $\flat$VI), as was common in Haydn's late music (see below). Usually final closure is subverted, often at the moment of the structural cadence, where a deceptive cadence to VI or an augmented sixth chord appears instead, soon returning to the dominant (which may be briefly prolonged before the fermata). The only exceptions are in remote keys. In Trio No. 14, an ABA movement comes to its appointed end (m. 50) and is followed by a formal transition back to the home dominant. Trio No. 29 employs an unusual AA'BB' form: its final section modulates from C-flat back to and proceeds at length in the overall tonic E-flat, before a deflected cadence of the usual type; the movement thus changes, during its course, from a closed, lyrical form to a tonally progressive transition.

Except perhaps for Sonata No. 47 (whose cyclic pattern differs from the others), all the *attacca* solo sonatas date from the 1770s. Given Haydn's more or less continual cultivation of the genre from the 1750s through the second London visit, the reason for this chronological restriction is not clear. It bears no direct connection with his "Sturm und Drang" manner, which disappeared after 1772; nor, except for the slow movements themselves, are the run-on sonatas on average more expressive than the others. They appear in all three *opera* from the decade (Hob. XVI:21–26, 27–32, 35–39+20; on the latter conjunction, see *JHW* XVIII/2), but never more than twice in any given opus. Their finales are all "easy" movements in galant style, suggesting performance by amateurs: minuets or *tempi di menuetto* in Nos. 30, 33, 38, and 47; variations or simple rondos in Nos. 24, 31, 34, and 37. (Here and throughout this section, I use "connois-

---

[24] The remarks from here to the end of this paragraph are based on the scrupulously accurate editions in *JHW* XVII and XVIII.

seurs" and "amateurs" not so much in the sense of the somewhat different eighteenth-century distinction between *Kenner* and *Liebhaber* [and "dilettantes"], as to suggest the distinction between "difficult" and "easy" music, both technically and stylistically.) An attractive verbal symbol of this function is Haydn's unusual marking "innocentemente" for the finales of Nos. 34 and 37, a characterization he employed only for short movements in simple textures. (Other examples of this usage are the slow movement of Trio No. 29, the finale of Sonata No. 34, the opening movement of Sonata No. 40 in G ("innocente"), and the opening Andante of the string quartet in D Minor Op. 42.) All these principles are combined in Sonata No. 30 in A, Haydn's only entirely continuous multimovement instrumental composition (see Chapter 8).

In the 1780s and 1790s, by contrast, Haydn's run-on finales appear in the piano trios. And in this context he twice changed his view of *attacca* finales. Whereas those in the sonatas from the 1770s were amateurs' movements, from 1785 into 1794 every trio in question (Nos. 7, 14, 16, and 18) features a big, imposing sonata-form or rondo finale, fully on a par with those in the three-movement trios with an independent slow movement (Nos. 12, 15, 20–23, 27, and 28).[25] On the other hand, from 1795 (or late 1794) on, he reverted once more to easier finales in *attacca* trios. No. 24 in D (from the set XV:24–26, dedicated to Haydn's paramour Mrs. Schroeter, an amateur) concludes with a simple ABA movement, with the unusual marking "Allegro ma dolce." But even in the grand and original No. 29 in E-flat (from the set XV:27–29, dedicated to the first-rate professional pianist Therese Jansen-Bartolozzi), the finale, though in sonata form and quite difficult, is an Allemande-type ("in the German Style"); that is, dance-related. In the apparently later No. 30 in E-flat, it is an (admittedly elaborate) ABA movement. The latter two finales thus mediate between the amateur and connoisseur finale traditions.

Thus beginning in the mid-1780s – when he was at the height of his career as a composer of instrumental music destined for publication – Haydn favored large finales for connoisseurs even in keyboard music, so long as nothing spoke against it, but maintained the amateur type in works intended in the first instance for private use or non-professional dedicatees. Both types coexist in his post-1785 solo sonatas as well (which have no *attacca* movements): Nos. 49–51 end with simple movements in triple meter, but Nos. 48 and 52 with, respectively, a full-fledged sonata-rondo and a sonata form. Nor is the overall form a determinant: both finale-types occur in two-movement cycles (Nos. 48, 51) and in three-movement ones (Nos. 49, 50, 52). The critical point, again, was the "destination" of each work or opus. From the late 1780s, No. 48 in C, sold to the publisher Breitkopf, has a difficult sonata-rondo, while No. 49 in E-flat for Mme. Genzinger has a technically simple (if subtle) minuet movement. The same distinction can be observed in Nos. 52 and 51 in their entirety: the former, grand and difficult throughout, was dedicated to Jansen-Bartolozzi; the latter, a markedly "easy" work (and

---

[25] The date of XV:18–20, the latest set to include a big *attacca* finale, is uncertain (1793 or 1794); similarly with XV:24–26, the earliest with an easy *attacca* finale (1794 or 1795). See *JHW* XVII/3, vii; Brown, *Keyboard Music*, pp. 127–28.

hence difficult to understand today), was perhaps destined for Mrs. Schroeter.[26] (No scheme is perfect. The finale in the otherwise difficult No. 50 in C, which, according to the first edition, was also dedicated to Jansen-Bartolozzi, is more difficult and less unassuming than, but generically similar to, that in No. 51. But it also seems possible that this sonata is a pastiche; the Adagio, at least, originated separately from the rest of the work.)

Thus in many respects the run-on slow movements and finales in Haydn's keyboard works balance, *as a whole*, the opening sonata-form movements. To this extent, the works resemble an expanded two-movement pattern,

$$
\begin{array}{c|cc}
\text{F} & (\text{S}\;\text{------}) & \text{Fn} \\[4pt]
\text{I} & (\text{x}-\text{V}-) & \text{I}
\end{array}
$$

as much as any in three movements. Indeed, two-movement cycles were common throughout his life; nor were they necessarily "easy." This *attacca* pattern is itself a normal type within his keyboard style, not a mere "variant" of the three-movement cyclic form. His keyboard music was inherently supple and flexible, in ways foreign to the quartet and symphony. At the same time it always maintained its generic integrity.

Symphonies and quartets

Proportionally, Haydn composed fewer run-on movement pairs in his symphonies and string quartets than in his keyboard music. This is hardly surprising: from the late 1760s on, these genres had fixed four-movement cyclic patterns and a relatively formal, non-improvisatory style, and (especially symphonies after 1780) they were more likely to be performed at public social functions. Nevertheless, they occasionally exhibit through-composed tendencies, of three types: a loosening of the repetition structure in minuets and trios (discussed in Chapter 5), large compound movements, and actual run-on movement-pairs.

The twelve compound movements and four run-on movement-pairs in Haydn's symphonies and string quartets are listed in Table 6.2. The compound movements occur throughout his career and appear in all the principal non-minuet movement types (opening fast, interior slow, finale); hence despite their relative rarity, they deserve attention as a characteristic aspect of his art. They comprise numerous distinct subtypes, each of which, interestingly, is found in precisely two works that are related in other ways as well. Compound first movements based on an opening Adagio – not a slow introduction – and a very fast section are found in the early Symphonies 15 and 25; sophisticated Allegretto/Allegro movements open the two last quartets in Op. 76 (1797). We find concerto style featuring violin and cello in the slow movements of Symphonies 6 and 7, both from the *Matin–Midi–Soir* trilogy (1761); each is preceded by a long introduction

---

[26] In view of the difficulty and originality of all the works known to have been dedicated to Jansen-Bartolozzi, the traditional view that No. 51 also was destined for her, as if to make up an opus of three works (which these sonatas do not constitute in any case), is probably mistaken. See Feder's tentative suggestion in *JHW* XVIII/3, viii, and Brown's confident one in *Keyboard Music*, p. 122.

Table 6.2. Run-on and compound movements in Haydn symphonies and string quartets

Notes: Slow introductions are not cited with respect to initial fast movements.
In the column "Cyclic pattern," parts of single movements indicated in smaller type are structurally (not necessarily aesthetically) subsidiary to adjacent sections.

Work	Cyclic pattern	Remarks
Symphonies		
6 (D)	F (s–S–s) M Fn	Programmatic ("Le matin") Adagio (concertante violin) at beginning and end; frames main Andante (concertante violin and cello). Both joins end on dominant
7 (C)	F (s–S) M Fn	Programmatic ("Le midi") Adagio: First section in recitative (concertante violin) prepares double-concerto movement (violin/cello; concertante flutes). See pp. 241–42
15 (D)	(S–F–S) M S Fn	See also Chap. 8
25 (C)	(S–F) M Fn	See also Chap. 8
31 (D)	F S M Fn	Extramusical associations. Cf. No. 72. See p. 246
45 (F#)	F S M Fn_1 – Fn_2	See Part I
46 (B)	F S M (Fn–M–Coda)	See also Chap. 8
67 (F)	F S M (Fn–s–Fn)	Finale: ABA: exposition and recapitulation frame slow middle section
72 (D)	F S M Fn	Cf. No. 31
79 (F)	F (S–F) M Fn	Finale: Andante variation, 2/4; Presto coda, 6/8 (no thematic recall) Slow movement: Adagio cantabile – Un poco Allegro
String quartets		
20/2 (C)	F S–M FN	See also Chap. 8
54/2 (C)	F S–M (S–F–S)	See also Chap. 8
71/2 (D)	F S M F	Finale: Allegretto (ABA) – Allegro (A–Coda)
76/4 (Bb)	F S M F	Finale: Allegro ma non troppo – Più Allegro – Più Presto
76/5 (D)	(Mod–F) S M Fn	Opening:
		Allegretto Allegro
		1 || 29 41 49 | 58 || 76–127
		A || A/B C C(A) | A/B(C) || A ABC'
		I || i–$_b$III $_b$VI | $_b$VI–V | I–V || I
76/6 (Eb)	(Mod–F) S M Fn	Opening: Allegretto (theme and Vars 1–3) – Allegro (fugato and Var. 4)

featuring recitative passages for the solo violin. Both concertante four-horn symphonies from the mid-1760s, Nos. 31 and 72, have variation finales which feature numerous players as soloists in turn; each ends with a fast coda in a contrasting meter. Two late quartets, Op. 71 No. 2 (1793) and Op. 76 No. 4 (1797), have finales ending with *stretto* passages. Only the ABA finale of Symphony No. 67 (mid-1770s) and the two-part "slow" movement of No. 79 (*c.* 1782) fail to "pair" in this sense with a comparable movement from a related work. The four works with run-on movements are also paired. Symphony No. 46 is related to the "Farewell," not only by its unique manipulation of cyclic form, but by date (1772), the unusual sharp-side key, and extramusical associations. And two string quartets in C, Op. 20 No. 2 (1772) and Op. 54 No. 2 (1788), each feature a unique, expressive adagio in C minor which is run-on to the ensuing minuet in the major, and an unusual finale. We will examine these three works more closely in Chapter 8.

The compound and run-on movements usually fit into the conventional four-movement cyclic plans (see the second column in Table 6.2); indeed, as suggested above, these patterns determine the individual movement-types, as much as the movements create the pattern. Fast codas in finales, as in Symphonies 31 and 72, and Opp. 71 No. 2 and 76 No. 4, were a convention in their own right. In *Le matin*, we hear the Adagio which follows the first movement as an introduction to the ensuing sonata-form Andante, especially because it returns (varied) at the end, producing an ABA effect which is understandable only in the sense of a single movement. Even the two successive Adagios in *Le midi* function together as a single movement in this sense, notwithstanding their substantial contrast and the length, thematic independence, and firm final cadence of the first one: they follow a complete "first" movement which has come to a formal close, and they precede a minuet and finale which in this respect are entirely regular. Also, the first Adagio is unstable, modulating, in parts recitative-like, in contrast to the following double-concerto movement, which is formally and gesturally conventional and complete in itself. The former is thus typed as an introduction, and the movement-pair resembles a recitative and aria; that is, a single compound movement. In addition, to interpret each movement as a separate, independent entity would be to have five movements in all, including two successive "slow" movements – an unheard-of combination in an eighteenth-century symphony. (We return to *Le midi* in Chapter 7, pp. 238–41.)

Both tempo and form indicate that the Allegretto variations which begin Op. 76 Nos. 5 and 6 cannot be "slow" movements – even before we hear their concluding Allegro sections.[27] The generic point of the latter is rather to make it possible for the second movement to follow immediately as the true slow movement, while still preserving the principle of contrast. (This need presumably reflected in part the triumph, by the 1790s, of the ordering F–S–M–Fn as the only standard one, at the expense of the related pattern F–M–S–Fn.) Similarly, the cyclic position of the odd slow/fast second movement in Symphony No. 79 types it as functionally "slow," despite the fast second

---

[27] Landon (*Haydn*, vol. 4, pp. 304–05) applies the church sonata concept to these works; given the differences between their opening movements and cyclic forms, and those in Haydn's early symphonies with opening Adagio movements, this seems anachronistic.

part and the failure of the initial section to return; the triple meter and other differences in the ensuing minuet preserve the principle of contrast.

Of the two ABA movements, the fast–slow–fast which concludes Symphony No. 67 is unquestionably a single compound movement with the function "finale," despite the extent and independence of its middle Adagio. The latter section is framed by the Allegro di molto on either side, and the first Allegro section is incomplete to boot: it is a full exposition ending in the dominant and is balanced, following the Adagio, by a full recapitulation. (Fast–slow–fast finales were not uncommon; the best known are perhaps in Mozart's piano concertos in E-flat, K. 271 and 482 – another "pair"? These movements also relate to the so-called "da capo overture" form, although both the term – "reprise overture" seems preferable – and the nature of the historical relation are in dispute.[28] There is, however, reason to associate Symphony No. 67 with stage music; see Chapter 7.) A comparison of this finale with the "Farewell" is also decisive: in the latter, the Presto completes a sonata-form design (except for breaking off at the last moment), and the farewell movement, despite beginning and ending in different keys, executes a complete form as well. Neither movement is a frame for or subsidiary to the other. Even the in almost every other respect baffling ABA fourth movement in Op. 54 No. 2 unquestionably carries out the cyclic function "finale" (see Chapter 8). The upshot is that Haydn's only works whose cyclic form remains in doubt are the two early symphonies 15 and 25; we will return to them in Chapter 8 as well.

THEMATICISM

A fundamental aspect of Western art-music of the nineteenth and twentieth centuries (at least until very recently) has been the tendency for various ideas in a composition to be related to a single theme or motive or (in serial music) set of interval relations. Concomitantly, one of the most prominent theoretical traditions in this century is "thematicism" (German *Substanzgemeinschaft*, "commonality of material"); that is, the belief in the importance of thematic relations, and the pursuit of them in analysis.[29] But the status of thematicism in the analysis of eighteenth-century music is uncertain; there have been few substantial contributions, and these tend to lack methodological rigor.

Among thematicist analyses of tonal music, we may distinguish two basic orientations, whose votaries I call "strict constructionists" and "organicists." The former attempt to restrict the class of permissible relations to obvious features on the musical surface, by insisting that they be contextually associated, or "audible," or even "intentional"; and by excluding "coincidental" and "conventional" resemblances (for example, undifferen-

[28] "Da capo overture": LaRue, "Symphony," *The New Grove*, vol. 18, pp. 440–42; Churgin, "Italian Symphonic Background," pp. 331–32 (see the exchange between Churgin and Rosen, pp. 343–44). "Reprise overture": Stephen C. Fisher, "Haydn's Overtures and Their Adaptations as Concert Orchestral Works," Ph.D. diss., University of Pennsylvania, 1985, pp. 40–41, 57–66, 344, 351–53.

[29] An excellent survey of the literature on *Substanzgemeinschaft* up to World War II is Feder's contribution to the symposium "Das Problem der Substanzgemeinschaft in den zyklischen Werken," in *MJb* 1973–74, pp. 117–25; he cites (p. 118) Hans Mersmann as having coined the term. I have taken the English term "thematicism" from Kerman's recent survey in *Contemplating Music*, pp. 64–79.

tiated triadic motives). The relatedness they seek might be called common-sense, or technical, or even "compositional" (in the sense that they imagine the craftsman searching for
derived ideas). Prominent representatives include Tovey, Hans Mersmann, Ludwig Misch,
Karl H. Wörner, LaRue, and Meyer.[30] The organicists, on the other hand, tend to believe
that a single idea (a "germ" or "cell") "generates" the entirety of a work. They therefore
must seek "hidden" relations among musical ideas, probe "beneath the surface," and
pursue derivations among distant and conflated entities as well as local and immediate
ones. The ultimate goal is always to demonstrate "unity," and is in that sense not so
much analytical as theoretical, indeed metaphysical.[31] (Organicist beliefs in the distinction
between [mere] appearance and [higher] reality, and in the existence of unity within or
underlying diversity, derive from Plato and the Neoplatonists, respectively.[32])

The most influential "organic" thematicist has been Schoenberg, with his concepts
of "developing variation" and the *Grundgestalt*, or "basic idea." These concepts were hope-
lessly conflated in his own mind; indeed in his published writings he notoriously failed
either to define them clearly or to produce a sustained analysis of an entire work or
movement in these terms.[33] But it seems permissible to characterize them as dialectically
related aspects of *Substanzgemeinschaft*. Developing variation would then designate
ongoing development on the motivic level, primarily on the surface and involving
contiguous or nearby entities. However, it should not be restricted to or "privilege"
pitch-content (as Schoenberg tended to do), but rather embrace all relevant musical
processes, as they create and alter the identity and relations of foreground entities.
The *Grundgestalt*, on the other hand, is something protean, malleable; it informs all
musical domains, operates at a remove as well as locally, and penetrates into (or wells up
out of) the deepest levels of structure.[34] Neither can be understood without the other:
developing variation ensures cogency and intelligibility to the inexhaustibly various
manifestations of the foreground, while the all-pervasive *Grundgestalt* assures the unity of
the whole. The homology between this Neoplatonist orientation and Schenker's thought
is obvious. ("Thematic transformation" is yet another phenomenon: a variation of an
entire theme or idea, usually in a non-contiguous context, which is immediately apperceptible as a new *Gestalt*.) Schoenberg's best-known followers writing in English have
been Rudolph Réti and Hans Keller, followed at a more skeptical distance by younger
scholars.[35]

[30] Tovey, "Some Aspects of Beethoven's Art Forms," *Essays and Lectures*, pp. 274–80, 296; Meyer, *Explaining Music*,
chap. 4. For the others, see Feder's article cited in the previous note, and below.

[31] See Vernon L. Kliewer, "The Concept of Organic Unity in Music Criticism and Analysis," Ph.D. dissertation, Indiana
University, 1961; Ruth A. Solie, "The Living Work: Organicism and Musical Analysis," *19CMus* 4 (1980–81), 147–56.

[32] These origins of musical organicism are set forth in William Pastille, "*Ursatz*: The Musical Philosophy of Heinrich
Schenker," Ph.D. diss., Cornell University, 1985.

[33] See Dahlhaus, "What Is 'Developing Variation'?" in *Schoenberg and the New Music* (Cambridge, 1987), pp. 128–33.

[34] The best introduction to the *Grundgestalt* is Patricia Carpenter, "*Grundgestalt* as Tonal Function," *MTS* 5 (1983),
15–38, esp. 15–18.

[35] Réti, *Thematic Process*, and *Thematic Patterns in Sonatas of Beethoven* (New York, 1967). Keller, "The Chamber Music,"
in Landon and Donald Mitchell, eds., *The Mozart Companion* (London, 1956), pp. 90–137, and "KV 503: The Unity
of Contrasting Themes and Movements," *MR* 17 (1956), 48–58, 120–29. Recent contributions include the volumes by
Epstein and Frisch. (However, in common with most English-language analysts, they more or less ignore the
metaphysical aspect of Continental thought – represented here by the *Grundgestalt* – and hence offer a sanitized version
of Schoenberg's thinking that is actually closer to strict constructionism.)

The types of relation asserted by thematicists of these various persuasions are legion. A simplified list for pitch-relations alone would include (in order of increasing distance from the model) transposition, octave-displacement of individual notes, similarity of contour, variation in the ordinary sense, fragmentation and "liquidation," variation in the serial sense (inversion, retrograde, retrograde inversion, "interversion" [Réti]), all the way to complex manipulations of a "pitch-cell" (Réti) or a *Grundgestalt*. In the rhythmic domain, we have repetition, strict augmentation and diminution, alteration of the relative lengths of individual notes, subdivision of notes by repetition (or, less commonly, fusion of repeated notes into a longer one), the addition or suppression of upbeats and afterbeats, metrical displacement, change of meter and tempo, and so on. Dynamics, scoring, and phrasing can also create and subvert motives, and hence affect thematic processes. Thematicists assert five basic types of relation (listed in rough order from "strict" to "organic"): *thematische Arbeit*, thematic transformation, developing variation, motivic unity, and generation from a *Grundgestalt* or the equivalent. (We will characterize these types further below.)

With such wildly differing results on the table, it is hardly surprising that the thematicist enterprise has been controversial. Even the more liberal strict constructionists ridicule the tendency towards reductionism and obscurantism on the part of most unity-mongers,[36] who indeed often seem to take literally the Biblical injunction "Seek, and ye shall find." (Although Schenker was as organicist and reductionist as anyone, he was not a thematicist; indeed, in his late *Ursatz* phase he can only be called an anti-thematicist. Nevertheless, he allowed such relationships to slip in through the back door, in the form of his beloved "diminutions" and "hidden repetitions."[37]) But the strict constructionist position is equally suspect: "audibility" is notoriously subjective, "intentionality" usually speculative. As in the analogous case of Schenkerian analysis, almost any proposed relation between distant or different-sounding entities will seem arbitrary and forced to some, but to others will be testimony to the analyst's keen hearing. The issue is not so much whether such relations are "true" or "false" – they are almost always true in some sense – as their relevance to a given analytical intention and, in turn, the relevance of that intention to a given understanding of the work.

Even when one accepts the thematicist agenda in principle, however, a fundamental practical difficulty remains which, so far as I am aware, has never been explicitly acknowledged, let alone seriously studied. Responsible thematicist analysis is almost insuperably difficult. How does one determine, in a given context, which motives are related to or derived from individual prior ones, which are combinations, and which new? When does one look for "hidden" correspondences or "middleground motives," and when does one abstain? These difficulties are by no means restricted to incompatible

---

[36] E.g., Ludwig Misch, *Die Faktoren der Einheit in der Mehrsätzigkeit der Werke Beethovens: Versuch einer Theorie der Einheit des Werkstils* (Munich, 1958); Meyer, *Explaining Music*, pp. 59–79; Meir Wiesel, "The Presence and Evaluation of Thematic Relationship and Thematic Unity," *Israel Studies in Musicology* 1 (1978), 77–91.

[37] Two excellent discussions of these matters are Charles Burkhardt, "Schenker's 'Motivic Parallelisms,'" *JMT* 22 (1978), 145–75; John Rothgeb, "Thematic Content: A Schenkerian View," in David Beach, ed., *Aspects of Schenkerian Theory* (New Haven, 1983), pp. 39–60.

analyses by scholars of different persuasions, nor is it simply a matter of finding the "right" approach once a given context is known, or a specific intent decided. Given the complexity of relations between musical entities, the same person analyzing the same movement for the same purpose will (or at least should) change his mind again and again, regarding both the identity of given motives (and hence their groupings and relations, as well as the "levels" on which they function) and the proper degree of analytical detail, of motivic "density," suitable for a given context. The enterprise is subjective through and through – which is not to say that it should be abandoned.

In the later eighteenth century

The relative paucity of thematicist analyses of eighteenth-century music might at first seem unproblematical. In Haydn's time, contrasting ideas were not understood as constituents of binary and sonata movements; hence the "problem" of their potential relation did not exist, as it has in the nineteenth century and much of the twentieth. Of course, the character of the (single) main theme of a movement was decisive for its rhetoric and affective content. And many Baroque sonatas and suites incorporate related headmotives in different movements,[38] continuing a tradition going back at least to the Renaissance. But the few attempts to find "motivic unity," or even related headmotives, in Bach's prelude and fugue movements have been unconvincing.[39] Attempts to apply thematicist methods to Mozart have also been problematical.[40] The relationships adduced have generally been found fortuitous or conventional; thus Jan LaRue had little difficulty refuting a series of unpersuasive "transformations" proposed by Hans Engel.[41] (But perhaps it is merely that a properly nuanced approach to thematic relations in Mozart has not yet emerged.)

Two exceptions must be acknowledged. First, as always, Beethoven stands on a cusp: although thematic development and a "modern," psychological sense of progression towards climax were essential aspects of his music, he nevertheless always maintained the spirit of Haydn's and Mozart's compositional principles.[42] Hence as an exclusive approach to Beethoven's music, thematicism is bound to fail. This has not dissuaded the organicists! Schoenberg offers a freely developing analysis of various motives in the F Minor String Quartet; according to Patricia Carpenter, he applied his *Grundgestalt* concept to the first movement of the "Appassionata."[43] Réti, as we have seen, devoted an

---

[38] William S. Newman, *The Sonata in the Baroque Era* (Chapel Hill, N.C., 1959), pp. 78–79.

[39] For example, Wilhelm Werker, *Studien über die Symmetrie im Bau der Fugen und die motivische Zusammengehörigkeit der Präludien und Fugen des "Wohltemperierten Klaviers" von Johann Sebastian Bach* (Leipzig, 1922); Johann Nepomuk David, *Das Wohltemperierte Klavier: Der Versuch einer Synopsis* (Göttingen, 1962).

[40] For example, by David, *Die Jupiter-Symphonie: Eine Studie über die thematisch-melodischen Zusammenhänge* (Göttingen, 1953); Réti, *Thematic Process*, chap. 5 (the G-minor Symphony); Keller (as cited above); Karl Marx, *Zur Einheit der zyklischen Form bei Mozart* (Stuttgart, 1971); Christoph Wolff, "Musikalische 'Gedankenfolge' und 'Einheit des Stoffes': Zu Mozarts Klaviersonate in F-Dur (KV 533+494)," in Hermann Danuser et al., eds., *Das musikalische Kunstwerk: Festschrift Carl Dahlhaus* (Laaber, 1988), pp. 441–53.

[41] Engel, "Haydn, Mozart und die Klassik," in *MJb* 1959, pp. 46–79; LaRue, "Significant and Coincidental Resemblance between Classical Themes," *JAMS* 14 (1961), 224–34.

[42] On the latter point, see Rosen, *Classical Style*, chap. 7.

[43] *Style and Idea*, pp. 423–24; on the "Appassionata," see Carpenter, "*Grundgestalt*."

entire volume to *Thematic Patterns in Sonatas of Beethoven*. And many others have joined them to argue for thematic unity of all kinds – even, in the case of the late string quartets, across several independent, gigantic, multimovement compositions.[44] Indeed the strict constructionists' skepticism regarding thematicism in Beethoven is increasingly under attack – despite its having been shared by the two greatest, yet so different, analysts of this century, Tovey and Schenker. This turn must signal a sea-change in our view of Beethoven, which seems to have become, paradoxically, at once less organicist and more thematicist.[45] Be this as it may, eighteenth-century scholars have so far by and large remained in the strict-constructionist camp.

A second exception must be made for *thematische Arbeit*, a central component of the concept "Classical style." This term, coined by Adolf Sandberger around 1900, designates primarily the enrichment of accompanimental parts by the use of significant motives or submotives; secondarily, motivic development in a general sense (in effect, developing variation).[46] But it is not merely a question of enrichment; aesthetic and philosophical issues lie scarcely beneath the surface. Those who see *thematische Arbeit* as an essential constituent of "Classical style" (not merely as a common technique) are animated by a need to understand the elements of a musical work as interrelated, as mutually derived; in short, by the old desire for unity. Central in this context is its supposed historical and aesthetic role as a "synthesis" of homophony and counterpoint, in turn a prerequisite for "Classical style" itself; we return to this topic in the concluding chapter. In any case, *thematische Arbeit* is ordinarily understood as applying only within single movements; it has had little influence on the analysis of multimovement works.

Haydn

The most relevant thematicist approach to Haydn is Schoenberg's concept of "developing variation." Haydn developed musical ideas continually, not to say irrepressibly, in every movement he ever wrote.[47] But this is not merely a matter of themes and motives. Each and every parameter, including abstract ones like pitch-class content, rhythmic profile, and destabilizing intervals, is subject to variation at any time, whether independently or in conjunction with others, whether overtly or in the accompaniment. These processes not only foster Haydn's famous freedom and vitality but, when used in combination, are potentially form-defining as well. Nevertheless, analysts have tended to ignore these

---

[44] A sampling: Harry Goldschmidt, "Motivvariation und Gestaltmetamorphose," in *Festschrift Heinrich Besseler zum sechzigsten Geburtstag* (Leipzig, 1961), pp. 389–409; Deryck Cooke, "The Unity in Beethoven's Late Quartets," *MR* 24 (1963), 30–49; Emil Platen, "Über Bach, Kuhlau und die thematisch-motivische Einheit der letzten Quartette Beethovens," in Sieghard Brandenburg und Helmut Loos, eds., *Beiträge zu Beethovens Kammermusik: Symposion Bonn 1984* (Munich, 1987), pp. 152–64; Christopher Reynolds, "The Representational Impulse in Late Beethoven," *Acta Musicologica* 60 (1988), 43–61, 180–94. Many earlier contributions are discussed in Feder, "Substanzgemeinschaft."

[45] On Tovey in this regard, see Kerman, "Tovey's Beethoven," in Alan Tyson, ed., *Beethoven Studies*, vol. 2 (London, 1977), pp. 184–87.

[46] Sandberger, "Zur Geschichte des Haydnschen Streichquartetts" (1900), in his *Ausgewählte Aufsätze zur Musikgeschichte*, vol. 1 (Munich, 1921), pp. 224–65. The best modern description in English (albeit lacking the term "thematische Arbeit") is found in Rosen, *Classical Style*, pp. 116–19 (quoted p. 354 below).

[47] I have suggested the importance of this tendency in Haydn's earliest music in "Freedom of Form."

aspects of his art – not merely because they are so complex, but because the attitudes required to want to hear them have developed primarily with respect to nineteenth- and twentieth-century music. To be sure, LaRue has recently described what he calls Haydn's "multistage variance."[48] But this turns out to be merely a strict-constructionist neologism for "developing variation" – which concept, in company with almost all eighteenth-century thematicists, he simply ignores.

It is no better with respect to thematic continuity among different movements in works by Haydn. Studies of *thematische Arbeit* and "motivic unity" (the latter have on the whole had little influence) have been restricted to individual movements. The chief exception is merely the borderline case of slow introductions and allegros.[49] Many authorities find motivic connections between headmotives of different movements, endings of movements and beginnings of the next ones, and occasionally between slow introductions and *later* movements.[50] A fertile field, so far little tapped, comprises thematic relations between minuets and trios, especially the end of the minuet and the beginning of the trio. Among other things, this context relates closely to the rhythmic ambiguities of run-on trios and the formal complexities of blurred boundaries (see Chapter 5). Examples of such minuet–trio links in Haydn include the string quartets Op. 9 No. 5 in B-flat, Op. 20 No. 6 in A, and Op. 55 No. 3 in B-flat. (A familiar example in Mozart is the transformation of the pathetic concluding phrase of the minuet of the G-minor String Quintet into the sweetly consoling initial phrase of the trio.)

In general, however, the intermovemental motivic links adduced for Haydn are so elementary and local as to fail to support any claim of unity. But then Schoenberg and his disciples have paid no attention to Haydn; even Keller's recent *The Great Haydn Quartets* – surprisingly, in view of his earlier writings – almost entirely ignores thematicist issues. The only extended *Grundgestalt*-analyses of entire works known to me comprise J. K. Randall's eccentrically serialistic pursuit of "operations" on a "progression of tonicizations" in Op. 76 No. 5, and brief discussions of the "London" Symphony, No. 104, by Friedrich Heller and Ernest F. Livingstone.[51] Heller asserts that "the

[48] "Multistage Variance: Haydn's Legacy to Beethoven," *JM* 1 (1982), 265–74; "A Haydn Specialty: Multistage Variance," in *Haydn Congress Vienna 1982*, pp. 141–46.

[49] *Thematische Arbeit*: Egon Kornauth, "Die thematische Arbeit in Joseph Haydns Streichquartetten seit 1780," Ph.D. diss., University of Vienna, 1915; Therstappen; Wörner, pp. 76–86, 248–49; Bard, *Untersuchungen zur motivischen Arbeit in Haydns sinfonischem Spätwerk* (Kassel, 1982).

Introduction–allegro relations: Rudolf von Tobel, *Die Formenwelt der klassischen Instrumentalmusik* (Bern, 1935), pp. 131–40; Landon, *Symphonies*, pp. 408–10, 572–75; Joel Lazar, "Thematic Unity in the First Movements of Haydn's London Symphonies," M.A. thesis, Harvard University, 1963; Rosen, *Classical Style*, pp. 345–50; Danckwardt, pp. 106–18; Klinkhammer, pp. 43–57; Bard, *Untersuchungen*, pp. 85–89, 117–18, 128–30, 138–47.

Motivic unity: Lazar; Carl Hadley Reed, "Motivic Unity in Selected Keyboard Sonatas and String Quartets of Joseph Haydn," Ph.D. diss., University of Washington, 1966.

[50] Hermann Abert, "Joseph Haydns Klavierwerke," *ZfMw* 2 (1919–20), 558–59, 561, 572–73, and "Joseph Haydns Klaviersonaten," ibid., 3 (1920–21), 538, 539–40, 542; Frits Noske, "Le principe structural génétique dans l'œuvre instrumental de Joseph Haydn," *Revue belge de musicologie* 12 (1958), 35–39; Landon, *Symphonies*, pp. 408–10, 421–22, 572–75; Finscher, *Streichquartett*, vol. 1, pp. 206–07, 216, 227, 233–35, 264–66; Brown, *Keyboard Music*, pp. 291, 320, 340, 359, 363, 373–74.

[51] Randall, "Haydn: String Quartet in D Major, Op. 76, No. 5," *MR* 21 (1960), 94–105; Heller, "Haydns 'Londoner Symphonie', D-Dur: Eine Analyse," in Heller, ed., *Beiträge zur Musikgeschichte des 18. Jahrhunderts* (Eisenstadt, 1971), pp. 182–88; Livingstone, "Unifying Elements in Haydn's Symphony No. 104," in *Haydn-Studies*, pp. 493–96.

introductory bars [mm. 1–3] present the 'germ' [*Kern*] of the material used in the entire symphony." True to his word, he finds fifths and seconds in motives from all four movements, but only in random tonal and formal contexts and on the surface; he thus fails to substantiate his claim for their generative power. Livingstone merely offers two lists, titled "thematic unity" and "structural unity"; but the latter indiscriminately mixes proportional and structural/tonal relationships, and he never describes the relation between his two types of unity.

This leaves Karl Marx's 1976 study of the London symphonies as the only broadly based thematicist analysis of Haydn, and the only one with pretensions to methodological sophistication (particularly when read in conjunction with Feder's afterword).[52] Marx by and large limits himself to small-scale relationships of motive and contour. But occasionally he adopts the organicist viewpoint: the beginning of Symphony No. 96 is the "germ-cell" (*Keimzelle*) for other themes (p. 4), as is that of No. 103 for the entire first movement (p. 6); almost all the main themes in No. 101 are "derived" [*abgeleitet*] from the opening "unison-hexachord" or *Urthema* (p. 5). And he employs an entire battery of such concepts in saying of No. 104 (p. 7) that "it harbors [*birgt*] a wealth [*Fülle*] of relationships which are as fascinating as they are bewildering – bewildering, because there is no basic form [*Urgestalt*] at the beginning as in No. 101. The two-bar motive in the opening Allegro-theme (mm. 19–20) . . . proves to be the germ-cell for various themes in the other movements." This comical "bewilderment" at the absence of a clearly articulated "basic motive" at the beginning betrays the organicist belief that surface thematic relations alone are not sufficient, that only "deeper" processes can generate musical coherence.

Marx's musical examples deal primarily with important themes in the various movements (chiefly, but not exclusively, opening themes). He asserts a wide variety of types of relationship (many of them cited from earlier authors); their degree of persuasiveness runs the gamut from self-evident, through original and insightful, to far-fetched and specious. The persuasive ones fall into two types. (1) A few are "thematic transformations":[53] Symphony No. 91, introduction and minuet, beginnings; No. 86, Allegro spiritoso, mm. 195–96, and Largo, mm. 15–16; No. 93, second themes of first movement, minuet, and finale; No. 99, beginning of introduction and Adagio, second theme; No. 103, introduction fragments in the Allegro. (2) The majority of Marx's examples juxtapose numerous different ideas from different movements – themes, fragments, combined motives, and so forth – related by various factors (pitch succession, rhythm, contour, and so on) applied in an *ad hoc* manner. Some of these are eye-opening: in Nos. 93 and 96 the common descending triadic motives go far beyond mere conventional formulae (even allowing, *pace* LaRue, for the similarities of key and motive between the two works). In No. 101 many of the derivations from the "ascending hexachord" seem persua-

---

[52] "Über thematische Beziehungen in Haydns Londoner Symphonien," *H-S* 4 (1976–80), 1–19; Feder's afterword, pp. 19–20.

[53] Many of Marx's examples have multiple, *unlabeled* subparts, of widely differing character. My characterizations apply *only* to the passages specifically cited.

sive, and everyone agrees on Haydn's impressive motivic development in No. 104.[54]
However, Marx's presentation of these examples harbors an implicit contradiction.
In each group, most of the ideas are "transformations" of each other (prominent,
temporally separate themes, each with its own *Gestalt*), but his (implied) assertions of
relatedness depend instead on "developing variation" (manifold, multivalent relationships
among small motives). Admittedly, he shows classic examples of developing variation in
Nos. 103, first movement, and 104; but only there.

In addition, many of Marx's proposed relationships are dubious on their merits.
His thematic transformations often depend on imprecise or factitious criteria: contour,
vaguely defined; transpositions which alter the tonal function of ostensibly related
pitches; melodic patterns which violate the respective harmonic or rhythmic context,
and deny the very groupings of notes that must be the basis of any actual relationship.
Take for example his comparison of the trio and finale of Symphony No. 91 (shown
here as Example 6.1a). Indeed, both themes open with the same three triad pitches

Example 6.1 Symphony No. 91, trio and finale: motivic relations

(a) Marx

(b)

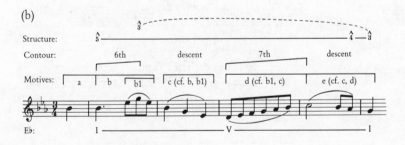

---

[54] Regarding No. 104, in addition to Marx's citations, see Heller and Livingstone (just cited); Wörner, pp. 83–86; Rudolf
Kelterborn, *Zum Beispiel Mozart*, 2 vols. (Kassel, 1981), text-volume, pp. 63–64, example-volume, No. 17.

(to skip over the initial eb² in the trio is legitimate); under favorable circumstances the upward transposition of d¹–c² to d²–c³ could pass muster; and the contours are similar. But the leisurely, upbeat trio-motives are unrecognizable in the hasty, downbeat, duple-meter finale phrase; the latter cadences abruptly onto bb², while the trio bb¹ is a weak-beat passing-note heading down to a cadence on g¹ in m. 47 (Marx in fact suppresses this note). Worst of all, this analysis ignores the shape of the finale theme (see my Example 6.1b). We intuitively grasp m. 2 (*x'*) as a variant of m. 1 (*x*), and especially the rising seventh d²–c³ as a complex, derived submotive (*x1/x2*): diastematically, a variant of the rising sixth bb¹–g² (*x1*); rhythmically, of the two quarter notes immediately preceding (*x2*). On the other hand, m. 2 as a whole varies the *entirety* of m. 1: the interval of a rising sixth occupies the same time-span and metric position (first to third quarter). While my analysis is excessively detailed (for the sake of the argument), it does not falsify the nature of the finale theme. (It would be better to interpret *both* themes as contrasting composings-out of different implications of a *Grundgestalt* – in short, as a multilayered developing variation, governing not only the internal structure of each theme, but also the complex represented by them both.)

The other inadequacy lies in the motivic analyses themselves (see Example 6.2a). That

Example 6.2 Symphony No. 88: motivic relations

(a) Marx

(b)

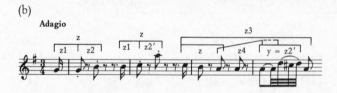

the two versions of motive x are similar, nobody will dispute; but in the absence of other linking events, it seems pointless to emphasize a relationship between a cadential figure in the first theme of a first movement (m. 22) and the initial phrase of the trio, two-and-one-half movements later. The two ys, on the other hand, are close in time (introduction and allegro), but their melodic, rhythmic and harmonic contexts are so different – m. 4 is a cadential afterbeat over a static harmony, m. 21 is moving towards a cadence – that to focus on this similarity for its own sake is merely pedantic. For if we believe in y as a motive at all, we must include its two-note upbeat (shown in my Example 6.2b as $z4$). Indeed, this motive not only adumbrates the headmotive of the Allegro itself (upbeat to 16), but develops out of the initial motive of the entire movement (z). The entire passage sparkles with multiple relationships: the sixteenth-upbeat ($z1$) is different on each occurrence (repetition, step up, step down), and the last of these, unlike the first two, *continues* down by step to a^1; the skip in m. 2 complements that in m. 1 from a third to a sixth; mm. 20–21 relate, in different ways, to mm. 1, 3–4, and 17–18 (as an exercise for the reader, I label an interesting puzzle in m. 20 with a question-mark); and so on indefinitely. This inexhaustible "developing variation" – Schoenberg would have reveled in it – Marx more or less ignores. But the root problem is more fundamental, and endemic among thematicists: in tonal music in sonata style, relations in the "material" domain alone tell us nothing, until they are placed in context: of the structural voice leading, rhythm (on both local and global levels), formal function, and rhetoric. Reductive thematicism is fragmented, sterile; it denies the most basic aspects of musical continuity. As Haydn would have said, "Nothing remains in the heart."

My own thematicist approach to Haydn's music is abundantly illustrated in the last section of Chapter 1, in Chapters 2–3 *passim*, and in Chapter 8. An *ad hoc* pursuit of his fluid, ever-changing complexes of motives seems more enlightening than an ostensibly exhaustive description of every individual motive. The only appropriate response to questions of strict construction vs. organicism, of the proper level of "density," of the derivation vs. independence of motives, is: "It depends"; the only rule is that, other things equal, the more fully one's thematicist results can be integrated into a comprehensive view of the composition – not to be confused with the search for "unity" – the more persuasive they will be. But thematic/motivic relations *are* central in Haydn; they cannot be ignored. To interpret the D-major interlude in the Farewell as an "insubstantial third-related key," without grasping how its motives both are, and are not, "consequences" of earlier ones; to revel in the structural descents from $\hat{5}$ to $\hat{1}$ in F-sharp major at the end, without realizing that mm. 82–85 transmit an extraordinary motivic condensation, or that mm. 103–05 are a thematic recapitulation, is to understand nothing.

But I must be as skeptical regarding my own analysis as anyone else's. In the Farewell Symphony, is m. 29 of the Allegro assai (see Examples 1.6 and 2.3) best understood as "triadic" (a) or as "offbeat" (c), or both? In the Adagio, is the "hybrid" label $a5/c$ (offbeat and triadic) for m. 1 in the bass an appropriate registration of complexity of derivation, or merely an easy way to avoid deciding whether it is better understood as one or the other – or as a new motive? In the farewell movement, does motive *j* (Example 3.8, mm. 1–2) really "sound new" (see p. 96)? If so, should not the listener be encouraged to continue hearing it as such, rather than as, "nevertheless, a compressed repetition of the essential motivic content of the main theme" of the Allegro assai? How incontrovertible is the "extraordinary synthesis" of "all three primary motivic complexes" at the end of the main theme (see p. 98); how "profound" the "motivic synthesis" in the recapitulation of the second theme (Example 3.12, mm. 82–85: p. 104)? Are the structural cadences (Example 3.13, mm. 94–95, 101–02) best understood as motivic variations of *a1* and *a2* from the main theme of the Allegro assai, last heard twenty minutes and four movements earlier, rather than simply as derived from this movement's opening theme? And what of the assertion regarding the main theme of the farewell movement (p. 97), that "these motivic parallels do not attract attention": is it that, since the majority of listeners will not suspect their existence, they are unimportant; or that Haydn is an unusually subtle composer (and the discoverer of these relations an unusually clever musicologist)? Although I pose these questions in the immediate context of the analyses in this volume, they are fundamental. It is a signal weakness of thematicist analysis that it has scarcely acknowledged their existence. But perhaps this is not so surprising: there seem to be no guidelines for answering them, save individual taste and experience.

TONAL ORGANIZATION

Two principles of tonal organization

There are essentially two means by which tonality can organize a multimovement work, and they are analogous to those mentioned earlier in connection with rhetoric: a series of unusual, but related, harmonic events in different movements, or a large-scale progression connecting them. The former entails repetition of a striking modulation, harmonic juxtaposition, tonal ambiguity, or sonority, with sufficiently pointed effect and in sufficiently prominent contexts – such as the beginnings and ends of movements and the joins between major sections within movements – that we associate the passages with each other, and hence interpret them as signs of an organizing relationship. Familiar examples include the Neapolitan (and its consequences) in Beethoven's C-sharp Minor String Quartet, and the submediant C (in conjunction with descending thirds) in Brahms's Fourth Symphony.[55] A modest but telling example in Mozart is found in the A-major concerto K. 488, where F-sharp minor (no less) appears towards the end of the ritornellos of both outer movements (Allegro, mm. 52ff; Allegro assai, mm. 52ff, 230ff, 508ff), and thus subtly extends the aura of the unique Adagio – his only movement in this key – over the entire work. The passages need not all be in the foreground, or of the same type; they may include contiguous sonorities, modulations and tonal juxtapositions (both within and between movements), and tonal spans reaching across an entire work. A classic example is the relationship between the opening interval of

[55] Beethoven: Tovey, "Beethoven's Art Forms." Brahms: Schoenberg, *Style and Idea*, pp. 405–06; Frisch, pp. 142–43; Jonathan Dunsby, *Structural Ambiguity in Brahms* (Ann Arbor, 1981), chap. 4.

Beethoven's E Major Sonata Op. 109, g#¹–b¹, and the structural role of both pitches;[56] to me, the work even seems to close on g#¹ in the background, with no descent to the tonic. (This tendency to relate detail to structure is another manifestation of organicist thinking in composition and analysis.) Our awareness of these tonal relationships often depends on their being associated with other kinds of events: an important theme or motive or a memorable sonority (both are common in Wagner),[57] or a prominent instability or discontinuity (for example, the "excessively" strong dominant E in the first, second, and fourth movements of Beethoven's Seventh Symphony). Especially common is an emphasis, at the end of a movement, on a note or sonority other than the tonic, which then links up by common-tone with a remote key in the next. (This extends a principle already familiar to us from introduction-allegro and minuet-trio relations, to the join between wholly separate movements.)

The other organizing principle is to initiate or imply a large-scale tonal progression at or near the beginning, but to postpone its conclusion until the last movement. Given the *de facto* necessity that an instrumental work had to begin and end in the same key, the only feasible way of doing this was to move from a minor tonic to the parallel major. (The converse move, from major to minor, almost never appears.[58]) The *locus classicus* was Haydn's Chaos–Light sequence at the beginning of *The Creation*, followed by numerous works of Beethoven, such as the *Egmont* Overture and the Fifth and Ninth Symphonies. (The Farewell Symphony had no comparable nineteenth-century influence.) The effect was not easy; even the greatest composers occasionally miscalculated it – to judge from critics' mixed reactions to Mozart's G-minor String Quintet and Beethoven's F-minor String Quartet. The progression from minor to major can be combined with other musical elements, whether motivic continuity (as in Beethoven's Fifth), additional structural tonalities (for example, B-flat within D minor–major in the Ninth), or instability moving to stability (as in the Fifth and the Farewell). Often, several "feints toward" or "promises of" the major precede the actual resolution, increasing the sense of progression towards coherence (see all three works just cited).

A merely conventional use of tonality cannot organize the cycle in this sense; to be effective, it must be unusual, difficult, destabilizing. No eighteenth-century symphony is "unified" merely because all its movements stand in closely-related keys and, internally, modulate to the dominant. (Nor does Haydn's set of lieder Hob. XXVIa: 13–24 constitute a cycle, merely because of his concern for the sequence of keys: "Please tell me," he wrote to his publisher Artaria, "what key the last song you printed is in, and how its text begins, so I can determine the keys of the next ones."[59]) To count, a harmonic progression or juxtaposition must go beyond these conventions, and must do so in a striking, memorable manner.

---

[56] Noted briefly by Schenker; see Nicholas Marston, "Schenker and Forte Reconsidered: Beethoven's Sketches for the Piano Sonata in E, Op. 109," *19CMus* 10 (1986–87), 24–42.

[57] See Robert Bailey on Wagner's "associative" tonality, in "The Structure of the *Ring* and its Evolution," *19CMus* 1 (1977–78), 51 ff.

[58] Tovey, "Haydn's Chamber Music," pp. 63–64.

[59] 3 February 1784; *Briefe*, No. 59, p. 133; Landon, *Haydn*, vol. 2, p. 486.

In Haydn's compositional development, these two types of tonal organization – similar, strikingly unusual harmonic events in different movements and an overall tonal progression – were related. The link seems to have been the minor mode. In major keys, he did not use remote tonal relations between movements until late in his career. On the other hand, as we have seen in Chapter 5, he began to juxtapose remote sonorities *within* single movements in the *major* as early as the "Sturm und Drang." In addition, however, he also began to use remote key relations *between* movements in works in the *minor* mode at the same time. Haydn's increasingly urgent tonal explorations towards the end of his life thus apparently resulted from a combination of these two earlier tendencies. But at the same time the minor mode was the basis of the other possible tonal plan, an overall progression from minor to major. A survey of this complex of topics will also refine our understanding of Haydn's supposed general tendency to end minor-mode works in the major, and the meaning of such works within his style. (In addition, as we have seen, destabilizing progressions of all types are found throughout his *oeuvre*. When combined with these tonal plans, such instability powerfully increases the need for eventual resolution, and hence the potential strength of the overall tonal organization.)

Destabilizing progressions

Strikingly unusual, related tonal events in different movements can have a powerful organizing effect. Op. 50 No. 5 in F begins, like so many Haydn string quartets, with violin(s) alone (compare Opp. 17 No. 4, 33 Nos. 1 and 3, and 64 No. 2, discussed in Chapter 5). When the viola and cello enter in m. 5, they disrupt the all-too-diatonic antecedent phrase with a dissonant, unfathomably low C♯. Once registered in the inner ear, this stroke cannot be forgotten; hence we inevitably relate it to the astonishing low D♭ at the beginning of the trio (see Example 5.5), and to many other things as well. In Symphony No. 103 in E-flat, the "Drum Roll," the recapitulation of the finale is prepared by an unmediated V/vi–I juxtaposition, of the type described at length in Chapter 5. This is not in itself unusual. But when we hear it as a "consequence" of the identical progression at the join between the slow introduction and the Allegro con spirito, and at the tonic restatement of the introduction theme in the middle of the development (m. 111) – aspects of Haydn's most extraordinary through-composed first movement – then the finale retransition acquires a larger structural significance. But these effects appear in earlier works as well, and in other genres. In the sonata Hob. XVI:38 in E-flat, the slow movement and finale are run-on; the slow movement is in the relative minor. This would be entirely unremarkable, were it not that, in the *first* movement, the recapitulation enters as an unmediated succession to the structural cadence of the development – in the relative minor (mm. 48–49). In itself, neither incident would seem more than locally significant; in combination, they create a significant degree of tonal organization.

Symphony No. 50 (1773) includes the most unusual trio, formally, in any Haydn symphony; it is entirely through-composed. (No other pre-London symphony deviates from the conventional two-part construction with both parts repeated – though those in

Nos. 57 and 81 "fool" with our expectations; see p. 158.) Although it is quiet and stands mainly in the subdominant, it begins with a loud transition phrase based on the headmotive of the minuet, which even begins in C, deviating towards F only at the last minute (see Example 6.3). The theme proper (mm. 63–68) is peculiar both melodically (ending an octave below the beginning and leaving e² hanging) and rhythmically (six bars, with an oddly redundant and unstable harmonic rhythm). The peculiarity is not ameliorated by its development through four statements into a double period (mm. 63–86) without so much as a change of scoring (the solo oboe is for example not withheld for the counterstatement, but plays along from the beginning). Hence mm. 63–86 sound like the first part of a regular two-part trio, with its repetition; the modulating continuation (m. 87), like the beginning of the second part. However, this section unexpectedly lands on the dominant of A minor (m. 94), which it prolongs as a pedal; astonishingly, the

Example 6.3 Symphony No. 50: trio

Ex. 6.3 (cont.)

[75-86=63-74]

Ex. 6.3 (*cont.*)

minuet follows directly (with the plaintive solo oboe trio motive – note the dynamics, *pianissimo* – as a bridge, analogous to the minuet headmotive at the beginning). The harmonic progression is our old friend, V/vi–I with common-tone $\hat{3}$. The modulating structure of mm. 87–102 transforms the trio from something merely eccentric into something unique: the entire trio is an unstable (re)transition, leading from the end of the minuet back to its own beginning: I–IV–V/vi–I.

In the finale, the recapitulation is prepared by the identical V/vi–I progression (see Example 6.4b). But a chord-label analysis of this join would completely miss the effect of the unassuming *piano* main theme beginning on E, following the brash high wind dissonances on the same note – the common tone itself. This retransition also relates to earlier surprises in the development: a false recapitulation, on the same progression a fifth lower (V/ii–IV, mm. 81–85), and the same *forte/piano* juxtaposition in the minor dominant (mm. 104–06). (This development section is the only one in Haydn's symphonies through 1774 with two descending major-third progressions of this type.) The two dissonant brass pedals on C and E (mm. 95–104, 120–26) – the sources of these two shocking juxtapositions – also incorporate the basic tonal material: the shy opening sonority of m. 1=127 (Example 6.4a) comprises the same two pitch classes. Although the minuet and finale of Symphony No. 50 are both in the tonic, separated from each other in the usual way, and begin and end without "incident," their common exploitation of the V/vi–I progression, both times in a shocking manner, creates a high level of mutual relatedness.

Even diatonic opening phrases can link one movement to another, if they are sufficiently provocative. The instability at the beginnings of Op. 33 Nos. 1 and 3

Example 6.4 Symphony No. 50, finale: mediant reprise

(a)

Ex. 6.4 (*cont.*)

(b)

(pp. 127–31) derives entirely from registral instability and tonal ambiguity. Nevertheless, these openings seem to relate to the openings of other movements in the same works. In No. 3 in C, all three movements in C open off the tonic: the scherzo like the first movement on I⁶, this time in the lowest register, the finale ambiguously: on the tonic (if the cello is the bass) or a six-four (if the viola is the bass).[60] In No. 1 in B minor, the second, third, and fourth movements all begin with rising triadic motives,[61] with the tonic in the bass on the initial downbeat. This is in itself unremarkable. But what nobody has pointed out is that this extreme tonal stability contrasts with the ambiguous opening movement, that it functions as a *resolution* – a tangible motivic projection of the quartet's underlying idea: the relationship between B and D in B minor. (The key succession of the quartet as a whole, it perhaps goes without saying, is the same as that in the opening movement: B minor enclosing D major.)

Remote tonal relations between movements

Beginning around 1790, and increasingly thereafter, Haydn employed remote key relations between contiguous movements.[62] (This was a general feature in instrumental music of the last decade of the century.) Such relations are found in Symphonies 99, 103, and 104; the string quartets Op. 74 Nos. 1–3, Op. 76 Nos. 5 and 6, and Op. 77 Nos. 1 and 2; the piano sonata Hob. XVI:52 in E-flat; and numerous keyboard trios, including the only example from before the London period, the slow movement of Hob. XV:14 in A-flat (1789–90). Otherwise, the earliest examples (Symphony No. 99 and Op. 74) date from 1793, when Haydn was living in Vienna between the two London sojourns – the very year, we note with interest, of Beethoven's instruction with him in counterpoint and (presumably) free composition.[63] Perhaps it is no coincidence that Beethoven's first works to employ remote keys in this way, the piano trio Op. 1 No. 2 in G and the sonatas Op. 2 No. 3 in C and Op. 7 in E-flat, were completed shortly thereafter. All three place the slow movement on the sharp side – which had also been Haydn's preference in three of the four 1793 works.

Haydn's chromatic juxtapositions between the end of one movement and the beginning of the next are not merely expressive, but structural as well. (By "structural" I mean, again, that they often relate to, and hence seem prepared by, events *within* individual

---

[60] Webster, "The Bass Part," pp. 402–06, 411.

[61] Finscher, *Streichquartett*, vol. 1, p. 265; Landon, *Haydn*, vol. 2, pp. 580–81.

[62] See Louise E. Cuyler, "Tonal Exploitation in the Later Quartets of Haydn," in Landon and Roger E. Chapman, eds., *Studies in Eighteenth-Century Music: A Tribute to Karl Geiringer on his Seventieth Birthday* (New York, 1970), pp. 136–50; Chapman, "Modulation in Haydn's Late Piano Trios in the Light of Schoenberg's Theories," in *Haydn Studies*, pp. 471–75; Haimo, "Remote Keys and Multi-movement Unity: Haydn in the 1790s," *MQ* 74 (1990), 242–68. My discussion differs in its distinction between major and minor tonics, its extension back before 1790, and its focus on through-composition.

[63] On Haydn's teaching of free composition, see Horst Walter, "On Haydn's Pupils," in *Haydn Studies*, p. 63, and "Kalkbrenners Lehrjahre und sein Unterricht bei Haydn," *H-S* 5 (1982–85), 23–41. On the likelihood of this having been the decisive aspect of Haydn's influence on Beethoven, see Douglas Johnson, "1794–1795: Decisive Years in Beethoven's Early Development," in Alan Tyson, ed., *Beethoven Studies*, vol. 3 (Cambridge, 1982), pp. 1–28. On Beethoven's personal relations with Haydn more generally, see Maynard Solomon, *Beethoven* (New York, 1977), chap. 7; Webster, "Falling-out."

preceding movements.) Even in the earliest example, the piano trio Hob. XV:14 in A-flat, the flat submediant key of the Adagio (enharmonically notated as E major/minor) relates to the prominent ♭III (notated as B major/minor) in the development of the first movement. The Adagio, in turn, is run-on to the rondo finale; thus all three movements are bound together, albeit by different methods. Similar principles animate the E-flat sonata Hob. XVI:52 (1794), which (owing to one of Tovey's greatest essays) is the work of Haydn's in which remote-key links are the most familiar. (Characteristically, Schenker's equally substantial essay says nothing about these intermovemental key relations.[64]) In the development of the first movement, an unexpected reprise of the second theme in E major prepares the unprecedented use of the same key as the tonic of the Adagio, whose B section is in the even more remote E minor. The opening motive of the finale (mm. 1, 9) then pointedly reinterprets G and G♯, the thirds of both E triads, as $\hat{3}$ and $\hat{4}$ of the tonic E-flat. Tovey might have added that the E-major event in the first movement is remotely prepared by a half-cadence on V/vi (G), which sounds like an indirect preparation for a *true* reprise – something that had long since become conventional! – and that this V/vi is linked both to the earlier opening of the development in the remote

Example 6.5 String Quartet Op. 77/1: tonal form

[64] Tovey, *Chamber Music*, pp. 93–105; Schenker, "Haydn: Sonata Es-Dur." See also Lawrence K. Moss, "Haydn's Sonata Hob. XVI:52: An Analysis of the First Movement," in *Haydn Studies*, pp. 499, 501; Ratner, *Classic Music*, pp. 415, 418.
[65] Tovey, p. 101; Schenker, p. 11.

C major and, in the development of the finale, to the outcome of the long arpeggio passage *in the tonic* (mm. 164–70). In addition, the B♭♭ in the recapitulation of the "long-note motive" in the first movement (mm. 109–10; cf. mm. 38, 44) is not only a respelling of ♯$\hat{4}$ (as Schenker points out), but an appoggiatura to A♭, and thus also prepares E major at the beginning of the Adagio, only half a minute later: B♭♭–A♭=A–G♯.[65]

Comparable relations among motives, destabilizing pitches, and keys are found in most of Haydn's other works involving remote tonics; for example, the two string quartets in Op. 77 (1799). In No. 1 in G (see Example 6.5), both the Adagio and the trio, exceptionally, are in the same remote key, the flat submediant (E-flat). Both are strongly linked to the tonic: the trio plunges in without a break, as a deceptive resolution of the final cadence of the minuet, and is led back by a retransition to the dominant (once again all modern printed sources are corrupt; see Somfai's facsimile, cited above); the Adagio ends on an important motive (*a*), rising in the violin's lowest register from g to e♭¹, which is followed directly by the minuet, beginning on the same g and rising to d¹. The structural relation between the two keys – ♭VI as a lowered $\hat{6}$ impinging on the dominant – is thus manifested by the foreground motives themselves. With a modicum of analytical zeal, one also notices that the same pitch classes, E♭ and G, are the first two notes of the Adagio; furthermore, its provocative opening phrase, in bare octaves, is bounded (in all senses) by E♭ and D – the very pitch classes whose relation to the overall tonic G is manifested across the break from the Adagio to the minuet. The finale also begins on an exposed, tonally ambiguous unison motive which connects $\hat{6}$ (now major) and $\hat{5}$. The function of $\hat{6}$ is explicitly problematized by the counterstatement (mm. 9ff), where it becomes a rude, unprepared dissonance (over the dominant; that is, $\hat{5}$!); this implied neighbor-relation remains important throughout the finale.

In No. 2 in F, Haydn uses both of the two commonest remote submediant keys, D-flat (♭VI) in the trio, and D (VI♯) in the Andante (see Example 6.6). In the context of F major, both keys can be suggested by C♯, which is at once the leading-tone of D minor (which can become D major) and the enharmonic equivalent of D♭. Haydn plants this pitch at the beginning, in the insistent chromatic d♭¹ in the viola (*sf*, mm. 11, 13). At the end of the Allegro moderato, he harps on a² ($\hat{3}$) in the melody, harmonizing it (among other ways) by V⁶/vi–vi (mm. 165–66, 168–69); that is, with C♯–D in the bass; the strained high octave in all four instruments (m. 165) and the final melodic note further emphasize A. The scherzo (in all but name) emphasizes a² almost as strongly, including the climax of the first phrase (m. 4) and, again, the final sonority – which immediately precedes both the trio and the Andante. Hence it is "consequential" that the trio is in D-flat (with the melody beginning and ending on f¹), and that the Andante is in D major (with the melody beginning and ending on f♯¹). The latter key has been prepared not only by the tonicizations of D minor at the end of the Allegro, but by its common-tone relation to F major, articulated by the continual emphasis on A. It therefore seems like conscious wit when, at the end of the finale, following the structural $\hat{3}$–$\hat{2}$–$\hat{1}$ in mm. 186–87 (and no fewer than six confirmations), Haydn emphasizes a² "one more time" at the final melodic cadence, m. 194.

Example 6.6 String Quartet Op. 77/2: tonal form

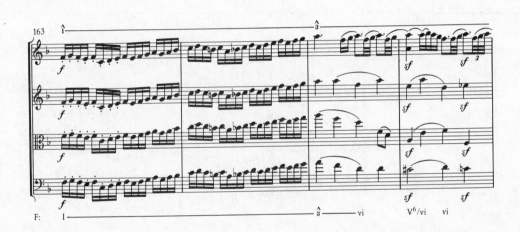

Ex. 6.6 (*cont.*)

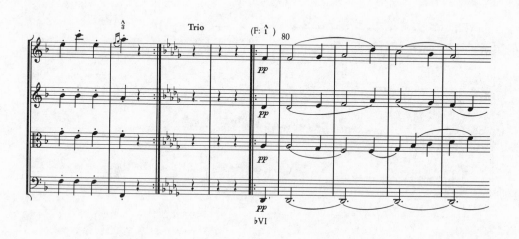

Ex. 6.6 (*cont.*)

Ex. 6.6 (*cont.*)

It is important to remember that what was novel in these late works was only the *particular* technique entailed: remote key relations. The idea of cyclic organization as such, as a general principle of composition, he had exploited throughout his life. We have already seen how he explored remote key relations at structural joins within individual movements from the late 1760s on. Again, as Rosen has shown, he created a sense of process within individual movements by beginning with ambiguous or destabilizing motives or intervals, and then composing out their implications. But Rosen, like Schenker, remains bound to the level of the single movement; as we have seen above and will examine in detail in Chapter 8, however, these principles can carry through the cycle as a whole. It is merely that in the absence of remote keys and run-on movements, they manifest themselves in less spectacularly obvious ways.

The minor mode

We may distinguish three different principles of overall tonal organization in the minor: "normal," "remote," and "monotonal." (All three occur with respect to a major tonic as well.) The first of these is analogous to the usual late eighteenth-century pattern in the major (closely related keys for the slow movement and, optionally, the trio); it is most common in Haydn's earlier music. The "remote" type substitutes an indirectly-related key in one or both of these locations; as with the major, it became normal only in Haydn's late music. Finally, in a "monotonal" work *only* tonic minor and the parallel major appear; this type is found throughout his life when the overall tonic is minor, whereas in the major it disappears about 1780 (except in two-movement and "light" three-movement works). The remote and monotonal types both offered possibilities for meaningful tonal organization – of opposed import, however: chromatically questing in the one case, sternly concentrated in the other.

Juxtapositions of tonic major with mediant and submediant Haydn's sense for remote tonal relations arose in the first instance from a special effect obtainable within the normal plan. A minor-mode tonic relates directly to two different classes of common major keys: the relative major and submediant (III and VI), and the parallel major (I♯). Taken independently, however, these major keys stand in a remote tonal relation to each other. (Theoretically, the analogous possibility exists in a major tonic; Haydn never exploited it.) Such sets of three keys – tonic minor, mediant or submediant, and tonic major – appear in seven minor-mode works from the late 1760s and the 1770s. In the string quartets Opp. 9 No. 4 and 20 No. 3, and the keyboard sonatas 34 and 36, one major key appears in the slow movement, the other in the trio; both are "framed" by the tonic minor, and no remote juxtaposition occurs. But the first movement of Symphony No. 26 in D minor ends in the parallel D major; the slow movement, based on a "lamentation" theme, follows directly in F. (This was Haydn's first use of a remote relation between successive movements; perhaps this tonal innovation was related to the extramusical association.) In Op. 17 No. 4 in C minor, the minuet, unusually, is in the tonic major, the trio in the minor (ordinarily a minor-mode work does the reverse); the slow movement in E-flat then creates the remote key-relation I♯–III. Finally, the Farewell Symphony demonstrates how pervasive and destabilizing this set of tonal relations could become over the span of an entire work (again, with programmatic associations).

From about 1780 on, Haydn often incorporated these remote juxtapositions in minor-mode works (see Table 6.3). The most common plan is that found in Symphony No. 26: the opening movement moves to the tonic major at the end, creating a remote relationship to the ensuing slow movement in III or VI. (Op. 42, like Op. 17 No. 4, creates the same relation between the minuet in second position and the slow movement in third position.) Or the minuet can be in the tonic major following a diatonically related second movement. In Symphony No. 83 and Op. 50 No. 4, the slow movement contrasts with the tonic major on both sides; that in Op. 74 No. 3, with the same disposition, is in an even more distant key (E major in relation to an initial G minor).

Table 6.3. *Haydn minor-mode works with remote juxtapositions between movements*[a]

	Opening	Slow	Minuet and Trio	Finale
Symphonies				
26 (d)[b]	i−I♯	**III**	i−I−i[b]	—[b]
45 (f♯)	i	**III**	I♯−I−I	i−V♯−**III**−I♯
78 (c)	i	**III**	I♯−I−I	i−I
80 (d)	i−I♯	**VI**	i−I−i	I
83 (g)	i−I♯	**VI**	I♯−I−I	I
95 (c)	i−I♯	**III**	i−I−i	I
Quartets				
Op. 17/4 (c)[c]	i	I−i−**I♯c**	**III**[c]	i
Op. 42 (d)[c]	i[d]	I♯−i−**I♯c**	**VI**[c]	i
Op. 50/4 (f♯)	i−I♯	**III**[e]	I♯−I−I	i
Op. 74/3 (g)	i−I♯	**♯VI♯e**	I♯−i−I	i−I
[Op. 103][f]	[i−I♯][f]	**VI**[e]	i−I♯−I	—
Piano trios (Hob. XV)				
19 (g)[g]	i−I♯g	**VI**	—	i−I
23 (d)[g]	i−I♯g	**VI**[e]	—	I♯

[a] The remote juxtapositions are shown in bold-face. I♯ designates raised $\hat{3}$ in minor as well as major.
[b] Order of movements: F−S−M.
[c] Order of movements: F−M−S−F.
[d] Andante ends I♯, but only as *tierce de picardie*.
[e] Interior key within slow movement even more remote.
[f] Assuming unwritten D-minor opening movement which, as usual in flat-side late Haydn, would have ended in the major.
[g] Order of movements: Var.−S−F.

Monotonal works: minor to major A surprising number of Haydn's works, including four-movement symphonies and string quartets, are *monotonal*; that is, every movement has the same tonic, and the only contrast is between major and minor. (I use Schoenberg's term "monotonal" in preference to Keller's "homotonal," but in a different sense from Schoenberg: to denote not the functional relatedness of all keys to a given tonic, but a work in which all the movements are in the tonic major and minor.) The majority of these works are in the major, and use the minor for interior slow movements and (sometimes) trios, apparently without "organizing" intentions or extramusical associations: Symphonies 3, 4, 12, 17, 18, 19, 25, 37 – all early – and 63; Quartets Opp. 17 No. 1, 20 No. 4, 33 No. 6, and 50 No. 6 (the last three all in D). Works with an opening slow movement are also monotonal: Symphonies 5, 11 (trio in IV), 21, 22; Quartet Op. 1 No. 3 (one trio in IV).[66] There are two borderline types. In one, *only* the trio stands outside the tonic (as already noted for Symphony No. 11 and Op. 1 No. 3); since

[66] Op. 9 No. 6, Op. 17 No. 3, and Op. 76 Nos. 5 and 6 do not begin with "slow" movements; see the discussion of genre above.

it remains framed by the minuet, there is no other tonic on the level of the independent movements (except for change of mode in interior slow movements). This is found in Symphonies 33 and 62, and the quartets Opp. 2 No. 4 and 20 No. 3. (The slow movement of No. 62, uniquely, remains in the tonic major; this is Haydn's only major-mode four-movement work with an opening fast movement that exhibits no variation of tonic whatever on the movement-level, not even major vs. minor. On the basis of Haydn's re-use of an overture as its first movement, and other features of style, Landon speculates that it may have been patched together from various pre-existing pieces, including incidental music for stage-plays.[67]) In the other borderline monotonal type, a work begins in the minor but gives no strong impression of through-composition (Symphony No. 34, also opening with a slow movement).

By contrast, most of Haydn's monotonal symphonies and quartets in the minor are so concentrated and intense as to suggest through-compositional intent; this is often confirmed by recurring unusual features. These comprise Symphonies 44, 49, and 52; and Opp. 20 No. 5, 55 No. 2, 64 No. 2, and 76 No. 2. (Several minor-mode works in three movements are also monotonal. Two of the earliest, the string trio Hob. V:3 in B minor and the piano trio XV:f1 in F minor, seem to be Haydn's only multimovement works *entirely* in the minor. They are correspondingly serious in tone.) In addition, a few monotonal works in the major are similarly concentrated: Symphonies 46 (see Chapter 8), 59 (widely suspected of deriving from incidental music), and 70; and two pairs of related quartets – Opp. 20 No. 2 and 54 No. 2 (both in C, with run-on Adagio-minuet pairs and unusual finales; see Chapter 8); and Opp. 17 No. 5 and 33 No. 5 (both in G, with recitative/arioso slow movements in the minor; see Chapter 7). Except for five quartets (Opp. 50 No. 6, 54 No. 2, 55 No. 2, 64 No. 2, 76 No. 2), all of these monotonal works date from 1781 or earlier. On the other hand, monotonal keyboard works appear throughout Haydn's career.

Minor-mode endings These considerations lead to an important general point. The conventional opinion, held even by Tovey, is that Haydn ordinarily ends minor-mode movements and works "cheerfully," in the major.[68] But this view applies only to his works in flat-side minor keys composed after 1780, not to pre-1780 works (in all keys) or works in sharp-side minor keys (in all periods) – not to mention the obvious fact that an ending in the major is scarcely "conventional" for that reason alone; see, for example, the first movement of Symphony No. 80, described in Chapter 5. From the 1750s through the 1770s, most of Haydn's minor-key works remain in the minor through the end (not counting *tièrce de picardie* cadences). Among the twenty-two extant pre-1780 minor-mode works in the main instrumental genres (symphony, string quartet, string trio,[69] baryton trio, keyboard trio, keyboard sonata), only four shift to the major:

---

[67] *Symphonies*, pp. 367–68; *Haydn*, vol. 2, p. 562. Compare Fisher, pp. 176–84, 295–96, 351–53, 382–85, 445–51.

[68] "Haydn's Chamber Music," pp. 60, 63–64. Cf. Fischer, "Entwicklungsgeschichte," p. 70; Geiringer, *Haydn*, pp. 368–69; Alfred Einstein, *Mozart: His Character, His Work* (London, 1945), p. 235.

[69] These important and little-known early works have recently become available in *JHW* XI/1.

Symphony No. 34 in D minor (middle 1760s) and the Farewell, and the sonatas Hob. XVI:47 in E minor (late 1760s?) and 44 in G minor (early 1770s?).[70] All eighteen others end in the minor: Symphonies 26 (D minor), 39 (g), 44 (e), 49 (f), and 52 (c); the string quartets Opp. 9 No. 4 (d), 17 No. 4 (c), and 20 Nos. 3 (g) and 5 (f); the string trio Hob. V:3 (b); the baryton trios Hob. XI:87 (a) and 96 (b); the keyboard trios Hob. XV:1 (g) and f1 (f); and the keyboard sonatas Hob. XVI:20 (c), 32 (b), 34 (e), and 36 (c-sharp). Similarly, only one individual sonata-form movement in the minor, the opening Allegro of Symphony No. 26, reverts to the major for the recapitulation of the second group, as became customary later; and this exception, again, seems to be linked to extramusical associations.

More important than the statistical predominance of these minor-mode endings is their musical weight. Of the eighteen just listed, fifteen maintain the scale and tone of the music that has preceded them: except for the concluding fugue of Op. 20 No. 5 (a formidable movement in every way), all are in sonata form or the equivalent. (The exceptions are minuet finales in the two baryton trios and Symphony No. 26, and the latter is no anticlimax; see pp. 243–44.) This is no accident: aside from the Farewell's, all three finales which do end in the major (cited in the preceding paragraph) are drastically simplified in form and texture. (To be sure, the complex and subtle Tempo di menuetto in Sonata No. 44 includes some "downright solemn thoughts" in the middle, as Tovey said in a different context.[71])

In short, Haydn composed two distinct types of endings in pre-1780 minor-mode works, which we may call "serious" and "galant." (Note the similarity of this distinction to that between the two finale types in keyboard music, described above with respect to run-on movements.) As a compositional principle, a galant ending is neither aesthetically deficient nor stylistically "immature." Unpretentious finales remained popular throughout the century, especially in keyboard music; they are found in several of Haydn's greatest late works, such as the sonatas Hob. XVI:49, 50, and 51, and the piano trios XV:6, 8, 11, 17, and 24. Furthermore, all three "easy" endings (Symphony No. 34 and Sonatas 44 and 47) date from the mid-1760s to c. 1772 – the very years of the "Sturm und Drang." (Even then, the vast majority of Haydn's works were in the major, a point underemphasized by Haydn scholars.) Admittedly, the group with connoisseurs' finales is larger and, on average, more imposing. In this context (like so many others), the Farewell Symphony is unique: it is Haydn's only pre-1780 minor-mode work with a large-scale, serious finale which resolves into the major.

In the second half of the eighteenth century, composers used sharp-side minor keys

[70] XVI:47 is in E minor, not F major as used to be thought; it has the movement-sequence Adagio (minor)–Allegro (major)–Tempo di menuet (major). On its date, see Feder in *JHW* XVIII/1, ix–x; Brown, *Keyboard*, pp. 71–73, 119–20. The earliest documentation for XVI:44 is the first edition (1788), but it is generally believed (on stylistic grounds) to date from the early 1770s.

[71] Tovey, "Haydn's Chamber Music," pp. 63–64. On XVI:44/ii, see Sisman, "Haydn's Variations," Ph.D. diss., Princeton University, 1978, pp. 315–18.

far less than flat-side keys. (This relationship is well known from the perhaps extreme case of Mozart; no tally of this sort has been published regarding Haydn.) Presumably, this reluctance stemmed from both intonational difficulties for string players and the notational difficulties entailed by double sharps, as well as beliefs of the time regarding "key characteristics" (see Chapter 4). Nevertheless, Haydn employed sharp-side minor-mode keys with some frequency: the six genres discussed above include twenty-four works on the flat side, but also thirteen on the sharp side, an "unremarkable" ratio of 2:1. (He used A minor only in baryton works, the trio Hob. XI:87 and the octet X:3 – genres in which, owing to the baryton's limitations, he desperately needed tonal variety.)

Haydn's thirteen minor sharp-side works form an impressive corpus, drawn from all the main genres and all the major periods: Symphony No. 44 (E minor) and the Farewell; the string quartets Opp. 33 No. 1 and 64 No. 2 (both in B minor) and Op. 50 No. 4 (f♯); the early string trio Hob. V:3 (b); the baryton trio Hob. XI:96 (b); the late piano trios XV:12 (e) and 26 (f♯); and the sonatas XVI:32 (b), 34 and 47 (e), and 36 (c♯). Moreover, and again contrary to the received view, Haydn ended sharp-side minor-mode works in the minor throughout his life. The only exceptions (other than the Farewell) are Sonata No. 47 and two late works: the piano trio Hob. XV:12 and Op. 64 No. 2. The remaining nine works close in the minor; furthermore, in all but one of these (Op. 50 No. 4), as well as the three works whose finales turn to the major, the sonata-form first movement likewise remains resolutely in the minor. The endings incorporate both aesthetic stances noted above: a serious finale in sonata form (or the equivalent) in Symphony No. 44, both B-minor string quartets, the string trio, and Sonata No. 32; a minuet or simple rondo in the other two sonatas, the baryton trio, and the piano trio XV:26. The quartet Op. 50 No. 4 is the most serious of all, ending with a fugal finale. (We return to the latter two works at the end of Chapter 8.)

One can see how Tovey came by his prejudice. Haydn's most familiar minor-mode works – late symphonies and quartets – do end in the major. Still, now that we increasingly value Haydn's early and middle periods, and the galant style of many of his keyboard works (including late ones), it is time to accept his minor-mode endings as essential aspects of his art. Their variety of mood is astonishing, ranging from the starkly foreboding (Symphony No. 26) and the tragic (Op. 50 No. 4), through vigorous passion (Symphony No. 44 and many others) and grim humor (Op. 33 No. 1), to pathos, both agitated (Sonata No. 20 in C minor) and melancholy (the F-sharp-minor Piano Trio). Nor is the contrast between minor and major merely a matter of good humor or *tièrce de picardie* convention; it is a fundamental aesthetic stance that could animate an entire multimovement composition. In works like Op. 74 No. 3 (see Chapter 8) and the Farewell Symphony, minor and major interpenetrate to such an extent that, were it not for the overall psychological progression, one might not talk of a "minor key" at all, but simply of "the tonic," understood as both minor and major.[72] Viewed in this light,

---

[72] As Keller suggests with respect to Op. 74 No. 3 (*The Great Haydn Quartets*, p. 205).

Haydn's late tendency to end minor-mode works in the major takes on a wholly different aspect. It is not only the chief technical basis of the remote relations just described, but the chief aesthetic basis of some of his greatest and most profound music, from the Farewell Symphony right through to the "Chaos–Light" sequence in *The Creation*. To describe such an art as merely "cheerful" is as patronizing as to call its creator "Papa Haydn."

EXTRAMUSICAL ASSOCIATIONS

AUSTRIAN INSTRUMENTAL MUSIC IN HAYDN'S TIME

Every late eighteenth-century musician believed in the expressive power of music. To be sure, the nature and effects of such expression were widely disputed, in large part because of changing ideas regarding the traditional aesthetic concepts of imitation and representation, especially as applied to music.[1] These changes were reciprocally linked to the gradually increasing autonomy of instrumental music, which eventually led to the novel Romantic belief in the superiority of what later came to be known as "absolute" instrumental music to all other art.

All this decisively altered the nature of what we today call "program music"; indeed, it effectively created the distinction between it and absolute music.[2] We need only recall the disputes over Haydn's uses of word-painting and other forms of associational representation in *The Creation* and (especially) *The Seasons* (disputes which have not been evaluated by contemporary scholars).[3] Beethoven's famous phrase regarding the Pastoral Symphony, "mehr Ausdruck der Empfindung als Malerey," was doubtless intended not merely as a succinct verbalization of complex aesthetic aims, but as a pre-emptive defense against criticism of his program as excessively literal. His insecurity on this score, and his preference for "feelings" over "pictorialisms," doubtless derived in part from his own ambivalence: although he was often inspired by extramusical associations, he mocked the word-painting in Haydn's late oratorios.[4] (His later tribulations with *Wellington's Victory* demonstrated that these fears were not unfounded.)

The prestige of absolute music still persists, most of all in current attitudes towards the "Classical period." Modern accounts of instrumental program music tend to ignore the late eighteenth century, leaping from earlier in the century (Biber, Kuhnau, Bach's *Capriccio*, Vivaldi's *Seasons*, Couperin's "portraits") directly to the radically different situation represented by the "Pastoral Symphony," and beyond; even C. P. E. Bach's

[1] The literature summarized in this paragraph has been cited in Chapter 5, in the second part of the section "Gesture and Rhetoric," and Chapter 6, at the beginning of the section "Cyclic Form?"

[2] On program music, see Frederick Niecks, *Programme Music* (London, [1906]); Suzanne K. Langer, *Feeling and Form* (New York, 1953), chap. 10; Wiora, pp. 124–56; Dahlhaus, *Esthetics*, chap. 10, and "Thesen über die Programmusik," in Dahlhaus, ed., *Beiträge zur musikalischen Hermeneutik* (Regensburg, 1975), pp. 187–204.

[3] The relevant materials will be found in Landon, *Haydn*, vol. 4, pp. 572–601; vol. 5, pp. 182–99. Compare, recently, Feder, "Die *Jahreszeiten* in der Vertonung von Joseph Haydn," in *Die Vier Jahreszeiten im 18. Jahrhundert* (Heidelberg, 1986), pp. 96–107.

[4] Webster, "Falling-out," pp. 17–18, 24, 27.

Empfindsamkeit is explained away as merely eccentric, or "pre-Classical."[5] At most, they glance at Dittersdorf's symphonies relating to passages from Ovid's *Metamorphoses*, Leopold Mozart's sleigh-ride, and of course the Farewell Symphony (but never taking it "seriously"). (Most of the few recent interpretative essays devoted to music from this period focus not on Haydn or Mozart, but on Beethoven; they tend to claim too much or, more precisely, to advance their claims uncritically.[6]) This inhibition perpetuates a scholarly tradition that goes back at least as far as the rejection of Arnold Schering's (admittedly untenable) programmatic interpretations from the 1930s.[7] In fact, however, Schering contributed the best single survey of Haydn's programmatic symphonies we have, based on extensive knowledge of the thought and music of the period, and marred only by a lack of attention to the distinction between authentic and inauthentic evidence and infelicities in the concrete interpretations.[8] The only noteworthy recent extramusical interpretations of Haydn's (outwardly) absolute instrumental music comprise writings by David P. Schroeder on possible meanings of Haydn's symphonies for contemporary audiences and by Elaine Sisman on possible theatrical origins of certain symphonies (cited below), and Somfai's brilliant, albeit speculative interpretations of the quartets Op. 76 Nos. 2 and 3.[9]

This bias against interpretation is fundamentally mistaken, for the simple reason that the supposed dichotomy between absolute and program music did not exist in the eighteenth century. First, as described in the introduction to Chapter 5, every eighteenth-century work was composed and understood within a context of genre, *Affekt*, "topoi," and rhetoric. And secondly, music having extramusical associations and literary programs was widespread in Haydn's milieu, especially symphonies; the aesthetic normalcy of such music was taken for granted. Widely available modern collections alone, such as *The Symphony 1720–1840*, transmit nearly a hundred works from Austria and Bohemia during the second half of the eighteenth century whose titles (or other features) mark them as extramusical.[10] Composers represented include Franz Joseph Aumann, Franz Anton von Beecke, Dittersdorf, Georg Druschetzky, Joseph and Michael Haydn, Hoffmeister, Leopold Hofmann, Kozeluch, Leopold Mozart, Mysliveček, Wenzel Pichl, Salieri, Süssmayr, Vanhal, Anton and Paul Wranitzky, and Anton Zimmermann. The champions were Dittersdorf, by whom at least nineteen works can be identified, including the twelve symphonies on Ovid's *Metamorphoses*, as well as (I translate the Italian originals) "The struggle of the human passions," "National Symphony according

[5] On Bach's extramusical orientation, see Eugene Helm, "The 'Hamlet' Fantasy and the Literary Element in C. P. E. Bach's Music," *MQ* 58 (1972), 277–96.

[6] For example, Owen Jander, "Beethoven's 'Orpheus in Hades': The *Andante con moto* of the Fourth Concerto," *19CMus* 8 (1984–85), 195–212; Peter Schleuning, "Beethoven in alter Deutung: Der 'neue Weg' mit der 'Sinfonia eroica,'" *AfMw* 44 (1987), 165–94; Reynolds, "The Representational Impulse in Late Beethoven." For a rejoinder to one of these, see Cone, "Beethoven's Orpheus – or Jander's?" *19CMus* 8 (1984–85), 283–86.

[7] *Beethoven und die Dichtung* (Berlin, 1936).

[8] Schering, "Haydns Programmsinfonien."

[9] "'Learned Style' in Two Late String Quartet Movements of Haydn," *SM* 28 (1986), 325–49.

[10] This paragraph is based in part on unpublished research by Richard Will. See also F. E. Kirby, "The Germanic Symphony in the Eighteenth Century: Bridge to the Romantic Era," *JMR* 5 (1984–85), 51–83, §IV. *The Symphony 1720–1840* is edited by Barry S. Brook, 61-vols.-in-60 plus 1 reference vol. (New York, 1979–86).

to the Style of Five Nations," and "The Composers' Delirium"; and Pichl (employed for a time by the Esterházy court), with at least sixteen works, including invocations of mythical gods, a "Sinfonia of Pichl in the style of Dittersdorf, or Symphony in the French Style," and eight (*sic*) symphonies on the muses (the *abbandonata* was Erato, the goddess of love poetry). To judge from the titles, the most common subjects were pastoral themes, military topics, the hunt, imitations of "national" and "ethnic" styles, and literary topics; religious associations seem to have been less common. As we will see, Haydn's own symphonies exploit the same topics. Indeed Paul Wranitzky's "Sinfonia Quodlibet" and Dittersdorf's "Il ridotto" or "le Carneval" were directly influenced by the Farewell Symphony: in the former, the players enter ("tuning up"), and leave, one by one; the latter concludes with a fast 3/8 movement which gradually slows down as the players leave, ending with two solo violins.[11] The following is only a brief survey, focusing on Haydn exclusively; I make no pretense of dealing with eighteenth-century program music as a general topic.

EXTRAMUSICALITY IN HAYDN'S AESTHETICS

Haydn's musical aesthetics agreed with those of his contemporaries: the foundations of music were imitation, expression, and rhetoric. Contrary to received opinion, he was by no means poorly-read or uninterested in literature and aesthetics.[12] He circulated among enlightened-conservative Viennese intellectuals. In addition to German, he read and wrote Latin and Italian fluently and, to a lesser extent, French; in the 1790s he added English. He took some care with the selection of texts for lieder and part-songs; the ones he set boast as high a proportion of worthy authors as those by any other eighteenth-century composer. He composed more than twenty operas (and arranged and conducted hundreds more), as well as incidental music to dramas both comic and serious. His library included not only works on music and many other subjects, but the complete works of Shakespeare in the original (with Johnson's commentary), and of the two great librettist-dramatists of the century, Metastasio and Goldoni, as well as works by Tasso, Pope, Klopstock, Wieland, and Gellert. He also owned books on philosophy and aesthetics, including, no less, Burke's *A Philosophical Inquiry into the Origin of our Ideas of the Sublime and Beautiful* (in English). He owned many engravings after famous paintings, and maintained an interest in architectural style. Although Haydn "was not actually a connoisseur of literature or art, . . . he was [as] interested in [them] as in all aspects of culture and human life"; for him, "belles-lettres meant everything it was possible for them to mean for a cultured middle-class social group in an enlightened age such as his own: a source of pleasure and edification, but most of all a helpmeet in his artistic and musical strivings."[13] Hence it is appropriate to inquire into his musical aesthetics.

[11] Wranitzky: LaRue, "A 'Hail and Farewell' Quodlibet Symphony," *Music and Letters*, 37 (1956), 250–59. Dittersdorf: Krebs 94; printed in *The Symphony 1720–1840*, vol. B1, ed. Badura-Skoda (New York, 1985).

[12] This paragraph is based on Feder, "Mensch und Musiker"; Maria Hörwarthner, "Joseph Haydns Bibliothek – Versuch Erlösers am Kreuze," in Anke Bingmann *et al.*, ed., *Studien zur Instrumentalmusik: Lothar Hoffmann-Erbrecht zum 60. Geburtstag* (Tutzing, 1988), pp. 253–60.

[13] Feder, "Mensch und Musiker," p. 48; Hörwarthner, p. 207.

The following passage from Griesinger transmits Haydn's views on the nature of good music:

[Haydn's] theoretical *raisonnements* were very simple: A piece of music ought to have a fluent melody; coherent ideas; no superfluous ornaments, nothing overdone, no deafening accompaniments; and so forth. But how to satisfy these requirements? That, he admitted, cannot be learned by any rules; it depends entirely on natural talent and the inspiration of inward genius. . . .

Haydn was informed of Albrechtsberger's opinion that all fourths should be banished from strict composition. "What good is that?" answered Haydn. "Art is free, and should not be inhibited by technical rules. The ear must decide – a trained ear, of course, – and I am as competent to make laws in this respect as anyone else. Such affectations are useless; I would rather that somebody tried to compose a really *new* kind of minuet."

Haydn always composed his works at the keyboard. "I sat down, began to fantasize [*phantasiren*]. . . . Once I had seized upon an idea, my whole endeavor was to develop and sustain it in keeping with the rules of the art. . . . This is what [many] younger composers lack: they tack one little idea onto another; they break off when they have scarcely begun. Hence nothing remains in the heart after one has heard it."

He also criticized the fact that now so many musicians compose who have never learned how to sing. "Singing must almost be reckoned one of the lost arts; instead of song, people allow the instruments to dominate."[14]

These precepts, uttered (or at least transmitted) with wonderful economy, are typical of the age. The purpose of a composition is to move the listener. In order to do this, it should have (1) good melodies, free from excessive ornamentation, and discreetly accompanied; (2) a viable basic "idea" – Haydn's term *phantasiren* is usually translated as "improvise," but this suppresses its *compositional* implications;[15] and (3) coherent development of that idea according to the "rules of the art" (understood as principles rather than prescriptions or proscriptions). Violation of these technical principles runs the risk of aesthetic failure: if the development is not logical and consistent, "nothing remains in the heart." The precepts also assume engaged listeners, who to be sure approach a composition with many preconceptions, but are prepared to follow its "argument," in a rhetorical sense. Haydn also agreed with late eighteenth-century musicians and aestheticians that, although musical technique could be taught, the more fundamental qualities of genius, taste, and originality could not be. (Kant's statement to this effect is quoted in the conclusion, p. 357; Griesinger himself, in another passage from the extract just given, cites Kant as authority for the same idea.) Within this context, there is neither an explicit nor an implicit bias against extramusical associations.

Vocal music and music dependent on verbal models

Haydn took the expressive character and extramusical significance of vocal music for granted. (Though self-evident, this point is relevant here, because it will lead directly to instrumental contexts.) Indeed, as implied by the last paragraph in the quoted extract,

---

[14] Griesinger, pp. 113–15 (Gotwals, pp. 60–61).
[15] See Schafer, "Wisely Ordered *Phantasie.*"

he adhered in many respects to the traditional belief in its superiority: "Haydn sometimes said that instead of the many quartets, sonatas, and symphonies, he should have written more vocal music." This conforms to the emphasis in his autobiographical sketch of 1776, where in describing his achievements he cited major vocal works first and by name, but mentioned instrumental music only afterwards and only under the general rubric "chamber style"; and in Gerber's biographical dictionary of 1790, in which, after describing the "sensation" aroused by Haydn's early quartets, he continues, "Meanwhile Haydn's great genius drove him from one stage of perfection to the next, until, around the year 1780, he attained the highest level of excellence and fame *through his church and theater works.*"[16] He even believed in its moral efficacy. In 1801, he replied to a plea for help from a schoolmaster who had been threatened with punishment for a "desecratory" performance of the *Creation* in the local church:

The [story of the] Creation has always been considered the sublimest [*erhabenste*] and the most awe-inspiring image [*Bild*] for mankind. To accompany this great work with appropriate music could certainly have no other result than to heighten these sacred emotions in the listener's heart, and to make him highly receptive to the goodness and omnipotence of the Creator. . . . It is not unlikely that the audience will have been far more touched by my oratorio than by [that cleric's] sermons. . . .[17]

Griesinger – perhaps reflecting this incident – wrote in a similar vein to the publisher Härtel in the same year:

No preacher [*Kanzelredner*] can portray the greatness of the Creator, of His works, and of His beneficence with *such* penetrating power, can *so* fill the soul with gratitude and awe and lift it above the sphere of common sensory nature, as has been achieved by the combined effect of poetry and music in the *Creation* and the *Seasons.*[18]

Apparently, Haydn even harbored feelings of a personal nature about certain numbers from the late oratorios. His one-time pupil Sigismund von Neukomm wrote,

[Haydn] tried to prevent me from expressing, now and then, my admiration at passages in his *Creation* and *Seasons*. For example, regarding the chorus "The Lord is Great" (*Creation*), in my enthusiasm I let fly the outburst, "Papa, you composed that about yourself! [*das haben Sie über sich selbst geschrieben*]" – whereupon he answered quite seriously (though with his customary kindness), "Don't say that! You flatter me – you know I can't stand that." . . . In response to my enthusiastic admiration of the great bass aria (*Seasons*, in "Winter"), "Behold, O weak and foolish man, Behold the picture of thy life," he said, "This aria refers to *me!*" And in this wonderful masterpiece he really did speak entirely from his inmost being [*aus seinem innersten Innern*], so much so that he became seriously ill while composing it, and one must assume that this was the decisive point when the Lord, Who giveth and Who taketh away, closed Haydn's glorious career, and allowed him to see "his life's image and his open grave."[19]

[16] Griesinger, p. 118 (Gotwals, p. 63); the autobiographical passage in *Briefe*, p. 77 (Landon, *Haydn*, vol. 2, pp. 398–99); Gerber, *Lexikon der Tonkünstler*, vol. 1 (Leipzig, 1790), col. 611 (emphasis added).

[17] *Briefe*, p. 373; Landon, *Haydn*, vol. 5, pp. 70–71.

[18] Günter Thomas, "Griesingers Briefe über Haydn," *H-S* 1 (1965–68), 82; Edward Olleson, "Georg August Griesinger's Correspondence with Breitkopf & Härtel," *HYb* 3 (1965), 32 (emphases there); Landon, *Haydn*, vol. 2, p. 91.

[19] Neukomm, as transcribed in Horst Seeger, "Zur musikhistorischen Bedeutung der Haydn-Biographie von Albert Christoph Dies (1810)," *Beiträge zur Musikwissenschaft*, 1/3 (1959), 30.

According to Fredrik Samuel Silverstolpe (who had extensive contact with the composer in 1797, the year of his main work on the *Creation*), Haydn described correspondences between musical "action" and the things represented:

[Haydn] showed me the aria in D [No. 6] from the *Creation*, which was intended to portray the motion of the sea and the rocks rising out of it. "Look–" he said in a joking tone, "see how the notes run up and down like waves? See too there the mountains, which rise out of the depths of the sea? One must enjoy oneself a little after one has been serious a long time." – But when thereafter we came to the clear stream, . . . oh! I was entirely carried away. . . . [He] sang at the piano with a simplicity that went straight to the heart.[20]

Haydn's sense of word-painting still reflects the common eighteenth-century notion of a link between the "motions" (activity) within a composition and the "motions of the soul" it arouses or reflects.[21] For this reason, even though his comments (like so many of those which have survived) come towards the end of his creative life, when he was often depressed about his failing health and his inability to continue composing, there is every reason to suppose that he always harbored similar attitudes regarding the expressivity and moral functions of sacred vocal music.

Haydn's beliefs were equally clear regarding instrumental music intended to function within a larger vocal work, or in conjunction with a program. The "Idea" or "Representation of Chaos" from the *Creation* is only the most familiar example. (The phrase *Vorstellung des Chaos* appears in Van Swieten's handwritten libretto, from which Haydn worked. But the Baron's often pedantically detailed marginal suggestions for musical treatment give here only "Picturesque features [*mahlerische Züge*]";[22] the responsibility for *this* music lay with Haydn alone.) According to Silverstolpe – if (again) the anecdote is not too good to be true – Haydn even addressed the issue of creating expressive value by technical means: "Haydn let me hear the introduction to his oratorio, representing Chaos. 'You have doubtless noticed how I avoided the resolutions which one would have most expected. The reason is that nothing has yet assumed form.'"[23] But this musical Chaos, like that which engendered the world, is to be imagined not as "chaotic," but as paradoxical; it is a product of art and accessible to thought (a point on which, again, Tovey and Schenker agreed).[24] And, again reflecting the nature of the world, it acquires meaning only in conjunction with the act of Creation: the ensuing vocal recitative and choral climax on "Let There Be Light / And There Was Light!" Haydn's Chaos is not merely a programmatic overture, but an intensification of his last symphonic

---

[20] C. G. Stellan-Mörner, "Haydniana aus Schweden um 1800," *H-S* 2 (1969–70), 26; Landon, *Haydn*, vol. 4, p. 256. Silverstolpe was writing long after the event and his anecdotes often seem too good to be true, but factually, at least, his remarks are generally accurate; cf. Mörner, pp. 30–31, note [g].

[21] Neubauer, pp. 157–67; Allanbrook, "Ear-Tickling Nonsense," pp. 6–8.

[22] Horst Walter, "Gottfried van Swietens handschriftliche Textbücher zu 'Schöpfung' und 'Jahreszeiten,'" *H-S* 1 (1965–67), 250. The libretto is published in facsimile in Landon, ed., *The "Creation" and the "Seasons": The Complete Authentic Sources for the Word-Books* (Cardiff, 1985).

[23] Mörner, p. 25; Landon, *Haydn*, vol. 4, pp. 251–52.

[24] *Essays in Musical Analysis*, vol. 5, *Vocal Music* (London, 1937), p. 115; *Das Meisterwerk in der Musik*, 2 (1926), 161.

introductions, from the years just preceding. Like those to the Oxford and the Drum-Roll Symphonies (see pp. 167–73, 330–31), it is the initial member of a larger process whose completion points beyond itself; it begins in dark mystery and ends in triumphant major. The invocation of the sublime has become explicit, and carries through *into* the major, uniting instruments and voices in expressing the idea of the origins of the universe and of history. This invocation still reverberated in the 1830s, as Gustav Schilling testifies:

The concept of the sublime transcends all physical reality. . . . In music too the sublime achieves its most perfect expression and greatest power when it links the finite and phenomenal, so to speak, with the indefinite and divine, thereby clothing the sublime with a miraculous radiance. Thus there is still no music of greater sublimity than the passage, "And There Was Light" which follows "and God said" in Haydn's *Creation*.[25]

In fact, Haydn's inspiration had broad and deep sources in European culture.[26] At the same time, however, it proves how thoroughly instrumental music had triumphed by the end of the century: the one truly unthinkable notion about the music of his "Chaos" would be that it originated as the setting of a verbal text!

Haydn's other prominent example of religious program music, almost as important for his career in the 1780s as *The Creation* in the 1790s, was the *Seven Last Words of the Savior on the Cross* (1786).[27] His description (1787) written to the English publisher Forster, though a sales pitch, leaves no doubt as to his intentions:

An entirely new work, consisting purely of instrumental music. . . . These sonatas are composed on, and appropriate to [*bearbeitet, und angemessen über*], the utterances [*die Wort(e)*] which Christ our Savior spoke on the Cross. . . . Each sonata, that is, each text is expressed [*ausgedr[ü]ckt*] purely by instrumental music, in such a way that it arouses the deepest impressions in the soul of [even] the most naive [*unerfahrenster*] listener. . . .[28]

Griesinger commented later,

It was undoubtedly one of the most difficult [imaginable] tasks to create seven Adagios following one another in a row, without text and freely invented [*ohne untergelegten Text, aus freyer Phantasie*], which would not tire the listener, and would arouse in him all [the] feelings corresponding to each and every utterance of the dying Savior. Indeed Haydn often stated that this work was one of his most successful.[29]

---

[25] "Erhaben," in *Encyclopädie der gesammten musikalischen Wissenschaften, oder Universal Lexikon der Tonkunst*, 7 vols. (Stuttgart, 1834–38), vol. 2, p. 617; tr. le Huray and Day, p. 474.

[26] See, recently, Hans-Jürgen Horn, "Fiat lux: Zum kunsttheoretischen Hintergrund der 'Erschaffung' des Lichtes in Haydns Schöpfung," *H-S* 3 (1973–74), 65–84; A. Peter Brown, "Haydn's Chaos: Genesis and Genre," *MQ* 73/1, 1989, pp. 18–59.

[27] Two recent studies are Theodor Göllner, *"Die Sieben Worte am Kreuz" bei Schütz und Haydn* (Bayerische Akademie der Wissenschaften, Philosophisch-historische Klasse, Abhandlungen, Neue Folge, 93; Munich, 1986); Peter Ackermann, "Struktur, Ausdruck, Programm: Gedanken zu Joseph Haydns Instrumentalmusik über *Die sieben letzten Worte unseres Erlösers am Kreuze*," in Anke Bingmann et al., ed., *Studien zur Instrumentalmusik: Lothar Hoffmann-Erbrecht zum 60. Geburtstag* (Tutzing, 1988), pp. 253–60.

[28] *Briefe*, p. 162; Landon, *Haydn*, vol. 2, p. 691.

[29] Griesinger, p. 33 (Gotwals, p. 21).

Indeed, its reception was not merely positive, but wholeheartedly enthusiastic regarding Haydn's program. For example, an anonymous reviewer wrote in 1788,

Herr Haydn has already given us numerous character-pieces, or, if one prefers, musical depictions; but none before now which could surpass this collection. . . . Even if the author had composed directly out of the soul of the dying Savior, he would scarcely have been able to portray these feelings more truly or solemnly. . . .

May Herr Haydn decide to give us more compositions of this type! The four ages of man: wouldn't that be a fine subject![30]

Haydn signaled the connection between the Biblical texts and his music not only by printing the seven "words" (phrases) at the head of each number, but "underlaying" them in the first violin part of each sonata (see *JHW* IV). (It was thus inaccurate of Haydn to imply, and of Griesinger to write, that Haydn had had no verbal stimuli, and had composed entirely "from free fantasy.") In the 1790s, Joseph Friberth, a Kapellmeister in Passau, arranged the work as a kind of oratorio by adding choral parts; Haydn felt constrained to revise parts of the work in this form (which he did with care), and to publish his version (see *JHW* XXVIII/2). In so doing, he himself authenticated the fusion of the "words" with his music, and thus transformed the implicit meaning of a set of programmatic sonatas with associated texts into an explicitly religious vocal work.

Still another type of instrumental music with extramusical overtones comprises "incidental" and related types of illustrative music intended in the first instance to accompany stage action.[31] Here too, the need to correlate the music with the exigencies of word- and action-painting often led to alterations in the associative *topoi*, specifics of rhythmic activity, sectional lengths, proportions, and so on, compared to what apparently would otherwise have been the case. Haydn often "recycled" such music into independent instrumental works. The most familiar example is Symphony No. 60 in C, known as "Il distratto," based on his incidental music to Jean François Regnard's *Il distrait* as produced at Eszterháza in 1774, and converted into a symphony the same year; the in part bizarre events reflect the contents of the drama.[32] A substantial number of Haydn's symphonies from the middle and late 1770s and early 1780s make use of pre-existing instrumental material from his operas; these certainly include, in addition to No. 60, Nos. 53, 62, 63, 73, and perhaps 59, 64, 65, 67, and others.[33] (No. 59 was called in some eighteenth-century sources "Feuer-Symphonie," apparently in the belief – which remains conjectural – that it accompanied a play titled "Die Feuersbrunst."[34])

[30] *Musikalische Realzeitung für das Jahr 1788*, No. 11 (5 March 1788), pp. 1–2 (signed "Zx").

[31] Sisman, "Haydn's Theater Symphonies," pp. 297–311.

[32] Landon, *Symphonies*, pp. 349–53; Rudolph Angermüller, "Haydns 'Der Zerstreute' in Salzburg (1776)," *H-S* 4 (1976–80), 85–93; Robert A. Green, "'Il Distratto' of Haydn and Regnard: a Re-examination," *HYb* 11 (1980), 183–95; Fisher, "Haydn's Overtures," pp. 181–83, 306–07; Sisman, "Haydn's Theater Symphonies," pp. 311–20.

[33] Fisher, pp. 161–214, 304–67.

[34] See Landon, *Haydn*, vol. 2, pp. 279–80. This play must not be confused with a *Singspiel* of the same name attributed to Haydn, whose authorship (*pace* Landon [*ibid.*, pp. 517–21]) remains very doubtful; see Thomas, "Haydns deutsche Singspiele," *H-S* 6/1 (1986), 53–61.

Instrumental music

But Haydn also believed in the expressiveness and extramusical significance even of instrumental music not dependent on vocal or textual models. (Again, only a brief survey can be given here.) In 1790, he wrote Marianne von Genzinger regarding the sonata Hob. XVI:49 in E-flat, "This sonata . . . is meant forever for your grace alone. . . . The Adagio . . . is very full of meaning [*hat sehr vieles zu bedeuten*], which I will analyze [*zergliedern*] for your grace at [the first] opportunity."[35] He thus not only "tailored" this work for the taste and the performing style of its dedicatee – so much was routine in his day – but endowed it with deep expressive content. A surprising indication, albeit in connection with an uncompleted project, appears in a letter to the Parisian publisher Sieber of August 1789: "Since I am now fully assured that the four symphonies which I am to compose are destined for you, I will do my best. . . . N.B. I would like one of these four symphonies to bear the title 'National'-Symphony."[36] Whatever Haydn had in mind (the symphonies were never composed), it must have incorporated an extramusical or programmatic component. (Bartha surmises that he wanted thereby to take advantage of the "political situation" in France, without inquiring whether it is plausible that any Austrian composer should have had such an intention as early as 1789, or whether it is compatible with Haydn's character. It would not necessarily have been a question of "sympathy for the revolution"; Haydn was fully capable of catering to, if not exploiting, the predilections of his customers, indeed of placing his art in the service of cultural politics, as the example of the "Emperor's Hymn" shows with brutal clarity.)

In London, Haydn noted down the following curious anecdote, relating to the solemn, hymn-like opening theme of the Andante of Symphony No. 75 (it resembles the more familiar Adagio theme from No. 98):

On 26 March [1792], at Mr. Barthelemon's concert, an English clergyman [*Pop*; i.e. "Father"] was present, who, upon hearing the following Andante [Haydn quotes the theme], fell into the most profound melancholy, because he had dreamed about this Andante the night before – as a premonition of his own death. He left the company at once and went to bed.

Today, 25 April, I heard from Mr. Barthelemon that this Protestant clergyman had died.[37]

Haydn tells this story without comment, and apparently without irony (except perhaps for the otherwise superfluous epithet "Protestant"); whether he took it as merely an astonishing coincidence, or as something more nearly supernatural, we cannot say. (The only contemporary commentary is that his biographer Dies has him ask rhetorically, "Is that not a strange [*wunderbar*] occurrence?"[38])

The following anecdote is indisputably linked to a programmatic movement. Until

[35] *Briefe*, p. 240; Landon, *Haydn*, vol. 2, p. 744.

[36] *Briefe*, p. 212; Landon, *Haydn*, vol. 2, p. 726.

[37] *Briefe*, p. 507; Landon, *Haydn*, vol. 3, p. 152; quoted with minor changes by Griesinger, p. 45, and Albert Christoph Dies, *Biographische Nachrichten von Joseph Haydn* (Vienna, 1810), pp. 124–25 (Gotwals, pp. 27, 151).

[38] Dies, pp. 124–25 (Gotwals, p. 151). Landon (*Haydn*, vol. 3, p. 152) asserts that the event made a profound impression on Haydn.

recently, its significance has been disputed, because the story itself is transmitted only by the often unreliable Dies, and because the work had not been identified:

In London [Haydn] was closely acquainted with a German amateur who had attained a skill on the violin bordering on virtuosity, but who had the bad habit of always getting in trouble on the highest notes, [by playing] too close to the bridge. Haydn decided to make an experiment and to see if it would be possible to break the dilettante of his habit and to give him a feel for a solid way of playing.

The dilettante often visited a certain Miss J. [Therese Jansen], who played the piano with great skill, while he usually accompanied. In great secrecy, Haydn composed a sonata for piano with accompaniment for the violin, titled it "Jacob's Dream," and had it delivered to Miss J. under seal and without signature. She did not delay trying out the apparently easy sonata in company with the dilettante. What Haydn had foreseen came to pass. The dilettante constantly got stuck in the highest registers, which were full of passage-work. Now as soon as Miss J. realized that the unknown composer had intended to represent [vorstellen] the ladder to heaven which Jacob saw in his dream, and then noticed how the dilettante was climbing up and down this ladder – now ponderous, insecure, and stumbling, now reeling and frisking – it seemed too funny to her, and she could not suppress her laughter. The dilettante, however, cursed the unknown composer, and angrily asserted that he did not know how to write for the violin.

Not until five or six months later was it discovered that Haydn was the author of the sonata, who then received a present from Miss J. in return.[39]

The piece in question was believed lost, until Alan Tyson identified it as the *second* movement (Allegro) of the piano *trio* (called "Sonata") in E-flat minor Hob. XV:31. This movement was indeed originally a separate composition, with the autograph title "Sonata / Jacob's Dream! by Dr Haydn / 1794."[40] Its violin part is indeed characterized by extensive passages in high registers, in part involving passage-work, and by repeated swoops from high to low and back – features we must now understand as incorporating both comic and pictorial elements.

Finally, one anecdote transmitted by both Griesinger and Dies suggests that Haydn thought of certain instrumental works as programmatic in a larger or more pervasive sense:

[Griesinger:] It would be very interesting to know from what motives [Veranlassungen] Haydn created his compositions, as well as the feelings and ideas [Empfindungen und Ideen] which he had in mind and which he strove to express in musical language. . . . He related . . . that he had often portrayed moral characters/characteristics [moralische Charaktere geschildert habe] in his symphonies. In one of his oldest, which he however was no longer able to identify precisely, "the dominant idea [is] how God speaks to an unrepentant sinner, and pleads with him to reform; but the sinner in his foolishness pays no heed to the exhortations."[41]

[Dies:] I had long intended to ask Haydn to what extent the assertion was true (which I had often heard and also read) that he tried in his instrumental music to treat this or that literary subject [wörtliche Aufgabe] of his own choosing, or whether he had ever intended to portray

---

[39] Dies, pp. 154–55 (Gotwals, pp. 170–71).
[40] *The Times Literary Supplement* No. 3973 (26 May 1978), p. 4, col. 5. Cf. *JHW* XVII/3, viii and 365 (with facsimile).
[41] Griesinger, p. 117 (Gotwals, p. 62).

[*ausdrücken*] a coquette, a prude, or the like in a symphony movement. "Rarely," answered Haydn. "In instrumental music I normally gave entirely free rein to my purely musical imagination [*bloß musikalische Phantasie*]. At this point [1806] only one exception occurs to me: in the Adagio of a symphony I chose the theme of a dialogue between God and a foolish sinner.". . . I asked Haydn to specify the theme of the Adagio for me, . . . but he no longer remembered in what symphony it was found.[42]

The expression "moralische Charaktere" has always been translated "moral characters"; but the alternative "characteristics," implying instead qualities or feelings, seems equally likely. It might even apply to Haydn's example of a dialogue between God and a sinner: rather than having simplistically intended to "portray" such figures, he could well have had in mind the sinner's shifting states of mind – a better subject for musical associations, in both eighteenth-century terms and ours. (The discrepancy as to how frequently Haydn worked on the basis of such associations – Griesinger has him say "often," Dies, "rarely" – may reflect the difference in the terms of the question. Griesinger asked about feelings and ideas, which Haydn would have taken for granted as relevant, but Dies asked about explicitly programmatic subjects, going on to specify coquettes and prudes, as if Haydn had been a kind of Couperin. These discrepancies confirm the newly controversial nature of musical representation at the dawn of "absolute music.")

The identity of Haydn's symphony has been much debated. Hermann Kretschmar's suggestion of the compound slow movement of No. 7, *Le midi*, with "God" as the subject of the recitative, the "sinner" as the cello part in the double-concerto movement, is now ignored by Haydn specialists (though Hartmut Krones has recently revived it).[43] Landon's conjecture, the opening movement of No. 22 in E-flat (1764), has much to recommend it.[44] This work *begins* with an Adagio, substantial and serious; Haydn might have recalled it more readily than most interior slow movements. The movement is extraordinary enough; the grand triadic *fortissimo* motive, thundering darkly in cors anglais and horns, might well be associated with the Lord militant (this is Haydn's only symphony with English horns); it contrasts decisively with both the constant eighth-note bass (the "wandering" sinner?) and the dissonant syncopated material for strings alone (his soul's confusion?). (The movement is not in chorale-prelude form, as Landon suggests, but in sonata form; nor is there reason to suppose that its theme was borrowed from a liturgical melody.) Sisman (pp. 337–38) suggests the "Lamentatione" slow movement of No. 26, with the liturgical tune in longer notes representing God, the curlicues in violins the foolish sinner; the religious associations and serious style of this work are pertinent, and the tune can be heard as "pleading" (Griesinger). (The tentative nature of these suggestions, and the undecidability of the question, demonstrate once again that the effectiveness of program music is dependent on prior knowledge of the requisite association, not primarily on "inherent" qualities of the music.)

---

[42] Dies, p. 131 (Gotwals, p. 155, who however translates the phrase "wörtliche Aufgabe" all too literally as "verbal problem").

[43] Kretschmar, "Die Jugendsinfonien Joseph Haydns," *JbP* 15 (1908), 85–86; Krones, "Rhetorik," p. 122 (without citing Kretschmar).

[44] Landon, *Haydn*, vol. 1, p. 566. (The familiar nickname "The Philosopher" is spurious; see below.)

A constant and intimate symbol of Haydn's religious attitude, finally, was his almost invariable habit of "framing" his musical autographs in prayer: "In nomine Domini" forms an integral part of his title; his postscript reads "Laus Deo." In the literature, this has been interpreted as mere piety. But might he not have also intended these inscriptions as a private expression of his feelings about the experience of creating such music? If so, he must have believed that his audiences would be vouchsafed at least a hint of the same feelings while listening to it.

HAYDN'S EXTRAMUSICAL SYMPHONIES

Types

Even in the absence of documentation, many of Haydn's symphonies – I continue to concentrate on this genre – exhibit programmatic or extramusical associations. A surprisingly efficient approach to this subject is the at first simplistic-appearing phenomenon of their nicknames.[45] ("Absolute" musicians are as uncomfortable with these as with other extramusical phenomena.[46] In a broader sense, however, the dissemination of musical nicknames in the eighteenth and nineteenth centuries would appear to offer a rewarding topic in "reception history"; there is no space to pursue it here.) As in every other aspect of Haydn studies, one must distinguish between authentic and spurious nicknames and, more generally, between contemporary and later ones. At most eight of the thirty-odd common nicknames for Haydn's symphonies are authentic; he himself may not have originated a single one.

He titled the autograph of Symphony No. 7 "Le midi";[47] the companion titles "Le matin" and "Le soir" for Nos. 6 and 8 (whose autographs are lost) also occur in early sources. According to a plausible if somewhat garbled account by Dies, however (he speaks of four times of day and of "quartets"), the idea for this trilogy of 1761 originated with Prince Anton Esterházy.[48]

No. 63 in C ("La roxelane"; late 1770s) is so designated in authentic sets of parts, albeit not by Haydn; it refers to the tune which is the basis of the Allegretto.

The meaning of the phrase "Tempora mutantur" for No. 64 in A (early 1770s) remains unclear, despite the plausible suggestion that it relates to a Latin moralizing poem familiar in Haydn's day ("The times change, and we change with them," etc.). Sisman, taking seriously the undocumented reports that Haydn composed incidental music to *Hamlet*, goes so far as to relate it to Hamlet's famous phrase "The time is out of joint." Indeed, the Largo manipulates musical time (and much else) in strange ways indeed,

---

[45] A useful overview appears in Hoboken, vol. 1, p. 5 (compare the comments on individual works); see also Landon, *Symphonies*, Appendix I; and the work-list by Feder in *The New Grove*, section J.

[46] See, for example, Guido Adler, "Haydn and the Viennese Classical School," *MQ* 18 (1932), 200.

[47] Published in facsimile, ed. Somfai (Budapest, 1972); the title-page is also reproduced in Landon, *Symphonies*, facing p. 241; Landon, *Haydn*, vol. 2, plate 20.

[48] Dies, p. 47 (Gotwals, p. 100).

and the rondo finale is peculiar as well.[49] Unfortunately, the designation itself is not original, appearing only on a later wrapper for the (authentic) parts.[50]

The nickname "Laudon" for No. 69 in C (mid-1770s) – the name of a famous Austrian field-marshal – probably originated with Haydn's publisher Artaria, for a much later keyboard arrangement made by a third party and published with Haydn's approval. But Haydn did (rather cynically) endorse it: "The last or fourth movement . . . is not practicable for the keyboard, nor do I find it necessary to include it; the word 'Laudon' will aid the sale more than any ten finales."[51] (Confusingly, early MS sources to Symphony No. 48, also in C – inappropriately known today as "Maria Theresia" – also transmit the name "Laudon.")

The title "La chasse" appears on the title page of Torricella's first edition (1782) of No. 73 in D, whose finale originated as the "hunting" overture to *La fedeltà premiata* (1780). However, although by rights any Viennese edition of this period should have been authorized, there is no direct evidence of Haydn's participation in this case, and hence his approval of this name remains conjectural.[52] The nickname technically applies only to the finale (as Torricella indicates); in other editions it soon became transferred to the entire work.

Finally, No. 100 was widely known as the "Military" Symphony while Haydn was still in London; he listed it thus in the (lost) fourth London notebook. This title too however seems not to have been original; the autograph and other authentic musical sources do not transmit it.[53]

A few other nicknames that have no known direct relation with Haydn were common during his lifetime in his own milieu and hence, at the least, bear witness to the more or less immediate reception of his music. These include "Lamentation" and/or "Passione" (Symphony No. 26 in D minor), "Alleluia" (No. 30 in C), "Feuer" (No. 59 in A, cited above), and "Surprise" (German "Mit dem Paukenschlag"; No. 94 in G). Although this last was not Haydn's, the anecdotes about drowsy audiences became so widespread that he felt compelled to deny them, asserting (what is more plausible) that the sudden outburst was intended as an especially brilliant effect in his first new symphony of the 1792 season, the one marked by his rivalry with Pleyel.[54] And, of course, "Farewell" (in various languages); as described on pp. 1–2, the nickname itself is not authentic.

No other nicknames for Haydn symphonies circulated in his own milieu[55] – a fact

---

[49] On this work see Jonathan Foster, "The Tempora Mutantur Symphony of Joseph Haydn," *HYb* 9 (1975), 328–29; James Atkins, letter to the editor, ibid., 11 (1980), 196–98; Sisman, "Haydn's Theater Symphonies," pp. 326–31. The ending of the Largo is discussed in Chapter 5 (see Example 5.4).

[50] Remark by Fisher (the editor of this work for *JHW*), annual meeting, American Musicological Society, Baltimore, November 1988.

[51] *Briefe*, p. 127; Landon, *Haydn*, vol. 2, p. 474. On the authorship of the arrangement, see *JHW* I/8, vi–vii and n. 10, and critical report, pp. 24–25.

[52] Larsen, *Die Haydn-Überlieferung* (Copenhagen, 1939), pp. 98, 109–10.

[53] *JHW* I/17, vi and n. 7; Griesinger, p. 53 (Gotwals, p. 31) paraphrases the lost notebook passage.

[54] Griesinger, pp. 55–56 (Gotwals, p. 33); Dies, pp. 94–95 (Gotwals, p. 130). See Landon, *Haydn*, vol. 3, pp. 149–51.

[55] For the dissemination of sources and titles for Symphonies 22, 31, 55, 83, 85, 101, 104, see Hoboken and *JHW* (whose results are incorporated in the following).

it is high time musicologists took seriously. Even though Imbault's first edition of
No. 85 was authorized by Haydn and based on the autograph, its having been dubbed
"La reine [de France]" (owing to its reputation as the favorite of Marie Antoinette)
hardly justifies a critic's prattling of the "elegant, 'queenly' leisure" of the first movement.
Even plausible-sounding names can be spurious: "The Philosopher" (No. 22 in E-flat),
"Hornsignal" (No. 31 in D), "Mourning" (No. 44 in E minor),[56] "Maria Theresia"
(No. 48 in C)[57] and "La passione" (No. 49 in F minor; see Chapter 8). Of these, only
those for Nos. 31 and 49 bear any relation to contemporary programmatic associations, and that mainly by coincidence: like the majority of Haydn symphony nicknames, they became firmly attached to the works they now designate only after his
death. And most of these – Mercury, Imperial, Schoolmaster, Bear, Hen, Queen,
Letter V, Oxford, Miracle, Salomon, Clock, London – are trivial or irrelevant, mere
labels, lacking expressive or associative relevance; if they do relate cogently to the musical
substance, they fasten merely on a detail: Surprise, Drum Roll. (The smaller repertory
of string-quartet nicknames – joke, bird, dream, frog, razor, lark – is no better; only
the "Emperor" and the "Sunrise," Op. 76 Nos. 3 and 4, suggest *topoi* that could have
meant very much to Haydn.) By contrast, almost all the eighteenth-century nicknames
for Haydn symphonies are potentially significant. The age of program music misunder-
stood Haydn's genuinely extramusical muse.

Individual symphonies

As noted above, extramusical associations were common in Austrian-Bohemian symphonies of the middle and late eighteenth centuries. Not surprisingly, the topics of Haydn's
symphonies of this type are the same: time and the seasons, religious observance,
"ethnically" significant melodic materials, the hunt, and associations with the theater or
literary sayings. (All of these concepts are found as explicit *sujets* in Haydn's vocal
music as well.) Most of these works are not programmatic in the nineteenth-century
sense (the "Farewell" is a distinct exception in this respect) and, *pace* Sisman, only a
few can be documented as having originated as incidental music. Rather, the majority
invoke traditional or "characteristic" *topoi* of the types just mentioned, and are to be
understood as associational, rather than as representations of tangible objects or ideas or
the telling of stories.

Haydn's trilogy *Le matin–Le midi–Le soir* (1761) exemplifies a common pair of related
topics for instrumental works: the times of day and the seasons of the year. Both invoke
natural cycles of fundamental importance to human culture, indeed metaphors for

---

[56] According to dubious tradition, Haydn wanted the Adagio of No. 44 performed at his funeral; I know of no evidence
for this, or for its having been performed at his memorial service in Vienna in June 1809. Carl Ferdinand Pohl,
Joseph Haydn, vol. 2 (Leipzig, 1882), p. 265, asserts (without documentation) that it was performed at a memorial
service in *Berlin* in September 1809.

[57] Long believed to have been composed for a festive visit of the Empress to Eszterháza in 1773, No. 48 is now known in
a copy dated 1769. (Current speculation regarding the symphony for 1773 centers on No. 50.)

life itself; and, although the correspondences are not always exact, all of these cycles incorporate the same structural progression:[58]

dawn/morning	midday	afternoon	evening/night
spring	summer	autumn	winter
germination	growth	harvest	decay/dormancy
birth/youth	adulthood	maturity	old age/death

By composing an instrumental cycle of this type, an eighteenth-century composer participated in one of the oldest and most meaningful artistic traditions in his culture: the pastoral, which even after 1800 remained strong enough to sustain one of Beethoven's most "characteristic" works.[59] (There were also many works with generic titles like "Sinfonia pastorale," which may or may not have shared these higher pretensions.) The "seasonal" version of this tradition was exemplified early in the eighteenth century by Vivaldi's famous four concertos from Op. 8; at the turn of the nineteenth, by Van Swieten's and Haydn's own *Seasons* – in a form which explicitly links the seasons and the ages of man, most powerfully in the final part, devoted to winter and death.[60] (Recall Neukomm's quotation of Haydn's self-identification with "Behold, O weak and foolish man," and the hope expressed by the reviewer of the *Seven Words* that Haydn compose the four ages of man; both are quoted above.)

Haydn's title "La tempesta" for the finale of *Le soir* recalls Vivaldi's "La tempesta del mare," used in both Op. 8 No. 5 in E-flat (RV 253) and the flute concerto Op. 10 No. 1 in F (RV 433). (All the Vivaldi works mentioned here were owned by the Esterházy court in 1740,[61] although it is not known if Haydn encountered them.) A work of which he must have been aware was the *Neuer und sehr curios-Musicalischer Instrumental-Calender* by G. J. Werner, his predecessor as Esterházy Kapellmeister (published 1748).[62] It contains twelve suites, one for each month of the year, each consisting of four or five tiny pieces provided with comic or picturesque titles. An unusual feature, at once programmatic and "organizational," is that all twelve minuets are precisely twenty-four bars long, and each one is in two parts, such that the number of measures in the first part corresponds to the number of hours of daylight in that month, and the second part to the length of the night: "January" is 9+15 bars, "February" is 10+14, and so forth. The cycle is full of verbal references to the seasons and depictions of natural events; for example, the opening movement is headed "Cold and Freezing Season at the New Year," and is full of wild, "stormy" modulations.

[58] See Northrop Frye, *Anatomy of Criticism* (Princeton, 1957), pp. 158–62.

[59] Adolf Sandberger, "Zu den geschichtlichen Voraussetzungen der Pastoralsinfonie," in Sandberger, *Ausgewählte Aufsätze zur Musikgeschichte*, vol. 2 (Munich, 1924), pp. 154–200; Kirby, "Beethoven's Pastoral Symphony as a *Sinfonia caracteristica*," MQ 56 (1970), 605–23.

[60] See, recently, Landon, *Haydn*, vol. 5, pp. 93–199; Zeman, "Von der irdischen Glückseligkeit: Gottfried van Swietens *Jahreszeiten*-Libretto – eine Utopie vom natürlichen Leben des Menschen," in *Die Vier Jahreszeiten im 18. Jahrhundert* (Heidelberg, 1986), pp. 108–20; Feder, "Die *Jahreszeiten*," ibid., pp. 96–107. (This volume gives a rich overview of the tradition in all fields.)

[61] János Harich, "Inventare der Esterházy-Hofmusikkapelle in Eisenstadt," HYb 9 (1975), 43, No. 50; 46, No. 20; Landon, *Haydn*, vol. 1, p. 555.

[62] Modern edition in *Das Erbe deutscher Musik*, 31.

Other Austrian–Bohemian composers wrote similar cycles; an example is Mysliveček's set of six symphonies on the months January–June.

But Haydn apparently had more immediate stimuli. As Daniel Heartz has shown, the opening theme of *Le soir* is an extended quotation of a very popular tune from the revival of Gluck's *Le diable à quatre*, premiered in the Vienna Burgtheater in April 1761; the conclusion of the opening movement works in Gluck's ritornello as well.[63] Haydn might well have seen this opera (he apparently left Count Morzin's service in 1760 and was again living in Vienna); so might Prince Anton Esterházy, whose contract of employment with Haydn is indeed dated the following month, 1 May 1761 – and who, according to Dies, himself gave Haydn this subject for a series of instrumental works. They could well have been Haydn's first major productions in his new position. Heartz also states that it is the first sustained use of the "times of day" as a programmatic subject in purely instrumental music – as opposed to the stage, for which he cites a 1756 Viennese program of four ballets, *Le Matin, Le midi, Le soir* – and *Le nuit*. (Contrary to Heartz, and notwithstanding Dies's inaccurate account, there is no evidence that Haydn ever composed a "Night" symphony.)

Many details of Haydn's trilogy relate both to traditional pastoral conventions and to programmatic gestures in his own later music.[64] The lightning stroke in the finale of *Le soir* – the jagged descending flute arpeggio (mm. 14–15, etc.) – recurs almost literally in the *Seasons*, at the precise moment when the almost unbearable gathering tension finally erupts into the summer thunderstorm (transition from No. 18 to No. 19). In 1761, Haydn's lightning was joined by dancing raindrops (opening theme), torrential downpours (mm. 16ff), and perhaps other as yet unidentified meteorological manifestations. (The "Chaos" also includes prominent slow arpeggios, which have been interpreted as ur-meteorological in significance.) The slow introduction to *Le matin* suggests a sunrise (at the very beginning of the cycle, of course). It has counterparts in the explicit sunrise-invocations in both the *Creation* (recitative No. 12) and *Seasons* (No. 12). The *topos* is unmistakable: all three passages are in the key of D and in a slow tempo, ascend by step in long, even notes from *pianissimo* (*piano* in the *Seasons*) to *fortissimo*, and are constructed as single long, undivided phrases. (Perhaps the "Sunrise" string quartet, Op. 76 No. 4, ought therefore to renounce its nickname: it is not in D, its opening theme remains *piano*, its melody is not in long notes, and it is a well-organized sentence, 6+6+10.)

The prominent flute-writing in these symphonies directly signifies the pastoral: see the main themes of both outer movements in *Le matin*; the paired flutes in the double-concerto slow movement of *Le midi*; "La tempesta," as described above; and the concertante flute writing in general. Perhaps the solo bassoon, which appears in the trio of *Le matin* and the Andante of *Le soir*, also had pastoral associations: independent bassoon parts are very unusual in Haydn before the mid-1770s. (But the violone [double-bass]

---

[63] Daniel Heartz, "Haydn und Gluck im Burgtheater um 1760: Der neue krumme Teufel, Le Diable à quatre und die Sinfonie 'Le soir,'" in Mahling and Sigrid Wiesmann, eds., *Bericht über den Internationalen Musikwissenschaftlichen Kongress Bayreuth 1981* (Kassel, 1984), pp. 120–35.
[64] See also Kretschmar, "Jugendsinfonien," pp. 82–87.

solos in all three trios were most likely not meant as grotesquerie, or personifications of "country bumpkins," as one often reads. Modern ears still have no sense of the sound of Haydn's light, five-string instrument, or of the normalcy of his solo violone writing,[65] and the music of these trios is no less finely wrought than the remainder of the works.)

These symphonies also include extramusical associations of other kinds: the "schoolmasterish" do-re-mi counterpoint in the opening and closing Adagio sections of the slow movement of *Le matin*;[66] the *topos* of majesty in the introduction to *Le midi*, unusual by 1761 Austrian standards; and, most impressively, the recitative for solo violin which precedes the double concerto Adagio of the same work. Instrumental recitative is an important feature in the instrumental music of the "Classical" period, largely unexplored except in late Beethoven, except for a single recent article by David Charlton.[67] Admittedly, such passages are often difficult to interpret. There are no theories regarding the construction of recitatives (nor were there then); and in instrumental contexts we tend to be unsure of their expressive import. A chief reason for this is that instrumental recitative employs the language of *recitativo accompagnato* – that is, of *opera seria*, a genre for which musicologists have by and large had an aesthetic blind spot. The recitative in *Le midi* seems to me neither a "parody" (as Landon calls it; and he changes his own mind in mid-paragraph), nor "comic irony, perhaps a domestic quarrel" (Charlton).[68] Rather, it is a straightforward invocation of the pathetic style, with abrupt changes of mood and material, gestures of despair, and an unstable key progression from C minor through G minor to B minor. And what of the ensuing double concerto movement in G, with the accompanying concertante flutes? If it is a version of pastoral, then the recitative can only be associated with Hades; the two movements together will have invoked Haydn's listeners' feelings about moving from a confrontation with death to salvation. (Landon thus has his reasons for the epithet "Elysian," with comparisons to Gluck's *Orfeo*.) Heard in this way, it relates to more general features of Haydn's style: in particular, the sublimity of his late Introduction-Allegro symphony movements, and the Creation of Light itself.

Instrumental recitatives are found elsewhere in Haydn: in a divertimento in C, Hob. II: 17 (*c*. 1761–62?); the London "Concertante" (Hob. I:105) for four soloists and orchestra; and a number of string quartets, including Op. 17 No. 5, Op. 20 No. 2 (see Chapter 8), and Op. 33 No. 5. That in the *Concertante* occurs as an interruption towards the beginning of the finale, before things have really gotten under way. (Such passages were a clearly defined type of finale gesture: see, for example, Mozart's Divertimento in B-flat, K. 287 (271H). This recitative is also often assumed to be parodistic, in part because the finale proper is based on a popular tune which lies very far indeed from "high" style,

---

[65] See Webster, "Violoncello and Double Bass in the Chamber Music of Haydn and his Viennese Contemporaries, 1750–1780," *JAMS* 29 (1976), 413–38; Sara Ann Edgerton, "The Bass Part in Haydn's Early Symphonies: A Documentary and Analytical Study," D.M.A. essay, Cornell University, 1989.

[66] Kretschmar, p. 84; Krones, "Rhetorik," p. 123 and n. 54.

[67] "Instrumental Recitative: A Study in Morphology and Context, 1700–1808," in *Comparative Criticism: A Yearbook*, vol. 4 (Cambridge, 1982), pp. 149–68.

[68] Landon, *Haydn*, vol. 1, p. 557; Charlton, p. 157 (a disappointing conclusion to an otherwise helpful interpretation).

but even this interpretation may be a modern prejudice.) The quartets from Haydn's Op. 17 and Op. 33 are both in G, with slow movements in the tonic minor. The former, Adagio, is explicitly cast as a recitative/scena (see Charlton, pp. 162–65). But the latter's associations with drama and the stage are equally clear: it is marked "Largo e cantabile" and is constructed as an arioso for the first violin, whose melodic phrases are punctuated by an ominous unison rhythmic figure.

Perhaps other unusual features in Haydn's trilogy had extramusical associations which we do not recognize. Almost begging for interpretation is the startling, unprepared deceptive cadence onto E-flat late in the opening movement of *Le soir* (m. 206) – the earliest example I know among dozens of similar surprises in this key and context during the next half-century. The odd dotted-note interjections in the Andante (mm. 4–5, etc.) also suggest an extramusical association. For that matter, the extraordinary concertante scoring of all three works – usually taken (reasonably enough) as Haydn's way of "introducing" himself to his many virtuosos, and the newly hired among them to their patron, and (more speculatively) as a reflection of Prince Anton's supposedly Baroque and Italian taste – could have had its programmatic side as well. At the least, the rhetorical immediacy required for Haydn's many extramusical ideas will have been more easily obtained through prominent soloistic writing than with the compact orchestra of his pre-Esterházy symphonies.

Finally – in Rosen's brilliant interpretation – Haydn's late symphonies also invoke pastoral ideals, but indirectly, by "purely musical" means (*Classical Style*, pp. 162–63):

> The symphonies of Haydn are heroic pastoral, . . . the greatest examples of their kind. . . . Their direct reference to rustic nature is accompanied by an art learned almost to the point of pedantry. . . . The pretension of Haydn's symphonies to a simplicity that appears to come from Nature itself is no mask but the true claim of a style whose command over the whole range of technique is so great that it can ingenuously afford to disdain the outward appearance of high art. Pastoral is generally ironic . . . but Haydn's pastoral style is more generous: it is the true heroic pastoral that cheerfully lays claim to the sublime, without yielding any of the innocence and simplicity won by art.

If this be accepted, a link is forged between Haydn's earliest Esterházy symphonies and his last London productions – a link more directly intelligible on the level of extramusical association than on any other.

Religious associations are present in numerous Haydn symphonies. (He employed these more often than has so far been demonstrated for the Austrian repertory as a whole. But it seems likely that the corpus of *identified* programmatic symphonies is skewed towards the secular and the picturesque; these works are more easily located today, by titles on sources and the like. Indeed, many of Haydn's religious associations have only recently been recognized; a systematic search might well produce similar results for his contemporaries.) No. 30 in C, "Alleluia" (1765), and No. 26 in D minor, "La passione" or "Lamentatione" (late 1760s), are unmistakably identified as religious by his use of pre-existing liturgical melodies. Both works are in the (by then) unusual form of three movements with a concluding minuet. (No. 25, described in Chapter 8, is also in three movements, with a "churchy" opening Adagio section and a minuet in the middle. But it would go too far to suggest a direct correlation between this cyclic form and religious import. Symphonies 9 and 18, which have no known religious associations, are also three-movement symphonies with concluding minuets; No. 9, it is speculated, may even have originated as an overture.)

In No. 30, the borrowed melody is an Alleluia for Easter Sunday.[69] It appears as the framework for the main theme in the first movement (but only in the second violins!), in the second group its initial phrase becomes the chief motive, and in the development its initial motive is split off to become the bass of a prominent sequence. In addition, the minuet quotes from a complex of widely disseminated melodies in seventeenth- and eighteenth-century Austria–Hungary, some of which had religious texts.[70] The style of the symphony is not inherently "religious" (at least not in any way that is intelligible today). But it was characteristic of mid-century Austria to wed such non-liturgical religious texts to popular melodies, in both instrumental and vocal contexts: one need only think of Haydn's own "Pastorellas," the Cantilena pro Adventu in D (Hob. XXIIId: 3) and "Ei, wer hat ihm das Ding gedenkt" (XXIIId:G1).[71]

The slightly later No. 26, also an Easter work, is by contrast serious throughout, in Haydn's best early "Sturm und Drang" style.[72] The opening Allegro and the Adagio both utilize material from traditional Austrian musical dramatizations of the Passion. The main idea of the latter movement, in fact, includes as its second phrase the same motive that begins the Trio of the Farewell Symphony; Haydn also employed it elsewhere, and many of his contemporaries used it as well. But the concluding minuet has posed a problem; Landon, for example, following excellent descriptions of the first two movements, dismisses it as a "whimsical anticlimax." This not only anachronistically assumes that finales must be culminations, but abandons any pretense of explaining its programmatic function. In fact, however, this austerely concentrated movement is in many ways the most intense in the symphony. (Recall as well that, as described in Chapter 5, in keyboard music Haydn associated serious endings with the minuet form throughout his life.) The interlocking rhythmic motives, the offbeat accompaniment, the Neapolitan in mm. 3–4, and the ambiguous phrase rhythm leading to the dominant arrival in the fifth bar, all create an oppressive mood. The unstable opening on a first-inversion triad is structural: no root-position tonic appears anywhere until the recapitulation (mm. 32–33). And even the latter event is destabilized: although the melodic reprise, the horn pedal, and the phrase rhythm imply that m. 32 is the final bar of the dominant pedal and m. 33 the reprise, the lower strings astonishingly break in "prematurely" in m. 32, *forte*, with the descending-fifth motive of the theme – itself a reprise. Hence, despite the perfect

[69] Landon, *Symphonies*, pp. 260–63; *Haydn*, vol. 1, pp. 569–70.

[70] Stephen Cushman, "Sources of Haydn's Melodic Material," in *Haydn Studies*, pp. 377–80, esp. ex. 24.

[71] Irmgard Becker-Glauch, "Haydns Cantilena pro adventu in D," *H-S* 1 (1965–67), 277–81; "Neue Forschungen zu Haydns Kirchenmusik," *H-S* 2 (1969–70), 194–99.

[72] Landon, *Symphonies*, pp. 285–93; *Haydn*, vol. 2, pp. 291–95.

cadence (which finally grounds the unstable opening harmony), the reprise remains divided between bass and melody, between mm. 32 and 33. And this disjunction now generates a remarkable rising canon built on that falling fifth, which dominates the recapitulation. (Landon hears the canon in relation to Mozart's Adagio and Fugue in C minor; I would add that the abrupt pause on a *forte* augmented sixth chord (mm. 41–42), just before the quiet final cadences, resembles the main ritornello cadence of the younger master's Piano Concerto, K. 466, mm. 67–71 – in the same key.) Even more clearly than in the minuet of the Farewell Symphony, the background progression is thus i⁶–V–i, not i–V–i; the only root-position tonic closure comes at the *piano/pianissimo* cadences in the final six bars. Although it would be witless to attempt to divine how an eighteenth-century listener might have understood the particulars of this minuet in terms of the Passion, there can be no doubt that it is more than earnest enough to serve the purpose, and to conclude this remarkable symphony.

Other Haydn symphonies with documentable religious associations are not known. (As noted above, No. 49 is known today as "La passione" by mistake, and the connection of No. 22 with "God and the sinner" remains speculative. One must also guard against the supposition that Haydn's symphonies with opening slow movements were necessarily performed in or associated with the church, or for that matter that instrumental music performed in church necessarily had "intrinsic" religious content.[73]) A famous late symphony, for example, is a borderline case: in No. 103, the first few notes of the ominous unaccompanied bass melody resemble the famous "Dies irae" plainchant. It is so exposed, so prominently set up by the introductory drum roll, and so important throughout the movement in unprecedented ways, that it would scarcely be surprising to find in it programmatic significance as well. Yet even David P. Schroeder, who argues for Haydn's deliberate infusion of "enlightened" moral content into his London symphonies, says of this theme nothing more specific than that it participates in a "fusion of opposing ideas."[74] In view of the somewhat subterranean nature of the melodies in Nos. 26 and 30, and the latter's outwardly "unreligious" style, as well as Haydn's stories of "moral characters" and his lifelong faith, it seems likely that there were other religious symphonies, whose associations (or hidden borrowings) have not yet been identified.

The pre-existing melodies in Haydn's religious symphonies link them to another pervasive aspect of his art (and that of his contemporaries): the use or adaptation of "folk" melodies. Although Haydn's (and others') specific intentions in this respect usually remain unclear, there seems little question that such melodies must have had some kind of extramusical significance.[75] Many of them are the pert, popular tunes used as the main

[73] See Neal Zaslaw, "Mozart, Haydn, and the *Sinfonia da Chiesa*," *JM* 1 (1982), 95–124.

[74] *Haydn and the Enlightenment: The Late Symphonies and their Audience* (Oxford, 1990), pp. 190–94; compare his "Audience Reception and Haydn's London Symphonies," *International Review of the Aesthetics and Sociology of Music*, 16 (1985), 71–72; "Melodic Source Material and Haydn's Creative Process," *MQ* 68 (1982), 496–515.

[75] See Landon, *Symphonies*, pp. 179, 254, 264–66, 278, 350–51, 357, 566–59 (with further references); Walter Deutsch, "Volkslied und Geniemusik: Ein Beitrag zur Darstellung ihrer Beziehungen im Werke J. Haydns," *Jahrbuch des österreichischen Volksliedwerkes*, 8 (1959), 1–9; Bartha, "Volkstanz-Stilisierung in Joseph Haydns Finale-Themen," in Ludwig Finscher and Christoph-Hellmut Mahling, eds., *Festschrift für Walter Wiora zum 30. Dezember 1966* (Kassel,

themes of variation movements, trios, and finales, such as "La roxelane" (Symphony No. 63); others invoke Balkan, Hungarian, Croatian, and other "exotic" cultures. (Prince Esterházy – an ethnic Hungarian – encouraged "folk" culture; he must have tolerated, and might have stimulated, Haydn's use of such materials in his art music. Several baryton works composed expressly for him include such materials.[76]) Haydn used most of these tunes only once each; in these cases, they may have had no associations more specific than the effect of local color. Even so, it seems likely that such quotations and thematic references were a central part of eighteenth-century listeners' understanding.[77] Schroeder suggests that Haydn may have intended the special ethos suggested by such adapted melodies to form part of what one might call the "psychological material" of a given work, to be developed along with other, contrasting ideas (analogous to the "purely musical" development of contrasting themes).[78] Especially when he repeatedly used a particular tune or invoked a particular *topos*, he probably intended it to be understood in some particular extramusical sense.

The most prominent example of such a tune is the so-called "Night Watchman's Song," which was widely disseminated in Central Europe and the Balkans from the sixteenth through the eighteenth centuries.[79] Among other contexts, it was commonly employed in popular "Pastorellas" (in effect, religious *Singspiele*), at the moment in the action when a night watchman announces the hour of midnight on Christmas Eve, preparatory to the arrival of the shepherds to worship the Infant Christ. The religious texts in question further associate this event with the idea of dawn. The melody thus "condenses" two powerful extramusical associations – the natural rhythm of night yielding to day and the Christmas story – into a single *Gestalt*. (Dawn itself is of course a primary symbol of Advent.) Haydn quoted or adapted this melody at least six times from the 1750s through the 1770s, in works from various genres and in various musical contexts: Symphony No. 60 ("Il distratto"), two divertimenti (Hob. II:17 and 21), two baryton works (the trio XI:35 and the cassation XII:19 No. 2), and the piano sonata in C-sharp minor XVI:36; and he returned to it towards the end of his life, in the vocal canon "Wunsch" (XXVIIb:43). In at least three cases, each of quite different import, extramusical references are clearly entailed: comically in "Il distratto," as part of a pastorella-imitation in the baryton trio, serious and moralizing in "Wunsch." The text of this canon reads, "Langweiliger Besuch macht Zeit und Zimmer enger; / O Himmel, schütze mich vor jedem Müßiggänger!" (Boring visits waste my time and make my room feel cramped; / O Heaven, protect me from all idlers!); it is in the minor, with striking augmented sixth and dominant ninth chords, which emerge only gradually,

1967), pp. 375–84; Cushman, "Joseph Haydn's Melodic Materials: An Exploratory Introduction to the Primary and Secondary Sources Together with an Analytical Catalogue and Table of Proposed Melodic Correspondence and/or Variance," Ph.D. diss., Boston University, 1973.

[76] Bence Szabolcsi, "Joseph Haydn und die ungarische Musik," *Beiträge zur Musikwissenschaft*, 1/2 (1959), 62–73.

[77] Helmut Rösing, "Gedanken zum 'Musikalischen Hören,'" *Mf* 27 (1974), 213–16.

[78] *Haydn and the Enlightenment*, chap. 11.

[79] Geoffrey Chew, "The Night-Watchman's Song Quoted by Haydn and its Implications," *H-S* 3 (1973–74), 106–24; the following paragraph is based primarily on this excellent study.

as the successive voices enter. Presumably Haydn had comparable intentions in his other quotations of the theme as well.

A related programmatic impulse, which did not necessarily entail actual or pretended melodic borrowings, was the invocation of "national styles." As we have seen, this was one of the most common *topoi* in Austrian symphonies of the time, and in 1789 Haydn himself offered a "National Symphony" to a French publisher. In his surviving works, a deliberate invocation of "ethnic" moods is found primarily in two contexts: "Turkish" elements in operas, and Balkan/Hungarian style in instrumental music. The two most prominent examples of the latter (among dozens) are the famous "Gypsy rondo" from the Piano Trio Hob. XV:25, composed for England, where the exotic style will perhaps have needed no justification beyond that of an attention-getter; and the extraordinary slow movement of the String Quartet Op. 54 No. 2 (discussed in Chapter 8).

Another common type of programmatic reference in eighteenth-century instrumental music is the *chasse*.[80] Like the other topics under discussion here, it appealed to Haydn throughout his life: from symphonies of the early 1760s, through Symphony No. 73 (see above), all the way to one of the most astonishingly original productions of his astonishingly original old age, the hunting chorus from "Autumn" in the *Seasons*. There, as Heartz has shown, Haydn and van Swieten incorporated an entire panoply of traditional hunting calls.[81]

The "Hornsignal" Symphony (No. 31, 1765) has recently been shown by Horst Walter to be based on two familiar *topoi*: a military courier's flourish and a posthorn signal.[82] Like the similar but probably slightly earlier Symphony No. 72, it includes four concertante horns, which are prominent throughout. Thus they announce the two borrowed themes in sequence at the very beginning of the work (courier, mm. 1–8; posthorn, mm. 9–15); so prominent a juxtaposition of contrasting but related extramusical references must be more than a mere quotation of traditional generic motives, especially in view of the work's many other unusual features. In the opening Allegro, the posthorn theme returns as a countermelody to the closing theme in the strings (mm. 54–62). The closing theme is immediately juxtaposed with the courier theme at the beginning of the development. At the reprise (m. 111), however, Haydn astonishingly brings it back yet again, in the strings alone, *piano*, in the minor – without either horn theme. (This recalls another *piano* reprise in the minor on a derived theme, in a much more eccentric movement, also in D, composed only one year before: No. 24, first movement. Could it also have had extramusical associations?) The posthorn theme soon follows in the major; the courier theme, however, is withheld for a codetta-like fanfare at the very end of the movement. Most remarkably, this formally unusual ending rhymes with the end of the entire symphony: the variation finale leads to a Presto 3/4 coda, which

[80] See Alexander L. Ringer, "The *Chasse* as a Musical Topic of the Eighteenth Century," *JAMS* 6 (1953), 148–59.

[81] "The Hunting Chorus in Haydn's *Jahreszeiten* and the 'Airs de Chasse' in the *Encyclopédie*," *Eighteenth-Century Studies*, 9 (1975–76), 523–39.

[82] "Das Posthornsignal bei Haydn und anderen Komponisten des 18. Jahrhunderts," *H-S* 4 (1976–80), 21–34.

culminates in a last reprise of the courier motive from the opening Allegro. The "cyclic" principle is thus the same one employed in Brahms's Third Symphony.

IMPLICATIONS

Haydn's symphonies with extramusical associations constitute a substantial repertory of imposing works. They invoke many different topics, including nature, the seasons, pastoral ideals, religious feelings and beliefs, ethnic identity, and the hunt and allied activities. These topics are impressive not merely because of their variety, but for their importance, their concern with vital human and cultural issues. Even by the most conservative eighteenth-century standards, these works (if listened to with the slightest degree of sympathy) will have been no mere "ear-tickling nonsense," but serious productions worthy of serious attention – as the record of their reception indeed indicates.

For this study, a crucial aspect of Haydn's extramusical associations is their potential for organizing a multimovement work as a whole. Indeed, a program or a consistently invoked association is in many ways a stronger binding force than thematic commonalities or tonal relations. (Nor should the lack of "objectivity" entailed necessarily compromise the relevance of this principle; we have seen that many links in the technical domains of music, even when presented in a positivistic manner, are in fact anything but objective.) In the case of the Farewell Symphony, this function of the program is so obvious as to need no further comment here. But in other works described in this chapter (the pastoral Matin–Midi–Soir trilogy, the cyclically constructed "Hornsignal," the Passion in No. 26) the extramusical topoi link otherwise independent movements equally clearly, if less consistently. The same is true for many other works cited above, as well as some of those discussed in Chapter 8, where both technical and associational viewpoints come into play.

Extramusical associations of these types are also linked to musical rhetoric more generally (compare Chapter 5). There is no distinction of principle between them and the rhythmic topoi, or the more "semantic" tonal-gestural suggestion of majesty, for example, by C major (or, in opera, D major) and dotted rhythms. If (unlike the rhythmic topoi) they are not ubiquitous, when present they are correspondingly more potent, more deeply "explanatory." The rhetorical sense of form (Chapter 5) persisted at least until 1800, in theory and in Haydn's music. All these types of association form a continuum, from the simplest motoric elements that animate every phrase and movement, to a unique and unrepeatable program such as that of the Farewell. Since every eighteenth-century instrumental composition originated within this system and within the culture of which it was a part, every composition had its extramusical aspect.

Finally, it will not have escaped some readers' attention that almost all of Haydn's explicitly characteristic symphonies date from before 1780. This might be taken to imply that, with the supposed triumph of what is traditionally taken as "mature Classical style" around 1781, the traditional, pre-modern need for extramusical crutches simply withered away. But the votaries of absolute music cannot have it so easy. Schroeder's hypothesis of "moral enlightenment," for example, suggests that after 1780 Haydn transferred his

earlier rhetorical/communicative impulse to the level of musical ideas and their development. Rosen's reading of the London symphonies as heroic pastoral creates an explicit
link between the subjects of Haydn's earliest and latest symphonies; though the former
were (in this sense) traditional and associational, and the latter metamorphosed into the
implicit content of a self-sufficient art, the continuity remains. Furthermore, Rosen's and
Schroeder's interpretations are structurally identical, and therefore permit the general
conclusion that, far from abandoning musical rhetoric after 1780, Haydn *transformed* it.
What had been external now became immanent; what had been projected by the material
now became an indivisible part of it. (Since Haydn's late instrumental music was in fact
early-Romantic in style and reception – see the concluding chapter – and indisputably
counts as absolute music as well, the organicism of these formulations is no contradiction, but essential.) The proof (if more were needed) is the late Haydn's invocation
of the sublime as a rhetorical category – a topic which, though not absent from descriptions of the symphony earlier in the century, seems first fully realized, among instrumental compositions, in Haydn's London symphonies (and Mozart's last four as well).
A skeptic need only think, at a remove of less than two years, of his recreation of the
"Chaos" and of Light itself.

The importance of Haydn's extramusical compositions would loom even larger if we
could identify all of them – which we cannot do. In most cases, we are dependent on
tangible external features to alert us to extramusical associations – original titles and
nicknames, religious melodies, ethnic tunes, and so on – which often have been recognized only by accident. Similar features, not yet noticed, must exist in other works. Still
less can we expect to understand compositions which were animated by a governing extramusical idea *without* overt signs, or a systematic exploitation of contrasts among *topoi*.
Haydn's own anecdote about "God and the sinner" points to such a case: without it,
no Haydn instrumental movement would ever have been interpreted in those terms;
even with it, we cannot decide to which work it applies. The Farewell Symphony itself
approaches this condition. Without the anecdotes, we would have no reasonable way
to understand the nickname (which is transmitted only in late, inauthentic sources, and
does not fit the mood of the finale), the autograph remark "nichts mehr" (which on
its face merely registers the conclusion of two individual parts before the work is over),
the note "geht ab" in early sources (already inauthentic), the unique D-major interlude,
the ethereal ending, and all the rest.

Even in those works which we do know harbored extramusical associations, we will
never locate all the relevant features, let alone interpret correctly all those we do find.
(Not to mention the opposite danger: that we will "locate" many works, and features
in works, which Haydn never dreamed of.) It follows that any attempt to understand
even an authentic programmatic work by Haydn *primarily* in terms of its program is
doomed to failure. Again: even in the Farewell, Haydn's most thoroughly programmatic
composition (except for the theatrical "Il distratto"), only a small proportion of the
events, especially of the details, can be explicated on this basis; in most extramusical
works, many entire movements and long passages bear no discernible relationship to

the topic, and may not have done so even for Haydn. Hence even in this context the claims of formalist analysis are stronger than its opponents seem to realize. Only close analysis can reveal "what happens"; only on that basis can one hope to achieve a systematic and comprehensive view. Whatever the biases and limitations of the analysis, whatever "story" it tells (every analysis tells a story), the results serve as a constraint, a framework, within which any interpretation must fit, or remain irrelevant. (This dialectical relation between formal and expressive coherence is of course characteristic of all the arts.[83]) No interpretation of the program alone could explain why the D-major interlude of the Farewell, in its context, is so potentially "right" and yet so unrealizable, why the recapitulatory F-sharp-major music at the end is at once so complex and so much a release, and so on. No homily on the meaning of Easter can explain the peculiar tension of the minuet of Symphony No. 26, with its off-tonic beginning, its strident canon, its *pianissimo* ending. Landon (I, 559) calls the finale of *Le soir* "a piece of straight program music," but at the same time it is in very clear sonata form; its musical ideas are no more unusual or extreme, no less well motivated or cogently developed, than those in many other Haydn movements. Indeed, notwithstanding the programs (and the rich concertante scoring), all six fast outer movements of Haydn's 1761 trilogy are in sonata form. This is not a problem for either analysis or interpretation, but an opportunity – one that has so far not been taken up.

On the other hand, extramusical associations decisively stimulated Haydn's push towards increased tonal range and increased instability during the 1760s and earlier 1770s (and perhaps thereafter as well). In those years, the majority of his structural innovations first appeared in programmatic symphonies. The first "recitative" symphony movements occurred in *Le matin* and *Le midi*, the first "cyclic" recall of an earlier movement in the "Hornsignal," the first (and only) subversions of generic form and the most radical degree of through-composition in the "Farewell" and the equally programmatic No. 46. Regarding key relations, the first remote juxtaposition in a development section is found in *Le midi*, the first chromatic fall of a major third across a caesura (which became so important) in the "Hornsignal," the first remote juxtaposition between movements in No. 26. Every one of these techniques then either became common or, as in the case of through-composition, was as it were sublimated into a general feature of style. Even the most die-hard formalist must pay his respects to Haydn's extramusical associations: they were an essential aspect of his art throughout his life.

---

[83] Langer, *Feeling and Form*; Kenneth Burke, "Formalist Criticism: Its Principles and Limits," in *Language as Symbolic Action: Essays on Life, Literature, and Method* (Berkeley, 1966), pp. 480–506.

INDIVIDUAL COMPOSITIONS

Having topically surveyed Haydn's principal techniques of through-composition – progressive form, cyclic integration, extramusical associations – we now return to individual compositions. In this chapter we examine a dozen works which are to a greater or lesser degree through-composed: Symphonies 15, 25, 46, 49, 99, and 103; the string quartets Opp. 20 No. 2, 50 No. 4, 54 No. 2, and 74 No. 3; the keyboard sonata Hob. XVI:30; and the piano trio Hob. XV:26 (Others could be added; some of these have been described briefly in Chapters 6 and 7.) These works are varied by genre, date (two very early, one 1768, two 1772, one mid-1770s, two late 1780s, four 1793–95), and mode (eight in the major, four in minor); they also vary as to their likelihood of having had tangible extramusical associations. This broad distribution not only confirms the status of through-composition as a normal (if not necessarily common) aspect of Haydn's art, but disproves any notion that his interest in it might have been restricted to a single genre, period, or stylistic orientation – for example, to overtly exceptional "Sturm und Drang" works such as the Farewell Symphony.

On the other hand, cyclic integration must not be made a criterion of value. The Farewell and Symphony 46 (see below) are not among Haydn's greatest works *because* they are through-composed; their tonal and thematic continuity and manipulations of genre-patterns are aspects of their particular genius, not signs of special quality. Anyone who supposes that Symphony No. 47 in G is not on the same level as the Farewell or No. 46 (all three date from 1772), merely because it does not include run-on movements, weird keys, or identifiable extramusical references; or that, because Op. 54 No. 2 includes run-on movements and a culmination-finale, it is better than Op. 54 No. 1, has no hope of understanding Haydn's art. In the eighteenth century, overt integration is found only in a minority of exceptional (primarily programmatic) compositions. In the absence of obvious features pointing in that direction, we have no obligation to search for it; indeed, the assumption that such a search is *ipso facto* relevant is anachronistic. My pursuit of this question here reflects no such bias, but rather my interest in the extent to which the Farewell Symphony, and its compositional techniques, are characteristic of Haydn's music in general, as well as (admittedly) my desire to redress the relative neglect of the through-compositional aspects of his music.

Many of these compositions exploit only one or two integrative techniques. Conversely, each technique predominates only in certain works: manipulation of generic patterns in Symphonies 25 and 46 and Op. 54 No. 2; thematic links in Nos. 15, 25, and

46; tonal organization (of differing types) in Nos. 49 and 99 and Opp. 50 No. 4 and 74 No. 3; run-on movements in Symphony No. 46, Opp. 20 No. 2 and 54 No. 2, and Sonata No. 30; culmination-finales in Opp. 20 No. 2 and 50 No. 4; and so forth. Only Symphony No. 46, Opp. 20 No. 2 and 54 No. 2, and Sonata No. 30 approach the level of "total" integration we have seen in the Farewell. Reflecting this variety, my discussions vary widely in length and character; some emphasize technical matters, others expressive and aesthetic aspects. This eclecticism is not merely a matter of convenience; it reflects my conviction that any global, theory-laden methodology applied to music like Haydn's falsifies more than it explains. Insofar as I have an overriding thesis, it is that every work by Haydn is an individuum. This will emerge clearly when we consider putative "pairs" of works: the Farewell and Symphony No. 46, Opp. 20 No. 2 and 54 No. 2, Symphonies Nos. 99 and 103; and the three works in F-sharp minor. In every case, their differences will prove more important than their similarities. Haydn's tendency to through-composition was based on no formula, no abstract notion; it was but one aspect of his general powers of composition, of creating individual and coherent musical artworks.[1]

TWO EARLY SYMPHONIES: CYCLIC PATTERNS AND THEMATIC LINKS

Symphonies 15 and 25 are both early works, dating from just before or just after Haydn's move to the Esterházy court in 1761.[2] Their opening movements feature long, independent Adagio sections that are neither slow introductions nor independent movements and therefore call the overall cyclic pattern into question (on this issue, see Chapter 6). Both also exhibit substantial thematic links among the movements. (Tonal and thematic continuities are common in Haydn's early music; see, in the concluding chapter, the section "Maturity," especially p. 358.)

Symphony No. 15 in D

Symphony No. 15 begins in a highly unusual fashion, with an ABA movement, slow–fast–slow. Despite the weight and importance of the A sections and the sonata form of the interior Presto, the return to A at the end makes it a single (compound) movement, not a run-on "triple." And the Presto is formally unstable, as is appropriate to its position as the interior member of an ABA movement. On the other hand, it is a fast movement in sonata style and thus fulfills the expectations associated with the generic function "opening movement of a symphony." (This combination of attributes is no inconsistency;

---

[1] This point is well expressed by Tovey on Op. 20 No. 2 ("Haydn's Chamber Music," quoted below) and by Rosen, *Classical Style*, p. 120.

[2] Landon, *Haydn*, vol. 1, pp. 241–42; Larsen, "Haydn's Early Symphonies," p. 127; Feder's work-list in *The New Grove*. Gerlach has recently suggested (on grounds of instrumentation) that No. 15 may date from the earliest Esterházy years ("Fragen zur Chronologie"); even if this should be correct, the larger chronological picture would not thereby be affected.

it is inherent in the dialectics of cyclic form. A given movement is both a representative of a particular type, with associated conventional characteristics, and a component of a cycle, in which its function is determined in part by its relations to the other movements. The Presto is in sonata form because it is the central, and only fast, component of the first movement of a symphony; it is unstable because it is the interior member of an ABA.)

Granted this point, the overall form emerges as normal, albeit unusual: (S–F–S)— M–S–Fn: that is, a four-movement cycle with the minuet and slow movement reversed (see Chapter 6). The remaining movements are of conventional types and observe the principle of contrast: minuet, sprightly 2/4 Andante in the subdominant, 3/8 Presto finale. (Haydn's observance of these conventions does not entail immaturity of technique or primitiveness of style; even the *da capo* finale is finely wrought.[3]) Tempo and (usually) meter change at each possible location. The Andante, though generically the "slow" movement, differs markedly from the opening Adagio: relatively fast instead of quite slow, duple rather than triple, different key and material, scoring for strings alone. The danger of having two independent "slow" movements in a cyclic work of fewer than six movements is mitigated both by these strong contrasts and because the Adagio sections of the first movement, despite their weight, do not stand alone. The minuet is logically placed between the slow ending of the first movement and the moderate third movement.

The initial Adagio section is not a slow introduction (its material is quoted in Example 8.1, discussed below), not so much because of length as of principles of construction (see pp. 162–63). An introduction comprises a large-scale half-cadence in the tonic; it can support neither an organized modulation to and cadence in the dominant (as in the first part of a binary form or a small-scale sonata exposition) nor closure in the tonic towards the end. This Adagio, however, is a closed form which ends with a perfect authentic cadence in m. 28 (followed by a final dominant phrase which prepares the Presto), and cadences strongly in A major halfway through (m. 15); see the diagram below.

Opening Adagio

Bars	1–8	9–15	16–20	21–28	(28) 29–33
Phrase	1+Cad$_1$	2+Cad$_2$	3	1+Cad$_{1+2}$	4
Key	I——I	(I) V–V	V^7	I——I	V/i
Binary?	⌐A	B	⌐ (Ext.)	⌐A (B) ⌐	
Ternary?	⌐A	⌐B	(Tr.) ⌐	⌐A	

Closing Adagio

Bars	112–19		120–24	125–32 (–34)
Phrase	1+Cad$_1$		3	1+Cad$_{1+2}$ (+ Ext.)
Key	I——I		V^7	I——I

[3] I survey Haydn's *da capo* finales in "D-Major Interlude," §II.

In addition, its uniform motion and rhetoric are uncharacteristic of slow introductions, especially those comprising more than a single phrase plus dominant extension. Furthermore, the oboes are silent, whereas every true Haydn introduction employs all the instruments that play in the ensuing fast movement.

Like many small pieces in four phrases of which the first cadences in the tonic and the second in the dominant, it can be understood either as a so-called "quatrain" (a version of binary form)[4] or as ternary (both possibilities are shown in the diagram). The former reading focuses on the parallel between the cadence in the dominant halfway through (m. 15) and that in the tonic in m. 28: mm. 26–28 are as much a recapitulation of mm. 13–15 from phrase 2 as of mm. 7–8 from phrase 1 (see the dotted motive in mm. 13 and 26, and the horns in mm. 14 and 27); that is, mm. 21–28 reprise not merely phrase 1 but the cadence of 2 as well. The ternary reading takes the first phrase, closing firmly in the tonic, as form-defining; phrase 2 starts over following a caesura, as is characteristic in ABA structures; and both middle phrases are oriented around the dominant, before the reprise (m. 21 ≈ 1). By either reading, this passage is a closed, symmetrical form; its character is not preparatory, but independent and self-contained. Hence – and this is the generic point – unlike an introduction, the Adagio can bear repetition; it returns intact at the end, except for the omission of 2 in the dominant (and therefore becomes an unambiguous antecedent-consequent period, with extension of the antecedent by 3).

The Presto has the rushing, breathless character of several early Haydn symphony first movements in D, among them the familiar No. 1; it is still closer in style to No. 4 (also a Presto), with which it even shares certain prominent motives.[5] It begins with a rising, pseudo-imitative passage, 5 (not shown in Example 8.1); the theme proper, 6, enters only in the fourth bar (m. 37; in Symphony No. 4 the related motive appears at the very beginning). This unique opening, almost a pure musical "process," is also the key to the unusual form. The Presto prescribes no repetition of its two structural parts. Instead, what appears to be the final cadence of the exposition (m. 61) is elided to a repetition of the initial process, 5, which cadences again at m. 64. Which of these is the structural cadence? Is this repetition of 5 a codetta, confirming the dominant and hence still part of the exposition, or the beginning of the development? Or is the entire four-bar phrase, with its pair of cadences, a higher-level rhythmic/tonal arrival? No unambiguous answer is possible; will the recapitulation help? Alas, the reprise (m. 81) omits 5 entirely; it appears only at the end of the recapitulation, as in the exposition (mm. 105–08, this time elided to a transition back to the Adagio). Is then the initial 5 merely a "frame" (mm. 34–37, 105–08) to the sonata form, whose main idea is the thematic 6? But then it would seem to have no business in mm. 61–64. Or is it a codetta after all, as implied by mm. 105–08 (and perhaps mm. 61–64)? Then its use as the opening idea is unintelligible.

The answer must lie in a different direction. This is Haydn's only sonata-form

[4] Bartha, "Song Form and Quatrain."
[5] Noted by Landon, *Symphonies*, p. 224; *Haydn*, vol. 1, pp. 289–90.

symphony movement which is "framed" by slow music on either side; we should hardly be surprised to find that it is formally and gesturally unique as well. (In the "Drum Roll" Symphony, the return of the introduction is an interruption *within* the second group; following it, mm. 213–18+222–28 recapitulate mm. 73–78+the closing theme, 87–93, which have hitherto not been accounted for.) Its opening theme is a process; its structural cadences are ambiguous. Both features deny that functional clarity that sonata-form movements (even Haydn's) ordinarily attain; this denial is appropriate for the middle member of a larger structure. (Similar strictures apply to Haydn's only other sonata-form symphony first movement without internal repeats, that of No. 2; it is equally unusual in both texture and form. Among other things, the recapitulation includes an unprecedented threefold reprise, in mm. 94, 113, and 134, of which each passage is treated differently.)

The opening Adagio is of fundamental importance in another sense: it introduces motives that develop throughout the symphony, one of Haydn's most remarkable early thematicist essays (see Example 8.1). The motives might seem too modest or common to support "thematic organization." Thus we have a pitch collection x, rising triadically $\hat{1}$–$\hat{3}$–$\hat{5}$, then descending by step to $\hat{4}$ across a barline (note also the leap of a seventh down to the low $\hat{5}$), over the progression I–V⁷; its variant x', which resolves the dissonant $\hat{4}$ down to $\hat{3}$; a three-note upbeat over a dominant leading to a tonic (y); the interval of the sixth (z); an important dotted motive (w), especially in the cadential phrase, where it combines with v (in the cadences to **2** and the reprise of **1** the dotted figure is inverted in "Scotch snap" rhythm, w'). The Presto adds the slashing sixteenth-note fifth-span in **6** (u; u and y make up the related theme in Symphony No. 4), and a dominant pedal (t). These elements develop and combine in unpredictable ways: as headmotives and their variants, through developing variation, as links between the end of one section and the beginning of the next, through association with identical harmonic progressions, and so forth. The number and variety of these continually novel combinations create a motivic "repertory," a literal commonality of material (*Substanzgemeinschaft*) animating the symphony.

The initial Adagio phrase (Example 8.1a, theme **1**) recurs in varied form at the reprise (Example 8.1b), where the pitch collection x, now in the horns, assumes the eighth-note rhythm of y; and, in dotted rhythm, as one of the most important ideas in the minuet. More indirectly (but very close in time), x governs the thematic motive **6** of the Presto (Example 8.1a), in the variant form x'; u rises a fifth from d² to a²; the ensuing eighth notes both incorporate y and complete the x-motion from $\hat{5}$ to $\hat{4}$ (and on to $\hat{3}$). (Motive u also occurs in the main theme of the finale.) Meanwhile, the initial long d² returns, much lengthened, as a dominant pedal t over the horn reprise (Example 8.1b); this relates (8.1c) to the three-note upbeat t/y over the transitional dominant idea **4** (which also includes an inverted "premonition" of the sixteenth-note motive u). Later, this complex echoes in the second-group theme **9** of the Presto, through the minor mode, the repeated a², and the scalewise eighth-note figure leading to a strong beat. (If, as seems appropriate, a half note of the Presto equals a quarter note in the Adagio, the latter motivic relation

Example 8.1 Symphony No. 15: motivic-tonal relations

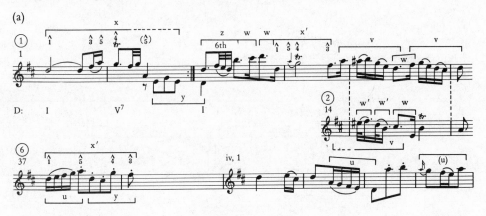

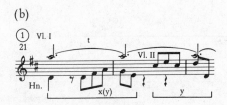

(b)

(c)

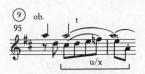

Ex. 8.1 (*cont.*)

(d)

(e)

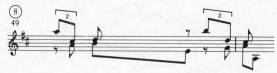

(f)

will be especially clear.) The little fragment from the second group of the Andante (shown to the right of Example 8.1c) is perhaps coincidental only; still, it is the only minor-mode inflection in the entire exposition, on the same bass-notes (s) and with the same harmonies as 4; and it is emphasized by being stated four times in succession and leading to a surprisingly big *fortissimo* climax.

Additional derivations from the headmotive x (some of them speculative) are shown in Example 8.1d. Meanwhile, the theme of the dominant section 2 from the Adagio (8.1e), including the sixth leap z, executes a four-bar harmonic progression I–ii²–V$^6_5$–I (a–g♯–a in the bass); this would be unremarkable, were it not that Haydn "quotes" it, 2+2 phrasing, sixth-leaps, bass line and all, in both the Presto and the finale, and both times in the first thematic group in the dominant – that is, in every location in the symphony having this harmonic and formal function. (The similarity is greater in the distant finale passage than in the immediate Presto one.) Finally, the ingeniously contoured headmotive of the Andante (Example 8.1f) is related to a prominent motive in the passage Haydn would have written down just before, the sighing *forte–piano* at the end of the trio – also in the subdominant (another example of "linkage technique"). Both motives prominently feature the sixth-contour.

Thus Symphony No. 15 exhibits many traits of through-composition. It opens with Haydn's only ABA symphony first movement; both the Adagio and Presto sections are correspondingly unique in form. Its cyclic pattern is unusual, while maintaining the principles of contrast between successive movements and balance among them all. And it boasts a rich and multifarious motivic continuity, whose intermovemental aspects in particular go far beyond what is customary in early Haydn. In another context, it would be tempting to speculate on possible extramusical associations for so unusual a work.

Symphony No. 25 in C

Symphony No. 25 also begins with a long Adagio which eventually leads to a sonata-form Allegro. But its generic function is ambiguous. It is serious, almost "ecclesiastical" in tone: the opening invokes trio-sonata style, unfolding contrapuntally over a "walking" bass, the second-violin melody imitated by the firsts at the fifth above, then by the bass in the tonic. The theme itself, leaping up to a high note which resolves down through a suspension chain to a cadence prepared by a trill, was a common type in mid-century Austrian church sonatas.[6] (Forty years later, in the Kyrie to the *Missa in tempori belli* – an overtly liturgical context in the same key – Haydn almost quoted mm. 17–19, a syncopated 6–5 progression rising from I⁶ to I$^5_3$; see the bottom system of Example 8.2, p. 261.)

But as the music proceeds, the harmonic rhythm, texture, and material change constantly:

[6] Kirkendale, *Fugue and Fugato*, pp. 89–94, 103–09.

Phrase	**1**			**2?**	**2**			**3**	**4**		
Bar	1	5	6	7	8b	10b	12b	15	17b	19	21–23
Motive	a	a+b	c	d (b)	a+b	e (b)	c' (b)	a'	a''+b	a'''	f
Harmony	I–V–I		V————		ii	ii^6	V	I–V	I^6	I	V

At each measure cited in this outline, a substantial alteration occurs: new sixteenth-note motive *b* (m. 5); rhythmically discontinuous unison half cadences (m. 6); *f–p* and the entry of the winds (m. 7); reversion to *a+b* (m. 8, theme in the bass); a halt on a long-prolonged ii^6, with new melodic motives (m. 10b); dominant pedal, with the winds again and a turn to the minor (m. 12b); return to the opening motive, now unison *forte* (m. 15); new variants of the headmotive (mm. 17b, 19), leading to a dominant pedal (mm. 21–23). Ordinarily, music such as the first five bars would have developed into a learned, continuously-textured movement that maintained the initial "churchy" propriety; here, however, the changes of topic and texture are so continual as to make discontinuity itself the leading principle.

In addition, this Adagio is formally and functionally ambiguous. It comprises four sections (identified with bold-face numerals at the top of the diagram), each beginning with a form of the headmotive *a* and ending with a strong half-cadence, considerably prolonged and emphasized by the winds (which play nowhere else). Except for the imitative exposition in mm. 2–3, V is always the home dominant, never a key in its own right. Hence, even though m. 15 returns to a variant of *a* in the tonic, it is a "second beginning" rather than a "recapitulation." The Adagio conveys no impression of binary or sonata form. On the other hand, the four half-cadences, each differently articulated, are too numerous for a slow introduction, which ordinarily has only two paragraphs and hence at most two structural dominants. Furthermore, the Adagio is too long (twenty-three bars of 4/4) for an early Haydn introduction: those to *Le matin* and *Le midi*, symphonies which as a whole are on a much larger scale, are but six and ten measures, respectively; indeed the opening Adagio of Symphony No. 15, which is unambiguously *not* an introduction, is virtually the same length (thirty-three bars of 3/4, compared to twenty-three of 4/4 here). In terms of Haydn's usual introductory rhetoric and proportions, the strong half-cadence in mm. 12–14 – already the second such arrival, prepared by ♯4 and extended two-and-one-half bars – would be the natural ending-point; the expected continuation would be the Allegro. Finally, as noted above, the use of the winds solely as reinforcing/sustaining instruments on the dominant violates the principle of meaningful exploitation of all instruments in a slow introduction. The Adagio fits no generic pattern.

By no coincidence, the overall cyclic form of the symphony is also ambiguous. If the Adagio were interpreted as a (long and strange) introduction, the cyclic pattern would be

$$\begin{array}{c} \text{(Intro–F)} - \text{M} - \text{Fn} \\ \text{I}\underline{\qquad\qquad}\text{I} \end{array}$$

that is, a "galant" three-movement form, with two fast movements enclosing a minuet in the middle but no slow movement, all in the tonic. Although this pattern is occasionally found in Austrian keyboard works and, less often, string quartets, it appears in almost no symphonies, and in none by Haydn. If on the other hand the Adagio were understood as an independent opening slow movement, the overall form would be

$$(S–F) – M – Fn$$
$$I————I$$

that is, the standard pattern for symphonies with an opening slow movement (see Chapter 6). But the Adagio is not a complete design or independent structure. Hence neither the concept of a single "compound" movement nor that of two "run-on" movements does justice to this unique opening Adagio or the work as a whole. Symphony No. 25 remains a generic anomaly.

However, like No. 15, it exhibits meaningful thematic continuities, albeit of a different type. The initial melodic motive, *a*, develops continually, both throughout the Adagio and in all three subsequent movements (see Example 8.2). It comprises a striking leap of a sixth from C up to A and a step down to G ($\hat{1}–\hat{6}–\hat{5}$), the latter gaining added significance from being a resolution of the dissonance created over the B in the bass. (Later, B itself becomes part of a variant of this motive, labeled *a'*; it combines with G to make a second, complementary leap of a sixth.) As always, Haydn varies the motive in different ways, often "subliminally." Obvious indeed, however, is the opening of the Presto finale precisely on the four notes of *a'* (g^2–a^2, b^1–c^2), a variant of the common contrapuntal finale motive most familiar from Mozart's "Jupiter" Symphony, which Haydn also used in three other early symphonies: in the finales of Nos. 3 and 13 and in the fast second movement of No. 11.

Thus both of these early symphonies (Nos. 15 and 25) exhibit a high degree of thematicist organization – as if in compensation for their formal ambiguity. Again, one posits an extramusical stimulus for No. 25; in view of the style of the opening, perhaps it was a religious association. (Of course, a "churchy" style in mid-century instrumental music does not imply a concrete liturgical association.[7] On the other hand, the apparently secular style of the remainder is no barrier; compare the 2/4 Andante and minuet-finale of the unquestionably religious No. 30, "Alleluia," described on p. 243.) If these two works were programmatic, it would confirm the hypothesis (see the end of Chapter 7) regarding the correlation between unconventional forms and extramusical associations – except that here the correlation is with unusual movement-types and cyclic patterns.

TWO EXPRESSIVE SYMPHONIES, C. 1770

Symphony No. 49 in F minor: monotonality

This work of 1768 is one of Haydn's earliest full-blown "Sturm und Drang" productions; it is also his last symphony with an opening slow movement. Despite its intense style and the familiar nickname "La passione," it has no documented programmatic associa-

---

[7] Zaslaw, "*Sinfonia da chiesa.*"

Example 8.2 Symphony No. 25: motivic-tonal relations

Ex. 8.2 (*cont.*)

Minuet

Trio

Presto

Adagio, 17–19

Missa in tempori belli, Kyrie, 17-18
Allegro moderato

tions; the nickname appears only in a single, late, peripheral source.[8] Indeed a strikingly different nickname, "The Good-humored Quaker," appears in other sources, one of which, apparently Viennese, includes the remark, "In his enthusiasm, the Good-humored Quaker; this symphony serves as a companion to that of the English Philosopher by the same author." The possibility mentioned by *JHW*, that Symphony No. 49 may have been performed at Easter and that this would explain the nickname, is based solely on Landon, *Symphonies*; he however provides no evidence for the proposition and was doubtless merely extrapolating from the nickname. Sisman's explorations of the importance of moralizing Quakers in European drama of the period, and her association of the "wide-leap style" of the second movement with Haydn's theatrical music, are provocative indeed; certainly the intensity and eccentricity of this work cry out for some kind of extramusical explanation. Nevertheless, the hypothesis that it was originally theatrical remains wholly speculative. (The "English philosopher" may refer to a play by Goldoni; perhaps he had something to do with No. 22, "The Philosopher."[9])

Like many other Haydn minor-mode works, Symphony No. 49 gives evidence of overall tonal organization. To be sure, its monotonal restriction to the tonic is not remarkable in the context of Haydn's symphonies with opening slow movements. But in addition, all the movements are linked by striking and unusual uses of the dominant, as both a melodic pitch-class and a harmonic degree. As shown in Example 8.3, the dominant is emphasized at the beginning by a double-neighbor headmotive, $\hat{5}$–$\hat{6}$–$\hat{4}$–$\hat{5}$. This configuration reappears (in varied forms) at the beginning of all five movements (counting the trio);[10] in the sense of a pitch-class motive, it appears in other contexts as well. In addition, all three sonata-form movements focus on the dominant minor key in the development: Adagio, mm. 60–61 (described below); Allegro di molto, mm. 63–71 and 85–94; Presto, mm. 73–84. A structural minor dominant is uncommon in Haydn developments (even in minor-key movements); its consistent use here qualifies as an organizing tonal gesture.

Furthermore, Haydn's handling of all three dominant retransitions is wilfully unusual. In the opening Adagio,[11] the development is quite short: only two paragraphs, 19 percent of the entire movement (eighteen bars of ninety-six), compared to Haydn's normal proportions of 23–31 percent. (The fact that this is an opening slow movement is irrelevant; as a group, these movements exhibit no significant differences in internal proportions from the norms.) It begins with the counterstatement of the opening theme **1'** (mm. 44–51=7–14, not 1–6); see the voice-leading diagram in Example 8.4a, which reads the movement as an interruption-structure, $\hat{5}$–$\hat{2}$||$\hat{5}$–$\hat{1}$; compare the equivalent background diagram in Example 8.4d. As in the exposition, the transitional theme **2** follows (m. 52=15), modulating through the tonic (m. 54) directly to the home dominant (m. 59), with a strong half cadence and caesura. As we have seen in Chapter 5,

---

[8] See *JHW* I/6, foreword; critical report, pp. 17–20.

[9] Sisman's comments on these works are in "Haydn's Theater Symphonies," pp. 331–36.

[10] Many of these are noted by Landon, *Haydn*, vol. 2, p. 290.

[11] Todd, "Haydn and the *Sturm und Drang*," pp. 177–79, makes many perceptive comments on this movement without, however, attempting to relate it to the remainder of the work.

Example 8.3 Symphony No. 49: *Grundgestalt* on $\hat{5}$?

Adagio

Allegro di molto

Minuet

Trio

Presto

so early a dominant ordinarily leads to a remote or otherwise unexpected continuation; indeed, it is supplanted by C minor, the dominant minor key (m. 60). Given its brevity to this point, we expect the development to continue. But the new phrase is only two bars long, abruptly pausing on its own dominant in first inversion (B♮ in the bass). Even though we may therefore focus on its material – a variant of the opening motive – the sequel is a shock: the recapitulation follows directly (m. 62=1), on a root-position tonic. The harmonic succession from the dominant of the dominant minor key to the tonic, with the tritone B♮–f in the bass, is arbitrary, almost inexplicable. In one sense, the two-bar phrase in C minor is an interpolation between the home dominant in m. 59 and the tonic reprise (see Example 8.4b). Or, perhaps one is meant to hear a linear succession from the e^2 of m. 59 to the eb^1 of m. 60, and on down by step from d^1 to c^1, the background headnote, *after* the reprise (8.4c). (Examples 8.4b and c are drawn in terms of an alternative reading of the voice-leading structure, in which $\hat{5}$ is prolonged undisplaced in the background until the recapitulation.) But this may miss the point as well: even for Haydn's minor-mode muse, this movement is unusually terse and intense; so baffling a succession at so important a formal join makes one search for a rhetorical explanation. Perhaps this recapitulation begins with an *ellipsis*, deliberately irregular and obscure – compare again Example 8.4a and d, in which this passage is notionally governed by the background G ($\hat{2}$) which, in the outer parts during the crucial bars (60–61), is nowhere to be heard. At the least, this abrupt, non-functional juxtaposition, V^6/v–i across a bass tritone, powerfully articulates the "missing" dominant, as chord, key, and scale degree – in keeping with its prominence in the whole symphony.

Furthermore, as in the Allegro assai of the Farewell, the recapitulation is prepared in so weak a fashion that the music cannot proceed normally: a strong V–i cadence is needed to restore the balance. But in the first large paragraph of the recapitulation (Example 8.4a, third system), the return of the root-position dominant (m. 67) is transformed in the foreground into the weaker $V^6_{[5]}$, moving by step to i (m. 70); the quiet pedal of mm. 76–78 resolves only to i^6 (m. 79); the cadence (82–83) is normal, but the winds have dropped out and it is only *piano*. In the final paragraph (mm. 83–96), the bass $\hat{5}$ is reinterpreted as a passing-note (m. 85) and as V^6_5/VI (mm. 87, 89), before an augmented sixth chord in m. 90 finally prepares the structural dominant of the entire recapitulation (m. 91).[12] But this dominant enters as a six-four; the resolution to V^5_3 and then to i, plus the important codetta (with two more dominants), are *piano* and for the strings alone. The dissonant six-four is left hanging – not tonally, but in register, instrumentation, and gesture. (Ordinarily, a quiet codetta *follows* the resolution onto the tonic on a strong downbeat.) Hence this dominant also remains in a meaningful sense unresolved – analogous to the elliptical "missing" $\hat{2}$ over C minor and the restoration of the tonic at the reprise. Astonishingly, there is no strong V–i in the foreground anywhere in the recapitulation. (Nor are these the only discontinuities in this movement; others are indicated in Example 8.4.)

---

[12] Landon's miniature score (Philharmonia 592) marks m. 90 *ff*, "partly in Frankfurt [Jos. Elssler]"; *JHW* I/6 (Mörner) gives no mark (leaving the prevailing *f* unchanged) and makes no comment in the critical report.

Example 8.4 Symphony No. 49: tonal form

Ex. 8.4 (cont.)

(b)

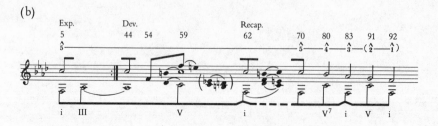

(c)

(d)

In the Allegro di molto, a remote tonal juxtaposition, V–III, occurs between the second, jagged first-group theme in the tonic (mm. 6–13) and the contrasting legato theme (m. 14) which, somewhat in the manner of a transition, begins the second group in A-flat. (In itself, this juxtaposition is normal in this location within minor-mode movements.) The development begins by restating the first group in the relative, but the jagged theme (m. 57) is extended, modulates into C minor, combines there in sequence with a motive from the opening theme (m. 64), and cadences on V/v (m. 71). This half-cadence proceeds, as in the exposition, down a third to the quiet legato theme in E-flat: V–III transposed to V/v–VII. The tonal cogency reaches further: C minor returns later – through its dominant (m. 85), linking up directly with m. 71 – and thus becomes the main key of the development as a whole. The reprise is again "weakly" prepared (see Example 8.3): a second-group theme (m. 91=37) moves, in a descending sequence of third-related keys articulated only by their leading-tones, from C minor (v) through A-flat

(III) to the tonic (mm. 97–98); the reprise enters at once (m. 100). There is no root-position home dominant.

In the development of the Presto finale, the minor dominant arrives in mm. 73–75. A sudden turn to *piano* (m. 79, Example 8.3) brings the headmotive, still in C minor, which gives way at the last moment to the home dominant (m. 85), the reprise following directly. But, as in the Adagio, the progression is elliptical: the dominant appears in root position only as a minor triad (mm. 79–84); at the moment of its yielding to the major (m. 85), the bass slips down to B♭, and proceeds down to the tonic by step. Indeed, as in the Allegro assai of the Farewell, the only root-position V–i cadence – and this is a finale! – occurs at the very end (mm. 119–21). Throughout the symphony, Haydn refuses to link a root-position home dominant to the tonic at every reprise. This apparent contradiction in the function of the dominant (it is by far the most important melodic and gestural pitch class, yet its structural role is always problematical) is a primary source of the consistently strained mood – a mood arising from other features as well: for example, in the Adagio, the provocative initial phrase ending on the dominant with introduction-like neighbors in dotted rhythm and a fermata; the syncopated motives with unexpected harmonic changes (mm. 4, 33, 57, 65–66, 78); the often strikingly irregular dynamics (mm. 19, 36 and 80 [compare 34 and 81!], 87); and so forth. In these respects Symphony No. 49 is genuinely through-composed.

Symphony No. 46 in B: the meaning of musical reminiscence

Symphony No. 46 in B is in many ways a "pair" to the Farewell Symphony. Both works were composed in 1772; both are set in unusual, "remote" sharp-side keys; both include horn parts requiring the special half-step crooks Haydn purchased in October of that year. And both massively disrupt symphonic conventions. In No. 46, the disruption is one of Haydn's most radical: the finale breaks off towards the end for a long reprise of the minuet, and then resumes and concludes.[13] This is Haydn's only substantial recall involving a previous movement; the only comparable case, the quotation from the first movement at the end of the "Hornsignal" Symphony (see Chapter 7), is much briefer and entails no change of tempo or meter. Even the return of the "Drum Roll" introduction towards the end of the Vivace, astonishing though it is, takes place within what, generically, remains a single movement. No comparable stroke was heard again until Beethoven's Symphony No. 5 (presumably an independent inspiration; Haydn's symphony did not circulate widely, and there is no evidence that Beethoven knew it). So unique an abrogation of normal generic procedures surely implies extramusical associations.

The first section of the minuet (see Example 8.5) is a complex eight-bar sentence (2+2+4), ending with a half-cadence; like many of Haydn's movements in this period (compare Chapter 5), it begins off the downbeat and off the tonic, on a I⁶ chord (D♯ in the bass). The second section, by contrast, comprises three six-bar phrases, of which the

---

[13] The published accounts are sketchy; they include Rosen, *Classical Style*, pp. 147–48; Landon, *Haydn*, vol. 2, pp. 303–04; Neubacher, pp. 235–36. I have received helpful comments on this section from Elizabeth Hudson, Roger Parker, Elaine Sisman, and Jessica Waldoff.

Example 8.5 Symphony No. 46: minuet

Ex. 8.5 (cont.)

first (mm. 9–14) prolongs the dominant to prepare the thematic reprise. This duly enters (m. 15) – but, as so often in Haydn minuets (even his earliest), in varied form. The winds drop out and the dynamics shift to *piano*, and the initial bass quarter rest is expanded to more than a measure. In this silence, the opening phrase appears in a free retrograde (noted by Rosen): mm. 1–2, motive *a*: long-note tonic followed by rising eighths over a dominant; 15–16, motive *d*: falling eighths over a dominant leading to a long note, and two bars later to a substitute tonic. When the bass does enter with its two-note offbeat motive *b*, it is rhythmically isolated, hesitant. Haydn plays with the form as well: the middle phrase of the second part (mm. 15–20) is linked to both the preceding and the following phrases. Although the "signs" of a reprise are strong and unambiguous (location partway through the second part, dominant preparation, motivic return), mm. 15–16 are still on the dominant, and the descent from $\hat{5}$ to $\hat{2}$ merely varies the middleground structure of mm. 9–14. Even the fact that mm. 15–20 are repeated in substance as the final phrase is not conclusive: only then do the sound and texture (if not the motivic forms) of mm. 1–8 return, and one could as well hear mm. 15–20 as a preparation for mm. 21–26, as mm. 21–26 a confirming repetition of mm. 15–20. The reprise phrase, mm. 15–20, is thus a large-scale elision: its dual function combines with the omission of the opening to create a progressive, non-symmetrical form for the minuet as a whole.

The trio (also in Example 8.5) exhibits numerous through-composed features. The repetition of the first part is written out, to accommodate the change in the violin parts from unisons to (very close) harmony. Motivically, it is based on m. 1 of the minuet, especially the offbeat two-note bass figure *b*. Having already become more prominent at the reprise, this now becomes an ostinato, animating one of Haydn's inimitable demonstrations that "less is more"; see not only the texture and lack of overt melodic content, but the continual four-bar phrases with their almost identical root-successions. The trio also invokes an "exotic" aura, by non-functional progressions such as VII–V (mm. 29–30) and VII–v (mm. 45–46), the heaping-up of harmonic, instrumental, and dynamic surprises in mm. 49–51, and the ambiguous tonality – the melody (such as it is) could be completely harmonized in either B minor or D major until the very last two bars. (This stripped-down ostinato was a distinct type of trio in Haydn; compare, both in related keys, Symphony No. 29 in E [1765; the trio is in E minor] and the String Quartet Op. 71 No. 2 in D [1793].)

Outwardly, the finale is typical of the period; indeed, it is similar in style to the Presto of the Farewell Symphony. However, the beginning (see Example 8.6) is "weak": it is scored for violins alone and again projects I⁶ (D♯ in the bass) until the cadence in m. 8 (whereupon the bass entry immediately reverts to I⁶); the entire theme is *piano*, even the horn entry – on the headmotive – and final cadence (mm. 13–18). More generally, the movement is rhythmically unsettled, almost hyperactive; even the occasional interruptions marked by G.P.s only mark the "opposite" tendency, as unmotivated in their silence as is the prevailing haste, and no more capable of restoring order. It is also unusually quiet for a finale; presumably, this feature is among those signaled by the heading "scherzando" (otherwise found, among "Sturm und Drang" symphony finales, only in the "easy"

Example 8.6 Symphony No. 46, finale: first group

Ex. 8.6 (*cont.*)

rondo of No. 42 in D). The counterstatement/transition (mm. 19–30) ends the first
group with reiterations of the headmotive, emphasized by the first G.P., on the
dominant; this gesture is trumped following the structural cadence (mm. 60–62; see
Example 8.9 below), as the codetta dies away in a joking/quizzical *pianissimo* based on
the headmotive tag *b'*, again followed by a G.P.

The very short development (Example 8.7) centers around V/vi and iii, again built on
D♯ in the bass. The violins descend by a stepwise circle of fifths to I⁶ (m. 95); the reprise
enters immediately, on the same sonority, still violins alone. This underarticulated
recapitulation (no root-position dominant; no contrast or break in the flow) is analogous
to the large-scale elision of the reprise in the minuet. (A similar reprise onto I⁶, also with
structural implications for the movement, is found in the Vivace of the chronologically
neighboring Symphony No. 51 [p. 144].) As in the Allegro assai of the Farewell, there is
no strong bass cadence onto a root-position tonic in the first-group recapitulation;
I⁶ drives directly into the secondary development (mm. 111ff); everything still seesaws
back and forth from I⁶ to V. In fact, from m. 19 to m. 152 the entire Presto articulates
only I⁶ and V; harmonically, the off-tonic opening generates (the word seems unavoida-
ble) most of the course of the movement. This matches the generic disruption to come:
the Presto can neither stand alone nor execute a complete background tonal progression;
it cannot be understood on its own terms. This instability correlates, on a subliminal
level, with its joking tone, its *piano* dynamics, its hyperactivity alternating with unmotivated pauses – in a word, its eccentricity.

Example 8.7 Symphony No. 46, finale: development and reprise

Ex. 8.7 (*cont.*)

The recall of the minuet (Example 8.8) is a literal repetition, except for an increase in the use of *piano* and the deceptive cadence at the end. Nevertheless – and this is the crucial point – it *begins with the internal reprise* (m. 15) which, as we have seen, is different from the initial phrase. It also replicates the tonal disposition: in the minuet, a dominant phrase (mm. 9–14) prepared a reprise beginning on the dominant (m. 15); here, a dominant pedal (mm. 142–52) leads to the same dominant reprise. From this point to m. 182, the recall consists of mm. 15–26 and then mm. 9–25; that is, the second and third phrases of the second part, and then the entire second part. The opening section is never heard. The recall thus further accentuates the progressive aspects of the minuet's construction.

The function of the recall within the finale becomes clear in the sequel. The deceptive cadence in m. 182 leads quickly to vii^4_3 (yet another dominant; note the high e^1 in the bass) and a fermata; then the Presto bursts in with the headmotive *d*, harmonized by a *forte*, root-position V–I cadence – the first and only such conjunction in the movement. This is the first event since m. 142 that could be an equivalent of the structural cadence at the end of the exposition (m. 62; this parallel passage is shown in Example 8.9). Indeed, it is followed immediately by a recapitulation of the codetta (mm. 189–200 ≈ 62–71), including the dying-away on the tag motive (also repeated in augmentation) and the two bars' rest. Structurally, the entire added passage mm. 142–88 is therefore an expansion of the single bar 61! The foreground confirms this: the added music begins with a dominant pedal (mm. 142–52) which is approached in the same way as the dominant in m. 61a; the recall, as we have seen, is oriented around the dominant; and the final tonic cadence (m. 182) is subverted by a deceptive resolution and another dominant, just before the resumption of the Presto (see Example 8.8), which finally brings the structural cadence (see the chart below, and compare Examples 8.8 and 8.9):

	Sequence I^6–IV–I	Cadence (headmotive) ii^6——V————————I	Codetta I–V–I etc.
Exposition	57–60	61a 61b 62	63–71
Recapitulation	137–40	141 142–52 + minuet + 188–189	190–200 (+ coda)

Hence the coda, with its pedal in the low horns, is not merely a good joke in the prevailing "scherzando" style; it also provides the minimum satisfactory degree of confirmation of the newly-won structural tonic.

Other movements in this period employ a massive interpolation at this point in a sonata form. A clear example from Mozart is the imitative climax of the opening movement of the String Quintet in C: mm. 320–52 expand m. 130 (a single bar, just as in the Haydn), prolonging the dominant just before the structural cadence (if the style were different, one would call this a written-out cadenza). The codetta is then literally recapitulated; only the single flashing viola B♭ in m. 353 intensifies its subdominant emphasis compared to the exposition, as is appropriate following such an expansion:

	Approach to cadence	Dominant	Cadential downbeat	Codetta
Exposition	124–130a	130b	131	132ff.
Recapitulation	314–319 + G.P.	321–52	353 (V^7/IV)	354ff.

Example 8.8 Symphony No. 46, finale: recall of minuet and coda

Ex. 8.8 (*cont.*)

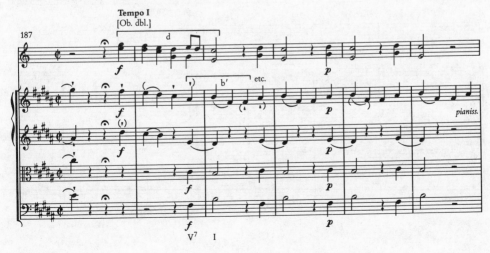

Ex. 8.8 (*cont.*)

Example 8.9 Symphony No. 46, finale: end of second group

The additional complexity of Haydn's stylistic discontinuity and generic disruption does not abrogate the similar function of these interpolations. Even the Scherzo recall in Beethoven's Symphony No. 5 is, structurally, the expansion of a single sonority: it further prolongs a dominant which has already prepared the recapitulation for twenty-one massive bars.

The minuet and the Presto are thus highly unusual, but in strikingly similar ways. Both begin on I⁶ and articulate this sonority and the dominant at the expense of the tonic; neither achieves a strong perfect cadence until the end. In both, the entry of the reprise is weak. (In all this, they resemble the Allegro assai and the minuet of the Farewell Symphony.) What is more, as Rosen points out (*Classical Style*, p. 148), they share important thematic elements: in particular, the unaccompanied descending phrase with which the minuet-recall begins (motive *d*) resembles the headmotive of the Presto. Both, in turn, are similar to the brief, unexpectedly contrasting phrase which answers the unison *forte* headmotive of the opening Vivace (compare Example 8.10 [p. 281], mm. 3–4, with Examples 8.5, mm. 15–18, and 8.6, mm. 1–2): all three are *piano* and descend from F♯ to B, with medial emphasis on C♯. But Rosen does not ask why this should be so. As we have just seen, however, the Presto headmotive *d* recurs at the very moment the *tempo primo* resumes. This thematic link is both rhetorically purposeful (it does not appear at the analogous place in the exposition; it is *new*) and of formal import (it brings about the only structural cadence in the recapitulation). The minuet exhibits a relatively subtle type of progressive form; the finale explodes into a massive disruption of both the closed form of the Presto and the conventions of the genre. In short, both movements constitute a single complex, which, as a whole, expresses the cyclic function "finale"; the recall of the minuet is merely the tangible manifestation of this interrelatedness. Or, one could understand minuet and Presto as variations of a single underlying compositional idea or *Grundgestalt* (not mere commonality of material). Given all this, Haydn's disruption of the symphonic proprieties is an appropriate gesture after all.

But this comfortable conclusion cannot be the end of the story. Why does the minuet abandon its own beginning? What is the point of recalling it in the Presto, and of fusing the two movements into a through-composed finale? What role does this "appropriate disruption" play in the symphony as a whole? What kind of work is it? Does it, as a whole, express "a single underlying compositional idea"? Or does it go *together* with its pair, the Farewell, in a symphonic "cycle" that expresses such an idea? (These questions are as much aesthetic as structural – one of the reasons they have never been asked.)

The cyclic form of Symphony No. 46 is suggestive: it is a monotonal work in the major mode. Haydn composed only four other such symphonies after 1764, all exceptional in relevant ways: No. 59 probably, and Nos. 62 and 63 certainly, are related to theater music, while No. 70 is indisputably integrated, on the basis of mutually reinforcing contrasts between major and minor and between galant and contrapuntal style.[14]

---

[14] On No. 70 see Landon, *Symphonies*, pp. 371–73; *Haydn*, vol. 2, pp. 563–64.

As one might expect, unusual features of the minuet and Presto of No. 46 have already appeared in the Vivace and Poco adagio. The latter, a conspiratorial/poignant *siciliano*, is as exotic as the trio; both are in B minor. Indeed this key, along with its dominant F-sharp minor, occurs in four lengthy passages in the Vivace (mm. 36–51, 76–81, 117–21, and 128–43), a far greater emphasis than usual even in Viennese works. The *forte* rising-arpeggio theme in m. 13 (see Example 8.10), for example, returns not only in the second group (mm. 36ff), with ominous syncopations recalling the Allegro assai in the Farewell, but also in the development, where, astonishingly, it once again stands in F-sharp minor.

Themes and tonality also link the Vivace to the final two movements. We have already noted that the central motive *d* is adumbrated at the beginning of the symphony. Regarding tonality, the crucial bass pitch class D♯ is emphasized in the opening Vivace motive *e* (Example 8.10), which skips *down* to it from the tonic; see also the cadence in m. 4. (Compare the beginning of Symphony No. 44 in E minor: although identical in rhythm and texture, it is much more stable, because the initial tonic is the lowest note.) Conse-

Example 8.10 Symphony No. 46, Vivace: first group

Ex. 8.10 (cont.)

quentially, the approach to the recapitulation is harmonically and gesturally "weak" as well (Example 8.11): without basses and in the two-foot register, descending merely by step in first-inversion triads from high g$^{\#1}$, with the dominant entering only at the last minute, and only as vii^6 ($\hat{2}$ in the bass). This retransition resembles that in the Presto

Example 8.11 Symphony No. 46, Vivace: retransition

(mm. 89–95; Example 8.7), which simply prolongs d♯¹. (It also resembles the retransition in the Allegro assai of the Farewell, where the dominant is articulated only at the last
minute, in a high register, and as vii⁶.)

But what is the point of these relationships? The melodic material of the minuet is based
largely on a two-note appoggiatura figure – that is, a sighing motive. At first, this *topos*
is not prominent, because the melody rises and is supported by a steady quarter-note bass.
Relevant, however, is a subtle change in the relation between the main notes and the
auxiliaries (see Example 8.12a), from anticipations in m. 2 (a♯¹, not b¹, belongs with f♯ in
the bass) to appoggiaturas in m. 4 (e², not d♯², belongs with g♯). (This recalls an
often-cited passage in the minuet of Mozart's "Dissonant" Quartet K. 465, mm. 17–20,
etc.) In m. 15, however, the sighs come to the fore: the two-bar phrase is a "dying fall."
Moreover, since it is unaccompanied, its ambiguity (just described) renders it indeterminate in melodic structure. Are the main notes those on the beat (Example 8.12b, upper
treble staff), starting with f♯² in m. 15 (prolonging the dominant of the preceding half
cadence) and descending by step on every beat as far as c♯² across the barline? (In this case,
the auxiliary notes are anticipations, as in m. 2, but this seems to contradict the sighing
Affekt.) Or are the on-beat notes appoggiaturas (lower treble staff), as the sigh figure

Example 8.12 Symphony No. 46, minuet, voice-leading:

(a) Beginning:

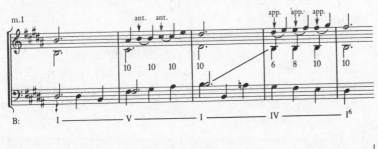

(b) Reprise

implies, with e² the initial main note in m. 15, reaching c#² on the third beat with a repetition across the barline? The former possibility seems to be confirmed when the theme is repeated in m. 21, where the accompaniment removes the ambiguity. But the latter one better fits the cadential descent in m. 19, where d#² is a dissonance and therefore sounds unmistakably like an appoggiatura moving to c#² on the same beat, and the quarter-note level moves entirely by step – except that such an appoggiatura could instead move on the *quarter-note* level (see the fragmentary interpretation above the staff); that is, it would conform to the upper line after all.

Now in the minuet proper, this melodically "undecidable" passage was already a varied, internal reprise. Hence the recall in the Presto is a reprise of a reprise – but that is not quite right. It is a "second-order" reprise: not merely the second appearance of this music as a reprise, but rhetorically two stages removed from the original model. It has therefore become music about a reprise; a "meta-reprise." To say the same thing in terms of a listener's psychology, it is music whose primary, first-order content is not a reprise in the ordinary sense, but the experience of hearing a reprise. It not only begins *in medias res*, on the dominant, with an incomplete, melodically indeterminate phrase; it is also generically shocking, unforeseeable; as it begins, we don't know what is happening; it takes a moment to get our bearings. Its character is not encompassed by the rhetorical concept of a "dying fall"; something simultaneously shocking and indeterminate can only be heard with mixed emotions. It is not merely a recall, but a *reminiscence* – a re-experiencing, tinged with nostalgia or regret.

This reminiscence may achieve something ordinarily not possible in instrumental music: it functions analogously to the past tense in fiction. (I do not mean mere references to past traditions, even ironic ones, as when Mahler apotheosizes the *Ländler* or Stravinsky reinterprets Pergolesi; nor mere intertextuality, as when a composer incorporates aspects of earlier works from his own immediate tradition; nor do I refer to the common nineteenth-century practice of "classicizing" or "problematizing" established forms or genres. And, obviously, I do not mean ordinary recalls within a given work. The latter are common events, which remain in the musical present; a verbalization of their effect would be, "We are now hearing again a passage we have heard before.") Haydn's passage is simultaneously a recall, and music "about" a recall; it incorporates its own past into its sounding present. In hearing it, we also learn what it "was," in an act of *recognition* (anagnôrisis). What we learn is both structural (the last two movements interpenetrate, as variations-in-common) and psychological (that which they have in common is absent, at least in part, and we regret that absence).

Furthermore, this meta-musical reminiscence arises in a context of generic disruption: it is removed from the world of ordinary symphonic music; it does not "belong." Now we have a concept for contextually distinct events that inform us about the past: *narrative*. Narratives are distinct from, separated off from, ordinary discourse; they inevitably entail the past. Paul Ricoeur writes, "What is essential to the narrated world is foreign to the immediate or directly preoccupying surroundings of the speaker."[15] As Peter Brooks put it (*Reading for the Plot*, pp. 4, 97):

---

[15] *Time and Narrative*, vol. 1 (Chicago, 1984), p. 68.

When we "tell a story," there tends to be a shift in the register of our voices, enclosing and setting off the narrative almost in the manner of the traditional "once upon a time" and "they lived happily ever after": narrative demarcates, encloses, establishes limits, orders. . . . Narrative [is] always in a state of repetition, as a going over again of ground already covered.

Several musicologists have recently considered possibilities of narrative in music.[16] I would like to contribute to this discussion by suggesting a distinction that, in general, has been ignored – primarily because it has been largely ignored by literary critics themselves. Theorists of narrative have focused largely on prose; or, more precisely, on species of narrative exemplified by self-contained works of fiction (thus including certain species of poetry, for example the ballad). But all such narratives must be distinguished from another type, namely spoken narratives *within a drama*: messengers reporting disaster, one character explaining or rationalizing earlier events to another, a character talking to himself (a soliloquy), and so forth. Notwithstanding the explosion of narratological theory in recent years, these have been little studied.[17] Like all narratives, their diction is distinct from that of their context (especially as regards verb tenses), and they are "framed" as well, by introductory phrases ("Now listen!") and by reactions at the end, which articulate the new dramatic state achieved by their performance. They also collapse the customary distinction between so-called *erzählte Zeit* and *Erzähl-zeit*, between the time of the events in the tale and the time of its telling, because a dramatic narrator informs his listeners, and us, of *past* events by the performative speech-act of telling the story *in the present*.

At least under certain conditions, this synthesis of past and present can also occur in the musical domain. The most obvious examples are found in opera. Consider Abbate's interpretation of what happens at the climax of Tannhäuser's narrative of his pilgrimage to Rome:

When Tannhäuser calls again on the ostinato [the prominent orchestral motive heard at the beginning of the narrative], presents it as a fragment, and pauses to say, "then I too drew near," he makes out of that ostinato motive a musical symbol: [it] mimics the halting resumption of motion as Tannhäuser takes his first steps towards the Pope. . . . The motive's *symbolic meaning is revealed to us*; and *at once we rehear and reinterpret* the Rome narrative's opening verses: what had seemed merely a "theme" . . . that could not comment on the text it accompanied, is *revealed* as a *secret sign* with a *secret meaning*.[18]

In principle, the same effects are obtainable in all opera. Early opera is full of narrative, from *Orfeo*'s messenger onwards. Mozart's and Da Ponte's clearest example is Donna

---

[16] A sampling: Peter Kivy, *Sound and Semblance: Reflections on Musical Representation* (Princeton, 1984), chap. 9, "Music as Narrative"; Anthony Newcomb, "Schumann and Late Eighteenth-Century Narrative Strategies," *19CMus* 11 (1987–88), 164–74, §§I–II; Abbate, "What the Sorcerer Said"; Maus, "Humanism," chap. 3, "Music as Narrative." I have found Abbate's and Maus's approaches the most helpful and have drawn on them in the following.

[17] An exception is Nina C. Ekstein, *Dramatic Narrative: Racine's Récits* (New York, 1986), pp. 1–10, 35–69, 139–60. (Keir Elam's useful *The Semiotics of Theatre and Drama* [London and New York, 1980] does not focus on formal narratives of this type.)

[18] Abbate, "Erik's Dream and Tannhäuser's Journey," in Arthur Groos and Roger Parker, eds., *Reading Opera* (Princeton, 1988), p. 161 (emphasis added).

Anna's account of Don Giovanni's attack on her at the beginning of the opera, told to
Don Ottavio just before "Or sai chi l'onore." Even more striking in its merging of past
and present is Count Almaviva's narrative in the Trio (No. 7) in Act I of *Figaro*: "Yester-
day, I suspected Cherubino of hiding under the table in Antonio's house, and found
him by pulling off the tablecloth, just . . . like . . . *this!*" – and poor Cherubino is discovered again, before our eyes, in the dramatic-musical present. Several narratives are
found in *Die Zauberflöte* as well.[19] Just as theory predicts, these narratives are "signaled,"
not merely verbally and dramatically, but musically as well: for example, the Count's narrative in *Figaro* begins in recitative style and is set off from the surrounding bustling
activity by reduced scoring and simpler textures and rhythms. Those in *Die Zauberflöte*
are marked by musical invocations of the symbolic, mythical aspects of past actions.

I see no reason not to extend this principle to instrumental music – at least under
conditions like those obtaining in Haydn's Symphony No. 46. The minuet recall is
"framed": by the gesture of breaking off, by the difference in style, by its self-reflexive
nature. And what is it that we hear? A dying fall, in the guise of a somewhat stately
minuet, which we know we have heard before, but at first cannot quite place. It conveys
a recognition, that could be verbalized as follows: "Once upon a time there was a happier
world, a world of ordered minuets, unlike this hurlyburly"; and it says this in a tone
of nostalgia and regret. It is also narrative-like in the larger senses of abrogating "ordinary" generic "discourse" and integrating the musical past into the musical present.

Comparable remarks are common with respect to Beethoven's recalls, not least the
analogous case of the scherzo in Symphony No. 5. Here is Tovey:

> The motto "Lest we forget" is an admirable summary of the effect which Beethoven produces
> when, [in the finale,] at the end of his development, he is preparing quite formally on the
> dominant for a return to his main theme. . . . But then comes the silence, measured, rather
> than broken, by the dying swing of the rhythm. [The Scherzo] has acquired a character for which
> it had no leisure in its original terrifying surroundings. It is a memory of the past, not a recapture
> of it. Without undue sentimentality, we can pity ourselves for past terrors, and even a hero's
> reference to them may take a pathetic tone. . . .[20]

I don't agree that Beethoven's scherzo-recall is only a memory, but the point here is
Tovey's implicit belief that music *can* invoke its own past. As he put it in another context,
"We are apt to forget or ignore the privilege of music to treat the time-direction in a
way of its own, retracing the past and grasping the future."[21] I don't mean merely that
Tovey is telling stories *about* the music, which we all do all the time; but that, at least in
contexts like these, instrumental music itself seems to tell a story – even though it may be,
as Maus argues, a story without referents or identifiable agents.

A number of music theorists who otherwise betray no direct influence of narratology
implicitly agree with this position. Jonathan D. Kramer distinguishes, in the first movement of Beethoven's F-major Quartet Op. 135, between "gestural time" and "piece-

---

[19] See Webster, "Cone's 'Personae' and the Analysis of Opera," *CMS* 29 (1989), 64–65.
[20] *Beethoven* (London, 1945), pp. 17–18.
[21] With respect to Brahms's *Schicksalslied*; *Essays*, vol. 5, p. 227.

time," in ways which are strikingly analogous to the narratologists' distinction between story and discourse, *Erzählzeit* and *erzählte Zeit*. Cone, in his somewhat notorious little essay "Schubert's Promissory Note" – not by coincidence, in a context of extramusical speculations – asserts that "formal repetitions are often best interpreted as representations of events rehearsed in memory."[22] (Note the complexity of this formulation.) In fact, Abbate's characterization of Tannhäuser's Rome narrative is pertinent to the recall in Symphony No. 46. We "at once rehear and reinterpret" the meaning of Haydn's minuet. It is yet another example of his music about music, of his irony.

Haydn's meta-musical reminiscence conflates past and present, minuet and Presto, into a complex presentation of the underlying idea of Symphony No. 46. What is that idea? As suggested above, the answer must lie in its manifold relationships with the Farewell Symphony. Surely No. 46 also had extramusical associations; surely two works composed at the same time, at once so extraordinary and having so much in common, were directly related – as a *pair* of programmatic works. (Haydn had long before composed a programmatic trilogy, the *Matin–Midi–Soir* sequence.) For example, the crucial unaccompanied minuet-recall phrase in No. 46, the key to its extramusical aspect, descends from F♯ to C♯, and is answered by a descent from F♯ to B – that is, the same motive (*e2*) which was the focus of the Farewell's attempts to achieve coherent melody, in the "motivic" form shown in Example 2.13. Hence Haydn must have intended the two works to be heard in a definite order. (Both were composed in the autumn of 1772; there is no known evidence bearing on their order of composition.) Did the B-major work come last? Do its slightly more familiar key and major mode invoke life back in Eisenstadt, with the minor mode of the Vivace and the Balkanisms in the middle reminders of the "wasteland" of Eszterháza, now happily left behind? Does the joking finale suggest that "they all lived happily ever after" in the tonic, after tribulations in the dominant? Or did it come first? Is it an image of life *at* Eszterháza (minor mode; Balkanisms); is the bittersweet minuet-reminiscence a reminder of happy, ordered times in Eisenstadt, still past, not yet regained? Do the two works progress from unhappy but bearable life in the present (with a minuet-reminiscence of happier times), through unbearable tension, to a vision of ethereal longing represented by the "action" of the musicians' departure from the hall? Such questions cannot be answered. But the search for such meanings – critically and skeptically pursued, to be sure, and in the first instance limited to contexts that give reason to suppose it relevant – is an essential aspect of any comprehensive understanding of Haydn's music. In this case it even suggests the astonishing possibility that he composed overarching "cycles" of two or more complete instrumental works.

[22] Kramer, "Multiple and Non-Linear Time in Beethoven's Opus 135," *Perspectives of New Music* 11/2 (Spring-Summer 1973), pp. 122–45; Cone, "Schubert's Promissory Note," *19CMus* 5 (1981–82), 240.

SONATA NO. 30 IN A: THE LIMITS OF
THROUGH-COMPOSITION

Sonata No. 30 in A major belongs to a set of six, Hob. XVI:27–32, composed apparently beginning in 1774 (following the Esterházy set XVI:21–26 of 1773) and disseminated in 1776. As a whole, the set is mixed in style: No. 27 in G is technically easy and "light" throughout; Nos. 28 in E-flat, 29 in F, and 31 in E mix easy and difficult, amateurs' and connoisseurs' music; No. 32 in B minor, notwithstanding its minuet in the middle, is uncompromisingly serious. (Five of the six works, all of which are in three movements, include a minuet.)

But nothing else in the set is remotely comparable to No. 30: this is Haydn's only instrumental work in three or more movements that is completely through-composed. It too is mixed in style. Although the interior Adagio invokes a connoisseurs' world, the outer movements suggest amateurs: the Allegro is in sonata form, but simple in texture and relatively easy; the finale is a minuet with six variations. The Allegro exposition ends (Example 8.13a) in Alberti-bass texture in both hands in octaves, cadencing into a dotted-rhythm fanfare (which recalls the half-cadence in the first group, mm. 13–16). In the recapitulation, however (8.13b), the second closing-theme statement diverges into an up-then-down sequence which eventually lands on a dominant seventh (m. 160), with a fermata on the downbeat of m. 162, followed by a rapid arpeggio breaking off on D (present since m. 157), with a second fermata over the ensuing rest. The second, conclusive cadence (equivalent to m. 55) and the fanfare have disappeared: closure is denied. (The technique is the same as in the Presto of the Farewell Symphony, mm. 45 and 53 vs. 136ff.)

Now follows the Adagio (Example 8.14), beginning abruptly on the dominant of F-sharp minor (V^6/vi).[23] Although one's initial impression is of an instrumental recitative (dotted motives, very short phrases, modulatory), from m. 165 on we hear a stylized, *Fortspinnung*-like improvisation based on a one-bar motive; it contrasts rising arpeggiated staccato eighths in the left hand with long-note, continually varied appoggiatura figures in the right. The restrainedly expressive style is markedly different from the Allegro; it recalls the Andante of the connoisseur-type Sonata No. 19 in D (1767; see Example 8.15). The impression of F-sharp minor also proves illusory: the music moves through B minor back to A, leading to half-cadences in m. 174 and, more strongly, mm. 180 and 182–83; the finale follows immediately. Even though its phrase structure is more or less regular – from m. 165 it proceeds by two-bar units, complexly grouped, (2+2)+ 2+4; 4+(2+2[+1]) –, the Adagio exhibits neither coherent themes nor closed form; it simply ruminates on its one-bar motive. Unlike Haydn's other run-on keyboard slow movements (see Chapter 6), it never implies closure (and hence cannot "deny" it as they do); it is not an independent movement at all. This is symbolized in the notation: at the beginning of the Adagio, there is no double-bar or other sign of separate status; at the end, no fermata. (The lack of the title "Finale," it must be acknowledged, is

---

[23] Brown, *Keyboard Music*, p. 308, briefly discusses the first two movements of this sonata (stating, however, that m. 162 is "on the tonic" and resolves "to C-sharp major").

Example 8.13 Sonata No. 30, Allegro:

(a) End of exposition

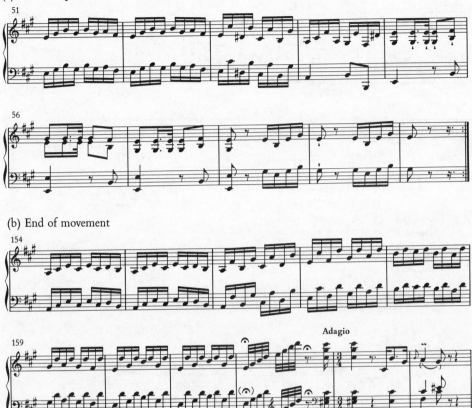

(b) End of movement

Example 8.14 Sonata No. 30: Adagio and finale theme

Ex. 8.14 (*cont.*)

Example 8.15 Sonata No. 19/ii, 67–73

common in Haydn's keyboard minuet/finales from the 1770s.) The entire sonata is a single structure, more in two movements than three, with a stylistically distinct, modulating transition which leads away from the dominant at the end of the Allegro and back again:

F   (Tr)   Fn

I–V——(V/vi–ii–I–)V——I

But of course the effect of the Adagio is hardly that of a mere transition. As described in Chapter 6, such mixed patterns hovering between two and three movements are characteristic of Haydn's keyboard music, and are strongly correlated with the presence of run-on movement pairs. But nowhere else did he so systematically pursue the through-composed ideal.

As one might expect, the Adagio is linked to the other movements tonally and thematically. The dotted rhythm, especially at the two joins (mm. 162–63 and even more 182–83), seems to account for the "missing" fanfare at the end of the Allegro. Tonally, the deceptive resolution to V/vi at the beginning of the Adagio relates to the development of the Allegro, which centers around F-sharp minor virtually throughout. Note especially the fermata on V^7/vi in m. 96 (Example 8.16a), with extremes of both high and low register which the continuation, though tonally a resolution, signally fails to notice; indeed, the first later gesture that resembles this striking event is precisely the fermata on V^7 and the high V^6/vi which lead into the Adagio itself. (Both passages are prepared by the octave-arpeggio closing theme.) A strange passage in the second group (Example 8.16b), in which the alto at first fails to resolve (see m. 130), also emphasizes F-sharp minor in the recapitulation.

Example 8.16 Sonata No. 30/i

(a) 91–98

Ex. 8.16 (*cont.*)

(b) 129–36

Further continuity derives from C♯, which is the leading melodic pitch in much of the second-group recapitulation (mm. 129–34, 141–46), at the join to the Adagio, and at both tonic cadences within the Adagio (mm. 170 and 178). The minuet theme itself begins on c♯² and circles around it. Indeed, Adagio and minuet have the same middleground "motive": a descending third spread out over four bars, 2+2 (shown in Example 8.14). It opens the Adagio (mm. 165–68), on f♯¹–d¹; more importantly, the last four bars preceding the half-cadence (mm. 175–78) return to it, descending chromatically from e² to c♯². The minuet not only begins by rising directly from c♯² back to e², but its opening four-bar phrase almost literally repeats mm. 175–78 from the Adagio, the last three bars harmonically as well as melodically;[24] even the ornaments – F♯ in the second bar (mm. 176, 2), C♯/E in the fourth (mm. 178, 4) – are the same. (In the final reprise of these bars in the last variation, mm. 105–08, the left hand recalls the rising eighths of the Adagio.) The Adagio thus introduces both motivic content and middleground structure of the finale theme.

Moreover, the background tonal structure similarly carries through all three movements (see Example 8.17). The Allegro first group appears to establish e² as a headnote (mm. 1–3, 9–11, 16–18 and, in the recapitulation, mm. 108–10 and 117–19), implying a background 5̂-line; but in the recapitulation d² is conspicuous by its absence in prominent descending contexts; indeed (as described above) c♯² seems to govern the second group. However, in ways that are now familiar to us, all the perfect cadences in the second-group recapitulation are too weak to achieve closure. Hence, when the closing theme reverts to e² (mm. 150, 154), it has the effect of the recapture of a still-undisplaced background headnote – which is immediately connected in the most forceful manner to the very

---

[24] The connection between the Adagio, mm. 165–68, and the beginning of the finale was noted by Abert, "Haydns Klaviersonaten," pp. 539–40.

Example 8.17 Sonata No. 30: structural voice-leading

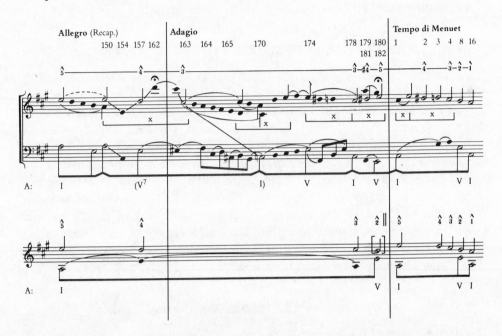

strong D over the climactic dominant seventh (mm. 157–62). Thus the resolution to
C♯ at the beginning of the Adagio finally sounds like part of a potentially background
melodic descent, but it is too late! – in the "wrong" movement, and over a chromatic,
off-tonic harmony. The entire Adagio (Examples 8.14 and 8.17) now plays with the
relation between C♯ and E; at the join to the finale, instead of descending to the tonic
($\hat{2}$–$\hat{1}$), we *rise* back to e² through its leading-tone d♯² (♯$\hat{4}$). The finale theme begins again
on a structural e² but, for the first time in the sonata, brings the line down (through
d♯² as well as d²) to clear and strong closure on the tonic. The unassuming minuet theme
articulates the only complete background structure in the sonata: indeed, it provides the
tonal resolution of the entire work – especially owing to its strong motion through
b¹ ($\hat{2}$, in mm. 8 and 15), which was studiously avoided in the last five bars of the Adagio.
(Its sixfold repetition in the variations gives it more than sufficient weight to carry out
this function.) As in the double finale of the Farewell Symphony, this entire three-
movement sonata projects a single tonal structure.

But its aesthetic and rhetorical import remains obscure. On the one hand, the Adagio's
invocation of high style (improvisatory recitative) does not match the easy tone of the
two movements it links; on the other, it seems odd to associate the minuet's tonal resolution of the entire sonata with such an unassuming style. Brown coyly implies that Haydn
deliberately kept the opening movement simple, in order to "set up" the surprise of the
transitional middle movement. This is plausible enough; but until the finale is included
in the picture, and the point of the whole clarified, it does not explain very much.
One also speculates (as always in such cases) about extramusical associations; none

come to mind. If Sonata No. 30 is Haydn's most thoroughly through-composed work, it also remains something of an enigma.

TWO C-MAJOR QUARTETS: THE FINALE AS CULMINATION

Haydn's String Quartets Op. 20 No. 2 (1772) and Op. 54 No. 2 (1788) are his most extensively through-composed works in the genre. In addition, they have many unusual features in common. Both are monotonal works in C major, with the tonic minor in slow movement and trio; in both, the slow movement is an Adagio with prominent fantasy elements, and is run-on to the minuet; each has a unique finale, which functions as a culmination of the entire work. (Of course, they remain individual artworks in a greater number of other respects.) Unlike most of the other "pairs" described in this chapter, they date from different periods: Op. 20, along with the Farewell and Symphonies 46 and 47 (composed the same year), represents the climax of the "Sturm und Drang"; Op. 54/55, along with Opp. 50 and 64, Symphonies 88–92, and Sonatas 48 and 49, the high-water mark of Haydn's instrumental composition during the last years (1787–90) of his tenure at the Esterházy court.

Op. 20 No. 2 and the "problem" of the fugal finale

Op. 20 No. 2 is one of three quartets in this set with fugal finales. As Kirkendale emphasizes (pp. 141–45), the long and honorable tradition of such finales in Viennese chamber music was still very much alive in 1772; their appearance in Op. 20 entailed no overt disruption of genre expectations. This has not prevented musicologists from criticizing them as inadequate "solutions" of two supposed "problems" of the genre: the synthesis of strict and free style in instrumental music, and the role of the finale in the string quartet.[25] (I treat these topics in detail in the concluding chapter.) Whether because of this prejudice, or the profession's discomfort with freely developing, non-periodic forms, no detailed analyses of these fascinating and original fugues have been published[26] – nor can I attempt them here; my subject is their function within the works they conclude.

As is well known, the three fugues in Op. 20 contrast markedly with each other; each conforms to the style of the quartet it concludes (especially that of the opening movement). That in F minor (No. 5) is based on traditional fugal *topoi*, developed in a virtuoso display of contrapuntal devices (stretti, canon, simultaneous statement of the theme and its inversion). It is at once serious and passionate; for Tovey (p. 47), it matches the "astonishing depth of thought" of the opening Allegro moderato, creating "the most nearly tragic work Haydn ever wrote." It is thus a classic example of cyclic culmination,

---

[25] See especially Sandberger, "Streichquartett," pp. 257–63; Finscher, *Streichquartett*, vol. 1, pp. 220, 231–37, 266–67.

[26] Some comments are found in Tovey, "Haydn's Chamber Music," pp. 43–46; Finscher, pp. 231–32; Kirkendale, pp. 141–45. (Kirkendale's original German edition [Tutzing, 1966] contains schematic diagrams, not included in the English translation, but still no full-dress analysis.)

a common generic role for fugal finales (see Chapter 6); at the same time, its traditional *topoi* mark it as a connoisseurs' movement – severe, forbidding, bristling with
contrapuntal artifice. It includes a lengthy exploration of remote flat-side keys centering
around the Neapolitan G-flat (mm. 61–78), which has virtually no parallel in the Austrian
fugal repertory (Kirkendale, p. 143). This creates a tonal link with the remarkable coda of
the first movement, which passes through G-flat to the *minor* Neapolitan, G-flat minor
(mm. 142–45), a very rare key relation indeed in the eighteenth century. One can also
hear the ensuing fourfold cello motive, c–C (mm. 148–51) – a dominant pedal in the
lowest two registers – as related to the very long, climactic pedals in the fugue, on the
same two notes in the same order (mm. 103–11, 135–44).

In the A-major Quartet (No. 6), the "capricious" fugue (as both Finscher and Kirkendale characterize it) recalls the tone of the Allegro di molto (which Haydn marks
"di scherzando"). Finscher also points out a similarity between the headmotives of
the Allegro di molto and the minuet. Notwithstanding its playful high spirits, the
level of contrapuntal artifice in its fugue is nearly as high as in that in F minor; perhaps
Haydn intended this to be understood as a deliberate incongruity. Nevertheless, its
tone marks it, stylistically, as a "light" or "galant" finale. Thus these two works, and
specifically their fugues, incorporate the two basic – and opposed – stylistic orientations of the time.

But the C-major fugue is more difficult to "locate" in this regard. The theme with
its countersubject (see Example 8.18) is mixed in style; Kirkendale (p. 144) describes it

Example 8.18 String Quartet Op. 20/2, finale, 1–5

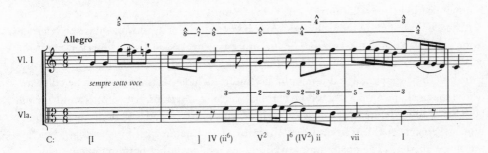

as "a new world . . . [of] elegance and charm. . . . The graceful upbeat introduces, for
the first time in a fugue subject, the chromatic passing-notes familiar from Viennese
classical melody." Finscher (p. 232) writes as follows:

The main theme . . . with its 6/8 dance-like rhythm, its veiled periodic structure, its precious
chromaticism . . . captures the relaxed-playful character of a Classical finale in the strictness of
a fugue, but no longer has anything much to do with the academic fugue tradition. It corresponds
to this new tone . . . that *motivische Arbeit* plays an almost greater role in the construction of
the movement than contrapuntal thematic development, that the episodes . . . increase in length
. . . [and] suspend strict [four-part] part-writing over long stretches.

But the "periodic structure" (which Kirkendale also mentions) is an illusion. The middle of the phrase includes no root-position dominant or cadential articulation: the g^1 on the downbeat of m. 3 (the source of this interpretation) continues seamlessly down through F to E, in both octaves, and the viola proves the point by entering on f^1, which the melodic g^1 transforms into a dissonance, forcing both lines downwards in an unbroken 3–2–3 contrapuntal chain. Nor is the part writing significantly more relaxed in the contrapuntal sections than in the other fugues.

The episodes, to be sure, are longer and more homophonic. But this feature relates in a more general way to all three fugues' manner of ending, which is indeed their most significant "generic" aspect. Here is Tovey (pp. 44–45):

[The] fugues are directed to be played *sotto voce* [actually "sempre sotto voce"] until, at or near the end, a sudden *forte* winds them up in a coda which more or less abandons fugal polyphony so as to end the work in sonata style. . . . These fugues . . . effectively establish fugue texture from henceforth as a normal resource of sonata style. Here and hereafter Haydn knows not only how to write a whole fugue for instruments, but how to let a fugue passage break out in a sonata movement and boil over quickly enough to accomplish dramatic action instead of obstructing it.

No later writer has grasped as clearly that the reason for Haydn's abandonment of strict counterpoint and four-part writing towards the end of these fugues is that they function as finales of works in sonata style. In this sense, they are indeed analogous to Haydn's (and Mozart's) later fugato passages, used in preference to full-blown fugal finales (see pp. 184–85). A further point is relevant to the C-major fugue in particular. As we have seen, each of the other two is intelligible from the beginning as a particular stylistic type. Consequently, their turn to *forte* and to sonata style comes relatively late: in F minor, periodic phrasing in m. 161, *forte* not until m. 179 (six bars from the end); in A major, unison texture in m. 92 (only four bars from the end; the *forte* must be inferred from the context and the example of the other two works).[27] In C, however, the *forte* comes much sooner (m. 129 of 162); the windup is correspondingly longer, internally varied, both contrapuntal and homophonic, and it includes several intermediate climaxes before the final unison phrase, whose chromatics, suddenly transformed into an image of power, *rise* towards the final cadence. In short, this is a true coda, the only one in these fugues; perhaps for this reason, it seems to provide closure not just for the finale, but for the entire quartet. (The final phrase strikingly resembles another homophonic windup to a concluding fugue in the key of C: the "Drinking" chorus at the end of Autumn in *The Seasons*. The latter, in turn, sounds like nothing so much as the rousing conclusion to yet another work whose fugal finale raises inebriation to the highest sphere of comedy: the final orchestral phrase in *Falstaff*. Could this have been a bit of playful *omaggio* on Verdi's part?)

More difficult to "read," however, is the function of the C-major fugue as the conclusion of the work as a whole, one of Haydn's most unusual. The two interior movements of Op. 20 No. 2 are run-on; the "Capriccio" Adagio is unique in style and form. Finscher sensibly attempts to relate the fugue's mixed character to other features in

---

[27] As always, only the texts in *JHW* are to be trusted.

the quartet, but (following Friedrich Blume) he cannot repress an uneasy feeling that Haydn has gone too far:

The first movement, through the obbligato three-part writing of its main theme, prepares for a pronounced level of counterpoint; the C-minor Capriccio . . . strengthens our expectation of the unusual through its Baroque associations. . . . Through its *attacca*-transition, the minuet is . . . at least outwardly linked to that movement, though in style it is more closely related to the first movement. . . . The fugue . . . intensifies the character of the first movement from unspecific play to specifically capricious counterpoint. Discreet archaism on the one hand, transformation of the academic fugue into a characteristic finale on the other, are brought into a balance of part-writing, such that at least the fugue no longer acts like a foreign body. Admittedly, the complications of this solution make the danger of spinning oneself into an esoteric web of artificial and overcomplex forms . . . especially clear.[28]

This passage illustrates the dangers of interpreting a composer on Haydn's level *primarily* on the basis of notions of genre, style, and movement-type; they lead to the absurdity that the F-minor fugue in No. 5 is a "foreign body"! (This is the tacit comparison in Finscher's phrase, "no longer acts like a foreign body" [see his p. 235; as we will see in the concluding chapter, this notion derives from Sandberger].) Compare Tovey:

Op 20, No. 2 . . . begins with a cantabile for the 'cello which tersely achieves a fine spaciousness by the way in which it repeats its figures and adds a "dying fall," which latter strain, repeated, gains energy to move to the dominant, in which key the violin takes up the theme [m. 7]. But for the translucent string-quartet tone, such an opening might not have been inconceivable in the old Neapolitan music; yet here there is no reversion to an old style, but the rediscovery of an ancient truth in a modern light. And this opening is no mere case of a 'cello solo; the discovery that the instrument can warble away in the tenor clef is not more important than the discovery that its fourth string can, with good economy, sound unfathomably deep, and that a not too rapid arpeggio ranging over all four strings *pesante* [mm. 16–17] is one of the most sonorous possibilities of quartet style. . . . Yet . . . this movement, so rich and so uniquely romantic in sound, . . . is not normal. . . . Haydn teaches a stern lesson: this movement is without sin or blemish; yet he never scored so gorgeously for string quartet again!   (pp. 41–42)

Tovey's phrase "the old Neapolitan music" (that is, the trio-sonata) circumscribes the slightly old-fashioned tone of the first movement, its initially contrapuntal texture, and its presentation of the main-theme complex almost in the manner of a fugal exposition: cello in the tonic, first violin in the dominant, second violin in the tonic (mm. 1, 7, 15). (The opening paragraph of Op. 20 No. 1 in E-flat is similarly constructed, notwithstanding its lack of overt counterpoint.) Historically naive though it may be, Tovey's account captures the peculiar style of this movement, leisurely yet dense, contrapuntal yet galant. Most important, he is not inhibited by a preoccupation with "types." The scoring of this movement is "rich," "sonorous," "luxurious," "lush," "gorgeous," even "romantic" – in a word, unique. "It is without sin or blemish"; nevertheless, what is decisive is Haydn's rigor: both his consistency in exploiting these special effects here, and his "stern lesson" in never repeating them.

---

[28] Finscher, pp. 235–36; cf. Blume, "Haydns Persönlichkeit," pp. 37–39.

Even better is Tovey's account of the "Capriccio"; alone in the literature, it reflects an unbiased appreciation of its development through time into an individual form:

Haydn takes a lingering farewell of all operatic idioms in a grand fantasia beginning with a noble, tragic unison theme which moves in vast sequences, expanding now and then into ruminating and declamatory passages for the first violin, shared in due course by the other instruments. This plan is nobly conceived, and executed with accurate dramatic sense; with the result that when eventually a pause on the dominant, *pp* [actually *piano assai*], is reached [m. 33], one is prepared for some such event as the opening of a lively or impassioned finale. What happens instead is a continuation of the adagio in a stream of consoling melody in the relative major. . . . Haydn shows here that he has clearly grasped the principles of composition on a larger scale than sonata form permits: it is manifestly inconceivable that this cantabile should behave as a "second subject," or that the first theme ever had any intention of confining itself to the function of a "first subject." It would take twenty minutes to work the material out in that way, and then there would be no sense of freedom and expansion. But Haydn is here able to make his melody ruminate and rhapsodize, to interpolate several ominous interruptions in the former tragic style, and finally to drift, in three solemn steps of gigantic sequence [mm. 54, 57, 59], down once more to the dominant of C. And now, in C major, the minuet begins, in a hesitating syncopated rhythm, like an awakening gaze dazzled by the sunlight – after which all is sunshine, with just the right shadow in the trio. Haydn shows in this pair of movements what Mozart showed later in his C minor Fantasia (K. 475), that if composition within the time-scale of the sonata had not absorbed his interest, he could easily have produced a music that moved like a modern [1929] symphonic poem. His art of composition is a general power that creates art-forms, not a routine derived from the practice of *a priori* schemes.   (pp. 42–43)

The master critic of sonata form here acknowledges that the basis of Haydn's formal genius was his general powers of composition, *independent of sonata style* (and, one could add, of historical "types"). It amounts to a manifesto of flexibility in analysis, appropriate to Haydn's compositional flexibility, and a warning against all analysis according to mechanical principles or reductive methods.

With this guidance, we can attempt a scenario for Op. 20 No. 2. In the first place, like Symphony No. 46, it at once commands attention as a rare monotonal work in the major mode (see the end of Chapter 6). Combined with the extraordinary nature of all four movements, especially the Capriccio/minuet pair, we can have every expectation that Haydn intended it to be understood as "through-composed." Sandberger and Finscher are not wrong to invoke the issues of counterpoint vs. freedom, tradition vs. novelty. But what they see as a "problem" – the apparent incompatibility of style within the generic context – is precisely Haydn's governing idea.

Blume, in his impressionistic-metaphysical description of Haydn's development towards cyclic integration – "to force the quartet, as a whole as in its several parts, into a unity, to subsume it under *one* idea" – comes closer:

With its *pianissimo* ending, the sonata-form [first] movement pulled the storm-cloud of the slow movement in its train like a force of nature. The slow movement dissolves in the spray . . . [and] without a [full] cadence glides into the minuet. But minuet and trio repeat, attenuated and in miniature, the conflict of the first two movements, . . . C major against C minor, . . . the unisons of the trio [and] the [*pianissimo*] dying-out of the minuet, so that even at the end of the third movement there has still been no decisive interruption in the overall structure. . . . The highest summit of possible unity is achieved, the cycle shaped with all possible consistency – how could this cycle attain a final culmination, if not in the strictest form of musical thought: the fugue?[29]

We can refine this account by pursuing more consistently Haydn's confrontation of contrapuntal and galant writing. The Moderato begins with a pseudo-fugal exposition, but is in sonata form and otherwise not overtly contrapuntal. Indeed it is almost demonstratively galant in tone; its leisure and its luxurious scoring represent free as opposed to strict style, and they are nowhere more in evidence than during the contrapuntal exposition itself: the cello lingers on high g^1 and "repeats its figures and adds a 'dying fall'" (Tovey). The Capriccio invokes a quite different tradition: a *scena* in pathetic style, combining threatening instrumental majesty (the dotted-rhythm theme in the bass), recitative, and aria. However, this scene is not self-contained; it does not even imply a coherent form, let alone achieve closure (Blume gives no sense of this); it can become complete only "outside" itself, by being run-on into the minuet. But the minuet is thoroughly modern – homophonic, melody-dominated, binary-like in its move to and cadence in the dominant in the first part, and so forth. Nevertheless, continuity is maintained: the trio in the minor not only distantly reminds us of the Capriccio, but is likewise run-on to the repetition of the minuet, which ends, in turn, with an intangible reminiscence of the *pianissimo* end of the Moderato.

All this Blume understands; he does not exaggerate the extent to which the finale has been set up to function as a culmination. But he says nothing about this fugue! Nor, despite his frequent invocations of Haydn's governing "idea," does he specify what this idea might actually have been. And yet, precisely the "confrontation of styles" would seem to qualify.[29a] The Moderato begins with a combination of contrapuntal texture and galant style; although the contrapuntal opening returns several times, it is never meaningfully developed, and the movement ends without any concluding reference to it. The expressive *scena* in high *seria* style moves without self-sufficiency or closure to the galant minuet, itself shadowed by the trio. The main part of the fugue combines "chromatic elegance and charm" (Kirkendale) with contrapuntal fireworks, but it moves to and concludes in sonata style even more decisively than the other fugues in this opus. As a whole, Op. 20 No. 2 thus progresses *from* counterpoint (admixed with the galant) and tradition (never self-sufficient), *to* the galant and sonata style.

Why should this be so? Within Op. 20, Haydn grouped the three fugal quartets together, in the order F minor, A major, C major (most likely reflecting their order of composition).[30] This also entails a systematic progression of the three fugues: the F-minor

[29] "Haydns Persönlichkeit," pp. 37, 39.

[29a] On this point see also Dahlhaus, *Analysis and Value Judgment* (New York, 1983), pp. 66–71.

[30] The primary evidence is the order of Haydn's entries of the incipits for Op. 20 in *EK*, which in other cases demonstrably reflects his intended ordering; see *JHW* XII/3, [vii]. That these three works belong together as a subgroup is further implied by the autograph: not only by differences in the ink (ibid., critical report, p. 9) but also, more objectively, by the fact that the three fugal quartets were written exclusively on one paper type, the other three primarily on another (this distinction is not reported in *JHW*). (This observation emerged from my examination of the autograph [Vienna, Gesellschaft der Musikfreunde] in 1986; I thank Dr. Otto Biba, the director of the archive, for his exemplary cooperation.) In view of these consistent documentary indications, Somfai's speculations regarding a different temporal ordering ("Vom Barock zur Klassik"; "Opus-Planung und Neuerung") are unpersuasive.

fugue is composed on two "soggetti" (in Haydn's autograph nomenclature), the A-major on three, the C-major on four. Given the demonstratively unusual nature of these quartets, all this implies that they actually constitute a loose "cycle" of three complete works (in the sense often asserted of Beethoven's Op. 59 and, especially, Opp. 130/133, 131, and 132; – and which we have just seen may apply to Haydn's Symphonies 45 and 46 as well). The keys are compatible with this hypothesis: in the order proposed here, they rise in thirds through a triad; as a set, they "frame" C major with a distinctly flat-side key and a distinctly sharp-side one. And if this be granted, we must surely suppose that Haydn intended his "cycle" to be understood extramusically. The F-minor quartet (which is also monotonal) would signify traditional, serious style and despairing passion; the A-major, galant wit and playful exuberance. (These meanings would be compatible with eighteenth-century notions of key characteristics.[31]) But if we hear the works in order, the cycle *progresses*: from traditional and severe, through the galant, to a mixture in which the galant eventually predominates. It would remain an open question whether Haydn intended the quartet in C to stand for the coexistence of the two styles in his art, or the triumph of the galant over the traditional. The former hypothesis is more in keeping with eighteenth-century thought (which was largely free from evolutionism); the latter, with traditional twentieth-century notions of the course of musical history.

Thus the fugues in Op. 20 do not stand for traditional musical culture as opposed to the galant; they conclude works in both styles. In a different sense – present in all three quartets – they are among Haydn's strongest articulations of the finale as a culmination: equally exceptional, equally conclusive as the run-on, generically disruptive finales in the linked programmatic symphonies of the same year, Nos. 45 and 46. The "stern lesson" which Tovey invokes with respect to Haydn's never again having scored so gorgeously as in the C-major quartet applies to every aspect of his art: Haydn never repeated himself. By never again composing quartet fugues (with the single exception of Op. 50 No. 4), Haydn teaches the same lesson. Far from being the "dead-end of an exaggerated radicalism" (Blume), Op. 20 No. 2 – like the Farewell Symphony itself – is precisely radical enough.

Op. 54 No. 2 and the dialectic of listeners' expectations

Op. 54 No. 2 is also a monotonal work in C major, with the tonic minor in slow movement and trio, a slow-movement fantasy which is run-on to the minuet, and a unique culmination-finale. But this finale is utterly different from the fugue in Op. 20 No. 2; it is "about" musical form itself, whose conventions it manipulates as powerfully as any movement by Haydn (which is to say, any movement in Western music). Just these characteristics drew Cone's attention more than twenty-five years ago, in a discussion designed to provide a context for remarks devoted primarily to Stravinsky; it has remained relatively unfamiliar among Haydn scholars.[32] His account wonderfully focuses

---

[31] See Steblin, *A History of Key Characteristics.*

[32] "The Uses of Convention: Stravinsky and his Models," *MQ* 48 (1962), 287–99, §II. See also Keller. *The Great Haydn Quartets*, pp. 123–24.

on the aesthetics of genre, and on the paradoxical nature of our experience in hearing this movement. On the other hand, it is brief and impressionistic, and in some respects lacks historical perspective; a more significant limitation (characteristic of all musicology in the 1960s) is that Cone says nothing about the rest of the quartet. My interpretation expands on his (especially regarding the other movements) and differs in numerous particulars, without denying the essential "rightness" of his approach.

As Cone suggests, the key to understanding this remarkable movement is listeners' expectations. (The surviving authentic sources give nothing away; it is merely headed "Finale.") These Haydn systematically undermines, creating "a series of mistaken interpretations . . . cleverly ordered in such a way that the subsequent correction of each merely exposes the listener to the next error." Over the course of the movement, these continual reversals create a chain of defeated expectations, reinterpretations, and contradictions, which reaches stability only at the very end. The process resembles that described by Leonard B. Meyer under the concept "implication–realization,"[33] with this important difference: Meyer describes single melodies and other short spans and limits himself to tonal and motivic patternings, whereas here we must deal with an entire movement, whose audition entails the most complex aspects of musical understanding: genre, formal plan, and cyclic form. (As such, the discussion must again conflate the expectations of Haydn's listeners with our own.) Also, the majority of the mental processes described in Cone's and my accounts are intuitive, indeed largely unconscious; nevertheless, they remain decisive for our musical experience. (A formal diagram of the movement and a chart of expectations and reinterpretations are given in Table 8.1; the principal musical passages, in Example 8.19.)

In analysis, we can distinguish at least nine stages of expectation and reversal in our experience of the form of this movement (see the lower part of Table 8.1). The first stage occurs in silence – following the minuet, during which we anticipate that the music to follow will be the finale, and that it will be fast, lighter in style and texture than the opening Vivace, and (if we go this far) most likely a sonata or sonata-rondo. (Variations, simple rondos, and minuets had disappeared from Haydn's string-quartet finales after Op. 33.) The very opening gesture (theme 1) is thus a shock: the movement begins slowly, formally. In many contexts, the unison dotted figure would suggest majesty, or something ominous; the ensuing melody, divided subtly between lower and upper strings, is distinctly elevated in tone. Hence we interpret it as a slow introduction (not unheard of in finales; Mozart's G-minor String Quintet had been composed just the preceding year); that is (Stage 2), we expect that it will be asymmetrical and incomplete and head for the dominant, and that the body of the movement will be fast. But as we hear the passage develop into an antecedent-consequent period, and even more upon its repetition, we realize that it cannot be an ordinary introduction (see pp. 162–63), and therefore take it as the "main" section of the movement.

We now expect (Stage 3) that the movement as a whole will be an ABA or, possibly, a theme and variations or a compound (slow–fast) form. But the opening theme leads

[33] *Explaining Music*, Part II.

Example 8.19 String Quartet Op. 54/2: finale

Ex. 8.19 (*cont.*)

Ex. 8.19 (*cont.*)

Table 8.1. *Op. 54 No. 2 Finale*

Bars	1-8	9-40	41-56	56-122	123-130	+131-140
Section	1	2	3	4	1	+2 (Coda)
Rhetoric/idea	Period/a	Melody/b	Melody/b	Action/c	Period/a	(Melody)/b
Tempo	Adagio			Presto	Adagio	Adagio
Internal form	4 + 4 $\quad$ I–V V–I	||8|| 8+8 $\quad$ I–V V–I	8 + 8 $\quad$ i–♭III ♭III–V	||8|| ||8+8|| (+10) $\quad$ I–V V–I –V^6_5	8 $\quad$ I–V V–I	10 $\quad$ iv–v–I
Key	I	I	i	I	I	I

Stage	Expectation	Event (keyed to sections above)	Reinterpretation
1	Finale (fast; "light")	1: Adagio; elevated in tone	Slow introduction to fast finale
2	To V; "preparatory"	Eight-bar period; repeated	1 is (slow) main section
3	Next: Variation? Contrast?	2: Flows continuously from 1	Entire Adagio through-composed
4	2 will be comparable to 1	Real melody; articulated form	1 is introduction; 2 main section
5	Contrast	3: Minor; flows from and develops 2; to half-cadence and fermata	Disorientation
6	??	4: Presto!	Adagio slow introduction after all
7	Presto: main section	Theme only; deceptive cadence; to V^6_5 and fermata	Presto is only an episode
8	Adagio melody (Section 2)	1!	1 is a main section
9	1+2 to be recapitulated; form ABA (slow–fast–slow)	Only 1 (2 merely coda [V/IV])	1 is the generating idea; form is a b c a/b

seamlessly into the next section (theme **2**, mm. 9–40); this is neither a contrast nor a variation, but a "pure" melody for the first violin, supported by "slow creeping arpeggios of the 'cello [rising] from the depths right into the region of the melody, combining with the simple repeated chords of the accompaniment in one of the finest tone-colours in any quartet" (Tovey, "Haydn's Chamber Music," p. 57). This melody is related to the opening theme by its dotted-upbeat g–c motive (*x*), but otherwise distinct in content and phrasing. Is the movement then going to be through-composed? Apparently not: the melody develops (Stage 4) into a complete thirty-two-bar song form. This, combined with its expressive character, makes it sound like a "main" section, suggesting, in yet another reinterpretation, that section **1** was an introduction after all. (Note the increasingly complex and ineluctably retrospective character of each successive reinterpretation.) We therefore expect (Stage 5) a contrasting section following the expressive theme; but although the melody turns surprisingly to the minor (m. 40; section **3**), it continues to develop without additional change, confirming our impression that the movement is a through-composed Adagio. More important, however, lulled by the continually developing melody and the striking flat-side modulations (note the barely disguised parallel fifths in mm. 42–43), we cease following the outward form, at least until the eventual drift towards the home dominant (mm. 54–56) and the *pianissimo* dying-away. Here (Stage 6) we indeed actively expect "something new," although by now we no longer have any concrete idea what it might be.

It is a rollicking Presto! – precisely the sort of music which, before the finale began, we supposed we would hear, but which in the meantime we have entirely forgotten. Perhaps the Adagio, despite its length and squareness, is merely a slow introduction (as the move to the dominant and the fermata imply); perhaps (Stage 7) the finale will be generically "fast" after all? But the main part of the Presto (mm. 57–112; section **4**) is merely a single (large-scale) theme, again in stable, closed form (a|b–a, with a written-out repetition of the second half). And as Keller points out, it comes so late, and after so much complex action, that it does not sound like the large-scale opening theme of a rondo (as it would have done if it had opened the movement). In fact, if one bar of the Presto is taken at approximately one eighth-note of the Adagio (four bars equal one), the entire section will last no longer than sixteen bars of Adagio – equal to the opening eight-bar period and its repetition, or the first half of the violin melody. (Compare the Presto windup of the opening movement of the piano trio in G minor, Hob. XV:19; as Rosen demonstrated, and Sisman confirmed on the basis of eighteenth-century notions of form, this is an expansion of the earlier G-major variation.[34] To these arguments one could add that it takes scarcely longer than the Andante theme in performance.) On both counts, the Presto theme in Op. 54 No. 2 turns out to be comparable to, not hierarchically superior to, each individual section of the preceding Adagio. This impression is confirmed by the deceptive cadence at the end of the theme proper (m. 112) and the hasty extension to V^2 and its surprising inversion to V^6_5 (note the dramatic

---

[34] Rosen, *Classical Style*, pp. 83–88; Sisman, "Small and Expanded Forms: Koch's Model and Haydn's Music," *MQ* 68 (1982), 463–70.

"hanging" high f³), and another fermata. In short, the Presto is only another episode. But (Stage 8) what will follow *this* fermata? The expressive violin melody **2**?

The Adagio indeed returns – but in the form of the original antecedent-consequent period **1**. As it now "bears the weight of the recapitulation" (Cone), it must be a main constituent of the movement after all. (The word "recapitulation" claims too much, for there has been neither a second group in the dominant nor a development; "reprise" would be more accurate.) Having returned unexpectedly to the beginning, we now (Stage 9) expect the entire Adagio, including the violin melody **2**, to be repeated (at least in essentials), to produce an ABA form, slow–fast–slow. This is Haydn's last deception. Only **1** is functionally recapitulated, with strong harmonic progressions; **2** recurs only after the structural cadence (m. 130), and only over a tonic pedal: "The apparently introductory period of the first statement assumes full thematic stature on its return; while the melody originally developed most fully is relegated to the coda" (Cone). Poetically, those wonderful cello arpeggios now rise from this very tonic pedal, the sounding symbol of stability; and the violin theme **2** recaptures the hanging f³ (m. 134) and cadences from it.

What then is the form of this movement? In order not to prejudice the issue (and to encourage multiple interpretation), the upper portion of Table 8.1 includes only "objective" criteria: the sections are merely numbered (**1, 2, 3, 4, 1+2**), not named, and characterized only in terms of their tempo, key, and gesture. In particular, except for the conflation of sections **1** and **2** at the end, the table privileges no particular grouping of the sections – the prerequisite to any sense of the form as a whole. In fact, each musical domain suggests a different grouping. The most audible pattern is doubtless that of the mutually reinforcing parameters fermata and tempo-change: this implies an ABA form, with the Presto the contrast in the middle. But the key structure suggests a different ABA, with the minor mode the primary contrast. And the rhetorical (thematic) distinctions suggest a four- (or even five-) part form:

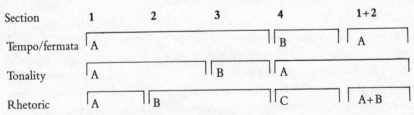

Section	1	2	3	4	1+2
Tempo/fermata	A			B	A
Tonality	A		B	A	
Rhetoric	A	B		C	A+B

Cone concludes, "The design of the whole is established as a ternary Adagio with a Presto interlude" (that is, ABCA); this slights the contrasts in tempo and tonality, and it seems problematical to downgrade the Presto **4** to a mere "interlude." It is not only the most prominent contrast, especially if the rhetoric of the two Adagio sections is thought to be more similar than different (as is after all implied by the final section), but its arrival is the only demarcation point that entails an essential contrast in all three principal domains. More to the point, however, as we have seen in other contexts (notably the D-major interlude of the Farewell Symphony), no one scheme, no single meaning, no formal "type" can account for the experience of hearing this movement.

(Cone himself elsewhere emphasizes this: "It is useless to ask of this movement, 'What "form" is it in?'") The question posed at the beginning of this paragraph is irrelevant.

The essential aspect of this finale is its continuity; this is not merely experiential, but involves both the individual section-forms and the actual motives. Each section is based on a stable formal type (see Table 8.1, top): antecedent-consequent period in **1**; song form (rounded binary) in **2**, **4**, and even **3** (broken off just before the putative cadence in the tonic). Despite the change of tempo, the Presto is thus a variation of the Adagio violin melody[35] – like the example from the G-minor Piano Trio (cited above) – except that it is not a thematic variation, but a structural one. This consistency of form in the small provides a substrate of intelligibility for this otherwise baffling movement. Also, there are subtle but telling motivic relationships (see Example 8.19). As noted above, the violin melody (m. 9) begins with the same dotted motive (x) as the opening. But the Presto begins with a clear allusion to the first melodic gesture in the movement (motive y), rising from e^1 through a two-note upbeat to g^1; it is thus motivically as well as structurally consequential. (These relations, which in many contexts would seem trivial, are meaningful here because they entail the initial motives of all three principal ideas.) The emphasis on y in the Presto legitimizes a Schenkerian "hidden repetition" in the internal reprise of Section 2 (mm. 33ff): the melody, which in mm. 9–13 had filled in the earlier gap between $\hat{1}$ and $\hat{3}$ (see m. 1) but halted on $\hat{3}$, now moves right on up $\hat{3}$–$\hat{4}$–$\hat{5}$, in a structural augmentation of mm. 1–2a. The initial period (Section **1**) thus provides a material basis for both of the other musical ideas, and in the same order (x then y). These correspondences confirm the formal effect of the reprise of **1** following the Presto: we return not merely to the beginning, but to a source of everything we have heard in the meantime.

This finale is one of Haydn's most stunning examples of progressive form. It proceeds by a kind of developing variation, whose stages are however more suggestive, fleeting, abstract, than the usual manipulations encountered under that banner. Only at the end do we realize that the initial idea has led to all the others. Similarly, its implication–realization structure obtains not so much in the domain of thematic material and completion, as in the more complex, larger-scale realm of form-as-experienced; because of the continual reinterpretations entailed in listening to it, we understand it only in retrospect. (On a much simpler scale, the same principle animates Haydn's manipulation of conventional small-scale forms, for example the trios of Symphonies 57 and 81 and Op. 9 No. 5, discussed on p. 158.) And yet, paradoxically, each individual section projects (or implies) a simple, unambiguous, closed formal pattern. Far more even than usual, the form of this movement resides in our experience alone.

Op. 54 No. 2 is in many respects Haydn's most unusual string quartet. Many strange features in the other movements – the contrast between C major and minor, the air of

---

[35] Noted by Rosen, *Classical Style*, p. 140; Keller, *The Great Haydn Quartets*, p. 124.

exoticism, the extravagant use of register – relate directly to the baffling finale; some of these are shown in Example 8.20. The opening Vivace employs C minor only in conventional ways, but it features a striking tonal clash of submediants, based on major/minor mixture. Following the initial twofold statement of the main theme on tonic and dominant, the third entry (m. 13) follows on A-flat (the flat submediant). Even if the "pregnant" G.P.s have aroused our suspicions, this is an astonishing stroke: all has been regular and diatonic, and remote harmonizations of a main-theme headmotive are hardly ever encountered in the first group. But in another sense this A-flat is a deceptive cadence from the massive cello dominant (the timid viola c^1 in m. 11 is no effective resolution); it is prolonged for ten bars until the dominant returns (m. 24) and, further elaborated, cadences twice (mm. 25, 29). A-flat plays a larger role in the movement as well: the return

Example 8.20 String Quartet Op. 54/2

(a) Vivace, first group

Ex. 8.20 (*cont.*)

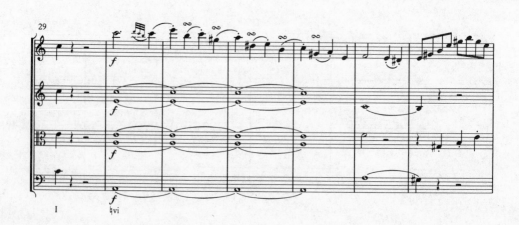

(b) End of minuet and beginning of trio

of this passage in the recapitulation engenders a "secondary development" (mm. 146–62), and still later it is the takeoff-chord for a very long extension within the second-group recapitulation (mm. 185–213). More important, the unexpected stroke at m. 13 establishes the principle of deceptive resolutions to VI as a compositional idea.

When a first group cadences strongly in the tonic, the transition often begins with a counterstatement of the opening theme. So it is here – but harmonized, astonishingly, by the *diatonic* submediant A minor. A structural dissonance between major and minor could be more vividly articulated only by direct confrontation of the two tonics, as in the opening movement of Schubert's G-major String Quartet; even Beethoven, in the "Appassionata" Sonata, reserves his comparable stroke for the recapitulation (m. 17 vs. m. 152). It is a fine irony that Haydn thus transforms the most conventional of all pivot chords, vi=ii, into the greatest harmonic shock of the movement. And that provisional first-group cadence (m. 25) testifies to his remarkable sense of tonal balance. Although it almost cries out for a deceptive resolution to vi, Haydn withholds this, so as not to steal the thunder of the A-minor thematic entry five bars later. But the real point comes in the recapitulation. The cadences from mm. 24–29 are suppressed in favor of the secondary development, but they return towards the end (mm. 206–13) – when, now that all mixture based on $\hat{6}$ is past, m. 209 grants us precisely that deceptive cadence onto A minor that was withheld at m. 25.

These surprises based on the two submediants A minor and A-flat major prepare, as it were, the unmediated major/minor contrasts in the remainder of the quartet. The Adagio in C minor is one of Haydn's strangest creations: a rhapsody for the first fiddle in gypsy style, whose fantastic roulades seemingly take no notice of the regularly-phrased, homophonic accompaniment (the actual melody remains in the second violin). As in the equally fantastic Capriccio in Op. 20 No. 2, such unbridled exoticism cannot stand alone: at the end, the Adagio deviates to the dominant and is run-on to the minuet. The trio again reverts to the minor (Example 8.20b). Its most prominent sonority (mm. 51–54, 65–68) reflects the exoticism of the Adagio: in refusing to move off eb for four full bars, the second violin produces the illusion of an A-flat-minor triad in first inversion (or a seventh-chord with root f). Hence the turn to the minor in the finale (section **3**), though surprising in the immediate context, is consequential (to invoke Cone's concept); its insinuating yet insistent tone (especially strong at the *unheimlich* parallel fifths at the turn to D-flat) recalls the exoticism of the Adagio and trio.

The idea of deceptive cadences onto vi and ♭VI – the gestural context of the initial major/minor contrast in the Vivace – is also maintained. The decisive formal moment of the Adagio, the turn towards the final dominant, is introduced by a cadence onto A-flat (m. 52, with Haydn's always-significant *pianissimo*). And the decisive moment in the Presto, the sign that it is not to be "the" finale but merely a section within it, is the deceptive cadence onto vi in m. 112. (Even the minor mode enters [Example 8.19, m. 40] with the equivalent of a deceptive cadence, substituting for the expected major arrival.) These two structural deceptive cadences, to A-flat in the gypsy Adagio and to A minor in the Presto, are additional "consequences" of the confrontation between the same two sonorities at the very beginning of the quartet.

Another aspect of cyclic organization in Op. 54 No. 2 comprises its continual gestures of extravagance, such as the gypsy Adagio (with its echo in the trio). The majority incorporate extremes of register as well. The turn-spangled opening theme of the Vivace establishes this *motif* at the very beginning, plunging down through tonic and dominant before exploding into the submediant confrontations described above. Such headlong juxtapositions of high and low, turn and triad, occur again and again in this movement, linked with dizzy ascents and eccentric descending-leap motives (mm. 39–54, 61ff, 73–78, 177ff, 185–201, 213–18). This complex returns in the explosion at the end of the minuet (Example 8.20b), in which the ensemble mounts in triple octaves through the entirety of musical space. And it recurs yet again in one of the decisive passages of the finale: the juxtaposition of the excruciatingly high Presto climax on a long-held V_5^6 (mm. 121–22) with the return of the original Adagio theme in the lowest possible register. (These recurrent linkings of high and low also provide a gestural context for those strange, wonderful rising cello arpeggios in section 2.) Another consequence of that triple-octave ascent in the minuet, meanwhile, is a new prominence of octave-textures as such. The trio begins with an ominous rising motive on low g and c^1 – the very pitches of the crucial dotted motive which opens the finale. (See as well the plunge from c^4 to g in mm. 44–45, just preceding; a diehard thematicist would relate all this back to the opening g^2–c^3 motive of the Vivace.) These are only the most prominent among many gestural and textural links throughout the quartet.

Finally, the entire work is remarkable for its absence of "development." The development section of the Vivace occupies only 16 percent of the movement (38 bars of 233), by far the lowest proportional length of a fast opening sonata-form movement of any Haydn string quartet or symphony. (The next-lowest figure, 20 percent, is found in the "Oxford" Symphony; that is, again in the context of a thoroughly unusual treatment of form.) The Adagio in its entirety (up to the deceptive cadence) is merely a thirty-two bar song form:

$$\|: 8 \qquad :\| \ 8 \qquad + \ 8$$
$$\|: \text{i–v(V)} :\| \ \text{III–V} \quad \text{i}$$

but this has been overlooked in the excitement over its wild gypsy style, in part because the first strain receives a written-out repetition (first without the rhapsody, then with it). The minuet and trio are (in this sense) small, non-developmental forms by definition. And as we have seen, the finale comprises a series of small, closed units which nevertheless create a progressive form in the large. But this is precisely the formal principle of the quartet as a whole. Each movement eschews or severely curtails the process of development (as this applies to large sections); yet the work is so unusual in style, so terse and concentrated, so single-minded in its confrontations of major and minor, that it is as if literally through-composed. So strong is this effect that its most obviously striking features – the run-on Adagio and minuet, the form of the finale – ultimately seem hardly more than surface manifestations of this pervasive, underlying continuity. The nature of that continuity is not easily expressed in words, except with the formula that in Op. 54 No. 2 Haydn's overriding aesthetic aim was the integration of the cycle.

TWO MASTERWORKS OF 1793

Op. 74 No. 3: minor into major

Op. 74 No. 3 in G minor occupies the final position among the quartets Op. 71/74, a single set of six composed in Vienna in late 1792 and 1793 and, notwithstanding Haydn's dedication to the local Count Appony, doubtless intended primarily as novelties for his second London visit. As we have seen in Chapter 5, it was in 1793 that Haydn first used remote key relationships among independent movements as a normal resource, in the last three quartets of this set and Symphony No. 99. Since he apparently began the quartet opus in late 1792 with Op. 71 Nos. 1 and 2,[36] and apparently composed all six works in the order now familiar to us (on which all the surviving authentic sources agree), and whereas the symphony belongs with Nos. 100 and 101 (completed in early 1794, in London), he most likely composed these four works in the order: Op. 74 Nos. 1, 2, 3, Symphony No. 99. This order conforms to his use of remote keys, which becomes increasingly bold and pervasive in each successive work. In Op. 74 No. 1 in C, A major (VI$^{\sharp}$) appears only in the trio of the minuet, with a primarily local and ex-pressive effect. In No. 2 in F, D-flat ($\flat$VI) is also used only in the trio; but its equivalent C$\sharp$ is tonally and motivically crucial in the first movement, at the joins between ex-position and development (where the enharmonic relationship is explicit) and between development and recapitulation (C$\sharp$ as part of V/vi). (Related effects are found in all the other late F-major quartets: within movements in Opp. 50 No. 5 and 55 No. 2; within and between them in Op. 77 No. 2; see pp. 159, 214.) In Op. 74 No. 3, the remote key appears in the more prominent location of the slow movement, and is fundamental to the overall plan. Symphony No. 99, finally, uses remote keys in both locations, and as a whole is even more highly organized in this respect. But whereas in the symphony all six movements (counting introduction and trio) are in the major mode, Op. 74 No. 3 begins in the minor, and the governing idea is its gradual transformation into the tonic major. Keller goes so far as to call this quartet "musical history's first work centred on a home tonality rather than a home key: it is, in fact, in G – or [if you say] 'in G' when you mean 'in G major', you'd have to say that it's in G minor-major."[37] However, he does not describe the transformation entailed, or the quartet's many through-compositional effects, or its ending with a culmination-finale. In these respects it resembles the much earlier Farewell Symphony – which is "centred on a home tonality rather than a home key" to at least as great an extent. Another distinguishing feature (which it shares with all the quartets in Op. 71/74) is that many of its ideas are presented abruptly and in compressed form or, if contrasting, are often juxtaposed without mediation.

The tonal relationships that govern Op. 74 No. 3 are shown in Example 8.21a. Each movement is based on a structural contrast between tonic major and minor: both outer movements are in G minor but move to G major in the recapitulation;

---

[36] *JHW* XII/5, [vii].   [37] *The Great Haydn Quartets*, p. 205.

Example 8.21 String Quartet Op. 74/3

(a) Tonal form

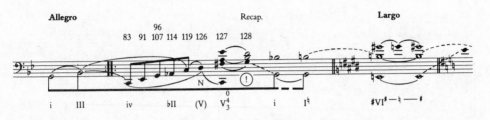

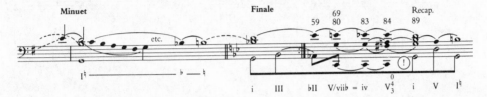

(b) Motivic relations

Ex. 8.21 (*cont.*)

(c) Allegro, retransition

(d) Finale, retransition

Ex. 8.21 (*cont.*)

(e) Largo assai, 5–14

both inner movements are major-mode ABA forms with the B section in the minor. The famous Largo is set astonishingly in E major, remote enough following the ending of the Allegro in G major, but positively bewildering in its implied relationship to the putative overall tonic G minor, from which ♭VI♯ is a doubly remote key, six steps removed on the circle of fifths. (In Sonata No. 52 in E-flat, most likely composed the following year, Haydn directly juxtaposed the slow movement in the Neapolitan with the tonic E-flat; see p. 213.) The middle section of the Largo is in E minor, locally the parallel minor, but also the relative minor of G major – in which key the minuet begins, G minor being reserved for the trio. (It was unusual but not unprecedented to have a major-mode minuet and a minor-mode trio in a work which begins in the minor: see Op. 17 No. 4, Op. 42, and Op. 50 No. 4.) Each join between movements is expressed locally by a common tone (described below).

The G-minor outer movements share other unorthodox structural harmonies. Both development sections center around the flat side, including the Neapolitan A-flat (Allegro, mm. 110–22; finale, mm. 57ff) and vii♭, F minor (finale, mm. 67–82, including its own subdominant B-flat minor). Even more remarkable are the retransitions. Once again, Haydn avoids the root-position dominant; both movements employ V_3^0, built on his favorite open low C in the cello – combining, in a sense, the functions of dominant and subdominant, and a "consequence" of the flatside orientation of the development sections. The Allegro, admittedly, reaches the dominant (m. 126; see Example 8.21c), but only in the upper octave; it then moves *fortissimo* to the diminished seventh, with fermata; the first violin also moves to a more exposed pitch. Only later is the dominant recaptured and transferred downwards (mm. 134ff). But the finale tops this with ease (Example 8.21d). The F-minor passage in the development eventually prolongs its dominant, C major (mm. 80–82), *piano* and with a high bass – when, without warning, the entire ensemble erupts *fortissimo*, first on C minor (m. 83), then for four bars (mm. 84–87) on V_3^0; the recapitulation follows directly. The violent contrast in texture, dynamics, register, and rhythm matches the harmonic shock whereby V/vii♭ unexpect-edly turns into the home subdominant. The cello insists on that C–c octave for five bars; even the ensuing very strong dominant, also five full bars long (mm. 95–99, just before the turn to the major), is confined above middle C. In fact, there is no low dominant D anywhere in the recapitulation, whereas low C recurs twice more (mm. 121, 142). Thus many aspects of the finale (and to a lesser extent the Allegro) diminish the primacy of the dominant; this seems compatible with the unusual, and unusually prominent, remote keys throughout the quartet, as well as with its single-minded concentration on the relation between tonic major and minor. (Haydn's other G-minor quartet, Op. 20 No. 3, also includes prominent low Cs at the expense of the dominant: in mm. 93–94 of the first movement, also a retransition, and 244–47, where the ensuing dominant drops to *piano*. The greater prominence of C here, especially its use at the same formal point in different movements, justifies interpreting it as "tonal organization.")

In addition, Op. 74 No. 3 includes meaningful motivic links, which relate to the abrupt theme in octaves at the very beginning. Unlike the "out-of-context" opening gestures in the other quartets in Op. 71/74,[38] this sounds like a real theme. But it cannot be the main theme in the ordinary sense: it is never heard again, except as a topic for contrapuntal elaboration in the development. On the other hand, although its gestural quality is that of an introduction, marching up to a half cadence on the dominant and followed by a two-bar G.P., it is not a normal introduction either: it is already in the prevailing fast tempo and, unlike the comparable theme in Op. 74 No. 2, is repeated along with the rest of the exposition. Its function is rather to set out the primary tonal material of *both* outer movements (see Example 8.21b). It rises triadically from the tonic up to D ($\hat{5}$), then to the upper neighbor E♭ ($\hat{6}$), and eventually (still rising) back to D, further embellished by its leading-tone C♯ ($\sharp\hat{4}$). The underlying tonal relations are shown on the right-hand portion of the same staff; note the double-neighbor configuration around D and the overlapping rising sixths. The finale headmotive (penultimate staff) has the identical structure, except that the rising sixth, $\hat{5}$–$\hat{3}$, has become more prominent. (But it was already prominent at the crucial destabilizing moment, when the closing theme of the Allegro entered in the tonic major; see the bottom staff of Example 8.21b.) The ensuing "main" theme of the opening movement (mm. 11ff, 128ff [Example 8.21b and c]) is also closely related in structure. Tonally as well as gesturally, the opening theme can thus be best understood as an introduction to the entire quartet.

On a larger scale, this emphasis on $\hat{6}$ links up with the Largo, whose remote tonic E major is after all built on $\hat{6}$ of G major, just heard at the end of the first movement. In addition, the joins on either side of the Largo are mediated by implied common-tone progressions. The raised mediant, B, prominent from the second-group recapitulation of the first movement, is emphasized one last time by the (admittedly conventional) after-beat gesture at the very end; it is of course the common tone between the two tonic triads, G major and E major. The minuet, in G major (not minor), actually begins on an upbeat e², descending to d² over the barline; this creates a common-tone link to the Largo and, in foregrounding the $\hat{6}$–$\hat{5}$ relation, recalls the structural disposition of the opening gesture and prepares the finale theme to come. The most important motives, common-tone links among remote keys, and the overall tonal plan all relate to the opening gesture, and to the governing idea of minor turning into major.

But how can this idea "govern" an entire quartet in which the opening Allegro closes in the major and both middle movements begin and end in major keys? The Allegro moves to G major for the contrasting *piano* closing theme: mm. 168–97 = 54–78 + 5 bars codetta. (In itself, this is an example of Haydn's tendency to postpone the primary contrast until late in the exposition or recapitulation; see p. 166.) When Haydn introduces the major within a recapitulation, the change usually arrives at the beginning of the second group, if not earlier (for example, Symphony No. 95, first movement, mm. 129ff = 29ff; Op. 76 No. 3, finale, mm. 152ff recompose mm. 21ff, then mm. 161ff =

[38] Tovey, "Haydn's Chamber Music," p. 63; Somfai, "Haydn's London String Quartets," in *Haydn Studies*, p. 390.

34ff). Here, however, it comes at the last possible moment (the second-group recapitulation has begun long before) and, except for the few extra bars at the end, merely repeats the closing theme. The effect is perfunctory: the Allegro ends before we have adjusted to the major. This lack of closure is the very opposite of a flaw (as it has been called); its purpose – like the D-major interlude in the Farewell – is to force us to listen "beyond" the end of the movement. This G major is only a promise; we expect that it will eventually be made good, by a strong, extended cadential passage which relates cogently to what has come before.

And then the Largo begins in E! This "overshooting" of the implied goal of G major drastically expands the process by which minor is transformed into major, so that it can govern the entire quartet. First, E major is elaborated by its parallel minor, which is G's relative minor. (Nor is the beauty of the Largo theme entirely self-contained: its only *fortissimo* and *pianissimo* [mm. 8, 12] occur on G-major sonorities; see Example 8.21e. Indeed, the remarkable juxtaposition of C-sharp minor and G major triads in mm. 11–12 is almost a tonal microcosm of the entire quartet.) Then, although G major itself becomes the tonic in the minuet, this movement begins tentatively off-tonic and (in the trio) is troubled by the minor mode. (Minuet and trio are motivically linked as well, by the triadic figures in mm. 23ff and 28–33, and 55–61 and 70–73.) In the finale, however, the major not only enters at the beginning of the second group (mm. 100–129+144–46=19–53, with mm. 120–22 a compression of 39–43), but the second group itself includes a massive, coda-like expansion towards the end (mm. 130–43). This is based on a complex passage from the development (mm. 63ff), but adds a prominent sixteenth-note motive (cello, m. 131) from the main theme itself (m. 2). The last appearance of this motive was in the first-group recapitulation, on the dominant and still in the minor (mm. 95–99); now, still on the dominant, it forms part of a climax that immediately leads to final closure in the tonic major (it has not been heard in the tonic major in this form). But as we have seen, the motive is also linked to the abrupt introductory theme that begins the opening Allegro. This rollicking climax rounds off not merely the finale, but the quartet as a whole, by grounding its basic tonal material in the tonic major. Although it has no run-on movements, it is through-composed. As pointed out at the end of Chapter 6, the notion that Haydn's major-mode endings connote mere "cheerfulness" could hardly be more inappropriate.

Symphony No. 99 and remote third relations

Symphony No. 99 in E-flat employs remote keys and sonorities so pervasively that they become the primary source of cyclic integration. This procedure is exceptional in Haydn; his only comparable works in this respect are Sonata No. 52 and a few piano trios (all from the second London period as well), and the even later Quartet Op. 77 No. 2 in F. Since the symphony begins and ends in the major, there can be no overall progression comparable to that in Op. 74 No. 3; indeed, all the structural remote sonorities are major (including, to be sure, the dominant of C minor). Instead, the introduction adumbrates a "system" of third-related keys, which recur again and again throughout the work. (Haydn avoided so strong an emphasis on structural remote keys in the five remaining London symphonies; only Nos. 103 and 104 employ them, and only in the slow movement and trio, respectively. Perhaps, after performing No. 99 – composed in Vienna but premiered in London – he concluded that they were less effective in the grand, public world of the symphony than in music destined primarily for connoisseurs.)

The introduction presents the governing tonal relations in compelling fashion (see Example 8.22, top). To be sure, the first paragraph is regular in harmony and phrasing: three widely spaced "hammerstrokes," I–V–I⁶ (mm. 1, 3, 5), alternating with a contrast-

Example 8.22 Symphony No. 99: motivic and tonal relations

Ex. 8.22 (*cont.*)

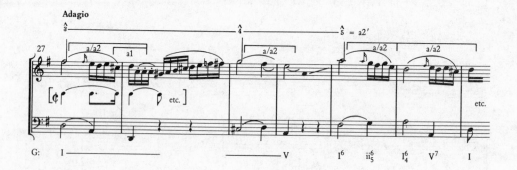

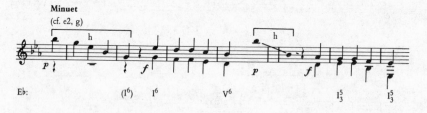

Ex. 8.22 (cont.)

ing *piano* melody based on a descending motive *a*, then moving to the dominant (m. 8). (This plan was especially characteristic of Mozart's introductions in E-flat: see the piano/wind quintet K. 452, the E-flat symphony K. 543, and the overture to *The Magic Flute*.) But the dominant is immediately prolonged by a chromatic descent to ab² in the melody and an unharmonized upper neighbor Cb (b6̂), emphasized by octave doublings in all registers and a long fermata ("*tenuto*"). At a stroke, regularity and normalcy vanish. (The technique is the by now familiar one of destabilization by a foreign pitch.) Clearly, we are being set up; even so, nothing can prepare the shock of hearing Cb turn into B♮ and behave like the dominant of E minor, or the paradoxical delicacy of the ensuing chromatic progression (based on motive *a*) through E minor and C minor to its dominant G (V/vi). (It seems to have affected Beethoven deeply; he was very familiar with this symphony, composed during the year of his close contact with Haydn. See the almost identical stroke towards the end of the finale of his first major E-flat composition thereafter, the Piano Sonata Op. 7; even the rise to the melodic B♮ is the same.[39] Less pointedly similar is the E-major second-theme statement at the beginning of the finale coda of the Piano Trio Op. 1 No. 1; in part because, by 1794–95, this had become a conventional location for Beethoven's surprise Neapolitans – which he probably also picked up from Haydn; see, for example, the finale of Symphony No. 90.[40] Perhaps Haydn's stroke in Symphony No. 99, or the several related ones in Sonata No. 52, subliminally stimulated Beethoven's later, even more famous association of E minor with E-flat in an opening symphony movement, that of the "Eroica" itself.)

The second paragraph of Symphony No. 99 is a true enharmonic progression: Cb enters as a neighbor to V, and the key of which it is the dominant is technically F-flat – that is, on the flat side. Nevertheless, "E minor" continues towards C minor – that is, still in the flat direction – and thus we traverse the entire circle of fifths, confirming that Cb is permanently equivalent to B♮. E minor itself is the minor Neapolitan of a major tonic, a doubly remote key relation ordinarily described as unknown before Schubert (although we have already seen it in the coda of the opening movement of the much earlier Op. 20 No. 5). All this relates to two basic tonal ideas (see Example 8.23a):

[39] See *JHW*, I/17, foreword, at n. 14; Beethoven's "citation" is noted by Marx, "Beziehungen," p. 7 and Ex. 21.

[40] On the date of Beethoven's Op. 1/1, see Douglas Johnson, *Beethoven's Early Sketches in the "Fischhof Miscellany": Berlin Autograph 28*, 2 vols. (Ann Arbor, 1980), vol. 1, pp. 304–05. Johnson cites other Neapolitans in Beethoven's finale codas, without mentioning Haydn in this connection.

Example 8.23 Symphony No. 99, tonal form

(a)

(b)

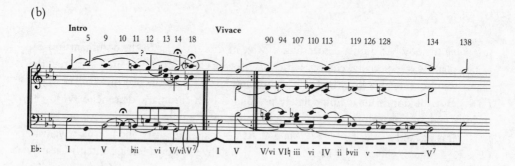

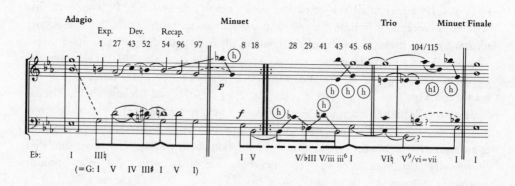

G (III♯ =V/vi) as a structural goal, and C♭=B♮ as a neighbor to the dominant. In combination, they not only establish the principles of key relations by thirds and chromatic half steps, but imply an overall harmonic progression by major thirds, symmetrically dividing the octave. No wonder the actual progressions sound Schubertian! – E minor to C minor; B/C♭ to G (the beginning and end of the enharmonic passage, emphasized by the basses and the fermatas); and, by implication, G to E-flat at the end. Because of the enharmonics, B is not merely a convenience of notation, but moves directly to C minor, and is a middleground constituent of the structural G-major chord (V/vi).

Ex. 8.23 (*cont.*)

(c)

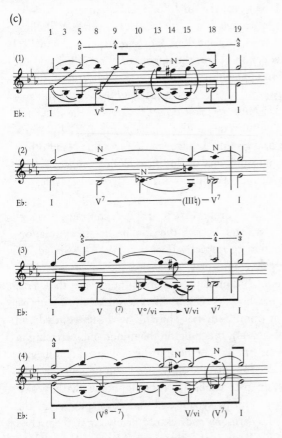

Given all this, Haydn's ending the introduction with his wonderful long wind chord creates a fundamental ambiguity as to the structural goal. Of course, it restates the dominant and directly prepares the tonic across the double bar, but is it hierarchically superior to the V/vi? If so, it must link up with the structural dominant in mm. 8–9; in this case, the entire chromatic passage is an expansion of the neighbor Cb (a common enough procedure), as suggested in the first two voice-leading graphs of Example 8.23c. But it is on a different "plane": for the winds alone, and ranging no lower than the Bb just below middle C, two octaves and a third above the absent double basses. The very long, very strong V/vi still reverberates mentally; is not this dominant seventh merely a foreground sonority, while the structural join remains V/vi–I? (In Haydn's next and last E-flat symphony, No. 103, the goal is unequivocally V/vi; see below. Such transitional dominants also occur at recapitulations; see pp. 142–43.) The Vivace assai itself (again not uncommonly) begins *piano* and without double basses, winds, or brass; hence the G can indeed be heard as remaining unresolved until the *forte* tonic of m. 27, which completes the circle of thirds from Cb in m. 10.

To illustrate the complexity, I show in Example 8.23c four possible voice-leading analyses of the introduction. The first two take the final dominant as superior to V/vi, linking up with m. 8. In No. 1, the upper voice is a 5̂-line and the chromatics prolong A♭, the texture as a whole prolonging the dissonant dominant seventh (a problematical procedure in orthodox Schenkerian theory); in No. 2, the upper voice is a 3̂-line, and the chromatics are understood as middleground neighbors in both parts, with V/vi subsidiary even to ♭6̂. No. 3, with a 5̂-line, shows the V/vi on the same level as both dominants (this is unorthodox), with B a subsidiary arpeggiation down to it (note the difference from No. 2 in this respect). No. 4, finally, subsumes both dominants to a I–III–I progression in the bass underneath a constant background 3̂. These various readings (and others could be added) reflect the complexity and ambiguity of this introduction, which, at least without taking the rest of the movement into account, is analytically "undecidable."

The Vivace assai is a superb example of Haydn's progressive form, with continual developing variation, additional remote-key play, and altered rhetoric in the recapitulation. The exposition has four paragraphs (beginning respectively at mm. 19, 34, 48, and 71), of which the second and third create a developmental "expansion section" (see p. 166). The main theme 1 (see again Example 8.22) dominates the first group, *piano* then *forte*; its chief motive *c'*, a half-step complete neighbor, derives by inversion from the disruptive C♭ in the introduction. The transition (mm. 34ff, not shown), with new dotted and syncopated motives, moves *through* V/V (m. 44), touching on the minor and increasing in energy, to a full cadence in the dominant (m. 48). Although the next paragraph begins with the main theme by elision, it develops irrepressibly, *forte* throughout: in part contrapuntal and syncopated (m. 54), in part exuberantly homophonic, with a new triadic motive (m. 59); the headmotive returns, syncopated and contrapuntal, in the minor (m. 63, compare m. 34), until the harmony and texture finally right themselves (m. 67) and prepare the cadence (mm. 70–71). But the cadence is subverted by a sudden drop to *piano* and a reduction of the ensemble to the accompanimental strings. (Compare the similar but more drastic effect in the finale of the "Surprise" Symphony, mm. 74 and 209.) Because of this subverted cadence, even the entry (at last) of the *piano* theme 2 (m. 71) provides no real relaxation (Example 8.22, quoted from the recapitulation). Nor, despite its lilt, is it inherently relaxed: the pert chromaticism of its upbeat motive *c1* (half-step motion to B♭; cf. mm. 9–10) and the continuing eighth-note accompaniment prevent it from settling down. Indeed, after only ten bars it yields to a *forte* closing theme 3 (m. 81), which combines motive *c1* with others from the expansion group, especially the descending-skip motive *e2* (compare mm. 58–60) and the *forzati* (compare 34ff, 64ff), both syncopated on the quarter-note level.

The development (shown in voice-leading outline in Example 8.23b) opens with two statements of the headmotive; both cadence on the dominant of C minor and are followed by fermatas. Except by an actual change of tempo, it would be difficult to advert more obviously to the end of the introduction. And so the development proper begins with the pert *piano* theme 2 (m. 94) – in the remote key of C major! This profound tonal wit brings out the latent sharp-side implications of E minor and the dominant of

C from the introduction, which we thought had tended towards the flat side exclusively. What is more, the new bright warm key manifests a hitherto latent rhetorical aspect of this theme: it is subtly expressive, particularly the chromaticism and the implied syncopations of its accented upbeat. And from this point on the closing group dominates the development: theme 2 in mm. 97–103 and 120–37, 3 in 104–19 (with the syncopated motive from m. 64); they even combine contrapuntally in mm. 104–06. Meanwhile, in what can only be called "middleground wit," Haydn reneges on the tonal implication of mm. 94–96, transforming C major into a dominant seventh and moving (like the introduction) constantly flatwards: to G minor for the outburst on theme 3, through C minor, A-flat, and F minor, all the way to D-flat (♭VII, m. 119), where 2 takes over again. D-flat moves down one more third, to the dominant, minor at first (m. 126) but then transformed into the major; the leading tone D (m. 128) is poetically combined with C♭, until the horns (m. 132) lead radiantly into the major and the structural dominant (m. 134). This retransition specifically recalls the introduction: not merely by the insistence on C♭ as neighbor to B♭, but by its wonderful transformation, precisely at the arrival of the dominant major, to the enharmonic equivalent b♮² (upbeat to m. 135). (This horn-call rise to the dominant is a nearly literal repetition of m. 7, the approach to the first structural dominant in the introduction.)

The development of theme 2 continues right into the recapitulation, which is thoroughly recomposed. Following the compressed transition (mm. 145–56), this theme enters immediately, as the *initial* idea of the second group (m. 157) – a "second theme" after all! (Compare, in Op. 33 No. 1, first movement, the change in function of the new theme in m. 11: in the exposition, it is the culmination of the first group; in the recapitulation, the beginning of the second; see p. 130.) It then leads into the tonic minor (m. 162); this indirectly recapitulates the very different minor-mode passages in the exposition (mm. 44–47, 63–66) – which, given the new emphasis on 2, there is no time for here. The *forte* theme 3 duly follows (m. 167), but detours once again to the dominant (m. 173), where, again colored by the minor, we hear theme 2 one last time – following yet another statement of the retransition (compare mm. 173–79 to mm. 128–34). Even now it has not had its final word; it also initiates the concluding *tutti* (m. 184, with an astonishing horn blast on e♭²) and leads it to the structural cadence of the entire movement (mm. 190–91), before yielding to the main theme for a brief coda.

In thus "taking over," theme 2 wonderfully alters the rhetoric of the movement.[41] The vigorous, foursquare, diatonic opening theme turns out to be only one of two main themes; indeed it must increasingly defer to its pert, chromatic, subtly expressive companion. The movement thus develops, both thematically and aesthetically, from beginning to end; this is the same principle we have already observed in a simpler sense in Symphony No. 80, and in a profoundly tonal sense in No. 92 (see Chapter 5). Haydn's forms remained dynamic – became more dynamic – throughout his life.

Many striking tonal events in later movements exploit the same third-related, chromatic harmonies. As so often – compare again Op. 33 No. 1 – Haydn reinterprets an originally

---

[41] This point is noted by Tovey, *Essays*, vol. 1, pp. 156–57, and Wolf, "Recapitulations," p. 73, but only in a formal sense.

witty idea on a higher level: thus C major, implied but revoked at the beginning of the Vivace development, becomes a structural key in the trio of the minuet. The minuet proper (see Example 8.22) is based on a descending triad motive (*h*), related to *e2* and *g* from the Vivace; as so often, it is at first unaccompanied, and thus only implies I^6; the root-position tonic does not arrive until m. 8. (The first two notes, b♭^{2}–g^2, fleetingly imply G minor, especially following the G major of the Adagio.) This emphasis on $\hat{3}$ is then taken seriously at the reprise, when a long-awaited cadence – in G minor (iii) – is undercut by the unexpected return of the headmotive in the bass, engendering a veritable orgy of overlapping *h*s, mainly implying first-inversion triads, which as a whole augment the initial pitch-descent $\hat{5}$–$\hat{3}$–$\hat{1}$. Most remarkably, the retransition from the trio to the minuet overtly recomposes the Adagio–Vivace join from the *first* movement. It moves to the dominant of C minor (mm. 101ff; the example picks up at m. 109) and transforms it into a ninth chord with a♭^{2} (m. 111), now on a fragmentary three-note motive *h1*; finally the bass and the leading tone (G/b) drop out, so that the last bars, A♭–F–D (still *h1*), suddenly sound like vii of E-flat, and the minuet enters directly on motive *h*. The harmonic progression, V^9/vi–(vii)–I, is analogous to the V/vi–(V^7)–I at the end of the introduction: a♭^{2} is the highest pitch in both "residual" dominant sonorities (the clarinets here standing for the full wind choir of the introduction), and the bass G (V/vi) drops out in both cases – here, linking directly to the bass entry on I^6 in the minuet (m. 2).

Meanwhile, the gorgeous and very full Adagio (Example 8.23b) fulfills another tonal implication of the introduction by being set in the key of G major. It also relates by common tone to the movements on either side, reflecting the afterbeat g^2 in mm. 200–01 of the Vivace assai and carrying over to the prominent G at the beginning of the minuet. What is more, within the Adagio the recapitulation is prepared by the same indirect progression (V/vi–I) that was implied at the end of the introduction – which is to say, by a sonority on B (III♯)! In a Schenkerian sense, the Adagio headnote seems to be $\hat{3}$, B; if, as seems likely, that of the other three movements is also $\hat{3}$, the set of tonics and headnotes for the four main movements comprises, again, a set of major thirds implying an augmented triad, E♭–G–B. Finally, although thematic connections are on the whole not central in this symphony, the second theme (m. 27) is a full-fledged thematic transformation of the opening theme of the introduction (see Example 8.22), on both the motivic level (*a*: long $\hat{3}$; dotted-note upbeat on $\hat{2}$ and $\hat{7}$; drop of a fourth, $\hat{8}$–$\hat{5}$, on the downbeat) and in the overall structure (*a2′*: steady two-bar rise from $\hat{3}$/I through $\hat{4}$/V^7 to $\hat{5}$/I^6).[42] Perhaps we can even hear what Kerman would call "thematic completion" in the fact that, while in the introduction this theme could not come to a cadence, it now leads to a very strong one indeed, three times during the course of the movement (mm. 33, 77, and 96).

The finale breaks off early in the recapitulation for an altered statement of the main theme, beginning on V/V (m. 185; see Example 8.22); the implied slowing-down becomes explicit in the next phrase, marked *adagio*. (The effect is not uncommon;

---

[42] Marx, p. 4 and Ex. 11 (citing a German edition of Geiringer; I find no such remark in the current [third] English edition).

compare, in other London symphony finales, No. 97, m. 304; No. 98, m. 321; No. 102, m. 261.) Haydn writes (m. 186) what looks like the diminished seventh of vi, with B♮ in the bass; but it sounds like the "home" diminished seventh, and indeed resolves down to the dominant – as if that note were really the upper neighbor C♭. It is a last, witty reflection of the momentously destabilizing C♭/B♮ of the introduction, and of the many striking harmonic events associated with it since.

Example 8.23b shows the principal tonal relations of the symphony. What emerges most clearly is the importance of the third scale-degree. We have not only the sharp-side G major as V/vi in several crucial passages and as the key of the slow movement, but the flat-side G-flat following the double bar of the minuet. Even more surprising, perhaps, is the prominence of the ordinary diatonic mediant, G minor. It predominates in the development sections of all three E-flat movements (Vivace, mm. 101–09; minuet, mm. 36–43; finale, mm. 146–61); the more common development tonalities ii, IV, and vi are conspicuously less important. It is motivically and structurally inscribed throughout the minuet. (The sixth degree, as C♭/B♮ and the key of C major, is not far behind.) All this is implied in the opening bars. So thorough and systematic an exploration, throughout a symphony, of tonal implications first presented in the slow introduction was not to be heard again until Beethoven's Seventh.

THE DIALECTIC OF "TYPE" AND UNIQUENESS

We have examined a number of Haydn compositions which alter or disrupt generic expectations, or exhibit overt cyclic integration. The techniques entailed are always the same: remote or indirect tonal progressions, a progression from minor to major, introduction-allegro continuities, progressive form, increasing importance of subsidiary material, run-on movements, and so forth. To conclude this chapter, I therefore return to the dialectic between the individuality of a work and its relatedness to others. My account has implicitly emphasized this topic by its organization primarily in terms of putative "pairs" of works: Symphonies 15 and 25, the Farewell and No. 46, Op. 20 No. 2 and Op. 54 No. 2; and so forth. I have touched on it in other chapters as well, with respect to central issues: for example, off-tonic introduction endings (Symphonies 90 and 92), destabilizing bassless openings on I⁶ (Op. 33 Nos. 1 and 3), remote tonal juxtapositions in symphonies of the late 1760s and early 1770s; and so forth. Similarly, we have often noted key-related similarities: the use of C♯/D♭ as a structural dissonance in all four quartets in F from Op. 50 No. 5 on; the remote A major in the trios of the two last C-major quartets, Opp. 74 No. 1 and 76 No. 3; preparations for the return of G minor on C, rather than D, in Opp. 20 No. 3 and 74 No. 3; and so forth. Nevertheless, each work remains unique, an individuum, without any trace of the merely conventional or of dependence on "types." To make this issue concrete: two of Haydn's most individual and tightly integrated symphonies are No. 99 and the Farewell. Even here, however, other works exhibit the very features I have claimed are responsible for their particular cyclic forms. Let us review this dialectic in more detail by comparing these two sets of related works.

Two E-flat symphonies with slow introductions on V/vi

Symphonies 99 and 103 have many things in common. Externally, both belong to the second set of London symphonies and are in E-flat (the only London symphonies in this key). Internally, both slow introductions move to G major (V/vi) as the overall tonal goal, and both works compose out implications of these progressions in later movements. Furthermore, as we have seen, the juxtaposition of V/vi and the tonic is perhaps Haydn's single most common "organizing" tonal move. Given all this, it would be easy to think of these two symphonies as a "pair," or as representatives of a "type." But it would be wrong.

In No. 103, as is well known, the main introduction theme dominates the Allegro con spirito as well,[43] to the point of its famous recall late in the recapitulation – apparently the first example of this in any symphony (anticipated by Mozart's String Quintet in D), and presumably the inspiration for the reprises of the Grave in Beethoven's "Pathétique" Sonata. What has not been described is the unusual form of the introduction itself, and its relation to the remote tonal preparation of the Allegro by common tone. It comprises a double statement of the long theme (mm. 2–25), itself an antecedent-consequent period, all firmly in the tonic; this extended formal and tonal stability is unusual in a slow introduction (see Chapter 5). It not only guarantees that we grasp the theme as a memorable *Gestalt* (which will be essential for understanding the Allegro), but provides an intelligible counterpart to its gestural mystery (low, bare octaves; initially undifferentiated slow rhythm). There follows merely a brief modulating sequence (mm. 25–31) to V/vi, which is prolonged for eight bars back down to the low register and the ominous octaves of the beginning. Although this harmonic shift is unexpected – except for passing hints of the tonic minor, common enough, there has been no hint of tonal instability – it too is directly intelligible, owing to the status of G as a triad pitch ($\hat{3}$). The common-tone basis of III$^\sharp$ and I has never been asserted more baldly than by the quotation of the final naked bass motive, G–A♭–G, in the melody at the beginning of the Allegro; even the implied accent on a♭^{2} (upbeat to m. 40, initiating a slur) is analogous to the *forzati* on A♭ in mm. 35–37. (That motive is in turn an inversion of the initial bass motive, E♭–D–E♭.)

Hence the main Allegro theme remains forever associated with the mysterious introductory world out of which it grew. It is thus highly consequential that the Adagio theme and its motives dominate the Allegro, and that the Adagio itself returns towards the end. The bass reprise in diminution in the middle of the development (m. 111) stands *in the tonic*; even this is logical, because it (not m. 39) is "the" main theme, and part of its character is to be in the tonic when stated in the bass. What is more, this tonic entry is also prepared by a V/vi–I cadence across a caesura. And in the finale, the same progression prepares the recapitulation itself (mm. 259–64). By implication, it also underlies the entry of C minor as the key of the Andante.

---

[43] Landon, *Symphonies*, pp. 574–75 and (more fully) *Haydn*, vol. 3, pp. 595–96; Wolf, "Recapitulations," p. 78; Marx, "Beziehungen," p. 6 and Exx. 17–18.

The differences between this symphony and No. 99 are far greater than the similarities. In No. 103, both outer movements begin with an abrupt gesture of annunciation, separated from what follows, almost like a frame: the drum roll at the beginning, and the horn-call theme of the finale (note the fermata in m. 4). Indeed, the unprecedented drum roll establishes the idea of annunciation so drastically – it is an introduction to the introduction (Haydn calls it "Intrada" in the autograph), so that this section becomes complexly multilayered – that it seems to introduce, not the Allegro con spirito alone, but the entire symphony. The remote introduction goal, V/vi, is not mediated by any dominant or contrasting timbre; the same is true of the V/vi–I progressions in the developments of the Allegro and finale. In No. 99, by contrast, V/vi–I progressions in E-flat are always mediated by the home dominant. On the whole, however, remote sonorities are less important in Symphony No. 103: the only structural key of this type is the C major that concludes the double-variation Andante. But this movement begins in the ordinary relative minor, the trio is in the tonic, and the development sections range only as far as D-flat. Unlike No. 99, this symphony includes no play with C♭=B♮ on the structural level, despite the V/vi goal of the introduction.

In this connection, one finds (at last) a possible compositional motive for Haydn's rejection of a mysterious interruptive passage towards the end of the finale (printed in *JHW* I/18 and by Landon): the entire band breaks off on V°/V; following a G.P. the strings three times intone a slow, ominous rising major third, C♭–E♭; only then follows the windup. The breaking-off at this point, the pauses, the slow tempo, the low strings, the lack of ornamentation and activity – all this invokes, not merely the general function "slow introduction," but specifically the *recall* of the introduction towards the end of the initial Allegro. It is all too portentous; we can only applaud Haydn's self-criticism in rejecting it. But there is a structural implication as well. The rejected passage would have introduced not only an "organizing" gestural link between the two outer movements, but also a powerful emphasis on ♭6̂, not now present anywhere in the symphony. It would have altered and augmented the meaning of every previous B♮ and C♭.

This would (I believe) have run counter to Haydn's artistic purpose, which was (or thus became) fundamentally different from what it had been in Symphony No. 99. That work exhibits few direct thematic links. All its movements (including the introduction) begin straightforwardly (the unpredictable events coming later); to a correspondingly great extent, it is "about" tonal relationships. But the primary idea of No. 103 comprises precisely its mysterious gestures of annunciation. The dramatic exploration of that idea motivates the thematic saturation in the opening movement. In contrast to No. 99, its primary *Affekt* is an invocation of the sublime; it explores the mutual implications of contrasting ideas; its intent, perhaps, is to provide moral enlightenment.[44] The effect of the sudden irruption of C♭ in No. 99 is sublime as well, but it seems on a smaller scale; from that point on, the work seems to explore its tonal implications more than its psychological ones. Despite their closeness in date, venue, and key, and their outward similarities of technique, these two symphonies inhabit different continents within Haydn's aesthetic world.

[44] Schroeder, *Haydn and the Enlightenment*, pp. 190–94.

F-sharp minor

The analysis of the Farewell Symphony in Part I emphasized the unusual and problematical aspects of the key of F-sharp minor: difficulties of intonation, notions of key character,
concepts of musical "distance," sheer infrequency. It would be tempting to infer that,
being thus "necessary" to the work's effect, the key itself would appear nowhere else.
But, although we admittedly know of no other symphonies in that key, Haydn himself
composed two additional works in F-sharp minor, the String Quartet Op. 50 No. 4
(1787) and the Piano Trio Hob. XV:26 (1794–95). By comparing these to the Farewell
Symphony, we can learn more about the relationship of individual composition and
"tonal type." Both later works are unusual in one relevant sense: they are Haydn's only
post-1781 minor-mode works which *end* in the minor (see Chapter 6); even the other
sharp-side works, Op. 64 No. 2 and the Piano Trio Hob. XV:12, turn to the major.
Conversely, the Farewell is one of his very few pre-1780 minor-mode works that ends in
the major, and the only one in a sharp-side key. Thus Haydn does seem to have regarded
the key of F-sharp minor as exceptional – as calling for special treatment. (As a tantalizing
sidelight on a different sort of relatedness, one should note his apparent quotation of
the Allegro assai headmotive in two later works: Symphony No. 60 ("Il distratto"), in the
development of the first movement, mm. 109ff, in A minor (compare the Farewell,
m. 38, in the same key); and No. 85 first movement, mm. 62ff, a dominant minor
outburst in the second group (F minor; compare the Farewell, m. 1). Both have been
noted in the literature, and have led to speculations as to possible extramusical or
self-referential meanings. These would perhaps seem more directly relevant to the
chronologically neighboring and overtly "stagey" No. 60 than to No. 85.)

Op. 50 No. 4 incorporates the same three-key system as the Farewell: F-sharp minor,
A major, and F-sharp major. (The dominant functions only within individual movements.) In the diagram below, the remote juxtapositions are shown in bold-face:

Spiritoso	Andante	Minuet+Trio	Allegro molto
Sonata form	Double variations		Fugue
f#–(III-V#)–f#–F#	**A–a–A**	**F#–f#–F#**	f#

But the distribution and functioning of these keys are very different here. The passionate,
motivically concentrated opening movement, unusually for a sharp-side work, transposes
the second-group recapitulation to the tonic major. (Aficionados of tonal instability
will enjoy working out the consequences of its violent unison opening motive, which
moves down from F# to low A; compare the opening of Symphony No. 46, described
above.) The remote A minor appears in the Andante, but only as the interior member
of a double-variation movement. The minuet returns to the tonic major, but is at
first completely diatonic, the obligatory mixtures coming in the second part (mm. 13ff,
25–29); the larger minor/major contrast, as is customary, is reserved for the trio. Finally,
the fugal finale is a severe essay in darkest F-sharp minor, wracked by *fortissimo* Neapolitans at the end, in a manner reminiscent of the second-group reprise of the Allegro assai
in the Farewell. Tovey, quoting that Neapolitan, called it "the quietest and deepest of
all the few instrumental fugues since Bach . . . so tragic that Beethoven's C sharp minor

Quartet is the first thing that one can connect with it" ("Haydn's Chamber Music," p. 61). Indeed, Op. 131 begins with a fugue, and employs the Neapolitan as a structural sonority; it seems likely that Tovey was also associating these two works because of their closely related, very unusual keys. In any case, he knew no higher praise.

This is Haydn's only fugal finale in any quartet after Op. 20. Like those earlier fugal quartets, Op. 50 No. 4 presumably also asks to be "read" as an essay in culmination, perhaps in an unusual way. The tonal plan itself is suggestive. The Spiritoso is Haydn's only sharp-side minor-mode opening fast movement which closes in the major (the entire second group is placed there). It is also unusual for a minor-mode work to place the minuet in the major. Indeed, F-sharp major seems to take over; this implies a major ending to the work as a whole (compare Op. 74 No. 3). Hence it is unexpected when the finale turns out to be in the minor, and a fugue at that – severe in style and technique, in a difficult key. It almost reverses the customary direction of modal change, as if a "major-mode" work had turned to the minor at the end. (This never actually happens in Haydn or Mozart.) The tone of the fugue matches that of the opening movement. Hence, unlike the Farewell and Op. 74 No. 3, which are about a change of being, Op. 50 No. 4 is (in this sense) a unified projection of a single state, which becomes even more intense and (if one wishes) hopeless towards the end. The striking and extended appearances of the major in the middle becomes a kind of *chiaroscuro*, or (if one wishes) an invocation of hope or yearning which remains unfulfilled. The overall tonal psychology is unique in Haydn.

The F-sharp minor Piano Trio, like many Haydn keyboard works in three movements, ends with a *Tempo di menuet* (see Chapter 6); like many such works, it is monotonal. The Allegro is impressively brooding, with Haydn's inimitable motivic concentration and an amazing development, the first half of which is one of the most sustainedly chromatic passages in his entire *oeuvre*. The gorgeous Adagio in F-sharp major, as is well known, has the same musical substance as the Adagio in Symphony No. 102 (the weight of recent opinion is that the trio came first).[45] The movement sounds in many respects like a delicately complex variant of the consoling language of the "farewell" movement, in the same key. But the finale begins roughly, on a dissonant dominant ninth, and this tonal instability is maintained, for there is no cadence on the tonic until the very last measure of the A section, just before the double bar. (In the reprise, even this cadence [m. 116] is deceptive, leading to a substantial coda.) And, as we have observed before (compare Symphony No. 26; pp. 243–44), such a minuet can be the opposite of an anticlimax. Rosen (*Classical Style*, pp. 361–62) does not exaggerate in speaking of its "intimate gravity . . . a melancholy so intense it is indistinguishable from the tragic." In Haydn's hands, even galant movement types were compatible with deep expressive value.

Despite the constraints of their unusual common tonic, these three F-sharp minor

---

[45] See Irmgard Becker-Glauch in *JHW* XVII/3, [vii] (1985); Brown's (1986) discussion of chronology (*Keyboard Music*, pp. 127–28) is ambiguous, but in another context (p. 378) he also assumes that the trio version came first.

works are utterly different from each other in both structure and style. The key scheme of Op. 50 No. 4 resembles that of the Farewell Symphony, but its opening movement ends in the major, and its culmination in a severe fugue could not be more unlike the symphony's distant hope of consolation. Structurally, the monotonal, three-movement trio has little in common with either. The minor mode itself has a different *tinta* in each: wild and untamed in the Farewell, densely passionate in the quartet, grave in the trio. The three endings alone – ethereal, tragic, melancholy – would suffice to make the point. It bears repeating: Haydn never repeated himself.

HAYDN'S MATURITY AND "CLASSICAL STYLE"

The high degree of cyclic integration in the Farewell Symphony and other works of Haydn has profound implications for our understanding of his compositional development, his position vis-a-vis Beethoven and the nineteenth century, and "Classical style" itself. It seems appropriate to conclude this study with a discussion of these historiographical topics.

ROSEN'S CRITICISM

Virtually the entire tradition of Haydn scholarship has assumed that he did not attain mastery or maturity (however this concept may be phrased) until the 1770s, in many accounts not until the 1780s. The corollary is that his "early" music – by some definitions more than half his output, up to his fiftieth year – was somehow lacking: in technique, in style, in degree of "synthesis," in emotional depth, or whatever. So that nobody will suppose that this discussion depends on straw men, I will focus initially on Rosen's *The Classical Style* which, regarding Haydn's music after *c.* 1780, offers arguably the most insightful writing in English since Tovey.

But Rosen's attitude towards Haydn's earlier music is highly ambivalent. While not denying its power, expressivity, and originality, he asserts that it lacks rhythmic cogency and large-scale coherence:

Taken on their own terms the works of the late 60s and early 70s inspire admiration; they are defective only when measured by the standards of Haydn's later works. . . Why then do we impose these standards?

In the twenty years between [J. S. Bach's] death and . . . the early 70s, [the] language had changed significantly: the syntax was less fluid, the relation between tonic and dominant more highly polarized. Haydn's style of 1770 . . . was not yet able to embrace its full implications. The higher degree of articulation of phrase and polarity of harmony raised problems for continuity that were difficult to solve: the shapes and rhythms move without transition from the squarely regular to the unsystematic, relying in the latter case almost entirely upon repetition or upon Baroque sequences to justify the sense of motion. . . . [In] the opening of the *Farewell* Symphony, . . . all the phrases are not only of the same length but of exactly the same shape, and [the] departure from this regularity (mm. 33 on) is almost entirely sequential in nature. The classical idea of balanced asymmetrical variation within a large period is only dimly foreshadowed.

There is . . . a genuine progress in style between early and late Haydn: the younger Haydn is a

great master of a style that only imperfectly realizes what the language of the time had to offer.
The greatest success of Haydn's early style, its fierce dramatic power, was inseparable there
from a harsh simplicity, a refusal of complex control, and a willingness at times to break almost
any rhythmic pattern for the sake of a single effect. It is difficult to see how a richer art could
have arisen from this often brutal contrast between a coarse but urgent regularity and a dazzling
eccentricity, except by abandoning the very virtues which made the style of the early 1770s so
compelling – which is, indeed, what Haydn did.   (pp. 146–47)

And regarding Symphony No. 46 in B, he asserts that its thematic links between
movements

are striking effects with little power to range beyond their immediate context. . . . [They]
have become events[, but] these events arrive unsupported by the rhythmic and harmonic conceptions, which allow them to take place but in no way reinforce them. The thematic logic
remains isolated.   (pp. 148–49)

But if this study has shown anything, it is that Haydn's music of the 1760s and 1770s
can be interpreted more positively. To begin on the level of detail: to see "exactly the
same shape" up to m. 33 of the "Farewell" Allegro assai is to ignore the changes in
texture and motivic contour in mm. 13–16, and the rhythmic/motivic fragmentation in
mm. 23–32 (see Examples 2.1 and 2.3 and the associated discussion). And Rosen does not
even ask whether Haydn might have had an artistic purpose in such single-minded
treatment, let alone attempt to relate these events to others elsewhere in the symphony.
(As we have seen, the differentiated motives of mm. 1–12 and 13–16 animate both the
main theme and the paired structural cadences in the farewell movement.) Similarly,
in view of the profoundly through-compositional character of Symphony No. 46
(see Chapter 8), the notion that its thematic links cannot "range beyond their immediate
context" and "remain isolated" can only be attributed to a kind of blindness – a
musicological manifestation, it would appear, of what Paul de Man insists is the inevitable
byproduct of critical insight.[1] In fact, like most postwar analysts (including both the
Schenkerians and such important figures as Meyer and Cone; see for example the latter's
account of Op. 54 No. 2, discussed in Chapter 8), Rosen's vision of "Classical style"
is largely restricted to single movements; he discusses through-composition and cyclic
integration but rarely, and never so much as mentions them with respect to Haydn. But
(again) if this volume has demonstrated anything, it is that this view now seems fatally
limited. (Even if some new "blindness" accompanies this insight, I must still insist on it.)

Rosen's harshest criticism is reserved for Symphony No. 43 in E-flat (c. 1770–71;
see Example 9.1):

The weakness of Haydn's early style . . . is not in its logical relations, nor in its moments of
drama and poetry, but in the passages of necessary prose. . . . It was at times difficult for him to
impart urgency or energy to [ordinary] material. . . . Even in . . . as fine a symphony as . . .
no. 43 . . . his struggles are apparent: The series of weak endings on the tonic is viable only if
one does not expect anything from the phrase which will imply an articulate shape and a neces-

---

[1] *Blindness and Insight* (New York, 1971).

Example 9.1 Symphony No. 43/i: first group

Ex. 9.1 (*cont.*)

sary continuation. The relaxed beauty . . . is evident, but a style which will accept it at the price of such a flaccid co-ordination between cadential harmonies and large-scale rhythm can reach a dramatic effect only through the extraordinary. . . . We can see Haydn beginning to struggle: not only the opening *forte* chords for each phrase but also the successive elongation of the phrase-length attempt to enforce a sense of growing energy. . . . But the faster rhythm of measure 27 is not persuasive because it is not what it would like to be: it is not faster at all, but only an extra excitement in the violins.   (pp. 149–50)

In fact, however, Haydn's opening eight bars are a perfectly clear period. More importantly, his apparently deviant procedures have a larger point. The ensuing quiet phrases indeed circle around I⁶, G in the bass always supporting $\hat{1}$ or $\hat{5}$ in the melody: they positively ruminate – *too* long, *too* demonstratively refusing to do anything; the longer they continue, the more we precisely do expect meaningful change. (The principle is again Meyer's implication–realization model, transferred to the domain of large-scale gesture; see the discussion of Op. 54 No. 2 in the preceding chapter.) And in mm. 27–31, action indeed takes over: with a sudden *forte*, the violins plunge down in tremolo sixteenths, as the bass accelerates the harmonic rhythm to eighth notes. (The violins' sixteenths are thus by no means mere "extra excitement.") This activity leads to the very strong cadence which closes the first group (mm. 30–31), in turn elided to the vigorous transition (on the same motive). To hear a "flaccid co-ordination between cadential harmonies and large-scale rhythm" in mm. 9–26 is a misreading, because these bars are not cadential at all (they come in the middle of the paragraph, and they avoid root-position V–I progressions, a descent to the tonic, and change of harmonic rhythm). By contrast, the actual cadence coordinates tonality and rhythm very strongly indeed.

The three elements of Haydn's paragraph – period, extension, cadence – cannot be dissociated. (Even the opening *forte* chords are relevant; they establish the contrasts between loud and soft, full orchestra and strings alone, root position and first inversion, which govern the paragraph as a whole.) The pitch content enhances the continuity. The high points of the overall rising line, eb²–g²–bb², coincide with the beginnings of the three parts (mm. 1, 9, 26); having achieved $\hat{5}$ in mm. 26–29, the cadence plunges directly down to the tonic. At the *forte* violin entry, the rushing scale bb²–bb¹ and the bass entry on G maintain the predominant pitch structure, $\hat{5}/I⁶$, of the ruminating phrases (compare the downbeat of m. 26); more subtly, the melodic progression B♮–C over I$^6_{3♮}$–IV (m. 28) replicates their initial harmonic move (mm. 9c–10). On the gestural level, the cadence provides long-awaited contrast and fulfillment; on the tonal level, it concludes a single, continuous process. (A symptom of Rosen's misreading is that his musical example breaks off at the downbeat of m. 28 – omitting the entire cadence!)

Furthermore, this opening resembles other triple-meter symphony first movements from the early 1770s. No. 41 in C (*c.* 1770) begins with a similar period, each phrase likewise marked by a single *forte* chord, followed by a fanfare continuation ending on a half-cadence and a repetition of the opening period; the active tremolo passage (texturally equivalent to the cadence in No. 43) begins the transition (m. 27). In No. 55 in E-flat (1774), the opening *forte* gesture is two bars rather than a single chord, the *piano* a brief four-bar period, leading to a fanfare on the dominant, a repetition of the *piano* theme, and a cadence; again, the tremolo initiates the transition (m. 23). And the Farewell itself opens with a four-phrase theme, with no contrast until the cadential phrase adopts the tremolo texture (as in No. 43, except in unison); owing to the single-minded violence of the whole movement, however, the transition reverts to the main theme. The familiar lesson applies: Haydn uses certain procedures again and again, but he does not repeat himself. The opening of No. 41 maintains periodic phrasing throughout; Nos. 45 and 55 assume those norms but manipulate them (each in a different way); in No. 43, mm. 9–26 overtly deny them. (This variety largely forestalls the potential objection that all these openings, being contemporaneous, could be "weak" in the same way; far more plausible is that Haydn, seeking (as always) new and unexpected effects, simply composed each work differently.) Furthermore, No. 41 chronologically precedes No. 43; the hypothesis that Haydn had not yet mastered periodic phrase-structure in the latter work is manifestly absurd – not to mention that he had already used periodic phrasing in hundreds of works, from the Quartet Op. 1 No. 1 on.[2] (This point illuminates yet another limitation of Rosen's position: his undifferentiated characterization of *all* of Haydn's music before 1780 as "early," as if there were no distinctions worth noting among hundreds of works composed over more than half his career.) Compare again the Farewell, in which Haydn "pointedly" contrasts non-periodic and periodic opening themes in the two F-sharp-minor movements, the Allegro assai and the Presto. (As we will see later, with the thesis of non-periodicity musicologists have been stalking bigger game.)

A different sort of similarity exists between Symphony No. 43's opening and that of Haydn's contemporary Quartet Op. 20 No. 1, also in E-flat. The stylized main theme of the latter is nothing if not leisurely in its triple presentation, I–V–I (mm. 1, 7, 11), as if it were going to be a trio-sonata (compare the opening movement of Op. 20 No. 2, described in the preceding chapter). But the real parallel is with the ensuing sequence (mm. 16–20), which again ruminates "too long" on the main theme in the tonic; the transition proper begins only in m. 21, *subito forte* – as if the performers suddenly "come to their senses" and initiate vigorous modulatory action. Perhaps this is another manifestation of Haydn's play throughout Op. 20 with old and new styles (compare Chapter 8); the effect here is witty, even ironic. The notion of insufficiency applied to this work seems as inappropriate as to the Farewell or No. 46. (Rosen [p. 118] criticizes the cello triplets in m. 4 as "purely transitional," taking no account of Tovey's citation of them as an example of Haydn's new sense of quartet scoring in Op. 20, or Keller's argument for their motivic continuity.[3])

My differences with Rosen regarding Haydn's early and middle years are not a matter of details alone. When so brilliant a critic misreads so egregiously, some deep-seated bias must be skewing perception. In this case, it seems to be a conflation of the supposed inadequacy of Haydn's individual technique with a hypothesized general development of style from "Baroque" to "Classical." (In an amusing demonstration of the persistence of these notions, Eric Weimer's otherwise intelligent criticism of Rosen's stance compromises its own argument by dismissing all of Haydn's early instrumental music as "light," and saying of No. 43 that it is one of the "weaker" Sturm-und-Drang symphonies![4]) As we will see, the argument against Haydn's early mastery always appeals to the notion of a general inadequacy in mid-century music, without which it would go up in smoke. To understand this (as it seems to me) untenable position, we must inquire into its origins: in the explanations of the purported distinction between Haydn's flawed production before 1781 and his consummate mastery thereafter; and in historiographical explanations of the development of "Classical style." (As we will see, both

---

[2] On Haydn's phrase-rhythm in Op. 1 No. 1, see Georgiades, "Zur Musiksprache der Wiener Klassiker."

[3] Tovey, "Haydn's Chamber Music," p. 40; Keller, "The String Quartet and Its Relatives," *MR* 26 (1965), 340–44 (repr. in *The Great Haydn Quartets*, pp. 31–32).

[4] *"Opera Seria" and the Evolution of Classical Style 1755–1772* (Ann Arbor, 1984), pp. 3–4; compare pp. 46–49.

notions are dependent on crudely reductive applications of the concept of evolution to stylistic development in the arts. I must therefore emphasize that the teleological and ideological agendas entailed have little in common with the ideas of Darwin and other nineteenth-century scientific thinkers, and still less with current theories of evolution. Thoughtful historians in the arts have long since distanced themselves from those reductive notions, without necessarily abandoning a nuanced and self-critical use of "evolution"; see, for example, James S. Ackerman's hypothesis that "what is called evolution in the arts should not be described as a series of steps towards a solution to a given problem, but as a succession of steps away from one or more original statements of a problem."[5] To make the distinction clear, I use the term "evolutionist" to designate the teleological/reductive sense of evolution found in many of the writers under discussion.[6])

SANDBERGER'S TALE

We begin with a story, first told by Adolf Sandberger in 1900. (All historical writing, we now believe, comprises narratives, selections from and shapings of the data according to the desires and needs of historians and their audiences; it has been argued that philosophy itself is a primarily narrative mode of discourse.[7]) Sandberger's tale deserves our attention, because it has decisively influenced almost all subsequent interpretations of Haydn's growth and maturity, as well as, indirectly, the concept "Classical style" itself. Sandberger focused on the principle of what he called *thematische Arbeit* (translated below as "thematic development"), claiming that Haydn more or less invented it, and first employed it systematically in his string quartets Op. 33 (1781). Despite its influence, his account has rarely been quoted in later writings (even in German), and so I begin with an extract long enough to establish both the narrative thread and the style:

[All of Haydn's string quartets before Op. 20] lack that principle which we today confess [*bekennen*] to be the primary and most important one by which quartets are shaped, which must be the most powerful impulse for a composer's imagination and artistic understanding: the *principle of thematic development*. . . .

The basic tone of all these works is still that of the old cassation; . . . a counterweight . . . to the attractive, harmless play of invention is still lacking. . . .

In this connection [Haydn] turned . . . to counterpoint; this served in the first instance for the increased stylization of his dance-movements. . . . But in the context of the work as a whole, these more strictly composed passages remained of minor importance. . . .

---

[5] In James S. Ackerman and Rhys Carpenter, *Art and Archeology* (Englewood Cliffs, N.J., 1963), p. 174. Leo Treitler, *Music and the Historical Imagination* (Cambridge, Mass., 1989), argues against the older reductive ways of thinking, of which evolutionism has been one of the most potent.

[6] I am grateful to Eugene K. Wolf for clarifying my original treatment of this topic, as well as other suggestions regarding this chapter.

[7] See, in a burgeoning literature, Hayden White, *Tropics of Discourse* (Baltimore, 1978), introduction; and "Interpretation in History," *New Literary History* 4 (1972–73), 281–314, repr. *Tropics*, pp. 51–80. Treitler's volume explores implications of this stance for musicology. On philosophy as narrative, see Jonathan Rée, *Philosophical Tales* (London and New York, 1987).

Then in 1771[8] the master suddenly has enough of this playful tone. And now it is . . . up to counterpoint to make things good. . . . Haydn resolves on a major campaign and introduces the heavy artillery of the great traditional art-forms. . . . [Op. 20 No. 2] receives as finale a fugue with four subjects, [No. 5] with two, [No. 6] with three. . . . This has led to [these works] being called "great quartets"; Gerber . . . emphasizes, "From this opus forward, Haydn appears in his entire greatness as a quartet composer." . . .

Nevertheless . . . Haydn here linked two things which stylistically have little in common in his quartet world . . . most clearly in [No. 5 in] F-minor. . . . Here cassation-quartet, there solemn counterpoint; here the fresh modern air, there the most profound resource in the musical arsenal – Haydn must have sensed these contradictions. And now . . . *Haydn entirely abandoned quartet composition for ten whole years.* . . .

What had been lacking was the *mediation* between strict and free musical form. The child of the marriage between counterpoint and freedom is *thematic development*. Counterpoint is the father. . . . But Haydn had as it were to reinvent it; he did this in the intervening years in the symphony. . . .

Now the master takes up quartet composition again and writes [Op. 33] *"in an entirely new special manner."* . . .

The principle of motivic development has taken possession of the string quartet; *the modern string quartet is invented.* . . .

In place of mere attractive *juxtaposition* of musical ideas, comes *organic development* of the motives. Thus the string quartet is at once homophonic and polyphonic. . . .

The Paris symphonies may have further extended the principle of thematic development; *but Haydn appears as its master first of all in the string quartet.*[9]

Although Sandberger does not use the expressions "Classical" or "pre-Classical," his story is based on analogous binary oppositions: modern vs. traditional, homophony vs. polyphony, freedom vs. strictness, complexity vs. simplicity ("harmless play"), completeness vs. limitation (the early quartets "lack" thematicism, which counterpoint must "make good"; Op. 20 "lacks" mediation), and so forth. The evolutionist metaphor is in full flower; he assumes an (inevitable) historical development from earlier, imperfect antecedents to a later synthesis of perfection; likewise organicism, in the distinction between mere "links" and "juxtapositions" of cassation and fugue in Op. 20 and the "organic development" of Op. 33. (In Sandberger's unintentionally comic description of the "marriage of freedom and counterpoint," their progeny – *thematische Arbeit* itself – becomes a "child" whom we revere! This was of course not blasphemous; possibly it was an unconscious parody of Wotan's procreative masterwork, the free hero Siegfried. But the issue of paternity was indeed crucial; the otherwise superfluous aside, "The father was counterpoint," reassured Sandberger's readers that the "law-giving" progenitor was the male. This must be one of the most egregious examples of "phallogocentrism" in the musicological literature.[10])

---

[8] Op. 20 dates from 1772; Sandberger inferred "1771" from Haydn's expression in the famous Op. 33 letters of December 1781, "I haven't composed any quartets for ten years."

[9] "Zur Geschichte des Haydnschen Streichquartetts," pp. 258–63 (all emphases in the original).

[10] For the concept "phallogocentrism," see Jonathan Culler, *On Deconstruction: Theory and Criticism after Structuralism* (Ithaca, N.Y., 1982), pp. 58–63.

Sandberger thus takes the underlying elements of what was about to become the prevailing sense of "Classical style" (perfection, synthesis, evolutionist teleology), associates them with a favorite composer and familiar compositions, and *dramatizes* them in a narrative. His account comprises six stages: (1) the naive simplicity of Haydn's early string quartets; (2) his recognition of an inadequacy; (3) his forcible, but fruitless, turn to counterpoint; (4) his abandonment of the quartet in favor of new experiments in the symphony; (5) invention of *thematische Arbeit*; and (6) its transfer back to the quartet, which is thereby perfected. This is neither more nor less than one of the oldest types of story known to man – the *quest*. Sandberger's structure is typical of such a tale: (1) an original state of innocence; (2) its disruption by a problem or threat; (3) an initial struggle to put things right, which fails; (4) a "trial": a period of labor, renunciation, pilgrimage, self-purification; (5) discovery of or winning the magic talisman; (6) final triumph. Perhaps a modest retelling will clarify the point:

Once upon a time there lived a talented young composer named Joseph Haydn. He composed cheerful string quartets, but they did not fully satisfy him; he attempted to enrich them contrapuntally, but only in minuets. Then one day, the ghost of Johann Sebastian Bach appeared to him, and said, "Young man: your mission is a higher one. Go and write fugues, and incorporate them into your string quartets." Haydn rushed to follow this advice; alas! his fugues did not go together with his cheerful tunes; his new quartets were failures. Heavy of heart, he wandered for ten long years in the wilderness of symphonic experimentation, until at last he discovered the secret of stylistic synthesis through *thematische Arbeit*. Then he returned home and began to compose Classical string quartets, and he continued to compose Classical string quartets the rest of his life. And everyone lived happily ever after.

In its own way, Sandberger's tale is as classic a fairy-tale as anything recorded by the brothers Grimm. (History – to repeat – is narrative; basic story types like the quest retain their power under the most varied manifestations.[11]) The proof is that it has dominated musicological discourse for close to a century, meeting people's need for an account of this confusing, crucial period in music history that is not only intelligible, but emotionally satisfying.

The central event in Sandberger's tale is the *crisis*: Haydn's coming under the sway of the contrapuntal muse, and his realization that the fugues in Op. 20 will not work, that the schematic linking of strict and free is a "contradiction." (Sandberger's sustained military imagery here – "resolves on a major campaign . . . heavy artillery . . . musical arsenal" – concretely invokes a hero in the midst of a grand struggle.) Less than ten years later, apparently by coincidence, Théodore de Wyzewa introduced another, equally influential notion of crisis into the Haydn literature: the so-called "Sturm und Drang" period, which he interpreted as reflecting a "crise romantique" in Haydn's personal life.[12] This (wholly imaginary) crisis quickly became a standard element in accounts both of Haydn's career and of musical style in the third quarter of the century. Wyzewa focused

[11] From (again) a vast literature, I have found Brooks, *Reading for the Plot*, most helpful.

[12] "A propos du centenaire de la mort de Joseph Haydn," *Revue des deux mondes*, 79th year, 5th period (vol. 51, 4th issue), 15 June 1909, pp. 935–46. On the "Sturm und Drang" generally, see the Introduction, note 7.

on the symphonies, not the quartets; nevertheless the common dates and comparable stylistic extremes of the two repertories quickly led to a conflation of the two accounts into a generalized hypothesis of crisis and radicalism in Haydn's music *c.* 1770–72. Thus Blume's influential essay of 1931 (which reflects the genuine crisis of its time of writing) portrayed Haydn as

feverishly working on, seeking the solution, so overenthusiastically that in Op. 20 the problem lost control of itself and flowed into the dead-end of an exaggerated radicalism. . . . [The] fugal finale . . . was merely the most extreme consequence of a consciously progressive process of development; . . . if, under the compulsion of a necessity having the force of law, Haydn here seized on the most radical means – all this should follow with total obviousness from the entire process [of Haydn's development]. . . . This phase represented an extreme beyond which Haydn had no possibility of developing further in the same direction.[13]

What in Sandberger had been a mere contradiction among stylistic incompatibilities is now interpreted as a general malaise, affecting the style and tone of entire works, and reflecting an even more thoroughgoing, indeed "radical," evolutionism.

For Finscher, writing in 1966 and publishing in 1974, the fugal finales themselves become the symptom of Haydn's crisis:

The three fugal quartets radically problematize the coherence of the cycle. . . . The fugal finales . . . are so distinct from the remaining movements . . . that they no longer have any persuasive function as finales. In the F-minor quartet . . . the fugue is to be sure vaguely related to the tone of the first two movements; but, owing to its schoolmasterly strictness and the fact that it appears entirely unprepared, it functions not as a conclusion but as an appendix. . . .

The total impression of Op. 20 . . . is very bewildering, above all because in it the most different imaginable tendencies clash. . . . The result . . . could have been nothing other than a crisis. . . .

From here, no path could lead further forward. The attempts to go beyond Op. 17 brought only experiments with extremes, not valid results. The crisis, which in [Haydn's] contemporary symphonies . . . was primarily a crisis of expression, became, in the quartet . . . a crisis of the genre itself. Nothing is more characteristic of this crisis than the fact that Haydn now turns his back on the genre for years . . . a pause which functions like a pause of helplessness and exhaustion.

(*Streichquartett*, vol. 1, pp. 235–37)

Finscher's concluding invocation of "a pause of helplessness and exhaustion" returns to the *motif* of the "trial," in language which recalls the fairy-tale aspect of Sandberger's narrative, just as his account of the "bewildering" stylistic "clashes" in Op. 20, particularly the supposed dysfunctionality of the fugue in No. 5 in F minor, reflects Sandberger's treatment (compare the discussion of Op. 20 No. 2 in chapter 8). Evolutionist "necessity" is fused with personal trauma, nowhere more clearly than in the last two sentences, where the magic word "crisis" appears no fewer than four times.

Sandberger's interpretation of Op. 33 has been even more influential. Alfred Einstein followed him in interpreting its "synthesis" in quasi-religious terms: "*Motivisch-thematische Arbeit* is [a] synthesis of homophony and counterpoint, the rescue [*Rettung*] of the concept of the symphonic, . . . the fusion, the reconciliation [*Schmelzung, Versöhnung*]

---

[13] "Josef Haydns künstlerische Persönlichkeit," pp. 38–39.

of . . . the galant and the learned."[14] Blume then took the decisive step of combining the idea of a style change with that of classicism itself:

The [ten-year] pause was thus no coincidence, but deeply motivated psychologically, and Op. 33 signified . . . a "consummation," insofar as it renounced exaggeration and confined the roaring currents into a new . . . classicism. . . .

What now followed was a gradually increasing and greater directedness towards a still stricter classicism.   (pp. 40, 43)

Finscher values above all else the elements of synthesis and the completion of a historical process:

Op. 33 is *the* epoch-making work in which the string quartet achieved its first classical realization . . . not only in the sense of a mature consummation of style . . . but in its fusion of the most extreme clarity of form with the greatest richness and malleability of detail. . . . [Its] "new art" . . . lies in the complete balance of its elements of the Classical style as such, which unites all the musical spheres – from the learned, through the galant, the expressive-*Empfindsam* and the divertimento-like, to the folk-like – into a new and [yet] . . . familiar whole. . . . Thereby was achieved the goal of a development which had begun with Op. 1: string-quartet style was discovered, the quartet defined as a genre. In all his later quartets, Haydn never again changed anything essential in this classical conception of the genre.[15]

But Sandberger's "Op. 33 hypothesis" (as we may call it) lacks sufficient historical foundation.[16] Following Pohl, he claimed that Haydn's early quartets comprised two separate genres, the serious "Quadro" and the light cassation. (This was necessary for the hypothesis of a synthesis of multiple antecedents.) In fact, however, their authentic sources, terminology, chronology, and style prove that all the early quartets belonged to a single, uniform repertory. Their historical and stylistic context was no stew of diverse influences, but indigenous Austrian/Bohemian chamber music.[17] They represented an intensification of one subspecies of this repertory, the "Divertimento a quattro" for four solo strings. His language offering Op. 33 for sale – "written in a new and entirely special manner" – was both a conscious declaration of stylistic novelty and an advertising slogan;[18] it does not imply that he was referring to anything that would justify our interpretation of it as the "achievement" of "Classical style."

The votaries of the Op. 33 hypothesis also ignore the actual chronology of Haydn's quartets (which has been obscured by the erroneous notion of his "continuous" production of them throughout his life). In fact, he cultivated the genre only during certain well-defined periods, which alternated with equally distinct pauses, often of five or ten years:

[14] "Haydns Sinfonie," *ZfM* 91 (1924), 173; quoted in Bard, *Untersuchungen*, p. 27.

[15] *Streichquartett*, vol. 1, pp. 266–67; compare pp. 18–20.

[16] This passage summarizes earlier discussions of mine: "The Chronology of Haydn's String Quartets," *MQ* 61 (1975), 44–46; "Haydn's String Quartets," in *Haydnfest* (Washington, D.C., 1975), pp. 13–17; a review of Finscher in *JAMS* 28 (1975), 543–49; and "Did Haydn 'Synthesize' the Classical String Quartet?" in *Haydn Studies*, pp. 336–39.

[17] See Larsen, "Some Observations," and "Der Stilwandel in der österreichischen Musik zwischen Barock und Wiener Klassik," in *Der junge Haydn*, pp. 18–30; Webster, "Towards a History," pp. 214–15.

[18] Feder, "Ein vergessener Haydn-Brief," *H-S*, 1 (1965–67), 114.

Middle or late 1750s   Opp. 1 and 2
1769/70–72   Opp. 9, 17, 20
1781   Op. 33
[1785   Op. 42]
1787–90   Opp. 50, 54/55, 64
1793   Op. 71/74
1797–99(–1803)   Opp. 76, 77, (103)[19]

By Sandberger's criteria, the last *early* quartets (Op. 2 Nos. 1 and 2) should also have represented a "crisis"; the long gap until Op. 9 (probably longer than that between Opp. 20 and 33) a licking of wounds and summoning of courage; Op. 9 itself the creation of a "classic" quartet style, further developed in Opp. 17 and 20. Worse still, the same logic could be applied to Haydn's "abandonment" of multiwork opera following Op. 33, with a "pause" of "six full years" until Op. 50 (the single, chronologically isolated, small Op. 42 does not compromise this larger pattern). In fact, the quartets in Op. 50 make a stronger claim to be Haydn's first that *intrinsically* embody "Classical style" as it has been traditionally understood: while retaining the virtues of Op. 33, they are on a larger scale; the slow movements more deeply felt, the finales more complex; and they reveal the influence of Mozart in their increased chromaticism and more earnest tone. And, again like Op. 9, Op. 50 inaugurated a uniform series of three six-work *opera* within a four-year period. (Nor, *pace* Blume and others, did Haydn's style become "fixed" in the 1780s; it continued to develop until the end of his career [see pp. 365–66].)

Finally, the "resonance" of Op. 33, of which Finscher makes so much, turns out on closer inspection to be rather thin: the dissemination of these works was no wider than that (say) of Op. 20. (Sandberger, who quotes Gerber [writing in 1810] in praise of Op. 20, does not mention that Gerber says nothing more about Op. 33 than "ever more glorious!", with no hint of registering a decisive arrival or turning point. To be sure, in 1790 Gerber did single out 1780 as the time when Haydn "attained the highest level of excellence and fame" – not in quartets, however, but "through his church and theater works"! This hardly supports the Op. 33 hypothesis.[20]) Op. 33 was one, admittedly very important, event within the explosive cultivation of quartets in Vienna during the 1780s. Insofar as the Classical string quartet exists at all, it arose precisely via this new general cultivation and dissemination; it included, but was not limited to, Haydn's quartets of the 1780s and Mozart's dedicated to him. During the later 1780s and the 1790s – when Koch and others crowned Haydn and Mozart as the first classics of the genre – Op. 33 was not specially singled out; indeed, Mozart's quartets dedicated to Haydn played a greater role in these accounts than any single opus of his own. The Classical string quartet was not a synthesis of pre-Classical genres from all over Europe, but a development within a single regional tradition, which became the central element in *later* explanations of the rise of the genre. "Classical" chamber music could arise only in the act of forgetting its own origins.

---

[19] Haydn intended the unfinished Op. 103 to go with Op. 77, to complete a standard set of three; see Webster, "Chronology," pp. 24–25.

[20] *Neues Lexikon*, vol. 2, col. 577 (his Op. 20 remark on col. 576); on "1780," *Lexikon* (1790), vol. 1, col. 611 (compare p. 229 above).

There is no basis in the record for the notion of a "crisis" centering around Op. 20. It makes sense only in terms of its function as the "other," the second half of a binary opposition whose leading term is Haydn's later achievement of his "goal" – as the mirror image of the triumph of Op. 33. Absent that apotheosis, there is no need for the crisis. It is high time we abandoned Sandberger's tale, crisis, trial, triumph, and all. To do this, however, we must examine the governing metaphor, the "master trope" of all musicological discourse about Haydn and his development: the notion of "Classical style" itself.

"CLASSICAL STYLE"

Although he does not use the term, the conceptual basis for Sandberger's tale was "Classical style." Regarding Haydn, this notion (in its traditional sense) is anachronistic, implicitly falsifies the nature of his music, misleads us as to his artistic development, and inhibits appreciation of his mastery before 1781 and outside the "central" instrumental genres. Historiographically, the related notion of the "Classical period" in music is equally problematical. Both concepts harbor covert, primarily conservative ideological implications for analysis and historical studies. (I will discuss certain recent revisionist views on these matters at the end of this section.)

Conflations of meaning

Leaving aside derived usages such as "classicistic," "Neo-Classical," and others, the central terms "classic" and "Classical" have a complex range of overlapping meanings.[21] We can distinguish the following principal senses (the first three are general; the last four apply specifically to music):

(1) [period-designation (e.g., "Classical antiquity")]
    (a) the civilization or art of ancient Greece and Rome; (b) any past civilization or art understood as comparable to ancient Greece and Rome; (c) any repertory understood as a historical climax or goal in an evolutionist sense
(2) [value-judgment (usually "classic," adj. and sb.)]
    (a) a work or author of the highest rank; (b) an exemplary member of its type or class; (c) having lasting influence; (d) belonging to a canon; etc.
(3) [style (description and evaluation)]
    (a) the style characteristic of ancient Greek and Roman arts; (b) regarded as having a style similar to that of ancient Greek and Roman arts; (c) the style of any repertory regarded as admirable or exemplary

---

[21] See, in addition to the *Oxford English Dictionary*, Blume, *Classic and Romantic Music* (New York, 1970), pp. 3–17; Finscher, "Zum Begriff der Klassik in der Musik," *Deutsches Jahrbuch der Musikwissenschaft*, 11 (1967), 9–34; Arno Forchert, "'Klassisch' und 'romantisch' in der Musikliteratur des frühen 19. Jahrhunderts," *Mf* 31 (1978), 405–25; Heartz, "Classical," *The New Grove*, vol. 4, pp. 449–54; Martin Zenck, "Zum Begriff des klassischen in der Musik," *AfMw* 39 (1982), 271–92; Wolf, "Classical," *The New Harvard Dictionary of Music* (Cambridge, Mass., 1986), pp. 172–73.

On the term and concept in literature and cultural history, see T. S. Eliot, *What Is a Classic?* (London, 1945); Frank Kermode, *The Classic* (New York, 1975); Rudolf Bockholdt, ed., *Über das Klassische* (Frankfurt am Main, 1987).

(4) Western art-music, as distinct from functional, popular, ethnic musics
     [compare (2cd)]
(5) ["classic" (compare 2ab)]
     An exemplary composer or work of a given type, etc.; e.g., Josquin or the *Missa Pange Lingua* as "classics" of Renaissance vocal polyphony; Schubert or *Die schöne Müllerin*, of the German Lied; the Beatles or "Got To Get You Into My Life," of Rock; etc.
(6) ["Classical period" (compare 1bc)]
     (a) a historical period in Western art-music, *c.* 1720–80 or *c.* 1750–1800 or *c.* 1780–1815; also, when viewed as dominated or characterized by the Austrian/Bohemian repertory of the time, "Vienna Classical period" (see (b))
     (b) ["Vienna/Viennese Classical period"; "Viennese Classics" (*Wiener Klassik*)] the Austro/Bohemian repertory of that period
(7) ["Classical style" (compare 2, 3bc)]
     (a) the style said to be characteristic of the Classical period;
        (1) described traditionally as exhibiting beauty, perfection, balance, symmetry; the union of form and content, of technique and expression; unity within diversity; a synthesis of earlier, local, imperfect styles, of traditional and modern, popular and learned; universality; appeal to audiences of many types and periods
        (2) described in some recent writings as exhibiting "poise, balance, proportion, simplicity, formal discipline and craftsmanship, and universal and objective (rather than idiosyncratic and subjective) expression"[22]
     (b) ["Vienna Classical style"] the same, applied specifically to the instrumental music of Haydn and Mozart after 1780, often extended to all their music after 1780, and/or all their music, and/or some or all of Beethoven's music, and/or the music of their Austrian contemporaries

The term thus has three primary meanings – period; value; style – which overlap substantially, especially in musicological usage. The traditional definitions of "Classical style" (that given above as 7.a1 is synthesized from Guido Adler and Finscher)[23] are unthinkable without favorable comparative value judgments. The concept suffers from a double conflation: between the style of an entire period or repertory and that of an individual work or artist, and between historical and descriptive investigation and aesthetic evaluation. The simple locution "Classic string quartet" can imply at least three different things: string quartets originating during the Classical period; string quartets which exhibit Classical style; classic (exemplary, canonical) string quartets. Even the ostensibly neutral historical term "(Viennese) Classical period" strongly (if covertly) incorporates the valuative concept "Viennese Classical style." Many musicologists perpetuate these conflations

[22] Wolf, "Classical," p. 172 (to be taken as representative only).
[23] Adler, "Die Wiener klassische Schule," in his *Handbuch der Musikgeschichte*, 2nd edn, vol. 2 (Berlin, 1930), p. 768; compare Volker Kalisch, *Entwurf einer Wissenschaft von der Musik: Guido Adler* (Baden-Baden, 1988), pp. 174–78; Finscher, "Klassik," §I, IV.

by using only one term (most often "Classic") for all the relevant senses: for example, William S. Newman (*The Sonata in the Classic Era*), Blume (*Classic and Romantic Music*), Leonard G. Ratner (*Classic Music*), and Eugene K. Wolf (*The Symphonies of Johann Stamitz: A Study in the Formation of the Classic Style*).[24] (Not merely the titles of these distinguished works, but their content, is affected.) But "classic music," for example, could imply any of the four musical definitions given above; "Classic style" is ambiguous as between "classic" (lower-case), that which is exemplary or canonized, and "Classic(al)" (a proper adjective) as a period-designation. If these meanings were systematically correlated with distinct lexical forms (such as I have suggested in the definitions), discussion of these topics – which are complex enough as it is – would become clearer.

Development of the concept

The concept "Classical style" did not exist in Haydn's time. To be sure, around 1800 he and Mozart, and certain of their works, were already becoming "classics" (definition 5).[25] But both composers thought of themselves, and were understood by their contemporaries, as *modern*: bold reformers, extenders of music's realm. (This explains Haydn's concern, in his old age, to inhibit the dissemination of juvenilia: it is not that he denigrated them as "antecedents," but that they no longer seemed modern, did not correspond to current taste.[26]) Nor did Haydn suppose that his music of the 1780s represented a historical climax, after which only mannerism and decay lay ahead. At the end of his career, he said the direct opposite: "How much remains to be done in this glorious art, even by such a man as I have been!"[27] And later still, "My *métier* is boundless; what could still be done in music is far greater than what has already been done; ideas often come to me through which my art could be developed much further, but my physical powers no longer permit me to work them out."[28] Indeed in the early nineteenth century Haydn and (even more) Mozart were understood as Romantics, as is clear not only from E. T. A. Hoffmann's criticism, but from the congruence between the early Romantics' literary and philosophical ideas and their reception of Haydn's and Mozart's music.[29]

Not until the second quarter of the nineteenth century did they (and later Beethoven) become "classics" as historical figures, or the sense arise that theirs had been a "classical" age.[30] The process was of a piece with the broad division, in German literary and intellectual circles, between "classical" and "Romantic" aesthetics; those who now called Haydn

---

[24] Wolf informs me that, in the meantime, he has come to prefer "Classical" in contexts such as his title.

[25] On the canonization of Haydn's and Mozart's late quartets, see Finscher, *Streichquartett*, vol. 1, pp. 129–36; Webster, "Towards a History," pp. 228–31.

[26] Larsen, *Die Haydn-Überlieferung*, pp. 139–40, 153–54.

[27] Griesinger, p. 122 (Gotwals, p. 65). This passage is not included in the surviving autograph of Haydn's letter, but it must have stood in another version, which Griesinger published in the *AMZ* and Härtel reprinted in his appendix to Griesinger's biography. See Bartha in *Briefe*, pp. 320–21; Landon, *Haydn*, vol. 4, p. 470, n. 2.

[28] Griesinger, p. 5 (Gotwals, p. 8).

[29] Dahlhaus, "Romantische Musikästhetik und Wiener Klassik," *AfMw* 29 (1972), 167–81.

[30] Blume; Finscher, "Klassik," §II–III; Zenck, pp. 281–85.

and Mozart classics were motivated not only by admiration and the desire to cultivate and preserve their music, but also by conservative, anti-Romantic feelings. Also in the 1830s, in analogy to the literary designation *Weimarer Klassik* for Goethe, Schiller, Herder, and others, the early musicologist Raphael Georg Kiesewetter and others began to describe Haydn, Mozart, and their contemporaries between *c.* 1780–*c.* 1800 as the "Vienna school" (*Wiener Schule*).[31]

Kiesewetter's work was decisive for later historiography; he invented many of the periods and subperiods, and sloganeering style- and "school"-designations, which have persisted to this day, including the "Netherlandish school" as the central repertory of Renaissance sacred vocal music[32] and the "Neapolitan school" as a designation for eighteenth-century Italian opera. In his *History of European-Western Music* (1834), he divided this vast repertory into seventeen chronological "ages" (*Epochen*), which he characterized in ways that will immediately register as familiar with students of music history. In order to indicate the nature of his criteria and the flavor of his formulations, I quote the last five of them here:

XIII. The age of [Alessandro] Scarlatti: 1680 to 1720. Fundamental development of recitative and dramatic melody. Initial development of an autonomous instrumental music.

XIV. The age of Leo and Durante: 1720 to 1760. The Neapolitan School. Reform of melody. Augmentation of instrumentation in the orchestra.

XV. The age of Gluck: 1760 to 1780. Reform of operatic style. Introduction of ensembles and finales [into the opera]. Increasing development of instrumental music.

XVI. The age of Haydn and Mozart. Vienna School. Perfection of instrumental music.

XVII. The age of Beethoven and Rossini: 1800 to 1832.[33]

Like early connoisseurs and scholars in art history, Kiesewetter thus establishes and perpetuates "periods" and "schools," characterized in the first instance by prominent individuals and neatly compartmentalized dates (which magically never overlap), but also by technical features (recitative, melody, instruments and instrumentation) and stylistic changes ("reform" of melody and opera). (The implied dates 1780–1800 for Haydn and Mozart may count as self-evident in the context; as we will see, Kiesewetter explicitly gives them elsewhere. His omission of any characterization for his most recent period will be criticized only by those who would feel confident in publishing a survey of Western music since 1945 organized around a single slogan.)

The fundamentally evolutionist aspect of Kiesewetter's historical sketch is evident in his peroration (pp. 98–99): "If we now gaze backwards . . . it is gratifying to observe how this most beautiful of the arts has risen, through a series of periods, stage by stage, slowly but surely, to that perfection which . . . we believe we have achieved"; few later

---

[31] Heartz, p. 450; Zenck, p. 283.

[32] Paula Higgins, review of Reinhard Strohm, *Music in Late Medieval Bruges*, in *JAMS* 42 (1989), 150–51.

[33] *Geschichte der europäisch-abendländischen oder unsrer heutigen Musik* (Leipzig, 1834), pp. 105–07. On Kiesewetter, see Herfrid Kier, *Rafael Georg Kiesewetter: Wegbereiter des musikalischen Historismus* (Regensburg, 1968); on the origins of the *History*, pp. 114–18.

utterances have equaled the "classic" perfection of this formulation. The steady progression of instrumental music to its appointed culmination in Haydn and Mozart can be
read directly from the outline quoted above; in another place (p. 95) he writes of Haydn,
"His glorious period falls principally in the years 1780 to 1800. . . . He raised the entirety
of instrumental music to a degree of perfection which had never before been imagined."
(Note the starting-date: 1780.) His conservative orientation emerges not only from the
peroration (p. 99), where he wonders aloud whether the "decay" of music may not
already be discernible, but in his introduction of the term "Vienna school" itself (p. 95):

Through Haydn and Mozart, music of every type developed to the greatest perfection. . . .
One must therefore designate them both as the founders of a new school, which one may
call the "German School," or – because in the meantime a side-branch, a sect, has arisen,
precisely in Germany, which enjoys allowing itself to be called by this name – perhaps better
the "Vienna School."

The fateful concept of a "Vienna School" centering around Haydn and Mozart thus
arose in conservative opposition to contemporary nationalistic and progressive trends.

   This complex of ideas (evolutionism, perfectionism, conservatism, the years 1780–1800
as the highpoint of Haydn's and Mozart's music, and the rise of autonomous instrumental
or "absolute" music) completed the conceptual prerequisites for the later concept "Vienna
Classical School." Only the term "Classical" itself was missing; indeed, it remained latent
for the rest of the century. To cite three standard late works, neither Pohl's biography of
Haydn (1875–82), Wilhelm Langhaus's general music history (1887), nor Otto Jahn's
biography of Mozart as revised by Hermann Deiters (1889–91) uses the term in this
sense.[34] It was thus left to Guido Adler and his student Wilhelm Fischer, in the first two
decades of this century, to establish the term and concept "Vienna Classical School/
Period," which has shaped the historiography of later eighteenth-century music ever since.
No more than Kiesewetter, however, were Adler and Fischer disinterested, "scientific"
historians. Adler was motivated not only by local patriotism, and the usual academic
procedure of legitimizing one's chosen repertory by making large claims for its cultural
value, but by the need to defend Vienna's historical role as the stylistic milieu in which
"Classical style" had arisen, against Hugo Riemann's rival claims on behalf of the
"Mannheim School."[35] In addition – we are in the first decade of this century – the
"Viennese classics," which had in the meantime become the greatest representatives of
the entire Western musical tradition, were now made to function as bulwarks against
the encroaching downfall represented by modernism and atonality. A conservative agenda
lay openly on the surface.[36]
   The notion of the "Classical period" arose in direct consequence. The newly canonized
"Classical school" was given historiographic status, and further legitimized, by being
made to stand for one of the great historical periods of Western music, comparable to the

---

[34] Langhaus, *Die Geschichte der Musik des 17., 18., und 19. Jahrhunderts*, vol. 2 (Leipzig, 1887); Jahn, *W. A. Mozart*,
   3rd edn, rev. Hermann Deiters (Leipzig, 1889–91).
[35] See Larsen, "Zur Bedeutung der 'Mannheimer Schule,'" in Heinrich Hüschen, ed., *Festschrift Karl Gustav Fellerer zum
   sechzigsten Geburtstag am 7. Juli 1962* (Regensburg, 1962), pp. 303–09.
[36] On Adler's musical conservatism, see Kalisch, pp. 178–83.

middle ages and the Renaissance, and complementary to the contemporaneously invented "Baroque" and the already familiar "Romantic." (At first, Adler and Fischer used the term "old-Classical" [*altklassisch*] for the Baroque, "new-Classical" for *c.* 1750–1815.) Adler's intention, in imitation of parallel activities in art history, was twofold: first, to establish style periods, whose characteristics could be investigated in an ostensibly objective manner; second, as was inevitable in that organicist and evolutionist age, to investigate the "life-history" of each style: its origins, growth, climax, and eventual decay or transformation.[37] (The problem of the relationship between the teleological intent of the latter and the positivistic methodologies of the former – were they complementary, or did they constitute an unacknowledged contradiction? – was not much discussed.) In this context, Sandberger's *thematische Arbeit* was a godsend. Although it seemed to reside objectively "in" the notes, and hence could be studied in a properly academic manner (as a glance at American and German dissertation lists will confirm), it simultaneously offered the prospect of a grand evolutionist synthesis: of homophony and counterpoint, traditional and galant, strict and free, *Kenner* and *Liebhaber*.

Soon thereafter (1915), Fischer propounded a second, equally influential technical "sign" of Classical style: the *Liedtypus* principle of melodic construction (balanced period-structure), as opposed to the earlier Baroque *Fortspinnungstypus* (continuous, often sequential composing-out of a headmotive towards a cadence).[38] Again, an ostensibly objective distinction was placed in the service of an evolutionist interpretation: Fischer's title was "On the *Evolutionary* History of Viennese Classical Style," and his introduction includes the teleological premise, "By far the largest part of the 18th century had the *mission* of *preparing* and *gradually developing* the new style" (p. 24; emphasis added). Again, the secret was a synthesis, as regards both technique and compositional levels. The *Liedtypus* did not replace the *Fortspinnungstypus*, so much as it incorporated and superseded it:

The eight-bar Bachian section [the first half of a binary dance-form] is to be regarded as equivalent to an entire Viennese classical first group [*Tuttisatz*]. . . .

A phrase which in the Baroque would have provided the basis of an entire *Fortspinnung*-melody is now provided with an identical consequent . . . constructed according to the principle of periodicity. . . . The *Fortspinnung* type becomes the form of an entire sonata-exposition. . . . The architectonic principle of closed Classical-period melodies around 1780 is bilateral symmetry. . . .

Within the framework of the *Fortspinnung* type . . . are constructed *Liedtypus* melodies . . . melody types which [previously] were found only in dance-movements.   (pp. 50, 52, 62–63)

Quite apart from its congruence with Kiesewetter, Fischer's date "1780" was no accident. In the "official" context of Adler's compendious handbook of music history, he suggested the following periodization: "I: the pre-Classical transitional period (until *c.* 1760); II: the early Classical period (*c.* 1760–1780); III: the high Classical period (*c.* 1780–1815)".[39]

---

[37] Adler, "Style Criticism," *MQ* 20 (1934), 172–76. Compare Warren Dwight Allen, *Philosophies of Music History*, 2nd ed. (New York, 1962), chaps. 9–11; Dahlhaus, *Foundations*, pp. 13–19.

[38] "Zur Entwicklungsgeschichte des Wiener klassischen Stils." Blume criticized the distinction on conceptual-historical grounds in "Fortspinnung und Entwicklung," *JbP* 36 (1929), 56–57.

[39] Adler, ed., *Handbuch*, vol 2, p. 795.

Thus 1780 stood on the threshold of mature Classicism. And where might Fischer have drawn this notion? His periodization of Haydn's music (in still another context) gives the answer: "[1] up to 1761 (before Eisenstadt; development within tradition); [2] 1761–81 (until the consummation of *motivische Arbeit*; development of individual style); [3] after 1781 (consummate mastery [*höchste Meisterschaft*]; consummation of individual style)." Elsewhere in the same account he writes, "In his 49th year [1781], Haydn began his highest ascent."[40] Not only does Fischer equate his proposed "three periods" for Haydn's career with those for European instrumental music as a whole (dividing-points at 1760–61 and 1780–81), but the dominant criterion for the entire structure – the only technical feature mentioned, the prerequisite for "consummate mastery" – is our old friend *thematische Arbeit* (here called *motivische Arbeit*). These links between "Classical style," Haydn's mastery, and *thematische Arbeit* and periodic phrasing after 1780 – and hence, fatefully, between the absence of those technical features, the supposedly transitional styles of music, and Haydn's supposed lack of mastery (or his immaturity) before 1780 – have dominated the literature ever since.[41]

Adler's notion of the "Classical period" as an objective construct of historical investigation was an illusion, and not merely because of the inevitable arguments as to whether its chronological limits were 1720 to 1780 or 1750 to 1800 or 1780 to 1815, or whether it should be understood as Viennese or European-wide. It was no less inseparable from evolutionist teleology and normative aesthetics than "Classical style" itself. Consider the following summary by Finscher, its most prominent postwar exponent:

The concepts [of the nineteenth century] do not suffice to encompass the *unique qualities* which for the last 130 years . . . have *raised* Viennese Classicism *above every other period in the history of Western music.* . . . [These concepts] are too vague unequivocally to designate *the truly "classical"* in Viennese Classicism. . . .

It influences later history in a more comprehensive sense than any earlier period, *not only on account of its special qualities,* but equally *on account of its historical position* at the beginning of our historicizing age. . . .

The musical *process of development* at whose *end* stands Viennese Classicism is a *process of maturation,* with respect to which [Viennese Classicism] is the point of *highest maturity.* At this point of maturity, the stylistic elements of this development appear *completely developed, each in its own fashion* . . . [but] at the same time *unified into a "necessary" unity.*

("Klassik," pp. 25–26; emphasis added)

The interpenetration of history, evolution, and aesthetic valuation is complete.

Thus we come full circle to Rosen, whose title *The Classical Style: Haydn, Mozart, Beethoven* provocatively identifies the period style with that of the triumvirate as individuals. His opening sentence, "I have not attempted a survey of the music of the classical period, but a description of its language" (p. 9), sounds like a sober, "objective"

---

[40] "Stilkritischer Anhang," in Alfred Schnerich, *Joseph Haydn und seine Sendung,* 2nd edn. (Zurich, 1926), pp. 248, 253.

[41] For example, in Ernst Bücken's influential *Die Musik des Rokoko und der Klassik* (Postdam, 1927). Compare Blume, "Haydns Persönlichkeit," pp. 38, 41; Finscher, *Streichquartett,* vol. 1, pp. 220, 246.

historiographer. (Indeed, in a later revisionist mood [1975], he said, "Haydn was not creating 'Classical style'; he never heard of it. Insofar as Classical style exists (and of course it does not exist at all), it was invented by people like Koch in the 1790s."[42]) But two sentences later we read, "I have restricted myself to the three major figures . . . it is in terms of their achievements that the musical vernacular can best be defined." And he soon declares his allegiance:

"Classical" . . . style . . . is *exemplary and normative* . . . a *standard by which* the rest of our *musical experience is judged*. . . .

  The relation of the classical style to the "anonymous" style of the late eighteenth century is that it represents not only a *synthesis* of the artistic possibilities of the age, but also a *purification of the irrelevant residue of past traditions*.   (pp. 10, 22; emphasis added)

His sense of the stylistic watershed around 1780 is comparable to Sandberger's and Finscher's:

During [the years 1750–1775] a composer had to choose between dramatic surprise and formal perfection, between expressivity and elegance; he could rarely have both at once. Not until Haydn and Mozart . . . created a style in which a dramatic effect seemed at once surprising and logically motivated, in which the expressive and the elegant could join hands, did the classical style come into being.   (p. 44)

Not surprisingly, Rosen agrees with the traditional interpretations of Op. 33: "I take seriously Haydn's claim that . . . Op. 33 [was] written according to entirely new principles" (p. 23). Indeed, without mentioning the term, or indicating awareness of the origins of his perspective, he offers the best description of *thematische Arbeit* ever published (the passage to which he refers, from Op. 33 No. 1, is given above as Example 5.1):

The opening page . . . is a manifesto[43] . . . [and] represents a revolution in style. The relation between principal voice and accompanying voices is transformed before our eyes. In measure 3, the melody is given to the cello and the other instruments take up the little accompanying figure. In measure 4, this accompanying figure has become the principal voice – it now carries the melody. [But] no one can say just at what point [the change occurs]. All that one knows is that the violin starts measure 3 as accompaniment and ends measure 4 as melody.

  This is the true invention of classical counterpoint. . . .

  Op. 33 [is] the first application of this principle – i.e., the accompaniment conceived at once as thematic and as subordinate – on any scale and with any consistency. . . . The texture of the string quartet is incomparably enriched without disturbing the late eighteenth-century hierarchical scheme of melody and accompaniment.   (pp. 116–17)

His view of the supposed defects of "aperiodicity" in Haydn's pre-1780 music (see the first section of this chapter) is equally dependent on this unacknowledged tradition, specifically Fischer's distinction between *Fortspinnung* and *Liedtypus*. Again, the other side

---

[42] "'Classical Period' and 'Classical Style' in Eighteenth-Century Music" (Round Table), in *Haydn Studies*, p. 345.

[43] Rosen erred in interpreting the opening page of the B minor quartet in Op. 33 as a "manifesto"; in the authentic printed edition and (presumably) the MSS Haydn sold to subscribers, the G-major work we know as No. 5 occupied the first position. See *JHW* XII/3. (He acknowledged the error in the preface to a reprint edition [1972], while maintaining his view of the revolutionary significance of Op. 33.)

of the coin animates his positive description of Haydn's style after 1780, about which he writes that

the clearest [element] in the formation of the early classical style . . . is the short, periodic, articulated phrase. . . .

Articulated, periodic phrasing brought about two fundamental alterations: one was a heightened, indeed overwhelming, sensitivity to symmetry, and the second was a rhythmic texture of great variety. . . . The dominance of symmetry came from the periodic nature of the Classical phrase: a period imposes a larger, slower pulse on the rhythm, and . . . symmetry of phrase structure was necessary to hear and feel the larger pulse.   (pp. 57–58)

Criticism recapitulates historiography.

Thus the traditional concept of "Classical style" is anachronistic, inherently ambiguous, and shot through with conservative aesthetic-ideological baggage. As a period designation, it denies both the strong continuity of late eighteenth-century music with earlier musical cultures of the century (see below), and its (very different) continuity with that of the nineteenth. It is incompatible with the reception of Haydn, Mozart, and Beethoven by their contemporaries as moderns, and the early nineteenth-century reception of them as Romantics. As a concept of style, many of its supposed characteristics (perfection, unity, synthesis, universality, interpenetration of form and content) apply equally to many other "classic" arts; others (balance, symmetry, architectonic form, and the rest) are largely irrelevant, at least as far as Haydn and Beethoven are concerned. We should heed the following admonition of Donald J. Grout, given, not incidentally, in a symposium on "Classical style":

We've heard a great deal about "antecedents," "models," "influence," "stages," "development," "synthesis," and above all that great ghost of the late nineteenth century, "evolution." . . .

People who talk about the history of music should analyze the procedures of language in regard to [such words]. If we use these metaphors long enough and become fond enough of them, we endow them with a kind of artificial life, as though they existed somehow separately from our mental activity. The difficulty – and I say this meaning no disrespect to anyone – is one to which languages that capitalize nouns are particularly susceptible.[44]

Our current interest in rhetoric, narrative, and deconstruction makes these words from 1975 seem prescient indeed. Alas, evolutionist ideas still infect our discourse; nor are speakers of English, French, or Italian free of their taint.

Furthermore – see the analyses elsewhere in this volume – the traditional concept is at best an inaccurate and misleading metaphor for Haydn's music. With only occasional exceptions, he never intended to compose "absolute music" in the nineteenth-century sense.[45] All his vocal music, and a substantial portion of his instrumental music as well, explicitly or implicitly incorporates extramusical associations. Although its coherence is

---

[44] "'Classical Period' and 'Classical Style,'" *Haydn Studies*, pp. 342, 346.

[45] On "absolute music," see Dahlhaus, *The Idea of Absolute Music*, and *Esthetics of Music*, chap. 4, "Emancipation of Instrumental Music"; Treitler, "Mozart and the Idea of Absolute Music," in *Music and the Historical Imagination*, pp. 176–85, 212–13.

unsurpassed and unsurpassable, this is not the same as the organicist shibboleth of "unity," nor has it much in common with the trivializing notions of "balance" and "symmetry." Haydn's dynamic form and through-compositional tendencies explode the comfortable view of him as "Classical" on the level of large-scale form, as surely as his surprises, wit, capriciousness, eccentricity, and irony do so in the small. Worse still, the valuative component of the concept banishes Haydn's early and middle music, indeed all pre-1780 music, to a pre-Classical ghetto. It is time to replace these notions with – what?

Alternatives?

Numerous recent writers have attempted to develop a different musicological narrative which removes "Viennese classicism" from its pedestal. In its place, they emphasize the roots of late eighteenth-century music in Italian opera and the galant. This is in part a generational distinction (younger scholars vs. tradition), in part a cultural one (Anglo-Saxon empiricism and Latin rationalism vs. German idealism). Regarding Haydn's and Mozart's milieu, Ratner asserts that

[many] meanings of *classic* – objectivity, austerity, noble simplicity, purity of style, lack of disturbing irregularities or mixtures – do not apply. . . . According to late 18th-century views, [this period] would be called the *galant* style, possibly qualified as *late Franco-Italian galant*. . . . There is hardly a mention of Vienna throughout 18th-century comments on style. The music there drew upon elements of Italian, French, and German styles.

Similarly, Daniel Heartz emphasizes

the interpenetration of French, Italian and German music during the last part of the 18th century. . . . The high degree of musical homogeneity prevailing throughout Europe as the century drew to a close . . . did not obtain 50 years earlier, when critics could perceive only national differences. . . . The coining of this *lingua franca* . . . , its common denominator – the irreducible core of stylistic unity – would seem to rest upon the uncontested dominion of Italian opera.[46]

Even Dahlhaus (whom nobody will accuse of underplaying the Germanic or the philosophical) insists on the historical and social continuity between the traditional, official musical culture of Italian opera (and the galant) and that of Haydn and Mozart (although, inconsistently, he perpetuates the implicitly pejorative and methodologically suspect term *Vorklassik*, not to mention *Wiener Klassik* itself). A recent rethinking of these issues by Rudolf Bockholdt, who is no disciple of Dahlhaus, implies that the Germanic tradition is indeed beginning to approach them in a relatively nuanced and undogmatic manner.[47]

However, in their revisionist zeal these accounts run the risk of exaggeration. Heartz almost goes so far as to invert Rosen – asserting that traditional Italian musical culture

---

[46] Ratner, *Classic Music*, p. xv; Heartz, "Classical," p. 451. On the galant in particular see David A. Sheldon, "The Concept *galant* in the 18th Century," *JMR* 9 (1989–90), 89–108.

[47] Dahlhaus, introduction to *Die Musik des 18. Jahrhunderts* (Laaber, 1985); tr. in part as "The Eighteenth Century as a Music-Historical Epoch," *CMS* 26 (1986), 1–6; Bockholdt, "Über das Klassische der Wiener klassischen Musik," in *Über das Klassische*, pp. 225–59.

and the galant are the (vernacular) historical categories by which even "Viennese classical instrumental music," even Haydn and Mozart, are to be understood – before reverting to those two figures as unique individuals. But (as we have already seen) there were strong Austrian/Bohemian traditions, which influenced Haydn in particular more than all others combined, as well as the vigorous North German tradition centering around C. P. E. Bach. And, arguing in the other direction, the traditional concept of "Classical style" represents the after-the-fact reception of the triumvirate's music, from Vienna outward; in this context, the lack of eighteenth-century comment on Vienna is irrelevant. And more is found in Haydn's and Mozart's music than was dreamt of in the philosophy of the galant; "genius" is an equally authentic eighteenth-century concept. Kant – publishing one year before Haydn's first London symphonies and *The Magic Flute* – stated, "*Genius* is the . . . inborn creative capacity . . . *through which* nature provides art with rules. . . . It is not a capacity or skill for something that can be learned from some rule or other. Its primary quality, then, must be *originality*."[48] The greater the genius, the more legitimate it is in principle (however difficult in practice) to distinguish between period style and that artist's individual style, the less successful will be any attempt to circumscribe it by the conventions of the time. (Rosen discusses this issue at length.)

The revisionists know all this perfectly well. But their argument for a different sense of "Classical style," beginning around 1720 or 1730 and ending around 1780, and associated primarily with Italian opera and the galant, would be more persuasive if they *abandoned* the term as a label for Haydn's and Mozart's later instrumental music. This would be the ideal test of their nominalist orientation: their claim to be using "Classical" in a purely neutral or conventional manner, devoid of ideological and associative residues and of valuative implications (as "Baroque" has lost its original pejorative connotations). A different label would conform to the contemporary reception of Haydn's and Mozart's music as modern, pioneering, overwhelming, as well as consummately crafted and rhetorically persuasive – something like "First Viennese-European Modern Style." ("First," to distinguish it from the Schoenberg school; "modern," because it was so understood at the time, is the first major repertory to have remained continuously viable from its time to ours, and coincided with the beginnings of modern (post-revolutionary) history; "Viennese-European," to encompass both its origins and its later influence.) This is admittedly so unwieldy as to be almost comical. And of course any neologism – that is, any new historical narrative – will have defects of its own: no completely satisfactory term for this repertory will ever be found. The only other possibility would be the impracticable one of doing without style-period designations altogether. But those who continue to use "(Viennese) Classical style" should acknowledge its ideological origins and traditions, and should acknowledge as well that these have not been (and perhaps never will be) entirely dissipated.

"MATURITY"

We can now return to the issue of Haydn's maturity and stylistic development. In my

---

[48] *Kritik der Urteilskraft*, Part 1, Book 2, §46; tr. in le Huray and Day, pp. 227–28.

view, his music was masterful in every period of his life, including the earliest. At the same time – and this is no paradox – his art deepened throughout his life. To paraphrase a saying of Goethe's, his later works may have been "more so" – larger in scale, higher in pretension, more encompassing – but his early music was not thereby "outdone": *Das war vielleicht zu überbieten, aber nicht zu übertreffen.* Compare Gerber's remarks in 1790, referring to Haydn's music before 1780, that "his great genius drove him from one stage of perfection to the next" and that he was "great in the small and even greater in the large."[49] Haydn's earlier music was no mere "antecedent" phase along a path towards the achievement of some later "goal." In compensation for what may seem the narrative poverty of this interpretation, we can focus sympathetically on the character and qualities of all his music, in all genres. We can interpret differences in style not teleologically, but as the display of different facets of his musical persona, as responses to differing conditions and audiences. (These distinctions are not chronological alone. Haydn composed in different ways at the same time, even in the same genre: see, for example, the coexistence of galant and traditional style in his early instrumental music,[50] and in Op. 20 (described in Chapter 8); of connoisseurs' and amateurs' music in his late keyboard works (described in Chapter 6); and of his baryton trios with large-scale, extroverted quartets and symphonies during the late 1760s and early 1770s. In these and many similar cases, the assumption that the "lighter" works are necessarily inferior to the others is a Romantic/early-modernist prejudice.)

With very few exceptions, Haydn's earliest works are in full command of musical technique, appropriate in style and adequately varied according to generic and social context, and (once one forgets about "Classical style") richly expressive. The very early Symphonies 15 and 25, for example, exhibit considerable thematic integration and offer unique and convincing manipulations of symphonic form (see Chapter 8). The divertimento Hob. II:8 for flutes, horns, and strings (*c.* 1762–63?) is based on a pervasive thematicist logic, which embraces not only developing variation but also a kind of *Grundgestalt*, and concludes with perhaps Haydn's first (and one of his best) "ending" jokes. The apparently routine da capo finales in his early symphonies and quartets harbor a rich variety of formal solutions; even the young Haydn did not "repeat himself." From the early and middle 1760s, the *Matin–Midi–Soir* trilogy and the "Hornsignal" Symphony (see pp. 238–42, 246–47) unite rich programmatic associations with virtuoso instrumentation and impressive formal rigor and originality, comparable to, if less spectacular than, the Farewell and No. 46. And in general, notwithstanding its frequent small scale and lack of outward pretension, Haydn's earliest instrumental music exhibits the imaginative, resourceful, varied responses that characterize mature artists. In addition, notwithstanding the similarities of style, it far surpasses the music of other Austrian composers of the 1750s such as Albrechtsberger and Wagenseil – in at least the same proportion as his late music surpasses that of Clementi and Pleyel.[51]

---

[49] *Lexikon*, vol. 1, p. 611.

[50] Feder, "Die beiden Pole." I also thank Prof. Feder for suggesting many years ago in conversation the pertinence of Goethe's saying, in a related context.

[51] This paragraph summarizes previous studies of mine on Haydn's early instrumental music: "Haydns frühe Ensemble-Divertimenti" (on Hob. II:8); "D-major Interlude," §2 (on da capo finales); "Freedom of Form." See also Vinton;

But if all this is so, why is his early music described as "immature"? The most important reason is precisely the ideology of "Classical style." As we have seen, Haydn's career has been identified with the historical development of "Classical style" itself, such that the perfection of the latter has been directly equated with his works of the 1780s and after. The inevitable corollary has been that whatever came before was "marginalized": seen as immature (or experimental), analogously to the lower status of "social" or "occasional" music like divertimenti and baryton trios, compared to the "central" genres symphony, string quartet, and piano sonata. The result has been a blindness to the value of his earlier music, and misinterpretations of his development. In order to elucidate these matters further, we must survey the periodizations which have been proposed for Haydn's career.

Periodizations of Haydn's career

Any attempt to organize an artistic repertory (whether the *oeuvre* of a single figure or the production of an entire century) into chronological periods is an act of interpretation: still another species of historical narrative. A periodization is not so much true or false, as a "reading," a way of making sense of complex data, which serves the needs and desires of those who make and use them. In the nineteenth century, Haydn's career stimulated no paradigmatic narratives comparable to the notion of Beethoven's "three periods," which remains so important even today.[52] Pohl's biography simply follows the outward course of Haydn's life, marking divisions at his entry into Esterhazy's service in 1761, the opening of Eszterháza castle in 1766 (the dividing point between Pohl's two completed volumes), and his release from active duty and departure for London in 1790. The first two volumes of Landon's monumental biography do the same. But for a satisfyingly explanatory periodization, purely biographical events seem insufficient; such turning-points, we feel, ought to be correlated with fundamental changes in the artist's style as well. Now "1761" and "1790" unquestionably qualify in this sense (as does Haydn's return to Vienna in 1795). But his thirty-year tenure at the Esterházy court, when biographical data are scanty and many of his compositions cannot be securely dated, poses more difficult problems.

The only serious overall attempt at a periodization to date was worked out by Larsen and Landon in the 1950s and published in several places, severally and jointly (each time with slight variations),[53] most recently by Larsen in *The New Grove*:

Feder, "Die Bedeutung der Assoziation und des Wertvergleichs für das Urteil in Echtheitsfragen," in Henrik Glahn *et al.*, eds., *International Musicological Society: Report of the Eleventh Congress Copenhagen 1972*, vol. 1 (Copenhagen, 1974), pp. 365–77; Fillion, "The Accompanied Keyboard Divertimenti of Haydn and his Viennese Contemporaries (*c.* 1750–1780)," Ph.D. diss., Cornell University, 1982, pp. 10, 290, 304–06, 329.

[52] Maynard Solomon, "The Creative Periods of Beethoven," *MR* 34 (1973), 30–38; Kerman and Tyson, "Beethoven," *The New Grove*, vol. 2, pp. 376–78 (repr., pp. 89–91).

[53] *Die Musik in Geschichte und Gegenwart*, vol. 7, s.v. "Haydn" (Larsen and Landon); Landon, *Symphonies* (with alterations to accommodate his focus on a single genre); Larsen, "Zu Haydns künstlerischer Entwicklung," in Hans Zingerle, ed., *Festschrift Wilhelm Fischer zum 70. Geburtstag* (Innsbruck, 1956), pp. 123–29; *The New Grove*, vol. 8, p. 350 (repr., p. 86).

1	Vienna, early years	to c. 1761
2	Eisenstadt	1761–66
3	Eszterháza, years of expansion	1766–c. 1775
4	Operatic activity	c. 1775–84
5	Foreign commissions	1785–90
6	London	1791–95
7	Vienna, late years	1795–1809

The effort is laudable in its freedom from cliché and schematicism, its thorough knowledge of the data, and its inclusion of external as well as internal criteria. Nevertheless, of the three suggested division points between 1761 and 1790, the only one marked by fundamental changes both externally and internally, and therefore potentially period-defining, is "1765–66" (as I would circumscribe it). These years were marked externally by the death of Kapellmeister Werner (Haydn had originally been hired only as vice Kapellmeister), Haydn's promotion, the opening of Eszterháza castle, and Haydn's beginning his thematic catalogue (the *Entwurf-Katalog* or "EK"). (The latter initiative can be assumed to have had real significance for him; it may have been a reaction to a letter of reprimand from the prince in late 1765, whose final passage began: "*Kapellmeister* Haydn is urgently enjoined to apply himself to composition more industriously than hitherto."[54]) Stylistically, the mid-1760s also saw important changes, including a new concentration on opera and sacred vocal music, the baryton, and (as of c. 1769) the string quartet, as well as the beginnings of his expressive "Sturm und Drang" manner (his earliest true minor-mode symphony, No. 39, probably dates from 1765–66).

But the next two divisions are problematical. "1775" is suspect because Haydn's "expressive" or "expansive" phase ended in 1772 (not later), and the putative event "resumption of opera" stretches from 1773 (*L'infedeltà delusa* and *Philomen und Baucis*) to the inauguration of the new opera house in 1776; in any case, "operatic activity" is far too narrow a characterization of his *compositional* output, especially after 1780. Regarding "c. 1785," an even more fundamental (and analogous) external change had already taken place in 1779–80, when Haydn initiated the direct sale of music to publishers and rapidly developed his public career as a composer of instrumental music independently of the court;[55] the effects on his style were at least as profound as those of 1785–86. Conversely, no known biographical events correlate with Haydn's remarkable climax of expressiveness c. 1770–72 (Wyzewa's "romantic crisis" being a figment of his imagination). Perhaps it reflected in part his suspension of operatic composition after *Le pescatrici* of 1769–70 and its resumption in 1773 – as if his "dramatic" tendencies, refusing to be suppressed, migrated to the main instrumental genres.[56] (We still have no general study of the stylistic relations between Haydn's instrumental music and his operas. With the

---

[54] *Briefe*, No. 5, p. 50; Landon, *Haydn*, vol, 1, p. 420. The hypothesis regarding Haydn's motive for beginning *EK* is again Landon's and Larsen's; see Landon, p. 421; *The New Grove*, vol. 8, p. 334 (repr., pp. 23–24).

[55] See Larsen in *The New Grove*, vol. 8, p. 339 (repr., p. 43); Webster, "Prospects for Haydn Biography After Landon," *MQ* 68 (1982), 490.

[56] For the hypothesis that many of Haydn's "Sturm und Drang" symphonies actually originated as theatrical music, and in any case reflect that style, see Sisman, "Haydn's Theater Symphonies," pp. 340–45.

exception of the early *Der Krumme Teufel*, *Acide*, and other fragments, and the ill-fated *Orfeo* in London, they span the years 1766 to 1784 – precisely those for which we have no clear periodization, and during which his most enigmatic symphonies originated, from the late 1760s, and the mid-1770s through the early 1780s.)

I therefore propose an alternative periodization for Haydn's Esterházy years, shown in Table 9.1. (The argumentation is of course drastically compressed; the possibility of smaller subperiods is not addressed; the data regarding chronology, genres, and style are generalizations, which admit of many exceptions. Because Haydn composed symphonies in all these periods, they are not mentioned.) The point is not to "improve on" Larsen; this (or any other) periodization remains an interpretation, subject to revision. It is rather that precisely these years, so hard for us to make sense of, witnessed the changes in Haydn's style invoked by those who would deny his maturity before 1770, or 1781, or 1785. In fact, however, no division points except 1765–66 (and perhaps 1779–80) are strong enough, on both external and internal grounds, to serve as the basis for such a fundamental event as "achievement of maturity." Even supposing that one were interested in locating such a thing, 1779–80 is wildly too late (and, I would argue, so is 1765). More to the point, the very idea of wanting to do this for Haydn's music seems to me misguided.

"Experimentation"

Like Sandberger's tale, the traditional musicological view of Haydn's development is a narrative, which conforms to (and confirms) deeper beliefs. It too begins with the "immature" Haydn, naively composing according to models he found around him, and ends with his "maturity" or "mastery." In between, however, comes a period of – stylistic "experimentation." This notion is so ubiquitous that we may interpret it as analogous, at those deeper levels, to Sandberger's "trial," Haydn's wandering in the symphonic wilderness. The narrative not only exemplifies the common organicist equation of the chronological development of an artist's *oeuvre* and the life-history of an individual, but is strongly moralistic as well: one does not deserve maturity as a young man; one must earn one's syntheses through restless, unceasing labor.

Regarding Haydn's pre-Esterházy years, Geiringer writes, "Haydn developed with *the utmost slowness*. . . . *Hardly any* of the young musician's first *attempts* pointed to *future* greatness. His first period is characterized by *youthful immaturity and dependence on the models of other composers*" (pp. 204–05; emphasis added). Landon calls Haydn's earliest symphonies "primitive," characterized by "rudimentary treatment of form, melodic structure and orchestration" and "a certain instrumental confusion." In his recent biography, this prejudice is displaced to the realm of expression: "One of the principal traits of Haydn's style . . . until the middle of the 1760s [was] to show no deeper emotions of any kind, to avoid any question of personal involvement with the music he was writing."[57] These examples could be multiplied at will.

---

[57] Landon, *Symphonies*, pp. 174, 203; compare pp. 213, 215 ("rudimentary" three times on the latter page alone); *Haydn*, vol. 1, p. 82.

Table 9.1. *Periods in Haydn's career, 1761–1790*

	External turning-points	Changes of genre and style
1761–1765/66	1761: Vice-Kapellmeister (nominally under Werner)	Concerto; secular cantata *Style:* courtly-expressive
1765/66–1772	1765–66: Werner dies; EK; Kapellmeister; Eszterháza castle	*Add:* sacred vocal; opera (–1769); quartet (1769–); baryton; sonata; (incidental music?) *Drop:* cantata; (concerto) *Style:* personally expressive
1773–c. 1779	1773: operas 1776: new opera house; duties as impresario	*Drop:* sacred; quartet; baryton *Add:* opera; incidental music *Style:* "light"; "theatrical"
c. 1779–c. 1784	1779: new contract; Polzelli; compositional independence 1780: publications in Vienna 1783: publications abroad	*Add:* quartet; lieder *Drop:* incidental music; (sonata) *Style:* "popular artistry"; modest scale
c. 1785–1790	1785: foreign commissions; Mozart's "Haydn" quartets 1787: job/tour offers c. 1788–89: Mme. Genzinger	*Drop:* opera; lieder; (sonata) *Add:* piano trio *Style:* larger-scale; more deeply felt

The literature has treated Haydn's music of the early and middle 1760s more favorably – primarily, however, as a period of "experimentation," on the way towards the "Sturm und Drang." No general account of his development interprets these works as objects of compelling interest in their own right. Geiringer damns the entire decade with faint praise, calling it "the preparatory period," a "phase of transition" during which "Haydn succeeded in finding a *way toward* the expression of his *true* self" (pp. 224–25; emphasis added). Landon's narratives exude the metaphors of journey and arrival, struggle and fulfillment, so strongly that the occasional slight inconsistency seems inconsequential:

The [1760s] saw . . . a succession of novel and often daring experiments. . . . If not all the movements in each symphony . . . are of equal value, this may be attributed . . . to the fact that the composer had not yet reached maturity. . . .

Opus 9 is . . . uneven but highly talented. . . . Opus 17 . . . has changed into near-maturity. . . . The new quartet form which Haydn had been seeking for so long is finally presented to us in the magnificent six quartets of Opus 20. All the inspiration of which we have had a foretaste during the past half decade seems to surge into and fill up . . . this set.

With the year 1771 we reach Haydn's full maturity.[58]

Finscher describes the symphonies as presenting

an unusually heterogeneous picture, which seems confusing . . . and . . . permits no consistently progressive development towards a clear stylistic goal to be discerned. Nevertheless there is a basic tendency . . . the character of experimentation, of restless searching, again and again striking out anew, aiming each time at an entirely different goal. Only in . . . the years of crisis, 1766–70, did he find a truly individual style and tone. (p. 161)

Even the sober and ostensibly objective Larsen concludes that

the instrumental music . . . shows an interesting diversity . . . the merging of a number of prototypes of different kinds . . . a variety of possibilities. . . . But it was only in the great expansion of a few years later that he arrived at a complete synthesis of the heterogeneous elements.[59]

The same conceptual field can be found throughout the literature. Haydn scholarship has been in thrall to the evolutionist dogma that privileges later repertories for exhibiting the composer's "true" self, "maturity," a "synthesis," or "individual style and tone," while damning earlier ones with faint praise: "preparation" and "restless experimentation," with an "interesting diversity" and "heterogeneous variety" among mere "prototypes."

The "Sturm und Drang" is also interpreted variously. Scholars who concentrate on the symphony (Larsen, Landon) tend to value it more highly than those who focus on the string quartet (Sandberger, Blume, Finscher). The latter, obsessed with the supposedly central role of Op. 33 and the preparatory "ten-year pause," interpret the quartets of 1770–72 as flawed (not only experimental, but unintegrated, extreme, conflict-ridden, the products of crisis); their opinions have been quoted above. The symphonists, on the other hand, are less ambivalent, owing in part to Haydn's continuing production

---

[58] *Symphonies*, pp. 242, 308–09, 307.   [59] *The New Grove*, vol. 8, p. 351 (repr., p. 90).

throughout the 1770s and 1780s and the absence of any later stylistic division point before the "Paris" Symphonies and the *Seven Last Words* of 1785–86. Indeed they often overtly reject the Op. 33 hypothesis and invoke "Classical style" itself. Thus Larsen:

The three quartet series Opp. 9, 17, and 20 . . . together with a number of important symphonies, stand out as a landmark in the creation of the Haydn-Mozart classical style. . . . Haydn at last got tired of the worn-out style of midcentury music, and realized how much more expansive force was to be found in the traditions of Baroque music. . . . In the resulting synthesis . . . the development of a specific classical style was so far primarily the work of Haydn.[60]

Sandberger's notions of Haydn's early simplicity and later synthesis remain active; they are merely displaced back ten years. Landon is blunter: "The Viennese classical style arrived at its full maturity *not* with the Quartets, Op. 33 . . . but with Op. 20" (*Haydn*, vol. 2, p. 324). (I pass over here the symphonists' ambivalence regarding Haydn's music from the middle 1770s through the early 1780s,[61] and their renewed pleasure in his more obviously serious productions of the middle and late 1780s, which they unanimously praise as "mature Classicism."[62] The principles of explaining away a given repertory as "experimental" or "transitional," a way-station towards the next "goal," remain the same. This conceptual field also governs Brown's and Somfai's accounts of Haydn's keyboard sonatas before the middle or late 1760s.)

Critique

These views on Haydn's "experimentation" during the 1760s, and to a lesser extent from *c.* 1773 to 1781 (or 1785), are speculative and implausible. To be sure, Haydn himself might seem to have raised the point (in Griesinger's familiar account):

"My prince was satisfied with all my works; I received approval. As head of an orchestra I could try things out [*Versuche machen*], observe what creates a [good] effect and what weakens it, and thus revise, make additions or cuts, take risks. I was cut off from the world; nobody in my vicinity could upset my self-confidence [*mich an mir selbst irre machen*] or annoy me; and so I had no choice but to become original [*so mußte ich original werden*]."[63]

But this passage refers to *compositional* experimentation within an institutional framework (a secure position in a well-appointed court *Kapelle*); it focuses primarily on technical matters (instrumental balance, the means of writing "effectively," rhythmic and proportional relations, texture), and on the issue of "originality," in the general sense of not following models or belonging to a school. It does not imply that Haydn experimented in the senses beloved of musicologists: that he contemplated global style-changes, or the wholesale incorporation (or abandonment) of contrapuntal texture, or anything of the sort.

Although the prince demanded in 1765 that Haydn compose more, there is no evidence

---

[60] "Vienna Classical Instrumental Music," pp. 123, 129–30.

[61] Landon, *Symphonies*, pp. 341, 344, 353, 367, 383; Larsen, *The New Grove*, vol. 8, p. 354 (repr., p. 101).

[62] Landon, *Symphonies*, pp. 397, 405; Larsen, *The New Grove*, vol. 8, p. 355 (repr., p. 105).

[63] Griesinger, pp. 24–25 (Gotwals, p. 17; altered in the passages for which I provide the original).

that he was dissatisfied with the quality or character of Haydn's music of the 1760s. Indeed Haydn stated precisely the opposite (see the preceding quotation). Similarly, his own account of his compositional beginnings contradicts the interpretation of insufficiency in the 1760s: "I wrote diligently, but not quite correctly, until I had the good fortune to learn the true fundamentals of composition from the famous Porpora (who was then in Vienna)."[64] Since Porpora arrived there in 1753, and by 1757 at the latest (possibly 1755) Haydn was already writing accomplished string quartets for Baron Fürnberg, he "learned the true fundamentals of composition" not later than the mid-1750s. No evidence indicates that he had any doubts as to the level of his achievement at any time thereafter – as if the *Matin–Midi–Soir* trilogy of 1761 were merely "transitional," soon to be superseded by Symphonies 21 in A and 22 in E-flat (1764), or they by the masterful No. 35 in B-flat (1767), or it by the Farewell. The notion of Haydn's experimentation in the 1760s is simply the mirror image of the fundamental metaphor that at some later time he "achieved" his "goal." Whether it is called maturity, mastery, a synthesis, or a breakthrough to expression, it is always understood, by binary opposition, as something greater than what preceded it, as permanent, stable, self-sufficient – in short, as "Classical style" itself. What came before must therefore be "pre-Classical": immature, limited, inexpressive, transitional – or a period of restless experimentation. Like the "crisis" of 1772, this notion is part and parcel of an evolutionist interpretation according to which his maturity and "Classical style" are linked, as the foreordained results of a teleological historical process.

In place of this notion of Haydn's development, I would argue that experimentation was a fundamental aspect of his musical personality, throughout his life. The "Sturm und Drang" witnessed not only unprecedented expressive force, but hitherto unimagined essays in through-composition. In the middle and late 1770s, he infused operatic style into his instrumental music. Op. 33 is indeed composed in an "entirely new and special manner"; in the middle and late 1780s, however, he not only deepened the expression and enlarged the scale of his symphonies and quartets, but also essayed novel and disruptive experiments in keyboard music and other genres.[65] In London he focused on the public aspects of the prevailing idioms to an unprecedented degree, and intensified his compositional virtuosity to undreamed-of new heights. And in his last years he concentrated, in a way that nobody could have predicted (or so it seems to us), on monumental vocal works and the sublime. Every one of these departures can legitimately be called experimental – at least as much as the varied cyclic patterns and concertante instrumentations in his symphonies of the early 1760s.

Still more ludicrous is the notion that Haydn ever stopped experimenting with the technical aspects of composition. This is most obvious with respect to his creation of ever-novel formal and tonal structures. But consider his late music alone. Where are the

[64] Autobiographical sketch of 1776; see *Briefe*, No. 21, p. 77; Landon, *Haydn*, vol. 2, p. 398.
[65] See Brown, "Critical Years for Haydn's Instrumental Music: 1787–1790," *MQ* 62 (1976), 374–94 (with the proviso that, as there was nothing unusual about the level of "experimentation" or eccentricity in Haydn's music during those years, there was probably no "crisis" either).

precedents in his *oeuvre* for his integration of slow introductions and allegros in the symphonies from 1788 on? for the wonderful Part-Songs (*Mehrstimmige Gesänge*) of 1796–99? his explorations of remote key relations? the "repayment" of the earlier influence of opera on his symphonies by the influence of the symphony on his last six masses? the compound, non-sonata-form opening movements, the emphasis on a central remote-key slow movement, and the Beethovenian scherzos of Op. 76 Nos. 5 and 6 and Op. 77? the "Representation of Chaos," or the hunting and drinking choruses of the *Seasons*? for the violent conclusion of his last completed movement, the minuet in Op. 103? And (as quoted above) Haydn would surely have continued to develop beyond 1802, if only he had had the strength to keep on composing. In technique and expression, in compositional details and the conception of entire works, all his music was "experimental."

The corollary is that, in principle, all his works are mature. The qualification "in principle" acknowledges that a few are not in every respect above criticism. They occur only in limited and as it were excusable categories (and comprise only a miniscule minority even within these), including "occasional" works, those composed in extreme haste and, admittedly, very early ones as well. Haydn himself acknowledged, in his account (quoted above) of having learned how to compose from Porpora, that some of his earliest compositions were not up to standard. My own suggestions in this direction would include the *Missa brevis* in F, the divertimenti Hob. II:2 and 11, and the string quartet Op. 1 No. 6 in C. But the more rigorously we exclude spurious and doubtful works – and the better we know the genuine early ones – the more we are persuaded of their technical competence and their generic and rhetorical adequacy. All the other early string quartets, the C-major Cello Concerto, the *Salve regina* in E, and many other pre-Morzin works are fully achieved (on their own terms) and without substantive blemish; this applies with greater force to the early symphonies. Of course, other things equal, a later work of Haydn will probably be richer and more complex, more concentrated, than an earlier one; nor would it be out of place to speak of his increasing maturity as he grew older and gained more (and more varied) compositional experience. But his music was never in any intrinsic sense "immature" – least of all his programmatically through-composed masterpieces of 1772.

THE FAREWELL SYMPHONY, THROUGH-COMPOSITION, AND BEETHOVEN

And so we have returned to the starting point of this study. In conclusion, let us briefly consider the implications of Haydn's through-composed music, as represented by the Farewell Symphony, for our historical understanding of Beethoven, and by implication for nineteenth-century music in general. (In this context we need not raise the issue of their personal relations.[66]) I have in mind not merely the unquestioned influence of

[66] See Walter, "Die biographischen Beziehungen zwischen Haydn und Beethoven," in Dahlhaus, *et al.*, eds., *Bericht über den Internationalen musikwissenschaftlichen Kongreß Bonn 1970* (Kassel, [1973]), pp. 79–83; Solomon, *Beethoven*, chap. 7; Webster, "Falling-out."

Haydn (and Mozart) on Beethoven in the early Vienna years up to *c.* 1802,[67] nor their less well-known but substantial influence in the middle period, especially on the string quartets,[68] nor even Beethoven's tendency, learned (as we have seen) from Haydn, to create dynamic large-scale forms by composing out the implications of an initial destabilizing gesture, by running-on the lead back from trio to minuet, and so forth. My concern is rather Haydn's integration of the cycle, and how this alters our views of what is generally taken to be one of the most revolutionary characteristics of Beethoven's music. As before, the task is not to "correct" former "errors," but to adumbrate a new historical narrative in place of a traditional one that no longer seems satisfactory. Instead of seeing Beethoven (to put it crudely) as "the man who freed music," we may view Haydn as the central figure in the "First Viennese Modern School," the inventor of a rhetoric of through-composition, the composer of the first paradigmatic works of this type – works which have never been surpassed – and Beethoven as his follower (and eventually his equal). In so doing, we can also review many of the topics treated in this study, from a somewhat different perspective.

Joseph Kerman's account of Beethoven's cyclic and through-composed music well represents current formulations of the traditional narrative. He invokes what he terms the "symphonic ideal," which

Beethoven perfected at a stroke with his Third Symphony and further celebrated with his Fifth, Sixth, Seventh and Ninth. The forcefulness, expanded range and evident radical intent of these works sets [*sic*] them apart from symphonies in the 18th-century tradition. . . . More than this, they all contrive to create the impression of a psychological journey or a growth process. In the course of this, something seems to arrive or triumph or transcend. . . . This illusion is helped by . . . "evolving" themes, transitions between widely separated passages, actual thematic recurrences from one movement to another, and last but not least, the involvement of extramusical ideas by means of a literary text, a programme, or (as in the "Eroica") just a few tantalizing titles.

In technical terms, this development may be viewed as the projection of the underlying principles of the sonata style on the scale of the total four-movement work, rather than that of the single movement in sonata form. . . .

Another aspect of the "symphonic ideal," one that is less technical but probably no less essential, [is that] the combination of his musical dynamic . . . and extra-musical suggestions invests his pieces with an unmistakable ethical aura. . . .

The conception of this symphonic ideal, and the development of technical means to implement it, is probably Beethoven's greatest single achievement. It is *par excellence* a Romantic phenomenon. . . .[69]

Regarding the paradigmatic work of this type, the C-sharp minor Quartet, he writes that it is

[67] Haydn and Beethoven: Gustav Becking, *Studien zu Beethovens Personalstil: Das Scherzothema* (Leipzig, 1921); Feder, "Stilelemente Haydns in Beethovens Werken," *Kongreß Bonn 1970*, pp 65–70; Johnson, "1794–1795."

[68] Webster, "Traditional Elements in Beethoven's Middle-Period String Quartets," in Robert Winter and Bruce Carr, eds., *Beethoven, Performers, and Critics* (Detroit, 1980), pp. 94–133.

[69] *The New Grove*, vol. 2, pp. 381–83 (repr. pp. 107–09).

the most closely integrated of all [Beethoven's] large compositions. . . . [It] may be seen as the culmination of [Beethoven's] significant effort as a composer ever since going to Vienna. The seven movements run continuously into one another, and for the first time in [his] music there is an emphatic and unmistakable thematic connection between the first movement and the last – not a reminiscence, but a functional parallel which helps bind the whole work together.

The uniqueness of this quartet lies exactly in the mutual dependence of its contrasted parts. . . . [It] is the most deeply integrated of all Beethoven's compositions. . . .

[The subdominant] ambiguity provides the last great binding force of organic interrelation. . . . The seven movements complete their perfect mutual trajectory.[70]

Kerman assumes not only the relevance of cyclic integration for Beethoven's music, but its status as a criterion of value – as unquestioningly as he assumes it had no role to play in earlier sonata-style music. It will be worth rehearsing in systematic order the features he claims Beethoven "perfected at a stroke" in the Eroica: (1) radical intent; (2) moral and rhetorical characteristics (the impression of a psychological journey towards triumph or transcendence; extramusical ideas; an ethical aura); (3) techniques designed to bring this about, comprising (a) evolving themes and thematic connections between movements; (b) run-on movements, functional and gestural parallels between movements; and (c) the mutual dependence of contrasted parts, the projection of the underlying principles of sonata style over an entire work, integration ("a perfect mutual trajectory"), and the function of the finale as a culmination.

The verdict is obvious. The Farewell Symphony incorporates every one of these features, and it integrates them in a through-composed, end-oriented work, as radical as any from Beethoven's middle period. Symphony No. 46 and Opp. 20 No. 2 and 54 No. 2 are in the same class. The notion that Beethoven invented this type of cyclic integration, or that it did not play a central role in earlier music, cannot withstand scrutiny. To begin with technique: thematicism, both within and among movements, is a fundamental aspect of Haydn's art (see Chapters 6 and 8); it is a chief basis of coherence in Symphonies 15, 46, and 49, and Op. 74 No. 3. Explicit recalls of earlier movements occur in Symphony No. 46, by implication in the Farewell, and in other Haydn works, for example Symphony No. 31.

Haydn composed movements in progressive form, which end in a different state from their beginnings or explode all sense of symmetry (for example, the opening movements of Symphonies 80, 92, 99 and 103). Symphonies 15, 25, 46, and the Farewell, and Opp. 20 No. 2 and 54 No. 2, have run-on movement pairs or compound movements which disrupt or problematize conventional genre patterns. Sonata No. 30 is continuous throughout; Beethoven's only comparable multimovement works are the E-flat "Quasi una fantasia" sonata Op. 27 No. 1 and the C-sharp minor Quartet itself. Regarding parallelism of gesture, Op. 20 No. 2 as a whole is "about" the issue of traditional style (contrapuntal or pathetic) vs. galant homophony, and Op. 54 No. 2 is "about" problems of musical form itself – not to mention the high, ethereal, *piano* passages in conjunction with F-sharp major in three different movements of the Farewell, or their central role in its progression towards resolution.

---

[70] Ibid., p. 389 (repr., p. 136); *The Beethoven Quartets* (New York, 1966), pp. 326, 349.

The "mutual dependence of contrasting parts" in the double finale of the Farewell, in the finales of Symphony No. 46 and Op. 54 No. 2, and throughout Op. 20 No. 2 and Sonata No. 30 is as strong as in any middle-period work of Beethoven. The role of discontinuity and dissociation in Beethoven's late music has recently attracted attention;[71] as in the case of his dynamic, off-tonic beginnings, he learned about such matters primarily from Haydn. In Symphony No. 46 and Opp. 20 No. 2 and 54 No. 2, not to mention the Farewell, tonality and large-scale rhythm combine with run-on movements so that "the underlying principles of sonata style" indeed govern the entire cycle; tonal coherence is equally strong in Symphony No. 99 and Op. 74 No. 3. In several of these works, the finale is a true culmination: in Op. 20 No. 2, it is a fugue, stylistically as well as gesturally a synthesis; in Op. 54 No. 2, an exploration of musical form itself; the major mode triumphs over the minor at the end of Op. 74 No. 3 (and of course the Farewell); Symphony No. 46 leads to a tonal and thematic "completion" and a psychological apotheosis. (In general, Haydn's sense of the relations among the movements in a cycle was more accurate than Beethoven's. The contrasts of tempo, length, style, material, and texture are almost always appropriate; nor does he strain unduly for effect, or compromise the whole through excessive length or complexity of individual movements, as Beethoven – in Kerman's own account – often does.) In the most thoroughly integrated of these works, furthermore, the resolution comes not merely at the beginning of the finale, or somewhere in the middle, but at or near the very end, at the last possible moment; and this resolution is articulated in all relevant musical domains. Their cyclic coherence, their sense of a "perfect mutual trajectory," could not be stronger.

Haydn's rhetoric also contributes to this integration. Extramusical associations were a fundamental aspect of his instrumental music; they comprised not only various conventional topics (religious associations, the pastoral, ethnic materials, and so forth), and the use of operatic and incidental music, but also what he called "moral character[istic]s." Because these topics provided a basis for relating otherwise separate movements, they contributed directly to cyclic coherence. Haydn's later instrumental music is suffused with what (combining Schroeder and Bonds) we may call the "rhetoric of enlightenment," as well as invocations of the sublime (in symphony introductions) and the "heroic pastoral" (Rosen). No more than the Eroica or Beethoven's Fifth and Ninth are these works "absolute music" in the nineteenth-century sense; nor are they the naive productions of a cheerful underling who happened to be a genius at witty tone combinations. The sense of tension yielding at last to resolution in the Farewell, the fusion of happy memory and troubled present at the end of Symphony No. 46, move beyond eighteenth-century norms of instrumental rhetoric; in listening to them attentively and with a sense of what they signify, one is uplifted, one feels transcendence, as much as when Chaos yields to Light. This transcendence was not a necessity for Haydn, any more than cyclic integration (see the introduction to Chapter 8), but to claim that Beethoven invented it is possible only by ignoring this aspect of Haydn's art.

[71] Kerman, *The Beethoven Quartets*, chaps. 8 and 10; David L. Brodbeck and John Platoff, "Dissociation and Integration: The First Movement of Beethoven's Opus 130," *19CMus* 7 (1983–84), 149–62; Agawu, "The First Movement of Beethoven's Opus 132 and the Classical Style," *CMS* 27 (1987), 30–45.

But the point is not merely the existence before 1803 of features on a list; it is a question of complete movements and works, and their effects. Let us therefore compare the Farewell Symphony with two relevant works of Beethoven, among the most famous and most highly through-composed from his entire middle period, and indubitably having extramusical associations as well: the Eroica (regarding one striking event) and the Fifth Symphony (as a whole work). (In neither case do I posit a direct or conscious influence from the Farewell in particular, which we are not certain Beethoven knew, although it seems not unlikely. I do assume a profound general influence of Haydn's style on his own, throughout his life.)

Regarding the Eroica, there are striking, hitherto unremarked similarities between its most notorious passage, the E-minor theme in the development of the Allegro con brio, and one of the most unusual features of the Farewell, the D-major interlude in the Allegro assai. Both enter in the middle of the development of a tumultuous sonata-form movement in very fast triple meter, in a new key (unexpected in Haydn; prepared but vastly remote in Beethoven), following the loudest and harshest music heard so far; both suddenly drop to *piano* in reduced scoring, leaving the preceding climax unresolved (harmonically in the Farewell; aesthetically in the Eroica). Both "change the subject" to what sounds like an entirely new theme, and yet both are intimately related to earlier material (for the interlude, see pp. 39–45; for the Eroica, Schenker's much-discussed derivation of the E-minor theme from the opening triadic motive).

Yet there is one crucial difference. Beethoven integrates his E-minor theme into his gigantic movement: he gradually leads it back to the tonic, repeating it in A minor (m. 292) and, later on, in the tonic minor (m. 322); and he diatonically grounds it in the coda by parallel statements in the ordinary supertonic F minor (instead of "F-flat" minor) and, again, the tonic minor (mm. 581, 589). (Both passages also move on to the home dominant (mm. 338, 603), in each case initiating a terrific preparatory passage leading to a huge climax in the tonic.) Perhaps in part because of this degree of integration, Beethoven's theme throws no shadows forward into the rest of his huge and rather heterogeneous symphony. Haydn, on the other hand, keeps his interlude a foreign body within his shorter and otherwise much more uniform movement, because its *lack* of integration forms part of his guiding purpose for the whole work, and it must remain mysterious and unresolved until the very end. The *ancien-régime*, "pre-Classical" composer thus achieved greater coherence in his symphony as a whole than the "revolutionary" of 1803. (This point admittedly takes some getting used to. I myself recently opined that it was "ironic" that Haydn should have outdone Beethoven in this respect.[72] But no irony is entailed; in his music, such integration was always possible.)

In the case of the Fifth Symphony, the similarities are perhaps even more striking, and affect both works as wholes. In both, the last two movements are run-on, destabilizing the usual four-movement pattern; both works are radical, "difficult" in style; both begin in the minor and end with a transcendent resolution into the tonic major. Many particular features coincide: tense and violent opening allegro, otherworldly

---

[72] "D-major interlude," final paragraph.

slow movement in the major, overtly "problematical" minuet/scherzo; culmination-finale. Furthermore, both employ comparable techniques of integration: destabilization in the earlier movements, forcing us ahead towards the ending; thematic links; prominent, yet unsatisfying, appearances of the major mode in earlier movements. (Every movement of the Fifth preceding the finale includes C major, but only in the middle and without real stability; in the Farewell, the Allegro assai and the minuet and trio "problematize" F-sharp major in ways that relate directly to the ending.) Nor would Haydn have hesitated to recall his minuet in his finale, if it had suited the overall progression or the program; see Symphony No. 46. And, of course, both works have extramusical associations. These relations are perhaps the most remarkable illustration of Solomon's dictum that Beethoven "learned too much from [Haydn] – more than he could acknowledge."[73]

But the relationships lie deeper as well. Consider Lawrence Kramer's recent interpretation of the Fifth, functioning as the peroration of his *Music and Poetry: The Nineteenth Century and After* (Berkeley, 1984). He describes it as

a re-thinking, a detailed problematizing, of the formal impulses that support the Classical symphony. . . . What is unprecedented about [the first movement] is its aggressiveness, the sheer vehemence with which it works and exhausts its motivic material, the intensity with which it turns the presence of a motive into an assault on the listener's nerves. . . . This ruthless expressivity is aimed at producing a crisis. . . . The major . . . is followed by a ferocious tonic-minor [ending] . . . that contain[s] the most emotionally violent music in the movement. . . . The startling vehemence of this gesture . . . becomes a testimony to the failure of the major to resolve the tensions produced by the music's sonata form. . . . A dialectical antagonism springs up between tonic minor and tonic major, a coiled tension that will have to be resolved through the totality of the work. The symphony as a whole thus acquires its widely recognized goal of the tonic major – but not just any tonic major; rather, one that is free of its dialectical vulnerability to the minor, a tonic major that *cannot be followed*. This projection of the . . . tension of the first movement onto the scale of the whole is what motivates – necessitates – the reappearance in each movement of [basic ideas from the first movement]. The symphony . . . is being redefined: it is no longer a sequence of integral movements . . . but a dynamic weaving-together of non-integral movements to form a whole that cannot be specified in advance. Procession gives way to process – which is also why the Fifth is the first symphony to violate the discreteness of its subdivisions, in the fusion of the third and fourth movements and the return of the third in the fourth.   (pp. 234–35)

And he continues with an urgent interpretation of the tonal, motivic, rhythmic, and instrumental continuities which create, at the end, "a tonic major cadence [which] is overpoweringly full. . . . Musical time appears as an impulse toward, a cathexis of, the tonic" (p. 240).

With the Farewell Symphony and No. 46 in our ears, we need not dwell on Kramer's error of supposing that Beethoven's Fifth was the first symphony to include run-on movements and recalls of earlier movements. The point is that every word of his description applies with equal justice to the Farewell. (In the quoted passage, Kramer writes

[73] *Beethoven*, p. 70.

"C minor" and "C major"; to facilitate the comparison, I have everywhere substituted "tonic minor" and, depending on the context, "tonic major" or "major.") The Farewell "problematizes" symphonic form. Its Allegro assai is "aggressive and vehement," its motivic and rhythmic concentration an "assault on the listener's nerves." The D-major interlude is a massive, unintegrated contrast: gesturally an unattainable distant realm, immediately abandoned; tonally, a stalking-horse for the tonic major (the chord which prepares it). It indeed "fails to resolve the tensions of the sonata form" and is followed by "ferocious minor, the most emotionally violent music in the movement" (the secondary development and the later Neapolitan passage). On all these levels (and others as well), the interlude can only be "resolved through the totality of the work," by a "projection of the harmonic and gestural tension of the first movement onto the scale of the whole that motivates – necessitates" the tonic major and motivic recalls in the minuet, and the through-composed double finale. And although the Farewell includes nothing comparable to Beethoven's transition between scherzo and finale, or his recall of the scherzo, Haydn's double finale indeed produces a "dynamic weaving together," in which "procession gives way to process": a single progression governing outwardly disparate movements, such that F-sharp minor, through the mediation of A major and the dominant, is transformed into F-sharp major and forever associated with the ethereal realm first hinted at by the D-major interlude, twenty-five minutes earlier. The resolution is withheld until the very end, until we hear "a tonic major that is free of its dialectical relation to the minor, a tonic major that *cannot be followed.*" (Admittedly, F-sharp as an apotheosis is different from C; see p. 127.) Haydn's symphony is as "ethical," as highly integrated, and as fully achieved as that of his sometime pupil.

It was not "Beethoven's achievement" to "conceive the symphonic ideal," let alone to "perfect it at a stroke" or to "develop the technical means to achieve it."[74] It was Haydn's, and it was from Haydn (and to a lesser extent Mozart) that he learned it. Nor is the Farewell less radical than Beethoven's symphonies. It is if anything more so; certainly its procedures and purpose have no parallel, and they have traditionally defied interpretation. Landon (*Symphonies*, p. 320), reflecting the traditions analyzed above, calls the unique formal features of the Allegro assai "experiments," "too radical," and therefore "never repeated"; this is the reverse of the truth. (Kramer himself refers to the "farewell" finale in passing as an "unrepeatable experiment" [p. 21].) The D-major interlude, the double second group, the minor close of the exposition, as well as the minuet's unaccompanied, off-tonic beginning and ending and major/minor conflicts, the run-on double finale, the progressive tonality of the final Adagio, not to mention the "farewell" procedure itself: all these features support and foster Haydn's overall musical and poetic conception. They were conceived and articulated in the service of a unique, and uniquely integrated, work – and therefore *inherently* unrepeatable. Like Op. 20 No. 2, the Farewell Symphony is precisely radical enough.

---

[74] Kerman himself recently wrote about the Fifth under the assumption that "disruption" and "defamiliarization" are musical categories absent from Haydn: "Taking the Fifth," in Hermann Danuser *et al.*, eds., *Das musikalische Kunstwerk . . . Festschrift Carl Dahlhaus* (Laaber, 1988), pp. 483–91.

Haydn's influence on Beethoven was not restricted to his personal example of comportment and careerism, the counterpoint instruction, and the transmission of the newly triumphant Viennese modern style to its eventual new standard-bearer. It also encompassed the art of projecting strong rhetorical impulses and deep ethical concerns (which Beethoven had from the beginning) in musical works which simultaneously exhibit the greatest craft and the profoundest coherence – which generate their rhetoric and their morality precisely by means of that coherence. It was this conjunction of the highest technique and the richest expression (not either alone) that, among late eighteenth-century composers, only Haydn and Mozart mastered. Within that historical context, it was first achieved by Haydn in works like the Farewell (I do not say this was his very first work of this kind), carried on by him and (from the 1780s) Mozart (including works as ethically uplifting as *The Magic Flute* and *The Creation*), and perpetuated (but not surpassed) in Beethoven's Eroica and the Fifth. Only towards the end of his life, if at all, did Beethoven "outdo" Haydn; even the *Missa*, the Ninth, the C-sharp minor Quartet live by the same conjunction. Their late style, partly hermetic, partly urgent, remains married to their novel techniques, "tantôt libre, tantôt recherchée," in part disjunctive, in part too simple for words. This ideal – the union, within an entire "modern" work, of technique and expression, of progressive form and coherence, of perfect individual movements and cyclic integration – led in an unbroken tradition at least as far as Brahms and Schoenberg. What the secret of that union was, we cannot say. But we can say that it originated before 1772 in the music of Joseph Haydn.

BIBLIOGRAPHY

Note. This bibliography lists only the substantive secondary literature cited in the present volume (including reprints of articles in book form). Original-language versions of works cited only in translation, and dictionary articles and the like, are included only if they are quoted or discussed in the text; other standard reference tools (e.g. Hoboken) are omitted. Editions of music, facsimile publications, book reviews, and most musical and literary sources from before *c.* 1850 are omitted (they are cited in the notes).

Abbate, Carolyn. "Erik's Dream and Tannhäuser's Journey." In *Reading Opera*, ed. Arthur Groos and Roger Parker. Princeton: Princeton University Press, 1988. Pp. 129–67
    "What the Sorcerer Said." *19CMus* 12 (1988–89), 221–30
Abbate, Carolyn and Parker, Roger. "Introduction: On Analyzing Opera." In *Analyzing Opera: Verdi and Wagner*, ed. Carolyn Abbate and Roger Parker. California Studies in 19th Century Music, 6. Berkeley: University of California Press, 1989. Pp. 1–24
Abert, Hermann. "Joseph Haydns Klaviersonaten." *ZfMw* 3 (1920–21), 535–52
    "Joseph Haydns Klavierwerke." *ZfMw* 2 (1919–20), 553–73
Abrams, Meyer H. *The Mirror and The Lamp.* New York: Oxford University Press, 1953
Ackerman, James S. and Carpenter, Rhys. *Art and Archaeology.* Humanistic Scholarship in America: The Princeton Studies. Englewood Cliffs: Prentice-Hall, 1963
Ackermann, Peter. "Struktur, Ausdruck, Programm: Gedanken zu Joseph Haydns Instrumental-musik über *Die Sieben letzten Worte unseres Erlösers am Kreuze.*" In *Studien zur Instrumental-musik: Lothar Hoffmann-Erbrecht zum 60. Geburtstag*, ed. Anke Bingmann *et al.* Frankfurter Beiträge zur Musikwissenschaft, 20. Tutzing: Schneider, 1988. Pp. 253–60
Adler, Guido. *Handbuch der Musikgeschichte.* 2 vols. 2nd. edn. Berlin: Keller, 1929–30
    "Haydn and the Viennese Classical School." *MQ* 18 (1932), 191–207
    "Style Criticism." *MQ* 20 (1934), 172–76
Agawu, V. Kofi. "Concepts of Closure and Chopin's Opus 28." *MTS* 9 (1987), 1–17
    "The First Movement of Beethoven's Opus 132 and the Classical Style." *CMS* 27 (1987), 30–45
    "Schenkerian Notation in Theory and Practice." *MusA* 8 (1989), 275–301
    Playing with Signs: A Semiotic Interpretation of Classic Music. Princeton: Princeton University Press, forthcoming
Allanbrook, Wye Jamison. "'Ear-Tickling Nonsense': A New Context for Musical Expression in Mozart's 'Haydn' Quartets." *The St. John's Review* 38 (1988), 1–24
    Rhythmic Gesture in Mozart: "Le nozze di Figaro" and "Don Giovanni." Chicago: University of Chicago Press, 1983
Allen, Warren Dwight. *Philosophies of Music History: A Study of General Histories of Music 1600–1960.* 2nd edn. New York: Dover, 1962
Andrews, Harold L. "The Submediant in Haydn's Development Sections." In *Haydn Studies*, ed. Larsen *et al.* Pp. 465–71

Angermüller, Rudolph. "Haydns 'Der Zerstreute' in Salzburg (1776)." *H-S* 4 (1976–80), 85–93

Atkins, James. [Letter to the Editor.] *HYb* 11 (1980), 196–98

Badura-Skoda, Eva, ed. *Joseph Haydn: Proceedings of the International Joseph Haydn Congress Wien, Hofburg, 5.–12. September 1982*. Munich: Henle, 1986

Bailey, Robert. "The Structure of the *Ring* and its Evolution." *19CMus* 1 (1977–78), 48–61

Bard, Raimund. "'Tendenzen' zur zyklischen Gestaltung in Haydns Londoner Sinfonien." In *Bericht über den Internationalen Musikwissenschaftlichen Kongress Bayreuth 1981*, ed. Christoph-Hellmut Mahling and Sigrid Wiesmann. Kassel: Bärenreiter, 1984. Pp. 379–83

Untersuchungen zur motivischen Arbeit in Haydns sinfonischem Spätwerk. Kassel: Bärenreiter, 1982

Barth, George Robert. "The Fortepianist as Orator: Beethoven and the Transformation of the Declamatory Style." D.M.A. essay, Cornell University, 1988

Bartha, Dénes. "Song Form and the Concept of 'Quatrain.'" In *Haydn Studies*, ed. Larsen *et al.* Pp. 353–55

"Volkstanz-Stilisierung in Joseph Haydns Finale-Themen." In *Festschrift für Walter Wiora zum 30. Dezember 1966*, ed. Ludwig Finscher and Christoph-Hellmut Mahling. Kassel: Bärenreiter, 1967. Pp. 375–84

Beach, David. "A Recurring Pattern in Mozart's Music." *JMT* 27 (1983), 1–30

Becker-Glauch, Irmgard. "Haydns Cantilena pro adventu in D." *H-S* 1 (1965–67), 277–80

"Neue Forschungen zu Haydns Kirchenmusik." *H-S* 2 (1969–70), 167–241

Becking, Gustav. *Studien zu Beethovens Personalstil: Das Scherzothema mit einem bisher unveröffentlichen Scherzo Beethovens*. Leipzig: Breitkopf und Härtel, 1921

Benary, Peter, "Die langsamen Einleitungen in Joseph Haydns Londoner Sinfonien." In *Studien zur Instrumentalmusik: Lothar Hoffmann-Erbrecht zum 60. Geburtstag*, ed. Anke Bingmann *et al.* Frankfurter Beiträge zur Musikwissenschaft, 20. Tutzing: Schneider, 1988. Pp. 239–51

Blume, Friedrich. *Classic and Romantic Music*. New York: Norton, 1970

"Fortspinnung und Entwicklung: Ein Beitrag zur musikalischen Begriffsbildung." *JbP* 36 (1929), 51–70

–Repr. in Friedrich Blume, *Syntagma Musicologicum: Gesammelte Reden und Schriften*. Kassel: Bärenreiter, 1963. Pp. 504–25

"Josef Haydns künstlerische Persönlichkeit in seinen Streichquartetten." *JbP* 38 (1931), 24–48

–Repr. in Friedrich Blume, *Syntagma Musicologicum: Gesammelte Reden und Schriften*. Kassel: Bärenreiter, 1963. Pp. 526–51

Bockholdt, Rudolf. "Über das Klassische der Wiener klassischen Musik." In *Über das Klassische*, ed. Rudolf Bockholdt. Suhrkamp Taschenbücher, 2077. Frankfurt am Main: Suhrkamp, 1987. Pp. 225–59

Bonds, Mark Evans. "Haydn's False Recapitulations and the Perception of Sonata Form in the Eighteenth Century." Ph.D. diss., Harvard University, 1988

Brodbeck, David L. and Platoff, John. "Dissociation and Integration: The First Movement of Beethoven's Opus 130." *19CMus* 7 (1983–84), 149–62

Brook, Barry S. "Sturm und Drang and the Romantic Period in Music." *Studies in Romanticism* 9 (1970), 269–84

Brooks, Peter. *Reading for the Plot: Design and Intention in Narrative*. New York: Knopf, 1984

Brown, A. Peter. "Critical Years for Haydn's Instrumental Music: 1787–1790." *MQ* 62 (1976), 374–94

"Haydn's Chaos: Genesis and Genre." *MQ* 73/1 (1989), 18–59

Joseph Haydn's Keyboard Music: Sources and Style. Bloomington: Indiana University Press, 1986

Bryan, Paul. "Haydn's Hornists." *H-S* 3 (1973–74), 52–58

Bücken, Ernst. *Die Musik des Rokoko und der Klassik*. Handbuch der Musikwissenschaft, 4. Potsdam: Musurgia, 1927; Athenaion, 1935

Burke, Kenneth. *Language as Symbolic Action: Essays on Life, Literature, and Method*. Berkeley: University of California Press, 1966

Burkhardt, Charles. "Schenker's 'Motivic Parallelisms.'" *JMT* 22 (1978), 145–75

Carpenter, Patricia. "*Grundgestalt* as Tonal Function." *MTS* 5 (1983), 15–38

Chapman, Roger E. "Modulation in Haydn's Late Piano Trios in the Light of Schoenberg's Theories." In *Haydn Studies*, ed. Larsen *et al.* Pp. 471–75

Charlton, David. "Instrumental Recitative: A Study in Morphology and Context, 1700–1808." *Comparative Criticism: A Yearbook* 4 (1982), 149–68

Chew, Geoffrey. "The Night-Watchman's Song Quoted by Haydn and its Implications." *H-S* 3 (1973–74), 106–24

Churgin, Bathia. "The Italian Symphonic Background to Haydn's Early Symphonies and Opera Overtures." In *Haydn Studies*, ed. Larsen *et al.* Pp. 329–36

"'Classical Period' and 'Classical Style' in Eighteenth-Century Music." [Round table] In *Haydn Studies*, ed. Larsen *et al.* Pp. 329–46

Cone, Edward T. "Analysis Today." *MQ* 46 (1960), 172–88
 –Repr. in *Problems of Modern Music: The Princeton Seminar in Advanced Music Studies*, ed. Paul Henry Lang. New York: Norton, 1962. Pp. 34–50
 –Repr. in Cone, *Music: A View from Delft: Selected Essays*, ed. Robert P. Morgan. Chicago: University of Chicago Press, 1989. Pp. 39–54

"Beethoven's Orpheus – or Jander's?" *19CMus* 8 (1984–85), 283–86

The Composer's Voice. Berkeley: University of California Press, 1974

Musical Form and Musical Performance. New York: Norton, 1968

"Schubert's Promissory Note." *19CMus* 5 (1981–82), 233–41

"Twelfth Night." [German.] *Mth* 1 (1986), 41–59
 –Tr. "Twelfth Night." *JMR* 7 (1986–88), 131–56

"The Uses of Convention: Stravinsky and his Models." *MQ* 48 (1962), 287–99
 –Repr. in Cone, *Music: A View from Delft: Selected Essays*, ed. Robert P. Morgan. Chicago: University of Chicago Press, 1989. Pp. 281–92

Cooke, Deryck. "The Unity in Beethoven's Late Quartets." *MR* 24 (1963), 30–49

Culler, Jonathan. *On Deconstruction: Theory and Criticism after Structuralism*. Ithaca: Cornell University Press, 1982

Cushman, Stephen. "Joseph Haydn's Melodic Materials: An Exploratory Introduction to the Primary and Secondary Sources Together with an Analytical Catalogue and Table of Proposed Melodic Correspondence and/or Variance." Ph.D. diss., Boston University, 1973

"Sources of Haydn's Melodic Material." In *Haydn Studies*, ed. Larsen *et al.* Pp. 377–80

Cuyler, Louise E. "Tonal Exploitation in the Later Quartets of Haydn." In *Studies in Eighteenth-Century Music: A Tribute to Karl Geiringer on his Seventieth Birthday*, ed. H. C. Robbins Landon and Roger E. Chapman. New York: Oxford University Press, 1970. Pp. 136–50

Dahlhaus, Carl. *Analysis and Value Judgment*. Tr. Siegmund Levarie. New York: Pendragon, 1983.

"The Eighteenth Century as a Music-Historical Epoch." *CMS* 26 (1986), 1–6

Esthetics of Music. Tr. William W. Austin. Cambridge: Cambridge University Press, 1982

"E. T. A. Hoffmanns Beethoven-Kritik und die Ästhetik des Erhabenen." *AfMw* 38 (1981), 167–81
 –Repr. in Dahlhaus, *Klassische und romantische Musikästhetik*. Laaber: Laaber, 1988. Pp. 98–111

Foundations of Music History. Tr. J. B. Robinson. Cambridge: Cambridge University Press, 1983

The Idea of Absolute Music. Tr. Roger Lustig. Chicago: University of Chicago Press, 1989

Die Musik des 18. Jahrhunderts. Neues Handbuch der Musikwissenschaft, 5. Laaber: Laaber, 1985

"Romantische Musikästhetik und Wiener Klassik." *AfMw* 29 (1972), 167–81
 –Repr. in Dahlhaus, *Klassische und romantische Musikästhetik*. Pp. 86–98

"Some Models of Unity in Musical Form." *JMT* 19 (1975), 2–30

"Thesen über die Programmusik." In *Beiträge zur musikalischen Hermeneutik*, ed. Carl Dahlhaus. Studien zur Musikgeschichte des 19. Jahrhunderts, 43. Regensburg: Bosse, 1975. Pp. 187–204

–Repr. in Dahlhaus, *Klassische und romantische Musikästhetik.* Pp. 365–85

"What is Developing Variation?" In Dahlhaus, *Schoenberg and the New Music.* Tr. Derrick Puffett and Alfred Clayton. Cambridge: Cambridge University Press, 1987. Pp. 128–33

Danckwardt, Marianne. *Die langsame Einleitung: Ihre Herkunft und ihr Bau bei Haydn und Mozart.* 2 vols. Münchner Veröffentlichungen zur Musikgeschichte, 25. Tutzing: Schneider, 1977

David, Johann Nepomuk. *Die Jupiter-Symphonie: Eine Studie über die thematisch-melodischen Zusammenhänge.* Göttingen: Deuerl, 1953

Das Wohltemperierte Klavier: Der Versuch einer Synopsis. Göttingen: Vandenhoeck und Ruprecht, 1962

De Man, Paul. *Blindness and Insight.* New York: Oxford University Press, 1971

Deutsch, Walter. "Volkslied und Geniemusik: Ein Beitrag zur Darstellung ihrer Beziehungen im Werke J. Haydns." *Jahrbuch des österreichischen Volksliedwerkes* 8 (1959), 1–9

Dies, Albert Christoph. *Biographische Nachrichten von Joseph Haydn nach mündlichen Erzählungen desselben entworfen und herausgegeben* [1810]. Modern ed. Horst Seeger. Berlin: Henschelverlag, 1959

[–For translation, see Gotwals.]

Dunsby, Jonathan. *Structural Ambiguity in Brahms.* Ann Arbor: UMI Research Press, 1981

Edgerton, Sara Ann. "The Bass Part in Haydn's Early Symphonies: A Documentary and Analytical Study." D.M.A. Essay, Cornell University, 1989

Einstein, Alfred. "Haydns Sinfonie." *ZfM* 91 (1924), 169–74

Mozart: His Character, His Work. New York: Oxford University Press, 1945

Ekstein, Nina C. *Dramatic Narrative: Racine's Récits.* New York: Lang, 1986

Elam, Keir. *The Semiotics of Theatre and Drama.* New Accents. London and New York: Methuen, 1980

Eliot, T. S. *What Is a Classic? An Address Delivered Before the Virgil Society on the 16th of October 1944.* London: Faber and Faber, 1945

Engel, Hans. "Haydn, Mozart und die Klassik." In *MJb* 1959. Pp. 46–79

Epstein, David. *Beyond Orpheus: Studies in Musical Structure.* Cambridge, Mass.: MIT Press, 1979

Feder, Georg. "Die Bedeutung der Assoziation und des Wertvergleichs für das Urteil in Echtheitsfragen." In *International Musicological Society: Report of the Eleventh Congress Copenhagen 1972,* ed. Henrik Glahn *et al.* Copenhagen: Hansen, 1974. Vol. 1, pp. 365–77

"Die beiden Pole im Instrumentalschaffen des jungen Haydn." In *Der junge Haydn: Wandel von Musikauffassung und Musikaufführung in der österreichischen Musik zwischen Barock und Klassik: Bericht der internationalen Arbeitstagung des Instituts für Aufführungspraxis der Hochschule für Musik und darstellende Kunst in Graz, 29.6–2.7 1970,* ed. Vera Schwarz. Beiträge zur Aufführungspraxis, 1. Graz: Akademische Druck- und Verlagsanstalt, 1972. Pp. 192–201

"Bemerkungen zu Haydns Skizzen." *Beethoven-Jahrbuch* 9 (1973–77), 69–86

"Die *Jahreszeiten* in der Vertonung von Joseph Haydn." In *Die Vier Jahreszeiten im 18. Jahrhundert: Colloquium der Arbeitsstelle 18. Jahrhundert, Gesamthochschule Wuppertal, Universität Münster, Schloß Langenburg vom 3. bis 5. Oktober 1983.* Heidelberg: Winter, 1986. Pp. 96–107

"Joseph Haydn als Mensch und Musiker." In *Joseph Haydn und seine Zeit,* ed. Gerda Mraz. Jahrbuch für österreichische Kulturgeschichte, 2. Eisenstadt: Institut für österreichische Kulturgeschichte, 1972. Pp. 43–56

"Das Problem der Substanzgemeinschaft in den zyklischen Werken [Mozarts]." In *MJb* 1973–74. Pp. 117–25

"Stilelemente Haydns in Beethovens Werken." In *Bericht über den Internationalen Musikwissenschaftlichen Kongreß Bonn 1970,* ed. Carl Dahlhaus *et al.* Kassel: Bärenreiter, [1973]. Pp. 65–70

"Ein vergessener Haydn-Brief." *H-S* 1 (1965–67), 114–16

[Work-list.] In "Haydn, Joseph." *The New Grove Dictionary of Music and Musicians,* ed. Stanley Sadie. London: Macmillan, 1980. Vol. 8, pp. 360–401

–Rev. ed. as *The New Grove Haydn*. New York: Norton, 1982. Pp. 122–208

Fillion, Michelle. "The Accompanied Keyboard Divertimenti of Haydn and his Viennese Contemporaries (c. 1750–1780)." Ph.D. diss., Cornell University, 1982

"Sonata-Exposition Procedures in Haydn's Keyboard Sonatas." In *Haydn Studies*, ed. Larsen *et al*. Pp. 475–81

Finscher, Ludwig. *Studien zur Geschichte des Streichquartetts*. Vol. 1. *Die Entstehung des klassischen Streichquartetts: Von den Vorformen zur Grundlegung durch Joseph Haydn*. Saarbrücker Studien zur Musikwissenschaft, 3. Kassel: Bärenreiter, 1974

"Zum Begriff der Klassik in der Musik." *DJbMw für 1966*, 11 (1967), 9–34

–Repr. in *Classic Music*. ed. Ellen Rosand. The Garland Library of the History of Western Music, 7. New York: Garland, 1985. Pp. 21–46

Fischer, Wilhelm. "Stilkritischer Anhang." In Alfred Schnerich, *Joseph Haydn und seine Sendung*. 2nd edn. Zurich: Almathea-Verlag, 1926

"Zur Entwicklungsgeschichte des Wiener klassischen Stils." *Studien zur Musikwissenschaft*, 3 (1915), 24–84

"Zwei neapolitanische Melodietypen bei Mozart und Haydn." In *MJb* 1960–61. Pp. 7–21

Fisher, Stephen Carey. "Haydn's Overtures and their Adaptations as Concert Orchestral Works." Ph.D. diss., University of Pennsylvania, 1985

Forchert, Arno. "'Klassisch' und 'romantisch' in der Musikliteratur des frühen 19. Jahrhunderts." *Mf* 31 (1978), 405–25

Foster, Jonathan. "The Tempora Mutantur Symphony of Joseph Haydn." *HYb* 9 (1975), 328–29

Fox, Pamela. "The Stylistic Anomalies of C. P. E. Bach's Nonconstancy." In *C. P. E. Bach Studies*, ed. Stephen L. Clark. New York: Oxford University Press, 1988. Pp. 105–31

Frisch, Walter. *Brahms and the Principle of Developing Variation*. California Studies in 19th Century Music, 2. Berkeley: University of California Press, 1984

Frye, Northorp. *Anatomy of Criticism*. Princeton: Princeton University Press, 1957

Geiringer, Karl. *Haydn: A Creative Life in Music*. 3rd edn. Berkeley: University of California Press, 1982

Georgiades, Thrasybulos. *Schubert: Musik und Lyrik*. Göttingen: Vandenhoeck und Ruprecht, 1967

"Zur Musiksprache der Wiener Klassiker." In *MJb* 1951. Pp. 50–59

–Repr. in Thrasybulos Georgiades, *Kleine Schriften*. Münchener Veröffentlichungen zur Musikgeschichte, 26. Tutzing: Schneider, 1977. Pp. 9–32

Gerlach, Sonja. "Die chronologische Ordnung von Haydns Sinfonien zwischen 1774 und 1782." *H-S* 2 (1969–70), 34–66

"Fragen zur Chronologie von Haydns frühen Sinfonien." Lecture, Joseph Haydn-Institut (Cologne), 1987. Unpublished typescript

"Haydns 'chronologische' Sinfonienliste für Breitkopf & Härtel." *H-S* 6/2 (1988), 116–29

"Haydns Orchestermusiker von 1761 bis 1774." *H-S* 4 (1976–80), 35–48

"Haydns Orchesterpartituren: Fragen der Realisierung des Textes." *H-S* 5 (1982–85), 169–83

"Welche stilistische Kriterien können zur genaueren Datierung von Haydns frühen Sinfonien beitragen?" *Jahrbuch für österreichische Kulturgeschichte*, 13. [In press]

Goldschmidt, Harry. "Motivvariation und Gestaltmetamorphose: Zur musikalischen Entstehungsgeschichte von Beethovens Violinkonzert." In *Festschrift Heinrich Besseler zum sechzigsten Geburtstag*, ed. Institut für Musikwissenschaft der Karl-Marx-Universität [Leipzig]. Leipzig: VEB Deutscher Verlag für Musik, 1961. Pp. 389–409

Göllner, Theodor. *"Die Sieben Worte am Kreuz" bei Schütz und Haydn*. Bayerische Akademie der Wissenschaften, Philosophisch-historische Klasse: Abhandlungen, Neue Folge, 93. Munich: Bayerische Akademie der Wissenschaften (Beck), 1986

Gotwals, Vernon. *Joseph Haydn: Eighteenth-Century Gentleman and Genius*. Madison: University of Wisconsin Press, 1963

[–Translations, with commentary, of Dies and Griesinger.]

Green, Robert A. "'Il distratto' of Haydn and Regnard: A Re-examination." *HYb* 11 (1980), 183–95

Gresham, Carolyn. "Stylistic Features of Haydn's Symphonies from 1768 to 1772." In *Haydn Studies*, ed. Larsen *et al.* Pp. 431–34

Griesinger, Georg August. *Biographische Notizen über Joseph Haydn*. Leipzig: Breitkopf & Härtel, 1810
[–For translation, see Gotwals.]

Großmann-Vendray, Susanne. *Felix Mendelssohn Bartholdy und die Musik der Vergangenheit*. Studien zur Musikgeschichte des 19. Jahrhunderts, 17. Regensburg: Bosse, 1969

Gülke, Peter. "Introduktion als Widerspruch im System: Zur Dialektik von Thema und Prozessualität bei Beethoven." *DJbMw für 1969*, 14 (1970), 5–40

Haimo, Ethan. "Haydn's Altered Reprise." *JMT* 32 (1988), 335–51

"Remote Keys and Multi-movement Unity: Haydn in the 1790s." *MQ* 74 (1990), 242–68.

Harich, János. "Inventare der Esterházy-Hofmusikkapelle in Eisenstadt." *HYb* 9 (1975), 5–125

Haydn, Joseph. *Gesammelte Briefe und Aufzeichnungen: Unter Benützung der Quellensammlung von H. C. Robbins Landon herausgegeben und erläutert von Dénes Bartha*. Kassel: Bärenreiter, 1965

Heartz, Daniel. "Classical." In *The New Grove Dictionary of Music and Musicians*, ed. Stanley Sadie. London: Macmillan, 1980. Vol. 4, pp. 449–54

"Haydn und Gluck im Burgtheater um 1760: Der neue krumme Teufel, Le Diable à quatre und die Sinfonie 'Le soir.'" In *Bericht über den Internationalen Musikwissenschaftlichen Kongress Bayreuth 1981*, ed. Christoph-Hellmut Mahling and Sigrid Wiesmann. Kassel: Bärenreiter, 1984. Pp. 120–35

"The Hunting Chorus in Haydn's *Jahreszeiten* and the 'Airs de Chasse' in the *Encyclopédie*." *Eighteenth-Century Studies* 9 (1975–76), 523–39

Heller, Friedrich. "Haydns 'Londoner Symphonie', D-Dur: Eine Analyse." In *Beiträge zur Musikgeschichte des 18. Jahrhunderts*, ed. Heller. Jahrbuch für österreichische Kulturgeschichte, I/2. Eisenstadt: Institut für österreichische Kulturgeschichte, 1971. Pp. 182–88

Helm, E. Eugene. "The 'Hamlet' Fantasy and the Literary Element in C. P. E. Bach's Music." *MQ* 58 (1972), 277–96

Horn, Hans-Jürgen. "Fiat lux: Zum kunsttheoretischen Hintergrund der 'Erschaffung' des Lichtes in Haydns Schöpfung." *H-S* 3 (1973–74), 65–84

Hörwarthner, Maria. "Joseph Haydns Bibliothek – Versuch einer literarhistorischen Rekonstruktion." In *Joseph Haydn und die Literatur seiner Zeit*, ed. Herbert Zeman. Jahrbuch für österreichische Kulturgeschichte, 6. Eisenstadt: Institut für österreichische Kulturgeschichte, 1976. Pp. 157–207

Hosler, Bellamy. *Changing Aesthetic Views of Instrumental Music in 18th-Century Germany*. Studies in Musicology, 42. Ann Arbor: UMI Research Press, 1981

Irving, Howard. "Haydn and Laurence Sterne: Similarities in Eighteenth-Century Literary and Musical Wit." *CM* no. 40 (1985), 34–49

Jahn, Otto. *W. A. Mozart*. 3d ed. rev. Hermann Deiters. 2 vols Leipzig: Breitkopf & Härtel, 1889–91

Jander, Owen. "Beethoven's 'Orpheus in Hades': The *Andante con moto* of the Fourth Concerto." *19CMus* 8 (1984–85), 195–212

Johnson, Douglas. "1794–1795: Decisive Years in Beethoven's Early Development." In *Beethoven Studies*, vol. 3, ed. Alan Tyson. Cambridge: Cambridge University Press, 1982. Pp. 1–28

Beethoven's Early Sketches in the "Fischhof Miscellany": Berlin Autograph 28. 2 vols. Studies in Musicology, 22. Ann Arbor: UMI Research Press, 1980

Jonas, Oswald. *Introduction to the Theory of Heinrich Schenker: The Nature of the Musical Work of Art*. Tr. John Rothgeb. New York: Longmans, 1982

Kalisch, Volker. *Entwurf einer Wissenschaft von der Musik: Guido Adler*. Sammlung musikwissenschaftlicher Abhandlungen, 77. Baden-Baden: Koerner, 1988

Keller, Hans. "The Chamber Music." In *The Mozart Companion*, ed. H. C. Robbins Landon and Donald Mitchell. London: Rockliff, 1956. Pp. 90–137

The Great Haydn Quartets: Their Interpretation. New York: Braziller, 1986

"KV 503: The Unity of Contrasting Themes and Movements." *MR* 17 (1956), 48–58, 120–29

"The String Quartet and Its Relatives." *MR* 26 (1965), 340–44; and 27 (1966), 59–62, 228–35

Kelterborn, Rudolf. *Zum Beispiel Mozart.* 2 vols. Kassel: Bärenreiter, 1981

Kerman, Joseph. *The Beethoven Quartets.* New York: Knopf, 1966

Contemplating Music. Cambridge, Mass.: Harvard University Press, 1985

"How We Got Into Analysis, and How to Get Out." *Critical Inquiry* 7 (1980–81), 311–31

"A Romantic Detail in Schubert's *Schwanengesang*." *MQ* 48 (1962), 36–49

"Taking the Fifth." In *Das musikalische Kunstwerk: Geschichte, Ästhetik, Theorie: Festschrift Carl Dahlhaus zum 60. Geburtstag*, ed. Hermann Danuser *et al.* Laaber: Laaber, 1988. Pp. 483–91

"Tovey's Beethoven." In *Beethoven Studies*, vol. 2, ed. Alan Tyson. London: Oxford University Press, 1977. Pp. 172–91

Kerman, Joseph and Tyson, Alan. "Beethoven, Ludwig van." In *The New Grove Dictionary of Music and Musicians*, ed. Stanley Sadie. London: Macmillan, 1980. Vol. 2, pp. 354–94

–Rev. edn. as *The New Grove Beethoven.* New York: Norton, 1983

Kermode, Frank. *The Classic: Literary Images of Permanence and Change.* New York: Viking, 1975

The Sense of an Ending. New York: Oxford University Press, 1967

Kier, Herfrid. *Rafael Georg Kiesewetter (1773–1850): Wegbereiter des musikalischen Historismus.* Studien zur Musikgeschichte des 19. Jahrhunderts, 13. Regensburg: Bosse, 1968

Kiesewetter, Rafael Georg. *Geschichte der europäisch-abendländischen oder unsrer heutigen Musik: Darstellung ihres Ursprunges, ihres Wachthumes und ihrer stufenweisen Entwickelung. . .* Leipzig: Breitkopf & Härtel, 1834

Kirby, F. E. "Beethovens Gebrauch von charakterischen Stilen: Ein Beitrag zum Problem der Einheit in der Mehrsätzigkeit." In *Bericht über den Internationalen Musikwissenschaftlichen Kongreß Bonn 1970*, ed. Carl Dahlhaus *et al.* Kassel: Bärenreiter, [1973]. Pp. 452–54

"Beethoven's Pastoral Symphony as a *Sinfonia caracteristica*." *MQ* 56 (1970), 605–23

–Repr. in *The Creative World of Beethoven*, ed. Paul Henry Lang. New York: Norton, 1971. Pp. 103–21

"The Germanic Symphony in the Eighteenth Century: Bridge to the Romantic Era." *JMR* 5 (1984–85), 51–83

Kirkendale, Warren. *Fugue and Fugato in Rococo and Classical Chamber Music.* 2nd rev. edn. Tr. Margaret Bent and the author. Durham, N.C.: Duke University Press, 1979

[–Orig. German *Fuge und Fugato in der Kammermusik des Rokoko und der Klassik.* Tutzing: Schneider, 1966.]

Kivy, Peter. *Sound and Semblance: Reflections on Musical Representation.* Princeton: Princeton University Press, 1984

Kliewer, Vernon L. "The Concept of Organic Unity in Music Criticism and Analysis." Ph.D. diss., Indiana University, 1961

Klinkhammer, Rudolf. *Die langsame Einleitung in der Instrumentalmusik der Klassik und Romantik.* Kölner Beiträge zur Musikforschung, 65. Regensburg: Bosse, 1971

Kornauth, Egon. "Die thematische Arbeit in Joseph Haydns Streichquartetten seit 1780 (Studie zur Entwicklungsgeschichte der Wiener klassischen Schule)." Ph.D. diss., University of Vienna, 1915

Kramer, Jonathan D. "Multiple and Non-Linear Time in Beethoven's Opus 135." *Perspectives of New Music* 11/2 (Spring-Summer 1973), 122–45

Kramer, Lawrence. *Music and Poetry: The Nineteenth Century and After.* California Studies in 19th Century Music, 3. Berkeley: University of California Press, 1984

Kretschmar, Hermann. "Die Jugendsinfonien Joseph Haydns." *JbP* 15 (1908), 69–90

Krones, Hartmut. "Das 'hohe Komische' bei Joseph Haydn." *Österreichische Musikzeitschrift*, 38 (1983), 2–8

"Rhetorik und rhetorische Symbolik in der Musik um 1800: Vom Weiterleben eines Prinzips." *Mth* 3 (1988), 117–40

Landon, H. C. Robbins, ed. *The "Creation" and the "Seasons": The Complete Authentic Sources for the Word-Books*. Cardiff: University College Press, 1985

Haydn: Chronicle and Works. 5 vols. London: Thames and Hudson; Bloomington: Indiana University Press, 1976–80

The Symphonies of Joseph Haydn. London: Barrie and Rockliff, 1955

Langer, Susanne K. *Feeling and Form: A Theory of Art Developed From "Philosophy in a New Key."* New York: Scribner, 1953

Langhaus, Wilhelm. *Die Geschichte der Musik des 17., 18., und 19. Jahrhunderts*. Vol. 2. Leipzig: Leuckart, 1887

Larsen, Jens Peter. "Haydn, Joseph." *The New Grove Dictionary of Music and Musicians*, ed. Stanley Sadie. London: Macmillan, 1980. Vol. 8, pp. 328–360

–Rev. edn. as *The New Grove Haydn*. New York: Norton, 1982

"Haydn's Early Symphonies: The Problem of Dating." In *Music in the Classic Period: Essays in Honor of Barry S. Brook*, ed. Allan W. Atlas. New York: Pendragon, 1985. Pp. 117–31

–Repr. in Jens Peter Larsen, *Handel, Haydn, and the Viennese Classical Style*, tr. Ulrich Krämer. Studies in Musicology, 100. Ann Arbor: UMI Research Press, 1988. Pp. 159–70

Die Haydn-Überlieferung. Copenhagen: Munksgaard, 1939

–Rev. edn. Munich: Kraus, 1980

"Some Observations on the Development and Characteristics of Viennese Classical Instrumental Music." *SM* 9 (1967), 115–39

–Repr. in Larsen, *Handel, Haydn, and the Viennese Classical Style*. Pp. 227–49

–Repr. in *Classic Music*, ed. Ellen Rosand. Pp. 47–71

"Sonatenformprobleme." In *Festschrift Friedrich Blume zum 70. Geburtstag*, ed. Anna Amalie Abert and Wilhelm Pfannkuch. Kassel: Bärenreiter, 1963. Pp. 221–30

–Tr. "Sonata Form Problems," in Larsen, *Handel, Haydn, and the Viennese Classical Style*. Pp. 269–79

"Der Stilwandel in der österreichischen Musik zwischen Barock und Wiener Klassik." In *Der junge Haydn: Wandel von Musikauffassung und Musikaufführung in der österreichischen Musik zwischen Barock und Klassik: Bericht der internationalen Arbeitstagung des Instituts für Aufführungspraxis der Hochschule für Musik und darstellende Kunst in Graz, 29.6–2.7 1970*, ed. Vera Schwarz. Beiträge zur Aufführungspraxis, 1. Graz: Akademische Druck- und Verlagsanstalt, 1972. Pp. 18–30

–Tr. "The Style Change in Austrian Music between the Baroque and Viennese Classicism," in Larsen, *Handel, Haydn, and the Viennese Classical Style*. Pp. 301–13

"Zu Haydns künstlerischer Entwicklung." In *Festschrift Wilhelm Fischer zum 70. Geburtstag überreicht im Mozartjahr 1956*, ed. Hans Zingerle. Innsbrucker Beiträge zur Kulturwissenschaft, Sonderhefte, 3. Innsbruck: Sprachwissenschaftliches Seminar der Universität, 1956. Pp. 123–29

–Tr. "On Haydn's Artistic Development," in Larsen, *Handel, Haydn, and the Viennese Classical Style*. Pp. 109–15

"Zur Bedeutung der 'Mannheimer Schule.'" In *Festschrift Karl Gustav Fellerer zum sechzigsten Geburtstag am 7. Juli 1962*, ed. Heinrich Hüschen. Regensburg: Bosse, 1962. Pp. 303–09

–Tr. "On the Importance of the 'Mannheim School,'" in Larsen, *Handel, Haydn, and the Viennese Classical Style*. Pp. 263–68

"Zur Entstehung der österreichischen Symphonietradition (ca. 1750–1775)." *HYb* 10 (1978), 72–80

–Tr. "Concerning the Development of the Austrian Symphonic Tradition (*circa* 1750–1755)," in Larsen, *Handel, Haydn, and the Viennese Classical Style*. Pp. 315–25

Larsen, Jens Peter, Serwer, Howard, and Webster, James, eds. *Haydn Studies: Proceedings of the International Haydn Conference, Washington, D.C., 1975*. New York: Norton, 1981

LaRue, Jan. "Bifocal Tonality: An Explanation for Ambiguous Baroque Cadences." In *Essays on Music in Honor of Archibald Thompson Davison by his Associates*. Cambridge, Mass.: Harvard University Press, 1957. Pp. 173–84

A Catalog of 18th-Century Symphonies. Vol. 1, *Thematic Identifier*. Bloomington: Indiana University Press, 1988

Guidelines for Style Analysis. New York: Norton, 1970.

"A 'Hail and Farewell' Quodlibet Symphony." *Music and Letters*, 37 (1956), 250–59

"A Haydn Specialty: Multistage Variance." In *Joseph Haydn, International Congress Wien, 1982*, ed. Badura-Skoda. Pp. 141–46

"Multistage Variance: Haydn's Legacy to Beethoven." *JM* 1 (1982), 265–74

"Significant and Coincidental Resemblance between Classical Themes." *JAMS* 14 (1961), 224–34

Lazar, Joel. "Thematic Unity in the First Movements of Haydn's London Symphonies." M.A. thesis, Harvard University, 1963

Le Huray, Peter and Day, James, eds. *Music and Aesthetics in the Eighteenth and Early Nineteenth Centuries*. Cambridge: Cambridge University Press, 1981

Levy, Janet M. "Gesture, Form, and Syntax in Haydn's Music." In *Haydn Studies*, ed. Larsen *et al.* Pp. 355–62

"Texture as a Sign in Classic and Early Romantic Music." *JAMS* 35 (1982), 482–531

Lewis, Christopher. "Mirrors and Metaphors: Reflections on Schoenberg and Nineteenth-Century Tonality." *19CMus* 11 (1987–88), 26–42

Livingstone, Ernest F. "Unifying Elements in Haydn's Symphony No. 104." In *Haydn Studies*, ed. Larsen *et al.* Pp. 493–96

MacIntyre, Bruce C. *The Viennese Concerted Mass of the Early Classic Period*. Studies in Musicology, 89. Ann Arbor: UMI Research Press, 1986

Mahling, Christoph-Hellmut. "Zur Frage der 'Einheit' der Symphonie." In *Über Sinfonien: Beiträge zu einer musikalischen Gattung: Festschrift Walter Wiora zum 70. Geburtstag*, ed Christoph-Hellmut Mahling. Tutzing: Schneider, 1979. Pp. 1–40

Marco, Guy A. "A Musical Task in the Surprise Symphony." *JAMS* 11 (1958), 41–44

Marston, Nicholas. "Schenker and Forte Reconsidered: Beethoven's Sketches for the Piano Sonata in E, Op. 109." *19CMus* 10 (1986–87), 24–42

Marx, Karl. "Über thematische Beziehungen in Haydns Londoner Symphonien." *H-S* 4 (1976–80), 1–19

Zur Einheit der zyklischen Form bei Mozart. Stuttgart: Ichthys, 1971

Maus, Fred Everett. "Humanism and Musical Experience." Ph.D. diss, Princeton University, 1990

"Music as Drama." *MTS* 10 (1988), 56–73

Menk, Gail Ellsworth. "The Symphonic Introductions of Joseph Haydn." Ph.D. diss., University of Iowa, 1960

Meyer, Leonard B. *Explaining Music: Essays and Explorations*. Chicago: University of Chicago Press, 1973

Misch, Ludwig. *Die Faktoren der Einheit in der Mehrsätzigkeit der Werke Beethovens: Versuch einer Theorie der Einheit des Werkstils*. Veröffentlichungen des Beethovenhauses in Bonn, Neue Folge, 4. Reihe: Schriften zur Beethovenforschung, 3. Munich: Henle, 1958

Moe, Orin, Jr. "The Implied Model in Classical Music." *CM* no. 23 (1977), 46–55

Morgan, Robert P. "The Delayed Structural Downbeat and its Effect on the Tonal and Rhythmic Structure of Sonata Form Recapitulation." Ph.D. diss., Princeton University, 1969

Mörner, C. G. Stellan. "Haydniana aus Schweden um 1800." *H-S* 2 (1969–70), 1–33

Moss, Lawrence K. "Haydn's Sonata Hob. XVI:52 (ChL. 62) in E-flat Major: An Analysis of the First Movement." In *Haydn Studies*, ed. Larsen *et al.* Pp. 496–501

Neubacher, Jürgen. *Finis coronat opus: Untersuchungen zur Technik der Schlußgestaltung in der Instrumentalmusik Joseph Haydns, dargestellt am Beispiel der Streichquartette: Mit einem Exkurs: Haydn und die rhetorische Tradition.* Mainzer Studien zur Musikwissenschaft, 22. Tutzing: Schneider, 1986

Neubauer, John. *The Emancipation of Music from Language: Departure from Mimesis in Eighteenth-Century Aesthetics.* New Haven: Yale University Press, 1986

Newcomb, Anthony. "Schumann and Late Eighteenth-Century Narrative Strategies." *19CMus* 11 (1987–88), 164–74

Newman, William S. *The Sonata in the Baroque Era.* Chapel Hill: University of North Carolina Press, 1959

The Sonata in the Classic Era. Chapel Hill: University of North Carolina Press, 1963

Niecks, Frederick. *Programme Music in the Last Four Centuries: A Contribution to the History of Musical Expression.* London: Novello, [1906]

Noske, Frits. "Le principe structural génétique dans l'oeuvre instrumental de Joseph Hadyn." *Revue belge de musicologie* 12 (1958), 35–39

Olleson, Edward. "Georg August Griesinger's Correspondence with Breitkopf & Härtel." *HYb* 3 (1965), 5–53

Oster, Ernst. "The Dramatic Character of the *Egmont* Overture." *Musicology*, 2 (1949), 269–85
–Repr. in *Aspects of Schenkerian Theory*, ed. David Beach. New Haven: Yale University Press, 1983. Pp. 209–22

Pandi, Marianne and Schmidt, Fritz. "Musik zur Zeit Haydns und Beethovens in der Preßburger Zeitung." *HYb* 8 (1971), 165–293

Pastille, William. "*Ursatz*: The Musical Philosophy of Heinrich Schenker." Ph.D. diss, Cornell University, 1985

Platen, Emil. "Über Bach, Kuhlau und die thematisch-motivische Einheit der letzten Quartette Beethovens." In *Beiträge zu Beethovens Kammermusik: Symposion Bonn 1984*, ed. Sieghard Brandenburg and Helmut Loos. Veröffentlichungen des Beethovenhauses in Bonn, Neue Folge, 4. Reihe: Schriften zur Beethovenforschung, 4. Munich: Henle, 1987. Pp. 152–64

Pohl, Carl Ferdinand. *Joseph Haydn.* 2 vols. Leipzig: Breitkopf & Härtel, 1878–82

Randall, J. K. "Haydn: String Quartet in D Major, Op. 76, No. 5." *MR* 21 (1960), 94–105

Ratner, Leonard G. *Classic Music: Expression, Form, and Style.* New York: Schirmer, 1980

Ratz, Erwin. *Einführung in die musikalische Formenlehre: Über Formprinzipien in den Inventionen J. S. Bachs und ihre Bedeutung für die Kompositionstechnik Beethovens.* Vienna: Österreichischer Bundesverlag für Unterricht, Wissenschaft und Kunst, 1951

Rée, Jonathan. *Philosophical Tales.* London and New York: Methuen, 1987

Reed, Carl Hadley. "Motivic Unity in Selected Keyboard Sonatas and String Quartets of Joseph Haydn." Ph.D. diss., University of Washington, 1966

Réti, Rudolph. *Thematic Patterns in Sonatas of Beethoven.* New York: Macmillan, 1967

The Thematic Process in Music. New York: Macmillan, 1951

Reynolds, Christopher. "The Representational Impulse in Late Beethoven, I: An die ferne Geliebte; II: String Quartet in F Major, Op. 135." *Acta musicologica*, 60 (1988), 43–61, 180–94

Ricoeur, Paul. *Time as Narrative.* Tr. Kathleen McLaughlin and David Pellauer. 3 vols. Chicago: University of Chicago Press, 1984–88

Ringer, Alexander L. "The *Chasse* as a Musical Topic of the Eighteenth Century." *JAMS* 6 (1953), 148–59

Rosen, Charles. *The Classical Style: Haydn, Mozart, Beethoven.* New York: Viking; London: Faber and Faber, 1971

Sonata Forms. New York: Norton, 1980

Rösing, Helmut. "Gedanken zum 'Musikalischen Hören.'" *Mf* 27 (1974), 213–16

Rothgeb, John. "Thematic Content: A Schenkerian View." In *Aspects of Schenkerian Theory*, ed. David Beach. New Haven: Yale University Press, 1983. Pp 39–60

Rywosch, Bernhard. *Beiträge zur Entwicklung in Joseph Haydns Symphonik 1759–1780*. Turbenthal: Furrer, 1934

Sandberger, Adolf. "Zu den geschichtlichen Voraussetzungen der Pastoralsinfonie." In Adolf Sandberger, *Ausgewählte Aufsätze zur Musikgeschichte*, vol. 2, *Forschungen, Studien und Kritiken zu Beethoven und zur Beethovenliteratur*. Munich: Drei Masken, 1924. Pp. 154–200

"Zur Geschichte des Haydnschen Streichquartetts." *Altbayerische Monatsschrift*, 2 (1900), 41–64. Rev. repr. in Adolf Sandberger, *Ausgewählte Aufsätze zur Musikgeschichte*, vol. 1. Munich: Drei Masken, 1921. Pp. 224–65

Schachter, Carl. "A Commentary on Schenker's *Free Composition*." *JMT* 25 (1981), 115–42

"Motive and Text in Four Schubert Songs." In *Aspects of Schenkerian Theory*, ed. David Beach. New Haven: Yale University Press, 1983. Pp. 61–76

Schafer, Hollace Ann. "'A Wisely Ordered *Phantasie*': Joseph Haydn's Creative Process from the Sketches and Drafts for Instrumental Music." Ph.D. diss., Brandeis University, 1987

Schenker, Heinrich. *Free Composition*. Tr. Ernst Oster. 2 vols. New York: Longmans, 1979

"Haydn: Sonata Es-Dur." *Der Tonwille: Flugblätter zum Zeugnis unwandelbarer Gesetze der Tonkunst einer neuen Jugend dargebracht* no. 3 (1922), 3–21

Das Meisterwerk in der Musik. 3 vols. Munich: Drei Masken, 1925–30

Schering, Arnold. *Beethoven und die Dichtung: Mit einer Einleitung zur Geschichte und Ästhetik der Beethovendeutung*. Neue deutsche Forschungen, Abteilung Musikwissenschaft, 3. Berlin: Junker und Dünnhaupt, 1936

"Bemerkungen zu J. Haydns Programmsinfonien." *JbP* 46 (1939), 9–27

–Repr. in Arnold Schering, *Vom musikalischen Kunstwerk*, ed. Friedrich Blume. Leipzig: Koehler und Amelang, 1949. Pp. 246–77

Schleuning, Peter. "Beethoven in alter Deutung: Der 'neue Weg' mit der 'Sinfonia eroica.'" *AfMw* 44 (1987), 165–94

Schmitz, Arnold. *Beethovens "Zwei Prinzipe": Ihre Bedeutung für Themen- und Satzbau*. Berlin and Bonn: Dümmler, 1923

Schoenberg, Arnold. *Style and Idea: Selected Writings*. Ed. Leonard Stein. Tr. Leo Black. London: Faber and Faber, 1975

Schroeder, David P. "Audience Reception and Haydn's London Symphonies." *International Review of the Aesthetics and Sociology of Music* 16 (1985), 57–72

Haydn and the Enlightenment: The Late Symphonies and their Audience. Oxford: The Clarendon Press, 1990

"Melodic Source Material and Haydn's Creative Process." *MQ* 68 (1982), 496–515

Schulenberg, David. *The Instrumental Music of Carl Philipp Emanuel Bach*. Studies in Musicology, 77. Ann Arbor: UMI Research Press, 1984

Schwarting, Heino. "Ungewöhnliche Repriseneintritte in Haydns späterer Instrumentalmusik." *AfMw* 17 (1960), 168–82

Schwartz, Judith L. "Periodicity and Passion in the First Movement of Haydn's 'Farewell' Symphony." In *Studies in Musical Sources and Style: Essays in Honor of Jan LaRue*, ed. Eugene K. Wolf and Edward H. Roesner. Madison: A-R Editions, 1990. Pp. 293–338

"Thematic Asymmetry in First Movements of Haydn's Early Symphonies." In *Haydn Studies*, ed. Larsen *et al*. Pp. 501–09

Seeger, Horst. "Zur musikhistorischen Bedeutung der Haydn-Biographie von Albert Christoph Dies (1810)." *BzMw* 1/3 (1959), pp. 24–31

Seidel, Wilhelm. "Die ältere Zyklustheorie, überdacht im Blick auf Beethovens Werk." In *Beiträge zu Beethovens Kammermusik: Symposion Bonn 1984*, ed. Sieghard Brandenburg and Helmut Loos. Veröffentlichungen des Beethovenhauses in Bonn, Neue Folge, 4. Reihe: Schriften zur Beethovenforschung, 4. Munich: Henle, 1987. Pp. 273–82

"Schnell – Langsam – Schnell: Zur 'klassischen' Theorie des instrumentalen Zyklus." *Mth* 1 (1986), 205–16

Shamgar, Beth. "On Locating the Retransition in Classic Sonata Form." *MR* 42 (1981), 130–43

"Rhythmic Interplay in the Retransitions of Haydn's Piano Sonatas." *JM* 3 (1984), 55–68

Sheldon, David A. "The Concept *galant* in the 18th-Century." *JMR* 9 (1989–90), 89–108

Sisman, Elaine R. "Haydn's Theater Symphonies." *JAMS* 43 (1990), 292–352

"Haydn's Variations." Ph.D. diss., Princeton University, 1978

"Small and Expanded Forms: Koch's Model and Haydn's Music." *MQ* 68 (1982), 444–75

Smith, Barbara Herrnstein. *Poetic Closure: A Study of How Poems End*. Chicago: University of Chicago Press, 1968

Solie, Ruth A. "The Living Work: Organicism and Musical Analysis." *19CMus* 4 (1980–81), 147–56

Solomon, Maynard. *Beethoven*. New York: Schirmer, 1977

"The Creative Periods of Beethoven." *MR* 34 (1973), 30–38

–Repr. in Maynard Solomon, *Beethoven Essays*. Cambridge, Mass.: Harvard University Press, 1988. Pp. 116–25

Somfai, László. "Haydn's London String Quartets." In *Haydn Studies*, ed. Larsen *et al*. Pp. 389–91

Joseph Haydn: Sein Leben in zeitgenössischen Bildern. Budapest: Corvina; Kassel: Bärenreiter, 1966

"'Learned Style' in Two Late String Quartet Movements of Haydn." *SM* 28 (1986), 325–49

"Opus-Planung und Neuerung bei Haydn." *SM* 22 (1980), 87–110

"Vom Barock zur Klassik: Umgestaltung der Proportionen und des Gleichgewichts in zyklischen Werken Joseph Haydns." In *Joseph Haydn und seine Zeit*, ed. Gerda Mraz. Jahrbuch für österreichische Kulturgeschichte, 2. Eisenstadt: Institut für österreichische Kulturgeschichte, 1972. Pp. 64–72

Sponheuer, Bernd. "Haydns Arbeit am Finalproblem." *AfMw* 34 (1977), 199–224

Steblin, Rita. *A History of Key Characteristics in the Eighteenth and Early Nineteenth Centuries*. Studies in Musicology, 67. Ann Arbor: UMI Research Press, 1983

"Key Characteristics and Haydn's Operas." In *Joseph Haydn, International Congress Wien, 1982*, ed. Badura-Skoda. Pp. 91–100

Sutcliffe, W. Dean. "Haydn's Musical Personality." *The Musical Times* 130 (1989), 341–44

Szabolcsi, Bence. "Joseph Haydn und die ungarische Musik." *BzMw* 1 (1959), 62–73

–Repr. in *Bericht über die Internationale Konferenz zum Andenken Joseph Haydns, Budapest, 17.–22. September 1959*, ed. Bence Szabolcsi and Dénes Bartha. Budapest: Akadémiai Kiadó, 1961. Pp. 159–75

Therstappen, Hans Joachim. *Joseph Haydns sinfonisches Vermächtnis*. Kieler Beiträge zur Musikwissenschaft, 9. Wolfenbüttel: Kallmeyer, 1941

Thomas, Günter. "Griesingers Briefe über Haydn: Aus seiner Korrespondenz mit Breitkopf & Härtel." *H-S* 1 (1965–68), 49–114

"Haydns deutsche Singspiele." *H-S* 6/1 (1986), 1–63

Tobel, Rudolf von. *Die Formenwelt der klassischen Instrumentalmusik*. Berner Veröffentlichungen zur Musikforschung, 6. Bern: Haupt, 1935

Todd, R. Larry. "Joseph Haydn and the *Sturm und Drang*: A Revaluation." *MR* 41 (1980), 172–96

Tovey, Donald Francis. *Beethoven*. London: Oxford University Press, 1945

"Brahms's Chamber Music." In *Essays and Lectures on Music*, ed. Hubert J. Foss. London: Oxford University Press, 1949. Pp. 220–70

Essays in Musical Analysis. 6 vols. London: Oxford University Press, 1935–39

"Haydn: Pianoforte Sonata in E flat, No. 1." In Tovey, *Essays in Musical Analysis: Chamber Music*, pp. 93–105. London: Oxford University Press, 1944

"Haydn's Chamber Music." [Orig. publ. *Cyclopedic Survey of Chamber Music*, ed. W. W. Cobbett, vol. 1. London: Oxford University Press, 1929.] In Tovey, *Essays and Lectures*, pp. 1–64

"Musical Form and Matter." In Tovey, *Essays and Lectures*, pp. 160–82

"Some Aspects of Beethoven's Art-Forms." [Orig. in *Music and Letters*, 8 (1927), 131–55] In Tovey, *Essays and Lectures*, pp. 271–97

   –Repr. in *Classic Music*, ed. Ellen Rosand. Pp. 169–93

"Sonata Forms." In Tovey, *Musical Articles from the Encyclopaedia Britannica*, ed. Hubert J. Foss. London: Oxford University Press, 1944. Pp. 208–32

Treitler, Leo. "Mozart and the Idea of Absolute Music." In *Das musikalische Kunstwerk: Geschichte, Ästhetik, Theorie: Festschrift Carl Dahlhaus zum 60. Geburtstag*, ed. Hermann Danuser *et al.* Laaber: Laaber, 1988. Pp. 413–40

   –Repr. in Leo Treitler, *Music and the Historical Imagination*. Cambridge, Mass.: Harvard University Press, 1989. Pp. 176–214

Music and the Historical Imagination. Cambridge, Mass.: Harvard University Press, 1989

Tyson, Alan. "On Behalf of Haydn." *The Times Literary Supplement*, no. 3973 (26 May 1978), 589

Über das Klassische. Ed. Rudolf Bockholdt. Suhrkamp Taschenbücher, 2077. Frankfurt am Main: Suhrkamp, 1987

Valkó, Arisztid. "Haydn magyarországi müködése a levéltári akták tükrében." Second Series. In *Haydn Emlékére*, ed. Bence Szabolcsi and Dénes Bartha. Zenetudományi Tanulmányok, 8. Budapest: Akadémiai Kiadó, 1960. Pp. 527–668

Die Vier Jahreszeiten im 18. Jahrhundert: Colloquium der Arbeitsstelle 18. Jahrhundert, Gesamthochschule Wuppertal, Universität Münster, Schloß Langenburg vom 3. bis 5. Oktober 1983. Heidelberg: Winter, 1986

Vinton, John. "The Development Section in Early Viennese Symphonies: a Re-evaluation." *MR* 24 (1963), 13–22

Wallace, Robin. *Beethoven's Critics: Aesthetic Dilemmas and Resolutions During the Composer's Lifetime*. Cambridge: Cambridge University Press, 1986

Walter, Horst. "Die biographischen Beziehungen zwischen Haydn und Beethoven." In *Bericht über den Internationalen Musikwissenschaftlichen Kongreß Bonn 1970*, ed. Carl Dahlhaus *et al.* Kassel: Bärenreiter, [1973]. Pp. 79–83

"Gottfried van Swietens handschriftliche Textbücher zu 'Schöpfung' und 'Jahreszeiten.'" *H-S* 1 (1965–67), 241–77

"Kalkbrenners Lehrjahre und sein Unterricht bei Haydn." *H-S* 5 (1982–85), 23–41

"On Haydn's Pupils." In *Haydn Studies*, ed. Larsen *et al.* Pp. 60–63

"Das Posthornsignal bei Haydn und anderen Komponisten des 18. Jahrhunderts." *H-S* 4 (1976–80), 21–34

Webster, James. "The Bass Part in Haydn's Early String Quartets." *MQ* 63 (1977), 390–424

"Binary Variants of Sonata Form in Early Haydn Instrumental Music." In *Joseph Haydn, International Congress Wien, 1982*, ed. Badura-Skoda. Pp. 127–35

"The Chronology of Haydn's String Quartets." *MQ* 61 (1975), 17–46

"Cone's 'Personae' and the Analysis of Opera." *CMS* 29 (1989), 44–65

"Did Haydn 'Synthesize' the Classical String Quartet?" In *Haydn Studies*, ed. Larsen *et al.* Pp. 336–39

"The D-Major Interlude in the First Movement of Haydn's 'Farewell' Symphony." In *Essays in Honor of Jan LaRue*, Wolf and Roesner, eds. Pp. 339–80

"The Falling-out Between Haydn and Beethoven: The Evidence of the Sources." In *Beethoven Essays: Studies in Honor of Elliot Forbes*, ed. Lewis Lockwood and Phyllis Benjamin. Cambridge, Mass.: Harvard University Press, 1984. Pp. 3–45

"Freedom of Form in Haydn's Early String Quartets." In *Haydn Studies*, ed. Larsen *et al.* Pp. 522–30

"The General and the Particular in Brahms's Later Sonata Forms." In *Brahms Studies: Papers Delivered at the International Brahms Conference, The Library of Congress, Washington, D.C., 5–8 May 1983*, ed. George S. Bozarth. London: Oxford University Press, 1990. Pp. 49–78

"Haydns frühe Ensemble-Divertimenti: Geschlossene Gattung, meisterhafter Satz." Lecture, Conference on the Divertimento in the Eighteenth Century, Gesellschaft für Musikforschung, Eichstätt, 1988. Unpublished typescript

"Haydns frühe Ensemble-Divertimenti: Wandel einer Gattung von der Mitte des 18. Jahrhunderts zur Wiener Klassik." *Jahrbuch für österreichische Kulturgeschichte*, 13. [In press.]

"Haydn's String Quartets." In *Haydnfest: Music Festival, September 22–October 11, 1975; International Musicological Conference, October 4–11, 1975*, ed. [Jens Peter Larsen and Howard Serwer]. Washington, D.C.: The John F. Kennedy Center for the Performing Arts, 1975. Pp. 13–17

"Prospects for Haydn Biography After Landon." *MQ* 68 (1982), 476–95

"Schubert's Sonata Form and Brahms's First Maturity." *19CMus* 2 (1978–79), 18–35; 3 (1979–80), 52–71

"The Significance of Haydn's String Quartet Autographs for Performance Practice." In *The String Quartets of Haydn, Mozart, and Beethoven: Studies of the Autograph Manuscripts: A Conference at the Isham Memorial Library March 15–17, 1979*, ed. Christoph Wolff and Robert Riggs. Isham Library Papers, 3. Cambridge, Mass.: Harvard University Press, 1980. Pp. 62–95

"To Understand Verdi and Wagner We Must Understand Mozart." *19CMus* 11 (1987–88), 175–93

"Towards a History of Viennese Chamber Music in the Early Classical Period." *JAMS* 27 (1974), 212–47

–Repr. in *Classic Music*, ed. Ellen Rosand. Pp. 194–230

"Traditional Elements in Beethoven's Middle-Period String Quartets." In *Beethoven, Performers, and Critics: The International Beethoven Congress Detroit 1977*, ed. Robert Winter and Bruce Carr. Detroit: Wayne State University Press, 1980. Pp. 94–133

"Violoncello and Double Bass in the Chamber Music of Haydn and his Viennese Contemporaries, 1750–1780." *JAMS* 29 (1976), 413–38

"When Did Haydn Begin to Write 'Beautiful' Melodies?" In *Haydn Studies*, ed. Larsen *et al.* Pp. 385–88

Weimer, Eric. *"Opera Seria" and the Evolution of Classical Style 1755–1772*. Studies in Musicology, 78. Ann Arbor: UMI Research Press, 1984

Werker, Wilhelm. *Studien über die Symmetrie im Bau der Fugen und die motivische Zusammengehörigkeit der Präludien und Fugen des "Wohltemperierten Klaviers" von Johann Sebastian Bach*. Leipzig: Breitkopf und Härtel, 1922

Westphal, Kurt. *Der Begriff der musikalischen Form in der Wiener Klassik: Versuch einer Grundlegung der Theorie der musikalischen Formung*. Leipzig: Breitkopf & Härtel, 1935

–2nd edn. Schriften zur Musik, 11. Giebig über Prien am Chiemsee: Katzbichler, 1971

Wheelock, Gretchen A. "Wit, Humor, and the Instrumental Music of Joseph Haydn." Ph.D. diss., Yale University, 1979

White, Hayden. "Interpretation in History." *New Literary History* 4 (1972–73), 281–314

Tropics of Discourse: Essays in Cultural Criticism. Baltimore: The Johns Hopkins University Press, 1978

Wiesel, Meir. "The Presence and Evaluation of Thematic Relationship and Thematic Unity." *Israel Studies in Musicology* 1 (1978), 77–91

Willner, Channon. "Chromaticism and the Mediant in Four Late Haydn Works." *Theory and Practice* 13 (1988), 79–114

Winn, James Anderson. *Unsuspected Eloquence: A History of the Relations between Poetry and Music*. New Haven: Yale University Press, 1981

Wintle, Christopher. "Kontra-Schenker: *Largo e Mesto* from Beethoven's Op. 10 No. 3." *MusA* 4 (1985), 145–82

Wiora, Walter. *Das musikalische Kunstwerk*. Tutzing: Schneider, 1983

Wolf, Eugene K. "Classical." In *The New Harvard Dictionary of Music*, ed. Don Michael Randel. Cambridge, Mass.: Harvard University Press, 1986. Pp. 172–73

"The Recapitulations in Haydn's London Symphonies." *MQ* 52 (1966), 71–89

The Symphonies of Johann Stamitz: A Study in the Formation of the Classic Style. Utrecht/Antwerp: Bohn, Scheltema and Holkema; the Hague/Boston: Nijhoff, 1981

Wolff, Christoph. "Musikalische 'Gedankenfolge' und 'Einheit des Stoffes': Zu Mozarts Klaviersonate in F-Dur (KV 533 + 494)." In *Das musikalische Kunstwerk: Geschichte, Ästhetik, Theorie: Festschrift Carl Dahlhaus zum 60. Geburtstag*, ed. Hermann Danuser *et al.* Laaber: Laaber, 1988. Pp. 441–53

Wörner, Karl H. *Das Zeitalter der thematischen Prozesse in der Geschichte der Musik*. Studien zur Musikgeschichte des 19. Jahrhunderts, 18. Regensburg: Bosse, 1969

Wyzewa, Théodore de. "A propos du centenaire de la mort de Joseph Haydn." *Revue des deux mondes* 79th year/vol. 51 (15 June 1909), 935–46

Zaslaw, Neal. "Mozart, Haydn and the *Sinfonia da Chiesa*." *JM* 1 (1982), 95–124

Zeman, Herbert. "Joseph Haydns Begegnungen mit der Literatur seiner Zeit." In *Joseph Haydn und die Literatur seiner Zeit*, ed. Herbert Zeman. Jahrbuch für österreichische Kulturgeschichte, 6. Eisenstadt: Institut für österreichische Kulturgeschichte, 1976. Pp. 7–23

"Von der irdischen Glückseligkeit: Gottfried van Swietens *Jahreszeiten*-Libretto – eine Utopie vom natürlichen Leben des Menschen." In *Die Vier Jahreszeiten im 18. Jahrhundert: Colloquum der Arbeitsstelle 18. Jahrhundert, Gesamthochschule Wuppertal, Universität Münster, Schloß Langenburg vom 3. bis 5. Oktober 1983*. Heidelberg: Winter, 1986. Pp. 108–20

Zenck, Martin. "Zum Begriff des Klassischen in der Musik." *AfMw* 39 (1982), 271–92

INDEX

The Farewell Symphony is cited in two different ways: topically (both as a main entry and as a subentry in other main entries), and under Haydn, Symphonies, No. 45 (with respect to Part II and the conclusion only). Modern authorities are cited only when their research or opinions are substantively discussed.

Abbate, Carolyn, 285, 287
absolute music, 181, 225–26, 235
Adler, Guido, 9–10, 351–53
Albrechtsberger, Johann Georg, 228, 358
"Alleluia" (nickname), 237
amateurs, music for, 189–91, 222–23, 288, 293
ambiguity
    of background voice-leading, 167–70, 264–66, 324–26; in the Farewell Symphony, 66–67, 70–71, 96, 100–2, 108–10
    of form, 253, 258, 270, 301–08; in the Farewell Symphony, 64–71
    of phrase-construction, in the Farewell Symphony, 43–44
    of thematic/motivic relations, 196–204; in the Farewell Symphony, 20–24, 97–98, 104
    of tonal structure, 324–26
analysis
    and interpretation, 5–7, 112–13, 115–16, 179–82, 248–49; *see also* extramusical associations
    methodologies of, 4–5, 251
    multivalent, 4–5, 181, 307
    reductive, dangers of, 4–5, 196–97, 203, 298
    and taste, 204
    see also implication-realization; multivalence; narrative; Schenkerian analysis; thematicism
antiperiod, 44
Aristotle, 126
Artaria (publisher), 205, 237
audience, *see* expectations of listeners; Farewell Symphony; program music
Aumann, Franz Joseph, 226

Bach, Carl Philipp Emanuel, 225–26, 357
    cyclic organization in, 179, 182, 186
    not "Classical," 124
    Sonata, keyboard, F minor (Wq.57/6; Helm 173), 179, 182
Bach, Johann Sebastian, 197, 335
    Brandenburg Concerto No. 3 (G), 142
    Capriccio on the Departure of his Most Beloved Brother, 225
    Well-tempered Keyboard, 197n
background, *see* ambiguity; Schenkerian analysis
Bard, Raimund, 186n
Bartha, Dénes, 44, 233
Barthélémon, François Hippolite (clergyman), 233
bass
    absence of: in allegros following slow introductions, 163–64; at beginnings, 127–33, 206, 325; at endings, 149; in the Farewell Symphony, 14–15, 16, 43, 64–65, 67, 81, 110–12
    part-crossings in, 110, 143n, 146
Beatles (The), 348
    "Got To Get You Into My Life," 348
Becker-Glauch, Irmgard, 333n
Beecke, Franz Anton von, 226
Beethoven, Ludwig van, 115, 126, 163, 197–98, 226
    and "Classical style," 349–51, 355
    coda in, 166
    cyclic organization in, 179–84, 367–72
    extramusical associations in, 113
    influenced by Haydn, 10, 123, 144, 162, 172, 186, 212, 232, 367, 369, 372–73
    "three periods," narrative of, 359
    Missa Solemnis, 373